SOLUTIONS MANUAL

to accompany

PRINCIPLES AND APPLICATIONS OF ELECTRICAL ENGINEERING

Second Edition

Giorgio Rizzoni

Prepared by
Eugene Stuffle
Idaho State University
Linda Stuffle
Stuffle Engineering and Computer Consulting Services

WCB McGraw-Hill

Boston, Massachusetts Burr Ridge, Illinois Dubuque, Iowa
Madison, Wisconsin New York, New York San Francisco, California St. Louis, Missouri

WCB/McGraw-Hill
A Division of The McGraw-Hill Companies

Printed in the United States of America.

ISBN 0-256-20311-3

3 4 5 6 7 8 9 0 QPD 0 9 8

CONTENTS

Chapter 1 Instructor Notes

Chapter 1 is introductory in nature, establishing some rationale for studying electrical engineering methods, even though the students' primary interest may lie in other areas. The material in this chapter should be included in every syllabus, and can typically be thoroughly covered in a single-day introductory lecture. Oftentimes, reading of this material is left up to the discretion of the student.

Chapter 1 problem solutions

1.1

A few examples are:

Bathroom
- ventilation fan
- electric toothbrush
- hair dryer
- electric shaver
- electric heater fan

Kitchen
- microwave fan
- microwave turntable
- mixer
- food processor
- blender
- coffee grinder
- garbage disposal
- ceiling fan
- electric clock
- exhaust fan
- refrigerator compressor
- dish washer

Utility Room
- clothes washer
- dryer
- air conditioner
- furnace blower
- pump

Family Room
- VCR drive
- cassette tape drive
- reel-to-reel tape drive
- record turntable drive
- computer fan
- treadmill

Miscellaneous
- lawn tools
- power tools

1.2

Several examples are listed below for each system:

a) A ship

- Circuit Analysis
  - design of the ship's electrical system
- Electromagnetics
  - radar
- Solid-State Electronics
  - radio
  - sonar
- Electric Machines
  - pump
  - elevator
- Electric Power Systems
  - lighting
  - generators
- Digital Logic Circuits
  - elevator control
- Computer Systems
  - navigation
- Communication Systems
  - radio
  - telephone
- Electro-Optics
  - Morse light
  - bridge displays
- Instrumentation
  - compass
  - speed indicator
- Control Systems
  - rudder
  - HVAC

b) A Commercial Passenger Aircraft

- Circuit Analysis
  - Design of the plane's electrical system
- Electromagnetics
  - radar
  - microwave oven
- Solid-State Electronics
  - radio
- Electric Machines
  - turbines
  - fans
- Electric Power Systems
  - lighting
  - HVAC
- Digital Logic Circuits
  - seat belts
- Computer Systems
  - navigation
- Communication Systems
  - radio
  - telephone
- Electro-Optics
  - cockpit displays
- Instrumentation
  - compass
  - air speed indicator
  - inclinometer
  - altimeter
- Control Systems
  - rudder
  - flaps

c) Household

- Circuit Analysis
  - design of the home's electrical system
- Electromagnetics
  - microwave oven
  - stereo speakers
- Solid-State Electronics
  - television
  - stereo
  - VCR
- Electric Machines
  - appliances
  - power tools
  - fans
- Electric Power Systems
  - lighting
  - HVAC
  - receptacles
- Digital Logic Circuits
  - clocks
  - timers
- Computer Systems
  - microwave oven
  - programmable VCR
- Communication Systems
  - telephone
  - CB radio
  - television
  - radio
- Electro-Optics
  - digital clocks
- Instrumentation
  - electric meter
- Control Systems
  - thermostat

1.3

Some examples are:

a) HVAC
- lighting
- office equipment
  - typewriter
  - computer
  - copy machine
  - clock
  - stapler
  - shredder
- elevator

b) conveyor
- punch press
- lighting
- ventilation
- drill press
- hoist
- lathe

c) power saw
- drill
- lighting
- elevator
- pump
- compressor

Chapter 2 Instructor Notes

Chapter 2 develops the foundations for the first part of the book. Coverage of the entire Chapter would be typical in an introductory course. The Instructor will find that although the material is quite basic, it is possible to give an applied flavor to the subject matter by emphasizing a few selected topics in the examples presented in class. In particular, a lecture could be devoted to *resistance devices*, including the resistive displacement transducer of Example 2.7 and the resistance strain gauges of Example 2.8. The instructor wishing to gain a more in-depth understanding of resistance strain gauges will find a detailed analysis in [1].

Early motivation for the application of circuit analysis to problems of practical interest to the non-electrical engineer can be found in the Wheatstone Bridge examples (2.12 and 2.13). The latter of these can also serve as an introduction to a laboratory experiment on strain gauges and the measurement of force (see, for example, [2]). Finally, the material on practical measuring instruments can also provide a number of useful examples.

The homework problems include a variety of practical examples. Problem 2.6 illustrates a battery charging scheme; problem 2.36 discusses the thermistor, and problems 2.42 through 2.51 present a variety of problems related to ammeters, voltmeters and wattmeters.

It has been the author's experience that providing the students with an early introduction to practical applications of electrical engineering to their own disciplines can increase the interest level in the course significantly.

[1] Doebelin E. O., Measurement Systems, McGraw-Hill, Fourth Edition, 1987.
[2] Rizzoni, G., A Practical Introduction to Electronic Instrumentation, Kendall-Hunt, 1989

Chapter 2 problem solutions

EIT 2.1

a) Energy = Power × time

$$= (1A)(12V)(120hr)\left(\frac{60\,\text{min}}{hr}\right)\left(\frac{60\,\text{sec}}{\text{min}}\right)$$

$$\boxed{w = 5.184 \times 10^6 \text{ J}}$$

b) Assume that 150 W is the combined power rating of both lights; then,

$$w_{used} = (150W)(8hrs)\left(\frac{3600\,\text{sec}}{hr}\right)$$

$$= 4.32 \times 10^6 \text{ J}$$

$$\boxed{w_{stored} = w - w_{used} = 864 \times 10^3 \text{ J}}$$

EIT 2.2

a) Q = area under the current-time curve

$$Q = \int I dt$$

$$Q = \frac{1}{2}(4)(30)(60) + \frac{1}{2}(2)(90)(60) + $$

$$+ \frac{1}{2}(4)(60)(60) + 6(30)(60) + $$

$$4(90)(60)$$

$$= 48{,}600 \text{ C}$$

$$\boxed{Q = 48{,}600 \text{ C}}$$

b) $\frac{dw}{dt} = P$

$$w = \int p dt = \int v i dt$$

$v = 9 + \frac{3}{10800} t$ V $\quad 0 \le t \le 10800$ s

$i_1 = 10 - \frac{4}{1800} t$ A $\quad 0 \le t \le 1800$ s

$i_2 = 6\frac{2}{3} - \frac{2}{5400} t$ A $\quad 1800 \le t \le 7200$ s

$i_3 = 12 - \frac{4}{3600} t$ A $\quad 7200 \le t \le 10800$ s

where $i = i_1 + i_2 + i_3$

Therefore,

$$w = \int_0^{1800} v i_1 dt + \int_{1800}^{7200} v i_2 dt + \int_{7200}^{10800} v i_3 dt$$

$$= \left(90t + \frac{t^2}{720} - \frac{t^2}{100} - \frac{t^3}{4.86 \times 10^6}\right)\Bigg|_0^{1800}$$

$$+ \left(60t + \frac{t^2}{1080} - \frac{t^2}{600} - \frac{t^3}{29.16 \times 10^6}\right)\Bigg|_{1800}^{7200}$$

$$+ \left(108t + \frac{t^2}{600} - \frac{t^2}{200} - \frac{t^3}{9.72 \times 10^6}\right)\Bigg|_{7200}^{10800}$$

$$= 132.9\times10^3 + 380.8\times10^3 - 105.4\times10^3$$

$$+ 648\times10^3 - 566.4\times10^3$$

$$\boxed{\text{Energy} = 489.9 \text{ kJ}}$$

2.3

a) $i = \frac{4\times10^{-3}t}{1}$

$$Q_1 = \int_0^1 i\,dt = \int_0^1 4\times10^{-3}\,t\,dt$$

$$Q_1 = 4\times10^{-3}\frac{t^2}{2}\Big|_0^1 = 2\times10^{-3}\frac{amp}{\sec} = 2\times10^{-3}\ Coulombs$$

b) The charge transferred from $t=1$ to $t=2$ is the same as from $t=0$ to $t=1$.

$Q_2 = 4\times10^{-3}\ Coulombs$

The charge transferred from $t=2$ to $t=3$ is the same in magnitude and opposite in direction to that from $t=1$ to $t=2$.

$Q_3 = 2\times10^{-3}\ Coulombs$

$t = 4$

$$Q_4 = 2\times10^{-3} - \int_3^4 4\times10^{-3}\,dt$$

$$= 2\times10^{-3} - 4\times10^{-3}$$

$$= -2\times10^{-3}\ Coulombs$$

$t = 5,6,7$

$$Q_5 = -2\times10^{-3} + \int_4^5 2\times10^{-3}dt = 0$$

$$Q_6 = 0 + \int_5^6 2\times10^{-3}dt = 2\times10^{-3}\ Coulomb$$

$$Q_7 = 2\times10^{-3} + \int_6^7 2\times10^{-3}dt = 4\times10^{-3}\ Coulombs$$

$t = 8,9,10s$

$Q = 4\times10^{-3}\,Coulombs$

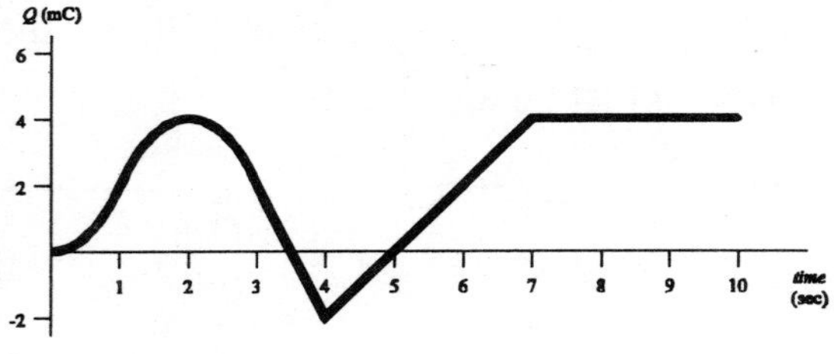

2.4

a) $100A\times1hr = \left(100\frac{C}{s}\right)(1hr)\left(3600\frac{s}{hr}\right)$

$= 360000\ C$

b) charge on electron $= 1.602\times10^{-19}\ C$

ॐ no. of electrons =

$$\frac{360\times10^3}{1.602\times10^{-19}} = 224.7\times10^{22}$$

2.5

$i = density(area)(velocity)q$

$$i_e = 2\times10^{19}\frac{e}{m^3}(50\times10^{-9}m^2)\left(0.5\times10^{-3}\frac{m}{s}\right)1.602\times10^{-19}\frac{C}{e}$$

$= 80pA$

$$i_h = \left(5\times10^{18}\frac{h}{m^3}\right)(50\times10^{-9}m^2)\left(0.2\times10^{-3}\frac{m}{s}\right)1.602\times10^{-19}\frac{C}{h}$$

$= 8pA$

a) Since $i_e > i_h$ the current is to the right (electron motion to the left)

b) $i_e - i_h = 72pA$

2.6

a) To find the charge delivered to the battery during the charge cycle we examine the charge-current relationship:

$$i = \frac{dq}{dt} \quad \text{or } dq = i\,dt$$

thus

$$Q = \int_{t_0}^{t_1} i(t)dt$$

$$Q = \int_0^{5hrs} 50mAdt + \int_{5hrs}^{10hrs} 20mAdt$$

$$= \int_0^{18000s} 0.05dt + \int_{18000}^{36000s} 0.02dt$$

$$= 900 + 360$$

$$= 1260C$$

b) To find the energy transferred to the battery, we examine the energy relationship

$$\frac{dw}{dt} = P \qquad dw = p(t)\,dt$$

$$w = \int_{t_0}^{t_1} p(t)dt = \int_{t_0}^{t_1} v(t)i(t)dt$$

observing that the energy delivered to the battery is the integral of the power over the charge cycle. Thus,

$$w = \int_0^5 0.05(1 + \frac{3t}{20})\,dt + \int_5^{10} 0.02(1 + \frac{t}{20})\,dt$$

$$= (0.05t + \frac{3}{800}t^2)\Big|_0^5 + (0.02t + \frac{1}{2000}t^2)\Big|_5^{10}$$

$$\boxed{w = 1732.5\ J}$$

EIT 2.7

Applying KCL at the node:

$$-i + 2 + 6 - 5 = 0$$

thus i = 3 A which means that a 3-A current is leaving the node.

2.8

Applying KCL at the node:

$$i + 6 - 5 + 2 = 0$$

thus i = -3 A which means that a 3-A current is leaving the node.

2.9

Applying KVL:

$$-5 + 3 + v_2 = 0 \Rightarrow v_2 = 2V$$

$$-5 + 3 - 10 + v_1 = 0 \Rightarrow v_1 = 12V$$

EIT 2.10

(a) Power delivered by source to load = power absorbed by load = 2×10 = 20 W

(b) P = (-9)×4 = -36 W; the source is actually absorbing power, thus the "load" must be a source!

2.11

Applying KVL:

$$-v + 11Ri + 11i = 0$$

therefore,

$$i = \frac{v}{11R + 11} = \frac{110}{11R + 11} = \frac{10}{R + 1}$$

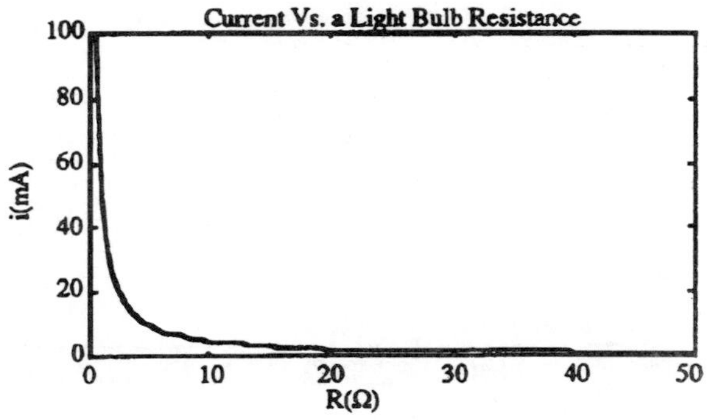

2.12

$$P = i \times v = i^2R = \frac{v^2}{R} = \frac{144}{3000} = 48 \text{ mW}$$

EIT 2.13

For circuit element A,

$$P = vi = (100V)(-12A) = -1200 \text{ W}$$

Therefore, circuit element A supplies 1200W to element B which dissipates (or absorbs) 1200W.

2.14

Element A:

$$P = - vi = -(-12 \text{ V})(25 \text{ A}) = 300 \text{ W}$$

(dissipating)

Element B:

$P = vi = (15 \text{ V})(25 \text{ A}) = 375 \text{ W}$ (dissipating)

Element C:

$P = vi = (27 \text{ V})(25 \text{ A}) = 675 \text{ W}$ (supplying)

2.15

Power absorbed by $R = (10 \text{ V})(3 \text{ A}) = 30 \text{ W}$

From Problem 2.9, $v_1 = 12V$. Therefore,

Power delivered by the current source =

$$(12 \text{ V})(3 \text{ A}) = 36 \text{ W}$$

2.16

By KCL, the current through element B is 5A, to the right.

By KVL, $-v_a - 3 + 10 + 5 = 0$.

Therefore, the voltage across element A is $v_a = 12V$ (positive at the top).

A supplies (12 V)(5 A) = 60 W

B supplies (3 V)(5 A) = 15 W

C absorbs (5 V)(5 A) = 25 W

D absorbs (10 V)(3 A) = 30 W

E absorbs (10 V)(2 A) = 20 W

Total power supplied = 60W + 15W = 75W

Total power absorbed = 25W + 30W + 20W

= 75W

Tot. power supplied = Tot. power absorbed

$\therefore$conservation of power is satisfied.

EIT 2.17

Headlight no. 1:

$$P = v\times i = 50\text{ W} = \frac{v^2}{R}$$

or,

$$R = \frac{v^2}{50} = \frac{144}{50} = 2.88\ \Omega$$

Headlight no. 2:

$$P = v\times i = 75\text{ W} = \frac{v^2}{R}$$

or,

$$R = \frac{v^2}{75} = 1.92\ \Omega.$$

The total resistance is given by the parallel combination:

$$\frac{1}{R_{TOTAL}} = \frac{1}{2.88\Omega} + \frac{1}{1.92\Omega}$$

or $R_{TOTAL} = 1.15\ \Omega$

2.18

The resistance corresponding to a 50-W headlight is

$$R_{50W} = \frac{v^2}{50} = \frac{144}{50} = 2.88\ \Omega$$

For each 10-W tail light we compute the resistance:

$$p = v\times i = 10\text{ W} = \frac{v^2}{R_{10W}}$$

or,

$$R_{10W} = \frac{v^2}{10} = \frac{144}{10} = 14.4\ \Omega$$

Therefore, the total resistance is computed as:

$$\frac{1}{R_{TOTAL}} = \frac{1}{2.88\Omega} + \frac{1}{2.88\Omega} + \frac{1}{14.4\Omega} + \frac{1}{14.4\Omega}$$

or $R_{TOTAL} = 1.2\ \Omega$

2.19

The current flowing clockwise in the series circuit is $i = \frac{20V}{20\Omega} = 1A$

The voltage across the 5 ✦ resistor, positive on the left, is $v_{5\Omega} = (1A)(5\Omega) = 5V$

Therefore, $P_{5\Omega} = (5V)(1A) = 5W$

2.20

(a) Using $I = \frac{15}{30+20}$ (clockwise current) :

$$I_1 = -0.3 \text{ A}; I_2 = 0.3 \text{ A}; V_1 = 6 \text{ V}$$

(b) The voltage across the 20 Ω resistor is $\frac{20}{4} = 5$ V; since the current flows from top to bottom, the polarity of this voltage is positive on top. Then it follows that

$$V_1 = 5 \text{ V, and } I_2 = -\frac{5}{30} = -0.167 \text{ A}$$

(the negative sign follows from the direction of I_2 in the drawing).

(c) Since -0.5A pointing upward is the same current as 0.5A pointing downward, the voltage across the 30 Ω resistor is

$$V_{30} = 15 \text{ V (positive on top);}$$

and $I_2 = \frac{15}{20} = 0.75$ A,

since V_{30} is also the voltage across the 20 Ω resistor. Finally,

$$I_1 = -(I_2 + 0.5) = -1.25 \text{ A,}$$

and $V_1 = -30 I_1 + 15 = 52.5$ V.

EIT 2.21

$$P = vi = 8 \text{ mW} \qquad \text{(Eq. 1)}$$

also,

$$v_1 = 4000i = \frac{v}{8} \qquad \text{(Eq. 2)}$$

From Eq.1 and Eq.2, we obtain:

$$i = 0.5 \text{ mA and } v = 16 \text{ V}$$

Applying KVL for the loop:

$$-v + 2000i + 4000i + Ri + 8000i = 0$$

or,

$$0.0005R = 9$$

Therefore,

$$R = 18\text{k}\Omega \text{ and } v_1 = 2V$$

2.22

Since the 3 resistors must have equal currents,

$$I_{30\Omega} = \frac{1}{3} \, 2.5 \text{ A}$$

$$I_{30\Omega} = 0.833A$$

2.23

Define a voltage, v, across the parallel circuit (positive at the top). Then, by KCL,

$$\frac{v}{2\Omega}+\frac{v}{3\Omega}+\frac{v}{6\Omega}=36A$$

and $v = 36V$

Therefore,

$$I_{2\Omega}=\frac{36V}{2\Omega}=18A\downarrow$$

$$I_{3\Omega}=\frac{36V}{3\Omega}=12A\downarrow$$

$$I_{6\Omega}=\frac{36V}{6\Omega}=6A\downarrow$$

2.24

Applying KVL:

$$(7\Omega)i_1+(3\Omega)i_1=20V$$

$$\therefore i_1=2A$$

$$(30\Omega)i_2+(50\Omega)i_2+(20\Omega)i_2=20V$$

$$\therefore i_2=0.2A$$

EIT 2.25

Let us refer to the current (down) through the 30Ω resistor as I_2.

Applying KCL, we have

$$I_1 + I_2 = 10\text{ A} \qquad \text{(Eq.1)}$$

Also, applying KVL and Ohm's law, we have

$$15\, I_1 - 30\, I_2 = 0 \qquad \text{(Eq.2)}$$

Solving Eq.1 and Eq.2, we obtain

$$I_1 = \frac{20}{3}\text{ A} \quad \text{and} \quad I_2 = \frac{10}{3}\text{ A}$$

2.26

a) 10% worst case: low voltage

$R_2 = 9000\ \Omega$, $R_1 = 11000\ \Omega$

$$v_{OUT_{min}}=\frac{9000}{9000+11000}5=2.25V$$

10% worst case: high voltage

$R_2 = 11000\ \Omega$, $R_1 = 9000\ \Omega$

$$v_{OUT_{max}}=\frac{11000}{9000+11000}5=2.75V$$

b) 5% worst case: low voltage

$R_2 = 9500\ \Omega$, $R_1 = 10500\ \Omega$

$$v_{OUT_{min}}=\frac{9500}{9500+10500}5=2.375V$$

5% worst case: high voltage

$R_2 = 10500\ \Omega$, $R_1 = 9500\ \Omega$

$$v_{OUT_{max}}=\frac{10500}{9500+10500}5=2.625V$$

2.27

(a) $$20 = \frac{R_a}{R_a + 15{,}000}(50)$$

$$R_a\,(50 - 20) = 20(15)\times 10^3$$

$$R_a = 10k\Omega$$

$$P_a = I^2R = \left(\frac{50}{25000}\right)^2 (10{,}000) = 40 \text{ mW}$$

$$P_{R_a} = \frac{1}{8}W$$

$$P_1 = I^2R = 60 \text{ mW}$$

$$P_{R_1} = \frac{1}{8}W$$

(b) $$2.25 = 5\times\left(\frac{270}{270+R_b}\right)$$

$$R_b = 330\Omega$$

$$P_{R_b} = \frac{1}{8}W$$

$$P_{R_2} = \frac{1}{8}W$$

c) $$28.3 = 110\times\left(\frac{2.7\times10^3}{2.7\times10^3 + 1\times10^3 + R_c}\right)$$

$$R_c = 6.8k\Omega$$

$$P_{R_c} = 1W$$

$$P_{R_3} = \frac{1}{8}W$$

$$P_{R_4} = \frac{1}{2}W$$

EIT 2.28

a) The equivalent resistance seen by the source is

$$R = 2 + 6 + 4 = 12\Omega$$

b) Applying KVL:

$$-6 + 12\,i = 0$$

Therefore, i = 0.5 A.

c) $P = vi = 6 \times 0.5 = 3$ W.

d) Applying Ohm's law:

$v_1 = 6\,i = 3$ V and $v_2 = -4\,i = -2$ V.

e) P_{min}(for R_1)= $i^2R_1 = 1$ W.

2.29

Starting from the right side, we combine the two resistors in series.

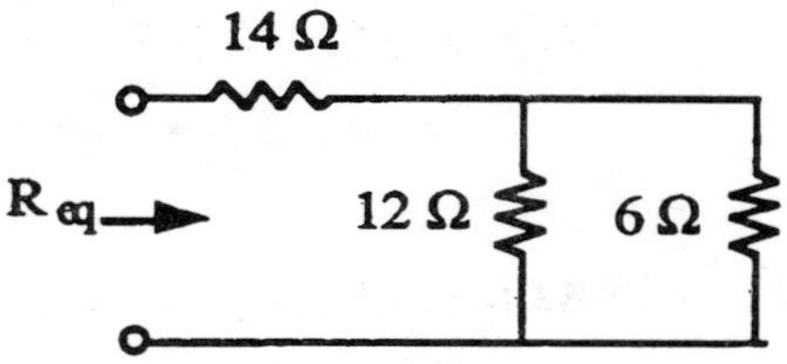

Then, we can combine the two parallel resistors, namely the 12 Ω resistor and 6 Ω resistor.

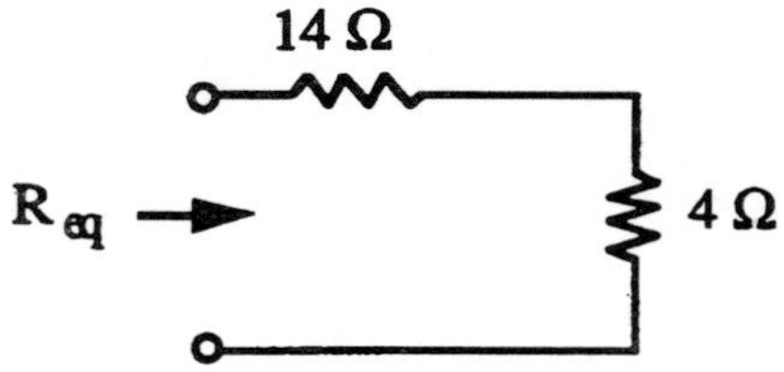

Therefore, $R_{eq} = 14 + 4 = 18\ \Omega$

2.30

$R_{EQ} = 2 + (9 \parallel 72) = 10\ \Omega$. Therefore,

$$i = \frac{9}{10} = 0.9 \text{ A}$$

By the current divider rule:

$$i_1 = \frac{72}{72+9}\, i = \frac{72}{81}(0.9) = 0.8 \text{ A.}$$

Also, since the 9 Ωand 72 Ω resistors are in parallel, we can conclude that

$$v = 9 i_1 = 7.2 \text{ V}$$

2.31

Step1: $(4 \parallel 4) + 22 = 24\ \Omega$

Step 2: $24 \parallel 8 = 6\ \Omega$

Therefore, the equivalent circuit is as shown below:

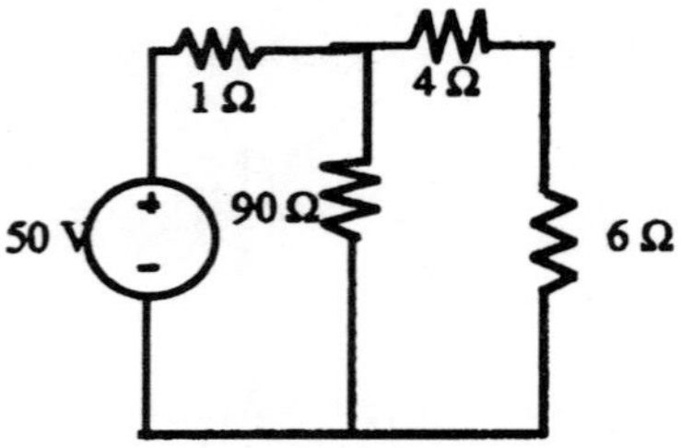

Further, $(4 + 6) \parallel 90 = 9$ ♦

The new equivalent circuit is shown below.

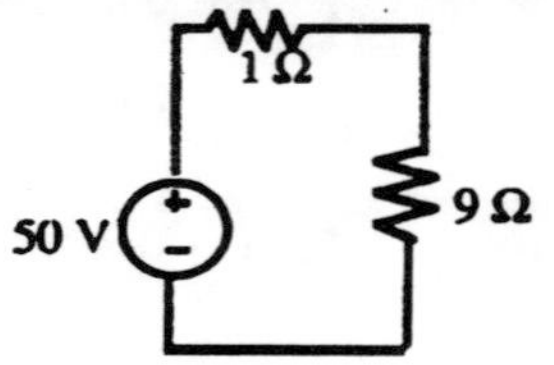

Thus, $R_{total} = 10\Omega$.

We can now find the current i by the current divider rule as follows:

$$i = \left(\frac{10}{10 + 90}\right)(5) = 0.5 \text{ A}$$

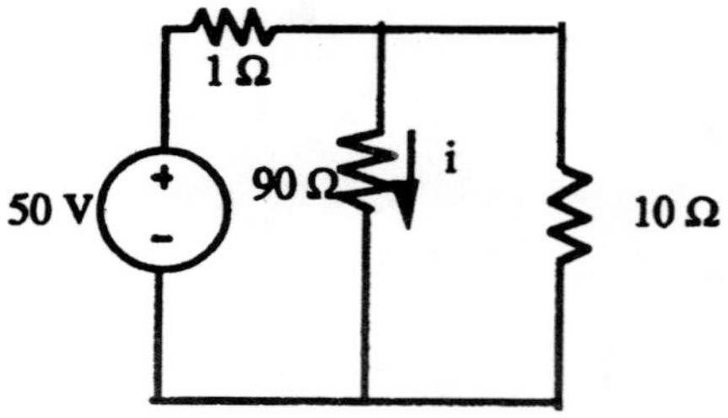

2.32

Combining the elements to the right of the 15 Ω resistor, we compute

$R_{eq} = ((4 \| 4) + 6) \| 24 + 4 = 10\ \Omega.$

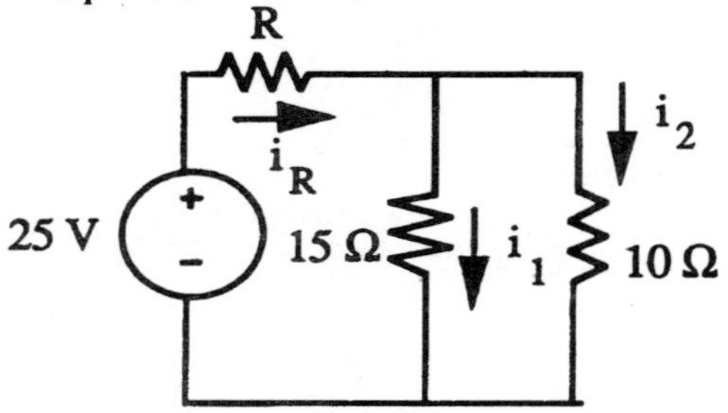

The power dissipated by the 15-Ω resistor is

$$P_{15\Omega} = \frac{v^2}{15} = 15\text{ W},$$

therefore,

$v_{15\Omega} = 15$ V and $i_1 = 1$ A.

Using the current divider rule:

$$i_2 = \frac{15}{10}(i_1) = 1.5\text{ A}.$$

Applying KCL, we can find i_R:

$$i_R = i_1 + i_2 = 2.5\text{ A}.$$

Using KVL:

$$-25 + 2.5R + 15 = 0$$

Therefore, R = 4Ω.

2.33

$2\Omega + 2\Omega = 4\Omega$

$6\Omega \| 12\Omega = 4\Omega$

$4\Omega \| 4\Omega = 2\Omega$

$4\Omega \| 4\Omega = 2\Omega$

$2\Omega + 2\Omega = 4\Omega$

$R_{eq} = 3\Omega + 4\Omega \| 4\Omega = 5\Omega$

2.34

(a)

$2\Omega + 1\Omega = 3\Omega$

$3\Omega \| 3\Omega = 1.5\Omega$

$4\Omega + 1.5\Omega + 5\Omega = 10.5\Omega$

$10.5\Omega \| 6\Omega = 3.818\Omega$

$R_{eq} = 3.818\Omega + 7\Omega = 10.818\Omega$

(b)

$$I = \frac{14V}{10.818\Omega} = 1.29A$$

$$P = (14V)(1.29A) = 10.12W$$

2.35

With terminals c-d open, R_{eq}= 400 Ω;
with terminals c-d shorted, R_{eq}= 390 Ω;
with terminals a-b open, R_{eq}= 360 Ω;
with terminals a-b shorted, R_{eq}= 351 Ω;

2.36

a) $R_{th}(T) = 100\, e^{-0.1T}$

b) $R_{eq}(T) = R_{th}(T) \| 100\ \Omega = \dfrac{100\, e^{-0.1T}}{1 + e^{-0.1T}}$

The two plots are shown below.

Thermistor Resistance vs. Temperature

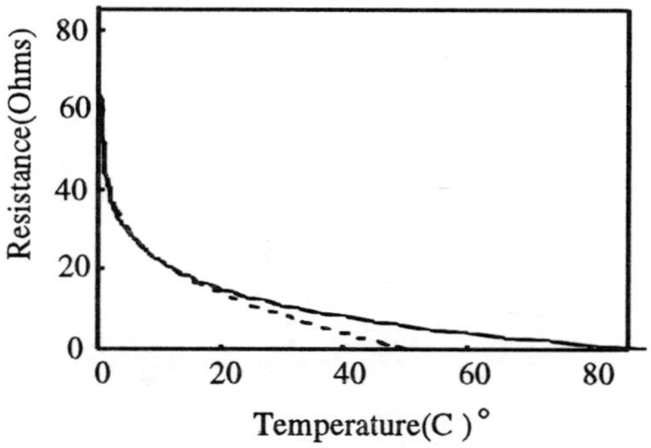

In the above plot, the solid line is for the thermistor alone; the dashed line is for the thermistor-resistor combination.

EIT 2.37

(a) $R_{Total} = 100\, e^{10} = 2.203\ M\Omega$ (Eq.1)

therefore,

$$v_{out}(x) = \frac{R(x)}{R_{Total}}(10)$$

$$= \frac{1000\, e^{x}}{2.203(10^{6})} =$$

$$\frac{e^{x}}{2203} \qquad \text{(Eq.2)}$$

b) $v_{out}(x) = 4$ V will therefore lead to:

$$e^{x} = 4\times 2203 = 8812$$

$$x = \log_e(8812) = 9.08\ \text{cm}$$

2.38

KCL at node 1 requires that

$$\frac{V_1}{R_2} + \frac{V_1 - 10\ V}{R_3} - 2\ A = 0$$

Solving for V_1 we have

$$V_1 = 11\ V$$

Therefore,

$$I_1 = \frac{-V_1}{R_2} = \frac{-11}{6}\ A$$

$$I_2 = \frac{10 - V_1}{R_3} = \frac{-1}{6}\ A$$

and the power delivered by the 2-A source is

$$P_{2\text{-}A} = (V_{2\text{-}A})(2)$$

Thus, we can compute the voltage across the 2-A source as

$$V_{2\text{-}A} = 2\times R_1 + V_1 = 2\times 32 + 11 = 75\ V$$

Thus,

$$P_{2\text{-}A} = (75)(2) = 150\ W$$

Similarly, the power supplied by the 10-V source is

$$P_{10\text{-}V} = (10)(I_{10\text{-}V})$$

We have $I_{10\text{-}V} = \frac{10}{R_4} + I_2 = 33.3$ mA,

thus

$$P_{10\text{-}V} = (10)(I_{10\text{-}V}) = 0.333\ W$$

Since the power dissipated equals the total power supplied:

$$P_{diss} = 150 + 0.333 = 150.333\ W$$

2.39

$$i = \frac{10V}{30\Omega} = \frac{1}{3}\text{ A}$$

$$i_{source} = 3\left(\frac{1}{3}A\right) = 1\text{ A}$$

The voltage across the dependent source (+ ref. taken at the top) can be found by KVL:

$$-V_D + (1A)(10\Omega) + 10V = 0$$

$$\therefore V_D = 20\text{ V}$$

$$P = (20V)(1A) = 20\text{ W}$$

2.40

By KCL,

$$\frac{v_{ab} - v_i}{10k\Omega} + \frac{v_{ab} - v_o}{20k\Omega} = 0$$

But $\quad v_{ab} = -\dfrac{v_o}{200{,}000}$

$$\therefore -\frac{v_o}{200{,}000}\left(\frac{1}{10k\Omega} + \frac{1}{20k\Omega}\right) - \frac{v_i}{10k\Omega} + \frac{v_o}{20k\Omega} = 0$$

or

$$v_i = -\left[\frac{v_o}{200{,}000}(1.5) + 0.5v_o\right]$$

$$= -0.5000025v_o$$

$$\therefore \frac{v_o}{v_i} \approx -2$$

2.41

a) $I_L = \dfrac{10}{0.05 + 0.45} = 20\text{ A}$

$$P_{Load} = I^2R_L = 180\text{ W}$$

b) With another source in the circuit we must find the new power dissipated by the load. To do so we write KVL twice using mesh currents to obtain 2 equations in 2 unknowns:

$$I_x(0.15) - I_y(0.05) = 0$$

$$-I_x(0.05) + I_y(0.5) = 10\text{ V}$$

Solving the above equations gives us

$$I_y = I_L = 20.69\text{ A}$$

$$P_{Load} = I^2R_L = 192.6\text{ W}$$

This is an increase of 7.0%

EIT 2.42

a) $\quad V_{out} = \left(\dfrac{10}{10 + r_B}\right)V_{oc}$

$$r_B = 10\left(\frac{V_{oc}}{V_{out}} - 1\right) = 10\left(\frac{1.64}{1.63} - 1\right)$$

$$= 0.061\Omega$$

b) $\quad r_B = 10\left(\dfrac{V_{oc}}{V_{out}} - 1\right) = 10\left(\dfrac{1.6}{0.17} - 1\right)$

$$= 84.1\Omega$$

2.43

We desire R_1, R_2, R_3 such that $I_a = 50$ mA for I = 1 mA, 10 mA, and 100 mA, respectively. We use conductances to simplify the arithmetic:

$$G_a = \frac{1}{R_a} = \frac{1}{2000} \text{ S} \quad G_{1,2,3} = \frac{1}{R_{1,2,3}}$$

By the current divider rule

$$I_a = \frac{G_a}{G_a + G_x} I$$

or

$$G_x = G_a\left(\frac{I}{I_a}\right) - G_a \text{ or } \frac{1}{G_x} = \frac{1}{G_a}\left(\frac{I_a}{I - I_a}\right)$$

$$R_x = R_a\left(\frac{I_a}{I - I_a}\right)$$

And we can construct the following table:

x	I	R_x(Approx.)
1	10^{-3} A	105 Ω
2	10^{-2} A	10 Ω
3	10^{-1} A	1 Ω

EIT 2.44

a) Assuming that $r_a \ll 10$ kΩ

$$i \approx \frac{10}{10000} = 1 \text{ mA}$$

b) With the same assumption as in part a)

$$i_{meter} = 0.43(10)^{-3} = \frac{R_p}{r_a + R_p}(1¢10^{-3})$$

or

$$0.43 = \frac{7}{r_a + 7}$$

Therefore, $r_a = 9.28\ \Omega$

2.45

Using the voltage divider rule:

$$V = 9.89 = \frac{r_m}{r_m + R_s}(10)$$

Therefore, $r_m = 899$ kΩ

2.46

By voltage division:

$$V = \frac{r_m}{r_m + R_s}(10)$$

R_s	V
$0.1r_m$	9.09 V
$0.3r_m$	7.69 V
$0.5r_m$	6.67 V
r_m	5 V
$3r_m$	2.5 V
$5r_m$	1.67 V
$10\ r_m$	0.91 V

For a voltmeter, we always desire

$$r_m \gg R_s$$

2.47

We develop first an expression for V_{R3} in terms of R_3. Next, using current division:

$$I_{R_3} = I_S\left(\frac{R_S}{R_S + R_1 + R_2 + R_3}\right)$$

$$V_{R_3} = I_{R_3}R_3$$

$$= \frac{R_3 R_S I_S}{R_S + R_1 + R_2 + R_3}$$

$$= \frac{9000V}{R_3 + 150k\Omega}$$

$$= 5.996V$$

a) $V_{R_3} = 5.996V$

b) $V_{R_3} = 59.6V$

c) $V_{R_3} = 562.5V$

d) $V_{R_3} = 3600V$

Now we must find the voltage drop across R3 with a 97 kΩ resistor across R3. This is the voltage that the voltmeter will read.

a)

$$V_{R_3} = R_3\|97\times10^3\left(\frac{9000}{R_3\|97\times10^3 + 150\times10^3}\right)$$

$$= 5.990V$$

b) $V_{R_3} = 59V$

c) $V_{R_3} = 512.9V$

d) $V_{R_3} = 2224V$

EIT 2.48

First we should find an expression for the current through R3 in terms of R3 and the meter resistance, R_m.

By the voltage divider rule we have:

$$V1 = \frac{R_1||(R_2 + R_3 + R_m)V_S}{R_1||(R_2 + R_3 + R_m) + R_S}$$

and

$$I_{R3} = \frac{V_1}{R_2 + R_m + R_3}$$

Therefore,

$$I_{R3} =$$

$$\frac{R_1||(R_2 + R_3 + R_m)V_S}{R_1||(R_2 + R_3 + R_m) + R_S} \quad \frac{1}{(R_2 + R_3 + R_m)}$$

$$= \frac{1000||(100 + R_3 + R_m)V_S}{1000||(100 + R_m + R_S) + 10} \times \frac{1}{100 + R_3 + R_m}$$

Using the above equation will give us the following table:

	with meter in circuit	without meter in circuit
a	8.61 mA	8.92 mA
b	39.6 mA	47.2 mA
c	61.9 mA	82.6 mA
d	65.6 mA	89.3 mA

2.49

With the full scale movement deflection current and voltage we can use Ohm's law to find the internal resistance.

$$R_m = \frac{V_m}{I_m} = \frac{0.01}{0.0005} = 20\Omega$$

Now we note that the meter acts as a voltage divider. The relationship at full scale is as shown below.

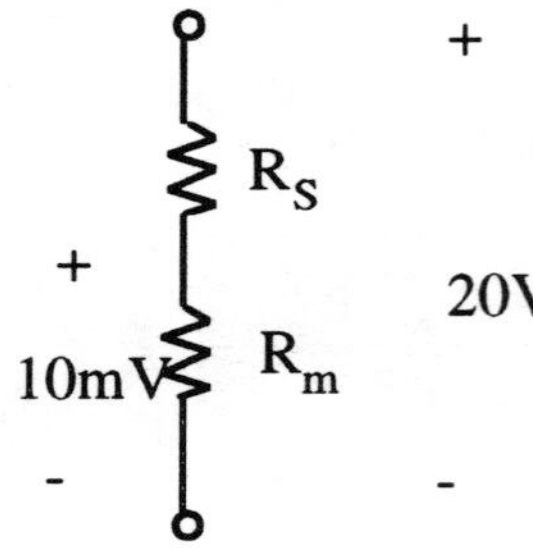

Therefore

$$0.01 = 20\left(\frac{R_m}{R_m + R_S}\right)$$

$$0.01(R_m+R_S) = 20R_m$$

$$R_S = \frac{20 - 0.01}{0.01} R_m$$

$$R_S = 39.98k\Omega$$

EIT 2.50

The full scale movement deflection rating, permits computation of the meter resistance by Ohm's law:

$$R_m = \frac{V_m}{I_m} = \frac{10\text{ mV}}{0.5\text{ mA}} = 20\Omega$$

Now we note that the meter acts as a current divider as shown below (for full scale currents).

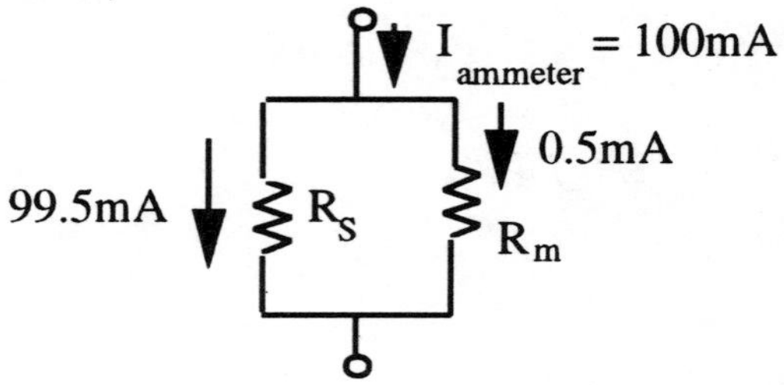

By current division:

$$I_m = \frac{R_s}{R_s + R_m} I_{ammeter}$$

Therefore,

$$5 \times 10^{-4}(R_s + 20) - R_s(100\times10^{-3}) = 0$$

or

$$R_s = 0.1005\ \Omega$$

2.51

Assuming an ideal voltmeter, the equivalent circuit of the wattmeter reduces to the one shown below.

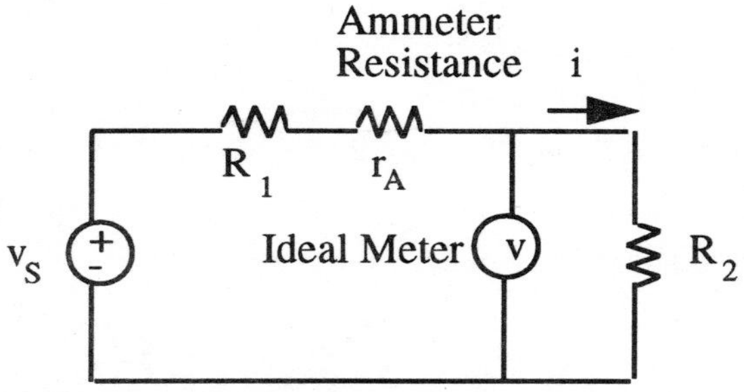

a) Applying KVL:

$$v_S = (R_1 + r_A + R_2)i$$

or

$$i = \frac{v_s}{R_1 + r_A + R_2}$$

$$p_{meter} = i^2 r_a = \left(\frac{v_s}{R_1 + r_a + R_2}\right)^2 r_A$$

b) The ideal power measurement ($r_A = 0$) corresponds to:

$$i = \frac{v_s}{R_1 + R_2}$$

$$P_{ideal} = i^2 R_2$$

$$= \left(\frac{v_s}{R_1 + R_2}\right)^2 R_2 =$$

$$\frac{10000}{(10050)^2}(v_s)^2$$

The actual power measurement (with r_A = 1.2 kΩ) is:

$$P_{actual} = i^2 r_A = \left(\frac{v_s}{R_1 + r_A + R_2}\right)^2 r_A$$

$$= \frac{10000}{(11250)^2}(v_s)^2$$

$$\%Error = \left(1 - \frac{P_{ideal}}{P_{actual}}\right) \times 100 = 25.3\%$$

2.52

(a) $\frac{(25V)^2}{R_L} = 5W \Rightarrow R_L = 125\Omega$

$v_s = 25.5V$, the open-circuit voltage

$$\frac{R_L}{R_S + R_L} v_S = 25 \Rightarrow \frac{125}{R_S 125} 25.5 = 25$$

$$\therefore R_S = \frac{(125)(25.5)}{25} - 125 = 2.5\Omega$$

(b)

$$v = \frac{R_L}{R_S + R_L} v_S = \frac{10}{2.5 + 10} 25.5 = 20.4V$$

(c) $i_{sc} = \frac{v_S}{R_S} = \frac{25.5V}{2.5\Omega} = 10.2A$

2.53

(a) For the parallel connection,

$P = 1500W$. Therefore,

$$1500 = \frac{(120)^2}{R_1} + \frac{(120)^2}{R_2}$$

$$= (120)^2\left(\frac{1}{R_1} + \frac{1}{R_2}\right)$$

or $$\frac{1}{R_1} + \frac{1}{R_2} = 0.104$$

For the series connection, $P = 200W$.

Therefore,

$$200 = \frac{(120)^2}{R_1 + R_2}$$

or $$\frac{1}{R_1 + R_2} = 0.01389$$

Solving, we find that $R_1 = 60.5\Omega$ and $R_2 = 11.43\Omega$.

(b) The power dissipated by R_1 alone is

$$P_{R_1} = \frac{(120)^2}{R_1} = 238W$$

and the power dissipated by R_2 alone is

$$P_{R_2} = \frac{(120)^2}{R_2} = 1260W$$

Chapter 3 Instructor Notes

Chapter 3 presents the principal topics in the analysis of resistive (DC) circuits. The presentation of node voltage and mesh current analysis is supported by several solved examples and drill exercises, with emphasis placed on developing consistent solution methods, and on reinforcing the use of a systematic approach. The aim of this style of presentation, which is perhaps more detailed than usual in a textbook written for a non-majors audience, is to develop good habits early on, with the hope that the orderly approach presented in Chapter 3 will facilitate the discussion of AC and transient analysis. A brief discussion of the principle of superposition precedes the discussion of Thèvenin and Norton equivalent circuits. Again, the presentation is rich in examples and drill exercises, because the concept of equivalent circuits will be heavily exploited in the analysis of AC and transient circuits in later chapters.

After a brief discussion of maximum power transfer, the chapter closes with a section on nonlinear circuit elements and load-line analysis. This section can be easily skipped in a survey course, and may be picked up later, in conjunction with Chapter 7, if the instructor wishes to devote some attention to load-line analysis of diode circuits. Finally, those instructors who are used to introducing the op-amp as a circuit element, will find that sections 11.1 and 11.2 can be covered together with Chapter 3, and that a good complement of homework problems and exercises devoted to the analysis of the op-amp as a circuit element is provided in Chapter 11.

The homework problems present a graded variety of circuit problems. Since the aim of this chapter is to teach solution techniques, there are relatively few problems devoted to applications. We should call the instructor's attention to a pair of problems on the Wheatstone bridge (3.40, 3.41), and to problem 3.53, which introduces thermistor circuits.

Chapter 3 problem solutions

3.1

Applying KCL at each of the two nodes, we obtain the following equations:

$$\frac{V_1}{3} + \frac{V_1 - V_2}{1} - 4 = 0$$

$$\frac{V_2}{2} + \frac{V_2}{2} + \frac{V_2 - V_1}{1} = 0$$

Rearranging the equations,

$$\frac{4}{3} V_1 - V_2 = 4$$

$$-V_1 + 2V_2 = 0$$

Solving the equations,

$$V_1 = 4.8 \text{ V and } V_2 = 2.4 \text{ V}$$

3.2

Applying KCL at each node, we obtain:

$$\frac{v_1 - 20}{30} + \frac{v_1}{20} + \frac{v_1 - v_2}{10} = 0$$

$$\frac{v_2}{30} + \frac{v_2}{30} + \frac{v_2 - v_1}{10} = 0$$

Rearranging the equations,

$$5.5v_1 - 3v_2 = 20$$

$$-3v_1 + 5v_2 = 0$$

Solving the two equations,

$$v_1 = 5.41 \text{ V and } v_2 = 3.24 \text{ V}$$

3.3

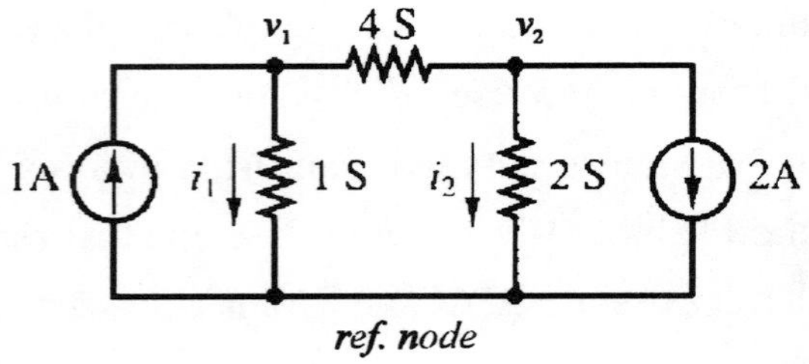

At node 1:

$$v_1(1+4) + v_2(-4) = 1$$

At node 2:

$$v_1(-4) + v_2(4+2) = -2$$

Solving, we find that

$$v_1 = -0.143V$$

$$v_2 = -0.428V$$

Then,

$$i_1 = v_1(1) = -0.143A$$

$$i_2 = v_2(2) = -0.856A$$

3.4

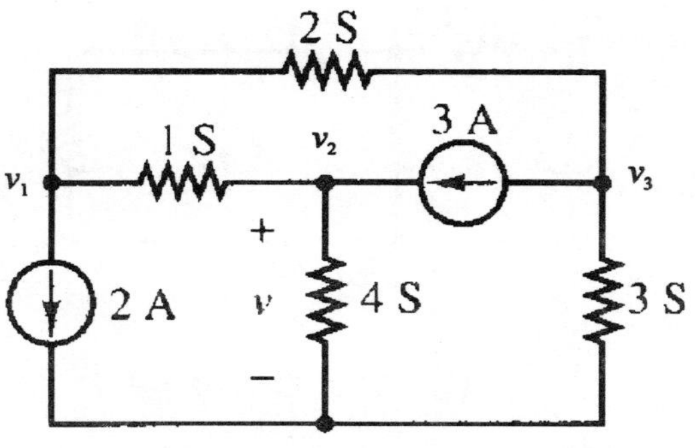

At node 1:

$$v_1(1+2) + v_2(-1) + v_3(-2) = -2$$

At node 2:

$$v_1(-1) + v_2(4+1) + v_3(0) = 3$$

At node 3:

$$v_1(-2) + v_2(0) + v_3(2+3) = -3$$

Solving for v_2, we find $v_2 = 0.34V$ and, therefore, $v = 0.34V$.

3.5

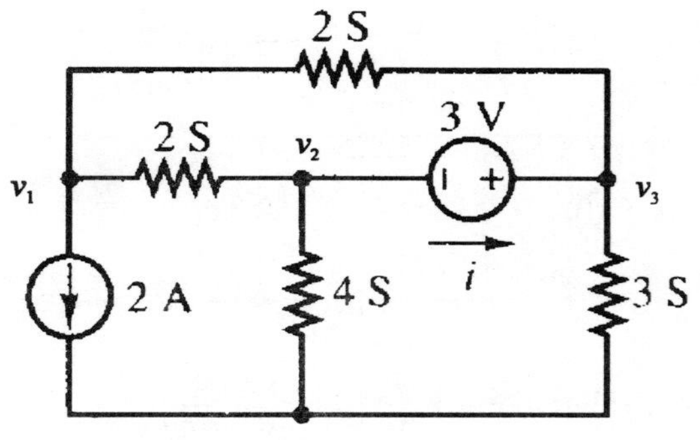

At node 1:

$$v_1(2+2) + v_2(-2) + v_3(-2) = -2$$

At the supernode:

$$v_1[-2+(-2)] + v_2(4+2) + v_3(2+3) = 0$$

For the voltage source:

$$v_1(0) + v_2(-1) + v_3(1) = 3$$

Solving for v_1 and v_3, we have

$$v_1 = -0.571V$$

$$v_3 = 1.428V$$

from which we find, by KCL, that

$$i = v_3(3+2) + v_1(-2) = 8.28A$$

3.6

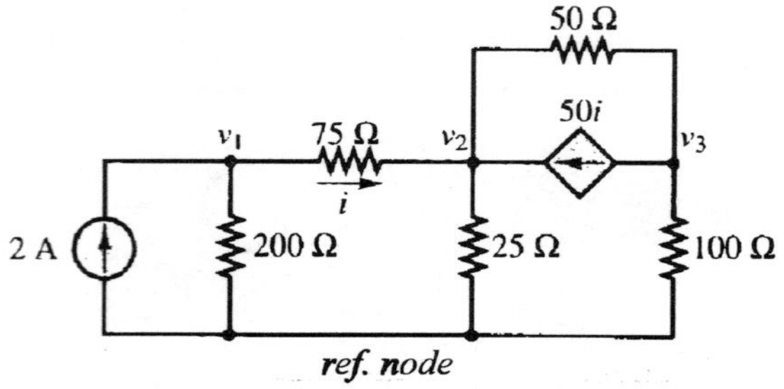

Note that $i = v_1\left(\frac{1}{75}\right) + v_2\left(-\frac{1}{75}\right)$

At node 1:

$$v_1\left(\frac{1}{200}+\frac{1}{75}\right) + v_2\left(-\frac{1}{75}\right) + v_3(0) = 2$$

At node 2:

$$v_1\left(-\frac{1}{75}\right) + v_2\left(\frac{1}{75}+\frac{1}{25}+\frac{1}{50}\right) + v_3\left(-\frac{1}{50}\right) = 50i$$

$$= v_1\left(\frac{50}{75}\right) + v_2\left(-\frac{50}{75}\right)$$

At node 3:

$$v_1(0) + v_2\left(-\frac{1}{50}\right) + v_3\left(\frac{1}{100}+\frac{1}{50}\right) = -50i$$

$$= v_1\left(-\frac{50}{75}\right) + v_2\left(\frac{50}{75}\right)$$

After some manipulation,

$$11v_1 - 8v_2 + 0v_3 = 1200$$

$$-408v_1 + 444v_2 - 12v_3 = 0$$

$$400v_1 - 412v_2 + 18v_3 = 0$$

Solving, we have

$$v_1 = 277.6V$$

$$v_2 = 231.7V$$

$$v_3 = -865.6V$$

3.7

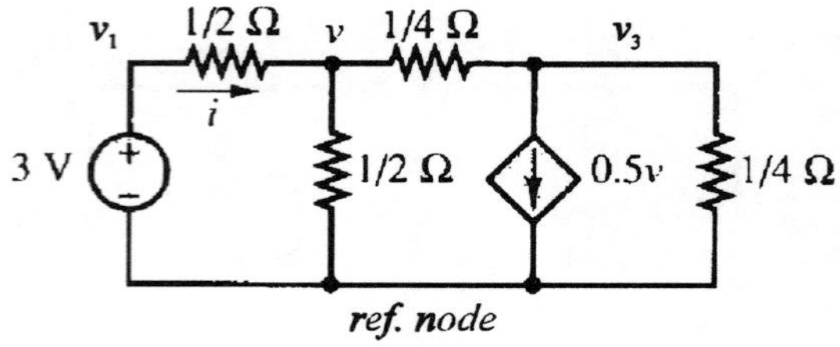

At node 1:

$$v_1(1) + v(0) + v_3(0) = 3$$

At node 2:

$$v_1(-2) + v(2+2+4) + v_3(-4) = 0$$

At node 3:

$$v_1(0) + v(-4) + v_3(4+4) = -0.5v$$

or

$$v_1(0) + v(-3.5) + v_3(4+4) = 0$$

Solving, we have

$$v_1 = 3V$$

$$v = 0.96V$$

from which

$$i = (3-0.96)2 = 4.08A$$

EIT 3.8

Using nodal analysis at the two nodes a and b, we write the equations

$$\frac{V_b - 15}{18} + \frac{V_b}{20} = 0$$

$$\frac{V_a - 15}{36} + \frac{V_a}{20} = 0$$

Rearranging the equations,

$$38\ V_b - 300 = 0$$

$$14\ V_a - 75 = 0$$

Solving for the two unknowns,

$$V_a = 5.36\text{ V and } V_b = 7.89\text{ V}$$

Therefore,

$$V_a - V_b = -2.54\text{ V}$$

EIT 3.9

KCL at node 1:

$$\frac{V_1}{R_I} + \frac{V_1 - V_s - V_2}{R_V} = 0.5$$

or

$$3\,V_1 - V_2 = 6 \qquad (\text{Eq. } 1)$$

KCL at node 2:

$$\frac{V_1 - V_s - V_2}{R_V} = \frac{V_2}{R_1 || (R_2 + R_L)}$$

or

$$14\,V_2 - 4\,V_1 = -16 \qquad (\text{Eq. } 2)$$

substitute Eq. 1 into Eq. 2

$$V_2 = -0.6316$$

and by voltage divider:

$$V_L = \left(\frac{R_L}{R_2 + R_L}\right) V_2 = -0.316V$$

$$P_L = \frac{V_L^2}{R_L} = 25mW$$

3.10

a) Using conductances, apply KCL at node 1:

$$(G_1 + G_{12} + G_{13})V_1 - G_{12}V_2 - G_{13}V_3 = I_s$$

Then apply KCL at node 2:

$$-G_{12}V_1 + (G_2 + G_{12} + G_{23})V_2 - G_{23}V_3 = 0$$

and at node 3:

$$-G_{13}V_1 - G_{23}V_2 + (G_3 + G_{13} + G_{23})V_3 = 0$$

Rewriting in the form

$$[G][V] = [I]$$

we have

$$\begin{bmatrix} G_1 + G_{12} + G_{13} & -G_{12} & -G_{13} \\ -G_{12} & G_2 + G_{12} + G_{23} & -G_{23} \\ -G_{13} & -G_{23} & G_3 + G_{13} + G_{23} \end{bmatrix} \begin{bmatrix} V_1 \\ V_2 \\ V_3 \end{bmatrix} = \begin{bmatrix} I_S \\ 0 \\ 0 \end{bmatrix}$$

b) The result is identical to that obtained in part a).

3.11

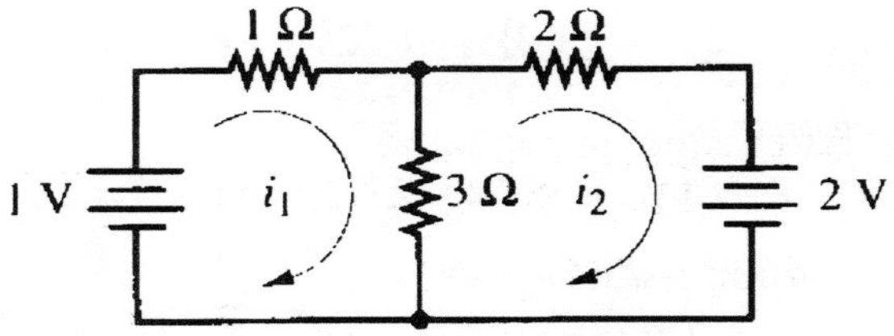

For mesh #1:

$$i_1(1+3) + i_2(-3)1$$

For mesh #2:

$$i_1(-3) + i_2(3+2) = -2$$

Solving,

$$i_1 = -0.091A$$
$$i_2 = -0.455A$$

EIT 3.12

Mesh #1 $(20 + 15 + 10)\ I_1\ - (10)\ I_2 = 0$

Mesh #2 $(10 + 40 + 10)\ I_2 - (10)\ I_1 = 50$

Therefore,

$I_1 = 0.1923$ A and $I_2 = 0.865$ A,

$v_{10\ \Omega} = 10(i_2 - i_1) = 6.727$ V (+ ref. at left)

3.13

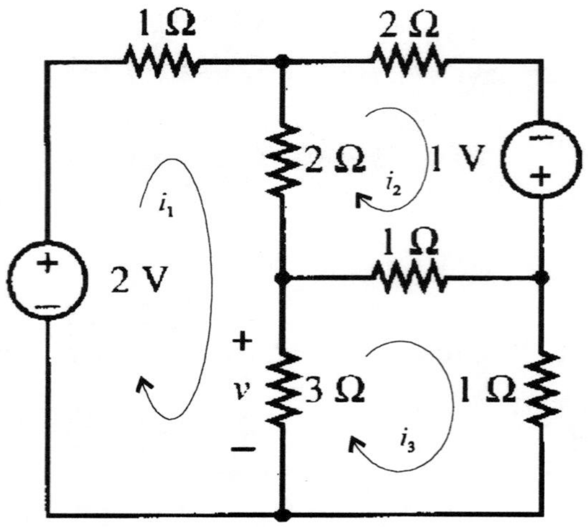

For mesh #1:

$$i_1(1+2+3)+i_2(-2)+i_3(-3)=2$$

For mesh #2:

$$i_1(-2)+i_2(2+2+1)+i_3(-1)=1$$

For mesh #3:

$$i_1(-3)+i_2(-1)+i_3(3+1+1)=0$$

Solving,

$$i_1 = 0.91A$$
$$i_3 = 0.69A$$

and $v = 3(i_1 - i_3) = 3(0.22) = 0.66V$

3.14

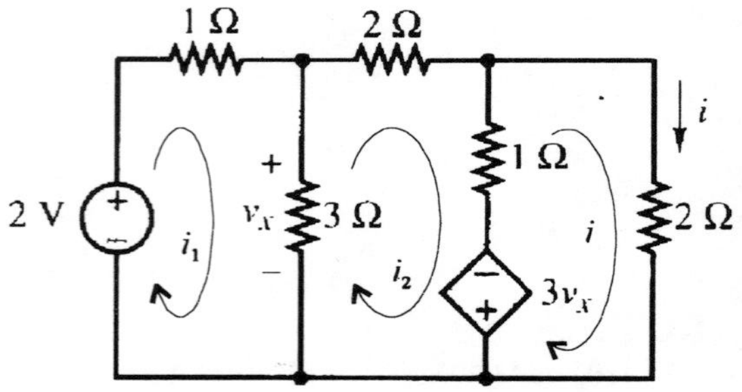

Note that $v_x = 3(i_1 - i_2)$

For mesh #1:

$$i_1(1+3)+i_2(-3)+i(0)=2$$

For mesh #2:

$$i_1(-3)+i_2(3+2+1)+i(-1)=3v_x$$
$$=9i_1-9i_2$$

or $\quad i_1(-12)+i_2(15)+i(-1)=0$

For mesh #3:

$$i_1(0)+i_2(-1)+i(2+1)=-3v_x$$
$$=-9i_1+9i_2$$

or $\quad i_1(9)+i_2(-10)+i(3)=0$

Solving, we find

$i = -0.508A$

3.15

Mesh #1

$(20 + 15 + 10)\ i_1 - 10\ i_2 - 15\ i_3 = 0$

Mesh #2

$-10\ i_1 + (10 + 40 + 10)\ i_2 - 40\ i_3 = 50$

Mesh #3

$-15\ i_1 - 40\ i_2 + (15 + 40 + 25)\ i_3 = 0$

Solving the system of equations:

$i_1 = 0.633$ A $\quad i_2 = 1.527$ A $\quad i_3 = 0.882$ A

Therefore,

$v_{40\ \Omega} = 40\ (i_2 - i_3) = 25.79$ V

3.16

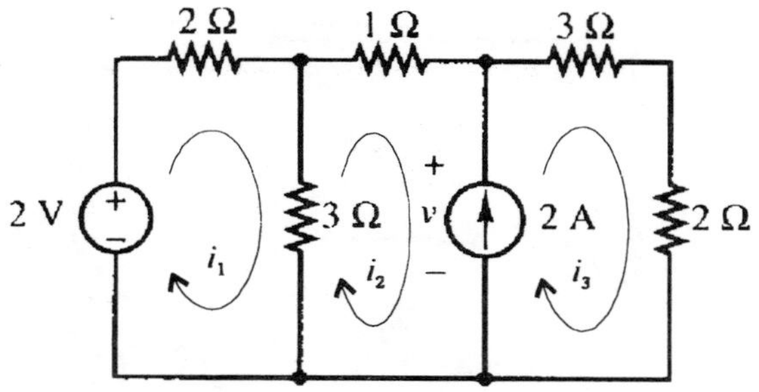

For mesh #1:

$$i_1(2+3)+i_2(-3)+i_3(0)=2$$

For meshes #2 and #3:

$$i_1(-3)+i_2(1+3)+i_3(3+2)=0$$

For the current source:

$$i_1(0)+i_2(1)+i_3(-1)=-2$$

Solving,

$$i_3 = 0.778A$$

and $\quad v = i_3(3+2) = 3.89V$

3.17

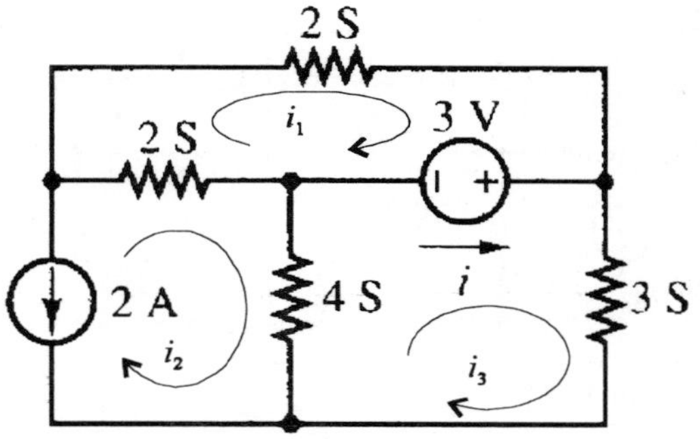

For mesh #1:

$$i_1\left(\frac{1}{2}+\frac{1}{2}\right)+i_2\left(-\frac{1}{2}\right)+i_3(0)=-3$$

For the current source:

$$i_1(0)+i_2(1)+i_3(0)=-2$$

For mesh #3:

$$i_1(0)+i_2\left(-\frac{1}{4}\right)+i_3\left(\frac{1}{4}+\frac{1}{3}\right)=3$$

Solving, we find

$$i_1 = -4A$$

$$i_3 = 4.29A$$

from which $\quad i = i_3 - i_1 = 8.29A$

3.18

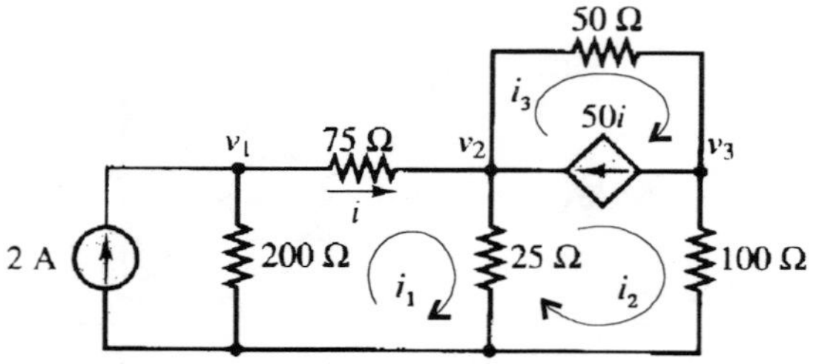

For mesh #1:

$$i_1(200+75+25)+i_2(-25)+i_3(0)=400$$

For meshes #2 and #3:

$$i_1(-25)+i_2(25+100)+i_3(50)=0$$

For the controlled source:

$$i_1(50)+i_2(1)+i_3(-1)=0$$

Solving for i_1, $\quad i_1 = 0.612A$

and, therefore, $\quad i = i_1 = 0.612A$

3.19

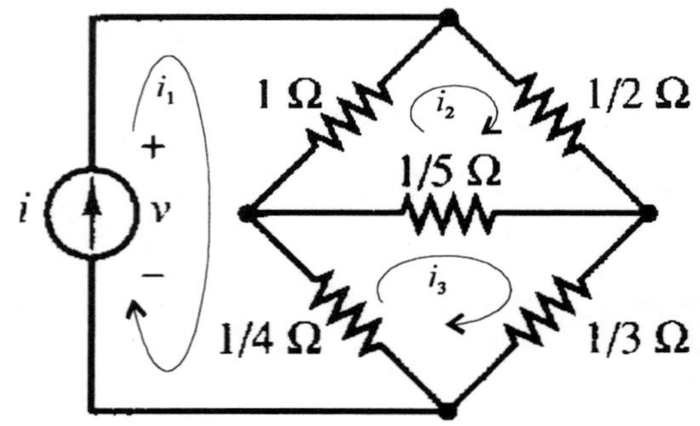

For mesh #1:

$$i_1(1)+i_2(0)+i_3(0)=i$$

For mesh #2:

$$i_1(-1)+i_2\left(1+\frac{1}{2}+\frac{1}{5}\right)+i_3\left(-\frac{1}{5}\right)=0$$

For mesh #3:

$$i_1\left(-\frac{1}{4}\right)+i_2\left(-\frac{1}{5}\right)+i_3\left(\frac{1}{4}+\frac{1}{3}+\frac{1}{5}\right)=0$$

Solving,

$$i_1 = i$$
$$i_2 = 0.645i$$
$$i_3 = 0.484i$$

Then,

$$v = 1(i_1 - i_2)+\frac{1}{4}(i_1 - i_3) = 0.484i$$

and

$$R=\frac{v}{i}=0.484\Omega$$

3.20

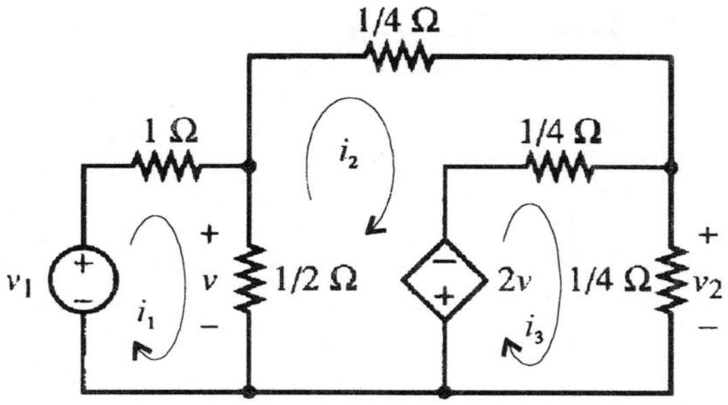

Note that $v = \dfrac{i_1 - i_2}{2}$

For mesh #1:

$$i_1\left(1+\frac{1}{2}\right)+i_2\left(-\frac{1}{2}\right)+i_3(0)=v_1$$

For mesh #2:

$$i_1\left(-\frac{1}{2}\right)+i_2\left(\frac{1}{2}+\frac{1}{4}+\frac{1}{4}\right)+i_3\left(-\frac{1}{4}\right)=2v$$

or

$$i_1(-1.5)+i_2(2)+i_3(-0.25)=0$$

For mesh #3:

$$i_1(0)+i_2\left(-\frac{1}{4}\right)+i_3\left(\frac{1}{4}+\frac{1}{4}\right)=-2v$$

or

$$i_1(1)+i_2(-1.25)+i_3(0.5)=0$$

Solving,

$$i_3=-0.16v_1$$

from which

$$v_2=\frac{1}{4}i_3=-0.04v_1$$

and

$$A_V=\frac{v_2}{v_1}=-0.04$$

EIT 3.21

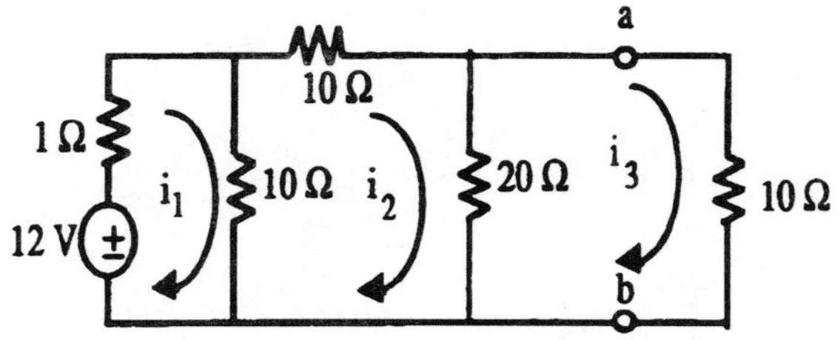

Using mesh analysis:

Mesh #1

$$(1+10)i_1 - 10i_2 = 12$$

Mesh #2

$$-10i_1 + (10+10+20)i_2 - 20i_3 = 0$$

Mesh #3

$$(20+10)i_3 - 20i_2 = 0$$

Rearranging and simplifying the equations,

$$11i_1 - 10i_2 = 12$$
$$-i_1 + 4i_2 - 2i_3 = 0$$
$$-2i_2 + 3i_3 = 0$$

Therefore,

$i_1 = 1.655$ A $\quad i_2 = 0.621$ A $\quad i_3 = 0.414$ A

$v_{1\Omega} = 1(i_1) = 1.655$ V (+ ref. at bottom)

3.22

Define mesh current i_1 (clockwise) equal to -I_x, and mesh current i_2 (clockwise) equal to I_2. Then:

$$(6+9)\,i_1 = -V_x$$
$$3\,i_2 = V_x - 12$$

Substitute the expression $V_x = 5(I_2 - I_x) = 5(i_2 + i_1)$ to obtain the equations

$$(6+9)\,i_1 = -5\,i_1 - 5\,i_2$$
$$3\,i_2 = 5\,i_1 + 5\,i_2 - 12$$

to obtain i_1=-4 A , i_2=16 A, and therefore I_x = 4 A and V_x =60 V.

EIT 3.23

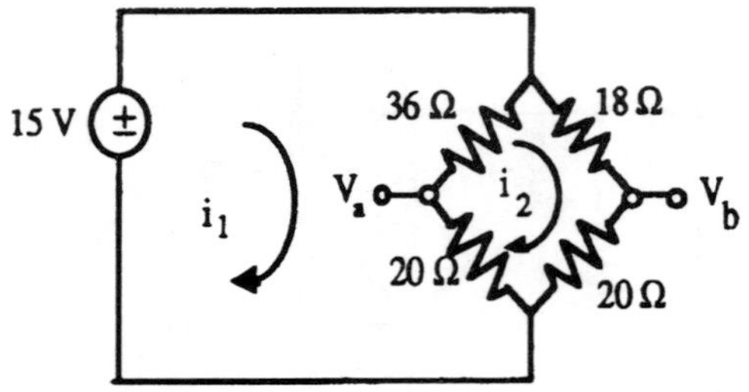

Using mesh analysis:

Mesh #1

$$(36 + 20)\, i_1 - (36 + 20)\, i_2 = 15$$

Mesh #2

$$-(36 + 20)\, i_1 + (36+20 +18 +20)\, i_2 = 0$$

Rearranging the equations:

$$56\, i_1 - 56\, i_2 = 15$$

$$-56\, i_1 + 94\, i_2 = 0$$

Therefore,

$$i_1 = 0.663 \text{ A} \quad i_2 = 0.395 \text{ A}$$

$$v_a = 20\,(i_1 - i_2) = 5.36 \text{ V}$$

$$v_b = 20\, i_2 = 7.895 \text{ V}$$

$v_a - v_b = -2.54$ V

***3.24**

a)

$$\begin{bmatrix} R_{12}+R_{13} & -R_{12} & -R_{13} \\ -R_{12} & R_{12}+R_2+R_{23} & -R_{23} \\ -R_{13} & -R_{23} & R_3+R_{13}+R_{23} \end{bmatrix} \begin{bmatrix} I_1 \\ I_2 \\ I_3 \end{bmatrix} = \begin{bmatrix} V_S \\ 0 \\ 0 \end{bmatrix}$$

b) same result as a).

3.25

By inspection, we can see that $V_T = V_{OC} =$ 10 V. To find R_T, we observe that in the circuit shown below $R_T = 0 \parallel 500 = 0\ \Omega$.

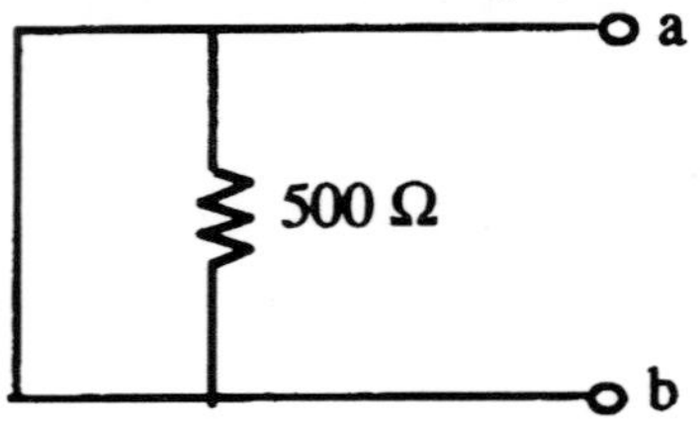

Therefore, the Thèvenin equivalent circuit is simply given by the voltage source, as shown below.

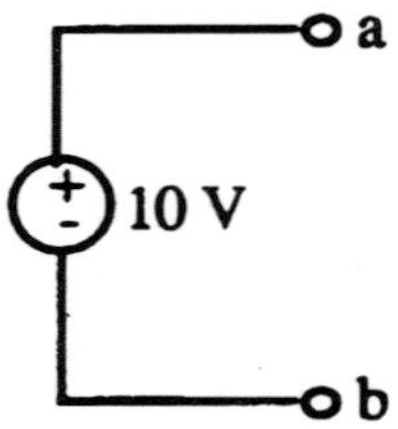

3.26

After removing the load: $I_{SC} = 1$A, $R_T = \infty$. Therefore, the equivalent circuit is as shown below. Note that the series 10Ω resistor does not appear in the equivalent circuit. This result is consistent with the definition of an *ideal* current source.

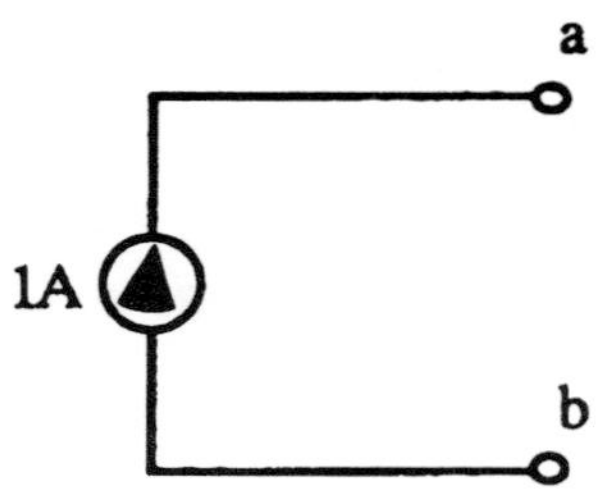

3.27

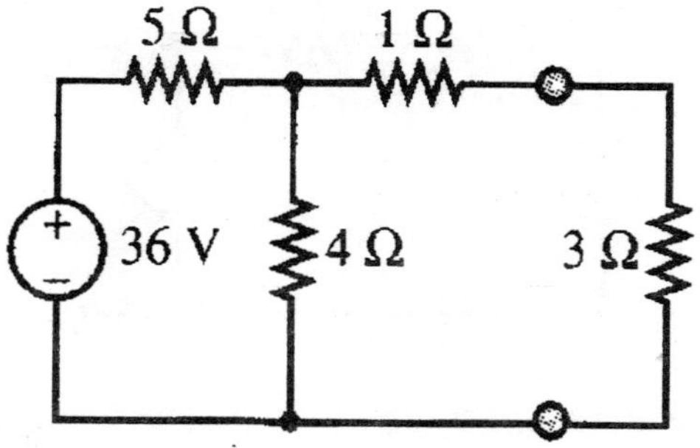

$$R_{TH} = 1\Omega + 4\Omega \| 5\Omega = 3.22\Omega$$

$$R_{TH} = 1 + \frac{1}{\frac{1}{5}+\frac{1}{4}} = 1 + \frac{20}{9}$$

$$= \frac{29}{9}\ \Omega = 3.222\ \Omega$$

Voltage divider gives

$$V = \left(\frac{4}{4+5}\right)36 = 16\text{ V}$$

KVL

$v_{oc} = -0(1) + v = v = 16$ V

3.28

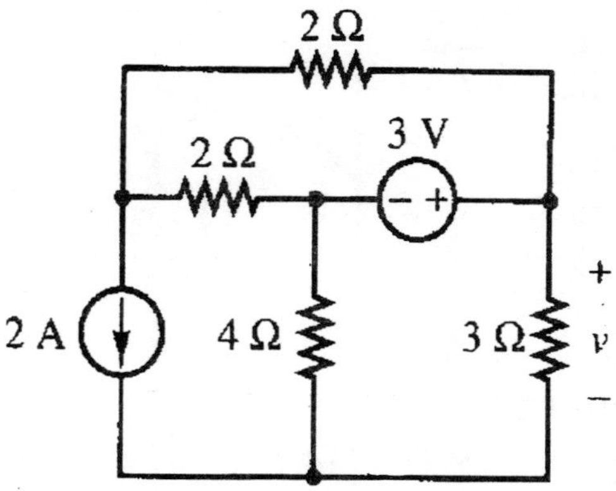

KVL: $v_3 = 3 + v_2$,

Find v_{oc} (3 Ω disconnected)

KCL Node 1:

$$2 + \frac{1}{2}(v_1 - v_2) + \frac{1}{2}[v_1 - (3 + v_2)] = 0$$

KCL Nodes 2 & 3:

$$\frac{1}{2}(v_2 - v_1) + \frac{1}{4}v_2 + \frac{1}{2}[(3 + v_2) - v_1] + 0 = 0$$

$$\left.\begin{aligned} 1v_1 - 1v_2 &= -\frac{1}{2} \\ -1v_1 + \frac{5}{4}v_2 &= -\frac{3}{2} \end{aligned}\right\} \Rightarrow \quad \begin{aligned} v_1 &= -\frac{17}{2} = -8.5\text{ V} \\ v_2 &= -8\text{ V} \Rightarrow v_{TH} = v_3 = v_2 + 3 = -5\text{ V} \end{aligned}$$

Set all independent sources to zero

$R_{TH} = 4\ \Omega$

$$v = \frac{3}{4+3}(-5) = -\frac{15}{7}\text{ V} = -2.14\text{ V}$$

3.29

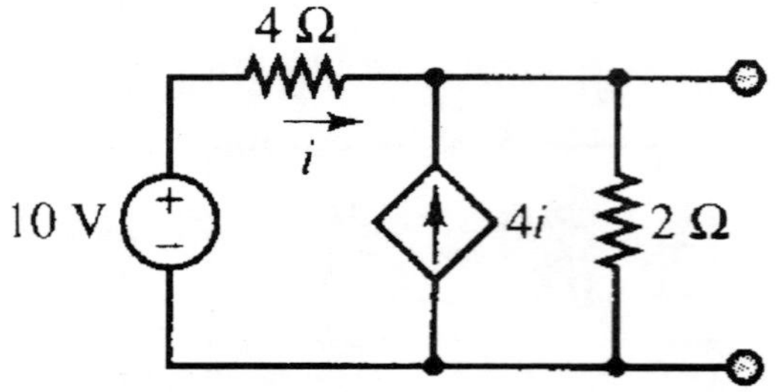

KVL around the outside loop:

$$10 - 4i - 2(5i) = 0$$

$$\Rightarrow i = 0.714A$$

$$\therefore V_{TH} = 10i = 7.14V$$

To find I_{SC},

$$10 - 4i = 0$$

$$\Rightarrow i = 2.5A$$

$$I_{SC} = 5i = 12.5A$$

$$\therefore R_{TH} = \frac{7.14V}{12.5A} = 0.57\Omega$$

3.30

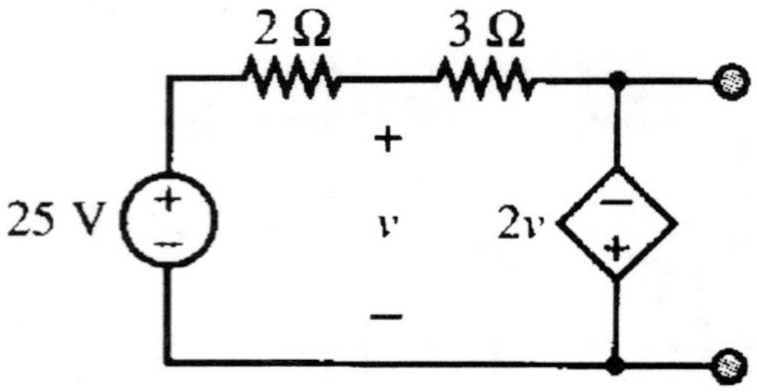

Define a current, i, flowing clockwise around the circuit. Then, from KVL, note that

$$-v + 3i + 2v = 0 \Rightarrow v = i$$

Also, from KVL,

$$-25 + 2i + 3i - 2v = 0$$

Solving, $v = i = 8.33A$, and

$$V_{TH} = -2v = -16.67V$$

To find R_{TH}, suppress the independent voltage source and apply a 1A current source. Under these conditions, by KVL,

$$3\left(\frac{v}{2}\right) + v + 2v = 0 \Rightarrow v = 0$$

$$\therefore R_{TH} = \frac{-2v}{1} = 0\Omega$$

3.31

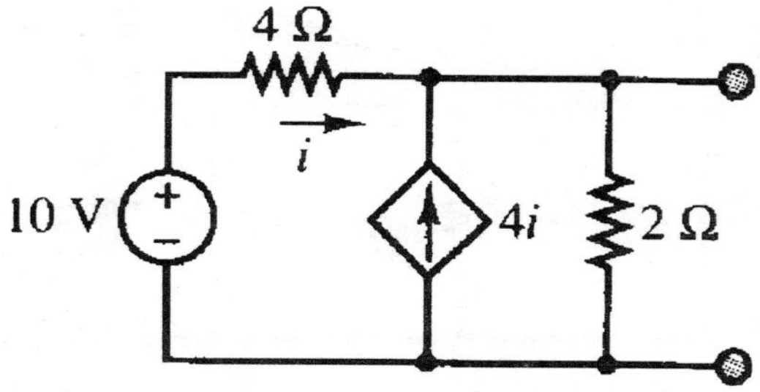

Under short-circuit conditions,
$$i_{SC} = 5i$$

where
$$i = \frac{10V}{4\Omega} = 2.5A$$
$$\therefore i_{SC} = 5(2.5A) = 12.5A$$

So, $I_N = i_{SC} = 12.5A$

From Problem 3.29, $R_N = R_{TH} = 0.57\Omega$

3.32

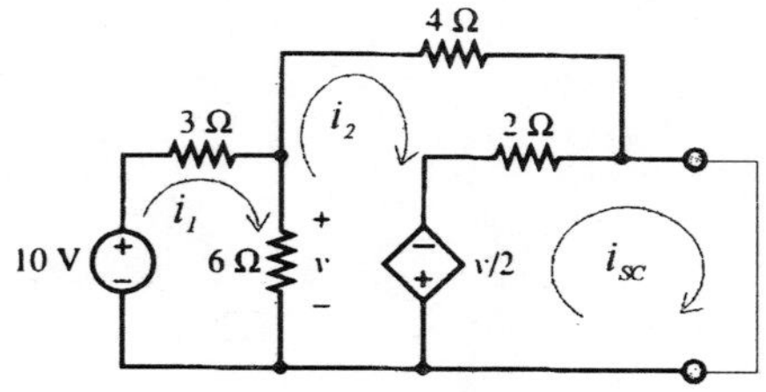

$$v = 6i_1 - 6i_2$$

Using mesh analysis,
$$9i_1 - 6i_2 = 10$$

$$-6i_1 + 12i_2 - 2i_{SC} = \frac{v}{2} = 3i_1 - 3i_2$$

or
$$-9i_1 + 15i_2 - 2i_{SC} = 0$$

and
$$\frac{v}{2} + 2i_{SC} - 2i_2 = 0$$

or
$$3i_1 - 5i_2 + 2i_{SC} = 0$$

Solving, $i_{SC} = 0 \Rightarrow I_N = 0$

To determine R_N, turn off the independent voltage source and apply a 1A current source at the output terminals. The resultant voltage across that current source is numerically equal to the Norton resistance.

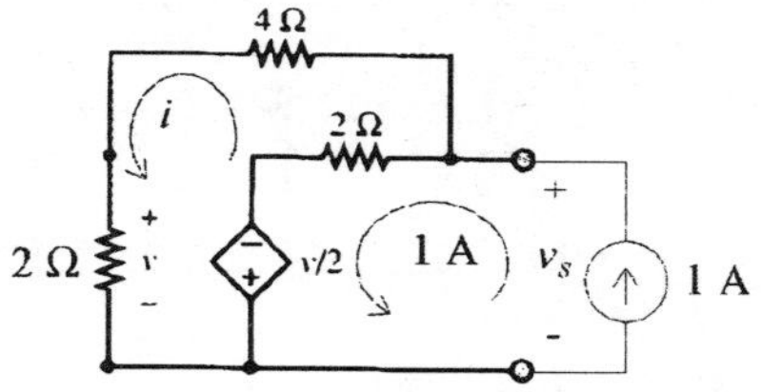

$$v = 2i$$
$$v_S = 2(1-i) - \frac{v}{2} = 6i$$
$$\Rightarrow 2 - 2i - i = 6i$$
$$\Rightarrow 9i = 2$$
$$\Rightarrow i = \frac{2}{9} A$$

$$v_S = 6\left(\frac{2}{9}\right) = \frac{12}{9} = \frac{4}{3}V$$

$$\therefore R_N = \frac{4}{3}\Omega$$

3.33

$R_N = 3\Omega + 1\Omega + (3\Omega \| 1\Omega) = 4.75\Omega$

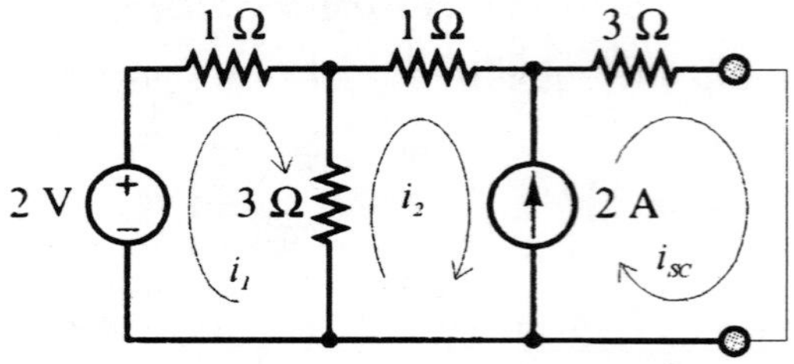

Using the mesh analysis approach

$$4i_1 - 3i_2 = 2$$

$$-3i_1 + 4i_2 + 3i_{SC} = 0$$

and

$$i_{SC} - i_2 = 2$$

Solving, $i_{SC} = \dfrac{20}{19} = 1.05\,A \Rightarrow i_N = 1.05$ A

3.34

$R_N = 5\Omega \| (3\Omega + 2\Omega \| 1\Omega) = 2.12\Omega$

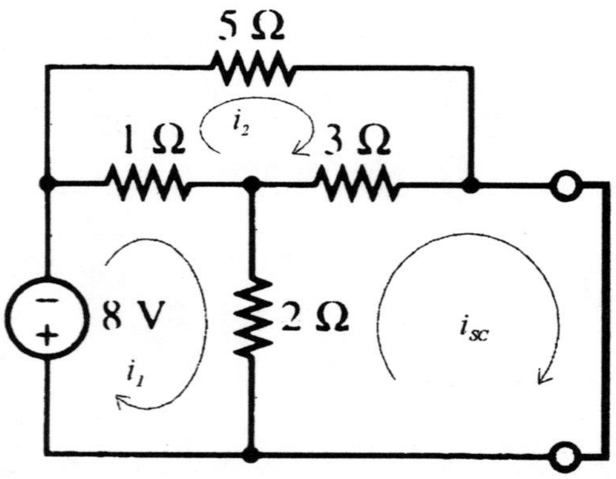

Using mesh analysis,

$$3i_1 - 1i_2 - 2i_{SC} = -8$$

$$-1i_1 + 9i_2 - 3i_{SC} = 0$$

and

$$-2i_1 - 3i_2 + 5i_{SC} = 0$$

Solving, $i_{SC} = -3.05\,A \Rightarrow I_N = -3.05\,A$.

EIT 3.35

To find R_T, we consider the circuit below:

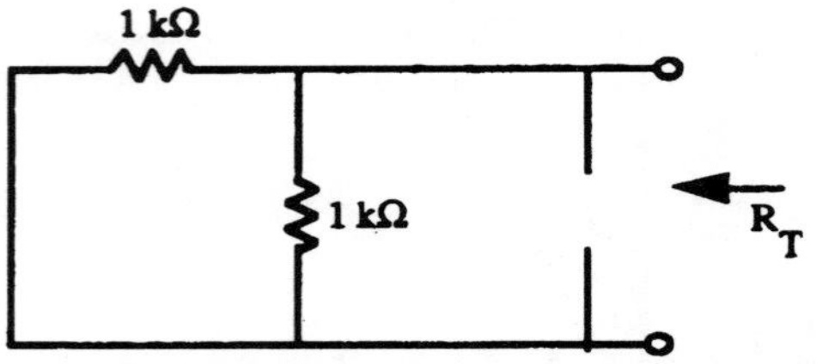

Therefore, R_T = 1,000 || 1,000 = 500 □.

To find v_{OC}, we apply nodal analysis.

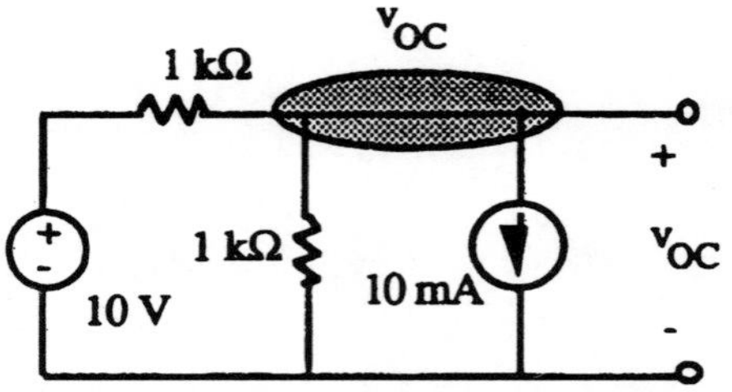

$$\left(\frac{1}{1000} + \frac{1}{1000} \right) v_{OC} - \frac{1}{1000}\, 10 + 0.01 = 0$$

Therefore,

$$v_{OC} = 0 \text{ V}$$

3.36

To find R_T, we need to make the current source an open circuit and the voltage sources short circuits, as follows:

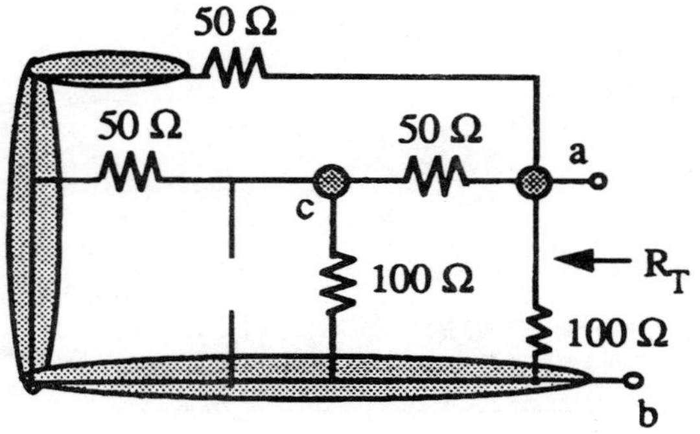

Note that this circuit has only three nodes. Thus, we can re-draw the circuit as shown:

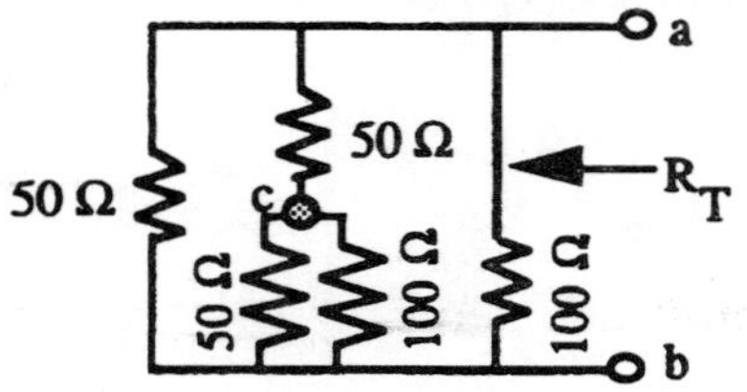

and combine the two parallel resistors to obtain:

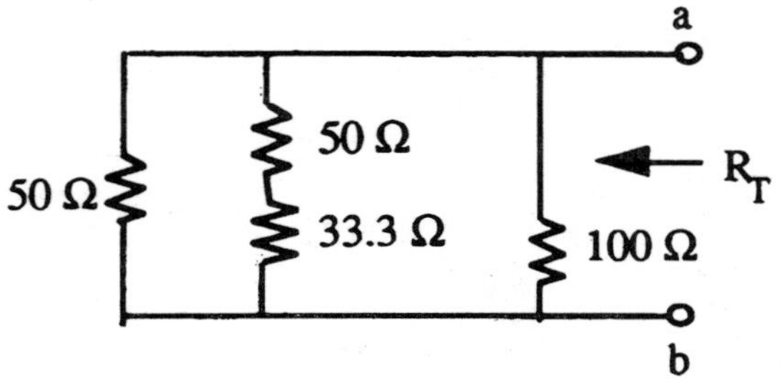

Thus,

$$R_T = 50 \parallel (50 + 33.3) \parallel 100 = 23.81\ \Omega$$

EIT 3.37

To find R_T,

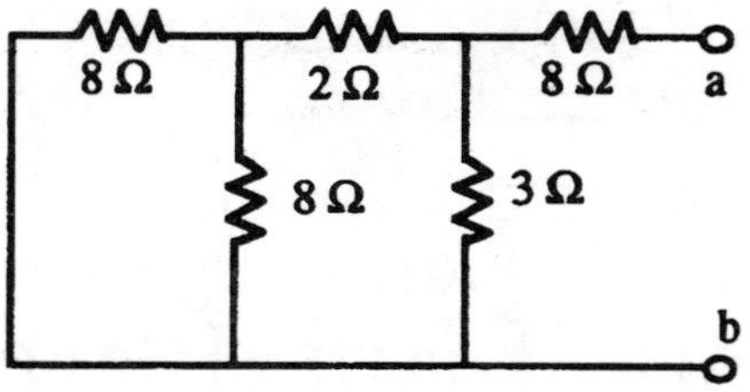

Therefore,

$$R_T = \{[(8 \parallel 8) + 2] \parallel 3\} + 8 = 10\ \Omega$$

To find v_{OC}, nodal analysis can be applied. Note that the 8 Ω resistor may be omitted because no current flows through it, and it therefore does not affect v_{OC}.

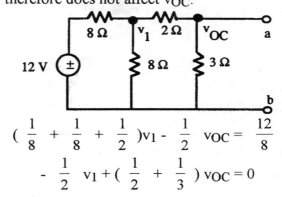

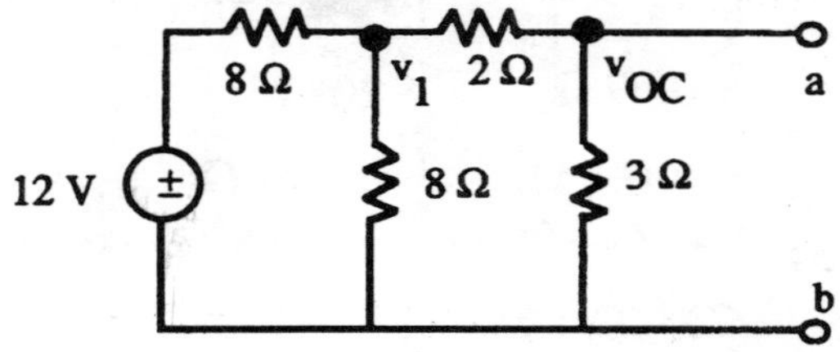

$$\left(\frac{1}{8} + \frac{1}{8} + \frac{1}{2}\right)v_1 - \frac{1}{2}v_{OC} = \frac{12}{8}$$

$$-\frac{1}{2}v_1 + \left(\frac{1}{2} + \frac{1}{3}\right)v_{OC} = 0$$

or

$$3v_1 - 2v_{OC} = 6$$

$$-3v_1 + 5v_{OC} = 0$$

Therefore, $v_{OC} = 2$ V

3.38

To find R_T, we short circuit the source

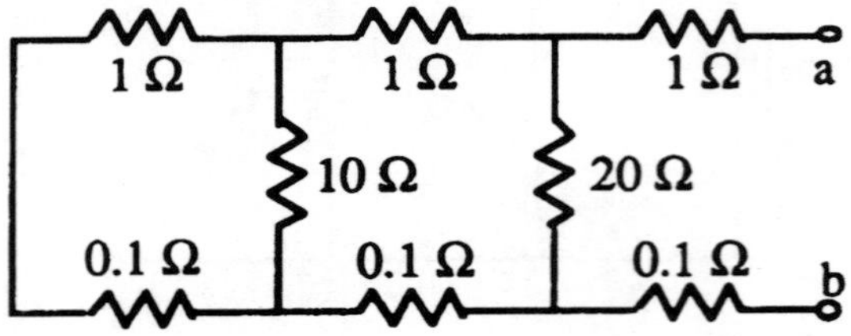

Starting from the left side,

$$(1 + 0.1) \parallel 10 = 0.99\ \Omega,$$

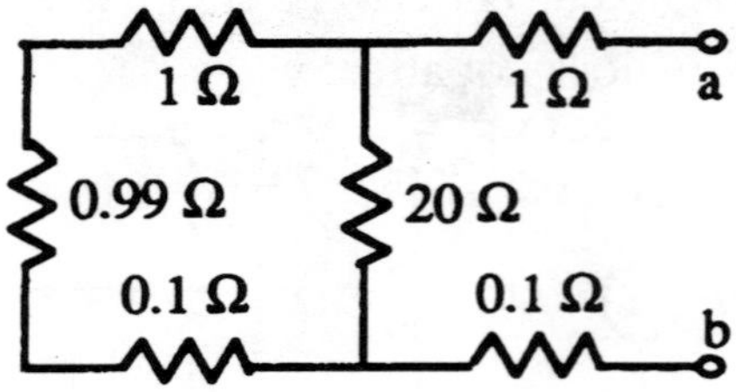

Then,

$$(1 + 0.99 + 0.1) \parallel 20 = 1.893\ \Omega$$

Therefore, we have

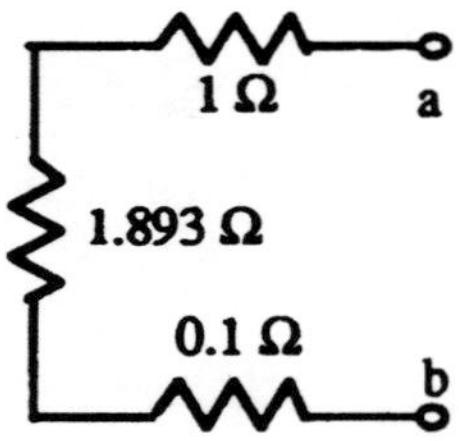

$$R_T = 1.893 + 0.1 + 1 = 2.993\ \Omega.$$

To find v_{OC}, we apply mesh analysis:

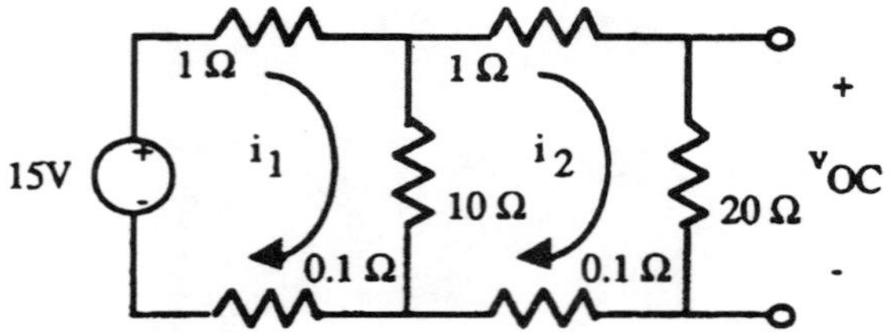

Two resistors are omitted because no current flows through them and they, therefore, do not affect v_{OC}.

$$(1 + 0.1 + 10)\, i_1 - 10\, i_2 = 15$$

$$(1 + 20 + 0.1 + 10)\, i_2 - 10\, i_1 = 0$$

Solving for i_2,

$$i_2 = 0.612 \text{ A}$$

we obtain,

$$v_T = v_{OC} = 20\, i_2 = 12.24 \text{ V}$$

EIT 3.39

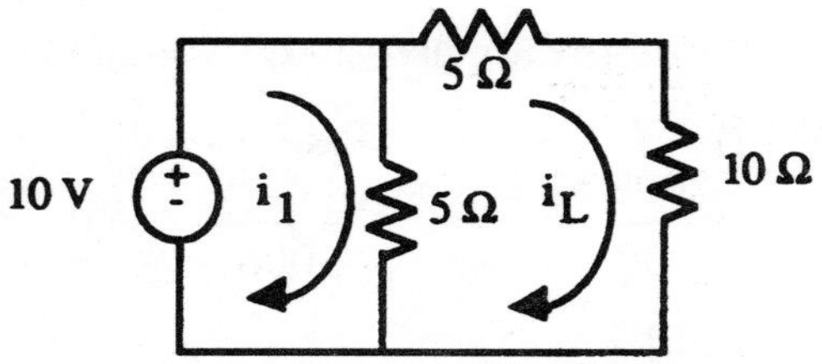

a) Applying KVL to the second mesh,

$$(5 + 10)\, i_L = 10$$

or $i_L = \frac{2}{3}$ A

$$P_{Load} = (i_L)^2 R_L = 4.44 \text{ W}$$

b) $P_{Source} = P_{5\,\Omega} + P_{5\,\Omega} = \frac{v^2}{R} + (i_L)^2 R$

$$= \frac{10^2}{5} + 5\left(\frac{2}{3}\right)^2 = 22.2 \text{ W}$$

c) By inspection, v_{OC} = 10 V and R_T = 5Ω:

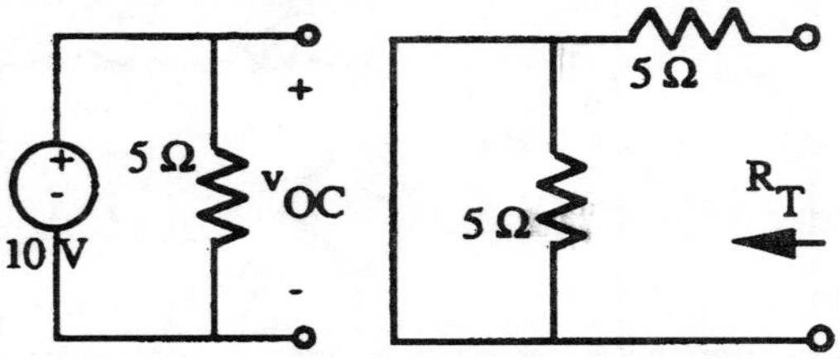

d)

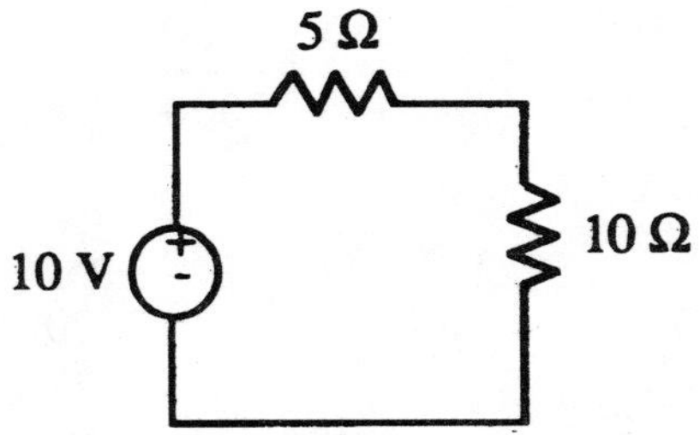

$$P_{RT} = 5\left(\frac{10}{15}\right)^2 = \frac{20}{9} \text{ W}$$

e) No, No. (This is a matter of interpretation. The total power delivered to the load, and therefore the total power delivered by the "source," ***is*** the same in both cases)

3.40

a) We have

$$V_{ab} = V_a - V_b = \frac{R}{R+R} V_S - \frac{R_x}{R+R_x} V_S$$

$$\boxed{V_{ab} = \frac{1}{2} V_S - \frac{R_x}{R+R_x} V_S}$$

b) For

R = 1 kΩ, V_S = 12 V, V_{ab} = 12 mV,

$$0.012 = 6 - \frac{R_x}{1000 + R_x} 12$$

$$R_x = 996\Omega$$

EIT 3.41

To find R_T, short circuit v_S. Thus,

$$R_T = (R_1 \parallel R_2) + (R_3 \parallel R_x) = 999\ \Omega$$

$$v_T = \frac{1}{2} v_S - \frac{R_x}{R + R_x} v_S = 12 \text{ mV}$$

b) Using the following circuit:

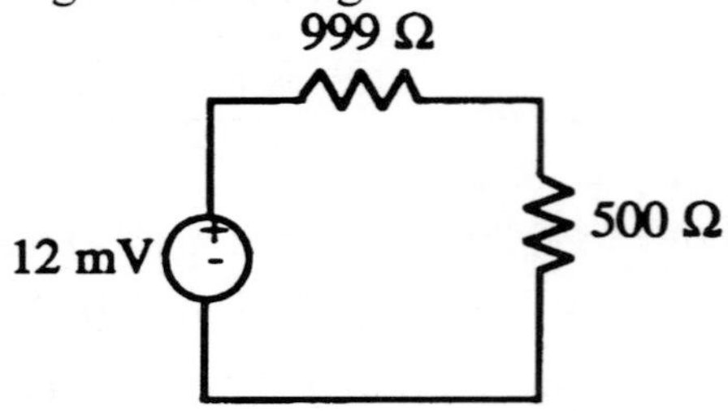

$$P_{500\ \square} = \frac{v^2}{R} = 32.04 \times 10^{-9} = 32 \text{ nW}$$

c) Using the previous circuit,

$$P_{RT} = \frac{v^2}{R_T} = 64 \text{ nW}$$

d) With no load resistor,

$$P_{dissipated} = \frac{12^2}{2000} + \frac{12^2}{1996} = 144.1 \text{ mW}$$

3.42

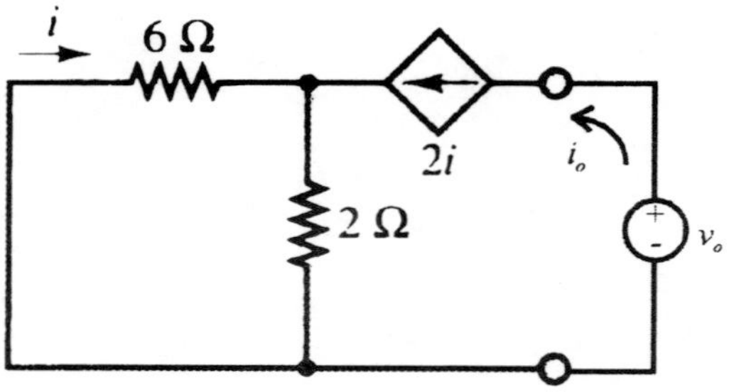

From KVL, $6i + 2(3i) = 0 \Rightarrow i = 0$

$i_o = 2i = 0 \Rightarrow R_N = \infty$ (an open circuit)

***3.43**

To determine the open circuit voltage we remove the load and apply KCL:

$$\frac{v_{oc} - 1000\ V_x}{70000} + \frac{v_{oc} + V_x}{3000} = 0$$

Eq.1

$$\frac{-V_x - 10}{2000} + \frac{-V_x - v_{oc}}{3000} + \frac{-V_x}{2000} = 0$$

Eq.2

Solving for the two unkowns, we obtain the following values:

$V_x = -0.34$ V and $v_{OC} = -13.64$ V

To find R_T, we connect a 1 A source to terminals a-b as shown below.

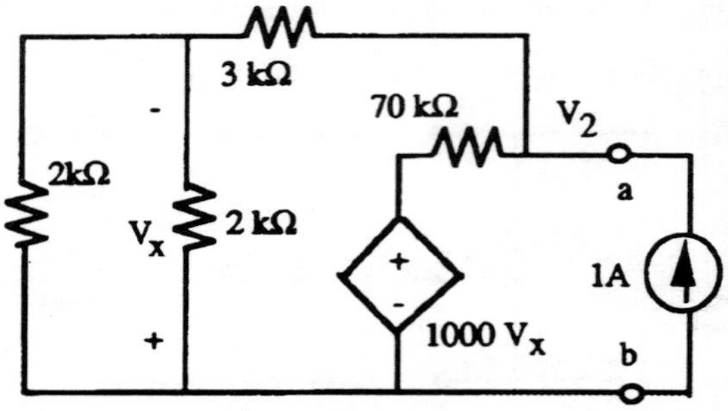

Then, applying KCL once again :

$$\frac{V_2 - 1000\ V_x}{70000} + \frac{V_2 - (-V_x)}{3000} = 1$$

Eq.3

$$\frac{-V_x}{2000} + \frac{-V_x - V_2}{3000} + \frac{-V_x}{2000} = 0$$

Eq.4

solving for V_2,

$V_2 = 260.7$ V

Thus, $R_T = \dfrac{V_2}{1} = 260.7\ \Omega$

***3.44**

Taking the bottom node as the reference,

$v_{O^-} = -4i_1,\ v_{O^+} = -4i_2$

Then,

$v_O = v_{O^+} - v_{O^-} = -4i_2 + 4i_1 = 4(i_1 - i_2)$

But,

$i_1 = \frac{1}{2}[v_1 - 5(i_1 + i_2)],\ i_2 = \frac{1}{2}[v_2 - 5(i_1 + i_2)]$

So,

$$v_O = 2(v_1 - v_2)$$

3.45

The Thevenin voltage from Problem 3.30 was -16.67V with a 25V source. Due to linearity of the circuit,

$$\frac{-2V}{-16.67V} = \frac{v_{S,new}}{25V} \Rightarrow v_{S,new} = 3V$$

***3.46**

$$11i_1 - 8i_2 - 3i_3 = 12$$
$$-8i_1 + 14i_2 - 6i_3 = 6$$
$$-3i_1 - 6i_2 + 13i_3 = 0$$

$$\begin{bmatrix} 11 & -8 & -3 \\ -8 & 14 & -6 \\ -3 & -6 & 13 \end{bmatrix} \begin{bmatrix} i_1 \\ i_2 \\ i_3 \end{bmatrix} = \begin{bmatrix} 12 \\ 6 \\ 0 \end{bmatrix}$$

Using Cramer's rule (see Appendix A),

$$i_1 = 6.9\ A$$
$$i_2 = 6.3\ A$$
$$i_3 = 4.5\ A$$

3.47

a) $V_L = V_T \dfrac{R_L}{R_T + R_L}$

$$P_L = \frac{V_{L^2}}{R_L} = (V_T)^2 \frac{R_{L^2}}{(R_T + R_L)^2} \frac{1}{R_L}$$

$$P_L = (V_T)^2 \frac{R_L}{(R_T + R_L)^2}$$

$$P_L = \frac{100\ R_L}{(500 + R_L)^2}$$

b) The expression obtained in part a) may be differentiated and set equal to zero to find that the maximum is at $R_L = 500\ \Omega$. The graph shown below is a plot of the load power vs the load resistance.

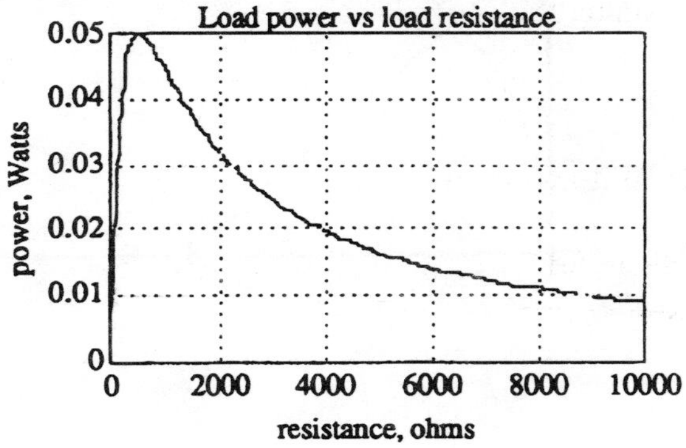

EIT 3.48

From KVL:

$$V_T = I\,R_T + V_2$$

$$V_2 = I^2R'$$

$$V_T = IR_T + I^2R'$$

$$12 = 20I + 10I^2$$

$$I^2 + 2I - 1.2 = 0$$

$$I = 0.483\text{ A} \quad \text{or} \quad -2.483\text{ A}$$

The second answer is physically impossible, so

$$\boxed{V_2 = 2.33\text{ V}}$$

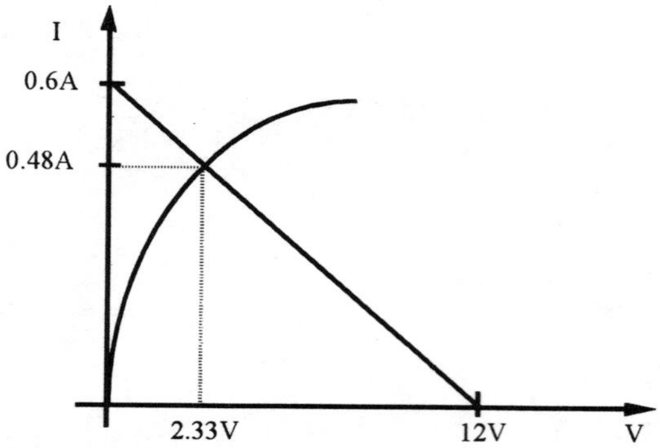

3.49

First, we find the Thèvenin equivalent of the source,

$$R_T = (2 \parallel 2) + 9 = 10\text{ k□}$$

By inspection,

$$v_{OC} = 15\text{ V}$$

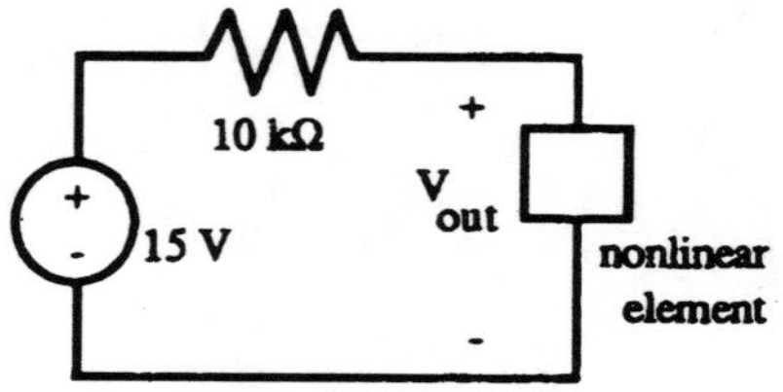

To find the load line, we apply KVL

$$20 = 10{,}000i + v_{out}$$

For $i = 0$

$$v_{out} = 15\text{ V}$$

For $v_{out} = 0$ V,

$$i = 1.5\text{ mA}$$

The resulting load line plot is shown below.

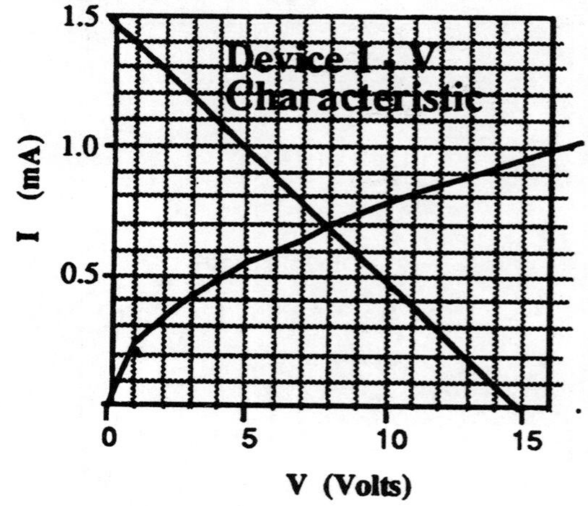

The intersection is at:

$$I = 0.7\text{ mA}$$

$$V = 8\text{ V}$$

Therefore, $V_{out} = 8$ V

EIT 3.50

First, we find the Thèvenin equivalent of the source,

$$R_T = (1{,}000 \parallel 500) + 333 = 666 \text{ □}$$

By inspection,

$$v_{OC} = 20 \text{ V}$$

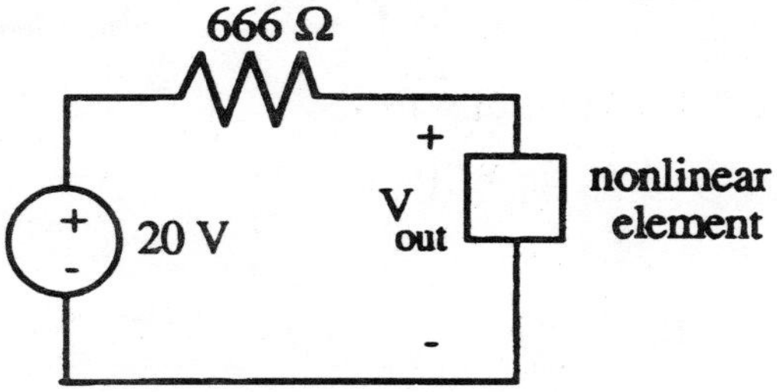

To find load line, apply KVL

$$20 = 666i + V_{out}$$

For i = 0, thus, $v_{out} = 20$ V

For $v_{out} = 0$ V, thus, i = 30 mA

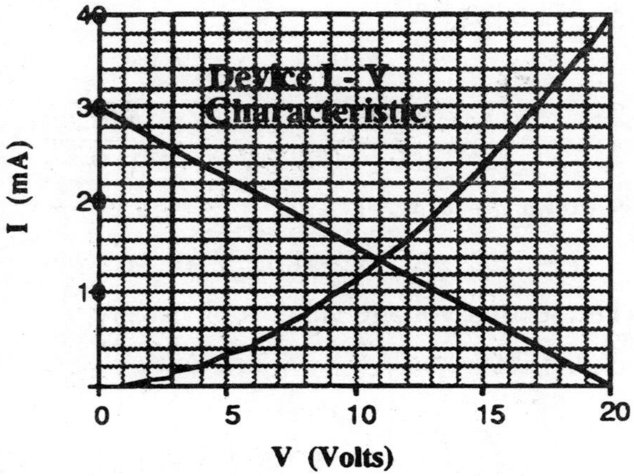

From the intersection,

$$I = 14 \text{ mA}$$

$$V = 11 \text{ V}$$

Therefore, $V_{out} = 11$ V

3.51

To find the load line, apply KVL:

$$20 = 40\,i + v_{out}$$

For i = 0, $v_{out} = 20$ V

For $v_{out} = 0$ V, i = 0.5 A.

From Figure 3.81 in the text, the resulting intercept is at Ix = 1.9 A, $V_x = 12.5$ V.

Therefore the output voltage is 12.5 V.

3.52

First, we find the Thèvenin equivalent of the source circuit:

$$R_T = (1 \parallel 2 \parallel 2) + 500 = 1 \text{ k}\Omega$$

and, by inspection,

$$v_{OC} = 5 \text{ V}$$

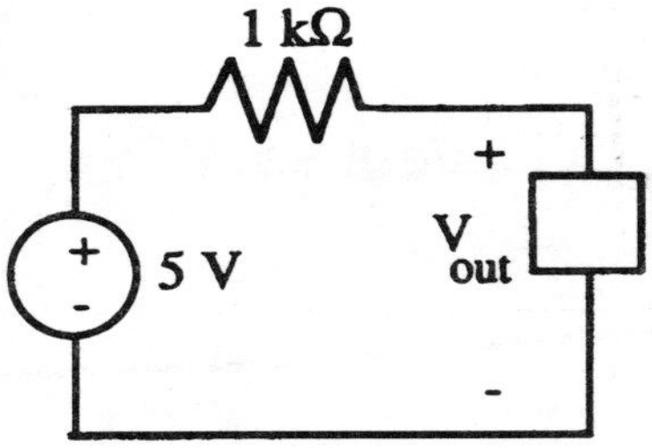

To find the load line equation, we apply KVL

$$5 = 1{,}000I + V_{out}$$

for I = 0, $V_{out} = 5$ V; for $V_{out} = 0$ V, I = 5 mA. Using these points, the load line intersects the device i-v curve at (approximately) I = 3 mA, V = 2 V. Thus, $V_{out} = 2$ V.

EIT 3.53

We need to obtain a Thèvenin equivalent and generate a load line. By inspection,

$$v_{OC} = 5\ \text{V}$$

$$R_T = (2\ \text{k}\Omega)\ ||\ (2\ \text{k}\Omega) = 1\ \text{k}\Omega$$

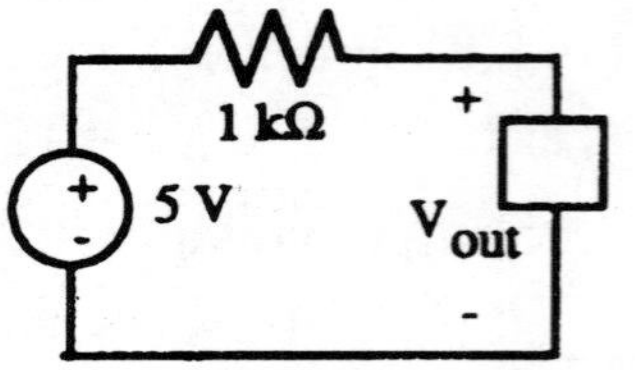

By KVL:

$$1{,}000i + V_{out} = 5$$

For i = 0, V_{out} = 5 V, and for V_{out} = 0 V, i = 5 mA. These values represent the i-v axes intercepts, and determine the load line.

a) T ≈ 0°

b) V_{out} ≈ 3.5 V

c)

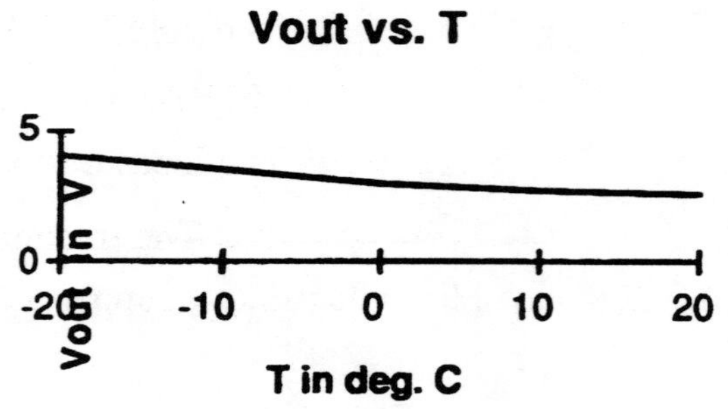

A few points from the curve are (T □C, V_{out} V): (-20, 4.1), (-10, 3.5), (0, 3), (10, 2.7), (20, 2.6).

3.54

At node 1,

$$\frac{v_1}{1} + i_a = 1 \Rightarrow v_1 + 2v_a^3 = 1$$

At node 2,

$$i_b - i_a = 26 \Rightarrow v_b^3 + 10v_b - 2v_a^3 = 26$$

But $v_a = v_1 - v_2$ and $v_b = v_2$. Therefore, the node equations are

$$v_1 + 2(v_1 - v_2)^3 = 1$$

and

$$v_2^3 + 10v_2 - 2(v_1 - v_2)^3 = 26$$

3.55

a) Applying KVL

$$-15 + 200\ I + V = 0$$

or

$$-15 + 200\ (0.0025\ V^2) + V = 0$$

Solving for V and I,

$$I = 52.2\ \text{mA}\ ;\ V = 4.57\ \text{V or } -6.57\ \text{V}$$

The second voltage value is physically impossible.

b)

$$R_{inc} = 10(0.0522)^{-0.5} = 43.8\ \Omega$$

c)

$$I = 73\ \text{mA} \quad V = 5.40\ \text{V}$$

$$R_{inc} = 37\ \Omega$$

Chapter 4 Instructor Notes

The chapter starts by developing the dynamic equations for energy storage elements. Though the treatment does not significantly differ from that encountered in most textbooks, an early example (4.4) on capacitive displacement and pressure transducers (microphones) will permit approaching the subject of capacitance in a pragmatic fashion, if so desired. The instructor wishing to gain a more in-depth understanding of such transducers will find a detailed analysis in [1]. The analogy between capacitors and inductors and equivalent mechanical elements is introduced early to permit a connection with ideas that may already be familiar to the student from a course in dynamics.

Next, signal sources are introduced, with special emphasis on sinusoids, and an intuitive introduction to Fourier Analysis (which may be bypassed if not deemed appropriate). The material in this section can also accompany a laboratory experiment on signal sources. The emphasis placed on sinusoidal signals is motivated by the desire to justify the concepts of phasors and impedance, which are introduced next. The author has found that presenting the impedance concept early on is an efficient way of using the (invariably too short) semester or quarter. The chapter is designed to permit a straightforward extension of the resistive circuit analysis concepts developed in Chapter 3 to the case of dynamic circuits excited by sinusoids. The ideas of nodal and mesh analysis, and of equivalent circuits, can thus be reinforced at this stage. The treatment of AC circuit analysis methods is reinforced by the usual examples and drill exercises, designed to avoid unnecessarily complicated circuits.

The capacitive displacement transducer example is picked up again to illustrate the use of impedances in a bridge circuit. This type of circuit is very common in mechanical measurements, and is likely to be encountered at some later time by some of the students. The homework problems in this chapter are mostly exercises aimed at mastery of the techniques, although problems 4.16 and 4.62 introduce practical applications of the capacitance and impedance concepts.

[1] Doebelin E. O., Measurement Systems, McGraw-Hill, Fourth Edition, 1987.

Chapter 4 problem solutions

EIT 4.1

The rms value of a waveform x is:

$$x_{rms} = \sqrt{\frac{1}{T}\int_0^T x^2(t\,dt}$$

Here, T=0.1s and x = V(t) = 20t,

$$v_{rms} = \sqrt{\frac{1}{0.1}\int_0^{0.1} 400t^2\,dt}$$

$$= \sqrt{10\,(\frac{0.4}{3})}$$

$$= 1.155\text{ V}$$

4.2

The rms value of v(t) is

$$v_{rms} = \sqrt{\frac{1}{T}\int_{t_0}^{t_0+t} V_{m^2}\,dt}$$

where t_0 is the left-hand side of the pulse.

$$v_{rms} = \sqrt{\frac{1}{T}V_{m^2}\,t}$$

$$= V_m\sqrt{\frac{t}{T}}\ \text{V}$$

4.3

The rms value of i(t) is

$$i_{rms} = \{\ \frac{1}{T}\int_0^{\frac{T}{4}} (\frac{8}{T}\,t)^2\,dt\ +$$

$$\int_{\frac{T}{4}}^{\frac{3T}{4}} (\frac{-8}{T}\,t + 4)^2\,dt$$

$$+ \int_{\frac{3T}{4}}^{T} (\frac{8}{T}\,t - 8)^2\,dt\ \}^{1/2}$$

$$= \{\ \frac{1}{T}\int_0^{\frac{T}{4}} (\frac{64}{T^2}\,t^2)dt\ +$$

$$\int_{\frac{T}{4}}^{\frac{3T}{4}} (\frac{64}{T^2}\,t^2 - \frac{64}{T}\,t + 16)dt$$

$$+ \int_{\frac{3T}{4}}^{T} (\frac{64}{T^2}\,t^2 - \frac{128}{T}\,t + 64)dt\ \}^{1/2}$$

$$= \left\{\frac{1}{T}\left(\frac{T}{3} + 9T - 18T + 12T - \frac{T}{3} + 2T - 4T + \frac{64}{3}T - 64T + 64T - 9T + 36T - 48T\right)\right\}^{1/2}$$

$$= \sqrt{\frac{1}{T}\,(\frac{4}{3}\,T)}$$

$$= \sqrt{\frac{4}{3}}$$

$$= \frac{2}{\sqrt{3}}$$

$$= 1.1547\text{ A}$$

4.4

We assume the circuit has reached a dc steady-state before the switch is opened, and, therefore, that

$$v_C(0) = \frac{5\Omega}{5\Omega + 5\Omega} 10V = 5V\ .$$

From KCL, for $t > 0$,

$$0.1\dot{v}_C + \frac{v_C}{5} = 0$$

or

$$\dot{v}_C + 2v_C = 0$$

This equation has a solution of the form

$$v_C(t) = v_C(0)e^{-2t}$$

Since $v_C(0) = 5V$,

$$v_C(t) = 5e^{-2t}\ V \quad \text{for} \quad t > 0$$

Other than our assumption that the circuit has reached a dc steady-state, we cannot describe the capacitor voltage for $t < 0$.

4.5

We assume the circuit has reached a dc steady-state before the switch is opened, and, therefore, that $i_L(0) = \frac{8V}{4\Omega} = 2A$.

From KVL, for $t > 0$,

$$2\frac{di_L}{dt} + 8i_L = 0$$

or

$$\frac{di_L}{dt} + 4i_L = 0$$

This equation has a solution of the form

$$i_L(t) = i_L(0)e^{-4t}$$

Since $i_L(0) = 2A$,

$$i_L(t) = 2e^{-4t}\ A \quad \text{for} \quad t > 0$$

Other than our assumption that the circuit has reached a dc steady-state, we cannot describe the inductor current for $t < 0$.

EIT 4.6

The rms value of v(t) is

$v_{rms} =$

$$= \sqrt{\frac{1}{0.004}\left[\int_0^{0.002} (-9)^2 dt + \int_{0.002}^{0.004} (1)^2\, dt\right]}$$

$$= \sqrt{250\,(0.162 + 0.004 - 0.002)}$$

$$v_{rms} = \sqrt{41} = 6.40\ V$$

4.7

The rms value of i (t) is

$$i_{rms} = \sqrt{\frac{1}{p}\int_0^p (10\sin^2 t)^2 dt}$$

$$= \sqrt{\frac{1}{p}\int_0^p 100\sin^4 t\ dt}$$

$$= \sqrt{\frac{1}{p}100\ (\frac{3p}{8})}$$

$$= \sqrt{\frac{300}{8}}$$

$$= \sqrt{\frac{75}{2}}$$

$$= 5\ \sqrt{\frac{3}{2}}$$

$$= 6.12\ \text{A}$$

4.8

The rms value of x (t) = 2sin (ωt) + 2.5 is

$$x_{rms} = \sqrt{\frac{w}{2p}\int_0^{\frac{2p}{w}} (2\sin\ (wt)\ +\ 2.5)^2\ dt}$$

$$= \{\ \frac{w}{2p}\int_0^{\frac{2p}{w}} [4\sin^2(wt + 10¢\sin wt + 6.25]$$

$$dt\}^{1/2}$$

$$= \sqrt{8.25}$$

$$= 2.87$$

4.9

(a) The rms value of $i(t)$ is

$$i_{rms} = \left\{\frac{1}{2\pi}\left(\int_0^{\theta_1}(10\sin t)^2\,dt + \int_\pi^{\theta_1+\pi}(10\sin t)^2\,dt\right)\right\}^{1/2}$$

$$= \left\{\frac{100}{2\pi}\left(\left(\frac{\theta_1}{2}-\frac{1}{4}\sin 2\theta_1 - 0 + 0\right)+\frac{1}{2}(\theta_1+\pi)-\frac{1}{4}\sin(2(\theta_1+\pi))-\frac{\pi}{2}+0\right)\right\}^{1/2}$$

$$= \left\{\frac{100}{2\pi}\left(\frac{\theta_1}{2}-\frac{1}{4}\sin 2\theta_1+\frac{\theta_1}{2}+\frac{\pi}{2}-\frac{1}{4}\sin 2\theta_1-\frac{\pi}{2}\right)\right\}^{1/2}$$

$$= \sqrt{\frac{100}{2\pi}\left(\theta_1-\frac{1}{2}\sin 2\theta_1\right)}$$

(b) For $\theta_1 = \frac{\pi}{2}$,

$$i_{rms} = \sqrt{\frac{100}{2\pi}\left(\frac{\pi}{2}-\frac{1}{2}\sin\pi\right)} = 5A$$

4.10

From KVL,

$$2i - v + 0.1\frac{d(v-2i)}{dt} = 0$$

EIT 4.11

a) $P_{10} = \frac{v^2}{R} = \frac{(10)^2}{10} = 10$ W

b) $P_{10} = 10$ W

For $\omega = 200\pi$ or f = 100 Hz,

we have $T = \frac{1}{f} = 0.01$s

The instantaneous power is

$$P_{10} = \frac{v^2(t)}{R} = \frac{100 \times 2\cos^2(200pt)}{10}$$

$$= 10\times 2\cos^2(200\pi t)$$

The average power can be found as

$$P_{10} = 20\ \frac{1}{T}\int_0^T \cos^2(200pt\ dt$$

$$= 20\times \frac{1}{0.01}(\frac{1}{2}T + \frac{1}{4}\sin 400pT)$$

$$= 20\times \frac{1}{0.01}(\frac{0.01}{2} + \frac{1}{4}\sin 4p)$$

$$= \frac{20}{2}$$

= 10 W (same as part (a))

4.12

$$Q = CV$$

$$C = \frac{Q}{V} = \frac{20¢10^{-3}}{60} = 333\ \mu F$$

$$W = \frac{1}{2}CV^2 = \frac{1}{2}333\times 10^{-6}\times 60^2 =$$

0.6 J

4.13

In an ideal capacitor,

$$i_c = C\frac{dv_c}{dt}$$

For $0 \le t \le 0.5$ s, the voltage is:

$$v_c = 30\,t$$

$$\therefore\ i_c = 0.01\times 30 = 0.3\ A$$

For $0.5 \le t \le 1$ s,

$$v_c = -30t + 30$$

$$\therefore\ i_c = -0.01\times 30 = -0.3\ A$$

For $1 \le t \le 1.5$ s,

$$v_c = 30t - 30\ V$$

$$\therefore\ i_c = 0.01\times 30 = 0.3\ A$$

For $1.5 \le t \le 2$ s,

$$v_c = -30t + 60\ V$$

$$\therefore\ i_c = -0.01\times 30 = -0.3\ A$$

Assuming the voltage is periodic, the waveform of $i_c(t)$ is shown below.

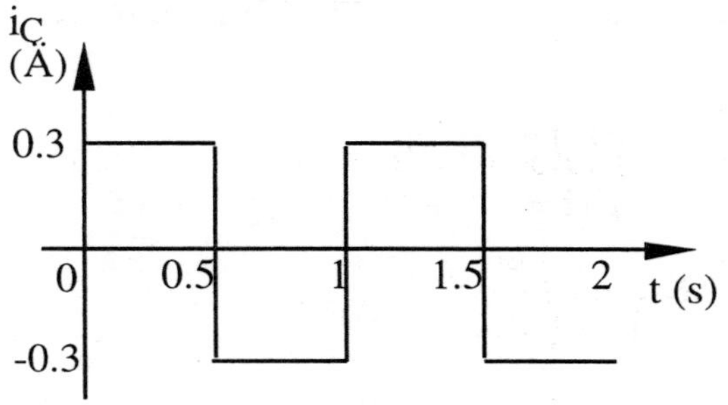

4.14

We assume the circuit has reached a dc steady-state before the switch is opened, and, therefore, that the current flowing from left to right through the inductor is

$$i_L(0^-) = \frac{5V}{10\Omega} = 0.5A$$

Since the energy stored in the inductor does not change instantaneously,

$i_L(0^+) = i_L(0^-) = 0.5A$

Therefore, $i(0^+) = -0.5A$ and $v(0^+) = 5V$.

From KVL, for $t > 0$,

$$5i + 10i + 1\frac{di}{dt} = 0$$

or

$$\frac{di}{dt} + 15i = 0$$

This equation has a solution of the form

$$i(t) = i(0^+)e^{-15t}$$

Since $i(0^+) = -0.5A$,

$$i(t) = -0.5e^{-15t} \ A \quad \text{for} \quad t > 0$$

Then,

$$v(t) = -10i = 5e^{-15t} \ V \quad \text{for} \quad t > 0$$

Other than our assumption that the circuit has reached a dc steady-state, we cannot describe either variable for $t < 0$.

4.15

$$v_L(t) = 0.5\frac{di_L}{dt}$$

$$= 0.5 \times \left[-377 \times 2\sin\left(377t + \frac{\pi}{6}\right)\right]$$

$$= 377\sin\left(377t + \frac{\pi}{6} - \pi\right)$$

$$= 377\sin\left(377t - \frac{5\pi}{6}\right) V$$

4.16

The capacitance is $C = \dfrac{eA}{d}$

Here, $A = \pi r^2 = \pi (0.01)^2$

and $\varepsilon = \varepsilon_0 = \dfrac{(10)^{-9}}{36p}$. Also, d = x.

Thus, C is a function of x:

$$C = \frac{\frac{10^{-9}}{36p}\, p\, (0.01)^2}{x} = \frac{(10)^{-13}}{36x}$$ F, (x in cm)

4.17

$$i_C(t) = 100\times10^{-6}\frac{dv_C}{dt} = 10^{-4}\frac{dv_C}{dt}$$

(a)

$$i_C(t) = 10^{-4}\left[-20\times40\sin\left(20t-\frac{\pi}{2}\right)\right]$$
$$= -0.08\sin\left(20t-\frac{\pi}{2}\right)$$
$$= 0.08\sin\left(20t-\frac{\pi}{2}+\pi\right)$$
$$= 0.08\sin\left(20t+\frac{\pi}{2}\right)\ A$$

(b)

$$i_C(t) = 10^{-4}[100\times20\cos100t]$$
$$= 0.2\cos100t\ A$$

(c)

$$i_C(t) = 10^{-4}\left[-80\times60\cos\left(80t+\frac{\pi}{6}\right)\right]$$
$$= -0.48\cos\left(80t+\frac{\pi}{6}\right)$$
$$= 0.48\cos\left(80t+\frac{\pi}{6}-\pi\right)$$
$$= 0.48\cos\left(80t-\frac{5\pi}{6}\right)\ A$$

(d)

$$i_C(t) = 10^{-4}\left[-100\times30\sin\left(100t+\frac{\pi}{4}\right)\right]$$
$$= -0.3\sin\left(100t+\frac{\pi}{4}\right)$$
$$= 0.3\sin\left(100t+\frac{\pi}{4}-\pi\right)$$
$$= 0.3\sin\left(100t-\frac{3\pi}{4}\right)\ A$$

4.18

$$v_L(t) = 250\times10^{-3}\frac{di_L}{dt} = 0.25\frac{di_L}{dt}$$

(a)

$$v_L(t) = 0.25[25\times5\cos25t]$$
$$= 31.25\cos25t\ V$$

(b)

$$v_L(t) = 0.25[-50\times(-10\sin50t)]$$
$$= 125\sin50t\ V$$

(c)

$$v_L(t) = 0.25\left[-100\times25\sin\left(100t+\frac{\pi}{3}\right)\right]$$
$$= -625\sin\left(100t+\frac{\pi}{3}\right)$$
$$= 625\sin\left(100t+\frac{\pi}{3}-\pi\right)$$
$$= 625\sin\left(100t-\frac{2\pi}{3}\right)\ V$$

(d)

$$v_L(t) = 0.25\left[10\times20\cos\left(10t-\frac{\pi}{12}\right)\right]$$
$$= 50\cos\left(10t-\frac{\pi}{12}\right)\ V$$

4.19

Solution Use passive sign convention

$$i_L = i_L(0) + \frac{1}{L}\int_0^t v(\alpha)d\alpha = 0 + \frac{1}{1}\int_0^t v(\alpha)d\alpha$$

For $0 < t < 0.2$

$$i_L = \int_0^t \left(0.5 - 0.5e^{-\frac{\alpha}{0.02}}\right)d\alpha = 0.5t + 0.01\left(e^{-\frac{t}{0.02}} - 1\right) \text{ A}$$

$$i_L(0.2) = 0.5(0.2) + 0.01\left(e^{-\frac{0.2}{0.02}} - 1\right) \text{ A} = 0.1 - 0.0100 = 0.0900 \text{ A}$$

For $0.2 < t < 0.3$

$$i_L = i_L(0.2) + \int_{0.2}^t \left(0.5e^{-\frac{(\alpha-0.2)}{0.02}}\right)d\alpha$$

$$= 0.0900 + 0.01\left[1 - e^{-\frac{(t-0.2)}{0.02}}\right] \text{A}$$

$$i_L(0.4) = 0.0900 - 0.01 = 0.1 \text{ A}$$

4.20

$$i_L(t) = \frac{1}{L}\int_{-}^{t} v_L(t\, d\tau$$

The current in the inductor is shown below:

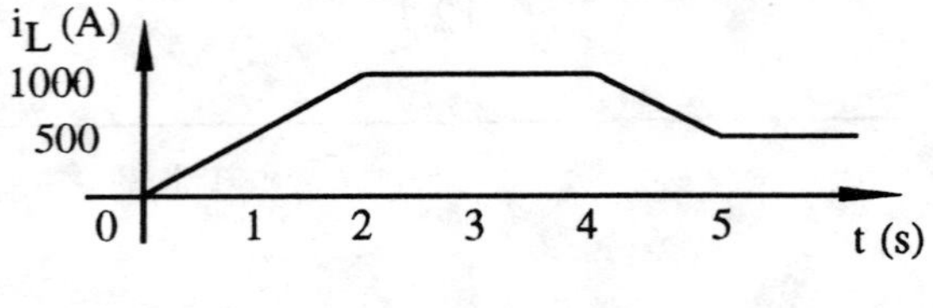

4.21

$$i(t) = \begin{cases} 4t - 15 \ mA & 0 < t < 5ms \\ 5 \ mA & t > 5ms \end{cases}$$

For a 2 H inductor, since $v_L = L\frac{di_L}{dt}$,

$$v_L(t) = \begin{cases} 8 \ V & 0 < t < 5ms \\ 0 & t > 5ms \end{cases}$$

The voltage waveform is sketched below

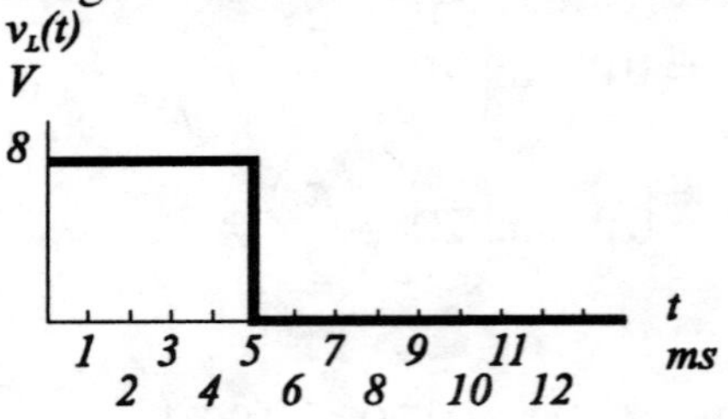

4.22

$$v_L(t) = L \frac{di}{dt}$$

$$= 0.01 \frac{d}{dt}(4e^{-t/10})$$

$$= 0.01 \times 4 \times (-\frac{1}{10})e^{-t/10}$$

$$= -4e^{-t/10} \text{ mV} \quad \text{for } t > 0$$

The resulting waveform is shown below.

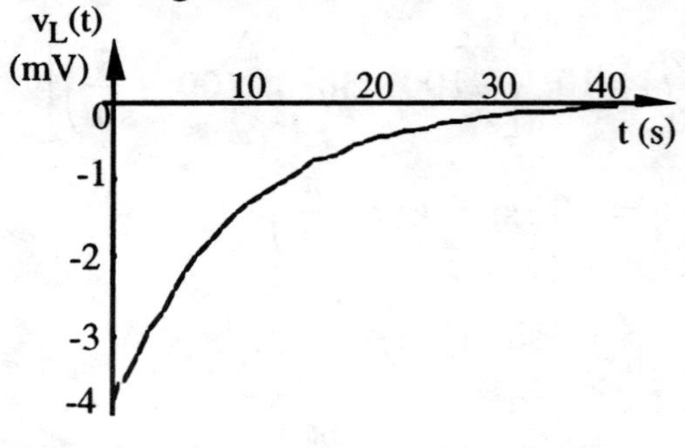

EIT 4.23

$$v(t)=\begin{cases}\dfrac{15}{0.004}t\ V & 0<t<4ms\\ 30-\dfrac{15}{0.004}t\ \ V & 4\text{ms}<\text{t}<8\text{ms}\end{cases}$$

$$=\begin{cases}3750t\ V & 0<t<4ms\\ 30-3750t\ V & 4ms<t<8ms\end{cases}$$

The capacitor current is

$$i_C=C\frac{dv}{dt}=500\times10^{-6}\frac{dv}{dt}$$

$$=\begin{cases}1.875\ A & 0<t<4ms\\ -1.875\ A & 4ms<t<8ms\end{cases}$$

The inductor current is

$$i_L=\frac{1}{L}\int_{-\infty}^{t}v(\tau)d\tau=i_L(t_0)+\frac{1}{L}\int_{t_0}^{t}v(\tau)d\tau=i_L(t_0)+10\int_{t_0}^{t}v(\tau)d\tau$$

Assume $i_L(0)=0$.

For $0<\text{t}<4\text{ms}$, we have

$$i_L=0+10\int_0^t3750\tau d\tau=37500\left.\frac{t^2}{2}\right|_0^t=18750t^2\ \ A$$

For $4\text{ms}<\text{t}<8\text{ms}$, we have

$$i_L=18750(0.004)^2+10\int_{0.004}^{t}(30-3750\tau)d\tau$$

$$=0.3+\left[300\tau-18750\tau^2\right]_{0.004}^{t}$$

$$=0.3+300t-18750t^2-300(0.004)+18750(0.004)^2$$

$$=300t-18750t^2-0.6\ \ A$$

The two functions are sketched below:

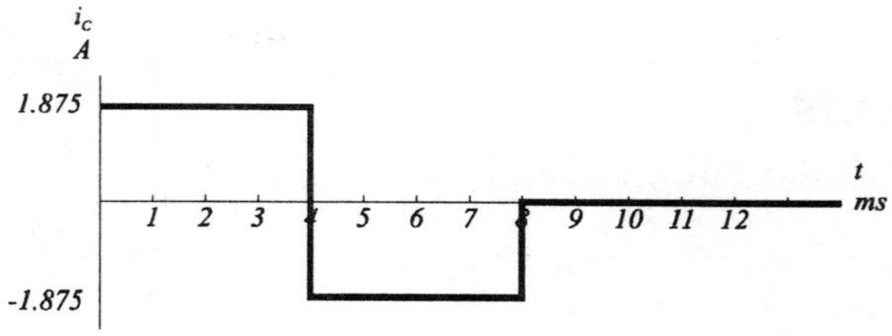

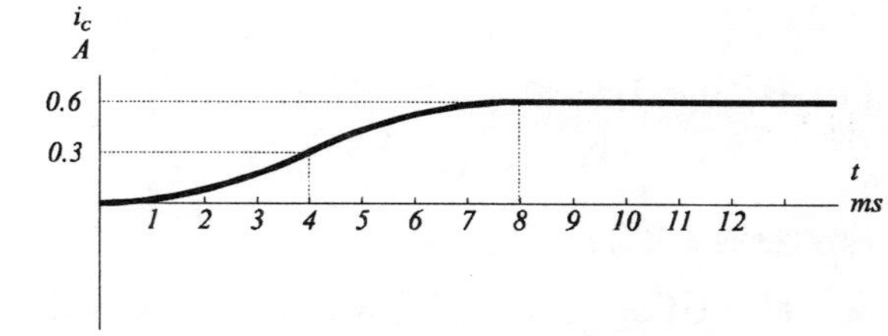

4.24

$$w_L(t)=\frac{1}{2}Li^2=\frac{1}{2}(2)i^2=i^2$$

For $-\infty<t<0$,

$$w_L(t)=0$$

For $0\le t<1s$

$$w_L(t)=t^2\ \ J$$

For $1s\le t<2s$

$$w_L(t)=\left[-(t-2)\right]^2=t^2-4t+4\ \ J$$

For $2s\le t<\infty$

$$w_L(t)=0$$

4.25

$$w_C(t) = \frac{1}{2}Cv^2 = \frac{1}{2}(0.1)v^2 = 0.05v^2$$

For $-\infty < t < 0$

$$w_C(t) = 0$$

For $0 \le t < 1s$

$$w_C(t) = 0.05(2t)^2 = 0.2t^2 \;\; J$$

For $1s \le t < 2s$

$$w_C(t) = 0.05[-(2t-4)]^2 = 0.2t^2 - 0.8t + 0.8 \;\; J$$

For $2s \le t < \infty$

$$w_C(t) = 0$$

4.26

Under steady-state conditions,

$$v_{2F} = (4\Omega)\left(\frac{\frac{1}{4}}{\frac{1}{4}+\frac{1}{8}}6A\right) = 16V \Rightarrow w_{2F} = \frac{1}{2}(2F)(16V)^2 = 256 \;\; J$$

$$v_{1F} = 0 \Rightarrow w_{1F} = \frac{1}{2}(1F)(0)^2 = 0$$

$$i_{2H} = \frac{\frac{1}{8}}{\frac{1}{4}+\frac{1}{8}}6A = 2A \Rightarrow w_{2H} = \frac{1}{2}(2H)(2A)^2 = 4 \;\; J$$

$$v_{3F} = (8\Omega)i_{2H} = 16V \Rightarrow w_{3F} = \frac{1}{2}(3F)(16V)^2 = 384 \;\; J$$

4.27

Under steady-state conditions,

$$v_{1F} = 12V \Rightarrow w_{1F} = \frac{1}{2}(1F)(12V)^2 = 72 \;\; J$$

$$i_{1H} = \frac{12V}{[6\Omega \| (3\Omega + 3\Omega)]} = 4A \Rightarrow w_{1H} = \frac{1}{2}(1H)(4A)^2 = 8 \;\; J$$

$$i_{2H} = \frac{1}{2}i_{1H} = 2A \Rightarrow w_{2H} = \frac{1}{2}(2H)(2A)^2 = 4 \;\; J$$

$$v_{2F} = \frac{1}{2}(6\Omega)i_{2H} = \frac{1}{2}(6\Omega)(2A) = 6V \Rightarrow w_{2F} = \frac{1}{2}(2F)(6V)^2 = 36 \;\; J$$

4.28

Define a current $i(t)$ flowing clockwise in the circuit. Then

$i(0^-) = 0 \Rightarrow i(0^+) = 0 \Rightarrow \dot{v}(0^+) = 0$

$v(0^-) = 0 \Rightarrow v(0^+) = 0$

For $t > 0$, from KVL,

$$16i + 4\frac{di}{dt} + v = v_S$$

But $i = \frac{1}{16}\dot{v}$ and $v_S = 1$, so

$$\dot{v} + \frac{1}{4}\ddot{v} + v = 1$$

or

$$\ddot{v} + 4\dot{v} + 4v = 4$$

The characteristic equation has a double root at -2, so the solution is of the form

$$v(t) = (A + Bt)e^{-2t} + C$$

where

$$4C = 4 \Rightarrow C = 1$$

and, therefore,

$$v(t) = (A + Bt)e^{-2t} + 1$$

Now, $v(0) = A + 1$ and $\dot{v}(0) = B - 2A$.

But $v(0) = 0$, and $\dot{v}(0) = 0$,

$\therefore\ A + 1 = 0 \Rightarrow A = -1$

and $B - 2A = 0 \Rightarrow B = -2$

and we have

$$v(t) = -(1 + 2t)e^{-2t} + 1\ V \qquad \text{for } t > 0.$$

EIT 4.29

Let the current in the loop be denoted by $i_c(t)$. Applying KVL we have:

$$v_S(t) = i_c(t)\,R_1 + i_c(t)\,R_2 + v_c(t)$$

For an ideal capacitor

$$i_c(t) = C\,\frac{dv_c(t)}{dt}$$

Thus, the differential equation for the circuit is:

$$v_S(t) = CR_1\frac{dv_c(t)}{dt} + CR_2\frac{dv_c(t)}{dt} + v_c(t)$$

or

$$\frac{dv_c(t)}{dt} + \frac{1}{C(R_1 + R_2)}v_c(t) = \frac{v_S(t)}{C(R_1 + R_2)}$$

$$\frac{dv_c(t)}{dt} + 1667\,v_c(t) = 1667v_S(t)$$

4.30

Applying KCL we determine that

$$i_S(t) = i_R + i_L$$

where $i_R = \frac{v_{out}}{R}$

$$i_L = \frac{1}{L}\int v_{out}\, dt$$

$$i_S(t) = \frac{v_{out}}{R} + \frac{1}{L}\int v_{out}\, dt$$

Differentiating the last equation, we have

$$\frac{d}{dt}(i_S(t) = \frac{1}{R}\frac{dv_{out}}{dt} + \frac{1}{L} v_{out}$$

$$\frac{d}{dt} i_S(t) = -\omega I_m \sin\omega t$$

or

$$\frac{dv_{out}}{dt} + \frac{R}{L} v_{out} = -\omega R I_m \sin\omega t$$

Assuming $v_{out} = D\cos(\omega t + \phi)$, we can write

$$\frac{dv_{out}}{dt} = -\omega D \sin(\omega t + .\phi)$$

and obtain the expression

$$-\omega D \sin(\omega t + \phi) + \frac{R}{L} D\cos(\omega t + \phi)$$

$$= -\omega R I_m(\sin\omega t)$$

Recalling that:

$\sin(\omega t + \phi) = \sin\omega t \cos\phi + \cos\omega t \sin\phi$

and

$\cos(\omega t + \phi) = \cos\omega t \cos\phi - \sin\omega t \sin\phi$

we obtain

$(-\omega D\cos\phi)\sin\omega t + (-\omega D\sin\phi)\cos\omega t +$

$+ \frac{R}{L} D\cos\phi \cos\omega t - \frac{R}{L} D\sin\phi \sin\omega t$

$= -\omega R I_m \sin\omega t$

Equating the coefficients of the sine and cosine terms, we have

1) $-\omega D\cos\phi - \frac{R}{L} D\sin\phi = -\omega R I_m$

2) $-\omega D\sin\phi . + \frac{R}{L} D\cos\phi = 0$

Solve for ϕ first, we obtain

$$\frac{\sin f}{\cos f} = \tan\phi = \frac{R}{wL}$$

$$\phi = \tan^{-1}\left(\frac{R}{\omega L}\right)$$

Then, $\sin\phi = \frac{R}{\sqrt{R^2 + (wL)^2}}$

and $\cos\phi = \frac{wL}{\sqrt{R^2 + (wL)^2}}$

Solving for D from 1), we have

$$\omega D\cos\phi + \frac{R}{L} D\sin\phi . = \omega R I_m$$

$$D\left(\frac{R}{L}\sin\phi + \omega\cos\phi\right) = \omega R I_m$$

$$D = \frac{\omega R I_m}{\frac{R}{L}\sin f . + w\cos f} = \frac{\omega R L I_m}{\sqrt{R^2 + (wL)^2}}$$

Finally, the output voltage is given by

$$v_{out}(t) = \frac{\omega R L I_m}{\sqrt{R^2 + (wL)^2}} \cos\left(\omega t + \tan^{-1}\left(\frac{R}{\omega L}\right)\right) \text{ V}$$

4.31

Using the voltage divider rule, we can write:

$$V_{out} = \frac{\frac{1}{jwC}}{R + \frac{1}{jwC}} V_{in}(\omega)$$

Substituting numerical values,

$$V_{out} = \frac{-j53{,}050}{40{,}000 - j53{,}050} 20\angle 0°$$

$$= 0.7985\angle -37° \times 20\angle 0°$$

$$= 15.97\angle -37°$$

Thus, $v_{out}(t) = 15.97 \cos(377t - 37°)$ V

EIT 4.32

Observing that $v_{out} = v_C$, and applying KCL, we have

$$I_m \cos\omega t = i_R + i_C$$

where

$$i_R = \frac{v_C}{R} \quad i_C = C\frac{dv_C}{dt}$$

$$I_m \cos\omega t = \frac{v_C}{R} + C\frac{dv_C}{dt}$$

or,

$$\frac{dv_C}{dt} + \frac{v_C}{RC} = \frac{I_m}{C}\cos\omega t$$

Assuming $v_C(t) = D\cos(\omega t + \phi)$,

$$\frac{dv_C}{dt} = -\omega D\sin(\omega t + \phi)$$

So, we have

$$-\omega D\sin(\omega t + \phi) + \frac{D}{RC}\cos(\omega t + \phi) = \frac{I_m}{C}\cos\omega t$$

Recalling that:

$\sin(\omega t + \phi) = \cos\phi \sin\omega t + \sin\phi \cos\omega t$

$\cos(\omega t + \phi) = \cos\phi \cos\omega t - \sin\phi \sin\omega t$

we can re-write the equation above as

$$-\omega D(\cos\phi \sin\omega t + \sin\phi \cos\omega t) + \frac{D}{RC}(\text{cosf coswt} - \text{sinf sinwt}) = \frac{I_m}{C}\cos\omega t$$

By grouping the sine and cosine terms, we have:

$$\left(-\omega D\cos\phi - \frac{D}{RC}\sin\phi\right)\sin\omega t + \left(\frac{D}{RC}\cos\phi - \omega D\sin\phi\right)\cos\omega t = \frac{I_m}{C}\cos\omega t$$

Equating the coefficients of like terms, we find that

1) $-\omega D\cos\phi - \frac{D}{RC}\sin\phi = 0$

2) 2) $\frac{D}{RC}\cos\phi - \omega D\sin\phi = \frac{I_m}{C}$

Solving 1) for ϕ, we obtain:

$$-\omega D\cos\phi = \frac{D}{RC}\sin\phi$$

$$\frac{\sin\phi}{\cos\phi} = \tan\phi = -\omega RC, \quad \phi = \tan^{-1}(-\omega RC)$$

Solving 2) for D, we obtain:

$$D\left(\frac{\cos\phi}{RC} - \omega\sin\phi\right) = \frac{I_m}{C}$$

$$D = \frac{\frac{I_m}{C}}{(\cos\phi - \omega RC\sin\phi)/RC}$$

$$= \frac{I_m}{C}\left(\frac{RC}{\text{cosf} - \text{wRCsin}\phi}\right)$$

$$D = \frac{I_m R}{\cos\phi - \omega RC\sin\phi} = \frac{I_m R}{\sqrt{1 + (\omega RC)^2}}$$

Finally,

$$v_{out}(t) = \frac{I_m R}{\sqrt{1 + (wRC)^2}}\cos(wt + \tan^{-1}(-wRC) \text{ V}$$

4.33

a) By KVL: $10\cos t = v_R + v_L + v_C$

where $v_R = R\,i = RC\frac{dv_C}{dt}$

$v_L = L\frac{di}{dt}$ and $v_C = \frac{1}{C}\int_{-}^{t} i(t)\,dt$

Substituting component values and these expressions into the KVL equation, we have:

$$10\cos t = i + \frac{di}{dt} + \int_{-}^{t} i(t)\,dt$$

Differentiating this expression, we obtain a second order differential equation:

$$\frac{d^2i}{dt^2} + \frac{di}{dt} + i = -10\sin t$$

Now, if $i(t) = A\sin t + B\cos t$ (Note that ω=1)

then $\frac{di}{dt} = A\cos t - B\sin t$

and $\frac{d^2i}{dt^2} = -A\sin t - B\cos t$

Substituting i(t) and its derivatives into the differential equation, we obtain:

$$-A\sin t - B\cos t + A\cos t - B\sin t + A\sin t$$
$$+ B\cos t = -10\sin t$$

Regrouping into sine and cosine terms:

$$(-A-B+A)\sin t + (-B+A+B)\cos t = -10\sin t$$

or $-B\sin t + A\cos t = -10\sin t$

By equating the coefficients of the sine and cosine terms we have

$$B = 10, \; A = 0$$

and can compute the current

$$i(t) = 10\cos t \text{ A}$$

b) $v_L(t) = L\frac{di}{dt} = \frac{di}{dt} = -10\sin t$ V

c) $v_R(t) = R\,i = 10\cos t$ V

4.34

$$-i_s + \frac{1}{40}v_{out} + 50\times10^{-6}\frac{d}{dt}v_{out} + 10\int v_{out}(t)dt = 0$$

$$-15\cos377t + \left[\frac{1}{40} + 50\times10^{-6}\frac{d}{dt} + 10\int dt\right]\cdot$$

$$(A\sin377t + B\cos377t) = 0$$

$$-15\cos377t + \frac{1}{40}A\sin377t + \frac{1}{40}B\cos377t$$

$$+0.01885A\cos377t - 0.01885B\sin377t$$

$$-0.02653A\cos377t + 0.02653B\sin377t = 0$$

$$-15\cos377t + (0.025A + 0.0076752B)\sin377t$$

$$+(-0.0076752A + 0.025B)\cos377t = 0$$

Equating coefficients on sin and cos gives

$$0.025A + 0.0076752B = 0$$

$$-0.0076752A + 0.025B = +15$$

Solve these two equations for

$A = -168.338$ $\quad$ $B = 548.319$

(a) $v_{out}(t) = -168.338\sin377t$

$+548.319\cos377t$ V

(b)

$$i_R(t) = \frac{1}{40}v_R(t) = -4.208\sin377t + 13.708\cos377t \text{ A}$$

(c)

$$i_L = \frac{1}{0.1}\int v(t)dt = 4.465\cos377t + 14.544\sin377t \text{ A}$$

4.35

Define the operators $D = \frac{d}{dt}$ and $\frac{1}{D} = \int dt$

KCL Node 1

$$\frac{1}{1}v_1 + \frac{2}{D}(v_1 - v_2) + \frac{4}{D}v_1 = 0 \Rightarrow \left(1 + \frac{6}{D}\right)v_1 - \frac{2}{D}v_2 = 0$$

KCL Node 2

$$-i_s + \frac{1}{2}v_2 + \frac{2}{D}(v_2 - v_1) = 0 \Rightarrow -\frac{2}{D}v_1 + \left(\frac{1}{2} + \frac{2}{D}\right)v_2 = i_s$$

Cramer's rule yields

$$\begin{vmatrix} 1+\frac{6}{D} & -\frac{2}{D} \\ -\frac{2}{D} & \left(\frac{1}{2}+\frac{2}{D}\right) \end{vmatrix} v_1 = \begin{vmatrix} 0 & -\frac{2}{D} \\ i_s & \end{vmatrix}$$

$$\left(\frac{1}{2} + \frac{5}{D} + \frac{8}{D^2}\right)v_1 = \frac{2}{D}i_s$$

Differentiate twice and multiply by 2 to obtain

$$(D^2 + 10D + 16)v_1 = 4Di_s$$

$$s^2 + 10s + 16 = 0 \Rightarrow s = -2, -8$$

$$v_{in} = AC^{-2t} + Be^{-8t}$$

Replace differentiation with multiplication by zero to calculate v_{1p}, because $i_s = 1$ for

$t > 0$

$$[(0)^2 + 10(0) + 16]v_{1p} = 4(0)(1)$$

$$\Rightarrow v_p = 0 \quad t > 0$$

The source is zero for t < 0, so $i_1(0^+) = 0$,
$i_1(0^+) = 0$

$v_1 = v_{1p} + v_{1n} = Ae^{-2t} + Be^{-8t}$

KCL gives

$$\frac{1}{1}v_1(0^+) + i_1(0^+) + i_2(0^+) = 0 \Rightarrow v_1(0^+)$$

$$v_1(0^+) = 0 = Ae^0 + Be^0 \Rightarrow A + B = 0$$

KCL also gives

$$-1 + \frac{1}{2}v_2(0^+) + 0 \Rightarrow v_2(0^+) = 2\text{ V}$$

Differentiate the first KCL equation and evaluate at t = 0^+

$$\frac{1}{1}\left[-2Ae^{-2t} - 8Be^{-2t}\right]\Big|_{t=0^+}$$
$$+2\left[v_1(0^+) - v_2(0^+)\right] + 4v_1(0^+) = 0$$

-2A - 8B + 2(0 - 2) + 0 = 0

A + 4B = -2

Solve for $A = \frac{2}{3}$ and $B = -\frac{2}{3}$

$$v(t) = v_1(t) = \left(\frac{2}{3}e^{-2t} - \frac{2}{3}e^{-4t}\right)u(t)\ \text{ V}$$

Where $u(t) = \begin{cases} 0 & t < 0 \\ 1 & t > 0 \end{cases}$

4.36

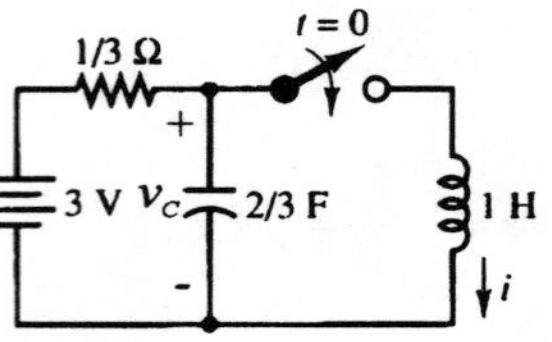

$$i(0^-) = 0 \Rightarrow i(0^+) = 0$$

$$v_C(0^-) = 3V \Rightarrow v_C(0^+) = 3V \Rightarrow \frac{di}{dt}\Big|_{t=0^+} = 3$$

For $t > 0$

$$\frac{1}{3}\left(\frac{2}{3}\dot{v}_C + 1\right) + v_C = 3$$

and $$v_C = 1\frac{di}{dt}$$

$$\therefore\ \frac{2}{9}\frac{d^2i}{dt^2} + \frac{1}{3}i + 1\frac{di}{dt} = 3$$

or

$$\frac{d^2i}{dt^2} + \frac{9}{2}\frac{di}{dt} + \frac{3}{2}i = \frac{27}{2}$$

The characteristic equation has roots at -0.363 and -4.137.

Therefore, the solution is of the form

$$i(t) = Ae^{-0.363t} + Be^{-4.137t} + C$$

where

$$\frac{3}{2}C = \frac{27}{2} \Rightarrow C = 9$$

So,

$$i(t) = Ae^{-0.363t} + Be^{-4.137t} + 9$$

and

$$\frac{di}{dt} = -0.363Ae^{-0.363t} - 4.137Be^{-4.137t}$$

$$i(0^+) = 0 \Rightarrow A + B + 9 = 0$$

$$\frac{di}{dt}\Big|_{t=0^+} = 3 \Rightarrow -0.363A - 4.137B = 3$$

Solving, A=-9.071 and B=0.071. Then,
$i(t) = -9.071e^{-0.363t} + 0.071e^{-4.137t} + 9\ A$ for t>0

EIT 4.34

By applying KCL: $i_S = i_R + i_C + i_L$ with

$$i_S = \frac{v_{out}}{R},\ i_C = C\frac{dv_{out}}{dt},\ i_L = \frac{1}{L}\int_{-\infty}^{t} v_{out}(\tau)\,d\tau$$

Differentiating, we have

$$\frac{di_S}{dt} = \frac{1}{R}\frac{dv_{out}}{dt} + C\frac{d^2v_{out}}{dt^2} + \frac{1}{L}v_{out}$$

Rearranging the equation:

$$\frac{d^2v_{out}}{dt^2} + \frac{1}{RC}\frac{dv_{out}}{dt} + \frac{1}{LC}v_{out} = \frac{1}{C}\frac{di_S}{dt}$$

$$\frac{d^2v_{out}}{dt^2} + 500\frac{dv_{out}}{dt} + 2\times10^5 v_{out} = 2\times10^4(-5{,}655\sin377t)$$

Assuming $v_{out} = A\sin\omega t + B\cos\omega t$

$$\frac{dv_{out}}{dt} = A\omega\cos\omega t - B\omega\sin\omega t$$

$$\frac{d^2v}{dt^2} = -A\omega^2\sin\omega t - B\omega^2\cos\omega t$$

with $\omega^2 = 142{,}129$ and substituting, we have

$$-142{,}129A\sin\omega t - 142{,}129B\cos\omega t$$
$$+ 500(377A\cos\omega t - 377B\sin\omega t) + 2\times10^5(A\sin\omega t + B\cos\omega t)$$
$$= -1.131\times10^8\sin377t$$

Grouping the sine and cosine terms we have:

$$(-142{,}129A - 188{,}500B + 200{,}000A)\sin\omega t$$
$$+ (-142{,}129B + 188{,}500A + 200{,}000B)\cos\omega t$$
$$= -1.131\times10^8\sin\omega t$$

This leads to the equations:

1) $57{,}871A - 188{,}500B = -1.131\times10^8$

2) $188{,}500A + 57{,}871B = 0$

From 2): $B = -\frac{188500A}{57871}$. Substituting into 1):

$$57{,}871A - 188{,}500\left(\frac{188{,}500}{57{,}871}\right)A = -1.131\times10^8$$

or $\quad -556{,}119.6A = -1.131\times10^8$

$$\boxed{A = 203.37352;\ B = -3.2572446\times A = -662.43729}$$

Therefore,

$$v_{out} = 203\sin377t - 662\cos377t\ \text{V}$$

4.35

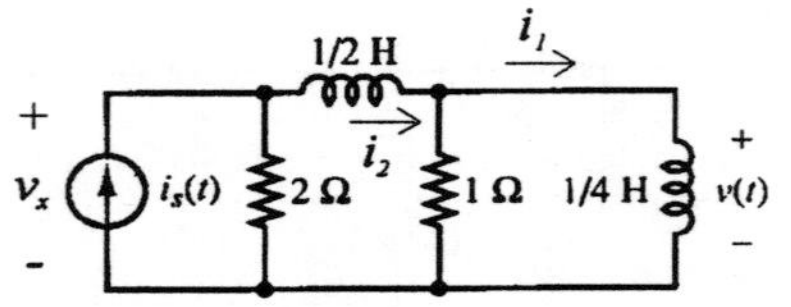

$$v = 1(i_2 - i_1) \Rightarrow \frac{dv}{dt} = \frac{di_2}{dt} - \frac{di_1}{dt}$$

$$v(0^+) = 0 \Rightarrow \left.\frac{di_1}{dt}\right|_{t=0^+} = 0$$

$$v_x(0^+) - v(0^+) = 2 - 0 = 2 \Rightarrow \frac{1}{2}\left.\frac{di_2}{dt}\right|_{t=0^+} = 2 \Rightarrow \left.\frac{di_2}{dt}\right|_{t=0^+} = 4$$

$$\therefore \left.\frac{dv}{dt}\right|_{t=0^+} = 4 - 0 = 4$$

By KCL, for $t > 0$,

$$-i_S + \frac{1}{2}v_x + 2\int_{-\infty}^{t}(v_x - v)d\tau = 0$$

and

$$2\int_{-\infty}^{t}(v - v_x)d\tau + \frac{1}{1}v + 4\int_{-\infty}^{t} v d\tau = 0$$

From the second equation,

$$2\int_{-\infty}^{t} v_x d\tau = 2\int_{-\infty}^{t} v d\tau + v + 4\int_{-\infty}^{t} v d\tau$$

$$= 6\int_{-\infty}^{t} v d\tau + v$$

or

$$2v_x = 6v + \frac{dv}{dt}$$

$$\Rightarrow v_x = 3v + \frac{1}{2}\frac{dv}{dt}$$

Substituting this into the first KCL equation,

$$\frac{1}{2}\left(3v + \frac{1}{2}\frac{dv}{dt}\right) + \left(6\int_{-\infty}^{t} v d\tau + v\right) - 2\int_{-\infty}^{t} v d\tau = 1$$

$$\frac{3}{2}v + \frac{1}{4}\frac{dv}{dt} + 6\int_{-\infty}^{t} v d\tau + v - 2\int_{-\infty}^{t} v d\tau = 1$$

$$\frac{1}{4}\frac{dv}{dt} + \frac{5}{2}v + 4\int_{-\infty}^{t} v d\tau = 1$$

or

$$\ddot{v} + 10\dot{v} + 16v = 0$$

This has a solution of the form

$$v(t) = Ae^{-2t} + Be^{-8t}$$

Given this, then

$$\dot{v}(t) = -2Ae^{-2t} - 8Be^{-8t}$$

Therefore

$$v(0) = A + B = 0$$

and

$$\dot{v}(0) = -2A - 8B = 4$$

Solving, $A = \frac{2}{3}$ and $B = -\frac{2}{3}$. Therefore,

$$v(t) = \frac{2}{3}e^{-2t} - \frac{2}{3}e^{-8t}\ V \quad \text{for } t > 0$$

4.36

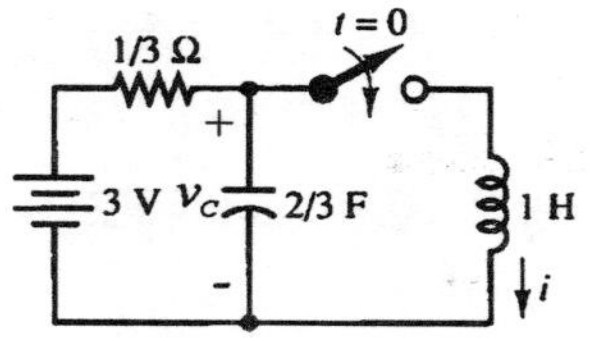

$i(0^-)=0 \Rightarrow i(0^+)=0$

$v_C(0^-)=3V \Rightarrow v_C(0^+)=3V \Rightarrow \left.\dfrac{di}{dt}\right|_{t=0^+}=3$

For $t>0$

$$\frac{1}{3}\left(\frac{2}{3}\dot{v}_C+1\right)+v_C=3$$

and
$$v_C=1\frac{di}{dt}$$

$$\therefore\ \frac{2}{9}\frac{d^2i}{dt^2}+\frac{1}{3}i+1\frac{di}{dt}=3$$

or

$$\frac{d^2i}{dt^2}+\frac{9}{2}\frac{di}{dt}+\frac{3}{2}i=\frac{27}{2}$$

The characteristic equation has roots at -0.363 and -4.137.

Therefore, the solution is of the form

$$i(t)=Ae^{-0.363t}+Be^{-4.137t}+C$$

where

$$\frac{3}{2}C=\frac{27}{2} \Rightarrow C=9$$

So,

$$i(t)=Ae^{-0.363t}+Be^{-4.137t}+9$$

and

$$\frac{di}{dt}=-0.363Ae^{-0.363t}-4.137Be^{-4.137t}$$

$i(0^+)=0 \Rightarrow A+B+9=0$

$\left.\dfrac{di}{dt}\right|_{t=0^+}=3 \Rightarrow -0.363A-4.137B=3$

Solving, A=-9.071 and B=0.071. Then,

$i(t)=-9.071e^{-0.363t}+0.071e^{-4.137t}+9\ A$ for t>0

EIT 4.37

a) $\mathbf{I}(\omega)=0.5\angle 45°$ A

b) The current waveform is shown below.

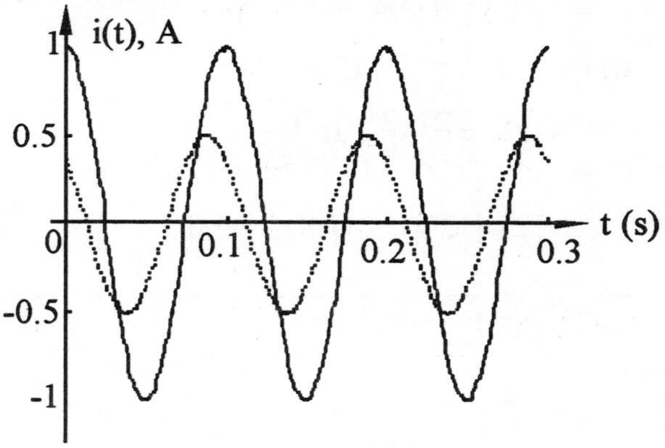

___ cos(2π10t)

..... 0.5cos(2π10t + 45°)

4.38

In phasor form:

a) $\mathbf{V}(\omega)=155\angle-25°$ V

b) $\mathbf{V}(\omega)=5\angle-130°$ V

c) $\mathbf{I}(\omega)=10\angle 63° + 15\angle-42°$

$= (4.54 + j8.91) + (11.15 - j\,10.04)$

$= 15.69 - j1.13 = 15.73\angle-4.12°$ A

d) $\mathbf{I}(\omega)=460\angle-25° - 220\angle-75°$

$= (416.90 - j194.40) - (56.94 - j212.50)$

$= 359.96 + j18.10 = 360.4\angle 2.88°$ A

4.39

a) $4 + j\,4 = 4\sqrt{2}\ \angle 45° = 5.66\angle 45°$

b) $-3 + j\,4 = 5\ \angle\ 126.9°$

c) $j + 2 - j\,4 - 3 = -1 - j\,3 = 3.16\ \angle-108.4°$

4.40

a) $(50 + j\,10)\,(4 + j\,8)$

$= 200 + j400 + j\,40 + j^2\,80 = 120 + j\,440$

$= 456.1\angle 74.7°$

b) $(j2 - 2)\,(4 + j\,5)\,(2 + j\,7)$

$= (-18 - j\,2)\,(2 + j\,7)$

$= -36 - j126 - j4 - j^2\,14$

$= -22 - j130 = 131.8\angle -99.6°$

EIT 4.41

a) $A = 4 + j\,4,\ \ A^* = 4 - j\,4$

$B = 2 - j\,8,\ \ B^* = 2 + j\,8$

$C = -5 + j\,2,\ \ C^* = -5 - j\,2$

b)

$$\frac{1 + j7}{4 + j4} = \frac{(1 + j7)\,(4 - j4)}{(4 + j4)\,(4 - j4)}$$

$$= \frac{4 - j4 + j28 - j^2\,28}{16 + 16} = \frac{32 + j24}{32}$$

$$= 1 + j\,0.75 = 1.25\angle 36.87°$$

$$\frac{j4}{2 - j8} = \frac{j4\,(2 + j8)}{(2 - j8)\,(2 + j8)}$$

$$= \frac{-32 + j8}{4 + 64}$$

$$= -\frac{32}{68} + j\frac{8}{68} = 0.485\angle 165.96°$$

$$\frac{1}{-5 + j2} = \frac{1\,(-5 - j2)}{(-5 + j2)\,(-5 - j2)}$$

$$= \frac{-5 - j2}{25 + 4}$$

$$= -\frac{5}{29} - j\frac{2}{29} = 0.1857\angle -158.2°$$

c) Repeat b) converting to polar form first:

$$\frac{1 + j7}{4 + j4} = \frac{7.071\angle 81.87°}{4\sqrt{2}\,\angle 45°} = 1.25\angle 36.87°$$

$$\frac{j4}{2 - j8} = \frac{4\angle 90°}{8.246\angle -75.96°} = 0.485\angle 165.96°$$

$$\frac{1}{-5 + j2} = \frac{1\angle 0°}{5.385\angle 158.2°}$$

$$= 0.1857\angle -158.2°$$

4.42

(a) From

$$\cos(\alpha+\beta) = \cos\alpha\cos\beta - \sin\alpha\sin\beta$$

$$10\cos(\omega t + 30°) = 10\cos 30° \cos\omega t - 10\sin 30° \sin\omega t$$

$$= 10\left(\frac{\sqrt{3}}{2}\right)\cos\omega t - 10\left(\frac{1}{2}\right)\sin\omega t$$

$$= 8.66\cos\omega t - 5\sin\omega t$$

$$20\cos(\omega t + 60°) = 20\cos 60° \cos\omega t - 20\sin 60° \sin\omega t$$

$$= 20\left(\frac{1}{2}\right)\cos\omega t - 20\left(\frac{\sqrt{3}}{2}\right)\sin\omega t$$

$$= 10\cos\omega t - 17.32\sin\omega t$$

$$v(t) = (8.66+10)\cos\omega t - (5+17.32)\sin\omega t$$

$$= 18.66\cos\omega t - 22.32\sin\omega t$$

Now, assume

$$v(t) = A\cos\phi\cos\omega t - A\sin\phi\sin\omega t$$

$$= A\cos(\omega t + \phi)$$

Since $\dfrac{A\sin\phi}{A\cos\phi} = \tan\phi$, we have

$$\phi = \tan^{-1}\left(\frac{22.32}{18.66}\right) = 50.1°$$

and

$$A = \frac{18.66}{\cos\phi} = 29.09$$

$$\therefore v(t) = 29.09\cos(\omega t + 50.1°)$$

(b) Using phasors,

$$V_1(\omega) = 10\angle 30° = 10\frac{\sqrt{3}}{2} + j10\frac{1}{2} = 8.66 + j5$$

$$V_2(\omega) = 20\angle 60° = 20\frac{1}{2} + j20\frac{\sqrt{3}}{2} = 10 + j17.32$$

$$V(\omega) = (8.66+10) + j(5+17.32)$$

$$= 18.66 + j22.32$$

$$= 29.09\angle 50.1°$$

$$\therefore v(t) = 29.09\cos(\omega t + 50.1°)$$

4.43

The series impedance of the circuit is

$$Z_{eq} = R + j\omega L + \frac{1}{j\omega C}$$

$$= 15 + j(0.001\omega - \frac{1}{10^{-6}\omega})$$

This impedance is purely resistive if its imaginary part (the reactance) is zero. Therefore, we solve for the frequency, ω, at which $0.001\omega = \dfrac{1}{10^{-6}\omega}$:

From this, $\omega^2 = \dfrac{1}{10^{-3}\times 10^{-6}} = 10^9$

and $\omega = 31{,}622.77$ rad/s

EIT 4.44

a) $Z_L = R + jX_L = 1 + j377 \times 13.26 \times 10^{-3}$

$= 1 + j5$

b) $Z_L' = Z_L \parallel Z_C, \qquad Z_C = \frac{1}{j\omega C} = \frac{1}{j377C}$

$$\therefore \; Z_L' = \frac{\frac{1}{j377C}(1 + j5)}{\frac{1}{j377C} + 1 + j5}$$

$$= \frac{1 + j5}{1 - 1885C + j377C}$$

The impedance angle is:

$$\phi_{ZL}' = \tan^{-1}(\frac{5}{1}) - \tan^{-1}\{\frac{377C}{1 - 1885C}\}$$

In order to have a strictly real impedance we set $\phi_{ZL}' = 0$, or:

$$5 = \frac{377C}{1 - 1885C}$$, which leads to:

$$C = \frac{5}{9802} = 510.1\ \mu F$$

c) $$Z_L' = \frac{1 + j5}{1 - 1885 \times \frac{5}{9802} + j377 \times \frac{5}{9802}}$$

$$= \frac{1 + j5}{\frac{377}{9802}(1 + j5)} = \frac{9802}{377} = 26\ \Omega$$

4.45

a) Let Z_1 denote the impedance of the parallel R_C-C combination:

$$Z_1 = R_C \parallel \frac{1}{j\omega C} = \frac{R_C \frac{1}{j\omega C}}{R_C + \frac{1}{j\omega C}} = \frac{R_C}{j\omega R_C C + 1}$$

Let $R_1=R_2=R/2$ and $L_1=L_2=L/2$. The total equivalent resistance, Z_{ab}, is given by:

$$Z_{ab} = R_1 + j\omega L_1 + Z_1 + R_2 + j\omega L_2$$

$$= R + j\omega L + \frac{R_C}{j\omega R_C C + 1}$$

$$= \frac{[R+R_C-\omega^2 L R_C C] + j[\omega(RR_C C+L)]}{1+j\omega R_C C}$$

$$\approx \frac{(R_C-\omega^2 L R_C C) + j\omega R R_C C}{1+j\omega R_C C}$$

$$= \frac{(10^8 - 2\times10^{-5}\omega^2) + j2\times10^{-4}\omega}{1 + j100\omega}$$

b) If we assume $R_C >> \frac{1}{\omega C}$ then

$$Z_1 \approx \frac{1}{j\omega C}$$

and $\quad Z_{ab} \approx R + j\omega L + \frac{1}{j\omega C}$

$$= R_{ab} + jX_{ab}$$

where $\quad R_{ab} = R$

and $\quad X_{ab} = \omega L - \frac{1}{\omega C}$

Now, $\quad X_{ab} > 10\, R_{ab} \Rightarrow \omega L - \frac{1}{\omega C} > R$

or $\quad \omega^2 LC - 1 > \omega RC$

But $\quad LC\omega^2 - RC\omega - 1 = 0$

$$\Rightarrow \omega = \frac{RC \pm \sqrt{(RC)^2 + 4LC}}{2LC}$$

$$= 2{,}236{,}073 \text{ rad/s}$$

(We drop the negative sign for physical reasons)

$\therefore \quad \omega \le 2{,}236{,}073$ rad/s

or $\quad f \le 355{,}882$ Hz

EIT 4.46

$$Z_{ab} = R_1 \parallel L_1 = \frac{R_1 (j\omega L_1)}{R_1 + j\omega L_1}$$

$$= \frac{(j\omega R_1 L_1)(R_1 - j\omega L_1)}{R_1^2 + (\omega L_1)^2}$$

$$= \frac{\omega^2 R_1 L_1^2 + j\omega R_1^2 L_1}{R_1^2 + (\omega L_1)^2}$$

$$R_2 = \frac{\omega^2 R_1 L_1^2}{R_1^2 + (\omega L_1)^2}$$

$$j\omega L_2 = \frac{j\omega R_1^2 L_1}{R_1^2 + (\omega L_1)^2}$$

$$L_2 = \frac{R_1^2 L_1}{R_1^2 + (\omega L_1)^2}$$

4.47

$$\omega = 3\frac{rad}{s}$$

$$V_S = 12\angle 0° V$$

$$Z_C = \frac{1}{j\omega C} = -j2\Omega$$

$$Z_L = j\omega L = j6\Omega$$

$$Z_{total} = 4 + j6 - j2 = 4 + j2\ \Omega$$

$$I = \frac{12}{4 + j4} = 1.5 - j1.5 = 2.12\angle -45°$$

$$\therefore\ i(t) = 2.12\cos(\omega t - 45°)\ A$$

4.48

$$\omega = 2\frac{rad}{s}$$

$$I_S = 10\angle 0°\ A$$

$$Z_L = j\omega L = j4\Omega$$

$$Z_C = \frac{1}{j\omega C} = -j\Omega$$

$$Z_{eq} = \frac{1}{\frac{1}{R} + \frac{1}{Z_L} + \frac{1}{Z_C}} = \frac{1}{0.5 - j0.25 + j}$$

$$= \frac{1}{0.5 + j0.75} = 0.615 - j0.923\ \Omega$$

$$V = I_S Z_{eq} = 10(0.615 - j0.923)$$

$$= 6.15 - j9.23 = 11.09\angle -56.3°\ V$$

$$v(t) = 11.09\cos(2t - 56.3°)\ V$$

4.49

$$Z_{eq} = \frac{1}{\frac{1}{5} + \left(\frac{1}{-j5}\right)} = 3.54\angle -45°\ \Omega$$

$$V_S = I_S Z_{eq} = (10\angle -45°)(3.54\angle -45°)$$

$$= 35.4\angle -90°\ V$$

$$I_1 = \frac{V_S}{R} = 7.07\angle -90°\ A$$

4.50

$$Z_L = j10\ \Omega$$

$$V_2 = \frac{3}{2 + j10 + 3} 25\angle 0° = \frac{75\angle 0°}{5 + j10}$$

$$= \frac{75\angle 0°}{11.18\angle 63.43°}$$

$$= 6.71\angle -63.43°\ V$$

4.51

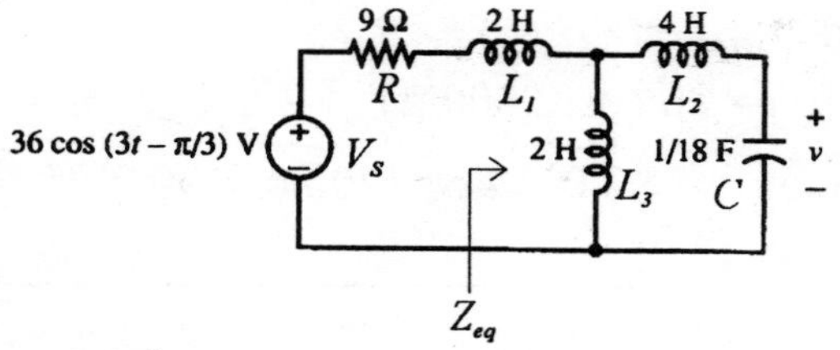

$$\omega = 3\frac{rad}{s}$$

$$V_S = 36\angle -60^\circ\ V$$

$$Z_{L_2} = j \times 3 \times 4 = j12\Omega$$

$$Z_C = \frac{1}{j \times 3 \times \frac{1}{18}} = -j6\Omega$$

$$Z_{L_2} + Z_C = j6\Omega$$

$$Z_{L_3} = j \times 3 \times 2 = j6\Omega$$

$$Z_{eq} = \frac{1}{\frac{1}{j6} + \frac{1}{j6}} = 3\angle 90^\circ\ \Omega$$

$$\begin{aligned} Z_T &= 9 + j \times 3 \times 2 + Z_{eq} \\ &= 9 + j6 + j3 \\ &= 9 + j9 \\ &= 12.73\angle 45^\circ \end{aligned}$$

$$I = \frac{V_S}{Z_T} = \frac{36\angle -60^\circ}{12.73\angle -105^\circ}$$

$$\begin{aligned} V_{eq} &= IZ_{eq} = (2.83\angle -105^\circ)(3\angle 90^\circ) \\ &= 8.49\angle -15^\circ\ V \end{aligned}$$

$$V = \frac{-j6}{j6} V_{eq} = -8.49\angle -15^\circ\ V$$

$$\begin{aligned} v &= -8.49\cos(3t - 15^\circ) \\ &= 8.49\cos(3t + 165^\circ)\ V \end{aligned}$$

4.52

Since the two sources are of different frequencies, we must use the superposition method.

1) For the 100 Hz current source, $\omega=200\pi$, and

$$\mathbf{I}_S(\omega=200\pi) = 0.5\angle 0° \text{ A}$$

Using the current divider rule, the inductor current is

$$\mathbf{I}_L(\omega=200\pi) = \frac{R_1}{R_1+j\omega L}\ 0.5\angle 0°$$

$$\text{Å } 0.5\angle 0° \text{ A}$$

since the impedance of the inductor has negligible magnitude at this frequency ($j\omega L = j0.063\ \Omega << 150\ \Omega$). Thus

$$\mathbf{V}_L(\omega=200\pi) = j\omega L \times \mathbf{I}_L(\omega=200\pi)$$

$$= 0.0314\angle 90° \text{ V}$$

Since R_1 and L are in parallel,

$$\mathbf{V}_{R1}(\omega=200\pi) = \mathbf{V}_L(\omega=200\pi)$$

$$= 0.0314\angle 90° \text{ V}$$

2) For the 1,000 Hz current source, $\omega=2{,}000\pi$, and

$$\mathbf{V}_S(\omega=2{,}000\pi) = 20\angle 0° \text{ V}$$

Using the voltage divider rule, the voltage across R_1 is

$$\mathbf{V}_{R1}(\omega=2{,}000\pi) = \frac{R_1}{R_1+j\omega L}\ 20\angle 0°$$

$$\approx 1\angle{-0.24°} \times 20\angle 0°$$

$$\approx 20\angle 0° \text{ V}$$

since even at the frequency $\omega=2{,}000\pi$ the inductor has negligible impedance. Thus, the voltage across the inductor is very nearly

$$\mathbf{V}_L(\omega=2{,}000\pi) = 0\angle 0° \text{ V}$$

Finally, the complete expressions for the voltages are:

$$v_L(t) = 0.0314 \cos(200\pi t + 90°) \text{ V}$$

and

$$v_{R1}(t) = 20 \cos(2{,}000\pi t) + 0.0314 \cos(200\pi t + 90°) \text{ V}$$

EIT 4.53

We have

$$j\omega_L = j(1000)(0.003) = j3$$

By voltage division:

$$V_L = \frac{j3}{4+j3}(24\angle 0°)$$

$$= 8.64 + j\,11.52 = 14.4 \angle 53.13°$$

Therefore

$$v_L(t) = 14.4\cos(1000t + 53.13°) \quad V$$

4.54

We have C = 100 μF, R = 100 Ω

By current division:

$$I_R = -\frac{\frac{1}{j\omega C}}{R + \frac{1}{j\omega C}} \times 1\angle 0°$$

$$= \frac{-1}{1 + j\omega RC} = \frac{-1}{1 + j2\pi}$$

$$= 157\times 10^{-3}\angle 99.04° \quad A$$

$$i_R(t) = 157\cos(200\pi t + 99.04°) \quad mA$$

4.55

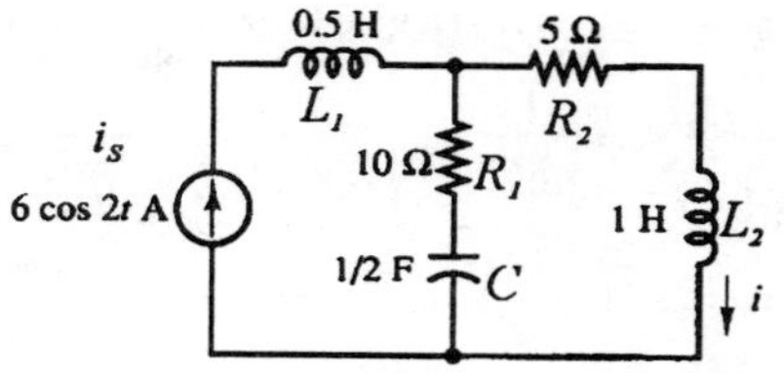

$$\omega = 2\frac{rad}{s}$$

$$Z_{L_2} = j2\Omega$$

$$Z_C = \frac{1}{j\times 2\times \frac{1}{2}} = -j\Omega$$

$$I = \frac{10-j}{(10-j)+(5+j2)} I_S$$

$$= \frac{10-j}{15+j} 6\angle 0°$$

$$= 4.01\angle -9.52° \; A$$

$$i = 4.01\cos(2t - 9.52°) \; A$$

4.56

$$V_{OUT}(\omega) = 10\times 10^{-3}\angle 90°(j1000 - j10000)$$

$$= 10\times 10^{-3}\angle 90° \times (-j\,9000) = 90\angle 0°$$

$$v_{OUT}(t) = 90\cos(\omega t) \quad V$$

EIT 4.57

(a) $Z_L = j\omega L = j1000\times10\times10^{-3} = j10\ \Omega$

$$Z_C = \frac{1}{j\omega C} = \frac{1}{j10^3\times0.1\times10^{-6}}$$

$$= -j10^4\ \Omega$$

The equivalent impedance is:

$$Z_{TH} = \frac{j10\times(-j10^4)}{j10 - j10^4} + 500$$

$$= 500 + j10.01\ \Omega$$

The equivalent Thèvenin voltage is:

$$\mathbf{V_T} = \mathbf{V_S} = 10\angle0°\ \text{V}$$

(b) $Z_L = j\omega L = j10^6\times10\times10^{-3} = j10^4\ \Omega$

$$Z_C = \frac{1}{j\omega C} = \frac{1}{j10^6\times0.1\times10^{-6}} = -j10\ \Omega$$

The equivalent impedance is:

$$Z_T = 500 - j10.01\ \Omega$$

4.58

$$Z_C = \frac{1}{j\omega C} = \frac{1}{j10\times100\times10^{-6}} = -j1000\ \Omega$$

The equivalent impedance is:

$Z_T = R \parallel Z_C =$

$$= \frac{1000\times(-j1000)}{1000 - j1000} = \frac{-j10^6}{1414\angle-45°}$$

$$= 707\angle-45° = 500 - j500\ \Omega$$

The Thèvenin voltage is

$$\mathbf{V_T} = \frac{-j1000}{-j1000 + 1000}\times12\angle0°$$

$$= 8.49\angle-45°\ \text{V}$$

EIT 4.59

$$\mathbf{V_S} = 2\angle0°\ \text{V}$$

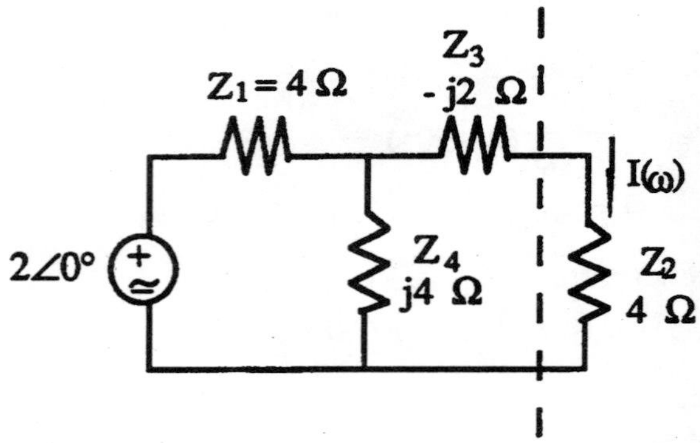

The Thévenin equivalent impedance of the circuit connected to Z_2 is:

$$Z_T = (Z_1 \parallel Z_4) + Z_3 = \frac{j16}{4+j4} - j2 = \frac{8+j8}{4+j4} =$$

$$\frac{11.314\angle45°}{5.657\angle45°} = 2\angle0°\ \Omega$$

The Thèvenin voltage is:

$$\mathbf{V_T} = \mathbf{V_S}\frac{Z_4}{Z_1 + Z_4} = 2\angle0°\times\frac{j4}{4+j4}$$

$$= \sqrt{2}\angle45°\ \text{V}$$

The current is:

$$\mathbf{I}(\omega) = \frac{\mathbf{V_T}}{Z_2 + Z_T} = \frac{\sqrt{2}\angle45°}{4 + 2\angle0°}$$

$$= \frac{\sqrt{2}}{6}\angle45°\ \text{A}$$

or:

$$i(t) = \frac{\sqrt{2}}{6}\cos(2t + 45°)$$

$$= 0.2357\cos(2t + 45°)\ \text{A}$$

***4.60**

In the phasor domain:

$$Z_C = \frac{-j}{1500(1\times10^{-6})} = -j\frac{2000}{3} = -j\,666.7$$

$$Z_L = j\,(1500)(0.5) = j\,750$$

By applying KVL in the first loop, we have

$$15\angle0° = 100\,I_1 + (-j\frac{2000}{3})(I_1 - I_2)$$

By applying KVL in the second loop, we have

$$0 = j\frac{2000}{3}\,I_1 + (75 + j\,(750 - \frac{2000}{3}))\,I_2$$

That is

1) $15\angle0° = (100 - j\frac{2000}{3})\,I_1 + j\frac{2000}{3}\,I_2$

2) 2) $0 = j\frac{2000}{3}\,I_1 + (75 + j\frac{250}{3})\,I_2$

By solving above equations, we have

$$\mathbf{I_1} = 3.3\times10^{-3}\angle52.7°$$

$$\mathbf{I_2} = 19.6\times10^{-3}\angle{-85.3°}$$

$i_1(t) = 3.3\cos(1500t + 52.7°)$ mA

$i_2(t) = 19.6\cos(1500t - 85.3°)$ mA

***4.61**

$$Z_C = \frac{-j}{100\times500\times10^{-6}} = -j\,20$$

$$Z_L = j100\times0.2 = j\,20$$

Applying KCL at node 1, we have

$$40\angle0° = \frac{\mathbf{V_1}}{10} + \frac{\mathbf{V_1} - \mathbf{V_2}}{-j20}$$

$$40\angle0° = (\frac{1}{10} + \frac{1}{-j20})\,\mathbf{V_1} - \frac{\mathbf{V_2}}{-j20}$$

1) $40\angle0° = (\frac{1}{10} + \frac{j}{20})\,\mathbf{V_1} - \frac{j}{20}\,\mathbf{V_2}$

Applying KCL at node 2, we have

$$\frac{\mathbf{V_1} - \mathbf{V_2}}{-j20} = \frac{\mathbf{V_2}}{40} + \frac{\mathbf{V_2}}{j20}$$

$$\frac{\mathbf{V_1}}{-j20} = \frac{\mathbf{V_2}}{40} + \frac{\mathbf{V_2}}{j20} + \frac{\mathbf{V_2}}{-j20}$$

$$\frac{\mathbf{V_1}}{-j20} = \frac{\mathbf{V_2}}{40}$$

2) $\mathbf{V_1} = \frac{-j20}{40}\,\mathbf{V_2} = -j\frac{1}{2}\,\mathbf{V_2}$

By replacing $\mathbf{V_1}$ in 1) we have

$$40\angle0° = (\frac{1}{10} + \frac{j}{20})(-j\frac{1}{2}\,\mathbf{V_2}) - \frac{j}{20}\,\mathbf{V_2}$$

$$= -\frac{j}{20}\,\mathbf{V_2} + \frac{1}{40}\,\mathbf{V_2} - \frac{j}{20}\,\mathbf{V_2}$$

$$40\angle0° = (\frac{1}{40} - \frac{j}{10})\,\mathbf{V_2}$$

$$\mathbf{V_2} = \frac{40\angle0°}{(\frac{1}{40} - \frac{j}{10})} = 388\angle75.96°$$

$$\mathbf{V_1} = -j\frac{1}{2}\,\mathbf{V_2} = 194\angle{-14.04°}$$

$v_1(t) = 194\cos(100t - 14.04°)$ V

$v_2(t) = 388\cos(100t + 75.96°)$ V

***4.62**

a) Assuming a balanced circuit, we have $v_{ab} = 0$, that is, $v_a = v_b$

From the voltage divider, we have

$$\frac{R_2}{j\omega L_3 - \frac{j}{\omega C_3} + R_2} = \frac{jX_4}{R_1 + jX_4}$$

Inverting both sides and equating imaginary parts, we have

$$R_1R_2 = \left(-\omega L_3 + \frac{1}{\omega C_3}\right)X_4$$

$$X_4 = \frac{R_1R_2}{\left(\frac{1}{\omega C_3} - \omega L_3\right)}$$

b) $$X_4 = \frac{100\times 1}{\frac{1}{2000\times 4.7\times 10^{-6}} - 2000\times 0.098}$$

$$= -\ 1.1158594$$

Negative reactance implies that the component is a capacitor.

From $\frac{1}{\omega C} = 1.1158594$, we have

$$C = \frac{1}{2000\times 1.1158594} = 448\ \mu F$$

c) If the reactances of L_3 and C_3 cancel, the bridge can not measure X_4. Thus, the condition to be avoided is:

$$\omega L_3 - \frac{1}{\omega C_3} = 0$$

$$L_3C_3 = \frac{1}{\omega^2} \Rightarrow \omega = \frac{1}{\sqrt{L_3C_3}}$$

For the component values soecified in (b),

$$\omega = \frac{1}{\sqrt{0.098\times 4.7\times 10^{-6}}} = 1473\ \text{rad/s}$$

or $$f = 234.5\ \text{Hz}$$

EIT 4.63

$$Z_T = (4\ \|\ j4) + (-\ j2)$$
$$= j2(1 - j) - j2$$
$$= 2 + j2 + (-j2) = 2\ \Omega$$

4.64

$$\mathbf{V}_T = 40\mathbf{I}_2$$

From the current division, we have

$$\mathbf{I}_2 = \frac{10}{(40 - j20) + 10}\ 40\angle 0°$$
$$= 7.4278\ \angle 21.8°\ \text{A}$$
$$\mathbf{V}_T = 40\ \mathbf{I}_2 = 297\angle 21.8°\ \text{V}$$
$$v_T(t) = 297\cos(100t + 21.8°)\ \text{V}$$

4.65

$$Z_L = j\Omega$$
$$Z_C = -j2\Omega$$
$$Z = Z_L + Z_C \| R$$
$$= j + \frac{1}{\frac{1}{-j2} + \frac{1}{2}}$$
$$= j + \frac{j2}{-1 + j}$$
$$= j + \frac{(j2)\ (-1-j)}{(-1+j)\ (-1-j)}$$
$$= j + \frac{j2(-1-j)}{1+1}$$
$$= j - j + 1$$
$$= 1\Omega$$

4.66

$$V_{TH} = \left(\frac{8+j8}{8+j8-j2}\right)5\angle -30^\circ$$

$$= \left(\frac{8\sqrt{2}\angle 45^\circ}{10\angle 36.87^\circ}\right)5\angle -30^\circ$$

$$= 5.66\angle -21.87^\circ\ V$$

$$Z_{TH} = \frac{(8+j8)(-j2)}{8+j8-j2}$$

$$= \frac{16\sqrt{2}\angle -45^\circ}{10\angle 36.87^\circ}$$

$$= 2.26\angle -81.87^\circ\ \Omega$$

4.67

$$Z_C = \frac{1}{j\times 5\times \frac{1}{10}} = -j2\Omega$$

$$Z_L = j\times 5\times \frac{4}{5} = j4\Omega$$

$$Y = \frac{1}{Z_C} + \frac{1}{R+Z_L}$$

$$= \frac{1}{-j2} + \frac{1}{3+j4}$$

$$= j\frac{1}{2} + \frac{(1)}{(3+j4)}\frac{(3-j4)}{(3-j4)}$$

$$= j\frac{1}{2} + \frac{3-j4}{9+16}$$

$$= j\frac{1}{2} + \frac{3-j4}{25}$$

$$= j\frac{1}{2} + \frac{3}{25} - j\frac{4}{25}$$

$$= 0.12 + j0.34\ S$$

EIT 4.68

From the voltage divider, we have

$$\mathbf{V_T} = \frac{j4}{4+j4}\,2\angle 0^\circ = (1+j)$$

$$= \sqrt{2}\,\angle 45^\circ = 1.414\angle 45^\circ\ \text{V}$$

$$v_T(t) = 1.414\cos(2t + 45^\circ)\ \text{V}$$

4.69

From the result of Problem 4.63, we have $Z_T = 2\ \Omega$. From the current divider, we have

$$\mathbf{I_N} = \frac{j4}{j4 - j2}\,\mathbf{I} = 2\mathbf{I}$$

and

$$j4 \parallel -j2 = \frac{(-j2)(j4)}{j2} = -j4$$

The current is

$$\mathbf{I} = \frac{2\angle 0^\circ}{4 - j4} = \frac{\sqrt{2}}{4}\angle 45^\circ = 0.35355\angle 45^\circ\ \text{A}$$

Therefore,

$$\mathbf{I_N} = 2\mathbf{I} = 2\left(\frac{\sqrt{2}}{4}\angle 45^\circ\right) = 0.707\angle 45^\circ\ \text{A}$$

Chapter 5 Instructor Notes

Chapter 5 surveys all important aspects of electric power. Coverage of Chapter 5 can take place immediately following Chapter 4, or as part of a later course on energy systems or electric machines. The material in this chapter will be of particular importance to Civil, Industrial, and Mechanical engineers, who are concerned with the utilization of electric power for civil and industrial applications in their designs.

The chapter permits very flexible coverage, with sections 5.1 and 5.2 describing the basic single phase AC power ideas. A survey course might only use this introductory material. The next two sections discuss transformers and three-phase power. Two descriptive sections are also provided to introduce the ideas of residential wiring, grounding and safety, and the generation and distribution of AC power. These sections can be covered independent of the transformer and three-phase material.

The homework problems present a few simple applications in addition to the usual exercises meant to reinforce the understanding of the fundamentals. For example, problem 5.10 approaches the calculation of the power factor of an electric machine from the nameplate data; problem 5.25 asks the student to estimate the specifications of an emergency generator for a household; problem 5.52 illustrates the billing penalties incurred when electric loads have insufficient power factors (this problem is based on actual data supplied by Detroit Edison).

A few advanced problems (5.40-5.42) discuss transformer test methods; these problems may be suitable in a second course in energy systems. Similarly, those instructors who plan to integrate the three-phase material into a course on electric machines, will find that problems 5.48 and 5.57 can be assigned in conjunction with the material covered in Chapter 16, as part of a more in-depth look at three-phase machines.

Chapter 5 problem solutions

5.1

The instantaneous power p(t) is

$p(t) = v(t)i(t) =$

$$= \frac{VI}{2}\cos(\theta) + \frac{VI}{2}\cos(2\omega t + \theta_V + \theta_I)$$

We have $\theta = \theta_V - \theta_I = 0$, V = 80 V,

$$I = \frac{V}{R} = \frac{80}{2\times 10^3} = 40\text{ mA}$$

Therefore,

$$p(t) = \frac{80\times 40\times 10^{-3}}{2} + \frac{80\times 40\times 10^{-3}}{2}\times\cos(2\times 377t)$$

The peak value is at t = 0:

$$p_{peak} = 1600\times 10^{-3} + 1600\times 10^{-3} = 3.2\text{ W}$$

The average power P is

$$P = \frac{VI}{2}\cos(\theta) = \frac{80\times 40\times 10^{-3}}{2} = 1.6\text{ W}$$

5.2

The power dissipated in the soldering iron is:

$$P = \frac{V^2}{R} = \frac{117^2}{391} = 35\text{ W}$$

EIT 5.3

The power dissipated in the electric heater is:

$$P = \frac{V^2}{R} = \frac{240^2}{10} = 5760\text{ W}$$

5.4

The instantaneous power p(t) is

$p(t) = v(t)i(t)$

$$= \frac{VI}{2}\cos(\theta) + \frac{VI}{2}\cos(2\omega t + \theta_V + \theta_I)$$

We have $\theta = \theta_V - \theta_I = 0$, V = 10 V,

$$I = \frac{V}{R} = \frac{10}{200} = 50\text{ mA}$$

Therefore,

$$p(t) = \frac{10\times 50\times 10^{-3}}{2} + \frac{10\times 50\times 10^{-3}}{2}\cos(2\times 10^5 t)$$

The peak value is at t = 0:

$$p_{peak} = 250\times 10^{-3} + 250\times 10^{-3} = 0.5\text{ W}$$

The average power P is

$$P = \frac{VI}{2}\cos(\theta) = \frac{10\times 50\times 10^{-3}}{2} = 0.25\text{ W}$$

5.5

The average power in a resistor is given by:

$$P = \frac{1}{T}\int_0^T \frac{v^2}{R}\,dt$$

For the voltage of part (a), T = 3 s, R = 5 Ω

$$P = \frac{1}{3}\int_0^3 \frac{v^2}{5}dt = \frac{1}{3}\left\{\int_0^1 \frac{10^2}{5}dt + \int_1^3 0dt\right\} = \frac{20}{3}$$

$$= 6.67 \text{ W}$$

For the voltage of part (b),

$$T = 2 \text{ s}, \quad v(t) = 20 \sin \pi t \quad 0 \le t \le 1$$
$$= 0 \quad 1 \le t \le 2$$

$$P = \frac{1}{2}\int_0^2 \frac{v^2}{5}\,dt = \frac{1}{2p}\left\{\int_0^p \frac{20^2\sin^2 x}{5}\,dx + 0\right\}$$

$$= \frac{400}{10\pi}\int_0^\pi \sin^2 x dx = 20W$$

EIT 5.6

The average power is

$$P_{av} = \frac{1}{2}\ I^2R$$

(a) $P_{av} = \dfrac{4^2 \times 100}{2} = 800 \text{ W}$

(b) $P_{av} = \dfrac{4^2 \times 100}{2} = 800 \text{ W}$

(c) By using phasor techniques,we have

$\mathbf{I} = 4\angle 0° - 3\angle{-50°}$

$= 2.0716 + j2.298 = 3.094\angle 47.97°$

$i(t) = 3.094\cos(100t + 47.97°)$

$$P_{av} = \frac{3.094^2 \times 100}{2} = 478.6 \text{ W}$$

(d) $v(t) = Ri(t) = 400\cos 100t - 300$

$p(t) = v(t)i(t)$

$= (400\cos 100t - 300)(4\cos 100t - 3)$

$= 800 + 800\cos 200t - 2400\cos 100t + 900$

Therefore, the average power is

$$P_{av} = 800 + 900 = 1700 \text{ W}$$

5.7

(a) $\frac{\sqrt{2}}{2} + \frac{\sqrt{2}}{2} = \sqrt{2} = 1.414$ A

(b) Using phasor analysis, we have

$\mathbf{I} = 1\angle 0° + 1\angle -90° = 1 - j = \sqrt{2}\ \angle -45°$

$i(t) = \sqrt{2}\ \cos(2t - 45°)$

Therefore, $I_{rms} = 1$ A

(c) $\sqrt{1^2 + \left(\frac{1}{\sqrt{2}}\right)^2} = \sqrt{\frac{3}{2}}$

(d) $\mathbf{I} = 1\angle 0° + 1\angle 135° = 1 - 0.707 + j0.707$

$= 0.765\angle 67.5°$; $I_{rms} = 0.5412$ A

(e) The minimum common period is 2π. Thus the current must be squared, then integrated from 0 to 2π. The resulting effective value is 1.

5.8

The average power drawn by the circuit is

$$P = \frac{VI}{2}\ \cos(\theta)$$

$$= \frac{220\sqrt{2} \times 10\sqrt{2}}{2}\ \cos(60°) = 1100\ \text{W}$$

The power factor is

$$pf = \cos 60° = 0.5 \text{ lagging}$$

EIT 5.9

(a) The power factor is

$$pf = \cos\theta = \frac{P}{V_{rms}I_{rms}} = \frac{800}{12 \times 120} = 0.56$$

(b) The phase angle θ is

$$\theta = \cos^{-1}0.56 = 56.25°$$

(c) The impedance Z is

$$Z = |Z|\ \angle\theta = \frac{V}{I}\ \angle \pm 56.25° = 10\angle \pm 56.25°$$

$$= 5.56 \pm j8.31\ \Omega$$

(d) The resistance is 5.56 Ω

5.10

The input power is

$$P = \frac{2¢746}{0.8} = 1865\ \text{W}$$

The power factor is

$$pf = \cos\theta = \frac{P}{V_{rms}I_{rms}}$$

$$= \frac{1865}{110 \times 24} = 0.706 \text{ lagging}$$

5.11

a) $P = \dfrac{650}{\sqrt{2}} \times \dfrac{20}{\sqrt{2}} \times \cos(10°) = 6401.25$

W

$Q = 1128.7$ VAR $S = 6500\angle 10°$ VA

b) $P = 4599.3$ W $Q = 4599.3$ VAR

$S = 6504.4\angle 45°$ VA

c) $P = 60$ W $Q = 857.91$ VAR

$S = 860\angle 86°$ VA

d) $P = 401.22$ W $Q = 260.56$ VAR

$S = 478.4\angle 33°$ VA

EIT 5.12

a) $pf = \cos(\theta_v - \theta_i) = \cos(-32°) = 0.848$

leading

b) $pf = \cos(\theta_v - \theta_i) = \cos(7°) = 0.9925$

lagging

c) $pf = \cos(\theta_v - \theta_i) = \cos(0° - 85°)$

$= 0.08716$ leading

d) $\theta = \tan^{-1} \frac{16}{48} = 18.43°$

$pf = \cos(18.43°) = 0.9487$ lagging

EIT 5.13

a) capacitive

b) capacitive

c) $i_L(t) = 4.2\cos(\omega t - 90°)$, inductive

d) resistive

5.14

a) average value $= \dfrac{(1\times 1) + (-3\times 1)}{2} = \dfrac{-2}{2} = -1$ V

rms value $= \sqrt{\dfrac{(1\times 1) + (9\times 1)}{2}} = \sqrt{\dfrac{10}{2}} = 2.24$ V

b) $P_{AVG} = \dfrac{V_{rms}^2}{R} = \dfrac{5}{10} = 0.5$ W

5.15

For load #1, we have

$\theta_1 = \arctan \dfrac{Q}{P} = \arctan \dfrac{1.4}{2} = 35°$

$\therefore\ |\mathbf{I}_1| = \dfrac{P}{V\cos\theta} \quad \dfrac{2000}{208 \times \cos 35°} = 11.74$ A

$\mathbf{I}_1 = 11.74\angle -35°$ A

For load #2, we have

$\theta_2 = \cos^{-1} 0.7 = 45.57°$ and

$|\mathbf{I}_2| = \dfrac{|S|}{|V|} = \dfrac{4000}{208} = 19.23$ A

$\therefore\ \mathbf{I}_2 = 19.23\angle 45.57°$ A

The total current is:

$\mathbf{I} = \mathbf{I}_1 + \mathbf{I}_2 = 23.1 + j7 = 24.14\angle 16.86°$ A

The total impedance is:

$Z = \dfrac{V}{I} = \dfrac{2080°}{24.1416.86°}$

$= 8.62\angle -16.86° = 8.25 - j2.5\ \Omega$

EIT 5.16

a) $P = V_S I_S \cos\theta$

$= 120\times1.94\cos(-40°) = 174.66$ W

$Q = V_S I_S \sin\theta$

$= 120\times1.94\sin(-40°) = -146.56$ VAR

$S = \mathbf{V}_S\mathbf{I}^*_S = 120\times1.94\angle{-40°}$

$= 232.8\angle{-40°}$ VA

b) $P_L = P = 174.66$ W

c) $Z_L = \dfrac{V_S}{I_S}$

$= \dfrac{120}{1.940°} = 63.16\angle{-40°}\ \Omega$

5.17

(a) $\mathbf{V}_{out} = \mathbf{V}_S \dfrac{R_2}{R_1 + R_2} = 20\angle 0°$

(b) $P = \dfrac{V_{out^2}}{R_2} = 100$ W

(c) $\mathbf{V}_{out} = \mathbf{V}_S \dfrac{R_2}{-j4 + R_2} = \dfrac{160}{5.66 - 45°}$

$= 28.28\angle 45°$

(d) P = 200 W

(e) The second circuit allows R_2 to dissipate more power.

5.18

$\omega = 3$

$Z_T = j6 - j6 + 4 = 4 + j0\ \Omega$

$I_{RMS} = \dfrac{10/\sqrt{2}}{4} = 1.77$ A

$P = I_{RMS}^2 R = 12.5$ W

$Q = I_{RMS}^2 X = 0$ VAR

5.19

(a) $jX_L = j\omega L = j377\times25.55\times10^{-3}$

$= j9.6\ \Omega,$

$jX_C = \frac{1}{jwC} = \frac{1}{j377¢265¢10^{-6}} = -j10$

Ω

$jX_L \parallel jX_C = j240\ \Omega$

The equivalent impedance Z is

$Z = jX_L \parallel jX_C + R = 10 + j240$

$= 240.2\angle 87.6°\ \Omega$

The current in the circuit is

$\mathbf{I} = \frac{V_S}{Z} = \frac{1200°}{24087.6°}$

$= 0.5\angle -87.6°\ A$

The real power P is

$P = I^2R = 0.5^2 10 = 2.5\ W$

The reactive power Q is

$Q = I^2X = 0.5^2 240 = 60\ VAR$

(b) $jX_L = j\omega L = j314\times25.55\times10^{-3} = j8\ \Omega$

$jX_C = \frac{1}{jwC} = \frac{1}{j314¢265¢10^{-6}}$

$= -j12\ \Omega$

$jX_L \parallel jX_C = j24\ \Omega$

The equivalent impedance Z is

$Z = jX_L \parallel jX_C + R$

$= 10 + j24 = 26\angle 67.38°\ \Omega$

The current in the circuit is

$\mathbf{I} = \frac{V_S}{Z} = \frac{1200°}{2667.38°}$

$= 4.6\angle -67.38°\ A$

The real power P is

$P = I^2R = 4.6^2\times10 = 211.6\ W$

The reactive power Q is

$Q = I^2X = 4.6^2\times24 = 507.8\ VAR$

5.20

$36\angle -60° = (8+j6)\ I_1 - j6\ I_2$

$-24\angle 36.9° = -j6\ I_1 + (6-j6)\ I_2$

$18 - j\ 31.2 = (8+j6)\ I_1 - j6\ I_2$

$-19.2 - j\ 14.4 = -j6\ I_1 + (6+j6)\ I_2$

$I_1 = 0.398 - j3.38\ A, \quad I_2 = 1.091 - j\ 0.911\ A$

$S_1 = V_{S1}I_1{}^* = 14.33\angle -60° + 121.68\angle 30°$

$P_1 = 112.5\ W, \quad Q_1 = 48.4\ VAR$

$S_2 = V_{S2}(-I_2{}^*)$

$= -26.18\angle 36.9° - 21.86\angle 126.9°$

$P_2 = -7.81\ W, \quad Q_2 = -33.2\ VAR$

EIT 5.21

$\mathbf{I}_S(\omega) = \frac{V_S}{R + Z_L} = \frac{230}{1 + 10 + j3}$

$= \frac{230}{11.415.26°} = 20.18\angle -15.26°\ A$

a) The average power delivered to the load:

$P_L = I_S{}^2R_L = 20.18^2\times10 = 4072.3\ W$

b) The average power absorbed by the line

$P_{line} = I_S{}^2R = 20.18^2\times1 = 407.23\ W$

c) The apparent power supplied by the generator is:

$S = \mathbf{V}_S\mathbf{I}_S{}^* = 230\times20.18\angle 15.26°$

$= 4641.4\angle 15.26°\ VA$

d) The load impedance angle

$\theta = \arctan \frac{3}{10} = 16.7°$

∴ The power factor of the load is

$pf = \cos(16.7°) = 0.9578$ lagging

e) The power factor of the line plus load is:

$pf = \cos(15.26°) = 0.9647$ lagging

5.22

$$\mathbf{Y}_{LD} = \frac{1}{R_L} + j\omega = \frac{1}{25} + j377\left(100 \times 10^{-6}\right)$$

$$= 0.04 + j0.0377 = 0.05497\angle 43.304°$$

$$\boldsymbol{Z}_{LD} = \frac{1}{\boldsymbol{Y}_{LD}} = 18.193\angle -43.304°\ \Omega$$

$$= 13.239 - j12.478\ \Omega$$

$$\mathbf{Z} = R + \mathbf{Z}_{LD} = 14.239 - j12.478\ \Omega = 18.933\angle -41.23°\ \Omega$$

$$\tilde{\boldsymbol{I}} = \frac{\tilde{\boldsymbol{V}}}{\mathbf{Z}} = \frac{230\angle 0}{18.933\angle -41.23°} = 12.15\angle 41.23°\ \text{A}$$

(a) Apparent power

$$\left|\boldsymbol{S}_{LD}\right| = \left|\boldsymbol{Z}_{LD}\left|\tilde{\boldsymbol{I}}\right|^2\right| = 18.193(12.15)^2$$

$$= 2686\ \text{VA}$$

(b) Apparent power

$$\left|\tilde{\mathbf{V}}_s\right|\left|\tilde{\mathbf{I}}\right| = 230(12.15) = 2794\ \text{VA}$$

(c) $\text{PF} = \cos\left[\arctan\frac{0.0377}{0.04}\right] = 0.728$ Leading

5.23

$$S = \frac{\left|\tilde{V}\right|^2}{Z^4} = \frac{50^2}{20 + j34.6} = 62.56\angle -59.97°$$

$$= 31.31 - j54.16\ \text{VA}$$

Apparent Power = |*S*| = 62.56 VA

$P = \text{R}_e\{S\} = 31.31$ W

$Q = \text{I}_m\{S\} = -54.16$ VAR

$\theta = -59.97° \cong -60°$

The power triangle is shown below:

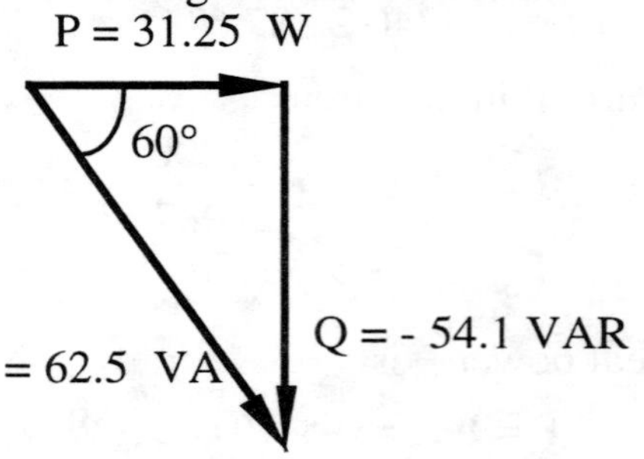

5.24

The magnitude of the current I is

$$I = \frac{P}{V\cos q} = \frac{220}{200¢0.8} = 1.375 \text{ A}$$

Therefore, $\mathbf{I} = 1.375\angle\text{-}36.87°$ A

The load impedance is

$$Z = \frac{V}{I} = \frac{200}{1.375\text{-}36.87°}$$

$$= 145.45\angle 36.87° = 116.36 + j87.27\ \Omega$$

The reactive power Q_L is

$$Q = VI\sin\theta = 200 \times 1.375 \times 0.6 = 165 \text{ VAR}$$

The reactance is

$$X_C = \frac{V^2}{Q} = \frac{200^2}{165} = 242.42\ \Omega$$

The required capacitor is

$$C = \frac{1}{wX_c} = \frac{1}{375¢242.42} = 11\ \mu\text{F}$$

EIT 5.25

The real power used by the air conditioner is

$$P_1 = 9.6 \times 120 \times 0.9 = 1036.8 \text{ W}$$

The reactive power is

$$Q_1 = 9.6 \times 120 \times \sin(\cos^{-1} 0.9) = 502.15 \text{ VAR}$$

The real power used by the freezer is

$$P_2 = 4.2 \times 120 \times 0.87 = 438.48 \text{ W}$$

The reactive power is

$$Q_2 = 4.2 \times 120 \times \sin(\cos^{-1} 0.87) = 248.5 \text{ VAR}$$

The real power used by the refrigerator is

$$P_3 = 3.5 \times 120 \times 0.8 = 336 \text{ W}$$

The reactive power is

$$Q_3 = 3.5 \times 120 \times \sin(\cos^{-1} 0.8) = 252 \text{ VAR}$$

The total real power P is

$$P = P_1 + P_2 + P_3 = 1811.28 \text{ W}$$

The total reactive power Q is

$$Q = Q_1 + Q_2 + Q_3 = 1002.65 \text{ VAR}$$

Therefore, the following power must be supplied

$$S = P + jQ = 1811.28 + j1002.65$$

$$= 2070.3\angle 28.97° \text{ VA}$$

5.26

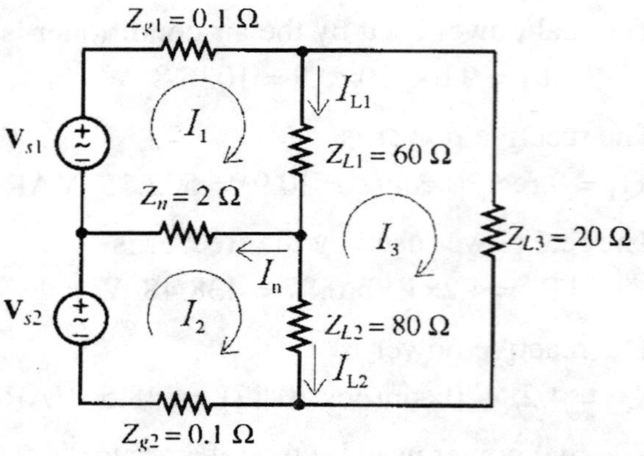

$I_1(62.1) + I_2(-2) + I_3(-60) = 115\angle 0°$

$I_1(-2) + I_2(82.1) + I_3(-80) = 115\angle 0°$

$I_1(-60) + I_2(-80) + I_3(160) = 0$

$I_1 = 13.25$ A

$I_2 = 12.8$ A

$I_3 = 11.37$ A

$I_{L1} = I_1 - I_3 = 1.88$ A

$I_{L2} = I_2 - I_3 = 1.43$ A

$I_n = I_1 - I_2 = 0.45$ A

a) $P_{L1} = I_{L1}^2 Z_{L1} = 212.1$ W

$P_{L2} = I_{L2}^2 Z_{L2} = 163.6$ W

$P_{L3} = I_3^2 Z_{L3} = 2585.5$ W

$P_T = 2961.2$ W

b) $P_{g1} = I_1^2 Z_{g1} = 17.56$ W

$P_{g2} = I_2^2 Z_{g2} = 16.38$ W

$P_n = I_n^2 Z_n = 0.405$ W

$P_T = 34.34$ W

c) $P_{S1} = V_1 I_1 = 1523.75$ W

$P_{S2} = V_2 I_2 = 1472$ W

5.27

(a) $P_{av} = VI\cos\theta = 120 \times 2.04 \times 0.672$

$= 164.5$ W

The total average power is

$P_{av} = 2 \times 164.5 = 329$ W

(b) At full load, $\cos\theta = 0.95$, $I = 6.8$ A,

$\eta = 0.8$

The electrical power P is

$P = 2 \times VI\cos\theta = 2 \times 120 \times 6.8 \times 0.95$

$= 1550.4$ W

$P_m = 0.8\ P = 1240.3$ W

(c) The current in motor 1 is

$I_1 = 6.8 \sqrt{0.9¢0.75 + 0.09} = 5.95$ A

and its power factor, pf_1, is

$pf_1 = 0.95 \sqrt{0.5¢0.75 + 0.5} = 0.89$

The real power, P_1, is

$P_1 = VI_1\cos\theta_1 = 120 \times 5.95 \times 0.89 = 635.5$ W

The reactive power Q_1 is

$Q_1 = VI_1\sin(\cos^{-1}0.89)$

$= 120 \times 5.95 \times 0.456 = 325.56$ VAR

The real power of motor 2 is

$P_2 = 120 \times 6.8 \times 0.95 = 775.2$ W

The reactive power Q_2 is

$Q_2 = 120 \times 6.8 \times \sin(\cos^{-1}0.95) = 254.8$ VAR

The total real power is

$P = P_1 + P_2 = 1410.7$ W

The reactive power Q is

$Q = Q_1 + Q_2 = 580.36$ VAR

The system power factor therefore is

$pf = \cos(\arctan \frac{Q}{P}) = \cos 22.36°$

$= 0.925$ lagging

EIT 5.28

The current is

$$\mathbf{I} = \frac{120}{12 + j377\times 20\times 10^{-3}}$$

$$= \frac{120}{14.1732.14°} = 8.47\angle\text{-}32.14° \text{ A}$$

(a) The average power dissipated in the load is

$$P_{av} = I^2R = 8.47^2\times 10 = 717.4 \text{ W}$$

(b) The power factor of the motor is

$$pf = \cos 32.14° = 0.847 \text{ lagging}$$

(c) $S_{NEW}\angle 25.84° = 717.4 \text{ W} + j(Q_L - Q_C)$

$$Q_L = 450.7 \text{ VAR}$$

$$S_{NEW} = 797.1$$

$$Q_{NEW} = 347.4$$

$$Q_C = 103.3 \text{ VAR}$$

$$Q_C = \frac{V^2}{X_C} = \frac{120^2}{X_C} = 103.3$$

$$X_C = 139.4 \ \Omega$$

$$C = \frac{1}{wX_C} = 19 \ \mu F$$

5.29

$$I_{L_{OLD}} = \frac{10\times 10^3}{(230)(0.5)} = 86.9\angle\text{-}60° \text{ A}$$

$$P_{LOST} = I_L^2(0.1) = 756.1 \text{ W}$$

$$I_{L_{NEW}} = \frac{10\times 10^3}{(230)(0.9)} = 48.3\angle\text{-}25.8° \text{ A}$$

$$P_{LOST} = I_L^2(0.1) = 233.4 \text{ W}$$

5.30

$$I_{OLD} = \frac{1000}{(120)(0.8)} = 10.4\angle\text{-}36.9° \text{ A}$$

$$I_{NEW} = \frac{1000}{(120)(0.95)} = 8.77\angle\text{-}18.2° \text{ A}$$

$$Q_{OLD} = 1000 \tan 36.9° = 750 \text{ VAR}$$

$$Q_{NEW} = 1000 \tan 18.2° = 328.8 \text{ VAR}$$

$$Q_c = 750 - 328.8 = 421.2 \text{ VAR}$$

$$X_c = \frac{120^2}{Q_C} = 34.2 \ \Omega$$

$$C = \frac{1}{(377)(34.2)} = 77.6 \ \mu F$$

5.31

(a) $Z_T = 10 \,||\, 100\times 10^3 \,||\, j50 \approx \frac{10\times j50}{10 + j50}$

$$\approx 9.6 + j2 \ \Omega$$

$$V_T = \frac{j5\times 10^6}{10^6 + j500 + j5\times 10^6} V_S = \frac{j5}{1 + j5} 20$$

$$= 19.22 + j3.84 = 19.6\angle 11.31° \text{ V}$$

(b) The load current can be computed from the Thèvenin equivalent as follows:

$$\mathbf{I} = \frac{19.611.31°}{2\times 9.6 + j4} = 1\angle\text{-}0.46° \text{ A}$$

The power dissipated by the load resistor is

$$P_L = 9.6 \text{ W}$$

(c) For maximum power transfer, we must have $Z_L = Z_T^* = (9.6 + j2)^* = 9.6 - j2 \ \Omega$

5.32

(a) $\mathbf{V}_{sec} = \dfrac{V_{prim}}{9} = 13.33\angle 32°$ V

$\mathbf{V}_{sec1} = \mathbf{V}_{sec2} = \dfrac{V_{sec}}{2} = 6.67\angle 32°$ V

(b) From $\dfrac{V_{prim}}{2V_{sec2}} = n$, we have

$n = \dfrac{208}{2 \times 8.7} = 11.95$

5.33

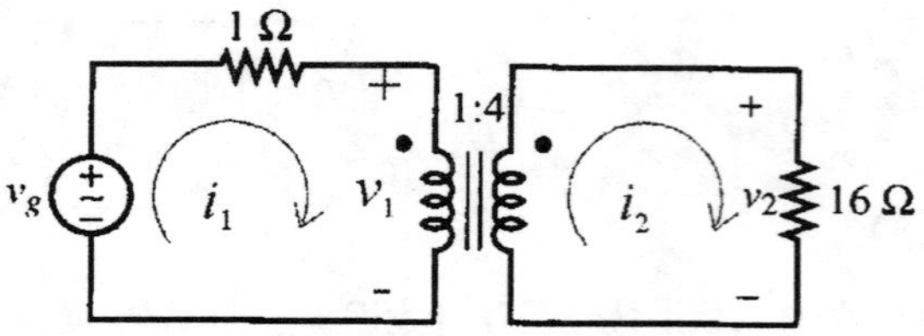

$v_g = i_1 + v_1 \qquad i_2 = v_2/16$

$v_2 = 4v_1 \qquad i_1 = 4i_2$

(a) $\dfrac{v_g}{i_1} = R_1 = \dfrac{v_g}{4i_2} = \dfrac{v_g}{v_2/4} = \dfrac{v_g}{2v_g}(4) = 2\Omega$

(b) $v_g = 4i_2 + \dfrac{v_2}{4} = \dfrac{v_2}{4} + \dfrac{v_2}{4} = \dfrac{v_2}{2} \Rightarrow \dfrac{v_2}{v_g} = 2$

(c) $R_S = 1\Omega$

$\dfrac{R_2}{R_1} = \dfrac{v_2/i_2}{v_1/i_1} = \dfrac{v_2/v_1}{i_2/i_1} = 16$

$R_L = 16R_2$

For maximum power transfer,

$R_L = R_S \Rightarrow R_2 = 16\ \Omega$

EIT 5.34

(a) From $S_{in} = V_1I_1 = V_2I_2 = S_{out}$,

$I_1 = \dfrac{S_{in}}{V_1} = \dfrac{400¢10^3}{460} = 869.57$ A

(b) For an ideal transformer, $P_{out} = P_{in} = V_LI_L\cos\theta$. With $\cos\theta = 1$,

$P_{out} = V_1I_1 = 400$ kW

(c) For $\cos\theta = 0.8$, the maximum power is

$P_{out} = V_1I_1\cos\theta = 400\times10^3\times0.8 = 320$ kW

(d) For $\cos\theta = 0.7$, the maximum power is

$P_{out} = V_1I_1\cos\theta = 400\times10^3\times0.7 = 280$ kW

(e) For $P_{out} = 300$ kW, the minimum power factor is

$\cos\theta = \dfrac{P_{out}}{400 \times 10^3} = 0.75$

5.35

The primary circuit is

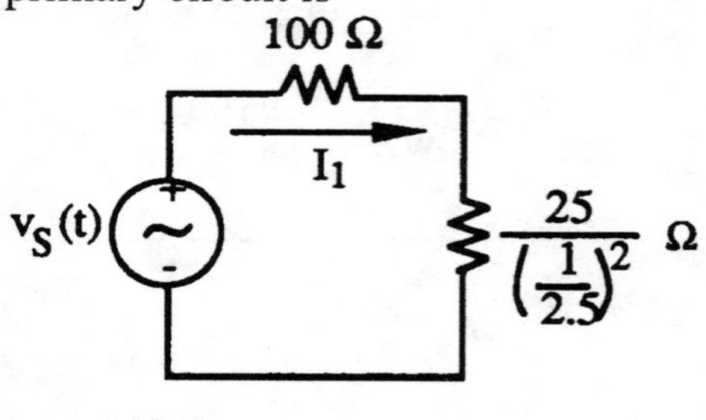

The current I_1 is

$I_1 = \dfrac{294}{156.25 + 100} = 1.15$ A

The secondary current I_2 is

$I_2 = \dfrac{I_1}{1/2.5} = 2.87$ A

The output voltage is

$V_o = I_2\times25 = 71.7$ V

That is

$v_o = 71.7\cos377t$ V

5.36

From Equation (5.48), we have

$$R_L = N^2 R_S$$

Therefore, the required turns ratio is

$$N = \frac{1}{n} = \sqrt{\frac{R_L}{R_S}} = 0.067$$

$$n = 15$$

5.37

From Equation (5.48), we have

$$R_L = N^2 R_S$$

Therefore, the required turns ratio is

$$N = \frac{1}{n} = \sqrt{\frac{R_L}{R_S}} = 0.5$$

$$n = 2$$

5.38

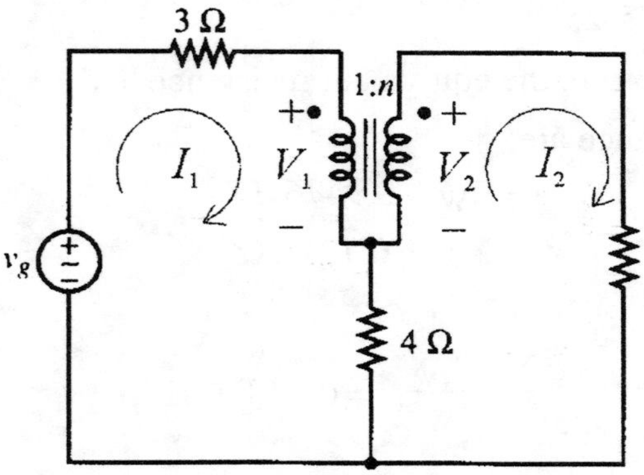

To maximize the power delivered to the 8 Ω resistance, select n to maximize the load current $I_b > 0$

Use $\boldsymbol{V}_a = \frac{1}{n}\boldsymbol{V}_b$ and $I_a = nI_b$

KVL Mesh "a"

$$-\boldsymbol{V}_g + 3n\boldsymbol{I}_b + \frac{1}{n}\boldsymbol{V}_b + 4(n\boldsymbol{I}_b - \boldsymbol{I}_b) = 0$$

KVL Mesh "b"

$$-\boldsymbol{V}_b + 8\boldsymbol{I}_b + 4(\boldsymbol{I}_b - n\boldsymbol{I}_b) = 0$$

$$(7n-4)\boldsymbol{I}_b + \frac{1}{n}\boldsymbol{V}_b = \boldsymbol{V}_g$$

$$(12-4n)\boldsymbol{I}_b - \boldsymbol{V}_b = 0$$

$$\boldsymbol{I}_b = \frac{\begin{vmatrix} \boldsymbol{V}_g & \frac{1}{n} \\ 0 & -1 \end{vmatrix}}{\begin{vmatrix} 7n-4 & \frac{1}{n} \\ 12-4n & -1 \end{vmatrix}} = \frac{-\boldsymbol{V}_g}{-7n+4-\frac{12}{n}+4}$$

$$= \frac{n}{7n^2-8n+12}\boldsymbol{V}_g$$

$$\frac{d}{dn}\boldsymbol{I}_b = \frac{(7n^2-8n+12) - n(14n-8)}{(7n^2-8n+12)^2}\boldsymbol{V}_g$$

$$= \frac{-7n^2+12}{(7n^2-8n+12)^2}\boldsymbol{V}_g = 0$$

$$-7n^2 + 12 = 0 \Rightarrow \quad n = \sqrt{\frac{12}{7}} = 1.30931$$

EIT 5.39

The voltage at j200 is

$$\mathbf{V}_S' = 240\times \frac{j200}{1 + j200.1} = \frac{4800090°}{200.189.7°}$$

$$= 239.88\angle 0.3° \text{ V}$$

The secondary side voltage is

$$\mathbf{V}_{secondary} = -\frac{1}{2}\mathbf{V}_S' = -119.94\angle 0.3° \text{ V}$$

***5.40**

we have

$$\mathbf{V}_W = 2\mathbf{V}_{secondary} = 220\angle 180° \text{ V}$$

$$\mathbf{I}_W = 25\angle 180° \text{ A}$$

$$\mathbf{I}_L = \frac{220180°}{20090°} = 1.1\angle 90° \text{ A}$$

$$\mathbf{I}_S = \mathbf{I}_L + \mathbf{I}_W = -25 + j1.1$$

The source voltage is

$$\mathbf{V}_S = (1 + j0.1)\mathbf{I}_S + \mathbf{V}_W = -245.11 - j1.4$$

$$= 245.1\angle -179.7° \text{ V}$$

***5.41**

The power factor during the open circuit test is:

$$pf = \cos\theta = \frac{P_{OC}}{V_{OC}I_{OC}} = 0.1398 \text{ lagging}$$

The excitation admittance is given by

$$Y_C = \frac{I_{OC}}{V_{OC}}\angle -\cos^{-1}pf = \frac{0.95}{241}\angle -81.96°$$

$$= 0.0005511 - j0.0039032$$

Therefore

$$R_C = 1.8 \text{ k}\Omega$$

$$X_C = 256.2\ \Omega$$

$$L = \frac{256.2}{377} = 0.68 \text{ H}$$

The power factor during the short circuit test is:

$$pf = \cos\theta = \frac{P_{SC}}{V_{SC}I_{SC}} = 0.9905$$

The series impedance is given by

$$Z_W = \frac{V_{SC}}{I_{SC}}\angle \cos^{-1}0.9905$$

$$= \frac{5}{5.25}\angle 7.914° = 0.9476 + j0.1311\ \Omega$$

Therefore, the equivalent resistance and reactance are:

$$R_W = 0.9476\ \Omega$$

$$X_W = 0.1311\ \Omega$$

and

$$L = \frac{X_w}{w} = 0.348 \text{ mH}$$

---

*5.42

The power factor during the open circuit test

$$pf = \cos\theta = \frac{P_{OC}}{V_{OC}I_{OC}} = 0.062 \text{ lagging}$$

The excitation admittance is given by

$$Y_C = \frac{I_{OC}}{V_{OC}} \angle\text{-}\cos^{-1}pf = \frac{0.7}{4600} \angle\text{-}86.45°$$

$$= 0.0000094 - j0.0001519$$

Therefore

$$R_C = 106.38 \text{ k}\Omega$$

$$X_C = 6583.38 \ \Omega$$

$$L = \frac{6583.38}{377} = 17.46 \text{ H}$$

The power factor during the short circuit test

$$pf = \cos\theta = \cos(\cos^{-1} \frac{P}{S}) \approx 0$$

The series resistance is given by

$$R_W = \frac{V_{SC^2}}{P_{SC}} = 0.54 \ \Omega$$

Therefore, the equivalent circuit is shown below.

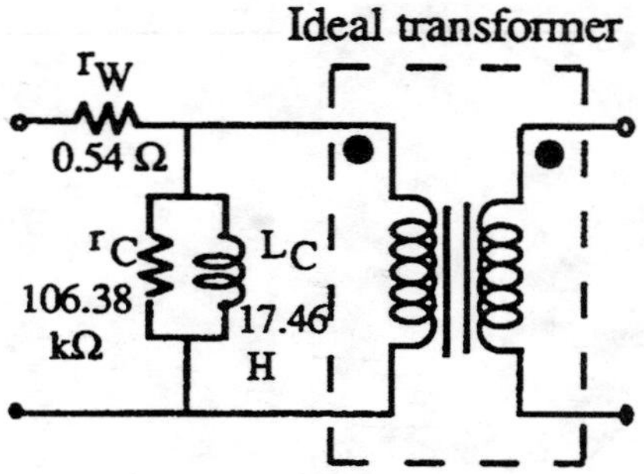

5.43

The phase voltages in polar form are:

$$\mathbf{V}_{an} = V_{an}\angle 0° = 100\angle 0° \text{ V}$$

$$\mathbf{V}_{bn} = 100\angle\text{-}120° \text{ V}$$

$$\mathbf{V}_{cn} = 100\angle 120° \text{ V}$$

The rectangular forms are:

$$\mathbf{V}_{an} = 100 \text{ V}$$

$$\mathbf{V}_{bn} = -50 - j86.6 \text{ V}$$

$$\mathbf{V}_{cn} = -50 + j86.6 \text{ V}$$

The line voltages in polar form are:

$$\mathbf{V}_{ab} = \sqrt{3} \ V\angle 30° = 173.2\angle 30° \text{ V}$$

$$\mathbf{V}_{bc} = \sqrt{3} \ V\angle -90° = 173.2\angle -90° \text{ V}$$

$$\mathbf{V}_{ca} = \sqrt{3} \ V\angle\text{-}210° = 173.2\angle 150° \text{ V}$$

The line voltages in rectangular form are:

$$\mathbf{V}_{ab} = 150 + j86.6 \text{ V}$$

$$\mathbf{V}_{bc} = -j173.2 \text{ V}$$

$$\mathbf{V}_{ca} = -150 + j86.6 \text{ V}$$

EIT 5.44

The neutral current is

$$\mathbf{I}_n = \mathbf{I}_{an} + \mathbf{I}_{bn} + \mathbf{I}_{cn}$$

$$= 10\angle 0° + 12\angle 150° + 8\angle 165°$$

$$= -8.12 + j8.07 = 11.448\angle 135.18° \text{ A}$$

5.45

The phase voltages are:

$$\mathbf{V}_R = 120\angle 0° \text{ V}$$
$$\mathbf{V}_B = 120\angle 240° \text{ V}$$
$$\mathbf{V}_W = 120\angle 120° \text{ V}$$

(a) $\mathbf{V}_{RW} = \mathbf{V}_R - \mathbf{V}_W$

$= 120\angle 0° - 120\angle 120°$

$= 120 + 60 - j103.92$

$= 207.8\angle -30° \text{ V}$

$\mathbf{V}_{WB} = \mathbf{V}_W - \mathbf{V}_B$

$= 120\angle 120° - 120\angle 240°$

$= -60 + j103.92 + 60 + j103.92$

$= 207.8\angle 90° \text{ V}$

$\mathbf{V}_{BR} = \mathbf{V}_B - \mathbf{V}_R$

$= 120\angle 240° - 120\angle 0°$

$= -60 - j103.92 - 120$

$= 207.8\angle -150° \text{ V}$

(b) $\mathbf{V}_{RW} = \mathbf{V}_R \sqrt{3} \angle -30°$

$= 120 \times \sqrt{3} \angle -30° = 207.8\angle -30°$ V

$\mathbf{V}_{WB} = \mathbf{V}_W \sqrt{3} \angle -30°$

$= 120 \times \sqrt{3} \angle 90$

$= 207.8\angle 90° \text{ V}$

$\mathbf{V}_{BR} = \mathbf{V}_B \sqrt{3} \angle -30°$

$= 120 \times \sqrt{3} \angle 210°$

$= 207.8\angle -150° \text{ V}$

(c) The two calculations are identical.

5.46

$$\mathbf{I}_R = \frac{\mathbf{V}_R}{50} = 2.2\angle 0° \text{ A}$$

$$\mathbf{I}_W = \frac{\mathbf{V}_W}{-j20} = 5.5\angle 210° \text{ A}$$

$$\mathbf{I}_B = \frac{\mathbf{V}_B}{j45} = 2.44\angle 150° \text{ A}$$

$\mathbf{I}_N = \mathbf{I}_R + \mathbf{I}_W + \mathbf{I}_B$

$= 2.2 + 5.5\angle 210° + 2.44\angle 150°$

$= -4.68 - j1.53 = 4.92\angle -161.9° \text{ A}$

EIT 5.47

$$\mathbf{I}_R = \frac{\mathbf{V}_R}{10} = 22 \text{ A}$$

$$\mathbf{I}_W = \frac{\mathbf{V}_W}{10} = 22\angle 120° \text{ A}$$

$$\mathbf{I}_B = \frac{\mathbf{V}_B}{10} = 22\angle 240° \text{ A}$$

$$\mathbf{I}_N = \mathbf{I}_R + \mathbf{I}_W + \mathbf{I}_B = 0 \text{ A}$$

***5.48**

The line voltages are:

$$V_{RW} = 416\angle{-30°}\ V$$

$$V_{WB} = 416\angle 90°\ V$$

$$V_{BR} = 416\angle 210°\ V$$

The phase voltages are:

$$V_R = 240\angle 0°\ V$$

$$V_W = 240\angle{+120°}\ V$$

$$V_B = 240\angle{-120°}\ V$$

The currents are:

$$I_R = \frac{V_R}{40 + j377¢5¢10^{-3}} = 6\angle{-2.7°}\ A$$

$$I_W = \frac{V_W}{40 + j1.885} = 6\angle 117.3°\ A$$

$$I_B = \frac{V_B}{40 + j1.885} = 6\angle{-122.7°}\ A$$

$$I_N = I_R + I_W + I_B = 0$$

5.49

(a) The power delivered to the motor is

$$P = 3V_R I_R \cos\theta = 3\times 240\times 6\times 0.9988$$

$$= 4315\ W$$

(b) The motor's power factor is

$$pf = \cos 2.7° = 0.9988\ \text{lagging}$$

(c) The circuit is balanced and no neutral current flows; thus the connection is unnecessary.

EIT 5.50

5.50

$$P = \sqrt{3}\tilde{V}\tilde{I}pf = \sqrt{3}(440)(40)(0.8) = 24{,}387\ W$$

Also $\theta = \arccos(pf) = \arccos(0.8) = 36.87°$

$$S = \sqrt{3}\tilde{V}\tilde{I}\angle\theta = \sqrt{3}(440)(40)\angle 36.87°$$

$$= 30{,}484\angle 36.87°\ VA = 24{,}387 + j18{,}290\ VA$$

$$= p + jQ$$

5.51

$$\tilde{V}_L = 120\sqrt{3}$$

$$S = 3\frac{\tilde{V}_L^2}{Z_\Delta^*} = 3\frac{(120\sqrt{3})^2}{(40 + j60)^*} = \frac{129{,}600}{40 - j60}\cdot\frac{40 + j60}{40 + j60}$$

$$= \frac{129{,}600}{5200}(40 + j60) = 996.9 + j1{,}495.4\ VA$$

$$= 1{,}797.2\angle 56.31°\ VA$$

Apparent Power = |S| = 1,797.2 VA

$$P = R_e\{S\} = 996.9\ W$$

$$Q = I_m\{S\} = 1{,}495\ VAR$$

Power Factor = pf =

cos(56.31°) = 0.555 lagging

5.52

(a) By virtue of the symmetry of the circuit, we can solve the problem by considering just one phase.

The current $\mathbf{I_R}$ is

$$\mathbf{I_R} = \frac{1200°}{5 + j6} = \frac{1200°}{7.8150.19°}$$

$$= 15.36\angle\text{-}50.19° \text{ A}$$

The total power supplied to the motor is

$$P = 3\times 120\times 15.36\times\cos(50.19°)$$

$$= 3541.3 \text{ W}$$

(b) The mechanical power is

$$P_m = 0.8\times P = 2832.23 \text{ W}$$

(c) The power factor is

$$pf = \cos(50.19)° = 0.64$$

(d) The company will face a 25 percent penalty.

5.53

$$\text{Let } V_{AN} = \frac{230}{\sqrt{3}}\angle 0° = 132.8\angle 0° \text{ V}$$

$$I_A = \frac{V_{AN}}{5\angle 53.1°} = 26.6\angle\text{-}53.1° \text{ A}$$

$$I_B = 26.6\angle\text{-}173.1° \text{ A}$$

$$I_C = 26.6\angle 66.9° \text{ A}$$

$$P_T = \sqrt{3}\,(230)(26.6)\cos(53.1°)$$

$$= 6362.5 \text{ W}$$

5.54

Assume that the voltages are line-to-neutral volts

(a)

$$\mathbf{S} = 3\frac{\tilde{\mathbf{V}}_{LN}^2}{\mathbf{Z}_{LN}^*} = 3\frac{120^2}{80 - j60} = \frac{3(120)^2}{100^2}(80 + j60)$$

$$= 345.6 + j259.2 \text{ VA} = 432\angle 36.87°$$

(b) $p = R_e\{S\} = 345.6$ W

(c)

$$\mathbf{S} = 3\frac{\tilde{\mathbf{V}}_L^2}{\mathbf{Z}_{LL}^*} = 3\frac{\left(120\sqrt{3}\right)^2}{80 - j60} = \frac{9(120)^2}{100^2}(80 + j60)$$

$$= 1{,}036.8 + j777.6 \text{ VA}$$

$$= 1{,}296\angle 36.87° \text{VA}$$

(d) $p = R_e\{S\} = 1{,}036.8$ W

5.55

$$Z_{Y'} = \frac{3 + j4}{3}$$

$$Z_T = (12 - j5)\,||\,(1 + j1.33) = 1.6\angle 46.3°\ \Omega$$

$$I_L = \frac{120/\sqrt{3}\angle 0°}{1.6\angle 46.3°} = 43.2\angle\text{-}46.3° \text{ A}$$

$$P_T = \sqrt{3}\,(120)(43.2)\cos(46.3°) = 6207.4 \text{ W}$$

p.f. = cos(46.3°) = 0.69 lagging

***5.56**

One method of solving the problem is to convert the wye load to an equivalent delta load. The circuit is shown below.

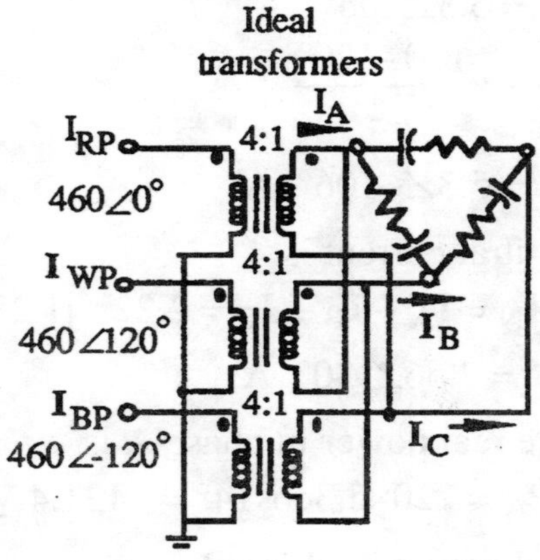

The delta load is

$$Z_\Delta = 3Z_Y = 30 - j21\ \Omega$$

The phase(line) voltage of the secondary side is $N|\mathbf{V}_R| = \dfrac{460}{4} = 115\ \text{V}$

For this connection of the secondary side of the transformer, the line voltage of the secondary leads that of the primary 30°(in the United States, it is customary to make the secondary lag the primary by 30°); the phasor diagram is shown below.

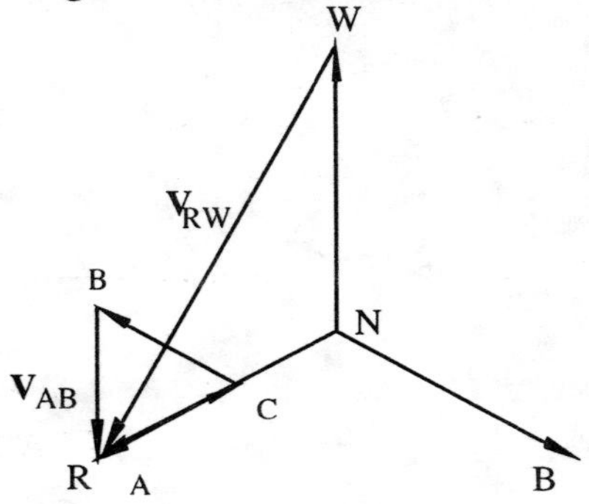

Thus, the primary line voltage is:

$$\mathbf{V}_{RW} = \sqrt{3}\ 460\angle -30° = 796.74\angle -30°\ \text{V}$$

and the secondary line voltage is

$$\mathbf{V}_{AB} = 115\angle 0°\ \text{V}$$

The phase currents are

$$\mathbf{I}_{AB} = \frac{V_{AB}}{Z_D} = 3.14\angle 35°\ \text{A}$$

$$\mathbf{I}_{BC} = 3.14\angle -85°\ \text{A}$$

$$\mathbf{I}_{CA} = 3.14\angle -205°\ \text{A}$$

The line currents are

$$\mathbf{I}_A = \mathbf{I}_{AB} - \mathbf{I}_{CA}$$
$$= 3.14\angle 35° - 3.14\angle -205°$$
$$= 5.42 + j0.47$$
$$= 5.44\angle 5°\ \text{A}$$

$$\mathbf{I}_B = 5.44\angle -115°\ \text{A}$$

$$\mathbf{I}_C = 5.44\angle -235°\ \text{A}$$

The currents on the primary side are

$$\mathbf{I}_{RP} = 0.785\angle -205°\ \text{A}$$

$$\mathbf{I}_{WP} = 0.785\angle 35°\ \text{A}$$

$$\mathbf{I}_{BP} = 0.785\angle -85°\ \text{A}$$

***5.57**

(a) For $t < t_1$, the line current $\mathbf{I}_R$ is

$$\mathbf{I}_R = \frac{120\angle 0^\circ}{40 + j30} = 2.4\angle\text{-}36.87^\circ \text{ A}$$

The circuit is symmetrical for $t < t_1$, therefore

$$\mathbf{I}_W = 2.4\angle 83.13^\circ \text{ A}$$

$$\mathbf{I}_B = 2.4\angle\text{-}156.87^\circ \text{ A}$$

The total power dissipated in the motor is

$$P = 3\times 120\times 2.4\cos 36.87^\circ = 691.2 \text{ W}$$

(b) The initial conditions at $t = t_1$ can be found as

$$i_R(t_1) = 2.4\cos(377t_1 - 36.87^\circ) \text{ A}$$

$$i_W(t_1) = 2.4\cos(377t_1 + 83.13^\circ) \text{ A}$$

$$i_B(t_1) = 2.4\cos(377t_1 - 156.87^\circ) \text{ A}$$

The steady state currents are

$$\mathbf{I}_R = \frac{120\angle 0^\circ - 120\angle\text{-}120^\circ}{80 + j60}$$

$$= \frac{207.8\angle 30^\circ}{100\angle 36.87^\circ}$$

$$= 2.078\angle\text{-}6.37^\circ \text{ A}$$

$$\mathbf{I}_W(\infty) = 0 \text{ A}$$

$$\mathbf{I}_B = -\mathbf{I}_R(\infty) = 2.078\angle 173.13^\circ \text{ A}$$

$$P = 2\times 1.2^2\times 40 = 115.2 \text{ W}$$

EIT 5.58

(a) $$\mathbf{I}_A = \frac{220}{40 + j10} = 5.3\angle\text{-}14^\circ \text{ A}$$

$$\mathbf{I}_B = \frac{110\angle 120^\circ}{20 + j5}$$

$$= 5.3\angle 106^\circ \text{ A}$$

$$\mathbf{I}_C = \frac{110\angle\text{-}120^\circ}{20 - j5}$$

$$= 5.3\angle -106^\circ \text{ A}$$

The neutral current is

$$\mathbf{I}_N = \mathbf{I}_A + \mathbf{I}_B + \mathbf{I}_C = 2.22 - j1.28$$

$$= 2.56\angle\text{-}30^\circ \text{ A}$$

(b) The real power in phase A is

$$P_A = 220\times 5.3\cos 14^\circ = 1131.4 \text{ W}$$

The real power in phase B is

$$P_B = 110\times 5.3\times\cos(120^\circ - 106^\circ)$$

$$= 565.68 \text{ W}$$

The real power in phase C is

$$P_C = 110\times 5.3\times\cos(-120^\circ + 106^\circ)$$

$$= 565.68 \text{ W}$$

The total real power dissipated in the load is

$$P = P_A + P_B + P_C = 2262.8 \text{ W}$$

Chapter 6 Instructor Notes

Chapter 6 introduces the system analysis aspects of electric circuits. The chapter devotes the first two sections to a discussion of frequency response and filters, focusing on first and second order circuits. Example 6.5 on the Wheatstone bridge filter can be tied to earlier application examples. Examples 6.8, describing a 60-Hz AC line interference filter, and 6.9 describing a seismic displacement transducer can also provide interesting application material. The latter example could fit well in those curricula where emphasis is placed on analogies between electrical and mechanical systems; further, this example emphasizes the importance of the concept of frequency response in other fields of application. The instructor who has already introduced the operational amplifier as a circuit element will find that section 11.3, on active filters, is an excellent vehicle to reinforce both the op-amp concept and the frequency response ideas. Another alternative (employed by this author for several semesters) consists of introducing the op-amp at this stage, covering sections 11.1 through 11.3.

The second half of the chapter generalizes the discussion of dynamic circuits begun in Chapter 4. The material is kept at an introductory level, focusing on solution methods for first and second order circuits. It has been this author's experience that time is usually too short, especially in a survey course, to deal with generalized solution methods based on the Laplace transform; thus, the solution oriented approach. The instructor who wishes to introduce the Laplace Transform will find that the material of Section 6.6 permits presentation of the basic ideas, and also includes solved examples. Practical examples and illustrations in the second half of the chapter include the pulse response of a long cable (Example 6.14), and analogies with heat and fluid flow systems. The problems present several filter and frequency response examples of varying difficulty, and permit the extension of the concept of an electrical filter to more useful circuits. The instructor who wishes to use one of the many available .software aids (e.g., MATLAB® or PSpice®) to analyze the frequency response of more complex circuits and to exploit more advanced graphics capabilities, will find that several advanced problems lend themselves nicely to such usage. Thus, problems that would be rather advanced for a student at this level of preparation (e.g., 6.24-6.27) could be used as a vehicle to introduce modern computer aids.

Chapter 6 problem solutions

6.1

(a) $$\frac{V_{out}}{V_{in}} = \frac{1/j\omega C}{R + 1/j\omega C} = \frac{1}{jwRC + 1}$$

$$\frac{V_{out}(\omega)}{V_{in}(\omega)} = \frac{1}{1 + j\omega/10}$$

$$\left|\frac{V_{out}}{V_{in}}\right| = \frac{1}{\sqrt{1 + 0.01\omega^2}}$$

$$\phi(\omega) = -\arctan(0.1\omega)$$

(b) The responses are shown below:

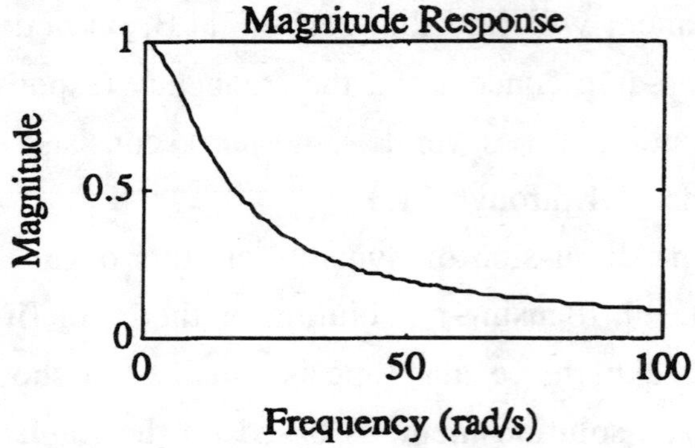

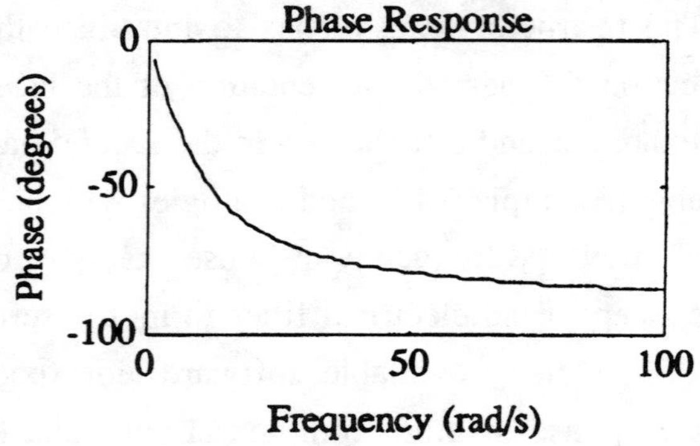

(c)

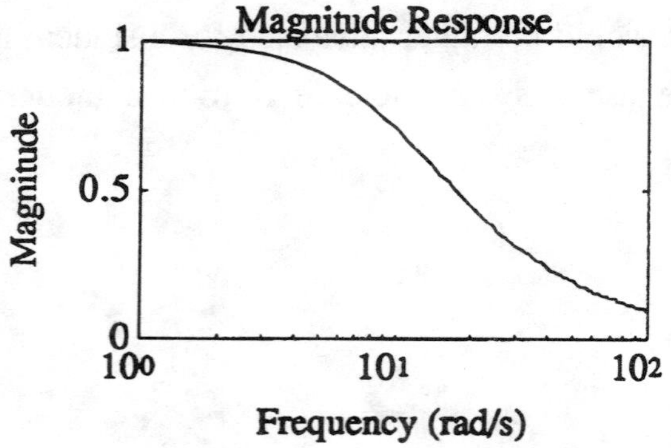

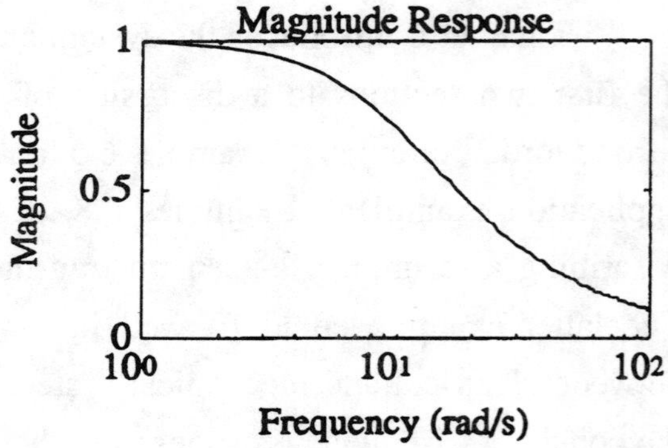

(d)

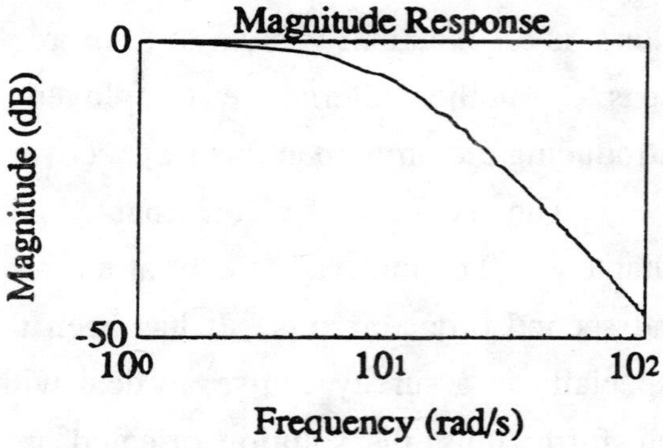

6.2

Assume $R = 1k\Omega$ and $L = 100mH$.

(a) $Y = \frac{1}{Z} = \frac{1}{R + j\omega L} = \frac{1}{1000 + j(0.1)\omega}$

$|Y|$ vs ω

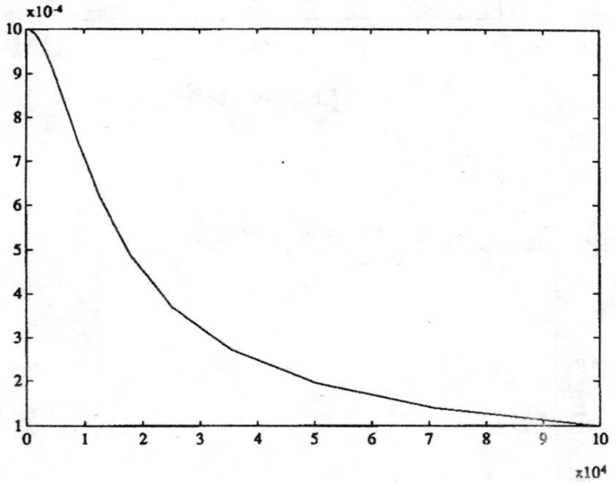

(b) $\frac{V_1}{V_S} = \frac{R}{R + j\omega L} = \frac{1000}{1000 + j(0.1)\omega}$

$\left|\frac{V_1}{V_S}\right|$ vs ω

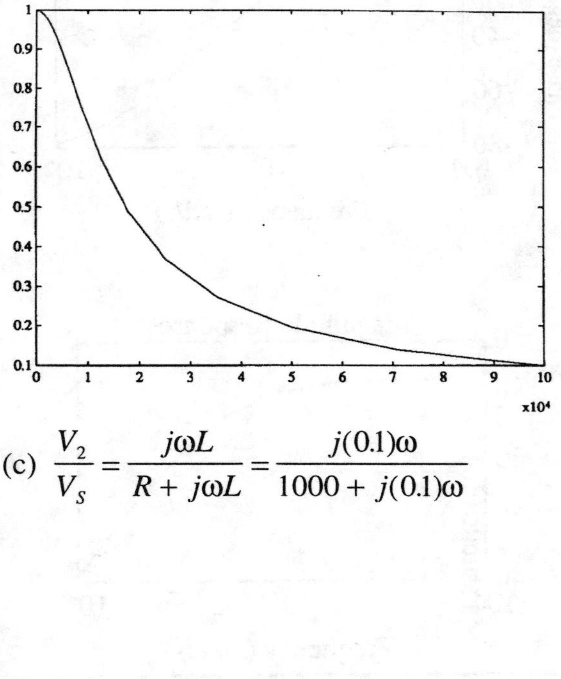

(c) $\frac{V_2}{V_S} = \frac{j\omega L}{R + j\omega L} = \frac{j(0.1)\omega}{1000 + j(0.1)\omega}$

$\left|\frac{V_2}{V_S}\right|$ vs ω

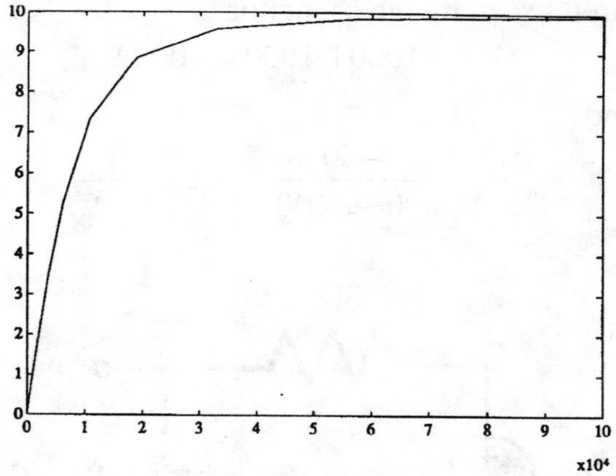

EIT 6.3

First, we find the Thèvenin equivalent circuit seen by the capacitor,

$$R_T = 1000 \parallel 1000 = 500\ \Omega$$

and

$$v_{OC} = \frac{1000}{1000 + 1000}\, v_{in} = \frac{v_{in}}{2}$$

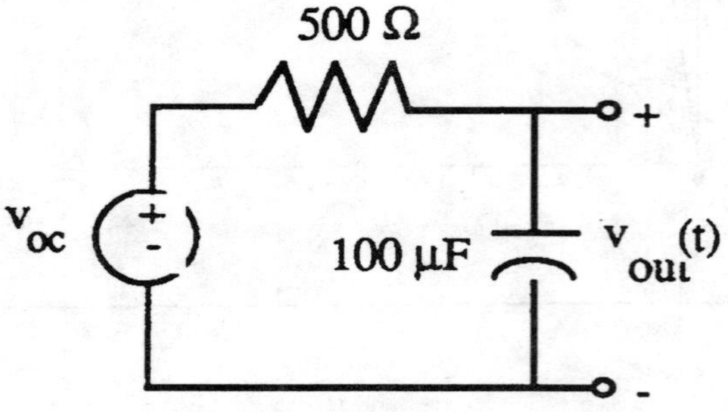

(a) $$\frac{V_{out}}{V_{oc}} = \frac{1/j\omega C}{R + 1/j\omega C} = \frac{1}{j\omega RC + 1}$$

$$\left| \frac{V_{out}}{V_{oc}} \right| = \frac{2}{\sqrt{4 + 0.01\omega^2}}$$

$$\left| \frac{V_{out}}{V_{in}} \right| = \frac{1}{2} \left| \frac{V_{out}}{V_{oc}} \right| = \frac{1}{\sqrt{4 + 0.01\omega^2}}$$

$$\phi(\omega) = -\arctan(0.05\omega)$$

(b)

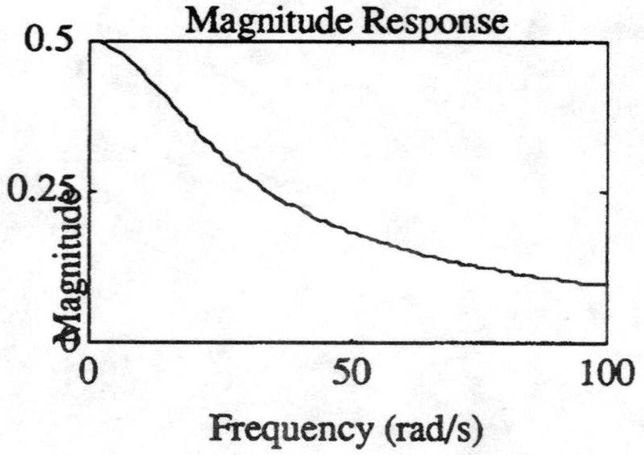

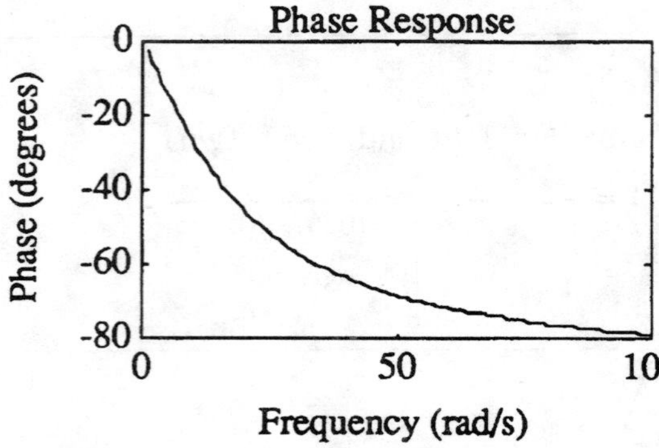

(c)

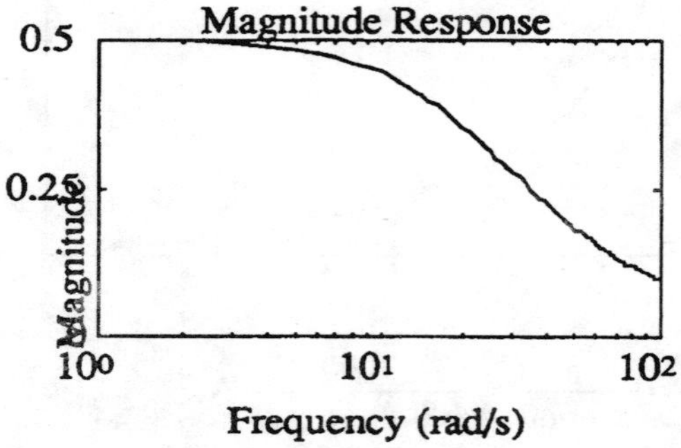

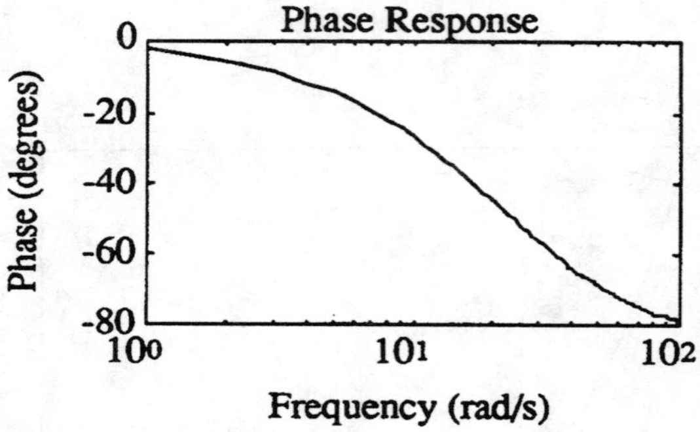

(d)

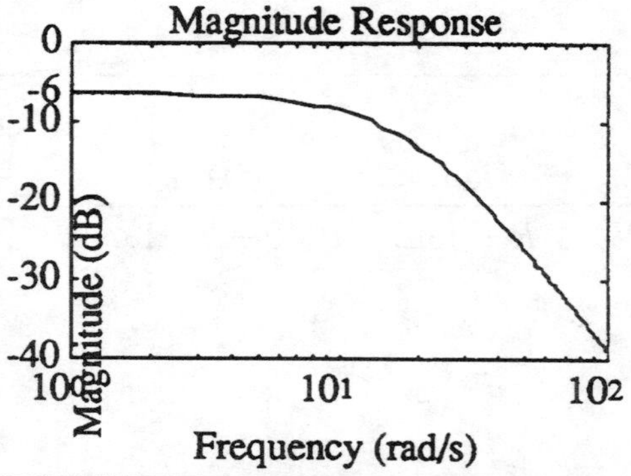

6.4

First, we find the Thèvenin equivalent circuit seen by the capacitor,

$$R_T = 1000 \parallel 1000 + 500 = 1000\ \Omega$$

and

$$v_{OC} = \frac{1000}{1000 + 1000} v_{in} = \frac{v_{in}}{2}$$

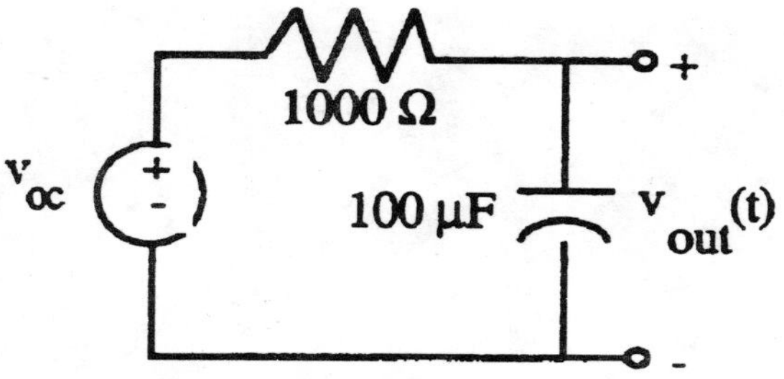

(a) $\dfrac{V_{out}}{V_{oc}} = \dfrac{1/j\omega C}{R + 1/j\omega C} = \dfrac{1}{jwRC + 1}$

$$\left| \frac{V_{out}}{V_{oc}} \right| = \frac{1}{\sqrt{1 + 0.01\omega^2}}$$

$$\left| \frac{V_{out}}{V_{in}} \right| = \frac{1}{2} \left| \frac{V_{out}}{V_{oc}} \right| = \frac{0.5}{\sqrt{1 + 0.01\omega^2}}$$

$$\phi(\omega) = -\arctan(0.1\omega)$$

(b)

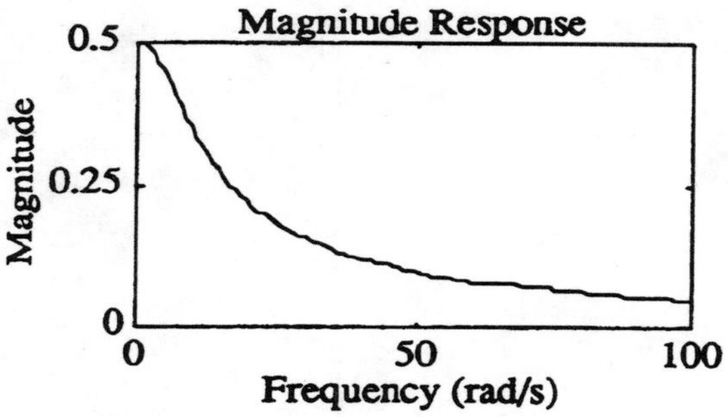

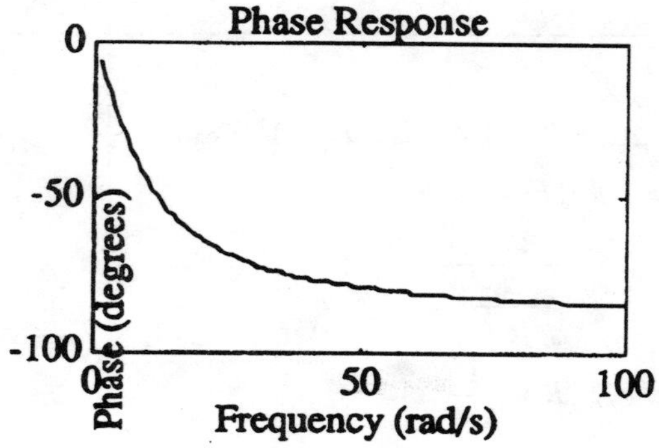

(c)

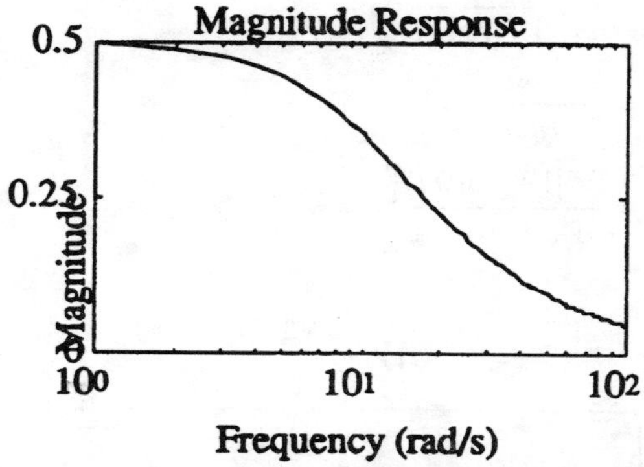

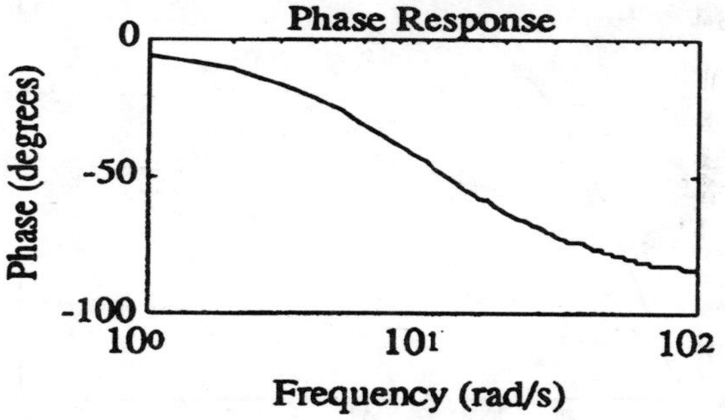

(d)

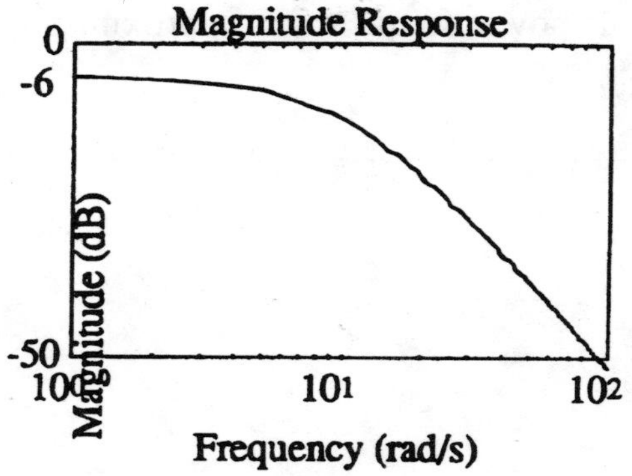

6.5

Assume $R_1 = 1000\ \Omega$, $R_2 = 1000\ \Omega$, $C = 100\mu F$.

$$\frac{V_2}{V_1} = \frac{R}{R + \dfrac{\dfrac{R}{j\omega C}}{R + \dfrac{1}{j\omega C}}}$$

$$= \frac{R}{R + \dfrac{R}{1 + j\omega CR}}$$

$$= \frac{1 + j\omega CR}{2 + j\omega CR}$$

$$= \frac{0.5[1 + j\omega(0.1)]}{1 + j\omega(0.05)}$$

$$\left|\frac{V_2}{V_1}\right| \text{ vs } \omega$$

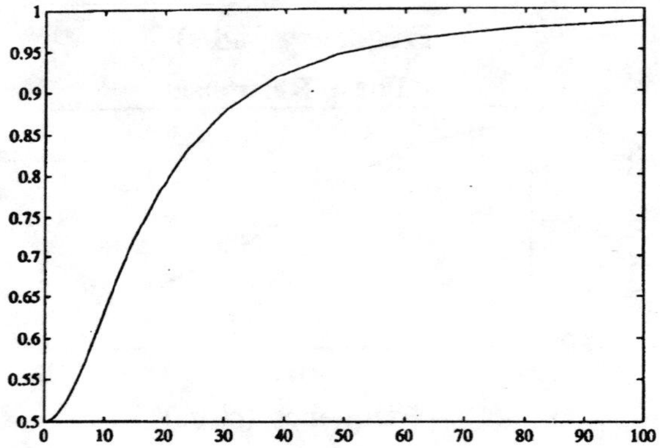

The half-power frequency is approximately 14 rad/s.

6.6

Assume $R = 1000\Omega$ and $C = 100\mu F$.

$$\frac{V_2}{V_1} = \frac{R + \dfrac{1}{j\omega C}}{R + \dfrac{1}{j\omega C}} = \frac{j\omega CR + 1}{j\omega 2CR + 1} = \frac{1 + j(0.1)\omega}{1 + j(0.2)\omega}$$

$$\left|\frac{V_2}{V_1}\right| \text{ vs } \omega$$

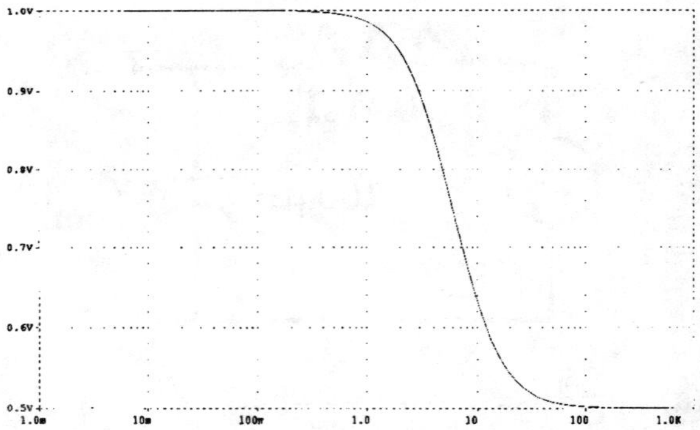

The half-power frequency appears to be about 7 rad/s.

EIT 6.7

(a) $$\frac{V_{out}}{V_{in}} = \frac{R}{R + j\omega L} = \frac{1}{1 + j\omega L / R}$$

$$\frac{V_{out}}{V_{in}} = \frac{1}{1 + j\omega / 10^6}$$

$$\left| \frac{V_{out}}{V_{in}} \right| = \frac{100000}{\sqrt{(100000)^2 + 0.01\omega^2}}$$

$$\phi(\omega) = -\arctan\left(\frac{0.1\omega}{100000} \right)$$

(b)

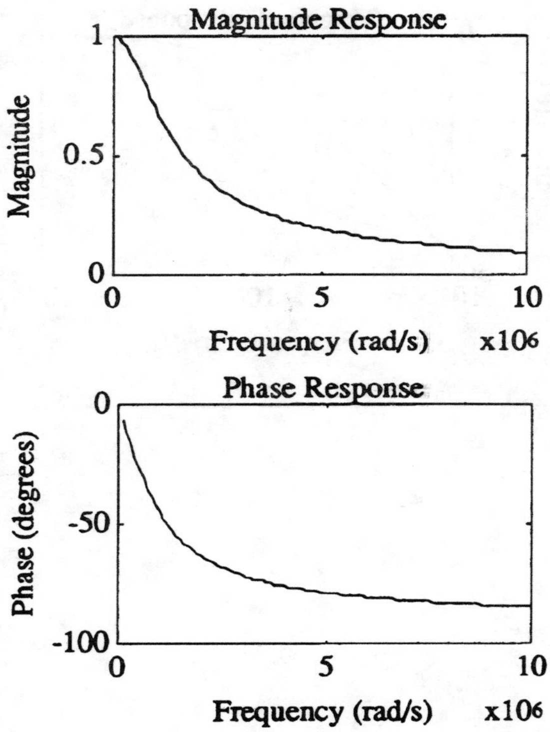

(c)

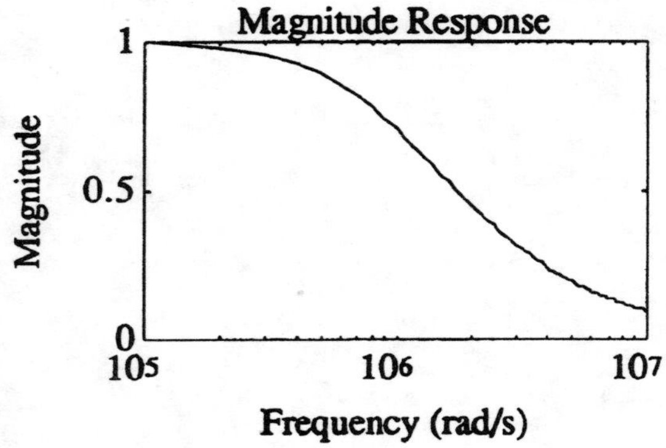

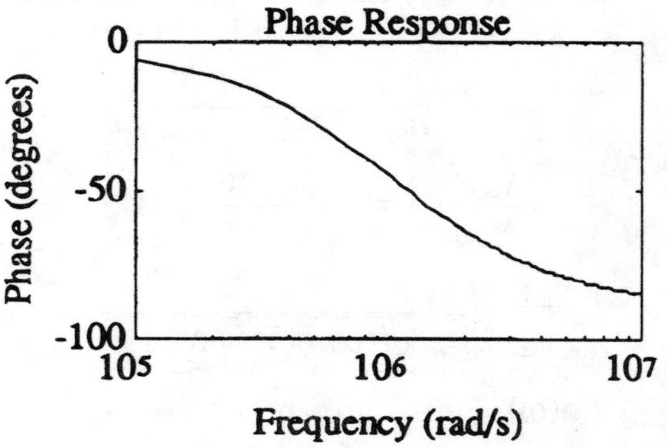

(d)

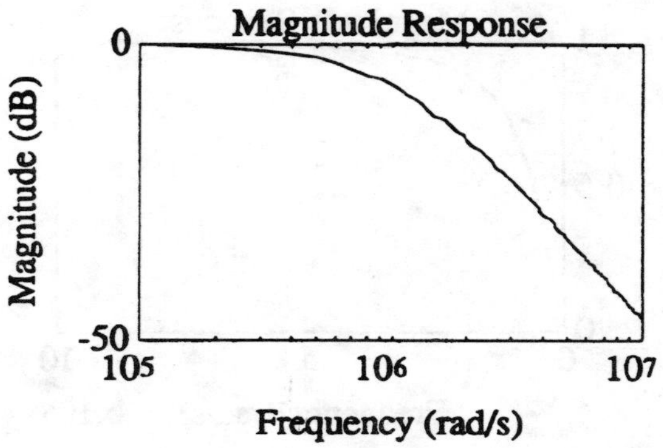

6.8

(a)

$$\frac{V_{out}(j\omega)}{V_{in}(j\omega)} = \frac{j\omega L}{R + j\omega L}$$

$$\frac{V_{out}(j\omega)}{V_{in}(j\omega)} = \frac{j\omega / 10^6}{1 + j\omega / 10^6}$$

$$\left| \frac{V_{out}}{V_{in}} \right| = \frac{0.1\omega}{\sqrt{(100000)^2 + 0.01\omega^2}}$$

$$\phi(\omega) = 90° - \arctan\left(\frac{0.1\omega}{100000} \right)$$

(b)

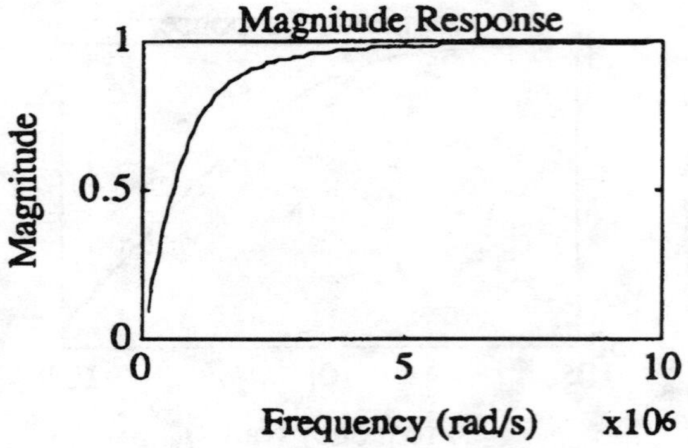

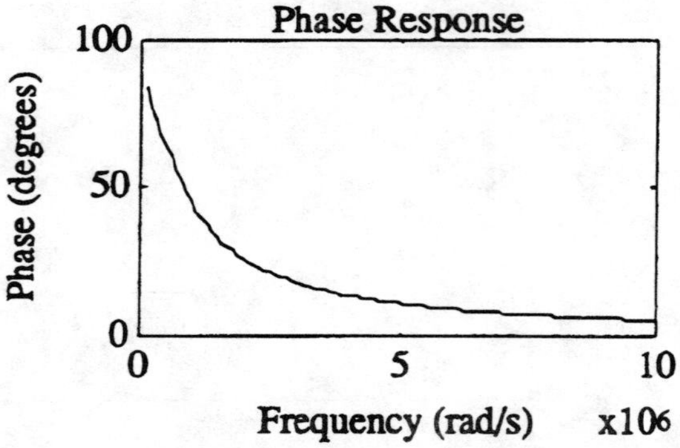

(c)

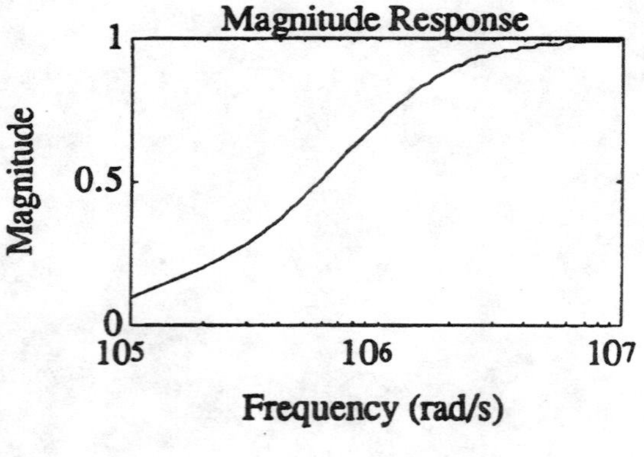

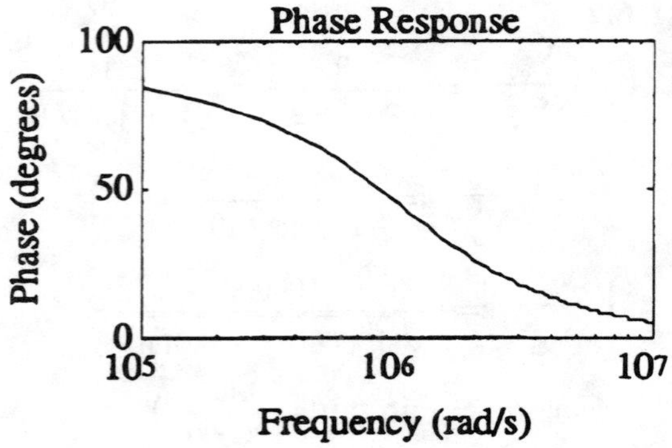

(d)

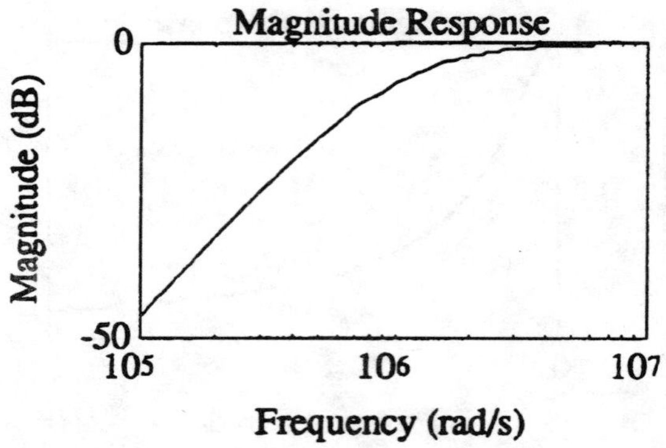

6.9

If $\left|\frac{V_{out}}{V_{in}}\right| \propto \frac{1}{\omega^2}$, it is seen that the amplitude is reduced by a factor of 100, or multiplied by $\frac{1}{100}$, every time the frequency increases by a factor of 10. Since $\frac{1}{100}$ is a -40dB gain, we speak of the transfer function rolling of at a $-40\frac{dB}{decade}$ slope. The term "decade" refers to a frequency factor of 10.

6.10

(a) By Ohm's law,

$$\mathbf{I}_L(\omega) = \frac{V_S(\omega)}{Z_{eq}}$$

$$\frac{I_L(\omega)}{V_S(\omega)} = \frac{1}{Z_{eq}}$$

$$Z_{eq} = 10\ \Omega + 20 \,||\, j\omega 0.2 + 10\ \Omega =$$

$$= \frac{400 + j\omega 8}{20 + j\omega 0.2}$$

Therefore,

$$\frac{I_L(\omega)}{v_s(\omega)} = \frac{20 + j\omega 0.2}{400 + j\omega 8}$$

$$\left|\frac{I_L}{V_s}\right| = \sqrt{\frac{(20)^2 + 0.04\omega^2}{(400)^2 + 64\omega^2}}$$

$$\phi(\omega) = \tan^{-1}\left(\frac{0.2\omega}{20}\right) - \tan^{-1}\left(\frac{8\omega}{400}\right)$$

6.11

(a) Given $|V| = \frac{A\omega}{\sqrt{B + C\omega^2}}$, this is seen to rise from zero at zero frequency to $\frac{A}{\sqrt{C}}$ at high frequencies, behaving like a high-pass filter. The corresponding complex phasor function is

$$V = \frac{j\omega A}{\sqrt{B} + j\sqrt{C}\omega} = \frac{j\omega\frac{A}{\sqrt{B}}}{1 + j\sqrt{\frac{C}{B}}\omega} = \frac{j\omega\frac{A}{\sqrt{B}}}{1 + \frac{j\omega}{\sqrt{\frac{B}{C}}}}$$

which we recognize to have a break frequency (or cutoff frequency, or half-power frequency) of

$$\omega_{CO} = \sqrt{\frac{B}{C}}$$

(b) At high frequencies the slope is zero, i.e., flat as in a high-pass filter.

(c) At low frequencies the Bode plot is sloping up at $20\frac{dB}{decade}$.

(d) At high frequencies, $|V| \rightarrow \frac{A}{\sqrt{C}}$

6.12

$$I_{HI} = \frac{V_S}{R_1 + \frac{1}{j\omega C}} = V_S \frac{j\omega C}{1 + j\omega C R_1}$$

$$I_{LO} = \frac{V_S}{R_2 + j\omega L} = V_S \frac{1}{R_2} \frac{1}{1 + \frac{j\omega L}{R_2}}$$

We want the cutoff frequencies of both the high-pass subcircuit and the low-pass subcircuit to be at

$$\omega = 2\pi \times 1200 = 7540 \frac{rad}{s}$$

$$\frac{1}{CR_1} = \frac{1}{8C} = 7540 \Rightarrow C = 16.57\mu F$$

$$\frac{R_2}{L} = \frac{8}{L} = 7540 \Rightarrow L = 1.06mH$$

EIT 6.13

$$\left| \frac{V_o}{V_i} \right| = \frac{\omega RC}{\sqrt{(1 - \omega^2 LC)^2 + (\omega RC)^2}}$$

(a) $$\left| \frac{V_o}{V_i} \right| = \frac{0.001\omega}{\sqrt{(1 - 10^{-6}\omega^2)^2 + 10^{-6}\omega^2}} \;)$$

(b) The center frequency may be found by differentiating the above expression with respect to ω, setting the derivative equal to zero, and solving for ω.

$$\omega_{center} = \frac{1}{\sqrt{LC}} = 1000 \text{ rad/s}$$

(c)

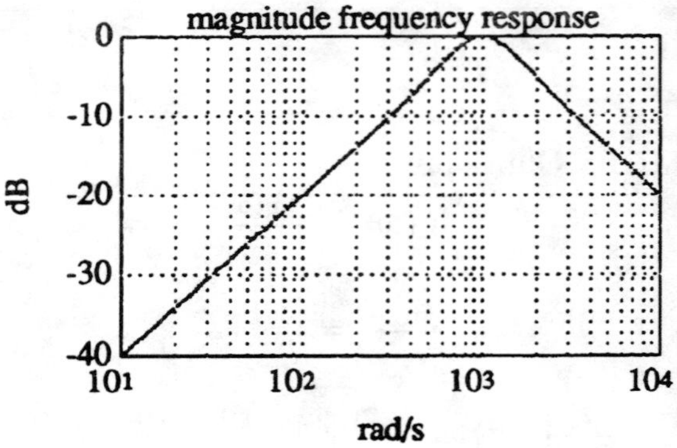

(d) Since an attenuation of -3 dB corresponds to a reduction by a factor of $1/\sqrt{2}$,we can find the desired frequency by solving the following equation:

$$\left| \frac{V_o}{V_i} \right| = \frac{0.001\omega}{\sqrt{(1 - 10^{-6}\omega^2)^2 + 10^{-6}\omega^2}} = \frac{1}{\sqrt{2}}$$

Solving for ω, we find solutions at

$\omega_1 = 618$ rad/s and $\omega_2 = 1{,}618$ rad/s

Thus, the 3-dB bandwidth is 1,000 rad/s

This is also confirmed by the graph.

6.14

Taking the output as the voltage across the parallel R-C subcircuit,

$$\frac{V_o}{V_{in}} = \frac{1}{\frac{j^2\omega^2}{32} + \frac{j\omega}{8} + 1}$$

The crresponding Bode plots are shown below:

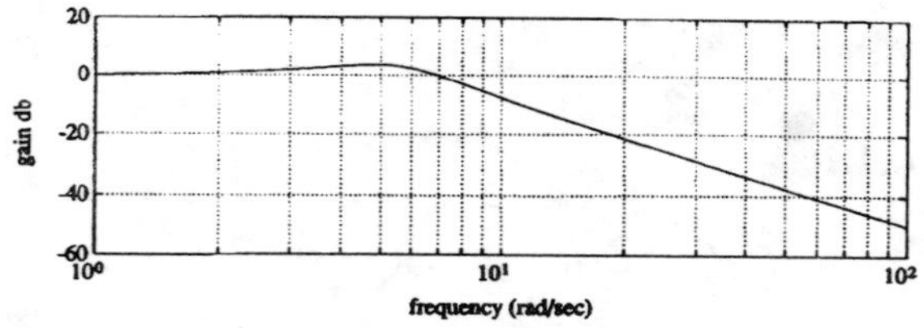

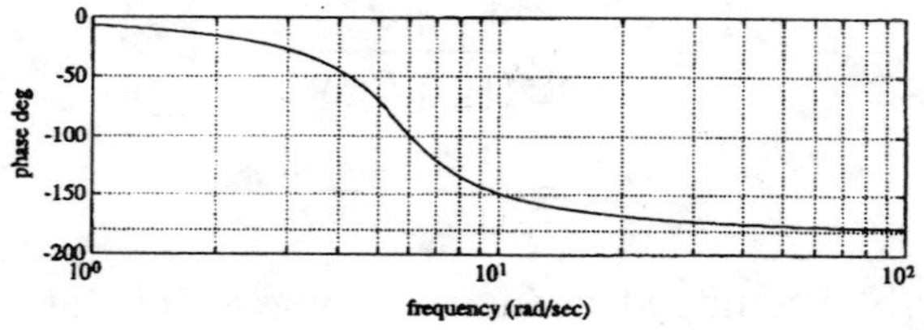

The peak gain occurs at the resonant frequency of 5.6 rad/s. The bandwidth, or frequency at which gain is down 3dB from the low frequency gain, is approximately 8 rad/s.

6.15

$$\left| \frac{V_o}{V_i} \right| = \frac{\omega RC}{\sqrt{(1 - \omega^2 LC)^2 + (\omega RC)^2}}$$

(a) $$\left| \frac{V_o}{V_i} \right| = \frac{0.01\omega}{\sqrt{(1 - 20(10^{-6})\omega^2)^2 + (.01\omega)^2}}$$

(b) $\omega_{center} \approx 223.6$ rad/s

(c)

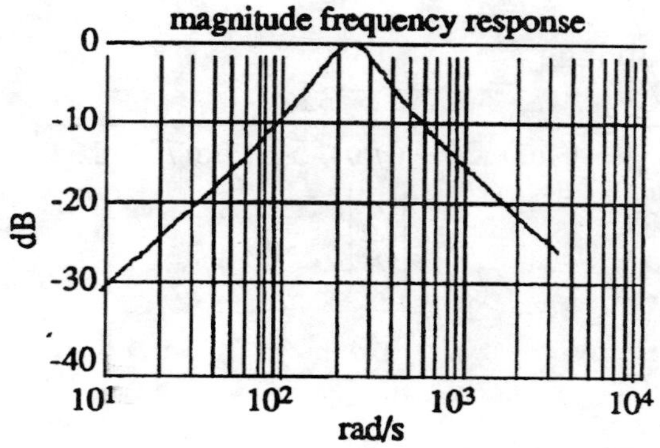

(d) Since an attenuation of -3 dB corresponds to a reduction by a factor of $1/\sqrt{2}$,we can find the desired frequency by solving the following equation:

$$\frac{1}{\sqrt{2}} = \frac{\omega RC}{\sqrt{(1 - \omega^2 LC)^2 + (\omega RC)^2}}$$

Solving for ω, we obtain $\omega_1 = 85.4$ rad/s and $\omega_2 = 585.4$ rad/s. Therefore, the 3-dB bandwidth is $\omega_2 - \omega_1 = 500$ rad/s, which is confirmed by the graph.

6.16

Take the output as the voltage across the capacitor. Define mesh currents I_1 flowing clockwise in the left-hand loop, and I_2 flowing clockwise in the right-hand loop. Then the corresponding mesh equations are:

$$(9 + j4\omega)I_1 - j2\omega I_2 = V_S$$

$$- j2\omega I_1 + \left(j6\omega - j\frac{18}{\omega} \right) I_2 = 0$$

Solving,

$$\frac{V_O}{V_S} = \frac{j32\omega}{(j\omega)^3 20 + (j\omega)^2 54 + j\omega 72 + 162}$$

$$\left| \frac{V_O}{V_S} \right| \text{ vs } \omega$$

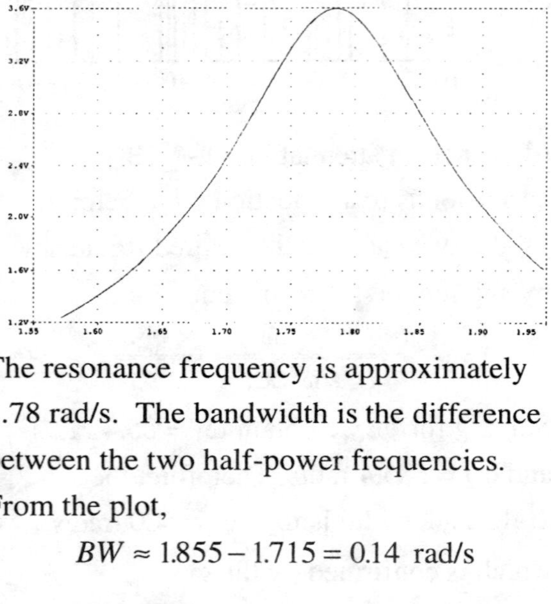

The resonance frequency is approximately 1.78 rad/s. The bandwidth is the difference between the two half-power frequencies. From the plot,

$$BW \approx 1.855 - 1.715 = 0.14 \text{ rad/s}$$

EIT 6.17

(a) $$Z_{ab} = j\omega L \parallel \frac{1}{j\omega C} = \frac{j\omega L / j\omega C}{j\omega L + \frac{1}{j\omega C}}$$

$$Z_{ab} = \frac{j\omega L}{1 - \omega^2 LC}$$

(b) The impedance will become infinite at

$$\omega = \frac{1}{\sqrt{LC}} = 10^6 \text{ rad/s}$$

6.18

(a) $$Z_{ab} = j\omega L \parallel \frac{1}{j\omega C} = \frac{j\omega L / j\omega C}{j\omega L + 1/j\omega C}$$

$$Z_{ab} = \frac{j\omega L}{1 - \omega^2 LC}$$

(b) The impedance will become infinite at

$$\omega = \frac{1}{\sqrt{LC}} = 31{,}622.8 \text{ rad/s}$$

6.19

$$\frac{V_{out}(\omega)}{V_s(\omega)} = \frac{R_L \parallel Z_{ab}}{R_L \parallel Z_{ab} + R_S}$$

$$R_L \parallel Z_{ab} = \frac{j\omega L R_L}{R_L - \omega^2 LCR_L + j\omega L}$$

$$= \frac{j\omega L}{1 - \omega^2 LC + j\omega L / R_L}$$

$$\frac{V_{out}(\omega)}{V_s(\omega)} = \frac{j\omega L / R_S}{j\omega(L / R_S + L / R_L) + 1 - \omega^2 LC}$$

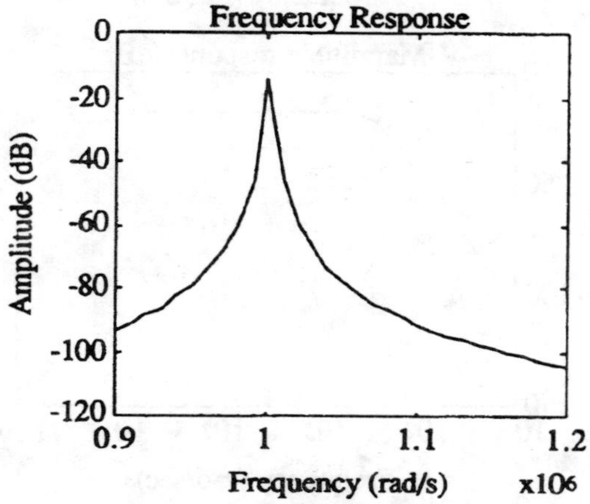

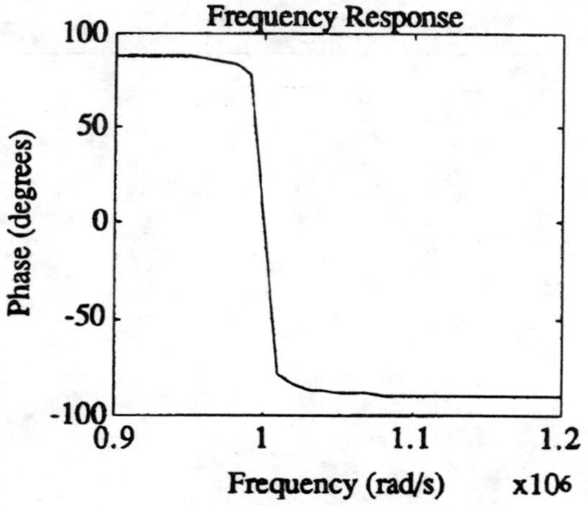

6.20

(a)

$$Z_f = \frac{1}{\frac{1}{R_L + j\omega L} + j\omega C + \frac{1}{R_C}}$$

$$= \frac{R_L + j\omega L}{1 + j\omega C(R_L + j\omega L) + \frac{R_L + j\omega L}{R_C}}$$

$$= \frac{R_L + j\omega L}{(j\omega)^2 LC + j\omega\left(R_L C + \frac{L}{R_C}\right) + \frac{R_C + R_L}{R_C}}$$

$$= \frac{j\omega(0.1) + 0.2}{(j\omega)^2 70.36 \times 10^{-7} + j\omega(7.2 \times 10^{-9} + 10^{-8}) + 1.0000002}$$

At 60Hz,

$$Z_f(377) = \frac{j37.7 + 0.2}{-1.00002 + j6.484 \times 10^{-6} + 1.0000002}$$

$$= 0.581 \times 10^6 - j30.8 \times 10^3$$

(b)

$$|V_O(377)| = \left| \frac{150}{200 + 0.581 \times 10^6 - j30.8 \times 10^3} \right| = 258\mu V$$

***6.21**

(a) $Z = (4 + j\omega L) \parallel (4 + \frac{1}{j\omega C})$

$$= \frac{(4 + j\omega L)(4 + 1/j\omega C)}{4 + j\omega L + 4 - j/\omega C})$$

$$= \frac{16 + L/C + j4(\omega L - 1/\omega C)}{8 + j(\omega L - 1/\omega C)} = 4\ \Omega$$

$Z_L = 4\Omega$ for all frequencies

(b) The power transfer is maximized and independent of frequency. Use the current divider.

$$\mathbf{I}_w = \frac{Y_w}{Y_L}\frac{V_L}{4} = \frac{Y_w}{Y_L}\frac{1}{8}\mathbf{V}_s = \frac{1/(R + j\omega L)}{1/4}\frac{1}{8}\mathbf{V}_s$$

$$= \frac{1}{2}\frac{1}{R + j\omega L}\mathbf{V}_s = \frac{1}{2}\frac{1}{4 + j\omega(2\times10^{-3})}\mathbf{V}_s$$

$$\mathbf{I}_w = \frac{1}{8}\frac{1}{1 + j\omega(5\times10^{-4})}\mathbf{V}_s = \frac{1}{8}\frac{1}{1 + j\left(\frac{\omega}{2\times10^3}\right)}\mathbf{V}_s$$

$$\mathbf{I}_T = \frac{Y_T}{Y_L}\frac{\mathbf{V}_L}{4} = \frac{Y_T}{Y_L}\frac{\mathbf{V}_s}{8} = \frac{j\omega C/(1 + j\omega RC)}{1/4}\frac{1}{8}\mathbf{V}_s$$

$$= \frac{1}{2}\cdot\frac{j\omega C}{1 + j\omega RC}\mathbf{V}_s = \frac{1}{2}\frac{j\omega(1.25\times10^{-4})}{1 + j\omega(5\times10^{-4})}$$

$$= \frac{1}{8}\frac{j\left(\frac{\omega}{2\times10^3}\right)}{1 + j\left(\frac{\omega}{2\times10^3}\right)}\mathbf{V}_s$$

For both the woofer and tweeter,
$\omega_o = 2\times10^3$ rad/s

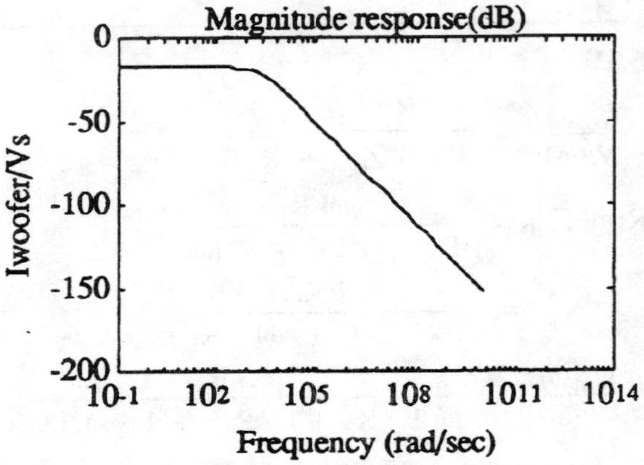

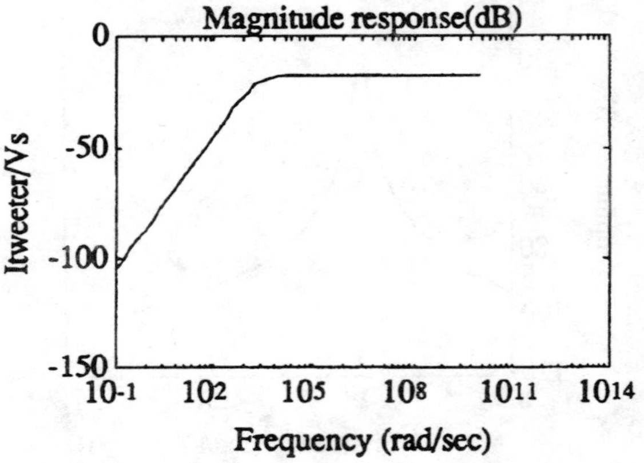

EIT 6.22

(a) The impedance of the L-C section is:

$$Z_{L\text{-}C} = j\omega L \parallel \frac{1}{j\omega C} = \frac{j\omega L}{1-\omega^2 LC}$$

Applying the voltage divider rule,

$$\mathbf{V}_{out}(\omega) = \mathbf{V}_S(\omega)\ \frac{R_L}{R_S + Z_{L\text{-}C} + R_L}$$

Thus,

$$\frac{V_{out}(\omega)}{V_s(\omega)} = \frac{R_L}{R_S + \dfrac{j\omega L}{1-\omega^2 LC} + R_L}$$

(b) The frequency response of this "notch" filter is plotted below.

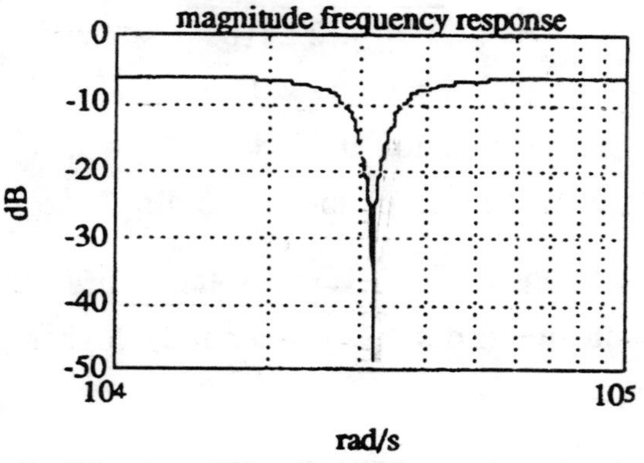

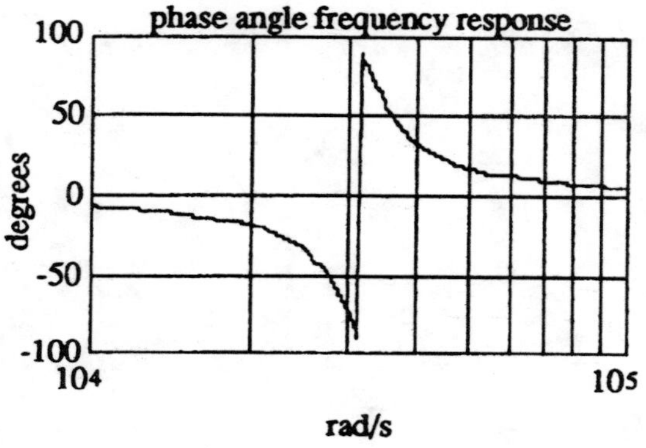

6.23

(a) $Z_{filter} = (r_L + j\omega L) \parallel \dfrac{1}{j\omega C}$

Therefore, $Z_{filter} = \dfrac{r_L + j\omega L}{(1-\omega^2 LC) + j\omega r_L C}$

(b) The center frequency of the filter impedance is approximately given by:

$$\omega_0 \approx \frac{1}{\sqrt{LC}} = 2\pi \times 60$$

Thus,

$$C = \frac{1}{w_0^2 L} = 7.04\times10^{-5}\ F = 70.4\ \mu F$$

The approximation given above is more accurate the smaller r_L is.

(c) The sharpness of the filter is maximum when r_L=0, and is reduced as the resistance of the inductor increases. The figure shows the magnitude of the filter impedance for r_L = 5, 15, 30 Ω, with the sharpest curve corresponding to the 5-Ω case.

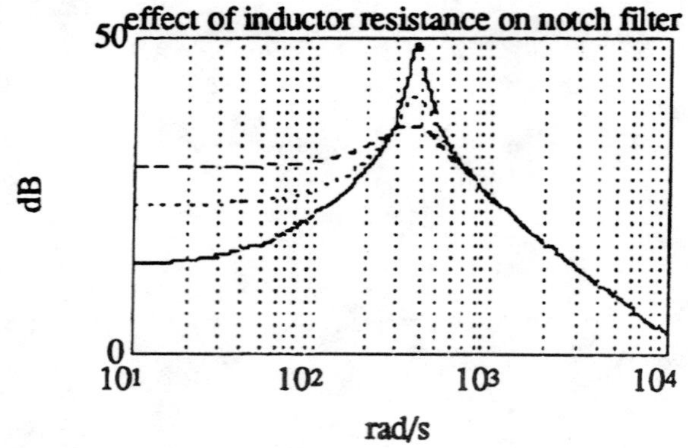

(d) $$\frac{V_L}{V_{in}}(\omega) = \frac{R_L}{R_L + r_g + Z_{filter}}$$

$$= \frac{300}{350 + \dfrac{(r_L + j\omega L)}{(1 - \omega^2 LC + j\omega r_L LC)}}$$

@ 60 Hz, $\dfrac{V_L}{V_n} =$

$$\frac{300(3)}{350 + \left(\dfrac{5 + j\,37.7}{1 - 1 + j\,0.013}\right)}$$

$$= \frac{300(3)}{350 + 2.92¢10^3\ -7.55°}$$

$$\approx 0.274\ \angle 0°$$

@ 1000 Hz,

$$\frac{V_L}{V_g} = \frac{300}{350 + \left(\dfrac{5 + j\,628.3}{1 - 278 + j\,0.22}\right)}$$

$$= \frac{300}{350 + 2.27180°}$$

$$\approx 0.863\ \angle 0°$$

(e) The attenuation at 60 Hz is -6.5 dB; at 1,000 Hz the attenuation is -1.3 dB. Note that $20\log_{10}\frac{300}{350} = -1.33$ dB; thus, no attenuation is due to the filter at the higher frequency.

***6.24**

(a) $\dfrac{V_O(s)}{V_S(s)} =$

$$\frac{\frac{1}{C_2 s} \parallel R_L}{\frac{1}{C_2 s} \parallel R_L + sL + R_S \parallel \frac{1}{C_1 s}}$$

We have $\dfrac{1}{C_2 s} \parallel R_L = \dfrac{R_L}{R_L C_2 s + 1}$

Therefore,

$\dfrac{V_O(s)}{V_S(s)} =$

$$\frac{\frac{R_L}{R_L C_2 s + 1}}{\frac{R_L}{R_L C_2 s + 1} + sL + \frac{R_S}{R_S C_1 s + 1}}$$

$$\frac{V_O(s)}{V_S(s)} = \frac{R_S C_1 s + 1}{s^3 K_1 + s^2 K_2 + s K_3 + K_4}$$

where

$$K_1 = C_2 R_S C_1 L$$

$$K_2 = C_2 L + C_1 L \frac{R_S}{R_L}$$

$$K_3 = R_S C_1 + R_S C_2 + \frac{L}{R_L}$$

$$K_4 = 1 + \frac{R_S}{R_L}$$

$$\frac{V_O(\omega)}{V_S(\omega)} = \frac{\frac{j\omega}{2000p} + 1}{\frac{j\omega^3}{(2000p)^3} - \frac{2\omega^2}{(2000p)^2} + \frac{3j\omega}{2000p} + 2}$$

(b)

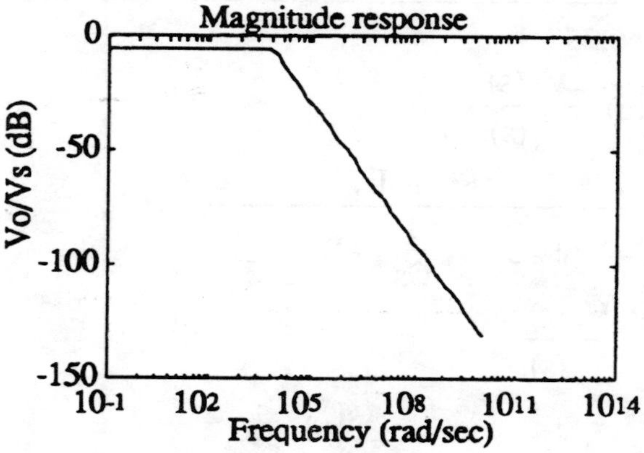

***6.25**

(a) $\frac{V_O(s)}{V_S(s)} =$

$$\frac{R_L \parallel sL_2}{R_L \parallel sL_2 + \frac{1}{Cs} + R_S \parallel sL_1}$$

$\frac{V_O(s)}{V_S(s)} =$

$$\frac{\frac{sL_2}{L_2 s / R_L + 1}}{\frac{sL_2}{L_2 s / R_L + 1} + \frac{1}{Cs} + \frac{sL_1}{sL_1 / R_S + 1}}$$

$$\frac{V_O(s)}{V_S(s)} = \frac{K_4 s^3 + s^2 L_2 C}{s^3 K_1 + s^2 K_2 + sK_3 + 1}$$

where

$$K_1 = \frac{L_1 L_2 C}{R_S} + \frac{L_1 L_2 C}{R_L}$$

$$K_2 = L_2 C + \frac{L_1 L_2}{R_S R_L} + L_1 C$$

$$K_3 = \frac{L_2}{R_L} + \frac{L_1}{R_S}$$

$$K_4 = \frac{L_1 L_2 C}{R_S}$$

$$\frac{V_O(j\omega)}{V_S(j\omega)} =$$

$$\frac{-j\omega^3 K - \omega^2 K^2}{-j\omega^3 2K - \omega^2 (2K^2 + \frac{1}{K^2}} + j\omega 2K + 1$$

where $K = 2000\pi$

(b)

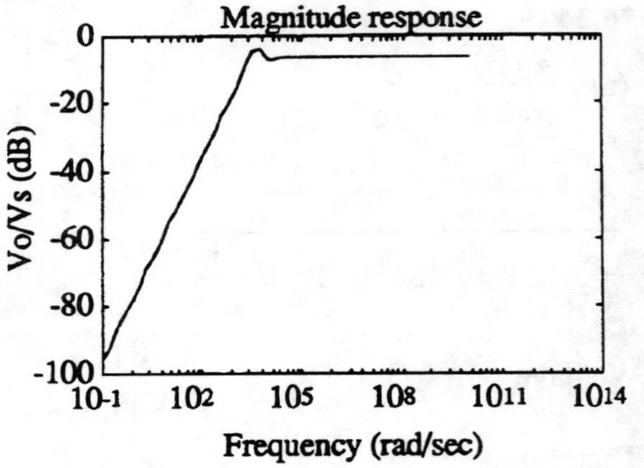

***6.26**

(a) <u>KVL mesh 1</u>

$$-\mathbf{V}_s + R_a\mathbf{I}_1 + \frac{1}{j\omega C_1}\mathbf{I}_1 + j\omega L(\mathbf{I}_1 - \mathbf{I}_2) = 0$$

<u>KVL mesh 2</u>

$$j\omega L(\mathbf{I}_2 - \mathbf{I}_1) + \frac{1}{j\omega C_2}\mathbf{I}_2 + R_L\mathbf{I}_2 = 0$$

$$(\mathrm{R_a} + \mathrm{j}\omega + \frac{1}{j\omega C_1})\,\boldsymbol{I}_1 - \mathrm{j}\omega\mathrm{L}\boldsymbol{I}_2 = \boldsymbol{V}_s$$

$$-\mathrm{j}\omega\mathrm{L}\boldsymbol{I}_1 + (\mathrm{R} + \mathrm{j}\omega\mathrm{L} + \frac{1}{j\omega C_2})\boldsymbol{I}_2 = 0$$

$$\mathbf{V}_o = R_L\mathbf{I}_2 = R_L \frac{\begin{vmatrix} R_a + SL + \dfrac{1}{SC} & \mathbf{V}_s \\ -SL & 0 \end{vmatrix}}{\begin{vmatrix} R_a + SL + \dfrac{1}{SC_1} & -SL \\ -SL & R_L + SL + \dfrac{1}{SC_2} \end{vmatrix}}$$

(b)

$$\frac{\mathbf{V}_o}{\mathbf{V}_s} = \frac{R_L LS}{(R_a + R_L)LS + \left(R_aR_L + \frac{L}{C_1} + \frac{L}{C_2}\right) + \left(\frac{R_L}{C_1} + \frac{R_a}{C_2}\right)\frac{1}{s} + \frac{1}{s^2C_1C_2}}$$

$$= \frac{R_LC_1C_2S^3}{(R_a + R_L)LC_1C_2 + (R_aR_LC_1C_2 + LC_1 + LC_2)s^2 + (R_LC_2 + R_aC_1)s + 1}$$

$$\frac{\mathbf{V}_o}{\mathbf{V}_s} = \frac{-j\omega^3R_LC_1C_2}{-j\omega^3(R_a + R_L)LC_1C_2 - \omega^2(R_aR_LC_1C_2 + LC_1 + LC_2) + j\omega(R_LC_2 + R_aC_1) + 1}$$

$$\frac{\mathbf{V}_o}{\mathbf{V}_s} = \frac{\left(\frac{S}{2000\pi}\right)^3}{2\left(\frac{S}{2000\pi}\right)^3 + 3\left(\frac{S}{2000\pi}\right)^2 + 2\left(\frac{S}{2000\pi}\right) + 1}$$

$$= \frac{\left(\frac{S}{2000\pi}\right)^3}{2\left[\left(\frac{S}{2000\pi}\right) + 1\right]\left[\left(\frac{S}{2000\pi}\right)^2 + \frac{1}{2}\left(\frac{S}{2000\pi}\right) + \frac{1}{2}\right]}$$

$$= \frac{\left(\frac{S}{2000\pi}\right)^3}{2\left[\left(\frac{S}{2000\pi}\right) + 1\right]\left[\left(\frac{S}{2000\pi}\right) + 0.25 + j\frac{1}{2}\sqrt{7}\right]\left[\left(\frac{S}{2000\pi}\right) + 0.25 - j\frac{1}{2}\sqrt{7}\right]}$$

$$\frac{\mathbf{V}_o(j\omega)}{\mathbf{V}_s(j\omega)} = \frac{\left(\frac{j\omega}{2000\pi}\right)^3}{2\left(\frac{j\omega}{2000\pi}\right)^3 + 3\left(\frac{j\omega}{2000\pi}\right)^2 + 2\left(\frac{j\omega}{2000\pi}\right) + 1}$$

$$\frac{\mathbf{V}_o(j2\pi f)}{\mathbf{V}_s(j2\pi f)} = \frac{-j\left(\frac{f}{1000}\right)^3}{-j2\left(\frac{f}{1000}\right)^3 - 3\left(\frac{f}{1000}\right)^2 + j2\left(\frac{f}{1000}\right) + 1}$$

$$= \frac{-j\left(\frac{f}{1000}\right)^3}{1 - 3\left(\frac{f}{1000}\right)^2 + j2\left[\left(\frac{f}{1000}\right) - \left(\frac{f}{1000}\right)^3\right]}$$

$$\left|\frac{\mathbf{V}_o(j2\pi f)}{\mathbf{V}_s(j2\pi f)}\right| = \frac{\left(\frac{f}{1000}\right)^3}{\sqrt{\left[1 - 3\left(\frac{f}{1000}\right)^2\right]^2 + 4\left[\left(\frac{f}{1000}\right) - \left(\frac{f}{1000}\right)^3\right]^2}}$$

$$dB = 20\log_{10}\left|\frac{\mathbf{V}_o(j2\pi f)}{\mathbf{V}_s(j2\pi f)}\right|$$

$\left|\frac{\mathbf{V}_o(j2\pi f)}{\mathbf{V}_s(j2\pi f)}\right|$ is plotted by hand on the next page. Plots of both the magnitude and phase were generated with the program Pspice and are shown on pages 5 and 6

***6.27**

(a) <u>KCL</u>

$$\frac{1}{SL_1+R_s}\left(\mathbf{V}_1-\mathbf{V}_s\right)+SC\mathbf{V}_1+\frac{1}{SL_2+R_L}\mathbf{V}_1=0$$

$$\mathbf{V}_1=\frac{L_2S+R_L}{L_1L_2CS^3+\left(L_1R_L+L_2R_s\right)CS^3+\left(L_1+L_2+R_sR_LC\right)S+\left(R_L+R_s\right)}\mathbf{V}_s$$

The voltage divider gives

$$\mathbf{V}_o=\frac{R_L}{SL_2+R_L}\mathbf{V}_1$$

$$\frac{\mathbf{V}_o}{\mathbf{V}_s}=\frac{R_L}{L_1L_2CS^3+\left(L_1R_L+L_2R_s\right)CS^3+\left(L_1+L_2+R_sR_LC\right)S+\left(R_s+R_L\right)}$$

$$=\frac{\dfrac{R_L}{R_L+R_s}}{\dfrac{L_1L_2C}{R_L+R_s}S^3+\left(\dfrac{L_1R_LC+L_2R_sC}{R_L+R_s}\right)S^3+\left(\dfrac{L_1+L_2+R_sR_LC}{R_L+R_s}\right)S+1}$$

(b)

$$\frac{\mathbf{V}_o}{\mathbf{V}_s}=\frac{1}{2}\,\frac{1}{\dfrac{L^2C}{2R}S^3+LCS^2+\dfrac{2L+R^2C}{2R}S+1}$$

$$=\frac{1}{2}\,\frac{1}{(LC)\left(\dfrac{L}{R}\right)\dfrac{1}{2}S^3+LCS^2+\left(\dfrac{L}{R}+\dfrac{1}{2}RC\right)S+1}$$

$$=\frac{1}{2}\,\frac{1}{\dfrac{1}{2}\left(\dfrac{1}{2000\pi}\right)^2\left(\dfrac{1}{2000\pi}\right)S^3+\left(\dfrac{1}{2000\pi}\right)^2S^2+\dfrac{3}{2}\left(\dfrac{1}{2000\pi}\right)S+1}$$

$$=\frac{1}{\left(\dfrac{S}{2000\pi}\right)^3+2\left(\dfrac{S}{2000\pi}\right)^2+3\left(\dfrac{S}{2000\pi}\right)+2}$$

$$=\frac{1}{\left[\left(\dfrac{S}{2000\pi}\right)+1\right]\left[\left(\dfrac{S}{2000\pi}\right)^2+\left(\dfrac{S}{2000\pi}\right)+2\right]}$$

$$=\frac{1}{\left[\left(\dfrac{S}{2000\pi}\right)+1\right]\left[\left(\dfrac{S}{2000\pi}\right)+\dfrac{1}{2}+j\dfrac{1}{2}\sqrt{7}\right]\left[\left(\dfrac{S}{2000\pi}\right)+\dfrac{1}{2}-j\dfrac{1}{2}\sqrt{7}\right]}$$

$$\frac{\mathrm{V}_o(j\omega)}{V_s(j\omega)}=\frac{1}{\left(\dfrac{j\omega}{2000\pi}\right)^3+2\left(\dfrac{j\omega}{2000\pi}\right)^2+3\left(\dfrac{j\omega}{2000\pi}\right)+2}$$

$$=\frac{1}{\left[2-2\left(\dfrac{\omega}{2000\pi}\right)^2\right]+j\left[3\left(\dfrac{\omega}{2000\pi}\right)-\left(\dfrac{\omega}{2000\pi}\right)^3\right]}$$

$$\frac{\mathrm{V}_o(j2\pi f)}{V_s(j2\pi f)}=\frac{1}{\left[2-2\left(\dfrac{f}{1000}\right)^2\right]+j\left[3\left(\dfrac{f}{1000}\right)-\left(\dfrac{f}{1000}\right)^3\right]}$$

$$\left|\frac{\mathrm{V}_o(j2\pi f)}{V_s(j2\pi f)}\right|=\frac{1}{\sqrt{4\left[1-\left(\dfrac{f}{1000}\right)^2\right]^2+\left[3\left(\dfrac{f}{1000}\right)-\left(\dfrac{f}{1000}\right)^3\right]^2}}$$

(b)

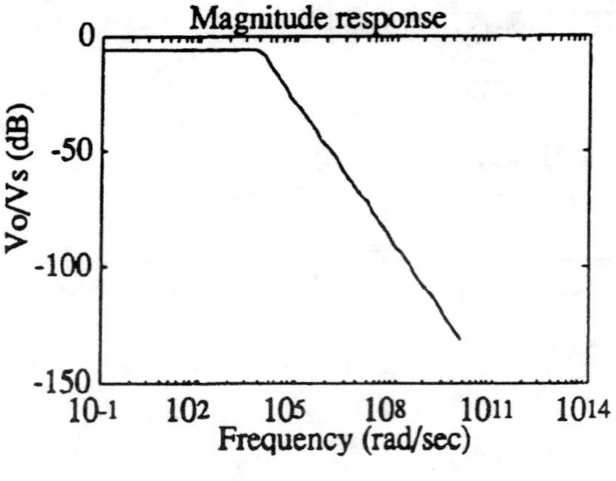

6.28

The characteristic polynomial is

$$0.01s^2 + 400 + \frac{10^8}{s}$$

which has factors

$$s = -2\times10^4 \pm j(9.79\times10^4)$$

leading to a solution of the form

$$v_C(t) = 10 + e^{-2\times10^4 t}\left[A\cos(9.79\times10^4 t) + B\sin(9.79\times10^4 t)\right]$$

From the initial conditions,

$10 + A = 0$

and

$-2\times10^4 A + 9.79\times10^4 B = 0$

Solving, we have $A = -10$, $B = -2.04$

The capacitor voltage for $t \ge 0$ is:

$$v_C(t) = 10 + e^{-2\times10^4 t}\left[-10\cos(9.79\times10^4 t) - 2.04\sin(9.79\times10^4 t)\right] V$$

6.29

Define clockwise mesh currents, I_1 in the lower loop, and I_2 in the upper loop. Then the mesh equations are:

$(5+5s)I_1 - 3I_2 = 0$

and

$$-3I_1 + \left(3 + \frac{1}{4s}\right)I_2 = 0$$

from which we determine that

$$(5+5s)\left(3+\frac{1}{4s}\right) - 9 = 0$$

or $s = -0.242 \pm j0.158$.

Therefore, the inductor current is of the form

$$i(t) = e^{-0.242t}\left[A\cos(0.158t) + B\sin(0.158t)\right]$$

From the initial conditions,

$$i(0) = \frac{6}{3} = 2 = A$$

and

$$L\left.\frac{di}{dt}\right|_{t=0} = 5\left.\frac{di}{dt}\right|_{t=0} = v_C(0^+) = -10$$

$$\Rightarrow \left.\frac{di}{dt}\right|_{t=0} = -2 = -0.242A + 0.158B$$

Solving, $A = 2$, $B = -9.59$

Therefore, the inductor current is

$$i(t) = e^{-0.242t}\left[2\cos(0.158t) - 9.59\sin(0.158t)\right] A$$

6.30

The first portion of the solution satisfies the conditions of Problem 6.29. Beginning with the solution to that problem, we continue to find the solution for v_C for the first 5 seconds. The solution will have the form

$$v_C(t) = e^{-0.242t}\left[A\cos(0.158t) + B\sin(0.158t)\right]$$

The initial conditions are

$$v_C(0) = 6 = A$$

$$\left.\frac{dv_C}{dt}\right|_{t=0} = \frac{1}{C}i_C(0) = 0 \Rightarrow -0.242A + 0.158B = 0$$

Solving, we have $A = 6,\ B = 9.18$, and

$$v_C(t) = e^{-0.242t}\left[6\cos(0.158t) + 9.18\sin(0.158t)\right]\ A$$

for $0 \le t \le 5s$.

From this equation, and the solution to Problem 6.29, $v_C(5) = 3.2807V$ and $i(5) = -1.641A$. These are the initial conditions for the solution after the switch recloses.

Now, for $t > 5s$, the mesh equations are:

$$(5s+3)I_1 - 3I_2 = \frac{6}{s} + 5i(5)$$

and

$$-3I_1 + \left(3 + \frac{1}{4s}\right)I_2 = -\frac{v_C(5)}{s}.$$

These lead to the characteristic polynomial

$$60s^2 + 5s + 3$$

from which $s = -0.041 \pm j0.220$.

Therefore, the inductor current has the form:

$$i(t) = 2 + e^{-0.041t}\left\{A\cos[0.220(t-5)] + B\sin[0.220(t-5)]\right\}$$

for $t > 5s$.

From the initial conditions,

$$2 + A = -1.641$$

and

$$\left.\frac{di}{dt}\right|_{t=5} = \frac{v_L(5)}{5} = \frac{6-3.28}{5} = 0.543 \Rightarrow -0.41A + 0.220B = 0.543$$

Solving yields $A = -3.641,\ B = 1.77$.

Thus, for $t > 5s$, the inductor current is

$$i(t) = 2 + e^{-0.041t}\left\{-3.641\cos[0.220(t-5)] + 1.77\sin[0.220(t-5)]\right\}\ A$$

This, together with the previous result, gives the complete solution to the problem.

6.31

This problem is the same as Problem 6.28, for $0 \le t \le 50\mu$, and therefore has the same solution during that time interval. For $t > 50\mu$, the solution will remain constant because the capacitor cannot discharge. The capacitor voltage after that point in time is

$$v_C(50\mu s) = 10 + e^{-2\times10^4 t}\left[-10\cos(9.79\times10^4 t) - 2.04\sin(9.79\times10^4 t)\right]\Big|_{t=50\mu s}$$

$$= 10.06V$$

6.32

This circuit has the same configuration during the interval $0 \le t \le 5s$ as the one for Problem 6.30 did for $t > 5s$. Therefore, the roots of the characteristic polynomial will be the same as those determined in that problem. They are

$$s = -0.041 \pm j0.220$$

and the general form of the capacitor voltage is

$$v_C(t) = 6 + e^{-0.041t}\{A\cos[0.220t] + B\sin[0.220t]\}$$

for $0 \le t \le 5s$.

The initial conditions are

$$v_C(0) = 0 \Rightarrow 6 + A = 0$$

and

$$\left.\frac{dv_C}{dt}\right|_{t=0} = \frac{1}{C}i_C(0) = 0 \Rightarrow -0.041A + 0.220B = 0$$

Solving, we have $A = -6,\ B = -0.904$, and

$$v_C(t) = 6 + e^{-0.041t}\{-6\cos[0.220t] - 0.904\sin[0.220t]\}\ V$$

for $0 \le t \le 5s$.

Note that $v_C(5) = 3.127\ V$, and for $t > 5s$ we have a simple RC decay

$$v_C(t) = 3.127e^{-\frac{t-5}{12}}\ V$$

EIT 6.33

(a) $v_C(0^-) = v_C(0^+) = 0$ V

(b) $\tau = 48$ s

(c)

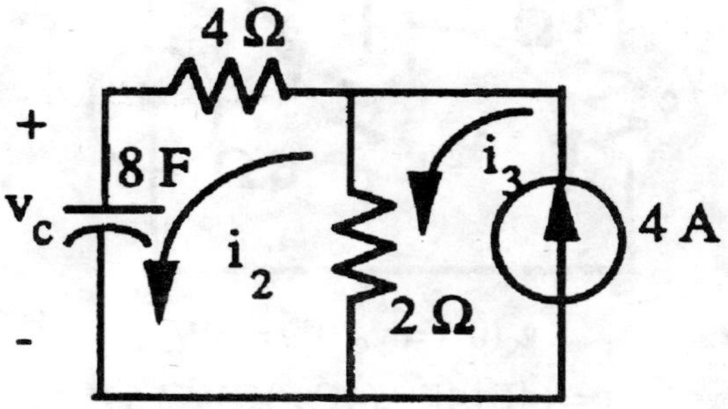

Applying KVL:

$$\frac{dv_c}{dt} + \frac{1}{48}v_C = \frac{1}{6}$$

Solving the differential equation:

$$v_C(t) = k_1 e^{-1/48\, t} + 8\ V \qquad t > 0$$

$$v_C(0^+) = 0\ V.$$

Thus,

$$v_C(t) = -8\, e^{-1/48\, t} + 8\ V \qquad t > 0$$

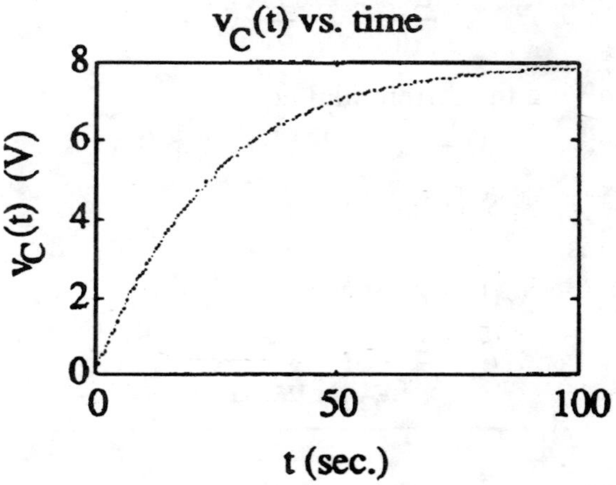

(d) $v_C(0) = 0$ V; $v_C(\tau) = 5.06$ V;

$v_C(2\tau) = 6.9$ V; $v_C(5\tau) = 7.95$ V;

$v_C(10\tau) = 8.0$ V

6.34

(a)

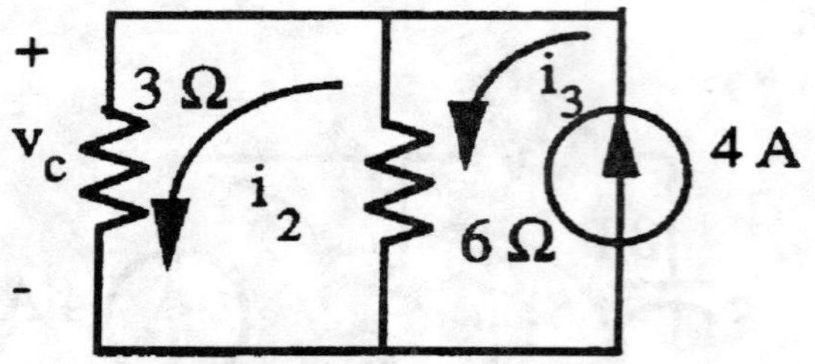

$$v_C(0^-) = v_C(0^+) = 8 \text{ V}$$

(b) $\tau = (4F+4F)\times(4\Omega+3\Omega) = 56$ s

(c)

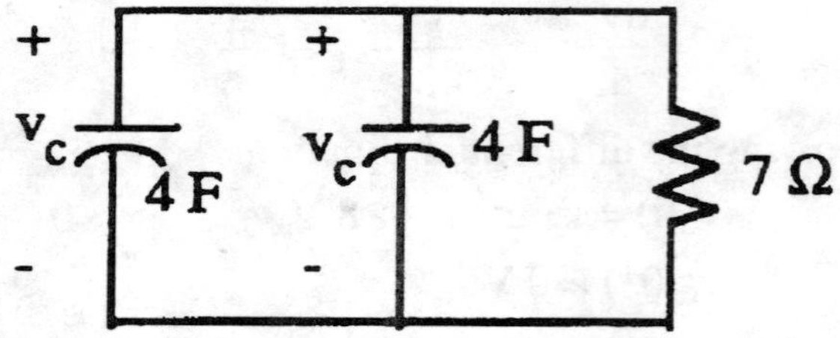

Applying KVL:

$$8\ \frac{dv_C}{dt} + \frac{1}{7}\ v_C = 0$$

Solving the differential eq.:

$$v_C(t) = k_1\, e^{-1/56\, t}\ \text{V} \qquad t > 0$$

$$v_C(0^+) = 8 \text{ V.}$$

Thus,

$$v_C(t) = 8\, e^{-1/56\, t}\ \text{V} \qquad t > 0$$

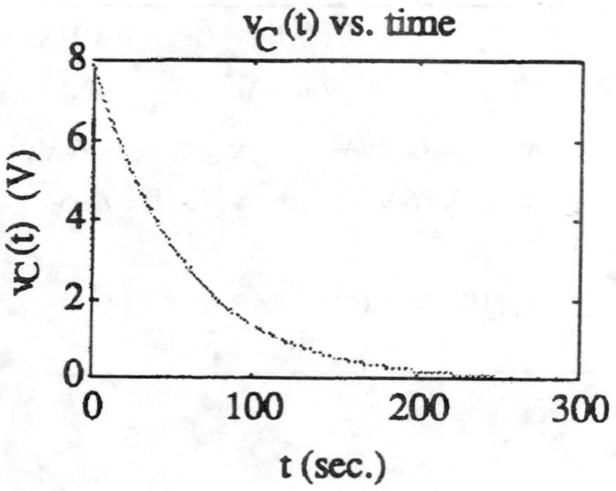

(d) $v_C(0) = 8$ V; $v_C(\tau) = 2.94$ V;

$v_C(2\tau) = 1.08$ V; $v_C(5\tau) = 0.05$ V;

$v_C(10\tau) = 3.6\times10^{-4}$ V

EIT 6.35

(a) S_1 has been closed for a long time. Thus, $v_c(0^-) = 20/12 \times 7 = 11.67$ V, at $t = t_1 = 3\tau$, the switch closes again. Thus, from 6.34

$$v_c(t) = k_1 e^{-1/56\, t} \text{ V} \quad t > 0$$

$$v_c(0^+) = 11.67 \text{ V.}$$

Thus,

$$v_c(t_1 = 3\tau) = 0.58 \text{ V}$$

(b)

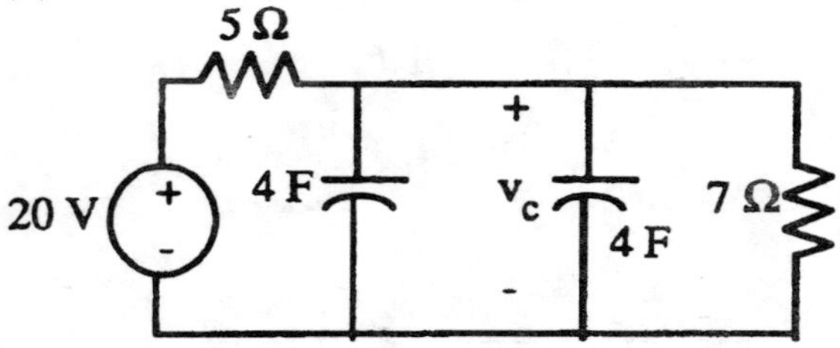

Applying KVL:

$$\frac{dv_c}{dt} + \frac{3}{70} v_c = \frac{1}{2}$$

Solving the differential eq.:

$$v_c(t) = k_1 e^{-3/70\, t} + 11.67 \text{ V} \quad t > 0$$

$$v_c(0^+) = 0.58 \text{ V.}$$

Thus,

$$v_C(t) = -11.09 e^{-3t/70} + 11.67 V \qquad t > 0$$

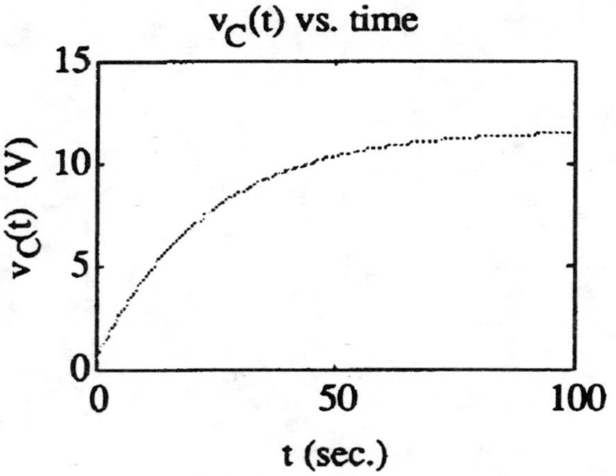

6.36

(a) $v_c(0^-) = v_c(0^+) = 0$ V

(b) $t = 21.8$ s

(c)

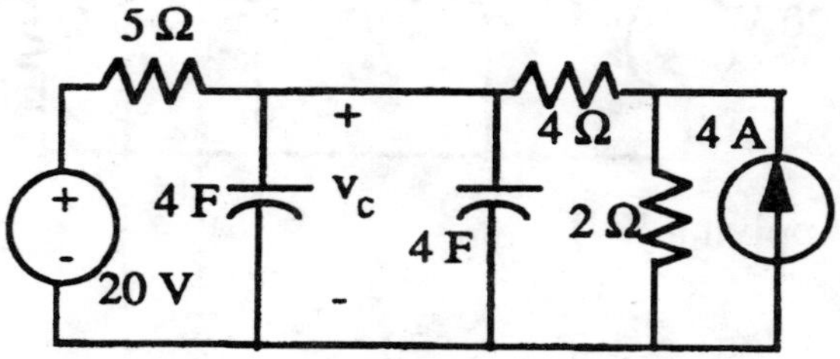

Applying KVL:

$$v_c(t) = k_1 e^{-11/240\, t} + 14.5 \qquad \text{for } t > 0$$

$v_c(0^+) = 0$, thus,

$$k_1 = -14.5$$

and

$$v_c(t) = -14.5\, e^{-11/240\, t} + 14.5 \text{ V for } t > 0$$

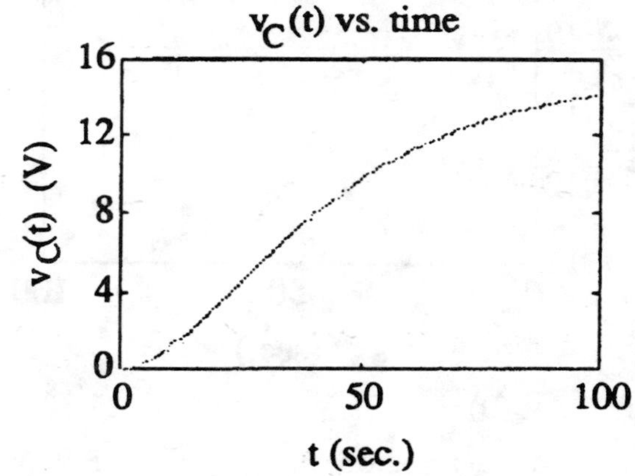

(d) $v_c(0) = 0$ V; $v_c(\tau) = 9.17$ V; $v_c(2\tau) = 12.5$ V; $v_c(5\tau) = 14.4$ V; $v_c(10\tau) = 14.5$ V

6.37

(a) $v_c(0^-) = v_c(0^+) = 14.55$ V

(b)

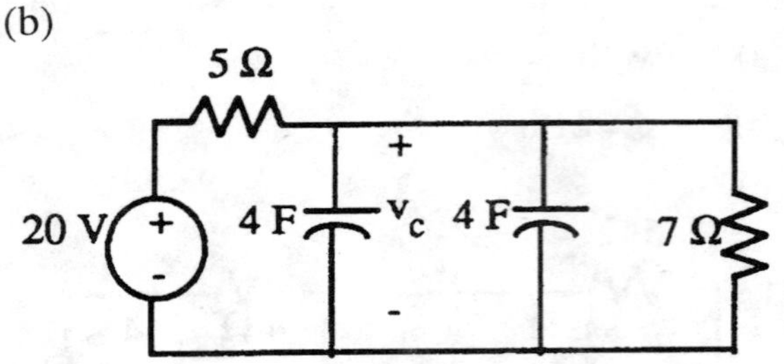

Applying KVL:

$$\frac{dv_c}{dt} + \frac{3}{70} v_c = \frac{1}{2}$$

Solving the differential equation:

$v_c(t) = k_1 e^{-3/70\, t} + 11.67$ V $\quad t > 0$

$v_c(0^+) = 14.55$ V

Thus, $v_c(t) = 2.88\, e^{-3/70\, t} + 11.67$ V $\quad t > 0$

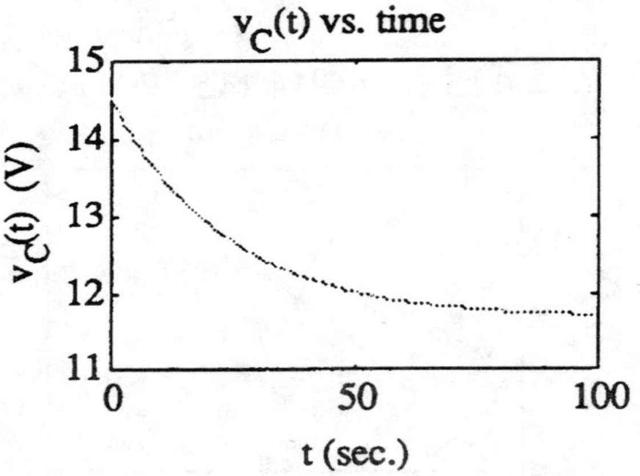

(c) $v_c(0) = 14.55$ V $\quad v_c(\tau) = 12.73$ V;

$v_c(2\tau) = 12.06$ V; $\quad v_c(5\tau) = 11.69$ V;

$v_c(10\tau) = 11.67$ V

EIT 6.38

Before: $R_T = R_S \parallel R_1 \parallel R_2 \parallel R_3 = 923\ \Omega$

$\tau = R_T C = 0.923$ ms

After: $R'_T = R_S \parallel R_1 = 1.333$ kΩ

$\tau' = 1.333$ ms

6.39

$\tau_{Burner} = R_S C_S = 1.5 C_S$

$V_{CSS} = R_S I_S,\ V_C(0) = 0$

$v_C(t) = R_S I_S (1 - e^{-t/\tau})$

$0.9 = 1 - e^{-t/\tau}$

$$-\frac{t}{t} = -2.3$$

$$\frac{10}{1.5 C_s} = 2.3$$

$C_S = 2.9$ F

6.40

(a) As t→∞, the capacitors become open circuits, and we can compute an equivalent circuit, as shown below.

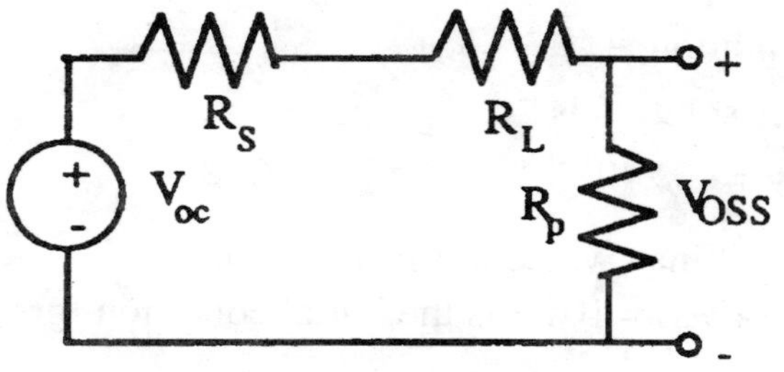

In the circuit above

$$V_{OC} = I_S R_S = 112.5 \text{ V}$$

$$R_S = 1.5\ \Omega \qquad R_L = 0.8\ \Omega$$

$$R_p = 2.5\ \Omega$$

Therefore,

$$V_{OSS} = 112.5\left(\frac{2.5}{2.5 + 0.8 + 1.5}\right) = 58.6 \text{ V}$$

(b) The Thèvenin equivalent seen by the capacitance, C_p, is shown:

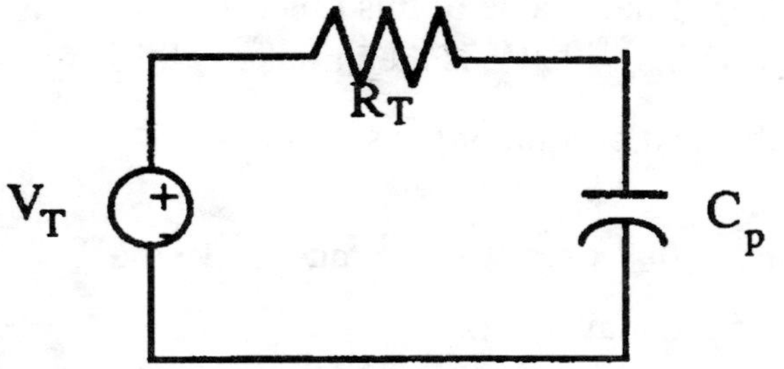

In the circuit above

$$R_T = (R_S + R_L) \,||\, R_p = 1.2\ \Omega$$

and the time constant for this circuit is:

$$\tau' = R_T C_p = 96 \text{ s}$$

To find the 80% time we set

$$0.8 = (1 - e^{-t/\tau})$$

and solve for t:

$$t = 155 \text{ s}$$

6.41

For $t > 0$, the steady-state portion of the solution can be found as follows:

$$10\angle 0^\circ = \left(j1 + \frac{1}{10} + \frac{1}{j}\right) V_{C_{SS}}$$

$$V_{C_{SS}} = \frac{10}{\left(j + \frac{1}{10} + \frac{1}{j}\right)} = 100$$

$$\therefore v_{C_{SS}}(t) = 100\cos(t)\ V$$

Now, we must determine the transient portion of the solution. The characteristic polynomial is given by

$$j\omega + \frac{1}{10} + \frac{1}{j\omega} \Rightarrow (j\omega)^2 + \frac{1}{10} j\omega + 1 \Rightarrow s^2 + \frac{s}{10} + 1$$

which means $s = 0.05 \pm j0.9987$ and the capacitor voltage has the form

$$v_C(t) = v_{C_{SS}}(t) + e^{-0.05t}\left[A\cos(0.9987t) + B\sin(0.9987t)\right]$$

The initial conditions are

$$v_C(0) = 2 \Rightarrow 100 + A = 2$$

and

$$1\left.\frac{dv_C}{dt}\right|_{t=0} = i_C(0) = 10 - 0.2 - 5 = 4.8$$

$$\Rightarrow 0 - 0.5A + 0.9987B = 4.8$$

Solving, we have $A = -98$, $B = -1$ and the capacitor voltage is

$$v_C(t) = 10\cos(t) - e^{-0.05t}\left[98\cos(0.9987t) + 1\sin(0.9987t)\right] V$$

for $t > 0$.

6.42

The equivalent circuit is shown below:

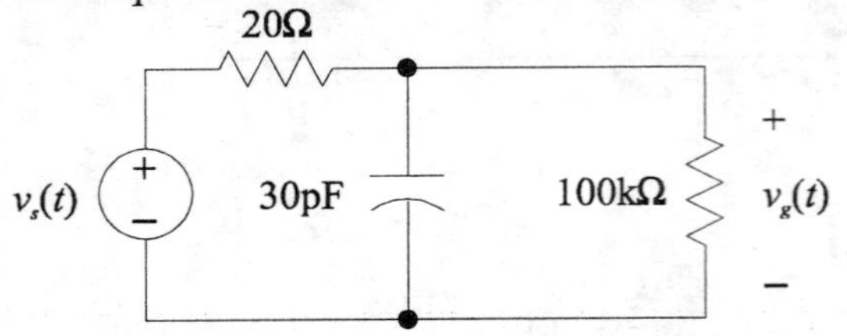

From KCL,

$$\frac{v_g - v_s}{20} + (30\times10^{-12})\frac{dv_g}{dt} + \frac{1}{100\times10^3}v_g = 0$$

or

$$(30\times10^{-12})\frac{dv_g}{dt} + \left(\frac{1}{20}+\frac{1}{100\times10^3}\right)v_g = \frac{1}{20}v_s$$

$$\frac{dv_g}{dt} + 1.667\times10^9 v_g \approx 1.667\times10^9 v_s$$

The input voltage is described by

$$v_s(t) = \begin{cases} 4\times10^8 t\ V & , 0<t<25ns \\ 10\ V & , 25ns<t<45ns \\ (100-2\times10^9 t)\ V, & 45ns<t<50ns \\ 0 & , 50ns<t<2\mu \end{cases}$$

For $0<t<25ns$, we must solve the differential equation

$$\frac{dv_g}{dt} + 1.667\times10^9 v_g \approx 1.667\times10^9\times4\times10^8 t = 6.668\times10^{17} t$$

subject to the initial condition $v_g(0)=0$.

The solution is

$v_g = 0.240e^{-1.667\times10^9 t} + 4\times10^8 t - 0.240\ V$.

The "final" value of this function, $v_g(25ns) = 9.76V$, is the initial condition for the next portion of the solution.

For $25ns<t<45ns$, we must solve the differential equation

$$\frac{dv_g}{dt} + 1.667\times10^9 v_g = 16.67\times10^9$$

subject to the above-mentioned initial condition.

The solution is

$v_g = -0.240e^{-1.667\times10^9(t-25ns)} + 10\ V$.

The "final" value of this function, $v_g(45ns) = 10V$, is the initial condition for the next portion of the solution.

For $45ns<t<50ns$, we must solve the differential equation

$$\frac{dv_g}{dt} + 1.667\times10^9 v_g = 1.667\times10^9(100-2\times10^9 t)$$
$$= 1.667\times10^{11} - 3.334\times10^{18} t$$

subject to the above-mentioned initial condition.

The solution is

$v_g = -1.2e^{-1.667\times10^9(t-45ns)} - 2\times10^9(t-45ns) + 11.2\ V$

The "final" value of this function, $v_g(50ns) = 1.2V$, is the initial condition for the next portion of the solution.

For $50ns<t<2\mu s$, we must solve the differential equation

$$\frac{dv_g}{dt} + 1.667\times10^9 v_g = 0$$

subject to the above-mentioned initial condition.

The solution is

$v_g = 1.2e^{-1.667\times10^9(t-50ns)}\ V$.

A sketch of the first 60ns of the solution is shown below. For $60ns < t < 2\mu$, the voltage is essentially zero and is, therefore, not shown in order to allow room to show more detail during the first 60ns.

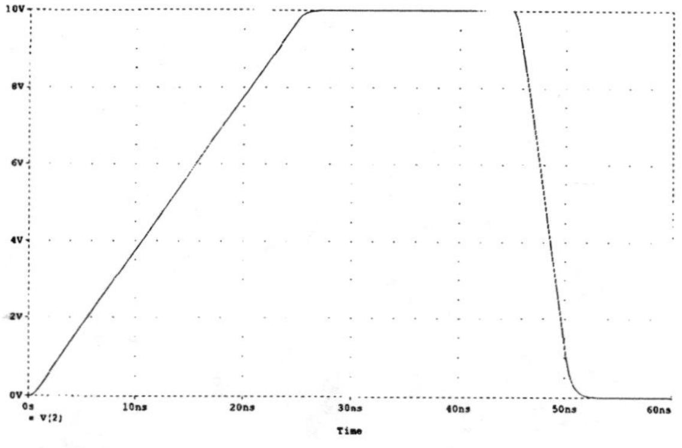

6.43

The circuit for t<0 is shown below:

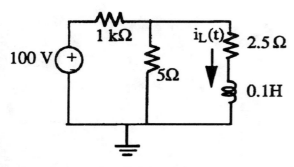

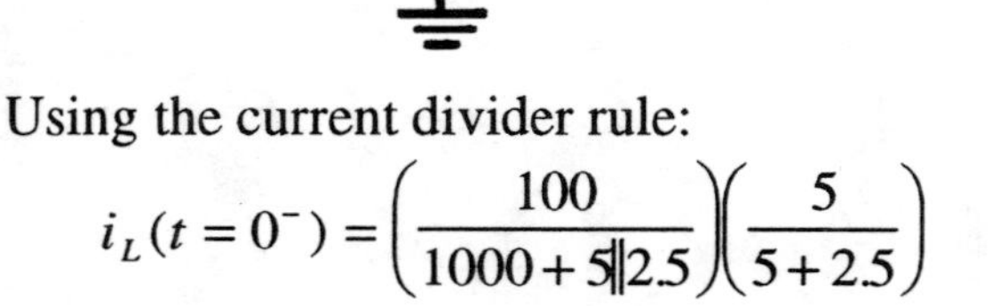

Using the current divider rule:

$$i_L(t=0^-) = \left(\frac{100}{1000+5\|2.5}\right)\left(\frac{5}{5+2.5}\right)$$

$i_L(t=0^-$ = 66.5 mA

For t > 0 we consider the following circuit

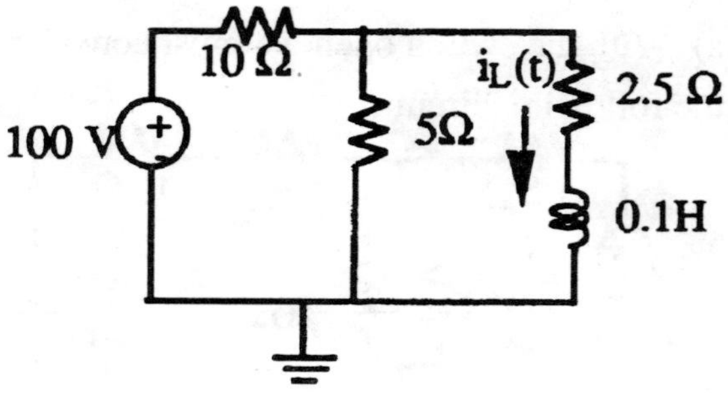

As $t \to \infty$ we can again apply the current divider rule:

$$i_L(\infty) = \left(\frac{100}{10+5\|2.5}\right)\left(\frac{5}{5+2.5}\right)$$

$i_L($ = 5.71 A

To find the time constant for the circuit we must find the Thèvenin resistance seen by the inductor:

$$R_T = 10\|5 + 2.5 = 5.83\ \Omega$$

$$\tau = \frac{L}{R_T} = \frac{0.1}{5.83} = 17.1\text{ ms}$$

Finally, we can write the solution:

$$i(t) = i(\infty) - (i(\infty)-i(0))e^{-t/\tau}$$

$$i_L(t) = 5.71 - (5.71 - 0.0665)e^{-t/17.1\text{ ms}}$$

$i_L(t$ = 5.71 - $5.64e^{-t/17.1\text{ ms}}$

EIT 6.44

a) With the switch open we must consider the following circuit.

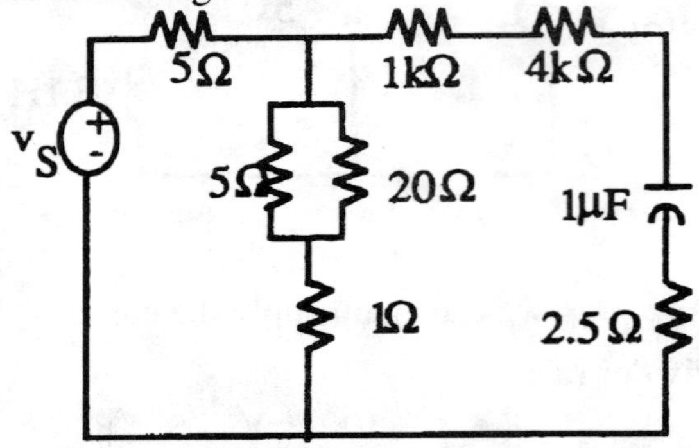

To find the time constant for this circuit we must find the Thèvenin resistance seen by the capacitor:

$R_T = 1000 + 4000 + 2.5 + 5||(5||20 + 1)$

$= 5005\ \Omega$

$\tau = R_T C = (5005\ \Omega)(1\ \mu F) = 5.005$ ms

b) With the switch closed, the 1-kΩ and 4-kΩ resistors are not included since there is a short circuit across them with the switch closed. The resulting circuit is shown below.

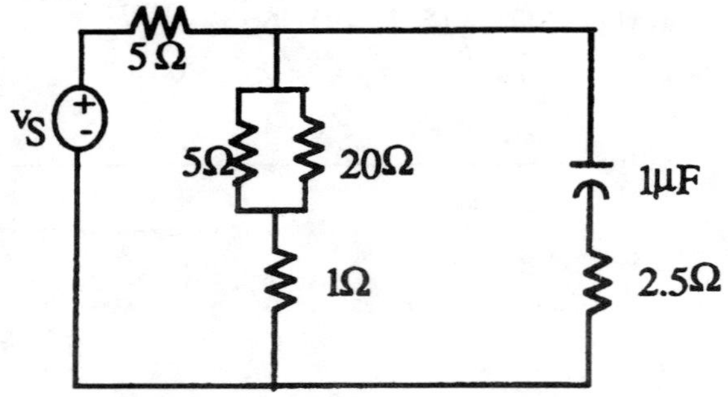

Now the Thèvenin resistance seen by the capacitor is:

$$R_T = 5||(5||20 + 1) + 2.5\Omega$$

$$= 2.5 + 2.5 = 5\ \Omega$$

and the time constant is,

$$\tau = R_T C = (5\Omega)(1F) = 5\mu$$

6.45

(a) With the switch open, we have the following circuit.

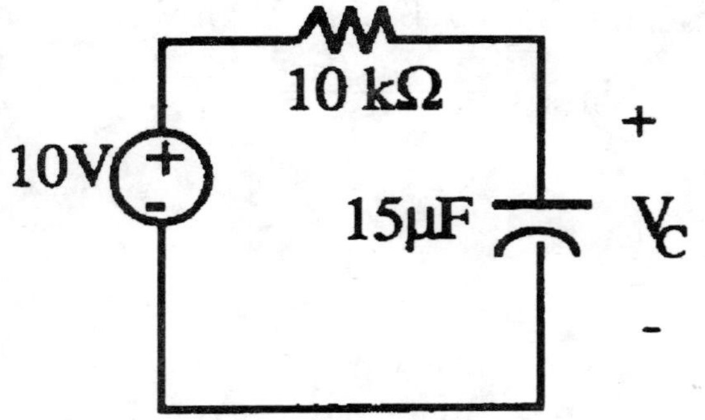

In the above circuit,

$$v_C(\infty) = 10 \text{ V}$$

$$\tau = RC = 0.15 \text{ s}$$

$$v_C(t) = v_C(\infty) - (v_C(\infty) - v_C(0))e^{-t/\tau}$$

$$v_C(t) = 10 - (10\text{-}0.5)e^{-t/0.15}$$

Now we must determine the time when

$$v_C(t) = 7.0 \text{ V}$$

Using the expression for the capacitor voltage,

$$7 = 10 - 9.5\, e^{-t0/0.15}$$

$$e^{-t0/0.15} = \frac{3}{9.5}$$

or

$$t_0 = 0.173 \text{ s}$$

Now the switch closes and we must consider the following circuit.

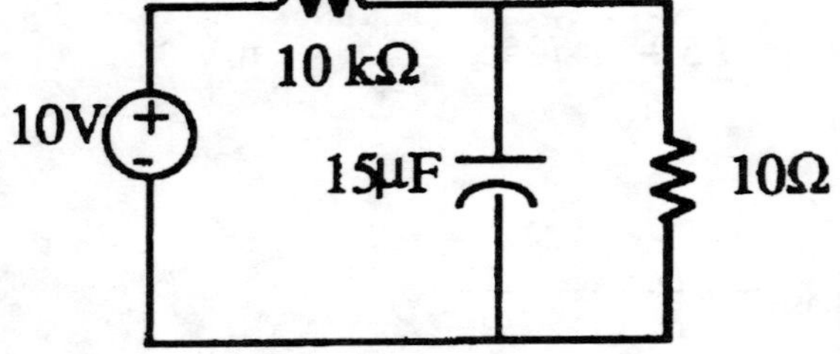

In the above circuit, the capacitor sees the Thèvenin equivalent defined by:

$$V_T = \frac{10}{10 + 10000}(10) \approx 1\times10^{-2} \text{ V}$$

$$R_T \approx 10\ \Omega$$

and the time constant is:

$$\tau = R_T C = 0.15 \text{ ms}$$

With these values we can write the expression for the capacitor voltage:

$$v_C(t) = v_C(\infty) - (v_C(\infty) - v_C(t_0))\, e^{-(t_1 - t_0)/\tau}$$

$$= 1\times10^{-2} + 6.99\, e^{-(t_1 - t_0)/0.15\times10^{-3}}$$

Using the initial condition,

$$v_C = 0.5 \text{ V} \qquad \text{at } t = t_1$$

we can set

$$0.5 \text{ V} = 10 \text{ mV} + 6.99\, e^{-(t_1 - t_0)/0.15ms}$$

$$0.49 = 6.99\, e^{-(t_1 - t_0)/0.15ms}$$

$$t_1 - t_0 = 399\ \mu\text{s}$$

$$t_1 = 399\ \mu\text{s} + 0.173 \text{ s} = 173.4 \text{ ms}$$

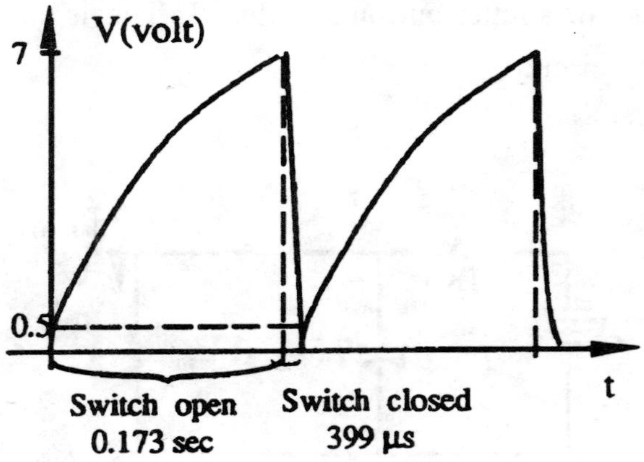

The period of the waveform is the same as the period of the capacitor voltage waveform:

$$T = 0.173 \text{ s} + 399\ \mu\text{s}$$

$$T = 0.173399 \text{ s}$$

EIT 6.46

(a) $v_C(t) = V_{batt} - V_{batt}\, e^{-t/\tau_a}$

$\tau_a = RC = (1000\Omega)(1500\mu F) = 1.5$ s

$v_C(t_{ready}) = 0.99 \times 7.5 = 7.5 - 7.5e^{-t_{ready}/1.5s}$

$$\frac{7.5 - 7.425}{7.5} = e^{-t_{ready}/1.5\text{ s}}$$

$t_{ready} = -1.5 \log_e(0.01)$

$t_{ready} = 6.9$ s

(b) We must find an expression for the voltage across the flash bulb (R_2) after the shutter button has closed. This is the circuit:

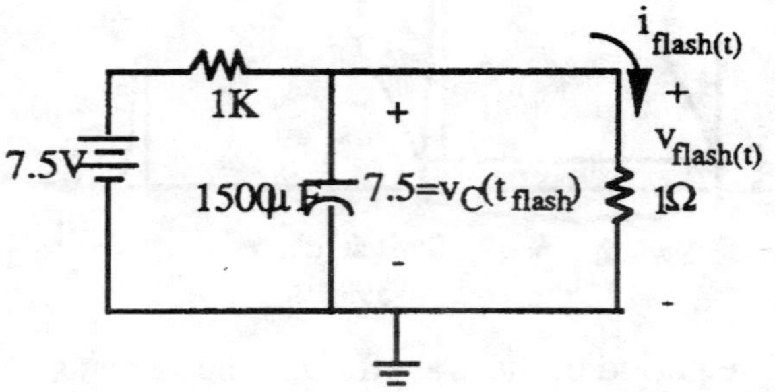

$\tau = R_T C = (1 \| 1000)\, C \approx 0.0015$ s

$\tau \approx 1.5$ ms

$$v_C(t) = v_C(\infty) - (v_C(\infty) - v_C(t_{flash}))\, e^{-\frac{t - t_{flash}}{t}}$$

$$v_C(t) = \frac{1}{1000+1}(7.5) - \left\{\frac{1}{1000+1}7.5 - 7.5\right\} e^{-\frac{t-t_{flash}}{1.5ms}}$$

$$= 7.5 - (0.0075 - 7.5)\, e^{-\frac{t-t_{flash}}{1.5ms}} \text{ mV}$$

$$v_{flash}(t) = 7.5 + 7.4925\, e^{-\frac{t-t_{flash}}{1.5ms}} \text{ mV}$$

$$i_{flash}(t) = \frac{v_{flash}(t)}{R_2} = \frac{v_{flash}(t)}{1\,\Omega}$$

$$W = \int_{t_{flash}}^{t_{flash}+\frac{1}{30}s} v_{flash}(t)\, i_{flash}(t)\, dt$$

$$W = \int_0^{1/30} (7.5 + 7.4925e^{-\lambda/1.5ms})(7.5 + 7.4925e^{-\lambda/1.5ms}) \times 10^{-6}\, d\lambda$$

$W = 42.27$ mJ

(c) In this case the capacitor has not fully charged but has achieved the value of

$v_C(t = 3\text{ s}) = 7.5 - 7.5e^{-3/1.5} = 6.48$ mV

after the shutter switch closes at t = 3 s. The voltage v_{flash} becomes:

$$v_{flash} = 7.5 - (7.5 - 6.48)e^{-\frac{t-3}{1.5ms}} \text{ mV}$$

$$= 7.5 + 6.4725e^{-\frac{t-3}{1.5ms}} \text{ mV}$$

$$i_{flash} = \frac{v_{flash}}{R_2} = \frac{v_{flash}}{1\Omega}$$

$$W = \int_{3}^{3+\frac{1}{30}} v_{flash}(\lambda) i_{flash}(\lambda) d\lambda$$

$$= \int_{0}^{\frac{1}{30}} (7.5 + 6.4725 e^{-\lambda/1.5ms})^2 \times 10^{-6} d\lambda$$

$$= (7.5\times10^{-3})^2 \lambda \Big|_{0}^{\frac{1}{30}}$$

$$- \frac{1.5ms}{2}(6.4725)^2 e^{-\frac{2\lambda}{1.5ms}}\Big|_{0}^{\frac{1}{30}}$$

$$- 1.5ms(2)(7.5\times10^{-3})6.4725 e^{-\frac{\lambda}{1.5ms}}\Big|_{0}^{\frac{1}{30}}$$

$$= 1.875\times10^{-6} + 31.5\times10^{-3} + 145.7\times10^{-6}$$

$$\boxed{W = 31.6 \text{ mJ}}$$

6.47

$$\frac{53.2-50}{70-50} = \frac{e^{-\alpha\times5\pi\times10^{-6}}}{e^{-\alpha\times\frac{5\pi}{3}\times10^{-6}}}$$

$$\Rightarrow \frac{3.2}{20} = e^{-\alpha\left(5\pi-\frac{5\pi}{3}\right)\times10^{-6}} = e^{-\alpha\times\frac{10\pi}{3}\times10^{-6}}$$

Solving for α, we have

$$\alpha = -\left(\ln\frac{3.2}{20}\right)\frac{3}{10\pi\times10^{-6}} = 175\times10^3$$

The period of the waveform is

$$T = 5\pi - \frac{5\pi}{3} = \frac{10\pi}{3} \Rightarrow \omega = \frac{2\pi}{T} = 0.6\times10^6$$

implying the characteristic polynomial for the circuit is

$$\left(s+175\times10^3\right)^2 + \left(0.6\times10^6\right)^2 = s^2 + 350\times10^3 s + 391\times10^9$$

Compare this with the standard form of the characteristic polynomial for a series RLC circuit:

$$s^2 + \frac{R}{L}s + \frac{1}{LC}$$

Matching terms
yields $L = 1.6mH$, $R = 560\Omega$.

6.48

Assuming we wish to retain the same peak amplitudes, we proceed as follows:

The new period is

$T = 15\pi \times 10^{-6} - 5\pi \times 10^{-6} = 10\pi \times 10^{-6}$

which means the new frequency is

$$\omega = \frac{2\pi}{T} = \frac{2\pi}{10\pi \times 10^{-6}} = 0.2 \times 10^{6}$$

In this case, the value of α is given by

$$\alpha = -\left(\ln\frac{3.2}{20}\right)\frac{1}{10\pi \times 10^{-6}} = 58.3 \times 10^{3}$$

The characteristic polynomial is

$$(s + 58.3 \times 10^{3})^{2} + (0.2 \times 10^{6}) = s^{2} + 116.6 \times 10^{3} s + 43.4 \times 10^{9}$$

Comparing with the standard form of the characteristic polynomial for a series RLC circuit,

$$s^{2} + \frac{R}{L}s + \frac{1}{LC}$$

we find $L = 14.4mH,\ R = 1680\Omega$.

Note that the frequency for this problem is one-third that of Problem 6.47, the inductance is 3^2 times that of Problem 6.47, and the resistance is 3 times that of Problem 6.47.

6.49

a) $i_L(t) = i_L(\infty) - i_L(\infty)\, e^{-t/\tau}$

$$\tau = \frac{L_{eq}}{R_T}$$

$$R_T = 10\ k\Omega$$

$$L_{eq} = L_1 + L_2 = 6H;\ \tau = 0.6ms$$

$$i_L(\infty) = 5\ \ A$$

$$i_L(t) = 5 - 5e^{-t/0.6ms}$$

b) $v_L(t) = L\dfrac{di_L(t)}{dt}$

$$= 1\frac{d}{dt}(5 - 5e^{-t/0.6ms})$$

$$= 5\left(\frac{1}{0.6ms}e^{-\frac{t}{0.6ms}}\right)$$

$$\boxed{v_L(t) = 8.333e^{-t/0.6ms}\ kV}$$

EIT 6.50

Applying KCL:

$$i_R = i_C + i_L$$

where

$$i_R = \frac{15 - v_C}{1000}, \quad i_C = 10^{-5}\frac{dv_C}{dt},$$

$$i_L = \int_{-\infty}^{t} v_C dt$$

$$\frac{15 - v_C}{1000} = 10^{-5}\frac{dv_C}{dt} + \int_{-\infty}^{t} v_C dt$$

Differentiating both sides,

$$\frac{d^2 v_c}{dt^2} + 100\frac{dv_c}{dt} + 100{,}000\ v_c = 0$$

6.51

Applying KVL:

$$10{,}000 i_L + v_L + v_C = 12$$

where

$$v_L = L\frac{di_L}{dt} \quad \text{and } i_L = C\frac{dv_C}{dt}$$

Substituting for i_L and v_L,

$$\frac{d^2v_C}{dt^2} + 10^6\frac{dv_C}{dt} + 10^6 v_C = 12\times10^6$$

6.52

The initial condition for the capacitor voltage is: $v(0^-) = 6$. Applying KCL,

$$i_R + i_C + i = 0$$

where

$$i_R = \frac{v}{1\Omega}, \quad i_C = 0.5\frac{dv}{dt}$$

Therefore,

$$i + v + 0.5\frac{dv}{dt} = 0$$

where

$$v = 2\frac{di}{dt} + 4i$$

Thus,

$$\frac{d^2i}{dt^2} + 4\frac{di}{dt} + 5i = 0$$

Solving the differential equation,

$$i(t) = k_1 e^{(-2+j1)t} + k_2 e^{(-2-j1)t} \quad t > 0$$

$$i(0) = k_1 + k_2 = 4$$

$$v(0) = 2\frac{di(0)}{dt} + 4\,i(0) = j2k_1 - j2k_2$$

$$= 6$$

Solving for k_1 and k_2 and substituting, we have

$$i(t) =$$

$$\left(2 - j\frac{3}{2}\right)e^{(-2+j1)t} + \left(2 + j\frac{3}{2}\right)e^{(-2-j1)t}\ \text{A}$$

for $t > 0$

EIT 6.53

$$v(0^-) = v(0^+) = 0$$

Applying KVL:

$$\frac{d^2v}{dt^2} + 4\frac{dv}{dt} + 4v = 48$$

Solving the differential equation;

$$v = k_1e^{-2t} + k_2t\,e^{-2t} + 12$$

$$v(0) = 0 \Rightarrow k_1 = -12$$

$$i_L(0) = c\frac{dv(0)}{dt} \Rightarrow 6 + \frac{k_2}{4} = 3 \text{ or } k_2 = -12$$

$$\therefore\ v(t) = -12\,e^{-2t} - 12t\,e^{-2t} + 12 \quad \text{V for } t > 0$$

6.54

In steady state, the inductors behave as short circuits. The resulting circuit is shown below.

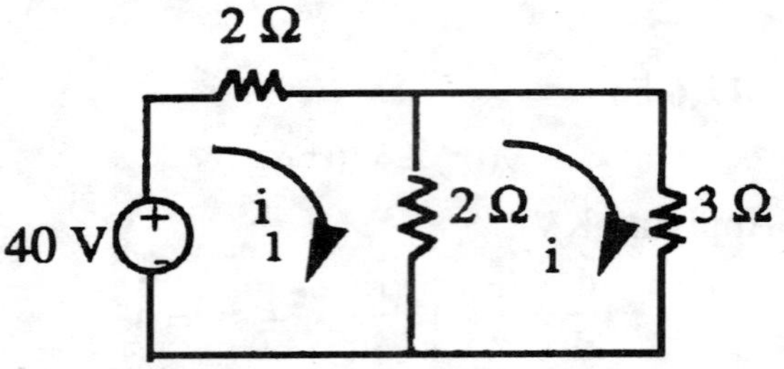

Using mesh analysis, we can find the initial conditions

$$i(0^-) = i(0^+) = 5 \text{ A}$$
$$i_1(0^-) = i_1(0^+) = 12.5 \text{ A}$$

After the switch is closed, the circuit is modified as shown:

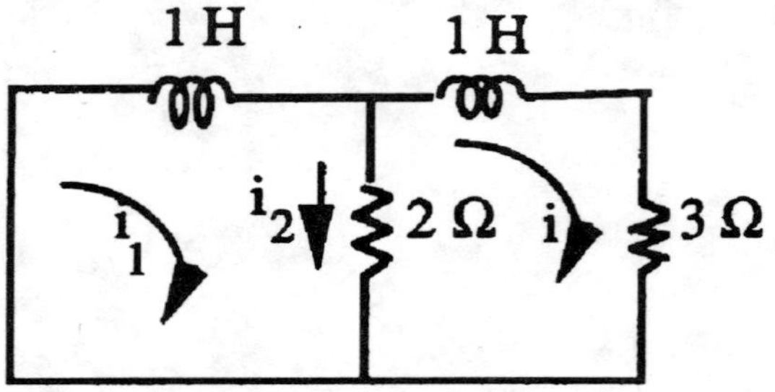

Applying nodal analysis,

$$\frac{d^2i}{dt^2} + 7\frac{di}{dt} + 6i = 0$$

Solving the differential equation:

$$i(t) = k_1 e^{-t} + k_2 e^{-6t} \quad t > 0$$

Solving for the unknown constants, using the initial conditions, we find.

$$i(t) = 6 e^{-t} - e^{-6t} \text{ A}, \quad t > 0$$

6.55

In steady state, the inductors behave as short circuits.

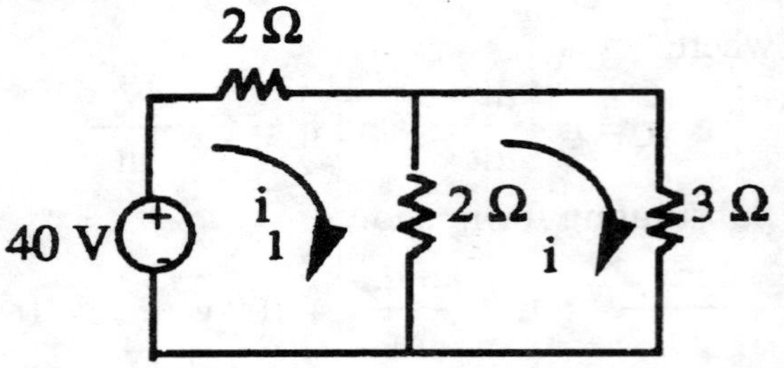

Using mesh analysis, we can find the initial conditions

$$i(0^-) = i(0^+) = 5 \text{ A}$$
$$i_1(0^-) = i_1(0^+) = 12.5 \text{ A}$$

After the switch is closed, the circuit is modified as shown:

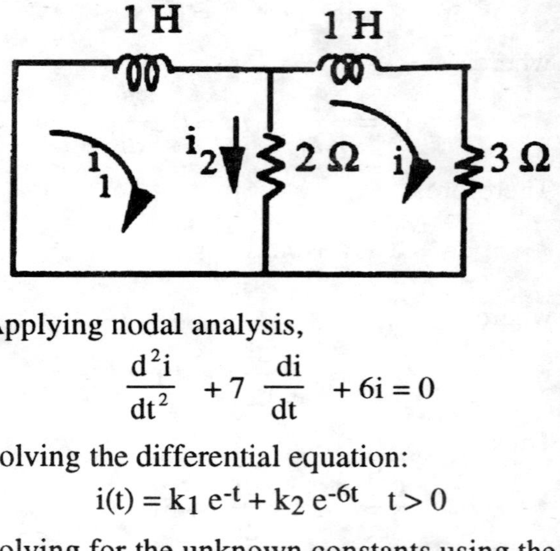

Applying nodal analysis,

$$\frac{d^2i}{dt^2} + 7\frac{di}{dt} + 6i = 0$$

Solving the differential equation:

$$i(t) = k_1 e^{-t} + k_2 e^{-6t} \quad t > 0$$

Solving for the unknown constants using the initial conditions, we find.

$$i(t) = 6 e^{-t} - e^{-6t} \text{ A}, \quad t > 0$$

EIT 6.56

The circuit is shown at $t=0^-$ with the inductors replaced by short circuits, and the capacitors by open circuits.

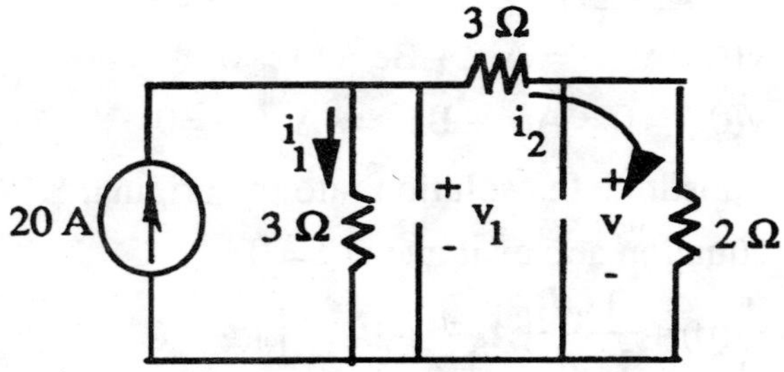

By current division:

$$i_2 = \frac{3}{3+5}(20) = 7.5 \text{ A}$$

$$v(0^-) = v(0^+) = 2i_2 = 15 \text{ V}$$

$$v_1(0^-) = v_1(0^+) = 5i_2 = 37.5 \text{ V}$$

After the switch opens:

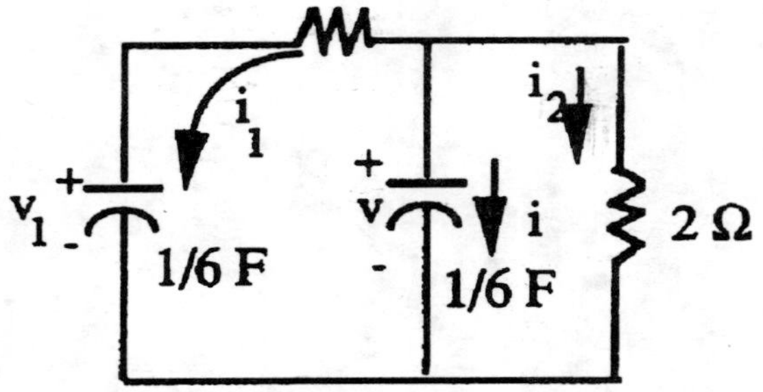

Applying KCL:

$$i + i_1 + i_2 = 0$$

$$i = C\frac{dv}{dt} = \frac{1}{6}\frac{dv}{dt}, \quad i_2 = \frac{v}{2}.$$

Therefore,

$$i_1 = -\frac{1}{6}\frac{dv}{dt} - \frac{v}{2}$$

Applying KVL:

$$v = 3i_1 + v_1 = 3\left(-\frac{1}{6}\frac{dv}{dt} - \frac{v}{2}\right) + v_1$$

or

$$v_1 = v - 3\left(-\frac{1}{6}\frac{dv}{dt} - \frac{v}{2}\right)$$

$$i_1 = \frac{1}{6}\frac{dv_1}{dt} = \frac{1}{12}\frac{d^2v}{dt^2} + \frac{5}{12}\frac{dv}{dt}$$

Applying KCL:

$$\frac{1}{12}\frac{d^2v}{dt^2} + \frac{5}{12}\frac{dv}{dt} + \frac{v}{2} + \frac{1}{6}\frac{dv}{dt} = 0$$

or

$$\frac{d^2v}{dt^2} + 7\frac{dv}{dt} + 6v = 0$$

Solving the differential equation,

$$v(t) = k_1 e^{-t} + k_2 e^{-6t} \quad t > 0$$

Solving for k_1, and k_2 using the initial conditions:

$$v(t) = 18\, e^{-t} - 3\, e^{-6t} \text{ V} \qquad t > 0$$

6.57

At t = 0⁻: $i(0^-) = i(0^+) = \dfrac{10}{5} = 2$ A,

$v(0^-) = v(0^+) = 0$ V.

After the switch is closed:

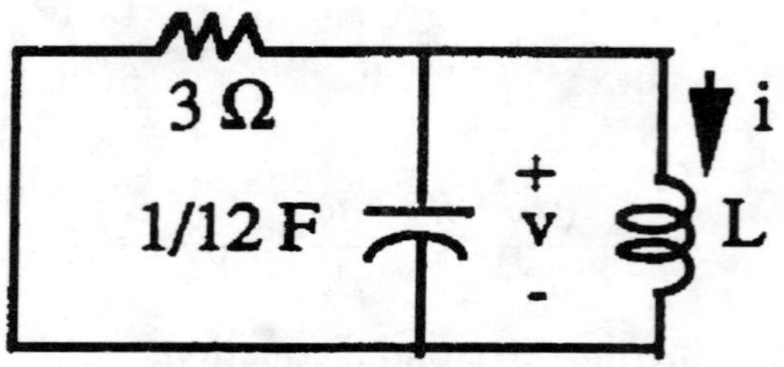

Applying KVL:

$$\frac{1}{L}\int_{-\infty}^{t} v\,dt + \frac{1}{12}\frac{dv}{dt} + \frac{v}{3} = 0$$

or

$$\frac{d^2v}{dt^2} + 4\frac{dv}{dt} + \frac{12}{L}v = 0$$

The particular response is zero for t > 0 because the circuit is source-free

(a) L = 2.4 ⇒ $s^2 + 4s + 5 = 0$

$s = -2 \pm j1$

$v(t) = v_n(t) = e^{-2t}(A\cos(t) + B\sin(t))$ t > 0

$v(0^+) = 0 = e^0(A\cos(0) + B\sin(0)) \Rightarrow A = 0$

Substitute the solution into the original KCL equation and evaluate at $t = 0^+$

$$\frac{1}{3}(0) + \frac{1}{12}\frac{d}{dt}\left[e^{-2t}(A\cos(t) + B\sin(t))\right]_{t=0} + 2 = 0$$

$$0 + \frac{1}{12}[B] + 2 = 0 \Rightarrow B = -24$$

$v(t) = -24e^{-t}\sin(t)$ V t > 0

(b) L = 3 H ⇒ $s^2 + 4s + 4 = 0$

$v(t) = v_n(t) = (A + Bt)e^{-2t}$ t > 0

$v(0^+) = 0 = [A + B(0)]e^0 \Rightarrow A = 0$

The original KCL equation evaluated at $t = 0^+$ is

$$\frac{1}{3}(0) + \frac{1}{12}\frac{d}{dt}\left[(A + Bt)e^{-2t}\right]_{t=0^+} + 2 = 0$$

$$0 + \frac{1}{12}\frac{d}{dt}\left[Be^{-2t} - 2Bte^{-2t}\right]_{t=0^+} + 2 = 0 \Rightarrow B = -24$$

$v = -24te^{-2t}$ V t > 0

(c) L = 4 H ⇒ $s^2 + 4s + 3 = 0 \Rightarrow s = -1, -3$

$v(t) = v_n(t) = Ae^{-t} + Be^{-3t}$ t > 0

$v(0^+) = 0 = Ae^0 + Be^{0+} \Rightarrow A + B = 0$

Substitute the solution into the original KCL equation and evaluate at $t = 0^+$

$$\frac{1}{3}(0) + \frac{1}{12}\frac{d}{dt}\left[Ae^{-t} + Be^{-3t}\right] + 2 = 0$$

$$0 + \frac{1}{12}[-A - 3B] + 2 = 0 \Rightarrow A + 3B = 24$$

Solve for A = -12 and B = 12

$v(t) = -12e^{-t} + 24e^{-3t}$ V t > 0

6.58

At $t = 0^-$, $v = 12$ V and $i_L(0^-) = i_L(0^+) = 6$ A. For $t > 0$, the circuit is as shown below, and:

$$0.8\frac{di_L}{dt} + 2i_L = 12$$

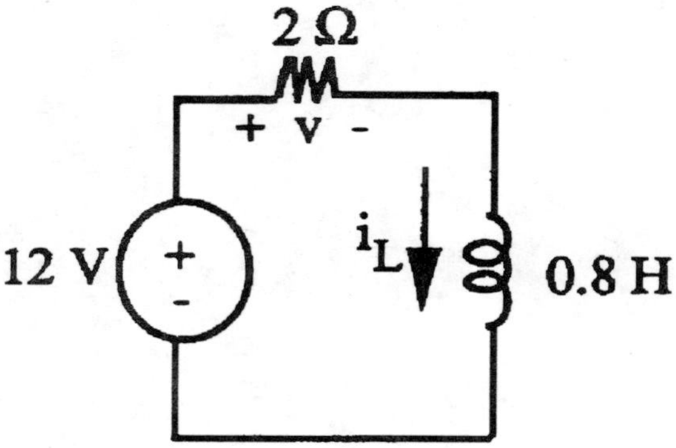

or

$$\frac{di_L}{dt} + 2.5i_L = 15$$

Solving the differential equation:

$$i_L(t) = k_1e^{-2.5t} + 6 \qquad t > 0$$

$$i_L(0) = 6 \Rightarrow k_1 = 0$$

Therefore,

$$i_L(t) = 6 \text{ A}, \qquad t > 0$$

$$v = 2i_L(t) = 12 \text{ V}, \qquad t > 0$$

6.59

(a) Since i(t) = constant we know that the element is a resistor.

$$V = I(R + 1)$$

$$I = 20 \text{ mA} \quad V = 5 \text{ V}$$

$$R = \frac{5\text{V}}{20\text{mA}} - 1\ \Omega$$

$$\boxed{R = 249 \text{ W}}$$

(b) Since the current through the element is decreasing from an initial value of 5 A, we can infer that the element must act as a short circuit at t=0. Thus, the element must be a capacitor.

$$v = 5e^{-\frac{1}{RC}t} \text{ V} \qquad t > 0$$

$$v(10\times10^{-3}) = 5e^{-\frac{1}{RC}(10\times10^{-3})} = 1.84$$

$$e^{-\frac{1}{RC}(10\times10^{-3})} = .368 \Rightarrow -\frac{1}{RC}(10\times10^{-3}) = \ln 0.368 = -1$$

$$C = \frac{1}{R}(10\times10^{-3}) = \frac{1}{1}(10\times10^{-3}) = 1\times10^{-3} \text{ F}$$

(c) Since the current is initially zero, the element must act as an open circuit at first. Thus it must be an inductor.

$$v = 5\left[1 - e^{-\frac{R}{L}t}\right] \text{V} \quad t > 0$$

$$v(2\times10^{-3}) = 5\left[1 - e^{-\frac{R}{L}(2\times10^{-3})}\right] = 3.16$$

$$e^{-\frac{R}{L}(2\times10^{-3})} = 0.368$$

$$-\frac{R}{L}(2\times10^{-3}) = \ln 0.368 = -1$$

$$L = (2\times10^{-3})R = (2\times10^{-3})(1) = 2\times10^{-3} \text{ H}$$

EIT 6.60

The desired time constant is:

$$\tau = RC_{eq} = 10{,}000 \times C_{eq}$$

$$C_{eq} = \frac{0.0375}{10{,}000} = 3.75\ \mu F.$$

The following combination of capacitors will result in the desired capacitance:

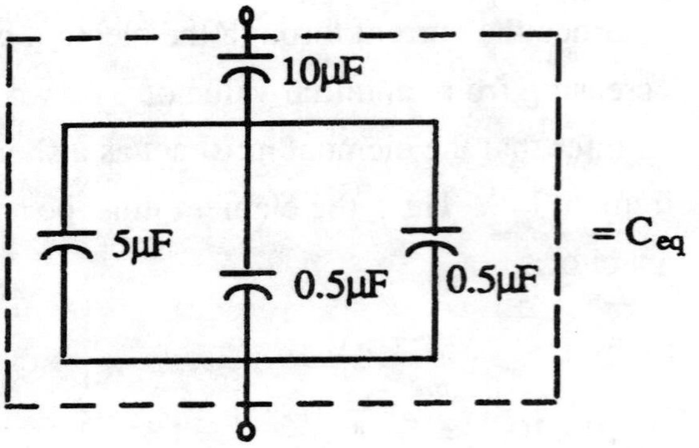

Semiconductors and Diodes

Chapter 7 Instructor Notes

Chapter 7 introduces the second part of the book with an introduction to semiconductor devices, followed by an intuitive discussion of the semiconductor diode. The emphasis is quickly shifted to a practical discussion of circuit models of the diode in increasing order of complexity, starting with the ideal diode on-off model, continuing with models including the diode offset voltage and forward and reverse resistances, and also including the exponential diode equation. The aim of the presentation is to illustrate how the elementary circuit models of Chapter 2 and 3 can be useful in the analysis of nonlinear circuit elements. The Instructor will find that a review (or perhaps first coverage) of the material on nonlinear circuit elements introduced in Chapter 3 (section 3.7) can be useful. The solution methods emphasize the use of simple circuit models for the diode, together with the use of Thèvenin equivalent circuits; this method is quite general, and will reinforce the importance (and understanding) of the concept of equivalent circuits.

Following the discussion of the different diode models, section 7.4 discusses various practical diode circuits, with special emphasis on rectification and on DC power supplies; Zener diode circuits and voltage regulation are also discussed here. This is a subject of practical interest to a large segment of the engineering community. Finally, the last section analyzes various signal processing circuits, and also introduces photodiodes and solar cells. The degree of coverage of the different sections depends on the nature of the course. For example, a survey or introductory course on electronics might end with the early topics of section 7.4, and skip the signal processing circuits and the material on optical devices. On the other hand, a second course with emphasis on electronic instrumentation could exploit the more advanced material on diode circuits and optical devices, especially in conjunction with one or more laboratory experiments.

The homework problems are a mixture of routine exercises, intended to reinforce the main concepts, and of more advanced applied problems. Problems 7.12 and 7.27 introduce diode OR and AND gates, and could be used to first approach the notion of logic circuits. Problem 7.17 approaches the temperature dependence of the diode characteristic, and proposes the application of the diode as a temperature sensing device. This problem is derived from the author's experience in developing a laboratory course; a laboratory experiment based on this concept can present many interesting ideas (see for example [1]). Problem 7.20 discusses the design of a DC power supply, and problem 7.39 illustrates the use of diodes in battery charging circuits. Two advanced problems on the design of a solar cell array, based on Example 7.15, are also included.

[1] Rizzoni, G., A Practical Introduction to Electronic Instrumentation, Kendall-Hunt, 1989

Chapter 7 problem solutions

7.1

Assuming the diode is conducting, the current is found to be

$$I = \frac{V_B - V_i}{5+10} = -\frac{2}{15} = -0.133 \text{ A}$$

The voltage across the diode is

$$V_D = (-10\,I + V_B) - (5I + V_i)$$
$$= -1.33 + 10 - 0.667 - 12 = -3.997 \text{ V}$$

This result contradicts the assumption, since the diode cannot conduct if V_D is negative. Thus, the diode must be off.

7.2

For $v_S < 0$, the diode is reverse biased, and $v_L = 0$. For $v_S > 0$, the diode is forward biased, and $v_L = v_S\left(\dfrac{R_L \| R_1}{R_S + R_L \| R_1}\right)$.

7.3

Replace the diode with an open circuit, and $v_{D_{oc}} = 3V$. Replace the diode with a short circuit, and $i_{D_{sc}} = \dfrac{1}{2}\dfrac{6V}{750\Omega} = 4mA$. These are the end points of the load line. The load line is superimposed on the diode characteristic in the sketch below:

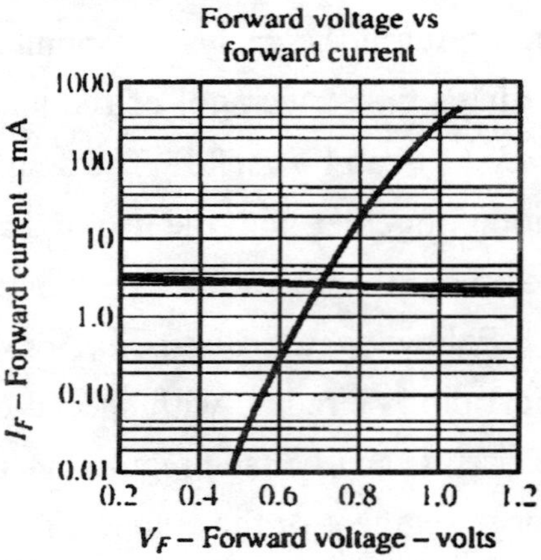

From the intersection of the load line and the diode characteristic, we see that $i_D \approx 3mA$ and $v_D \approx 0.7V$.

7.4

(a) $R = \dfrac{5-0.7}{5\times10^{-3}} = 860\Omega$

(b)

$$I = \frac{E_{min} - 0.7}{860} = 1\times10^{-3}$$
$$\Rightarrow E_{min} = 0.86 + 0.7 = 1.56V$$

7.5

(a) $I_{F_{max}} = \dfrac{50\sqrt{2} - 0.7}{220} = 318mA$

(b) $V_{rev_{max}} = 50\sqrt{2} = 70.7V$

7.6

(a) reverse-biased
(b) forward-biased
(c) reverse-biased
(d) forward-biased
(e) forward-biased

EIT 7.7

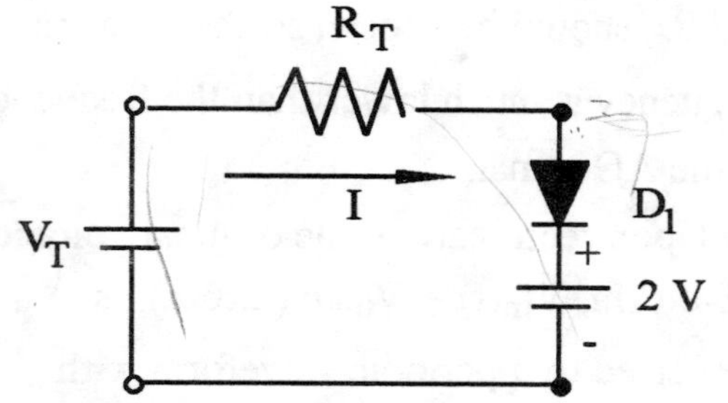

The Thèvenin equivalent resistance is

$$R_T = 500 \,\|\, 1000 = \frac{1000}{3} \;\; \Omega$$

The Thèvenin equivalent voltage is

$$V_T = \frac{V_{in}}{1500} \times 1000 = \frac{2}{3} \times V_{in}$$

The current I is

$$I = \frac{V_T - 2}{R_T} = \frac{\frac{2}{3} \times V_{in} - 2}{\frac{1000}{3}} = \frac{V_{in} - 3}{500}$$

To keep diode D_1 forward-biased, the current I must be greater than or equal zero. Therefore, the range of v_{in} is

$$v_{in} \geq 3 \text{ V}$$

7.8

If diode D_2 is conducting, the voltage at the node to the left of D_1 will be 5 V and D_1 will conduct. To ensure that D_2 is conducting, voltage V_{in} must be greater than 5 V.

Assume D_2 is cut off. D_1 will conduct as long as V_{in} is greater than zero. Thus, the value for D_1 to conduct is

$$V_{in} > 0$$

7.9

(a) D_2 and D_4 are forward biased; D_1 and D_3 are reverse biased.

$$v_{out} = -5 + 0.7 = -4.3V$$

(b) D_1 and D_2 are reverse biased; D_3 is forward biased.

$$v_{out} = -10 + 0.7 = -9.3V$$

(c) D_1 is reverse biased; D_2 is forward biased.

$$v_{out} = 5 - 0.7 = 4.3V$$

7.10

Assume diode D_1 is conducting; the diode current is

$$I = \frac{V_{in} - 2}{1500} \geq 0$$

Since the current is positive, the initial assumption was correct. Therefore, the range of V_{in} is: $V_{in} \geq 2$ V.

EIT 7.11

Assume D_1 is conducting; the diode current is

$$I = \frac{V_{in} - 2}{1500} = \frac{6}{1500} = 4 \text{ mA}$$

Since the current is positive, the initial assumption was correct. The output voltage V_o is

$$V_o = 500\, I + 2 = 4 \text{ V}$$

7.12

(a) Since no external voltage is present to forward bias the diodes, neither diode can conduct, and $V_{out} = 0$ V.

(b) With both inputs at 5 V, both diodes will conduct (if you are not sure, assume that they do and compute the diode currents). The resulting circuit is shown below:

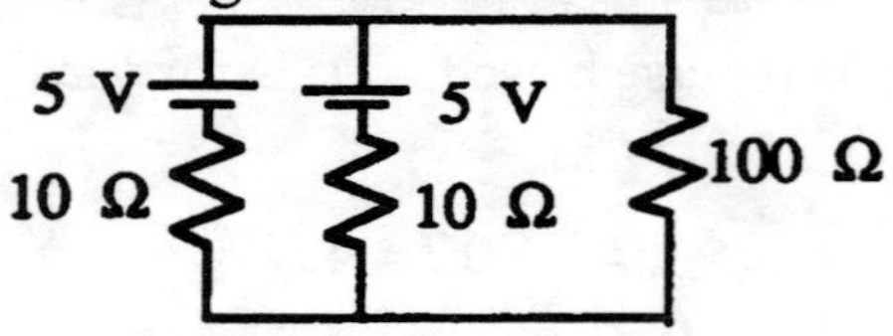

The Thèvenin equivalent resistance is

$$R_T = 10 \,\|\, 10 = 5 \ \Omega$$

The Thèvenin voltage is 5 V.

By applying the voltage divider, we have

$$V_{out} = 5 \times \frac{100}{100 + 5} = 4.76 \text{ V}$$

(c) In this case, D_1 is forward biased, while D_2 is reverse biased; thus only one of the two 5-V branches of part (b) exists:

$$V_{out} = 5 \times \frac{100}{100 + 10} = 4.545 \text{ V}$$

This circuit performs the function of a logic "OR" gate.

***7.13**

(a) The function of the capacitor is to act in concert with the load resistance as a low-pass filter to eliminate the AC component of the bridge rectifier output voltage. The filter cut-off frequency is:

$$\omega_0 = \frac{1}{R_L C}$$

and R_L should be chosen so that this cut-off frequency is much lower than the frequency of the AC signal.

(b) Upon rectification, the original voltage waveform, $V_{in}(t) = V_0 \sin(2\pi 60t)$, is converted to a periodic waveform with period equal to one half the original period; this waveform is shifted to a lower value by a voltage approximately equal to double the diode offset voltage, as explained on pp. 371-372: $V_{rect}(t) = V_0 \sin(2\pi 60t) - 1.4$ V with period $T = \frac{\pi}{60}$. To determine the average value of the rectified waveform, it is thus sufficient to integrate the input voltage between t=0 and $t = \frac{\pi}{60}$ and then subtract 1.4 V. The result of the integration is $\frac{V_i}{\pi}$; thus, we desire to have:

$$\frac{V_i}{\pi} - 1.4 = 5$$

or,

$$V_i = 11.31 \text{ V}$$

(c) If diode D_1 is destroyed, the rectifier becomes a halfwave rectifier and V_o will be approximately half of its original value.

EIT 7.14

The load-line equation is

$$i_D = -\frac{1}{R}\,v_D + \frac{1}{R}\,V_S$$

a) For $R = 1000\ \Omega$, $i_D = -v_D + 5$ mA

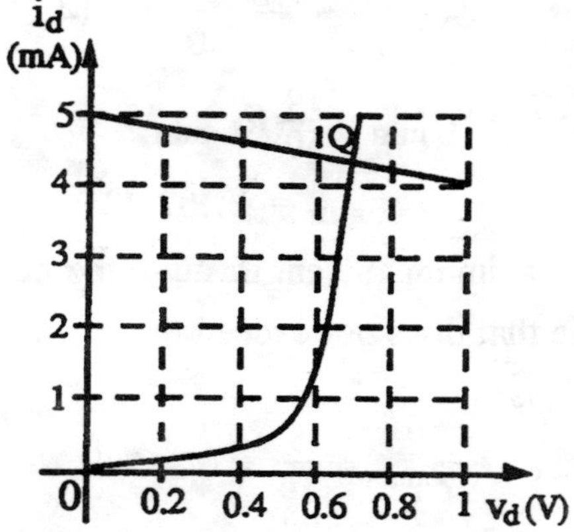

Using load line analysis, we find:

$$i_{DQ} \approx 4.3\ \text{mA},\quad v_{DQ} \approx 0.7\ \text{V}$$

The power dissipated by the diode is

$$P_D = i_{DQ} \times v_{DQ} = 4.3 \times 10^{-3} \times 0.7 = 3.01\ \text{mW}$$

(b) For $R = 5000\ \Omega$, $i_D = -\frac{1}{5}\,v_D + 1$ mA

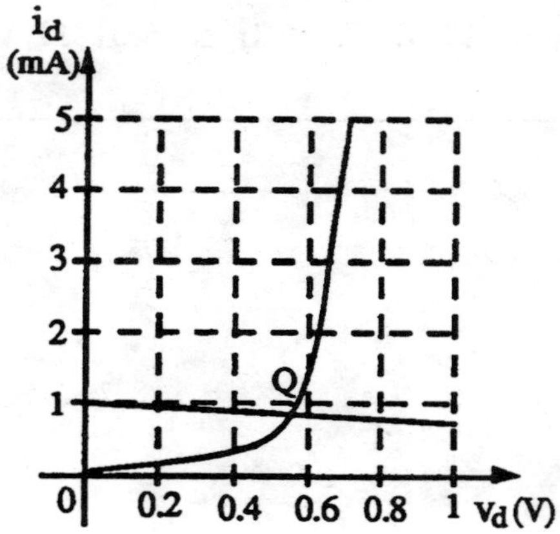

Using load line analysis we find:

$$i_{DQ} \approx 0.85\ \text{mA},\quad v_{DQ} \approx 0.58\ \text{V}$$

The power dissipated by the diode is

$$P_D = i_{DQ} \times v_{DQ} = 0.85 \times 10^{-3} \times 0.58 = 0.493\ \text{mW}$$

7.15

(a) The voltage across the diode is

$$V_Z = V_S\left(\frac{50+50}{100+50+50}\right) = 6 < 7.7\ \text{V}$$

Therefore, the Zener diode is off. Thus, the output voltage is:

$$V_{out} = 6\left(\frac{50}{100}\right) = 3\ \text{V}$$

(b) The voltage across the diode is

$$V_Z = 20\left(\frac{100}{200}\right) = 10 > 7.7\ \text{V}$$

In this case, the Zener diode is on and the output voltage is:

$$V_{out} = 7.7\left(\frac{50}{100}\right) = 3.85\ \text{V}$$

7.16

$$\frac{R_{L_{min}}}{R_{L_{min}} + 1800\Omega}(18V) = 5.6V$$

$$\Rightarrow 12.4R_{L_{min}} = 10080$$

$$R_{L_{min}} = 812.9\Omega$$

7.17

(a) The current i_D is

$$i_D = \frac{15 - v_D}{10}\ \text{mA}$$

For $v_D = 0.6$ V, $i_D = 1.440$ mA

For $v_D = 0.66$ V, $i_D = 1.434$ mA

The percent change in i_D is only 0.4%.

Thus, i_D is nearly constant.

(b) The diode voltage equation is

$$v_D(T) = -0.002T + 0.8$$

EIT 7.18

(a) The diode current, $i_D(t)$, is

$i_D = 1$ mA for $t < 10$ ms

$i_D = 0$ mA for $10 \text{ ms} < t < 20$ ms

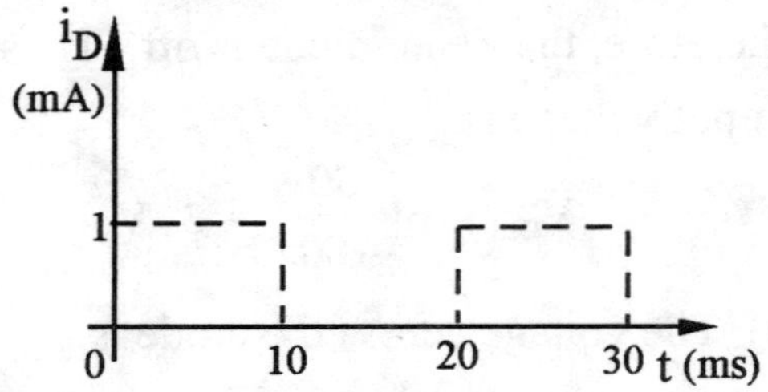

(b) The diode current, i_D, is

$$i_D = \frac{10 - 0.6}{10} = 0.94 \text{ mA for } t < 10 \text{ ms}$$

$i_D = 0$ mA for $10 \text{ ms} < t < 20$ ms

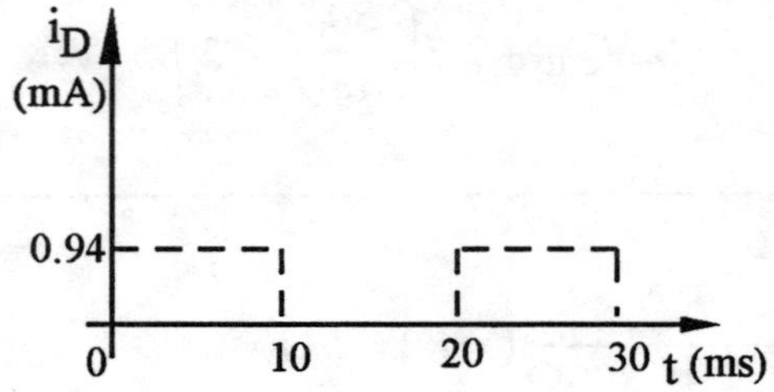

(c) The diode current, i_D, is

$$i_D = \frac{v_S - V_\gamma}{10 + r_D} = \frac{9.4}{11} = 0.85 \text{ mA}$$

for $t < 10$ ms

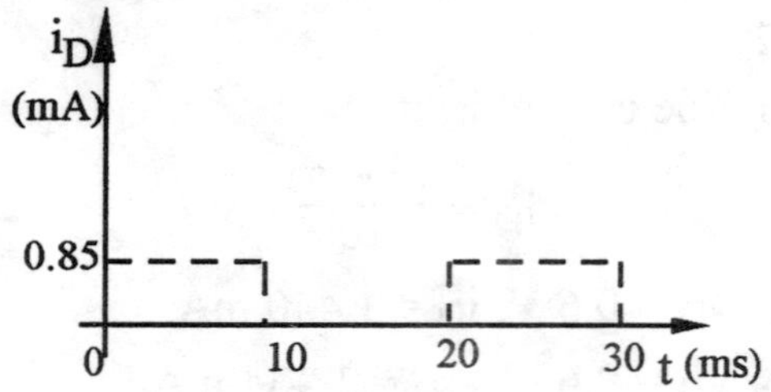

7.19

$v_S = 50$ V, Zener is rated $V_Z = 14$ V, 5W

The minimum load resistance for a regulated load voltage of 14 V is found from

$$50\left(\frac{R_{Lmin}}{R_{Lmin} + 30}\right) = 14$$

$$R_{L\,min} = \frac{14}{50}(R_{L\,min} + 30)$$

$$R_{L\,min} = 11.67 \ \Omega$$

The maximum current through the Zener diode that does not exceed the diode power rating is

$$i_{Zmax} = \frac{5}{14} = 0.357 \text{ A}$$

The source current is

$$i_S = \frac{50 - 14}{30} = 1.2 \text{ A}$$

So the maximum load resistance is

$$R_{L\,max} = \frac{14}{1.2 - 0.357} = 16.61 \ \Omega$$

Thus, the range of allowable load resistance:

$$11.67 \ \Omega \le R_L \le 16.61 \ \Omega$$

EIT 7.20

(a) The input source voltage is shown below, together with the rectified load voltage. (12 V rms = 16.97 V peak)

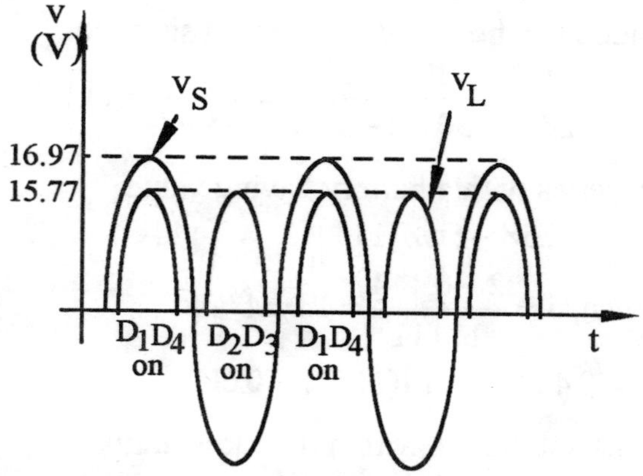

(b) The time constant, $\tau = CR$, is

$$CR = 1000 \times 8 \times 10^{-6} = 8 \text{ ms}$$

The period of the input sinusoid is

$$T = \frac{1}{60} = 16.7 \text{ ms}$$

Since the capacitor initial voltage is:
$v_C(0) = 16.97 - 1.2 = 15.77$ V,

and the final value is
$v_C(\infty) = 0$, $v_C(t)$ is given by

$$v_C(t) = 15.77e^{-t/\tau}$$

Therefore, at $t = T$, we have

$$v_C(T) = 15.77e^{-T/\tau} = 1.96 \text{ V}$$

The output waveform is shown below

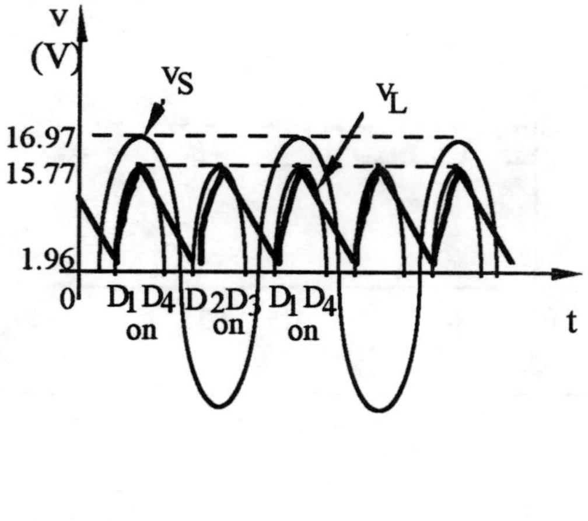

(c) The time constant is

$$CR = 1000 \times 100 \times 10^{-6} = 100 \text{ ms}$$

Since CR >> T.
$v_C(0) = 16.97 - 1.2 = 15.77$ V, $v_C(\infty) = 0$,
and

$$v_C(t) = 15.77e^{-t/\tau}$$

Therefore,

$$v_C(T) = 15.77e^{-T/\tau} = 13.34 \text{ V}$$

The output waveform is shown below.

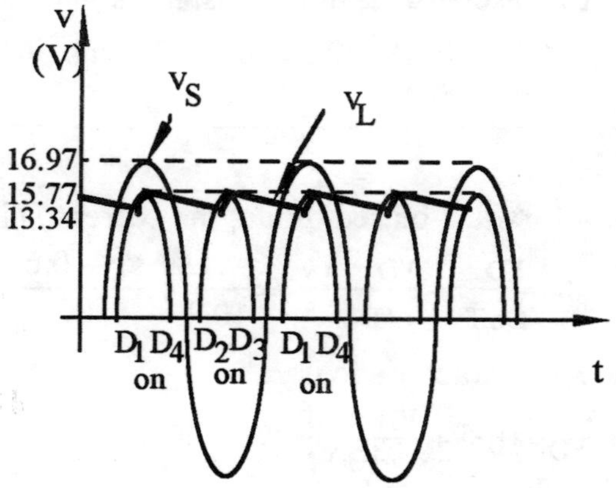

7.21

For the diode characteristic shown,

$$r_{Don} = \frac{\Delta v_D}{\Delta i_D} = \frac{0.6}{60} = 0.01\ \Omega$$

$$r_{Doff} = \frac{100}{0.2} = 500\ k\Omega >> 1\ k\Omega,$$

Therefore, the charging time constant is

$$CR = 2.2\times10^{-6}\times(20.01\ \|\ 1000)$$
$$= 43\ \ \mu s$$

and the discharging time constant is

$$CR \approx 1\times10^{3}\times2.2\times10^{-6} = 2.2\ ms$$

7.22

For a forward-biased diode, the current i_d is

$$i_d = \frac{v_D}{r_{Doff}} + \frac{v_D - V_\gamma}{r_{Don}} = \frac{v_D}{10^5} + \frac{v_D - 0.6}{100}$$

The i-v characteristic is:

$$i_d = v_D\times10^{-5} + \frac{v_D - 0.6}{100}$$
$$= v_D(10^{-5} + 10^{-2}) - 0.006$$
$$\approx 10\ v_D - 6 \quad mA$$

For a reverse-biased diode, the i-v characteristic is

$$i_d = \frac{v_D}{100} \quad mA$$

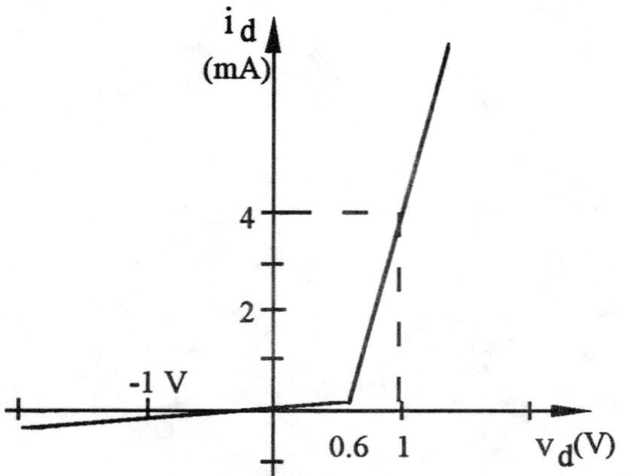

7.23

Assume that the diode is forward-biased, and operating in the region between (0.5V, 5mA) and (1V, 50mA). If this is true, then the diode can be modeled by the resistance

$$r_D = \frac{\Delta v_D}{\Delta i_D} = \frac{1V - 0.5V}{50mA - 5mA} = \frac{0.5V}{45mA} = 11.11\Omega$$

in series with a battery having value

$V_{bat} = 0.5V - 5mA(11.11\Omega) = 0.444V$.

Then, $i = \dfrac{2 - 0.444}{111.11} = 14mA$ and

$v = 0.444 + 0.014(11.11) = 0.6V$.

This solution is within the range initially assumed, justifying the assumption.

7.24

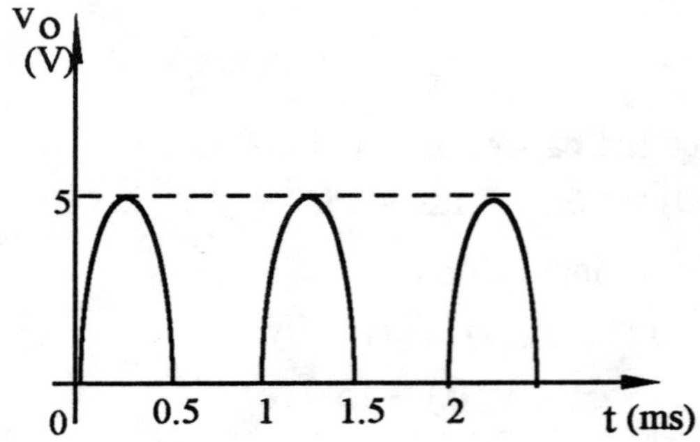

7.25

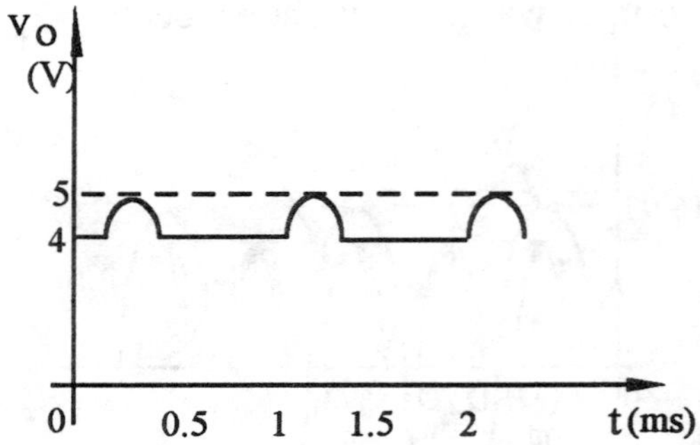

EIT 7.26

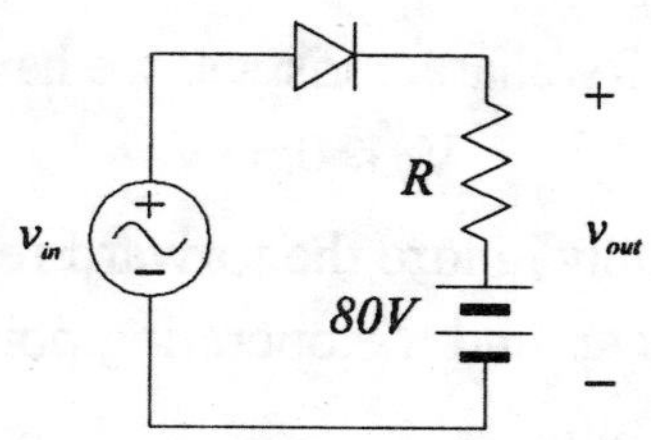

7.27

(a) With $r_{Don} = 20\ \Omega$, $v_{Don} = 0.6\ V$, we can draw the equivalent circuit shown below.

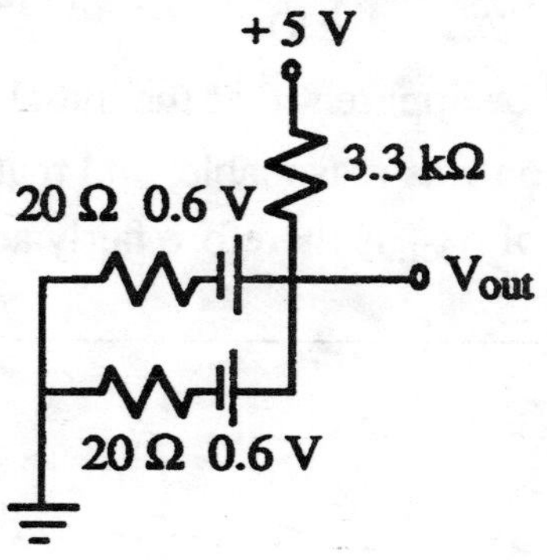

$$v_{out} = \frac{5 - 0.6}{3300 + 10} \times 10 + 0.6 \approx 0.61\ V$$

(b) $v_{out} = 5\ V$

(c) $v_{out} = \frac{5 \times 0.6}{3300 + 20} \times 20 + 0.6 = 0.63\ V$

(d) $v_{out} = 0.63\ V$

7.28

The capacitor will charge to $5V - 0.7V = 4.3V$ and, therefore, the input sine wave will be shifted up 4.3 volts to produce the output. As a result, after the cycle (the capacitor builds up its stored charge during the third quarter cycle), the average value of the output will be 4.3V.

7.29

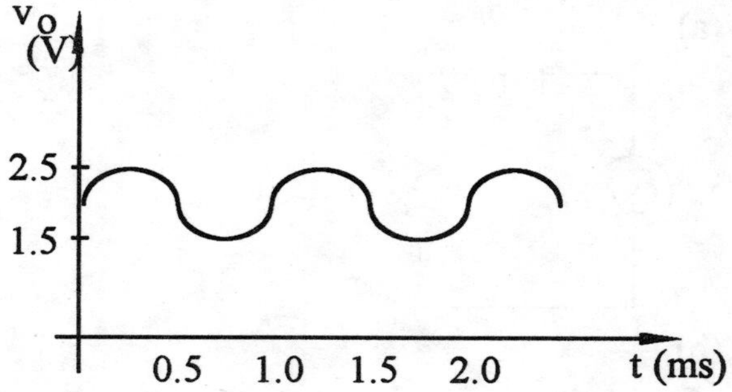

7.30

$$A_{min} \sin(5^\circ) = 0.7$$

$$\therefore A_{min} = \frac{0.7}{\sin(5^\circ)} = \frac{0.7}{0.0872} = 8.03V$$

EIT 7.31

(a)

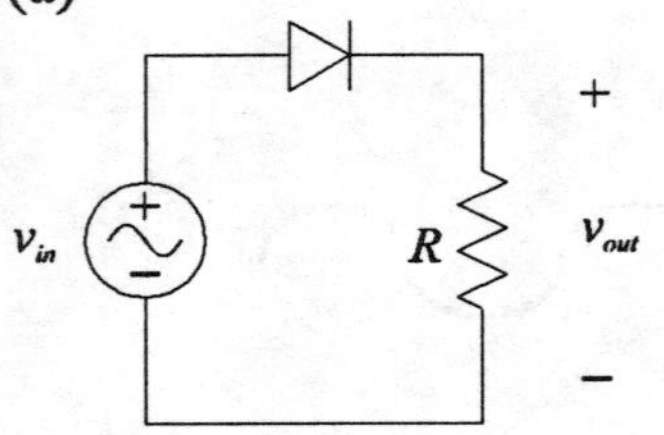

(b)

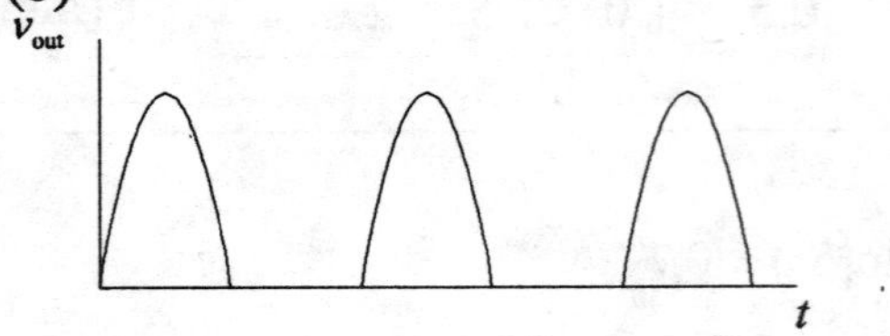

(c)

$$v_{ave} = 0.318 v_{peak} = 50 \Rightarrow v_{peak} = 157.2V$$

(d)

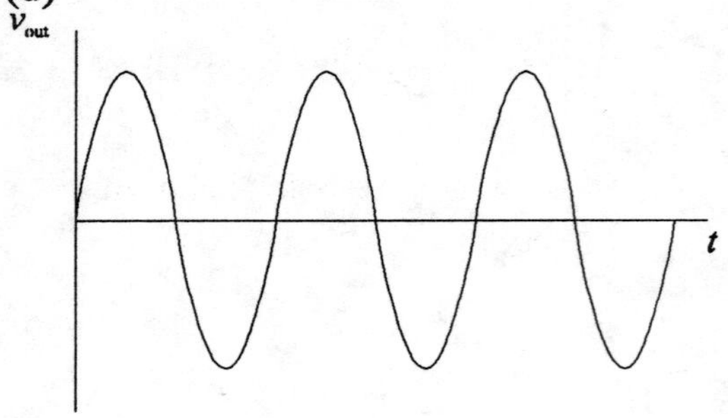

(e)

$$V_{in_{rms}} = \frac{157.2}{\sqrt{2}} = 111.2V$$

7.32

From the i-v characteristics, we have

$$V_{\gamma} \approx 0.5 \text{ V}$$

If we initially ignore the forward resistance, r_{Don}, we can find the operating point of the diode as follows:

$$i_{DQ} = \frac{2 - 0.5}{50 + 50} = 15 \text{ mA}$$

We can then estimate the diode forward resistance to be:

$$r_{Don} = \frac{25.6 \text{ mV}}{I_{DQ}} = 1.71 \ \Omega$$

It should be apparent that the initial assumption was reasonable, and that the estimate of r_{Don} is therefore fairly accurate.

***7.33**

(a) The dynamic diode resistance r_D is

$$r_D \approx \frac{25.6\text{ mV}}{I_{DQpoint}} = \frac{25.6}{7} = 3.66\ \Omega$$

(b) Considering only the AC, we have the following circuit.

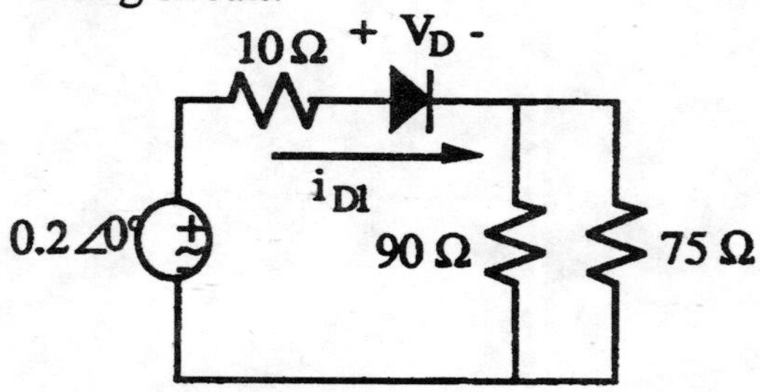

The equivalent resistance is

$$R = 10 + 3.66 + 90\ ||\ 75 = 54.57\ \Omega$$

The current i_{D1} is

$$i_{D1} = \frac{0.2}{R}\sin(2000\pi t)$$

$$= 3.7\sin(200\pi t)\ \text{mA}$$

Therefore, the peak value of the AC component of the diode current is 3.7 mA.

7.34

With the variables defined in the circuit below,

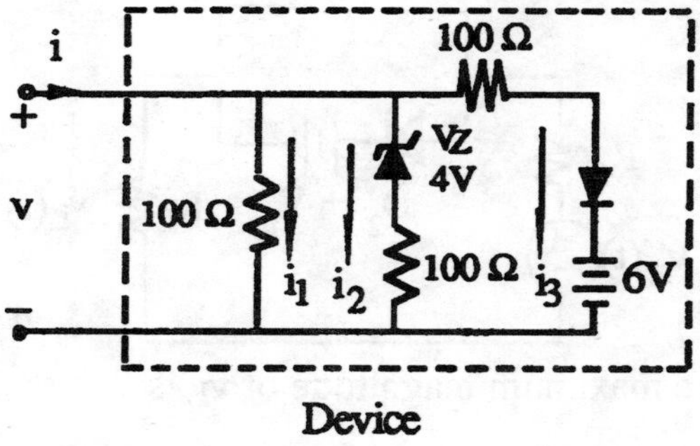

we can compute the following currents:

$$i_1 = \frac{v}{100}$$

$$i_2 = \frac{v - 4}{100} \qquad \text{for } v > 4\text{ V}$$

$$i_3 = \frac{v - 6}{100} \qquad \text{for } v > 6\text{ V}$$

For $0 < v < 4$ V, $i = 0.01v$

For $4 < v < 6$ V, $i = 0.02v - 0.04$

For $6 < v$, $i = 0.03v - 0.1$

The resulting i-v characteristic is shown below:

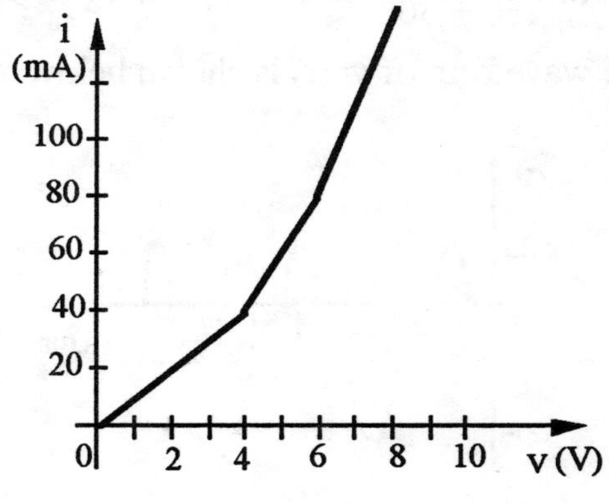

7.35

During the positive half cycle of v_S , the circuit may be modelled as shown below:

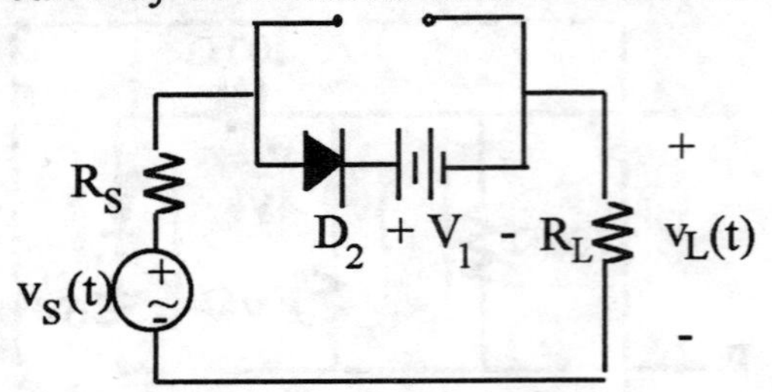

The maximum magnitude of v_L is

$$3\times\frac{150}{150+50} = 2.25 \text{ V, for } v_S > 12 \text{ V}$$

During the negative half cycle of v_S, the circuit is modeled as shown below.

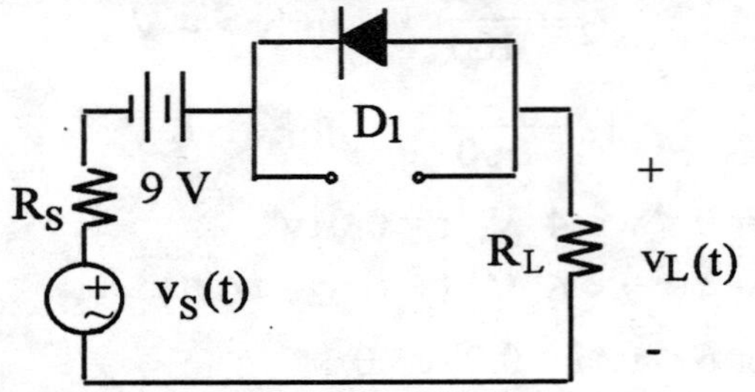

The maximum magnitude of v_L is

$$-6\times\frac{150}{150+50} = -4.5 \text{ V, for } v_S < -9 \text{ V}$$

The waveform of $v_L(t)$ is shown below

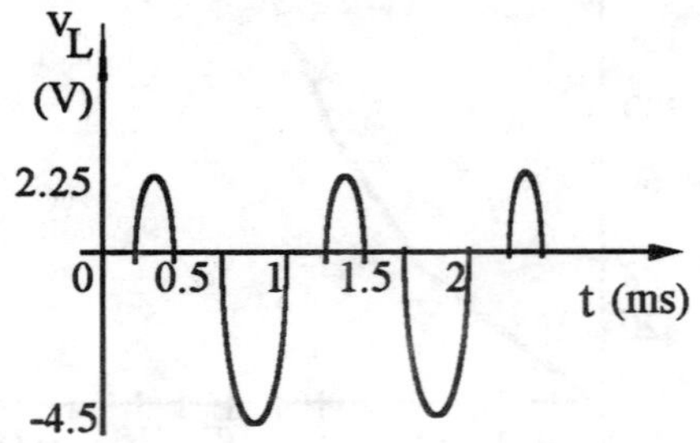

EIT 7.36

For $0 < v_S < V_2 = 12$ V, the circuit is shown below.

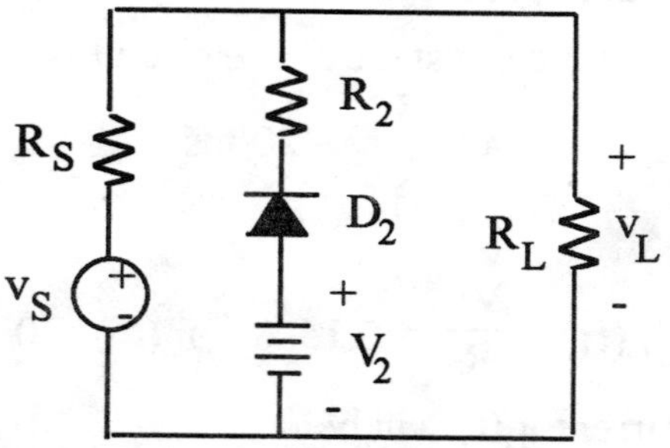

The Thèvenin equivalent circuit is the following:

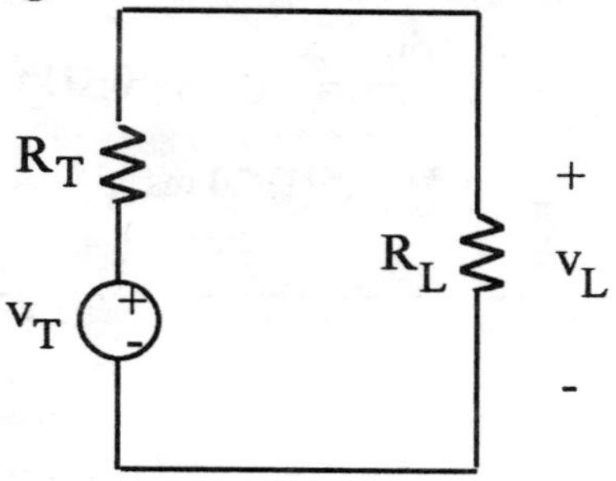

where,

$$V_T = \frac{v_S - V_2}{R_S + R_2} \times R_2 + V_2$$

$$= \frac{1}{3}\ v_S + 8 \ \text{V}$$

$$R_T = \frac{5 \times 10}{15} = \frac{10}{3} \ \Omega$$

Thus, the load voltage is given by the expression

$$v_L = \frac{R_L}{R_L + R_T} \times V_T = 0.3125 \ v_S + 7.5 \ \text{V}$$

For $12 < v_S < 15$, v_L is given by

$$v_L = \frac{5}{6}\ v_S = 0.833 \ v_S$$

For $15 < v_S < 20$, the equivalent circuit is shown below.

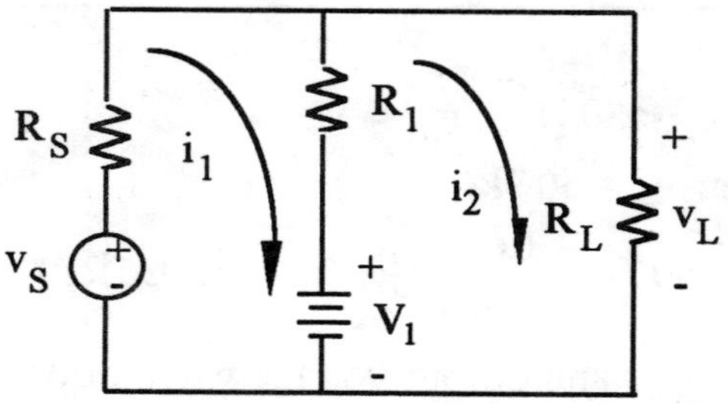

Applying mesh analysis,

$$i_1(R_S + R_1) - i_2 R_1 = v_S - V_1$$

$$i_2(R_1 + R_L) - i_1 R_1 = V_1$$

we find that

$$v_L = R_L \times i_2 = R_L \times \frac{v_S + 15}{110}$$

$$= 0.4545 \ v_S + 6.818$$

For $-20 < v_S < 0$, the circuit is the following:

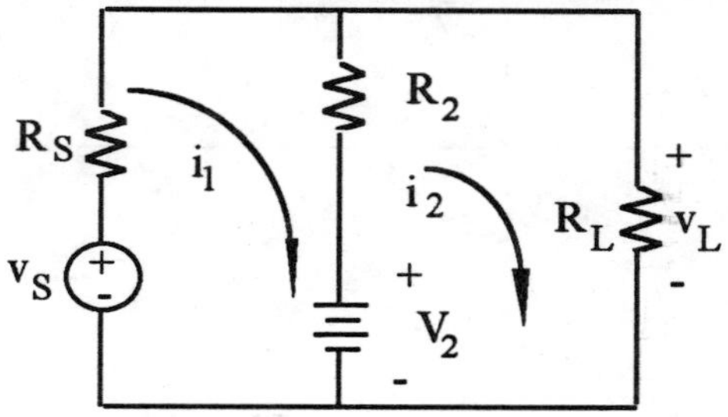

and

$$i_1(R_S + R_2) - i_2 R_2 = - V_2 + v_S$$

$$i_2(R_2 + R_L) - i_1 R_2 = V_2$$

so that $\quad v_L = i_2 \times R_L = \dfrac{24 + v_S}{160} \times 50$

$$= 7.5 + 0.3125 \ v_S$$

The v_L-v_S characteristic is shown below.

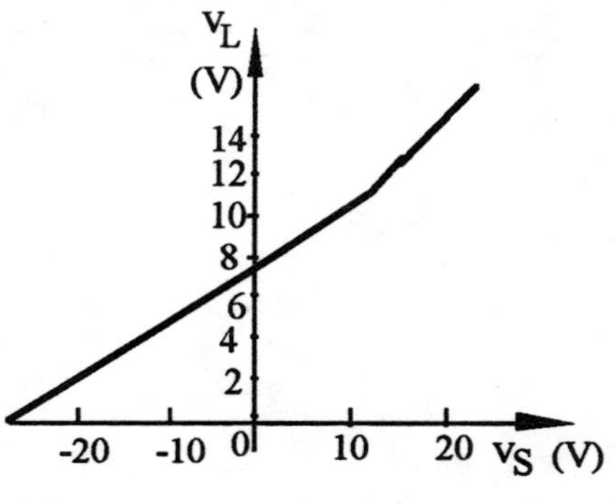

7.37

For $v_{in} < 50.7V$, $v_{out} = v_{in}$.

When $v_{in} \geq 50.7V$,

$$v_{out} = 50.7 + \frac{0.6}{98 + 0.6} v_{in} = 50.7 + \left(6.085 \times 10^{-3}\right) v_{in}$$

The input and output voltage waveforms are sketched below:

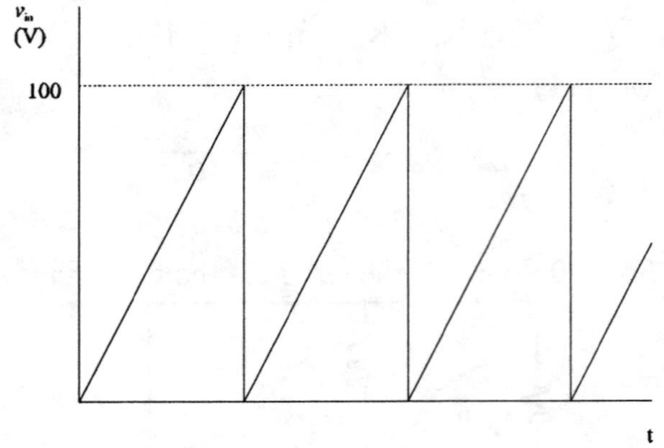

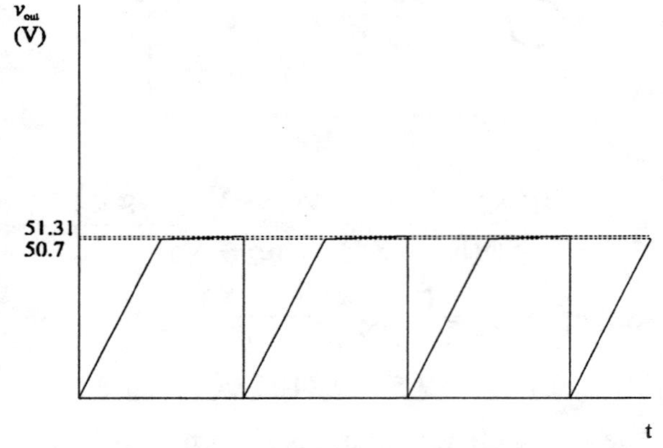

7.38

(a) The voltage across the inductor will be (theoretically) infinite.

(b) The time constant of the circuit is

$$\tau = \frac{L}{r_{on}} = 20 \text{ ms}$$

and

$$i_L(t_1) = \frac{V_S}{R} = 0.15 \text{ A}, \quad i_L(\infty) = 0$$

The current $i_L(t)$ will be

$$i_L(t) = 0.15e^{-(t-t1)/\tau} \text{ A}$$

Therefore, the voltage $v_L(t)$ is

$$v_L(t) = L\frac{di_L}{dt} = -0.75e^{-(t-t1)/\tau}$$

$$= -0.75e^{-(t-t1)/20 \text{ ms}} \text{ V}$$

EIT 7.39

For Figure P7.36 (a):

(a) At $t = t_1^-$, before the switch S_1 closes, we have

$$I_{SW} = 0$$

$$I_S = I_B = \frac{V_S - V_{battery}}{R_S + R_B}$$

$$= \frac{13 - 9.6}{11} = 0.31 \text{ A}$$

(b) At $t = t_1^+$, we have

$$I_S = 13 \text{ A}, I_B = -0.96 \text{ A}$$

$$I_{SW} = I_S - I_B = 13.96 \text{ A}$$

(c) The battery voltage will drop quickly because of the small resistance in the circuit.

For Figure P7.36 (b):

(a) At $t = t_1^-$, we have

$$I_{SW} = 0$$

$$I_S = I_B = \frac{V_S - V_{battery} - V_\gamma}{R_S + R_B}$$

$$= \frac{13 - 9.6 - 0.6}{11} = 0.25 \text{ A}$$

(b) At $t = t_1^+$, we have

$$I_S = I_{SW} = 13 \text{ A}, \quad I_B = 0$$

(c) The battery will not be drained, because of the large reverse resistance of the diode.

7.40

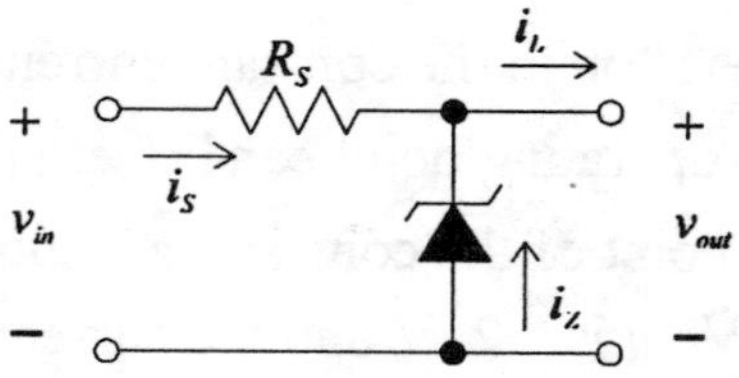

$$i_{S_{max}} = \frac{40-25}{R_{S_{min}}}, \quad i_{S_{min}} = \frac{35-25}{R_{S_{max}}}$$

$$i_{Z_{min}} = 0, \; i_{Z_{max}} = -250mA, \; i_L = 75mA$$

$$i_{S_{max}} = 250 + 75 = 325mA \Rightarrow R_{S_{min}} = \frac{15}{325\times10^{-3}} = 46.2\Omega$$

$$i_{S_{min}} = 0 + 75 = 75mA \Rightarrow R_{S_{max}} = \frac{10}{75\times10^{-3}} = 133.3\Omega$$

7.41

For $v_{in} = 6\sin\omega t$ V,

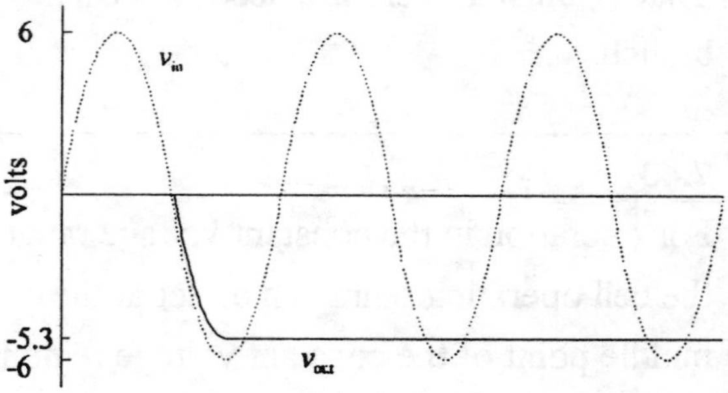

For $v_{in} = 1.5\sin\omega t$ V,

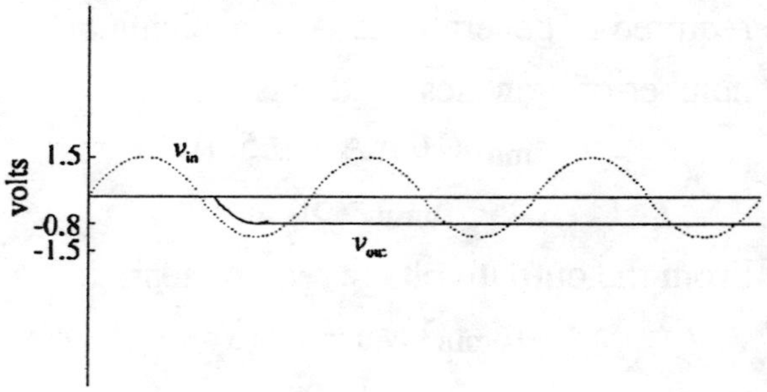

For $v_{in} = 0.4\sin\omega t$, the diode will never conduct, and the circuit will not function.

7.42

For operation in the constant current range, the cell operating point can be set at the middle point of the constant current region where V_{cell} is 0.2 V and the current is 20 mA (see Figure 7.82). Since the array is required to generate 0.5 A, the minimum number of branches needed is

$$n_{min} \times 20 \text{ mA} = 0.5 \text{ A}$$

$$n_{min} = 25$$

From the output voltage requirement, we have

$$m_{min} V_{cell} = 10 \text{ V}$$

$$m_{min} = \frac{10}{0.2} = 50$$

That is, 50 solar cells are needed in each branch.

7.43

For operation in the constant voltage range, the cell operating point can be set at the middle point of the constant voltage region where the current is 10 mA and V_{cell} is 0.515 V (see Figure 7.82). Since the array is required to generate 0.5 A, the minimum number of branches needed is

$$n_{min} \times 10 \text{ mA} = 0.5 \text{ A}$$

$$n_{min} = 50$$

From the output voltage requirement,

$$m_{min} V_{cell} = 10 \text{ V}$$

$$m_{min} = \frac{10}{0.515} = 20$$

That is, 20 solar cells are needed in each branch.

Transistor Fundamentals

Chapter 8 Instructor Notes

The first part of Chapter 8 introduces the fundamental ideas behind the operation of bipolar transistors, and of simple amplifier stages. The discussion of the properties of the BJT is centered around a description of the base and collector characteristics, and purposely avoids a detailed description of the physics of the device, with the intent of providing an intuitive understanding of the transistor as an amplifier and electronic switch. Thus, more emphasis is placed on the practical aspects of determining the operating state of the transistor than on explaining the detailed physical properties of the device.

Section 8.4 parallels the development of the previous sections for the metal-oxide semiconductor field-effect transistor (MOSFET). FET gates and switches are introduced at this point.

Several interesting homework problems are presented at the end of the chapter.

Chapter 8 problem solutions

8.1

(a) Since $V_{BE} = 0.8$ V, the BE junction is forward biased.

$V_{CB} = V_{CE} + V_{EB}$

$= 0.4 + (-0.8) = -0.4$ V

Thus, the CB junction is forward biased.

Therefore, the transistor is in the saturation region.

(b)

$V_{BE} = V_{BC} + V_{CE}$

$= -1.4 + 2.1 = 0.7$ V

The EB junction is forward biased.

$V_{CB} = 1.4$ V, the CB junction is reverse biased.

Therefore, the transistor is in the active region.

(c) $V_{CB} = 0.9$ V for a pnp transistor implies that the CB junction is forward biased.

$V_{BE} = V_{BC} - V_{CE}$

$= -0.9 - 0.4 = -1.3$ V

The BE junction is forward biased.

Therefore, the transistor is in the saturation region.

(d) With $V_{BE} = -1.2$ V, the BE junction is reverse biased. $V_{CB} = 0.6$: the CB junction is reverse biased. Therefore, the transistor is in the cut-off region.

8.2

V_1 is given by:

$$V_1 = V_{BE} + V_2 = 0.7 + 2.0 = 2.7 \text{ V}$$

The emitter current is

$$I_E = \frac{V_2}{R_E} = \frac{2}{3} \text{ mA}$$

The base current is

$$I_B = \frac{V_{BB} - V_1}{R_B} = \frac{4 - 2.7}{100}$$

$$= 0.013 \text{ mA} = 13 \ \mu\text{A}$$

The collector current is

$$I_C = I_E - I_B = \frac{2}{3} - 0.013 = 0.654 \text{ mA}$$

Therefore, β is found to be:

$$\beta = \frac{I_C}{I_B} = \frac{0.654}{0.013} = 50.3$$

and V_3 is

$$V_3 = V_{CC} - I_C R_C = 12 - 0.654 \times 5 = 8.73 \text{ V}$$

8.3

(a) $I_E = I_C + I_B = 1\text{ mA} + 20\mu\text{A} = 1.02\text{ mA}$

$V_E = 1000\, I_E = 1.02\text{ V}$

$V_{RC} = 5000\, I_C = 5\text{ V}$

$V_{CB} = 20 - V_{RC} - V_{BE} - V_E$

$= 20 - 5 - 0.7 - 1.02 = 13.28\text{ V}$

The CB junction is reverse-biased.
Therefore, the transistor is operating in the active region.

(b) $I_E = 3.2\text{ mA} + 0.3\text{ mA} = 3.5\text{ mA}$

$V_E = 3.5\text{ V}$

$V_{RC} = 16\text{ V}$

$V_{CB} = 20 - 16 - 0.8 - 3.5 = -30\text{ mV}$

The CB junction is forward-biased.
Therefore, the transistor is operating in the saturation region.

(c) $I_E = 3\text{ mA} + 1.5\text{ mA} = 4.5\text{ mA}$

$V_E = 4.5\text{ V}$

$V_{RC} = 22.5\text{ V}$

$V_{CB} = 20 - 22.5 - 0.85 - 4.5 = -7.85\text{ V}$

The CB junction is forward-biased.
Therefore, the transistor is operating in the saturation region.

8.4

(a) In the pnp transistor, $V_{BE} = -0.6\text{ V}$:
the EB junction is forward biased.

$V_{CB} = V_{CE} - V_{BE}$

$= -4 + 0.6 = -3.4\text{ V}$

The CB junction is reverse biased.
Therefore, the transistor is in the active region.

(b) For the npn transistor, $V_{CB} = 0.7\text{ V}$:
the CB junction is reverse biased.

$V_{BE} = V_{BC} + V_{CE}$

$= -0.7 + 0.2 = -0.5\text{ V}$

The BE junction is reverse biased.
Therefore, the transistor is in cut-off region.

(c) For the npn transistor, $V_{BE} = 0.7\text{ V}$:
the BE junction is forward biased.

$V_{BC} = V_{BE} - V_{CE} = 0.7 - 0.3 = 0.4\text{ V}$

The CB junction is forward biased.
Therefore, the transistor is in the saturation region.

(d) In the pnp transistor, $V_{CB} = -0.6\text{ V}$:
the CB junction is reverse biased.

$V_{BE} = V_{BC} + V_{CE}$

$= 0.6 - 5.4 = -4.8\text{ V}$

The EB junction is forward biased.
Therefore, the transistor is in the active region.

8.5

$V_{BE} = 0.6V$ and the BE junction is forward biased.

$$I_B = \frac{V_{CC} - V_{BE}}{R_1} = \frac{12 - 0.6}{820k} = 13.9\mu A$$

$I_C = \beta I_B = 1.39mA$

Writing KVL around the right-hand side of the circuit:

$$-V_{CC} + I_C R_C + V_{CE} + I_E R_E = 0$$

$$V_{CE} = V_{CC} - I_C R_C - (I_B + I_C) R_E$$
$$= 12 - (1.39mA)(2.2k\Omega) - (1.39 + 0.0139)mA(910\Omega)$$
$$= 7.664V$$

$V_{BC} = V_{BE} + V_{CE} = 0.6 + 7.664 = 8.264V$

$V_{CE} > V_{BE} \Rightarrow$ active region

8.6

$I_E = 6$ mA, $I_B = 0.1$ mA and $V_{EB} = 0.65$, $V_{CB} = 7.3$ V

(a) $V_{CE} = V_{CB} - V_{EB} = 7.3 - 0.65 = 6.65$ V

(b) $I_C = I_E - I_B = 6$ mA $- 0.1$ mA $= 5.9$ mA

(c) The total power dissipated in the transistor can be found to be:

$P \approx V_{CE} I_C = 6.65 \times 5.9 \times 10^{-3} = 39$ mW

8.7

Applying KVL to the right-hand side of the circuit,

$$I_E = -\left(\frac{V_{BE} + 15V}{30k\Omega}\right) = -\frac{(0.6 + 15))}{30k} = -520\mu A$$

Then, on the left-hand side:

$$-10 + I_C R_C + V_{CB} = 0$$

$$V_{CB} = 10 - I_C(15k\Omega)$$
$$= 10 - (-520\mu A)(15k\Omega)$$
$$= 17.8V$$

assuming $\beta >> 1$.

8.8

First, determine the Thevenin equivalent of the circuit connected to the base:

$$V_{BB} = \frac{R_2}{R_1 + R_2} V_{CC} = \frac{15k\Omega}{62k\Omega + 15k\Omega} 18V = 3.506V$$

$$R_{BB} = R_1 \| R_2 = \frac{62k \times 15k}{62k + 15k} = 12.08k\Omega$$

Then, applying KVL to the left-hand side of the circuit, we have:

$$-V_{BB} + I_B R_{BB} + V_{BE} + I_E R_E = 0$$

But $I_E = (\beta + 1) I_B$, so this equation becomes

$$V_{BB} = I_B R_{BB} + V_{BE} + (\beta + 1) I_B R_E$$

$$V_{BB} - V_{BE} = I_B [R_{BB} + (\beta + 1) R_E]$$

$$I_B = \frac{V_{BB} - V_{BE}}{[R_{BB} + (\beta + 1) R_E]} = \frac{3.506 - 0.6}{12.08k + (151)(1.2k)} = 15.04\mu A$$

$I_C = \beta I_B = 2.271mA$

Applying KVL to the right-hand side,

$$-V_{CC} + I_C R_C + V_{CE} + I_E R_E = 0$$

$$V_{CE} = V_{CC} - \beta I_B R_C - (\beta + 1) I_B R_E$$
$$= 18V - 150(15.04\mu A)(3.3k\Omega) - 151(15.04\mu A)(1.2k\Omega)$$
$$= 7.83V$$

Therefore, $I_{BQ} = 15.04\mu A$, $I_{CQ} = 2.271mA$ and $V_{CEQ} = 7.83V$.

8.9

Applying KVL to the right-hand side of the circuit,

$-V_{CC} + I_E R_E + V_{EB} = 0$

$I_E = \frac{V_{CC} - V_{EB}}{R_E} = \frac{20 - 0.6}{39k} = 497.4\mu A$

Since $\beta >> 1$, $I_C \approx I_E = 497.4\mu A$

Applying KVL to the left-hand side:

$V_{CB} + I_C R_C - V_{DD} = 0$

$V_{CB} = V_{DD} - I_C R_C$

$= 20V - (497.4\mu A)(20k\Omega)$

$= 10.05V$

8.10

$I_E = \frac{V_{CC} - V_{EB}}{R_E} = \frac{20 - 0.6}{22k} = 881.8\mu A$

$I_C \approx 881.8\mu A$

$V_{CB} = V_{DD} - I_C R_C$

$= 20V - (881.8\mu A)(20k\Omega)$

$= 2.364V$

8.11

$V_{CE} = V_{sat} = 0.2$ V, therefore, I_C is

$$I_C = \frac{10 - 0.2}{R_C} = 9.8 \text{ mA}$$

$V_{BE} = V_\gamma = 0.6$ V, therefore, I_B is

$$I_B = \frac{5.7 - 0.6}{50} = 102 \ \mu A$$

$$\frac{I_C}{I_B} = \frac{9.8 \text{ mA}}{102 \ \mu A} = 96 < \beta$$

8.12

The collector current is

$$I_C = \frac{12 - 0.1}{1} = 11.9 \text{ mA}$$

The base current is

$$I_B = \frac{I_C}{\beta} = \frac{11.9}{50} = 0.238 \text{ mA} = 238 \ \mu A$$

And since

$$I_B = \frac{V_{BB} - V_{BEsat}}{10} \text{ mA}$$

Therefore,

$$V_{BB} = 0.238 \text{ mA} \times 10 \text{ k}\Omega + 0.6 = 2.98 \text{ V}$$

8.13

The equivalent base supply voltage V_{BB} is

$$V_{BB} = \frac{R_2}{R_1 + R_2} V_{CC} = \frac{47}{147} 15 = 4.8 \text{ V}$$

The equivalent base resistance is

$$R_B = R_1 \| R_2 = \frac{100k\Omega \times 47k\Omega}{147k\Omega} = 32k\Omega$$

The base current is

$$I_B = \frac{V_{BB} - V_{BE}}{R_B + (\beta + 1)R_E}$$

$$= \frac{4.8 - 0.7}{32 + 76 \times 4} = 12.2 \ \mu A$$

The collector current is

$$I_C = \beta I_B = 0.915 \text{ mA}$$

The collector-emitter voltage V_{CE} is

$$V_{CE} = V_{CC} - I_C(R_C + \frac{\beta + 1}{\beta} R_E) = 9.46 \text{ V}$$

The Q-point of the transistor is:

$I_{BQ} = 12.2 \ \mu A$ $\quad$ $I_{CQ} = 0.915$ mA

$V_{CEQ} = 9.46$ V

and $V_{BEQ} = 0.7$ V (assumed)

8.14

(a) Since

$$I_E = I_B + I_C = (\beta + 1)\, I_B$$

we can compute

$$I_B = \frac{I_E}{\beta + 1} = \frac{4}{61} = 65.6 \ \ \mu A$$

(b) $V_{CE} = V_{CB} - V_{BE}$

$$= 7.2 - 0.6 = 6.6 \ \ V$$

8.15

(a) For $I_B = 100\ \mu A$ and $V_{CE} = 10$ V, from the characteristics, we have

$$I_C = 17 \ \ mA$$

The ratio of $\frac{I_C}{I_B}$ is 170.

For $I_B = 200\ \mu A$ and $V_{CE} = 10$ V, we find from the characteristic

$$I_C = 33 \ \ mA$$

The ratio $\frac{I_C}{I_B}$ is 165.

For $I_B = 600\ \mu A$ and $V_{CE} = 10$ V, from the characteristics, we have

$$I_C = 86 \ \ mA$$

The ratio $\frac{I_C}{I_B}$ is 143.

(b) For $I_B = 500\ \mu A$, and if we consider an average β from (a), we have

$$I_C = 159 \times 500 = 79.5 \ \ mA$$

The power dissipated by the transistor is $P = I_C\, V_{CE}$, therefore,

$$V_{CE} = \frac{P}{I_C} = 6.29 \ \ V$$

8.16

(a) From KVL:

$$-30 + I_{B1}(750k\Omega) + V_{BE1} = 0$$

$$I_{B1} = \frac{30 - 0.7}{750k} = 39.07\mu A$$

$$I_{C1} = \beta I_{B1} = 3.907mA$$

$$V_{C1} = 30 - (3.907mA)(6.2k\Omega) = 5.779V$$

$$V_{CE1} = V_{C1} = 5.779V$$

(b) Again, from KVL:

$$-5.779 + V_{BE2} + I_{E2}(4.7k\Omega) = 0$$

$$I_{E2} = \frac{5.779 - 0.7}{4.7k} = 1.081mA$$

$$I_{C2} = I_{E2}\left(\frac{\beta}{\beta + 1}\right) = 1.081mA\left(\frac{100}{101}\right) = 1.07mA$$

Also,

$$-30 + I_{C2}(20k + 4.7k) + V_{CE2} = 0$$

$$V_{CE2} = 30 - (1.07mA)(20k + 4.7k) = 3.574V$$

And,

$$I_{C2} = \frac{30 - V_{C2}}{20k}$$

$$\Rightarrow V_{C2} = 30 - (1.07m)(20k) = 8.603V$$

8.17

Construct a load line. Writing KVL, we have:

$-50+5000i_C+v_{CE}=0$

Then, if $i_C=0$, $v_{CE}=50V$; and if $v_{CE}=0$, $i_C=10mA$. The load line is shown superimposed on the collector characteristic below:

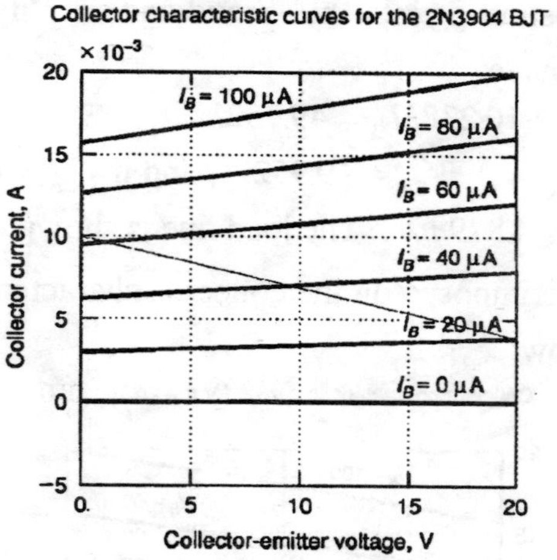

The operating point is at the intersection of the load line and the $I_B=20\mu A$ line of the characteristic. Therefore, $I_{CQ}\approx 4mA$ and $V_{CEQ}\approx 20V$.

Under these conditions, a $20\mu A$ increase in I_B yields an increase in I_C of approximately $7mA-4mA=3mA$. Therefore,

$$\beta\approx\frac{\Delta I_C}{\Delta I_B}=\frac{3mA}{20\mu A}=150$$

8.18

From KVL,

$-50+5kI_C+V_{CE}+5k(I_C+20\mu A)=0$

or

$V_{CE}+10kI_C=50-0.1=49.9$

If $V_{CE}=0$, $I_C=\dfrac{49.9}{10k}=4.99mA$, and if $I_C=0$, $V_{CE}=49.9V$. The load line is shown superimposed on the collector characteristic below:

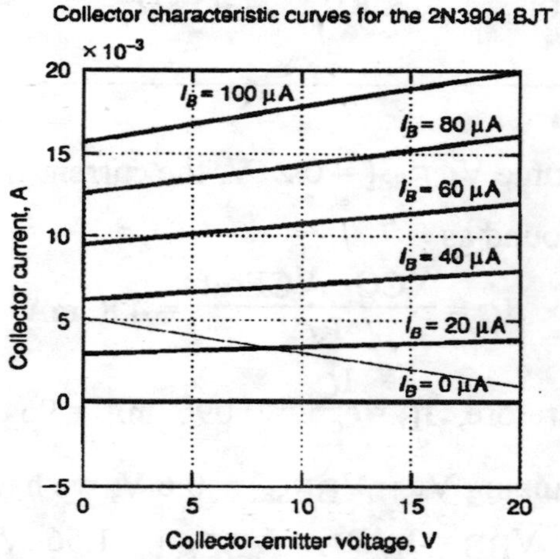

The operating point is at the intersection of the load line and the $I_B=20\mu A$ line of the characteristic. Therefore, $I_{CQ}\approx 3mA$ and $V_{CEQ}\approx 8V$.

Under these conditions, a $10\mu A$ increase in I_B yields an increase in I_C of approximately $5mA-3mA=2mA$. Therefore,

$$\beta\approx\frac{\Delta I_C}{\Delta I_B}=\frac{2mA}{10\mu A}=200$$

Addition of the emitter resistor effectively increased the current gain by decreasing the magnitude of the slope of the load line.

8.19

Assuming $V_{CEsat} = 0.2$ V, the current I_C is:

$$I_C = \frac{V_{CC} - V_{CEsat}}{R_C} = 9.8 \text{ mA}$$

Therefore, $I_B = \frac{I_C}{\beta} = 0.196$ mA

Assuming $V_\gamma = V_{BEsat} = 0.6$ V, we have

$$R_B = \frac{V_{BB} - V_{BE}}{I_B} = 22.45 \text{ k}\Omega$$

That is $0 \le R_B \le 22.45$ kΩ

8.20

Assume $V_{CEsat} = 0.2$ V, the current I_C can be found as

$$I_C = \frac{V_{CC} - V_{CEsat}}{R_C} = 4.8 \text{ mA}$$

Therefore, $I_B = \frac{I_C}{\beta} = 0.096 \text{ mA} = 96 \ \mu\text{A}$

Assuming $V_\gamma = V_{BEsat} = 0.6$ V, we have

$$V_{BB} = I_B R_B + V_{BEsat} = 1.56 \text{ V}$$

That is $V_{BB} > 1.56$ V

8.21

From KVL:

$$-2 + 100kI_B + 0.7 + 5k(I_C + I_B) = 0$$

and

$$-50 + 5kI_C + V_{CE} + 5k(I_C + I_B) = 0$$

From the first equation,

$$I_B = \frac{2 - 0.7 - 5kI_C}{100k + 5k} = \frac{1.3 - 5kI_C}{105k}$$

Substituting into the second and simplifying, we have:

$$V_{CE} + 10.238kI_C = 49.952$$

If $I_C = 0$, $V_{CE} = 49.952V$, and if $V_{CE} = 0$, $I_C = 4.879mA$. The load line is shown superimposed on the collector characteristic below:

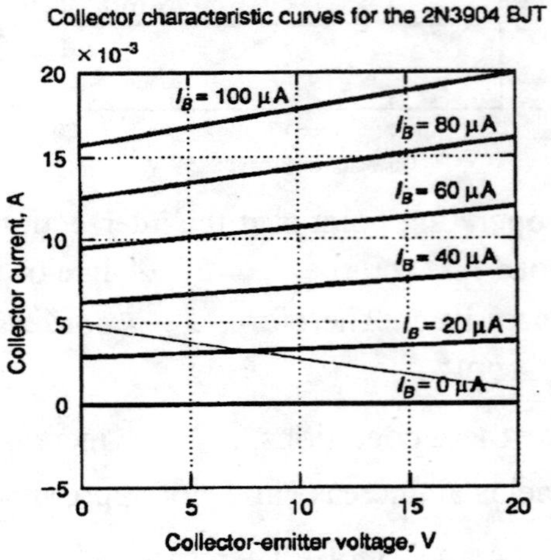

This figure is not significantly different from that of Problem 8.18. Thus, since it is still true that $I_B \approx \frac{2V}{100k\Omega} = 20\mu A$, the remainder of the solution is identical to that for Problem 8.18.

8.22

$I_C = \beta I_B = 100\times20\times10^{-6} = 2$ mA

$I_E = I_B + I_C = (\beta + 1)I_B$

$= 101\times20\times10^{-6} = 2.02$ mA

$V_{CE} = V_{CC} - I_C R_C = 10 - 2\times2 = 6$ V

Assume $V_{BE} = 0.6$ V,

$V_{CB} = V_{CE} - V_{BE}$

$= 6 - 0.6 = 5.4$ V

8.23

First, we find the operating point, and ΔV_B is assumed zero. Assume $V_{BE} = 0.6$ V:

$$I_B = \frac{V_{BB} - V_{BE}}{R_B} = \frac{3 - 0.6}{100}$$

$$= 0.024 \text{ mA} = 24 \ \mu\text{A}$$

$$I_C = \beta I_B = 100\times0.024 = 2.4 \text{ mA}$$

and

$$V_{CE} = V_{CC} - I_C R_C = 12 - 2.4\times3 = 4.8 \text{ V}$$

The small signal model is shown below:

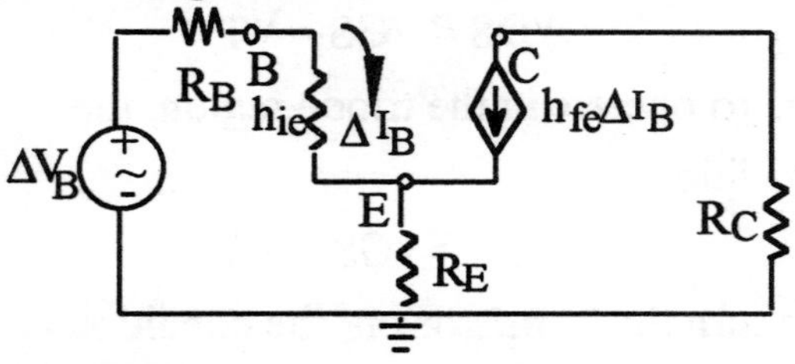

From the above model,

$$\Delta V_B = (R_B + h_{ie})\Delta I_B + R_E(h_{fe} + 1)\Delta I_B$$

$$\Delta V_C = - h_{fe} R_C \Delta I_B$$

The maximum AC voltage gain is obtained for $h_{ie} = 0$:

$$A_V = \frac{\Delta V_C}{\Delta V_B} = - \frac{h_{fe} R_C}{R_B + h_{ie} + (h_{fe} + 1)R_E}$$

$$\approx - \frac{100\times3\times10^3}{100\times10^3 + 101\times100} = - 2.725$$

8.24

(a)

$$V_{EB} = V_E - V_B = 0.7V$$

$$\Rightarrow V_B = V_E - V_{EB} = 1 - 0.7 = 0.3V$$

(b)

$$I_B = \frac{V_B}{20k\Omega} = \frac{0.3V}{20k\Omega} = 15\mu A$$

(c)

$$I_E = \frac{5 - V_E}{5k\Omega} = \frac{5-1}{5k} = 800\mu A$$

(d)

$$I_C = I_E - I_B = 800\mu A - 15\mu A = 785\mu A$$

(e)

$$\beta = \frac{I_C}{I_B} = \frac{785\mu A}{15\mu A} = 52.333$$

(f)

$$\alpha = \frac{I_C}{I_E} = \frac{785\mu A}{800\mu A} = 0.981$$

8.25

(a) This is an n-channel depletion MOSFET, with $V_T = -3$ V. To operate in the triode region, the condition is:

$$v_{DS} \leq v_{GS} - V_T;$$

to operate in the saturation region, the condition is:

$$v_{DS} \geq v_{GS} - V_T$$

To turn the transistor on, the condition is

$$v_{GS} > V_T$$

We can compute

$$v_{GS} = -2.5 \text{ V},$$

$$v_{DS} = 2.5 \text{ V},$$

$$v_{GS} - V_T = -2.5 + 3 = 0.5 \text{ V}$$

$$v_{GS} = -2.5 \text{ V} < v_{GS} - V_T = 0.5 \text{ V}$$

Therefore, the transistor is in the triode region.

(b) This is a p-channel depletion MOSFET with $V_T = 3$ V. To operate in the saturation region, the condition is

$$v_{DS} \leq v_{GS} - V_T$$

and to operate in the triode region, the condition is

$$v_{DS} \geq v_{GS} - V_T$$

To turn the transistor on, the condition is

$$v_{GS} < V_T$$

We can compute

$$v_{GS} = 2 \text{ V},$$

$$v_{DS} = -1 \text{ V},$$

$$v_{GS} - V_T = 2 - 3 = -1 \text{ V},$$

$$v_{GS} = 2 \text{ V} > v_{GS} - V_T = -1 \text{ V}$$

Therefore, the transistor is in the triode region.

(c) This is a p-channel enhancement mode MOSFET, with $V_T = -3$ V. To operate in the saturation region, the condition is

$$v_{DS} \leq v_{GS} - V_T$$

and to operate in the triode region, the condition is

$$v_{DS} \geq v_{GS} - V_T$$

To turn the transistor on, the condition is

$$v_{GS} < V_T$$

We can calculate

$$v_{GS} = -5 \text{ V},$$

$$v_{DS} = -1 \text{ V},$$

$$v_{GS} - V_T = -5 + 3 = -2 \text{ V}$$

$$v_{GS} = -5 \text{ V} < v_{GS} - V_T = -2 \text{ V}$$

Therefore, the transistor is in the saturation region.

(d) This is an n-channel enhancement MOSFET, with $V_T = 3$ V. To operate in the saturation region, the condition is

$$v_{DS} \geq v_{GS} - V_T$$

and to operate in the triode region, the condition is

$$v_{DS} \leq v_{GS} - V_T$$

To turn the transistor on, the condition is

$$v_{GS} > V_T$$

We have $v_{GS} = -2 \text{ V} < V_T$, therefore, the transistor operates in the cut-off region.

8.26

(a) To operate in the ohmic region, the condition is

$V_{DS} \leq V_{GS} - V_T$ and $V_T > 0$, $V_{DS} > 0$

The circuit for operation in the ohmic region, is shown below.

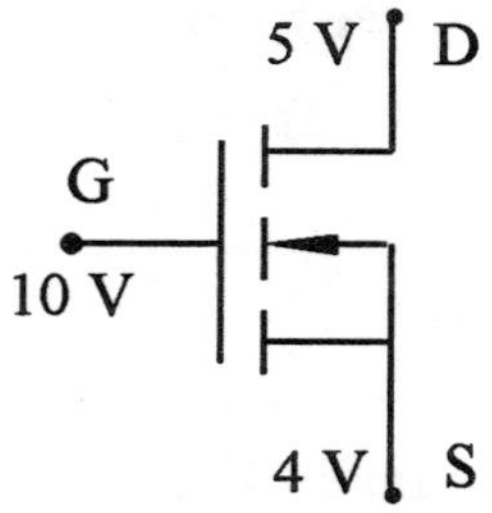

(b) To operate beyond pinch-off (in the saturation region), the condition is

$V_{DS} \geq V_{GS} - V_T$ and $V_T > 0$, $V_{DS} > 0$

The circuit for operation beyond pinch-off is shown below.

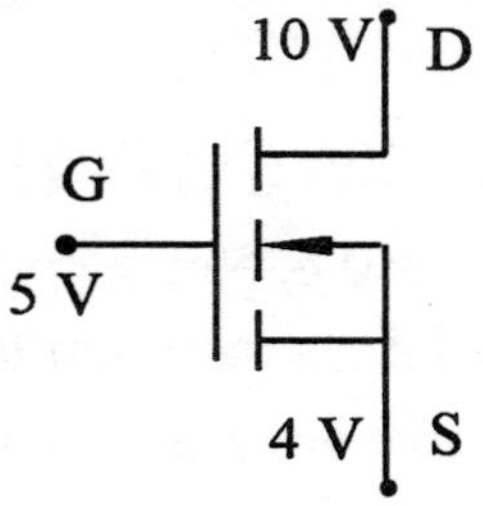

8.27

(a) $V_{DS} = V_D = 0.5$ V

$V_{GS} - V_T = 3 - 2 = 1$ V

$V_{DS} < V_{GS} - V_T$

The transistor is in the ohmic region.

(b) $V_{DS} = V_D = 1$ V

$V_{GS} - V_T = 3 - 2 = 1$ V

$V_{DS} = V_{GS} - V_T$

The transistor is either in the ohmic or in the saturation region.

(c) $V_{DS} = V_D = 5$ V

$V_{GS} - V_T = 3 - 2 = 1$ V

$V_{DS} > V_{GS} - V_T$

The transistor is in the saturation region.

8.28

(a) At $v_{DS} = 2$ V,

$v_{GS} - V_T = 3.5 - 1.5 = 2$ V

$i_D = K(v_{GS} - V_T)^2 =$

$= 0.1 \times 10^{-3} \times 2^2 = 0.4$ mA

(b) At $v_{DS} = 10$ V, $v_{DS} > v_{GS} - V_T$

$i_D = 0.1 \times 10^{-3} \times 4 = 0.4$ mA

8.29

Assuming

$$v_{DS} > v_{GS} - V_T$$

we can calculate the constants by the following method:

$$0.004 = K(10 - V_T)^2 \qquad (1)$$

$$0.001 = K(6 - V_T)^2 \qquad (2)$$

Equation (2) divided by equation (1) yields

$$4 = \frac{(10 - V_T)^2}{(6 - V_T)^2}$$

Solving the above equation, we have

$$V_T = 2\ \text{V}$$

Now,

$$I_{DSS} = \frac{i_D(V_T^2)}{(V_{GS} - V_T)^2} = \frac{1mA(2V)^2}{(6V - 2V)^2} = 250\mu A$$

8.30

The device shown is an n-channel enhancement-type MOSFET, with $V_T = 2$ V, $V_{DG} = 0$ V. To operate in the saturation region, we require:

$$V_{DS} \geq V_{GS} - V_T$$

Since

$$V_{DG} = V_{DS} - V_{GS} = 0 > - V_T = -2\ \text{V}$$

the transistor is in the saturation region. Knowing $K = 10\ \text{mA/V}^2$, we can write

$$0.4 = 10(V_{GS} - 2)^2$$

and determine

$$V_D = V_{DS} = 2.2\ \text{V}$$

R can be found as follows:

$$R = \frac{20 - V_D}{I_D} = \frac{20 - 2.2}{0.4} = 44.5\ \text{k}\Omega$$

8.31

Because $v_{DS} > v_{GS} - V_T$, the transistor is in the saturation region.

$$i_D = K(v_{GS} - V_T)^2 = K(3 - 2)^2 = 0.001$$

$$K = 0.001 \frac{\text{A}}{\text{V}^2} = 1 \frac{\text{mA}}{\text{V}^2}$$

For $v_{GS} = 4$ V, we have

$$i_D = 0.001(4 - 2)^2 = 0.004\ \text{A} = 4\ \text{mA}$$

8.32

Let $V_{GS1} = - 2.1$ V, represent the initial gate-source voltage. Then, $V_T = - 4$ V and $V_{GS1} - V_T = - 2.1 + 4 = 1.9$ V. With these values we can compute the operating state of the transistor:

$$V_{DS1} = 3\ \text{V} > V_{GS1} - V_T = 1.9\ \text{V}$$

Therefore, the transistor is in the saturation region. and

$$I_{D1} = K(V_{G1S} - V_T)^2 =$$

$$= 0.625 \times 1.9^2 = 2.26\ \text{mA}$$

Let $V_{GS2} = - 1.5$ V, represent the new value of the gate-source voltage. Then, $V_T = - 4$ V and $V_{GS2} - V_T = - 1.5 + 4 = 2.5$ V

$$V_{DS2} = 3\ \text{V} > V_{GS2} - V_T = 2.5\ \text{V}$$

Therefore, the transistor is in the saturation region, and the drain current is

$$I_{D2} = K(V_{GS2} - V_T)^2 = 0.625 \times 2.5^2$$

$$= 3.91\text{mA}$$

The change in I_D is: $\Delta I_D = 1.65$ mA

8.33

In the circuit of Figure P8.17,

$v_{DS} = 0.1 < v_{GS} - V_T = 14$ V,

therefore the transistor is in the ohmic region. We can compute the drain current to be:

$$i_D = K[2(v_{GS} - V_T)v_{DS} - v_{DS}^2]$$

$$= 0.5\times10^{-3}[2(15 - 1)\times0.1 - (0.1)^2] = 1.395 \text{ mA}$$

8.34

Since

$V_{DS} = 0.4 \text{ V} < V_{GS} - V_T = 5 - 3.2 = 1.8 \text{ V}$

the transistor is operating in the triode region.

The effective resistance is

$$R_{SD} = \frac{500}{5 - 3.2} = 277.78 \ \Omega$$

Since $R_{DS} = \frac{V_{DS}}{I_D}$, we have

$$I_D = \frac{V_{DS}}{R_{DS}} = \frac{0.4}{277.78} = 1.44 \text{ mA}$$

8.35

Since the transistor is in the saturation region and $I_D = 0.5$ mA, we have

$$I_D = K(V_{GS} - V_T)^2$$

$$0.5 = 0.5(V_{GS} + 1)^2$$

and $V_{GS} = -2$ V; $V_{GS} < V_T = -1$. Since the source is at 10 V, the gate voltage must be 8 V. Thus, we can select $R_1 = 1$ MΩ and $R_2 = 4$MΩ to obtain this operating condition.

(a) R_D can be found to be

$$R_D = \frac{V_D}{I_D} = \frac{8}{0.5} = 16 \text{ k}\Omega$$

(b) Saturation region operation would be maintained when V_D exceeds V_G by $|V_T|$,

$$V_{Dmax} = 8 + 1 = 9 \text{ V}$$

Therefore,

$$R_{Dmax} = \frac{V_{Dmax}}{0.5} = 18 \text{ k}\Omega$$

8.36

With $V_P = -2.8$ V, $i_D = 0.3$ mA, $V_{GS} = -1$ V and $V_{DS} = 0.05$ V, the JFET is operating in the ohmic region, and we can calculate I_{DSS} as follows:

$$0.0003 = I_{DSS}\left(2\times\left(1-\frac{-1}{-2.8}\right)\frac{0.05}{2.8}-\left(\frac{0.05}{-2.8}\right)^2\right)$$

$$I_{DSS} = 13.25 \text{ mA}$$

(a) The drain current is

$$i_D = 13.25\times10^{-3}\left(2\times\left(1-\frac{-1}{-2.8}\right)\frac{0.1}{2.8}-\left(\frac{0.1}{-2.8}\right)^2\right)$$

$$= 0.591mA$$

(b) The drain current is

$$i_D = 13.25\times10^{-3}\left(2\times\left(1-\frac{0}{-2.8}\right)\frac{0.1}{2.8}-\left(\frac{0.1}{-2.8}\right)^2\right)$$

$$= 0.930mA$$

(c) Since

$$V_{GS} = -3.2 \text{ V} < V_P$$

the transistor is cut off, and $i_D = 0$ mA.

8.37

(a) $V_{DS} = 3 > V_{GS} - V_T =$

$= 3.5 - 1.5 = 2$ V

$i_D = K(V_{GS} - V_T)^2 = 0.5\times10^{-3}\times4 = 2$ mA

(b) $V_{DS} = 10 > V_{GS} - V_T = 2$ V

$i_D = 0.5\times10^{-4}\times4 = 2$ mA

8.38

From the two operating points given, we can apply the following equation twice:

$$I_D = K(V_{GS} - V_T)^2$$

and compute the ratio of the two, to obtain:

$$\frac{0.006}{0.0015} = \frac{K(12 - V_T)^2}{K(6 - V_T)^2}$$

Solving the above equations, we find

$$V_T = 0$$

$$K = \frac{6\times10^{-3}}{144} = 4.17\times10^{-5} \text{ mA/V}^2$$

8.39

(a) $V_{DS} = 0.5 < V_{GS} - V_T =$

$= 4 - 2.5 = 1.5$ V

the transistor is in the ohmic region.

(b) $V_D = 1.5$ V $= V_{DS}$, the transistor is at the border of the saturation and ohmic regions.

8.40

From $0.001 = K(6 - 4)^2$, we have

$$K = \frac{1\times10^{-3}}{4} = 0.25\times10^{-3}$$

For $V_{GS} = 5$ V, and assuming saturated operation,

$$i_D = 0.25\times10^{-3}(5 - 4)^2 = 0.25 \text{ mA}$$

8.41

(a) Since $V_T = 1.5$ V, with

$$v_G = 0 \text{ V}, \ v_{GS} < V_T,$$

the transistor is cut off. Therefore,

$$V_D = 5 \text{ V}.$$

(b) When $v_G = 5$ V, and assuming that the transistor is in the saturation region:

$$I_D = K(V_{GS} - V_T)^2 = 0.4(5 - 1.5)^2$$

$$= 4.9 \text{ mA}$$

Therefore,

$$V_D = 5 - 4.9{\times}1 = 0.1 \text{ V}$$

8.42

(a) $$r_{DS} = \frac{-V_P^2}{2I_{DSS}(V_p - V_{GS})}$$

$$= \frac{-(-2)^2}{2(0.008)(-2-(-1))} = 250\ \Omega$$

(b) $$\frac{1}{2}\ 250 = \frac{-4}{2{\times}0.008{\times}(-2 - V_{GS})}$$

Therefore, $V_{GS} = 0$ V

8.43

Since the gate current is zero, the voltage at the gate is determined by the voltage divider formed by the two resistors:

$$V_G = \frac{1}{8+1}\ 10 = 1.11 \text{ V}$$

With this positive voltage at the gate the transistor will not be cut off. Assuming for the moment saturation region operation, we have

$$V_{GS} = 1.11 - 15\ I_D$$

$$I_D = K(V_{GS} - V_T)^2 = 0.5(1.11 - 15I_D + 1)^2$$

Solving the equations,we find

$$I_D = 0.1808 \text{ mA}$$

(The other solution of the quadratic equation is dropped because it does not satisfy our assumption of operation in the saturation region.) Then,

$$V_S = I_D{\times}15 = 1.642 \text{ V}$$

Therefore,

$$V_{GS} = 1.11 - 1.642 = -0.532 \text{ V}$$

$$V_D = 10 - 0.1808{\times}32 = 4.214 \text{ V}$$

$$V_{DS} = V_D - 1.11 = 8.655 \text{ V}$$

We can now confirm that, since

$$V_{DS} > V_{GS} - V_T = 0.468 \text{ V},$$

the transistor is operating in the saturation region.

8.44

With $I_D = 0.25$ mA, $V_G = 3$ V and $V_D = 10$ V, assuming saturated operation, we have

$$I_D = K(V_{GS} - V_T)^2$$

$$V_{GS} = \pm\sqrt{\frac{0.25}{0.2}} + 2$$

Selecting the negative solution (why?), we have

$$V_{GS} = 2 - \sqrt{1.25} = 882 \text{ mV}$$

Since $V_{GS} = V_G - V_S$,

$$V_S = V_G - V_{GS} = 3 - 0.882 = 2.118 \text{ V}$$

Because $V_{GS} < V_T = 2$ V, the transistor is in cut-off. Thus,

$$V_{out} = 0 \text{ V}$$

Transistor Amplifiers and Switches

Chapter 9 Instructor Notes

The concept of amplification is approached from the i-v characteristics, and small-signal models of BJT amplifiers are presented in an intuitive fashion. The small signal *h*-parameters are used as a vehicle to approach small signal models starting from the base and collector characteristics of the transistor.

The Common Emitter amplifier is then discussed in some detail, to introduce the ideas of voltage, current and power gain, as well as the notion of input and output resistance. The analysis method attempts to develop a systematic approach consisting of a separate analysis of the DC bias circuit and of the AC small signal circuit. The performance characteristics of the Common Base and Common Collector amplifiers are then summarized in a table.

A similar development is presented for the metal-oxide semiconductor field-effect transistor, and common-source and common-drain amplifiers are introduced. A brief discussion of frequency response and multistage amplifiers is then followed by an introduction to transistor gates and switching circuits. The Instructor who teaches a survey course will find that the first four sections permit an efficient overview of the material.

The homework problems reinforce and extend the examples presented in the chapter, and include several more advanced problems designed to permit a deeper exploration of the ideas discussed therein. In particular, these include a series of problems designed to allow the students to analyze the Common Base and Common Collector amplifier configurations using the same methods developed for the Common Emitter amplifier; other problems include the discussion of a driver for an automotive fuel injector (9.12) and relay driver circuits (9.13, 9.14).

Chapter 9 problem solutions

9.1

$h_{fe} = 350 \qquad h_{ie} = 1.4\ \text{k}\Omega$

$h_{oe} = 150\ \mu\text{S}$

The small signal model of the circuit of Figure 9.4 is shown below:

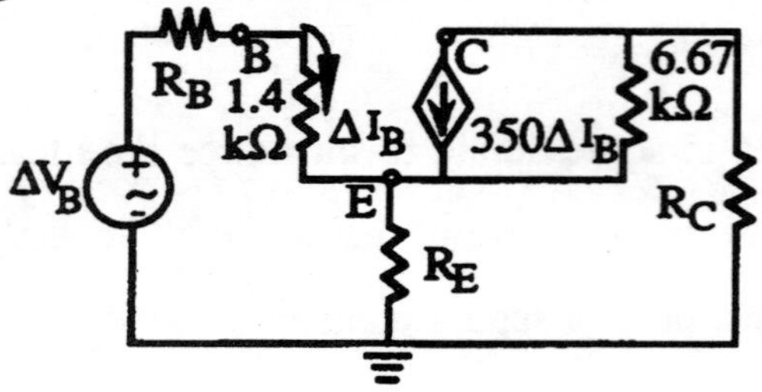

9.2

(a) Assume $V_{BE} = 0.7$ V; the emitter current is

$$I_E = \frac{5 - V_{BE}}{R_E} = \frac{5 - 0.7}{200} = 21.5\ \text{mA}$$

Therefore,

$$I_B = \frac{I_E}{\beta + 1} = 0.142\ \text{mA}$$

$$I_C = \beta I_B = 150 \times 0.142 = 21.3\ \text{mA}$$

The output voltage is

$$V_o = -I_C \times R_C = -8.52\ \text{V}$$

and

$$V_{CB} = V_o + 15 = 6.48\ \text{V}$$

Therefore, V_{CE} is

$$V_{CE} = V_{CB} - V_{EB} = 6.48 + 0.7 = 7.18\ \text{V}$$

(b) $h_{ie} = \left.\dfrac{\partial V_{BE}}{\partial I_B}\right|_{I_{BQ}}$

$$\approx \frac{0.7}{0.142 \times 10^{-3}} = 4.93\ \text{k}\Omega$$

$$h_{fe} \approx \beta = 150$$

The h-parameter model is shown below

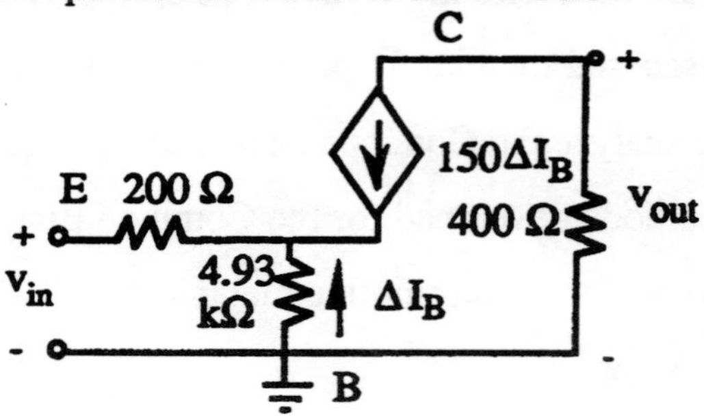

(c) We have

$V_{in} = -(150\Delta I_B + \Delta I_B)200 - \Delta I_B\, 4.93 \times 10^3$

$V_{out} = -150\Delta I_B \times 400$

Therefore, the AC voltage gain is

$$A_V = \frac{V_{out}}{V_{in}} = 1.71$$

9.3

From the figure in Table 9.2, we have

$$V_{in} = -R_E\Delta I_B + h_{ie}\Delta I_B$$

$$V_{out} = -h_{fe}\Delta I_B R_C$$

The voltage gain is

$$A_V = \frac{V_{out}}{V_{in}} = \frac{h_{fe}R_C}{R_E + h_{ie}}$$

The equation in the table indicates

$$A_V = \frac{h_{fe}R_C(R_E \parallel h_{ie})}{R_E h_{ie}}$$

where

$$R_E \parallel h_{ie} = \frac{R_E h_{ie}}{R_E + h_{ie}}$$

Therefore,

$$A_V = \frac{h_{fe}R_C \times \frac{R_E h_{ie}}{R_E + h_{ie}}}{R_E h_{ie}} = \frac{h_{fe}R_C}{R_E + h_{ie}}$$

Thus, the two results are the same.

9.4

To find the output resistance, we make the independent source $V_{IN} = 0$, causing the dependent source $h_{fe}\Delta I_b$ to be an open circuit. The actual resistance across the output is

$$R_{out} = \frac{1 + h_{fe}}{h_{oe}}$$

9.5

The small signal equivalent circuit is shown below:

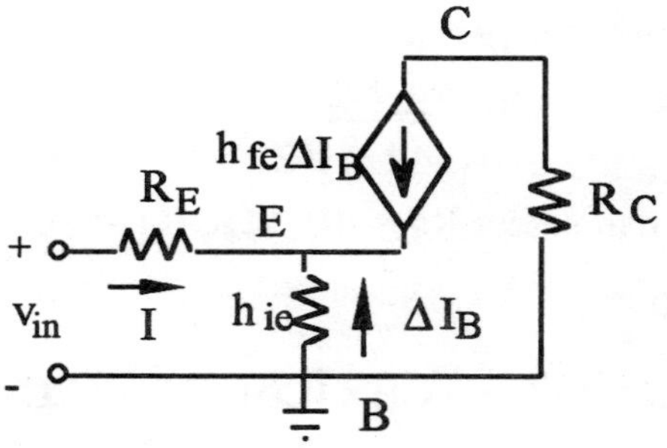

In the circuit,

$$I = -(\Delta I_B + h_{fe}\Delta I_B)$$

$$\Delta I_B = -\frac{I}{1 + h_{fe}}$$

$$V_{in} = I R_E - h_{ie}\Delta I_B = I R_E + h_{ie}\frac{I}{1 + h_{fe}}$$

Therefore, the input resistance is

$$R_{in} = \frac{V_{in}}{I} = R_E + \frac{h_{ie}}{1 + h_{fe}}$$

The result is the same as R_{in} Table 9.2.

9.6

For $V_{BB} = \frac{R_2}{R_1 + R_2} V_{CC} = \frac{1}{3} V_{CC}$

we must have

$$\frac{R_2}{R_1 + R_2} = \frac{1}{3}$$

We can select $R_2 = 10 \text{ k}\Omega$, $R_1 = 20 \text{ k}\Omega$.

Also

$$V_E = V_{CC} - V_{CE} - I_C R_C = \frac{1}{3} V_{CC} = 5 \text{ V}$$

and $\qquad I_E = 1 \text{ mA}$

Therefore,

$$R_E = \frac{V_E}{I_E} = 5 \text{ k}\Omega$$

Assuming $I_C \approx I_E$, we have

$$I_C R_C = \frac{1}{3} V_{CC} = 5 \text{ V}$$

$$R_C = \frac{5}{I_C} = 5 \text{ k}\Omega$$

9.7

(a) $V_{BB} = V_{CC}\dfrac{R_2}{R_1 + R_2} = 6.03\ \text{V}$

$R_{BB} = R_1 \parallel R_2 = 1158.35\ \Omega$

Applying KVL around the base-emitter loop:

$$V_{BB} = I_B R_{BB} + V_{BE} + I_E R_E$$

Substituting for I_B,

$$I_B = \frac{I_E}{\beta + 1}$$

We have

$$I_E = \frac{V_{BB} - V_{BE}}{R_E + R_{BB}/(\beta + 1)} = 48\ \text{mA}$$

The base current is:

$$I_B = \frac{I_E}{\beta+1} = \frac{I_E}{101} = 0.475\ \text{mA}$$

The base voltage is

$V_B = V_{BE} + I_E R_E =$

$= 0.6 + 48{\times}10^{-3}{\times}100 = 5.4\ \text{V}$

Assuming active-mode operation, the collector current is

$$I_C = \beta I_B = 47.5\ \text{mA}$$

The collector voltage can now be determined to be:

$$V_C = 10 - 47.5{\times}10^{-3}{\times}100 = 5.25\ \text{V}$$

Also

$$V_{CE} = V_C - V_E = 5.25 - 4.8 = 0.45\ \text{V}$$

b) The AC equivalent circuit is shown below

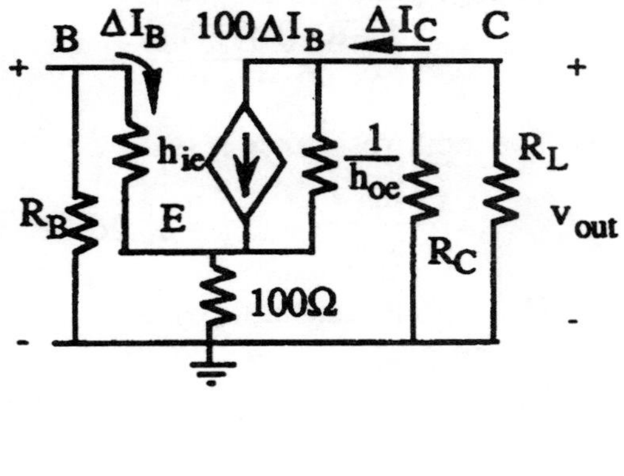

(c) $h_{ie} = \dfrac{\partial v_{BE}}{\partial i_B}\Big|_{I_{BQ}} \approx \dfrac{0.6}{0.475\times10^{-3}} = 1.26k\Omega$

$R_B = R_1 \parallel R_2 = 1158.35\ \Omega$

$R_C \parallel R_L = 60\ \Omega$

Solving for ΔV_{CE} and v_{in} (see Fig. 9.20):

$$\Delta V_{CE} = 10^5(\Delta I_C - 100\ \Delta I_B)$$

$$v_{in} = \Delta I_B 1258 + 100(\Delta I_B + \Delta I_C)$$

$$0 = 60\ \Delta I_C + \Delta V_{CE} + 100\ (\Delta I_B + \Delta I_C)$$

Rearranging the above equations, we have

$$v_{in} = 1358\Delta I_B + 100\ \Delta I_C$$

$$0 = 100160\ \Delta I_C - 9999900\ \Delta I_B$$

$$\Delta I_C = v_{in}/113.58$$

The output voltage is

$v_{out} = -\ \Delta I_C 60 = -\ 60\dfrac{v_{in}}{113.58} =$

$= -\ 0.528\ V_{in}$

The voltage gain is

$$A_V = \frac{v_{out}}{v_{in}} = -\ 0.528$$

(d) The input resistance is

$$r_i = \frac{v_{in}}{\Delta I_B} = 11.4\ \text{k}\Omega$$

(e) The output resistance is

$$r_o = R_C \parallel (1/h_{oe}) = 99.9\ \Omega$$

9.8

The small signal circuit is shown below.

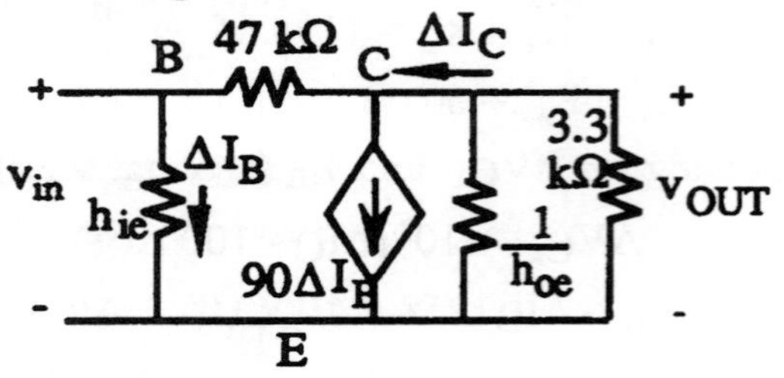

In the circuit

$$\Delta I_B = \frac{v_{in}}{h_{ie}}$$

$$\Delta I_C = -\frac{v_{out}}{3.3k\Omega \| \frac{1}{h_{oe}}}$$

Applying KCL at the collector, we have

$$\frac{v_{in} - v_{out}}{47\ k\Omega} = \frac{v_{out}}{2.36\ k\Omega} + 90\frac{v_{in}}{h_{ie}}$$

Solving the above equation, we have

$$A_V = \frac{v_{out}}{v_{in}} = \frac{1/47 - 90/1.3}{1/2.36 + 1/47}$$

$$= -155.5$$

9.9

(a) The voltage at the base is

$$V_B = \frac{R_{B1}}{R_{B1} + R_{B2}} V_{CC} = 1.58\ \text{V}$$

Assuming $V_{BE} = 0.6$ V, we have

$$V_{BE} = V_B - R_E(I_C + I_B) = 0.6\ \text{V}$$

Since $I_C = \beta\ I_B$,

$$I_B = \frac{1.58 - 0.6}{50\times(75 + 1)} = 0.258\ \text{mA}$$

$$I_C = \beta\ I_B = 75\times0.258\ \text{mA} = 19.35\ \text{mA}$$

The voltage at the collector is

$$V_C = V_{CC} - I_C R_L = 8.065\ \text{V}$$

and

$$V_{CE} = V_C - V_E = 8.065 - R_E I_E = 7.08\ \text{V}$$

(b) The AC equivalent circuit is shown below

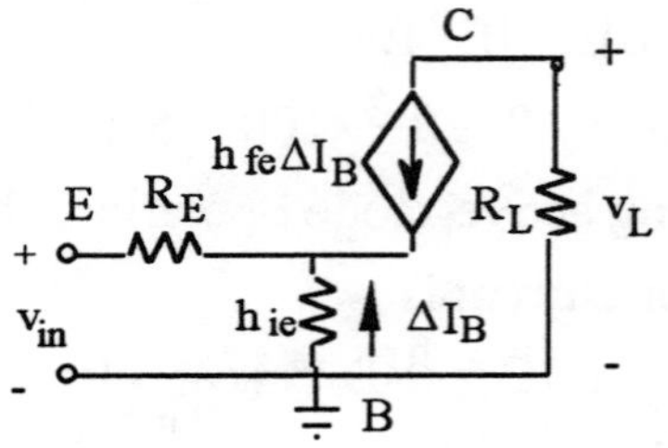

(c)

$$h_{ie} = \frac{\partial V_{BE}}{\partial i_B}\Big|_{I_{BQ}} \approx \frac{0.6}{0.258\times10^{-3}} = 2.3k\Omega$$

$$h_{fe} = \beta = 75$$

$$R_E \| h_{ie} = 48.94\ \Omega$$

The voltage gain is

$$A_V = \frac{h_{fe} R_L (R_E \| h_{ie})}{R_E h_{ie}} = 3.2$$

(d) The input resistance r_i is

$$r_i = \frac{h_{ie}}{h_{fe} + 1} + R_E = 80.26\ \Omega$$

(e) The output resistance r_o is

$$r_o = \frac{1 + h_{fe}}{h_{oe}} = \frac{76}{10\times10^{-6}} = 7.6\ \text{M}\Omega$$

9.10

(a) With $R_B = 60\ k\Omega$ and $V_B = 3$ V,

applying KVL, we have

$$3 = I_B R_B + 0.6 + (1 + \beta) I_B R_E$$

$$I_B = \frac{2.4}{60k\Omega + 101 R_E}$$

$$I_E = 101 \frac{2.4}{60k\Omega + 101 R_E} = 1mA$$

Therefore,

$$R_E = \frac{101 \times 2.4 - 60}{101} = 1.81\ k\Omega$$

(b) $V_{CE} = 15 - I_C R_C - I_E R_E$

From (a), we have

$$I_C = I_E \frac{\beta}{\beta + 1} = 0.99\ mA$$

Therefore,

$$R_C = \frac{15 - 5 - 1.81}{0.99} = 8.27\ k\Omega$$

(c) The small signal equivalent circuit is shown below

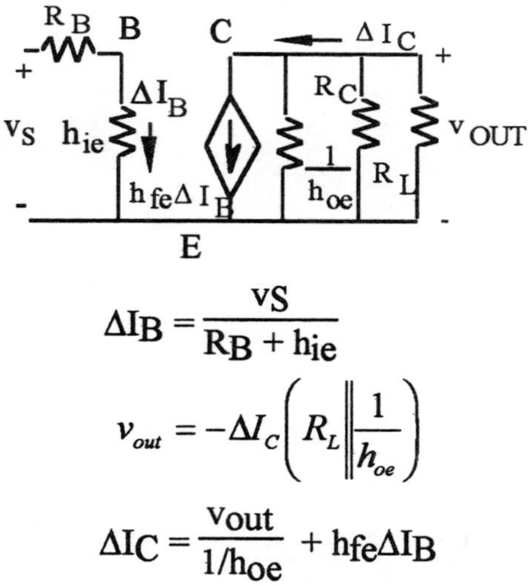

(d) $$\Delta I_B = \frac{v_S}{R_B + h_{ie}}$$

$$v_{out} = -\Delta I_C \left(R_L \middle\| \frac{1}{h_{oe}} \right)$$

$$\Delta I_C = \frac{v_{out}}{1/h_{oe}} + h_{fe} \Delta I_B$$

$$h_{ie} = \frac{\partial V_{BE}}{\partial i_B}\bigg|_{I_{BQ}} = \frac{0.6}{0.0099 \times 10^{-3}} = 60.6k\Omega$$

Since h_{oe} is not given, we can reasonably assume that $1/h_{oe}$ is very large. Therefore,

$$A_V = \frac{v_{out}}{v_S} = -\frac{100 \times R_L}{R_B + h_{ie}} = -4.15$$

9.11

(a) $V_B = V_{CC}\dfrac{R_2}{R_1 + R_2} = 6.1 \text{ V}$

$$R_B = R_1 \parallel R_2 = 3749.87\ \Omega$$

Assuming $V_{BE} = 0.6$ V, we have

$$V_E = V_B - V_{BE} = 5.5 \text{ V}$$

$$I_E = \frac{V_E}{R_E} = 22 \text{ mA}$$

$$I_B = \frac{I_E}{\beta + 1} = 0.088 \text{ mA}$$

and

$$V_{CE} = V_C - V_E = (V_{CC} - R_C I_C) - 5.5$$

$$= 15 - 200\times 21.912\times 10^{-3} - 5.5 = 5.12 \text{ V}$$

(b) The AC equivalent circuit is shown below

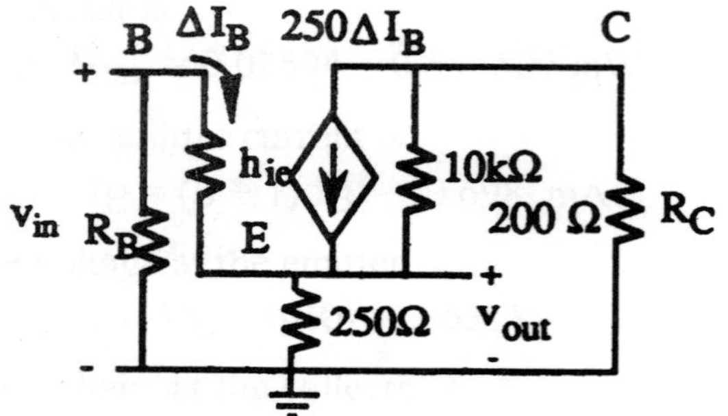

(c) $h_{ie} = \dfrac{\partial V_{BE}}{\partial_B}\Big|_{I_{BQ}} \approx \dfrac{0.6}{0.088\times 10^{-3}} = 6.82k\Omega$

$$v_{out} = R_E(\Delta I_B + \Delta I_C) = 250(250 + 1)\Delta I_B$$

$$v_{in} = \Delta I_B h_{ie} + v_{out} =$$

$$= \Delta I_B h_{ie} + 250\times 251\Delta I_B$$

Therefore, the voltage gain is

$$A_V = \frac{v_{out}}{v_{in}} = 0.902 \quad \text{and}$$

$$i_{out} = \Delta I_B + \Delta I_C = (\beta + 1)\Delta I_B$$

$$i_{in} = \Delta I_B + \frac{v_{in}}{R_B} =$$

$$= \Delta I_B + \frac{\Delta I_B h_{ie} + 250\times 251\Delta I_B}{R_B}$$

and the current gain is

$$\frac{i_{out}}{i_{in}} = \frac{(\beta+1)\Delta I_B}{\Delta I_B + \dfrac{\Delta I_B h_{ie} + 250\times 251\Delta I_B}{R_B}} = 12.84$$

(d) To find the input resistance we compute:

$$v_{in} = \Delta I_B h_{ie} + 250\times 251\Delta I_B$$

$$i_{in} = \Delta I_B + \frac{\Delta I_B h_{ie} + 250\times 251\Delta I_B}{R_B}$$

Therefore. the input resistance is

$$r_i = \frac{6820 + 250\times 251}{1 + \dfrac{6820 + 250\times 251}{3749.87}} = 3558\ \Omega$$

(e) To find the output resistance we compute

$$v_{out} = R_E(\Delta I_B + \Delta I_C) = 250(250 + 1)\Delta I_B$$

$$i_{out} = (\beta + 1)\Delta I_B$$

Therefore, the output resistance is

$$r_o = \frac{250(250 + 1)\Delta I_B}{(250 + 1)\Delta I_B} = 250\ \Omega$$

9.12

(a) With $V_{CE} = 0.3$ V, $V_{BE} = 0.9$ V and $V_{BATT} = 13$ V, $T_C = 100°$, from Figure P9.6(d), we have $K_C = 0$, $VCIT = \frac{16}{13} = 1.23$ ms. The signal duration is:

$$\tau = 1\times10^{-3}\times0 + 1.23\times10^{-3} = 1.23 \text{ ms}$$

When V_{signal} is applied, the base current is

$$I_B = \frac{V_{BATT}}{80} = 0.1625 \text{ A}$$

Thus, the transistor will be in the saturation region. Therefore,

$$V_{inj} = V_{BATT} - V_{CE} = 13 - 0.3 = 12.7 \text{ V}$$

The time constant of the injector circuit is:

$$\tau' = \frac{L}{R} = 0.1 \text{ ms} << \tau = 1.23 \text{ ms}$$

As $V_{signal} = 0$, the transistor is in the cut-off region. The differential equation governing the injector current is:

$$1\times10^{-3}\frac{dI_{inj}}{dt} + 10I_{inj} = V_{inj},$$

and $I_{inj}(0) = 0$. Thus,

$$I_{inj} = \frac{V_{inj}}{10} - \frac{V_{inj}}{10}e^{-10000t}$$

The time when $I_{inj} \geq 0.1$ is then found to be

$$t_{inj} = -\frac{\ln\frac{1.17}{1.27}}{10^4} = 8.2 \text{ } \mu s$$

That is, 8.2 ms after the V_{signal} is applied, the fuel will be injected into the intake manifold.

(b) From Figure P9.6(d), we have

$K_C = -\frac{1}{60}T_C + \frac{5}{3}$; at $T_C = 20$, $K_C = \frac{4}{3}$.

Also, $VCIT = \frac{16}{8.6} = 1.86$ ms

The signal duration therefore is

$$\tau = 1\times10^{-3}\times\frac{4}{3} + 1.86\times10^{-3} = 3.19 \text{ ms}$$

When V_{signal} is applied, the base current is

$$I_B = \frac{V_{BATT}}{80} = 0.1075 \text{ A}$$

Thus, the transistor will be in the saturation region. Therefore,

$$V_{inj} = V_{BATT} - V_{CE} = 8.6 - 0.3 = 8.3 \text{ V}$$

The time constant of the injection circuit is:

$$\tau' = \frac{L}{R} = 0.1 \text{ ms} << \tau = 3.19 \text{ ms}$$

When V_{signal} is 0, the transistor is in the cut-off region. Using the same differential equation and initial condition as in part (a),

$$I_{inj} = \frac{V_{inj}}{10} - \frac{V_{inj}}{10}e^{-10000t}$$

The time when $I_{inj} \geq 0.1$ can be found as

$$t = 12.84 \text{ } \mu s$$

That is, 12.84 μs after the V_{signal} is applied, the fuel will be injected into the intake manifold.

9.13

Applying KVL around the base-emitter circuit:

$$V_S = I_B(20 + 450) + 0.75 + (\beta + 1)I_B R_E$$

Assuming β is still valid for the transistor in the saturation region, we have

$$I_B = 0.898 \text{ mA}$$

When V_S is zero, the relay is open.

The collector current is

$$I_C = \beta\, I_B = 89.8 \text{ mA}$$

The power dissipated in the transistor is

$$P_t = I_C V_{CE} = 89.8\times 0.3 = 26.9 \text{ mW}$$

The power dissipated in the relay is 0.5 W, therefore, the maximum power dissipated in the circuit is

$$P_{max} = 0.02694 + 0.5 = 527 \text{ mW}$$

(b) The emitter current is

$$I_E = (\beta + 1)\, I_B = 90.698 \text{ mA}$$

The voltage at the emitter is

$$V_E = I_E R_E = 3.63 \text{ V}$$

The voltage at the collector is

$$V_C = 0.3 + 3.63 = 3.93 \text{ V}$$

Therefore, $V_R = V_{CC} - V_C = 8.07 \text{ V}$

The equation for the collector current is determined by the dynamic behavior of the inductor, and is therefore a differential equation, with initial and final conditions $i_C(0) = 89.8 \text{ mA}$, $i_C(\infty) = 0$:

$$L\frac{di_C}{dt} + i_C(R_{W1} + R_{W2}) = V_R$$

$$V_R = V_{CC} - 0.3 - i_C R_E$$

$$\frac{di_C}{dt} + 440 i_C = 117$$

Solving the differential equation, we find:

$$i_C(t) = 0.266 - 0.176e^{-440t}$$

When V_R is less than 2.4 V, the relay will be open. Therefore,

$$V_R = V_{CC} - 0.3 - i_C R_E$$

$$= 11.7 - 40\times(0.266 - 0.176e^{-440t}) < 2.4 \text{ V}$$

That is

$$e^{-440t} < 0.197$$

$$t > 3.69 \text{ ms}$$

Thus, it will take 3.69 ms for the relay to switch from closed to open.

9.14

From the power dissipation of the relay,

$$P = 0.5 = \frac{V^2}{R_W} \text{ W},$$

we can compute

$$R_W = 50\ \Omega$$

When v_S is 5 V, the transistor is in the saturation region and the relay current at steady state is:

$$I_R = \frac{5.5 - 0.2}{50} = 106 \text{ mA}$$

When v_S is 0 V, the transistor will be in cut off, and we have the following equation

$$0.005\frac{dI_R}{dt} + 50\ I_R = 0$$

That is

$$\frac{dI_R}{dt} + 10\times10^3 I_R = 0$$

Solving the above equation with $I_R(0) = 0.106$ A,

$$I_R(t) = 0.106e^{-10000t}$$

$$v_R(t) = -25\ I_R = -2.65e^{-10000t}$$

The relay will be cut-off as soon as v_S is 0.

Therefore, the switching frequency will be the frequency of the input signal v_S.

9.15

(a) The AC circuit is shown below

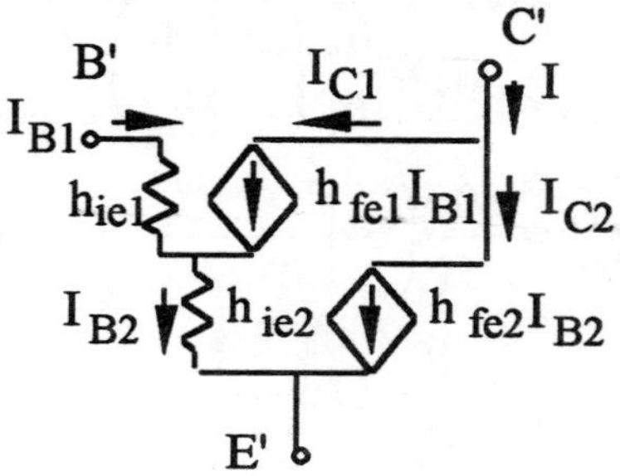

The current gain is

$$A_i = \frac{I}{I_{B1}} = \frac{I_{C1} + I_{C2}}{I_{B1}}$$

$$= \frac{I_{C1}}{I_{B1}} + \frac{I_{C2}}{I_{B2}}$$

$$= h_{fe1} + \frac{h_{fe2}I_{B2}}{I_{B1}}$$

$$= h_{fe1} + h_{fe2}\frac{I_{E1}}{I_{B1}}$$

$$= h_{fe1} + h_{fe2}(h_{fe1} + 1)\frac{I_{B1}}{I_{B1}} = 9300$$

(b) We have

$$V_{in} = I_{B1}h_{ie1} + (I_{B1} + h_{fe1}I_{B1})h_{ie2}$$

Therefore, the input resistance is

$$R_{in} = \frac{V_{in}}{I_{B1}} = h_{ie1} + (1 + h_{fe1})h_{ie2}$$

$$= 1500 + 131\times200 = 27.7\ \text{k}\Omega$$

9.16

(a) Using Table 9.2,

$$A_v = \frac{h_{fe}}{h_{ie}}\left(R_C \left\| \frac{1}{h_{oe}}\right.\right)$$

$$A_{v_{max}} = \frac{500}{15k}\left(6k \left\| \frac{1}{30\times10^{-6}}\right.\right) = 169.5$$

$$A_{v_{min}} = \frac{40}{1k}\left(6k \left\| \frac{1}{1\times10^{-6}}\right.\right) = 240$$

(b) Using Table 9.2,

$$A_i = h_{fe}\frac{R_B}{R_B + h_{ie}}$$

$$R_B = 10k \| 20k = 6.67k\Omega$$

$$A_{i_{max}} = 500\frac{6.67}{6.67+15} = 153.9$$

$$A_{i_{min}} = 40\frac{6.67}{6.67+1} = 34.78$$

9.17

For $V_{CEQ} = 5$, $V_{R_C} + V_{R_E} = 20V$.

Assume $I_C \approx I_E$.

$$I_C = \frac{20}{2.5k} = 8mA \Rightarrow V_E = 8V$$

$$V_B = 8 + 0.7 = 8.7V$$

For $\beta = 20$, $I_B = \frac{8}{20} = 0.4mA$.

For $\beta = 50$, and $I_C \le 8.8mA$,

$$I_B \le \frac{8.8}{50} = 0.176mA$$

$$V_B = 8.8 + 0.7 = 9.5V$$

$$V_B - 0.4\times10^{-3}R_B = 8.7$$

$$V_B - 0.176\times10^{-3}R_B = 9.5$$

Solving, $R_B = 5.35k\Omega$.

$$V_B = 9.84V$$

Since $V_B = \frac{R_1}{R_1+R_2}V_{CC} = \frac{R_1}{R_1+R_2}(25)$

and $R_B = \frac{R_1R_2}{R_1+R_2}$, we can solve for

$R_1 = 8.82k\Omega$ and $R_2 = 13.59k\Omega$.

9.18

Assume $V_{CE_{max}} \approx 23V$ and $V_{CE_{min}} \approx 3V$.
Then V_{CEQ} should be set to the middle of this range, or $V_{CEQ} = \frac{23+3}{2} = 13V$.

From KVL,

$$1000I_{EQ} + V_{CEQ} + 1500I_{CQ} = 25$$

or,

$$1000(\beta+1)I_{BQ} + V_{CEQ} + 1500(\beta)I_{BQ} = 25$$

Solving,

$$251000I_{BQ} = 25 - 13 = 12$$

$$\therefore I_{BQ} = 47.81\mu A$$

$$V_{EQ} = 1000(\beta+1)I_{BQ} = 4.829V$$
$$V_{BQ} = V_{EQ} + V_{BE} = 5.529V$$

Again from KVL,

$$R_1\left(I_{R_2} - I_{BQ}\right) = V_{BQ} \Rightarrow R_1(I_{R_2} - 47.81\mu A) = 5.529$$

and

$$R_2 I_{R_2} + V_{BQ} = 25 \Rightarrow R_2 I_{R_2} = 25 - 5.529 = 19.471$$

Choose a typical value for R_2, say $R_2 = 10k\Omega$. Then,

$$I_{R_2} = \frac{19.471}{R_2} = 1.947mA$$

and

$$R_1 = \frac{5.529}{1.947mA - 47.81\mu A} = 2911\Omega$$

9.19

Construct a load line. For $v_{DS} = 0$, $i_D = \frac{-30}{500} = -60mA$, and for $i_D = 0$, $v_{DS} = -30V$.

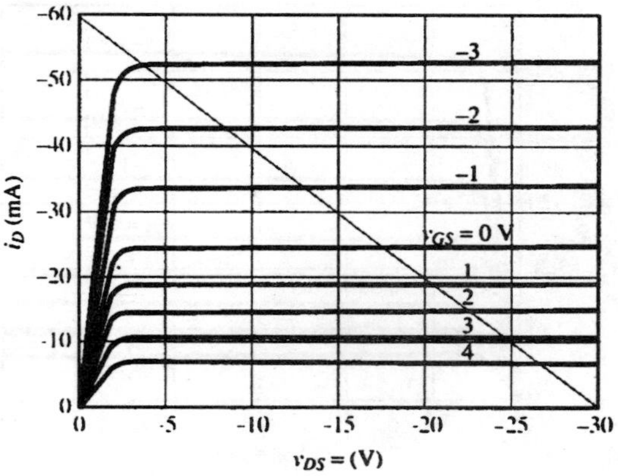

The intersection with $v_{GS} = 0$ occurs at $v_{DS} \approx -17.5V$, $i_D \approx -25mA$.

9.20

Construct a load line. For $v_{DS} = 0$, $i_D = \frac{-15}{330} = -45.4mA$, and for $i_D = 0$, $v_{DS} = -15V$.

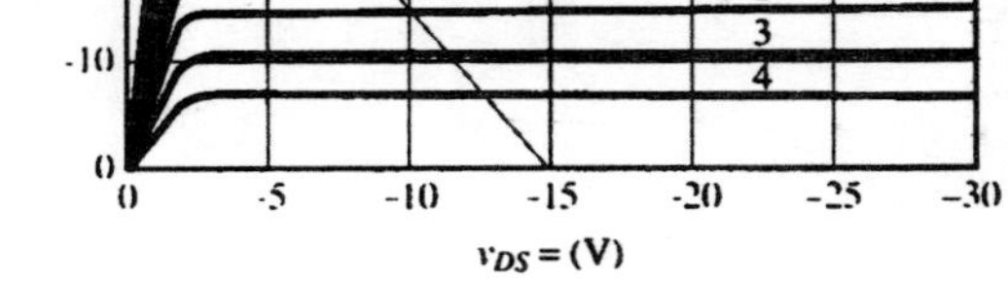

The intersection with $v_{GS} = 0$ occurs at $v_{DS} \approx -7V$, $i_D \approx -25mA$.

9.21

Construct a load line. For $v_{DS} = 0$,

$i_D = \frac{-50}{1.5k} = -33.3mA$, and for $i_D = 0$,

$v_{DS} = -50V$.

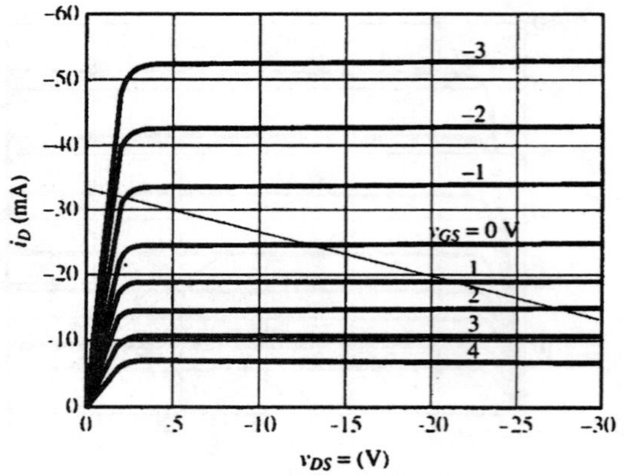

The intersection with $v_{GS} = 0$ occurs at $v_{DS} \approx -13V$, $i_D \approx -25mA$.

9.22

The load line must intersect $v_{GS} = 0$ at $v_{DS} = -12.5V$, $i_D = -25mA$. The slope of the line must be $-\frac{1}{R_D} = -\frac{1}{1k\Omega} = -1\frac{mA}{V}$.

The intersection with the v_{DS} axis will then occur at

$$V_{DD} = -12.5 + 25\left(-1\frac{V}{mA}\right) = -37.5V.$$

9.23

The load line must intersect $v_{GS} = 0$ at $v_{DS} = -12.5V$, $i_D = -25mA$. The slope of the line must be $-\frac{1}{R_D} = -\frac{1}{2k\Omega} = -\frac{1}{2}\frac{mA}{V}$.

The intersection with the v_{DS} axis will then occur at

$$V_{DD} = -12.5 + 25\left(-2\frac{V}{mA}\right) = -62.5V.$$

9.24

$v_{DSQ} = -17.5V$, $i_{DQ} = -25mA$ from Problem 9.19. When $v_{GS} = +1V$, $v_{DS} \approx -21V$, and $i_D \approx -19mA$. When $v_{GS} = -1V$, $v_{DS} \approx -13V$ and $i_D \approx -34mA$. The curves are sketched below.

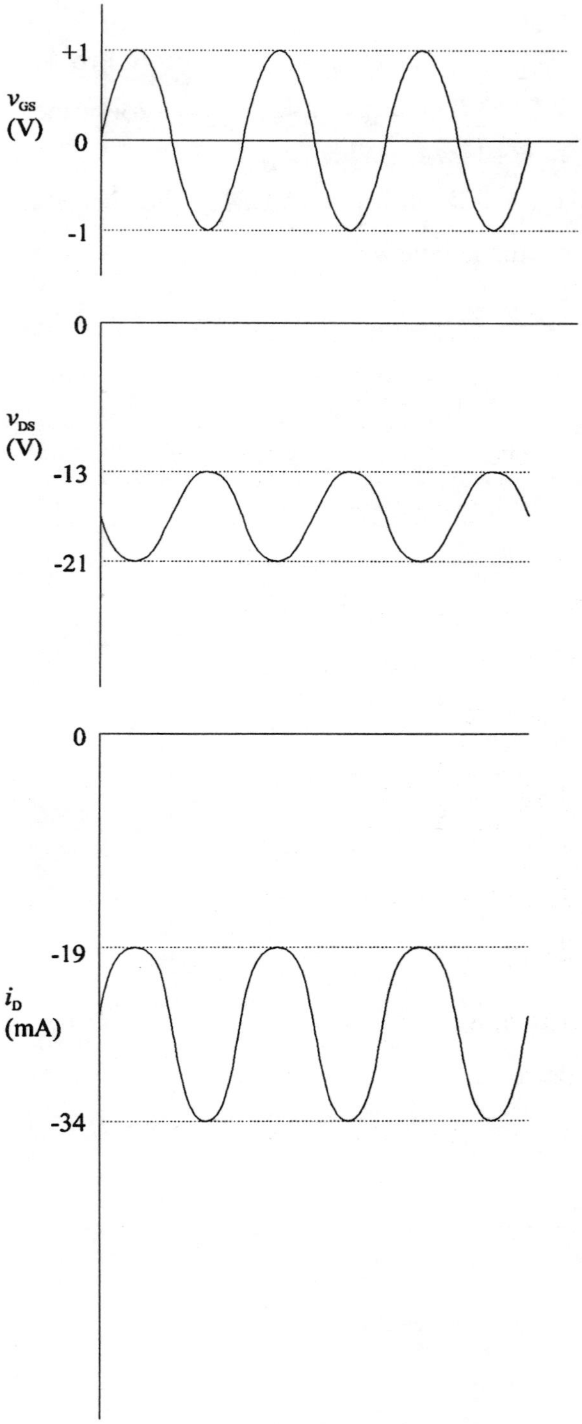

$$A_v \approx \frac{\Delta v_{DS}}{\Delta v_{GS}} = \frac{-13-(-21)}{1-(-1)} = \frac{8}{2} = 4$$

9.25

$v_{DSQ} = -17.5V$, $i_{DQ} = -25mA$ from Problem 9.19. When $v_{GS} = +3V$, $v_{DS} \approx -24V$, and $i_D \approx -11mA$. When $v_{GS} = -3V$, $v_{DS} \approx -3V$ and $i_D \approx -53mA$. The curves are sketched below.

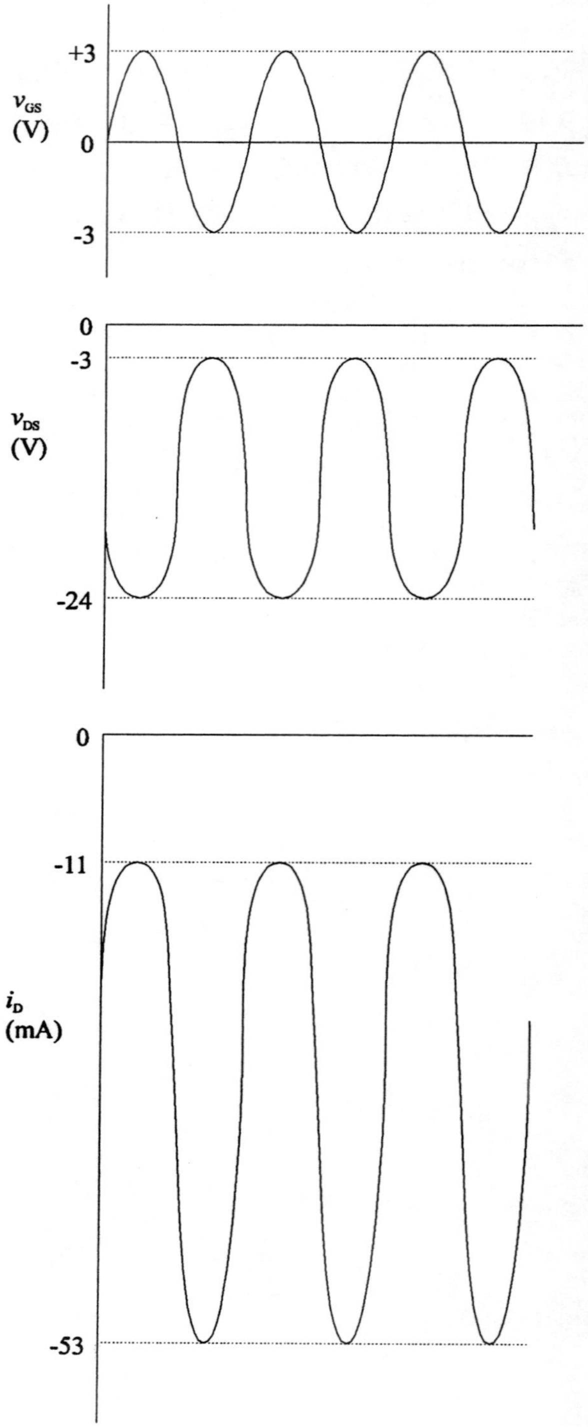

$$A_v \approx \frac{\Delta v_{DS}}{\Delta v_{GS}} = \frac{-3-(-24)}{3-(-3)} = \frac{21}{6} = 3.5$$

9.26

$v_{DSQ} = -7V$, $i_{DQ} = -25mA$ from Problem 9.20. When $v_{GS} = +1V$, $v_{DS} \approx -8V$, and $i_D \approx -19mA$. When $v_{GS} = -1V$, $v_{DS} \approx -3V$ and $i_D \approx -34mA$. The curves are sketched below.

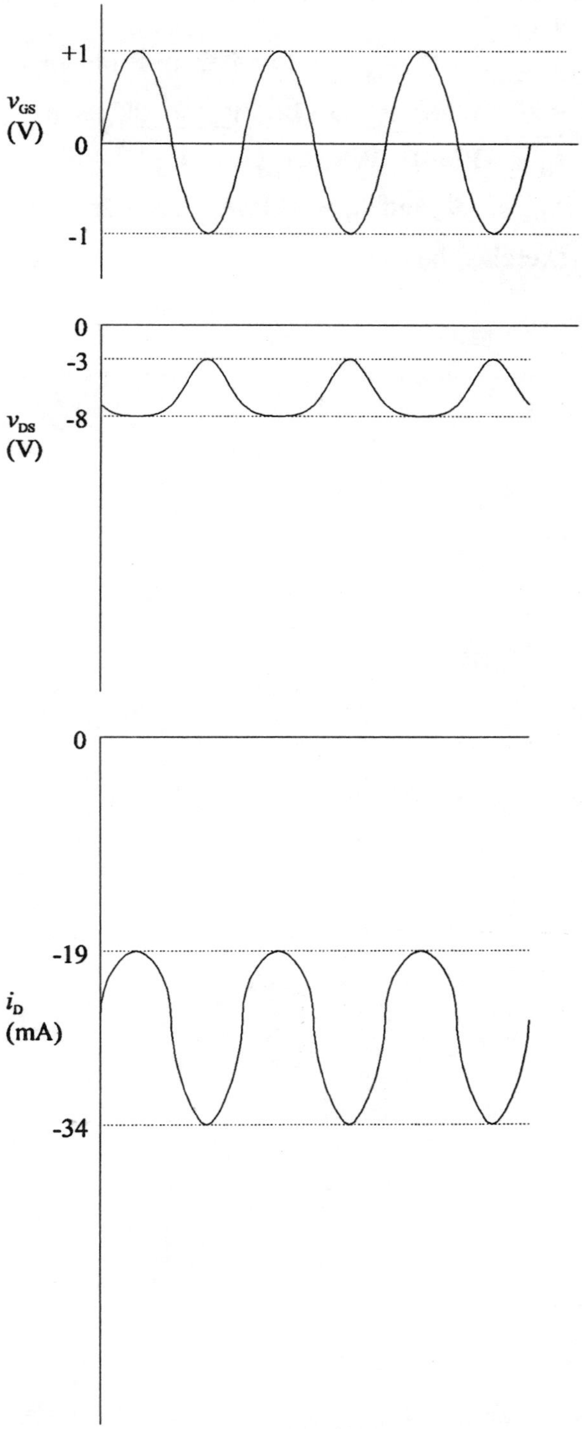

$$A_v \approx \frac{\Delta v_{DS}}{\Delta v_{GS}} = \frac{-3-(-8)}{1-(-1)} = \frac{5}{2} = 2.5$$

9.27

$v_{DSQ} = -7V$, $i_{DQ} = -25mA$ from Problem 9.20. When $v_{GS} = +1V$, $v_{DS} \approx -8V$, and $i_D \approx -19mA$. When $v_{GS} = -1V$, $v_{DS} \approx -3V$ and $i_D \approx -34mA$. The curves are sketched below.

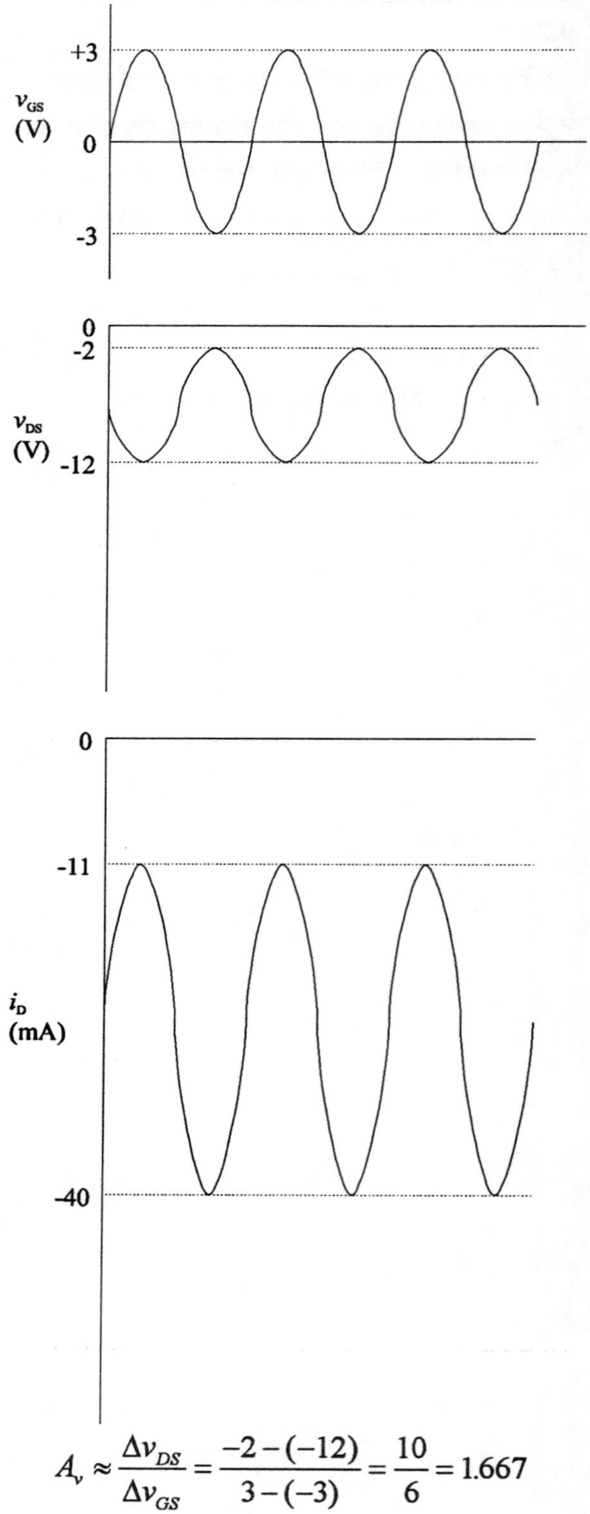

$$A_v \approx \frac{\Delta v_{DS}}{\Delta v_{GS}} = \frac{-2-(-12)}{3-(-3)} = \frac{10}{6} = 1.667$$

9.28

From the load line of Problem 9.19, we find that when v_{GS} increases from -1V to +1V, i_D increases from -34mA to -19mA.

Therefore,

$$g_m \approx \frac{\Delta i_D}{\Delta v_{GS}} = \frac{-19-(-34)}{1-(-1)} = \frac{15}{2} = 7.5mS$$

and

$$\mu = -g_m R_D = -(7.5\times 10^{-3})(500) = -3.75$$

9.29

Construct a state table:

v_1	v_2	Q_1	Q_2	Q_3	v_{o1}	v_{o2}
0	0	off	off	on	5V	0
0	5V	off	on	off	0	5V
5V	0	on	off	off	0	5V
5V	5V	on	on	off	0	5V

This table clearly describes an OR gate when the output is taken at v_{o2}.

9.30

See the state table constructed for Problem 9.29. This table clearly describes a NOR gate when the output is taken at v_{o1}.

9.31

Construct a state table:

v_1	v_2	Q_1	Q_2	Q_3	v_{o1}	v_{o2}
0	0	off	off	on	0	5V
0	5V	off	on	on	0	5V
5V	0	on	off	on	0	5V
5V	5V	on	on	off	5V	0

This table clearly describes an AND gate when the output is taken at v_{o1}.

9.32

See the state table constructed for Problem 9.31. This table clearly describes a NAND gate when the output is taken at v_{o2}.

9.33

$i_C = \frac{5 - 0.2}{2000} = 2.4$ mA, therefore, $i_B = i_C/\beta$ $= 0.24$ mA. $(v_{in})_{min} = 2.0$ V and $(v_{in})_{max} =$ 5.0 V, therefore, applying KVL:

$$-v_{in} + R_B i_B + 0.6 = 0$$

or

$R_B = \frac{v_{in} - 0.6}{i_B}$, substituting for $(v_{in})_{min}$ and $(v_{in})_{max}$, we find the following range for R_B:

$$5{,}833\ \Omega \le R_B \le 18{,}333\ \Omega$$

9.34

a) v_{in} is low $\Rightarrow$ Q1 is cutoff $\Rightarrow v_B = 5$ V $\Rightarrow$ Q2 is in saturation $\Rightarrow v_{out} = \text{low} = 0.2$ V.

b) v_{in} is high $\Rightarrow$ Q1 is in saturation $\Rightarrow v_B =$ 0.2V $\Rightarrow$ Q2 is cutoff $\Rightarrow v_{out} = \text{high} = 5$ V.

9.35

$i_{C2} = 5/R_{C2} = 2.5$ mA, therefore, $i_B = 2.5/\beta$ mA. Applying KVL:

$-5 + R_B i_{B1} + 0.6 + 0.6 + 0.6 = 0$, therefore, $i_{B1} = 0.64$ mA.

$i_{E1} = \beta_1 i_{B1} = 600/500 + i_{B2}$

or $\quad 0.64\,\beta_1 = 1.2 + 2.5/\beta_2$.

Choose $\beta_2 = 10 \Rightarrow \beta_1 = 2.27$

9.36

$i_{B1} = 3.2/4000 = 0.8$ mA $\Rightarrow i_{C1} = 3.2$ mA

Applying KCL:

$600/500 + i_{B2} = 3.2 \Rightarrow i_{B2} = 2$ mA

$i_{C2} = \beta i_{B2} = 8$ mA

Applying KVL:

$5 - 0.2 = .008\, R_{C2} \Rightarrow R_{C2} = 600\ \Omega$

9.37

This circuit performs the function of a 2-input NAND gate. The analysis is similar to Example 9.11.

9.38

Q_2 and Q_3 conduct, while Q_4 is cut off.

$v_{B1} = 1.8$ V, $v_{B2} = 1.2$ V, $v_{B3} = 0.6$ V, and $v_{C2} = v_{out} = 0.2$ V

9.39

v2	v1	Q1	Q2	Vo
L	L	L	L	L
L	H	H	L	H
H	L	L	H	H
H	H	H	H	H

L : Low; H : High

9.40

The two transistors at the top are cut off and the two at the bottom are on.

9.41

From the top two, the left transistor is off and the right transistor is on. From the bottom two, the last one is off, and the one before is on.

9.42

The output of Figure 9.59 is connected as an input to the circuit of Figure 9.55.

9.43

The output of Figure 9.66 is connected as an input to the circuit of Figure 9.55.

9.44

This is shown in Figure P9.20.

9.45

The output of the circuit of Figure 9.48 should be connected as an input to the circuit of Figure P9.15.

9.46

Construct a state table.

v_{in}	Q_1	Q_2	v_{out}
low	resistive	open	high
high	open	resistive	low

This table clearly describes an inverter.

9.47

Construct a state table.

v_1	v_2	Q_1	Q_2	v_{out}
0	0	off	off	high
0	high	off	on	low
high	0	on	off	low
high	high	on	on	low

This table clearly describes a NOR gate.

9.48

Construct a state table.

v_1	v_2	Q_1	Q_2	v_{out}
0	0	off	off	high
0	high	off	on	high
high	0	on	off	high
high	high	on	on	low

This table clearly describes a NAND gate.

Power Electronics

Chapter 10 Instructor Notes

This chapter introduces the subject of power electronics. This chapter can be covered immediately after section 8.3, if so desired, since it depends solely on material presented in Chapters 7 and 8. The importance of power electronics cannot be overemphasized, considering the widespread industrial application of electric motors, relays, and other high current loads in practical engineering applications. The chapter discusses the basic characteristics and limitations of power amplifiers, practical voltage regulators, inductive loads (such as electric motors), and SCRs. The aim is to give the student sufficient understanding of the device characteristics to be able to complete simple "order of magnitude" calculations to be able to size a device for a given application. This chapter is much more practically oriented than some of the others in the text.

Homework problems include two different voltage regulator circuits (10.2, 10.3) and a battery charging circuit (10.7), in addition to several other practical applications.

Chapter 10 problem solutions

10.1

Calculating the collector and base currents according to:

$$I_E = \frac{7 - 1.3}{10} = 0.57 \text{ A}$$

$$I_B = \frac{I_E}{11} = 51.8 \text{ mA}$$

We find

$$I_R = \frac{20 - 7}{47} = 0.277 \text{ A}$$

$$I_Z = I_R - I_B = 0.225 \text{ A}$$

$V_{CE} = 20 - V_L = 20 - 5.7 = 14.3 \text{ V} > 0.6 \text{ V}$

Thus, the transistor is in the active region.
The Zener power is $i_Z v_Z = 1.576$ W.

10.2

Assuming that the Zener voltage is V_Z, that $V_{BE} = V_\gamma = 0.6$ V, and that the required current is I, we have:

$$R_S = \frac{V_Z + V_{BE}}{I} = \frac{V_Z + 0.6}{I}$$

10.3

If the Zener diode is to be in the regulator mode, the CB junction must be forward biased; in this case, both the CB and the BE junctions are forward biased, since a substantial base current will be generated through the Zener diode (depending on the value of the shunt resistor in the output circuit). Thus, the collector-emitter voltage is equal to $V_{CEsat} \approx 0.2$ V, and the source current will be:

$$I_S = \frac{V_S - V_{CEsat}}{R_S} = I_C + I_Z$$

The voltage across the shunt resistor will therefore be V_γ, and the output voltage is:

$$V_{out} = V_Z + V_\gamma.$$

10.4

When the sinusoidal source voltage is in the positive half cycle, the series diode conducts, and the shunt diode is an open circuit; thus, the positive half cycle appears directly across the capacitor (assuming ideal diodes). During the negative half cycle, the series diode is open, and therefore the voltage across the capacitor remains zero, as shown in the sketches below.

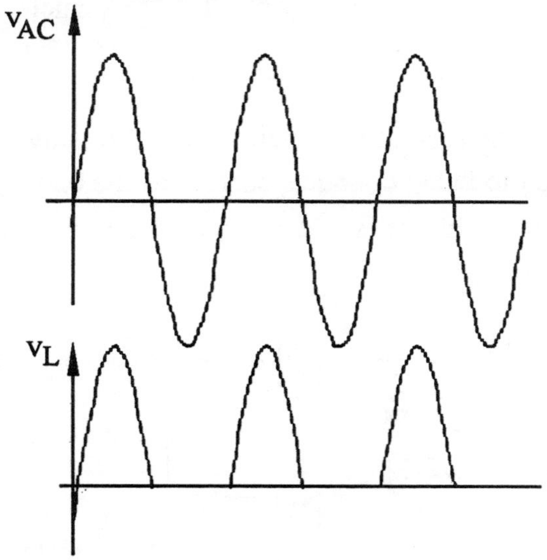

10.5

To obtain exact numerical values, we assume a 110 Vrms source, R = 10 Ω, and L = 2 H; then:

$$v_{AC}(t) = A \sin(\omega t) = 155.6 \sin(377\, t)$$

and from equation 10.6, the average load current is:

$$I_L = \frac{155.6}{\pi R} = 4.95 \text{ A}$$

Using the approximation

$$v_L(t) \approx \frac{A}{2} + \frac{A}{2} \sin \omega t$$

we have

$$v_L(t) \approx \frac{A}{2} + \frac{A}{2} \sin \omega t = 77.8 + 77.8 \sin(377\, t)$$

The waveform is shown below.

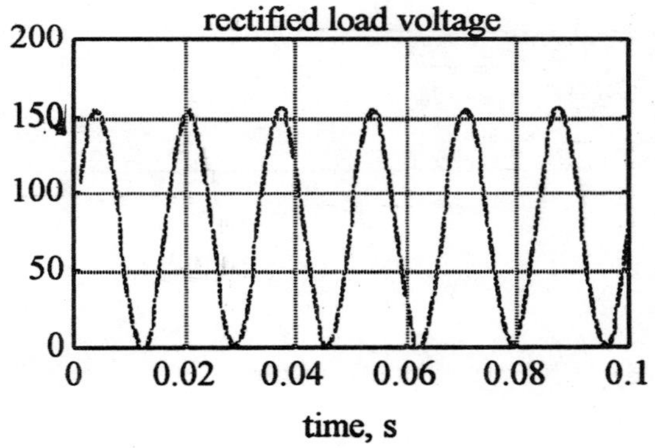

10.6

(a) Assume $v_{AC} = 10 \sin\omega t$ V

The output voltage is

$$v_L(t) = (10 - 0.7) \sin\omega t$$

The waveform is shown below.

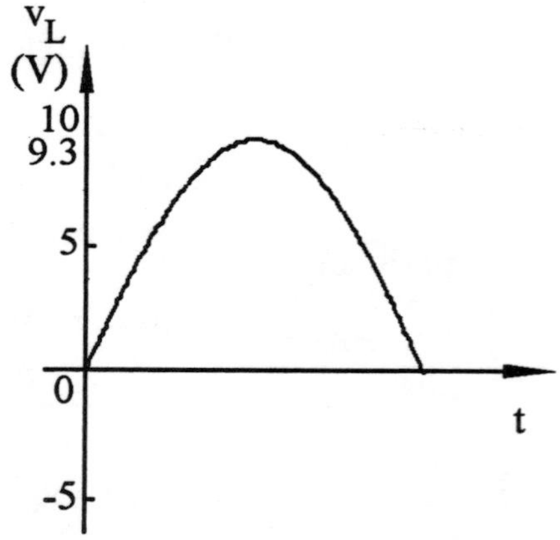

(b) $\langle v_L \rangle \approx \frac{1}{2\pi} \int_0^{\pi} 9.3 \sin(\omega t)\, d(\omega t)$

$$= \frac{9.3}{\pi} = 2.96 \text{ V}$$

10.7

(a) The positive half cycle from w1 is conducted by diode D_1. Diode D_2 does not conduct due to negative bias at w2. The first half cycle is passed through to the battery.

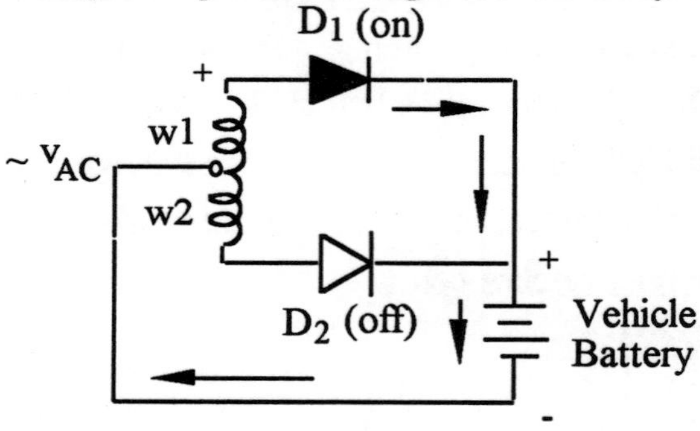

(b) The second half cycle finds w2 positive and diode D_2 conducts current to the battery while diode D_1 is negatively biased and is off.

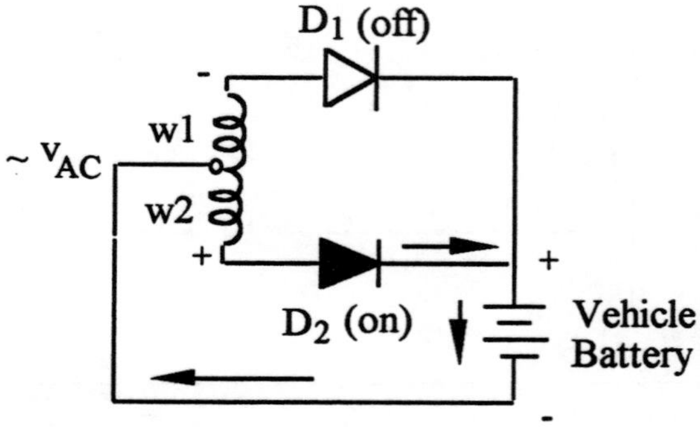

(c) The full-wave rectified output waveform is shown below.

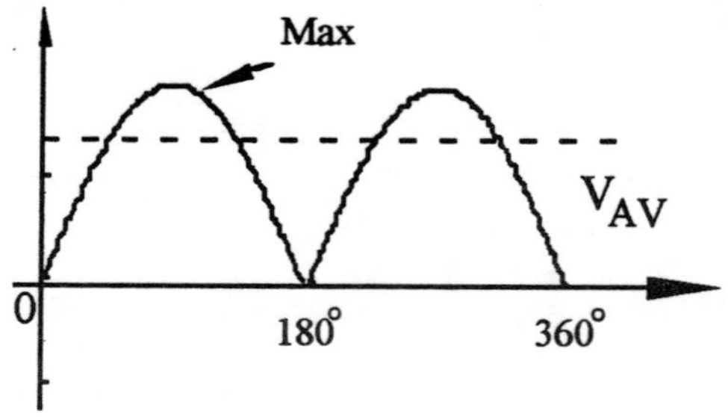

The average DC value V_{AV} is 63% of the peak value.

10.8

(a) For $\alpha = \frac{\pi}{3}$, we have

$$v_L\left(\frac{\pi}{3}\right) = \frac{120\sqrt{2}}{2}\sqrt{1-\frac{1}{3}+\sin\frac{2\pi}{3}} = 105V$$

The power is

$$P = \frac{vL^2}{R} = 45.94 \text{ W}$$

(b) For $\alpha = \frac{\pi}{6}$, we have

$$v_L\left(\frac{\pi}{6}\right) = \frac{120\sqrt{2}}{2}\sqrt{1-\frac{1}{6}+\sin\frac{\pi}{3}} = 110.6V$$

The power is

$$P = \frac{vL^2}{R} = 50.97 \text{ W}$$

10.9

(a)

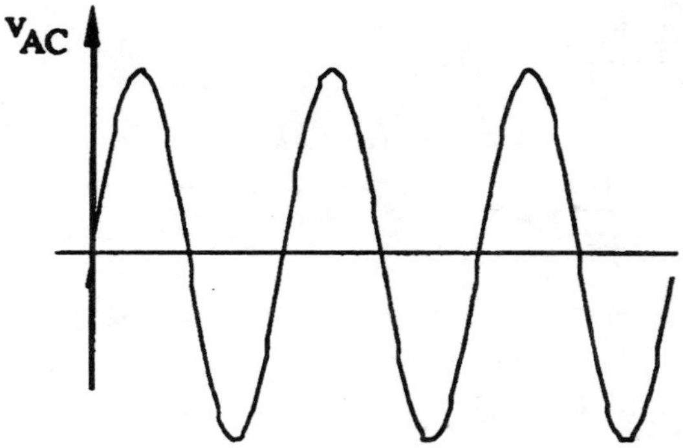

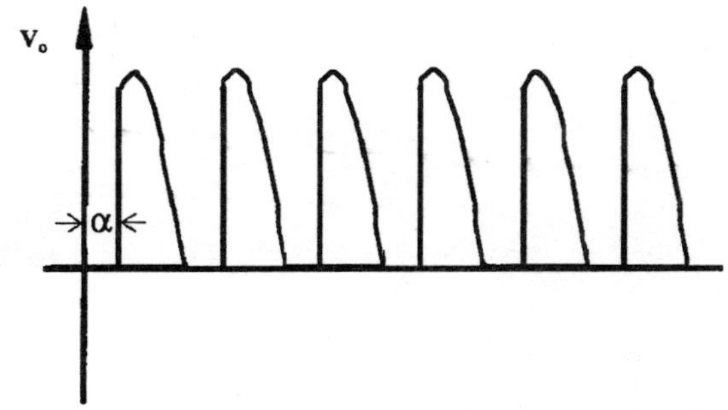

$$\alpha = 60 \times \frac{\pi}{180} = \frac{\pi}{3}, \quad R_a = 0.2\Omega$$

(b)

$$V_{o_{rms}} = \frac{120\sqrt{2}}{2}\left[1-\frac{1}{3}+\sin 120^\circ\right]^{\frac{1}{2}} = 105V$$

$$P_m = I_o V_{o_{rms}} = (20A)(105V) = 2.1kW$$

(c)

$$P_R = I_o^2 R_a = (20)^2(0.2) = 80W$$

$$P_S = P_m + P_R = 2180W$$

10.10

Back emf $= 0.055 \times 1000 = 55V$

$$I_{DC} = \frac{4000}{110} = 36.4A$$

$V = 110V$. Assume $R = 1\Omega$.

$$I_{DC} = \frac{1}{\pi R}\left[\sqrt{2}V(\cos\alpha) - V_B(\pi - \alpha)\right]$$

(a) $36.4 = \frac{1}{\pi}\left[\sqrt{2}(110)\cos\alpha - 55(\pi - \alpha)\right]$

Solving yields $\alpha \approx \frac{7}{12}\pi$ rad.

(b) With zero ripple, $I_{rms} = I_{DC} = 36.4A$.

10.11

Note that,

$$V_{L_{rms}} = \frac{120}{\sqrt{2}}\sqrt{1 - \frac{\alpha}{\pi} + \sin 2\alpha}\,, \quad \text{for } \alpha \le 90^\circ$$

and

$$V_{L_{rms}} = \frac{120}{\sqrt{2}}\sqrt{1 - \frac{\alpha}{\pi} + \frac{\sin 2\alpha}{2\pi}}\,, \quad \text{for } a > 90^\circ$$

α	$V_{L_{rms}}$	$P = \frac{V_{L_{rms}}^2}{R_{BULB}}$
0°	84.85	30
30°	110.60	50.98
60°	105.00	45.98
90°	60.00	15.00
120°	37.53	5.87
150°	14.41	0.87
180°	0	0

A sketch of power vs. firing angle is shown below:

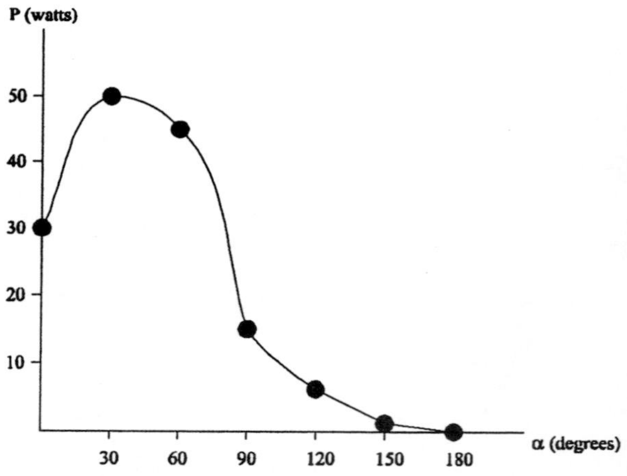

10.12

(a)

$$v_o = i_o R_a + E_a = (125)(0.15) + 6 = 24.75V$$

$$24.75 = \delta(120) \Rightarrow \delta = \frac{24.75}{120} = 0.2063$$

$$\delta = \frac{t_1}{T} \Rightarrow t_1 = \delta T = (0.2063)\left(\frac{1}{250}\right) = 825\mu s$$

(b)

$$P_m = E_a i_o = (6V)(125A) = 750W$$

$$P_R = R_a i_o^2 = (0.15)(125)^2 = 2.344kW$$

(c) $P_S = P_m + P_R = 3.094kW$

or

$$P_S = \delta V_S i_o = (0.2063)(120V)(125A) = 3.094kW$$

10.13

(a) Assume $R_a = 0.2\Omega$. Then,

$$v_o = E_a + i_o R_a = 240 + (-300)(0.2) = 180V$$

$$\delta = \frac{180V}{600V} = 0.300$$

(b)

$$P_m = E_a i_o = (240V)(-300A) = -72.0kW$$

$$P_R = R_a i_o^2 = (0.2\Omega)(-300A)^2 = 18kW$$

$$P_S = P_m + P_R = -54.0kW$$

or

$$P_S = \delta V_S i_o = (0.300)(600V)(-300A) = -54.0kW$$

10.14

$$\langle v_o \rangle = \frac{t_1}{T} V_S = \frac{t_1}{t \cdot t_1} V_S = \frac{1}{t} V_S = \delta V_S$$

The last section of the chapter is devoted to a discussion of the principal performance [illegible]its of the operational amplifier. Since the student will not be prepared to fully comprehend the [illegible]ason for the saturation, limited bandwidth, limited slew rate, and other shortcomings of practical [illegible]-amps, the section fo[illegible] desc[illegible] effects of these limitations, and on identifying the r[illegible]levant parameters o[illegible] of typical op-amps. Thus, the student is trained to r[illegible]gnize these limit[illegible] in the design of practical amplifier circuits. Since [illegible] of these limitat[illegible] low frequency app[illegible] (and extremely [illegible]ul) to supplement [illegible] laboratory exercises.

[illegible] homework [illegible] levels of [illegible]culty; many of thes[illegible] extensions of the circu[illegible] examples [illegible] will find that problem 11.41 [illegible] practical limitation of charge [illegible] and the charge amplifier [illegible] problem 11.41.

In a one-semester cou[illegible] stimulating curiosity [illegible] pursue further study in electronics or instrumentation [illegible] the chapter is the centerpiece of the book.

[1] Rizzoni, G., A Practical Introduction to Elect[illegible], Prentice-Hall, 199[illegible]
[2] Doebelin E. O., Measurement Systems, McGraw-Hill, Fourth Edition, 199[illegible]

Operational Amplifiers

Chapter 11 Instructor Notes

Chapter 11 introduces the notion of integrated circuit electronics through the most common building block of electronic instrumentation, the operational amplifier. This is, in practice, the area of modern electronics that is most likely to be encountered by a practicing non-electrical engineer. Thus, the aim of the chapter is to present a fairly complete ***functional*** description of the operational amplifier, including a discussion of the principal limitations of the op-amp and of the effects of these limitations on the performance of op-amp circuits employed in measuring instruments and in signal conditioning circuits. The material presented in this chapter lends itself particularly well to a series of laboratory experiments (see for example [1]), which can be tied to the lecture material quite readily.

After a brief introduction, in which ideal amplifier characteristics are discussed, open- and closed- loop models of the op-amp are presented in section 11.2; the use of these models is illustrated by application of the basic circuit analysis methods of Chapters 2 and 3, Thus, the Instructor who deems it appropriate can cover the first two sections in conjunction with the circuit analysis material. A brief, intuitive discussion of feedback is also presented to explain some of the properties of the op-amp in a closed-loop configuration. The closed-loop models include a fairly detailed first discussion of the inverting, non-inverting and differential amplifier circuits; however, the ultimate aim of this section is to ensure that the student is capable of recognizing each of these three configurations, so as to be able to quickly determine the closed loop gain of practical amplifier circuits. The section is sprinkled with various practical examples, introducing practical op-amp circuits that are actually used in practical instruments: the summing amplifier, the voltage follower (Example 11.2), an electrocardiogram amplifier (Example 11.3), the instrumentation amplifier (Example 11.4), the level shifter (Example 11.5), and a transducer calibration circuit (Example 11.6). In a survey course, the first two sections might be sufficient to introduce the device.

Section 11.3 presents the idea of active filters; this material can also be covered quite effectively together with the frequency response material of Chapter 6 to reinforce these concepts. Section 11.4 discusses integrator and differentiator circuits, and presents a practical application of the op-amp integrator in the charge amplifier (Example 11.9). This example is of particular relevance to the non-electrical engineer, since charge amplifiers are used to amplify the output of piezo-electric transducers in the measurement of strain, force, torque and pressure (for additional material on piezo-electric transducers, see, for example, [2]). A brief section (11.5) is also provided on analog computers, since these devices are still used in control system design and evaluation. Coverage of sections 11.4 and 11.5 is not essential to the material that follows.

The last section of the chapter is devoted to a discussion of the principal performance limits of the operational amplifier. Since the student will not be prepared to fully comprehend the reason for the saturation, limited bandwidth, limited slew rate, and other shortcomings of practical op-amps, the section focuses on describing the effects of these limitations, and on identifying the relevant parameters on the data sheets of typical op-amps. Thus, the student is trained to recognize these limits, and to include them in the design of practical amplifier circuits. Since some of these limitations are critical even in low frequency applications, it is easy (and extremely useful) to supplement this material with laboratory exercises.

The homework problems present a variety of interesting problems at varying levels of difficulty; many of these problems extend the ideas presented in the text, and present practical extensions of the circuits discussed in the examples. The instrumentation oriented instructor will find that problem 11.41 is a nice extension of Example 11.9, and illustrates a very important practical limitation of charge amplifiers. An entire lecture could be devoted to the ideal integrator and the charge amplifier by expanding the material in section 11.4 with an explanation of problem 11.41.

In a one-semester course, Chapter 11 can serve as a very effective closing of the course, by stimulating curiosity towards integrated circuit electronics, and by motivating the student to pursue further study in electronics or instrumentation. In many respects this chapter is the centerpiece of the book.

[1] Rizzoni, G., A Practical Introduction to Electronic Instrumentation, Kendall-Hunt, 1989
[2] Doebelin E. O., Measurement Systems, McGraw-Hill, Fourth Edition, 1987.

Chapter 11 problem solutions

11.1

(a) Using nodal analysis we can see that in the circuit of Figure P11.1(a)

$$\frac{v1}{3} + \frac{v1}{6} + \frac{v1 - vg}{6} = 0$$

or $$v1 = \frac{vg}{4}$$

(b) For the circuit of Figure P11.1(b),

$$v6k\Omega + v6k\Omega = vg$$

and the non-inverting terminal voltage is

$$v6k\Omega = \frac{vg}{2}$$

Since the circuit shown is a non-inverting amplifier with unity gain (see pp. 550-551), the output voltage, v_1, is equal to the non-inverting terminal voltage:

$$v1 = \frac{vg}{2}$$

11.2

From KCL and the properties of the ideal op-amp:

$$\frac{v_i}{R_1} + \frac{v_o}{R_2} = 0$$

From this equation, then:

$$\frac{v_o}{v_i} = -\frac{R_2}{R_1} \Rightarrow A_v = -\frac{R_2}{R_1}$$

11.3

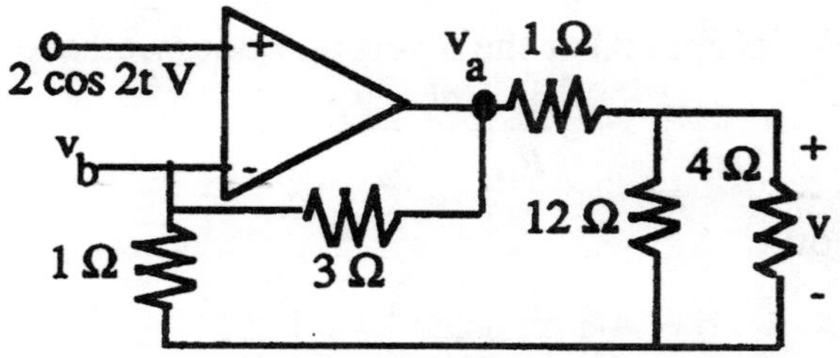

Since the op-amp attempts to maintain zero voltage difference between the inverting and the non-inverting terminal,

$$v_b = 2\cos 2t$$

But $v_b = v_a \frac{1}{1+3}$, and

$$v_a = 4\, v_b = 8\cos 2t$$

Using nodal analysis:

$$\left(1 + \frac{1}{12} + \frac{1}{4}\right) v = v_a$$

or $$v = \frac{12}{16}\, v_a = 6\cos 2t \text{ V}$$

11.4

From the properties of the ideal op-amp and KCL applied at the inverting node, we have:

$$\frac{v_i}{R_1} + \frac{v_i - v_o}{R_2} = 0$$

or

$$v_i\left(\frac{1}{R_1} + \frac{1}{R_2}\right) = v_o\left(\frac{1}{R_2}\right)$$

from which we have

$$\frac{v_o}{v_i} = \frac{\left(\frac{1}{R_2}\right)}{\left(\frac{R_2 + R_1}{R_1 R_2}\right)} = \frac{R_1}{R_2 + R_1}$$

Therefore,

$$A_v = \frac{R_1}{R_2 + R_1}$$

11.5

Using nodal analysis for the circuit shown:

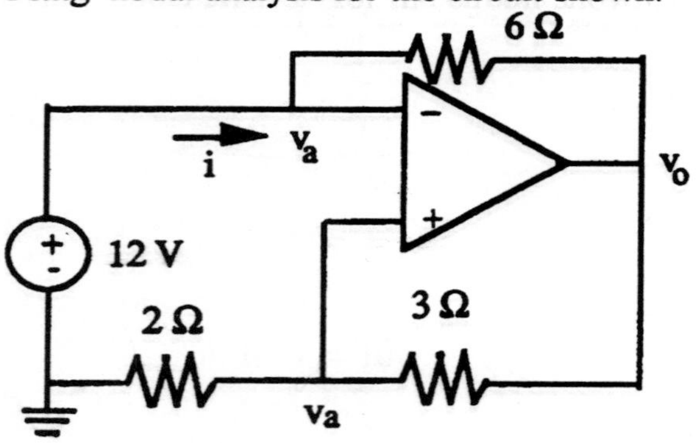

$$v_a = 12 \text{ V}$$

$$\left(\frac{1}{2} + \frac{1}{3}\right)v_a - \frac{1}{3}\, v_o = 0$$

or $\quad v_o = 30$ V

Thus $\quad i = \frac{12 - 30}{6} = -3$ A

EIT 11.6

Looking at the figure, we can immediately see that $v_2 = 0$ V. Using nodal analysis:

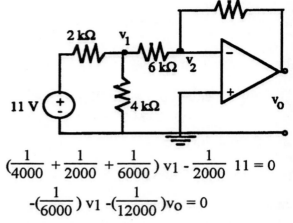

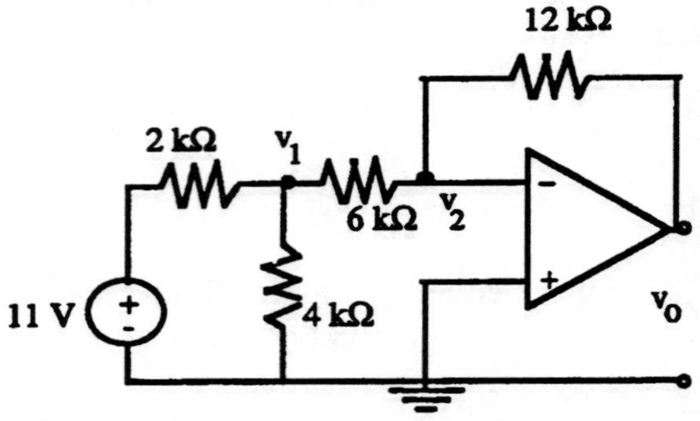

$$\left(\frac{1}{4000} + \frac{1}{2000} + \frac{1}{6000}\right) v_1 - \frac{1}{2000}\, 11 = 0$$

$$-\left(\frac{1}{6000}\right) v_1 - \left(\frac{1}{12000}\right) v_o = 0$$

Solving for v_1 and v_o,

$$v_1 = 6 \text{ V}$$

and $\quad v_o = -12$ V

EIT 11.7

Using nodal analysis:

$$-\left(\frac{1}{2}\right)10 - \left(\frac{1}{4} + \frac{1}{6}\right) v_o = 0$$

or $\quad v_o = -12$ V

Therefore,

$$i = -\left(-\frac{12}{6}\right) = 2 \text{ A}$$

11.8

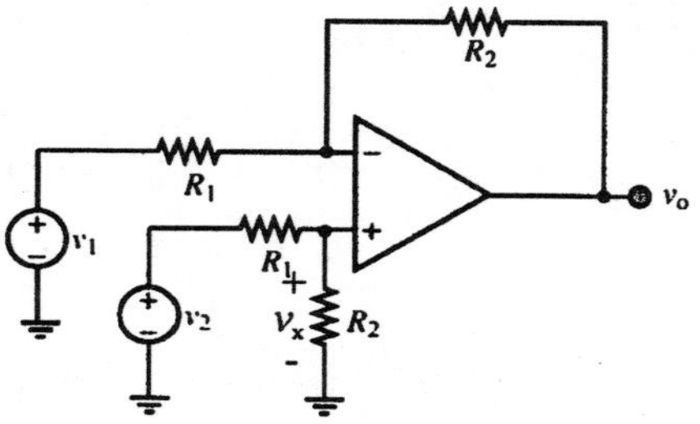

Define voltage v_x as shown. Then, applying KCL at the inverting node,

$$\frac{v_x - v_1}{R_1} + \frac{v_x - v_o}{R_2} = 0$$

or

$$v_x\left(\frac{1}{R_1} + \frac{1}{R_2}\right) = v_1\left(\frac{1}{R_1}\right) + v_o\left(\frac{1}{R_2}\right)$$

Applying KCL at the non-inverting node,

$$\frac{v_x - v_2}{R_1} + \frac{v_x}{R_2} = 0$$

or

$$v_x\left(\frac{1}{R_1} + \frac{1}{R_2}\right) = v_2\left(\frac{1}{R_1}\right)$$

Since the left-hand sides of these two equations are equal, the right-hand sides must be equal. Therefore,

$$v_2\left(\frac{1}{R_1}\right) = v_1\left(\frac{1}{R_1}\right) + v_o\left(\frac{1}{R_2}\right)$$

or

$$v_o = \frac{R_2}{R_1}(v_2 - v_1)$$

11.9

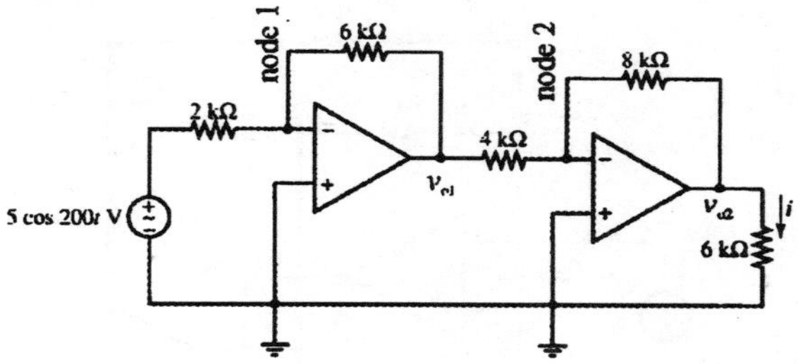

Applying KCL at node 1,

$$\frac{v_i}{2k\Omega} + \frac{v_{o1}}{6k\Omega} = 0$$

or

$$v_{o1} = -\frac{6}{2}v_i = -3 \times 5\cos 200t = -15\cos 200t \text{ V}$$

Applying KCL at node 2,

$$\frac{v_{o1}}{4k\Omega} + \frac{v_{o2}}{8k\Omega} = 0$$

or

$$v_{o2} = -\frac{8}{4}v_{o1} = -2 \times (-15\cos 200t) = 30\cos 200t \text{ V}$$

$$\therefore i = \frac{v_{o2}}{6k\Omega} = \frac{30\cos 200t}{6000} = 5\cos 200t \text{ mA}$$

11.10

Applying KCL at the inverting terminal:

$$v3 = (1 + \frac{Rf}{R})v^-$$

Applying KCL at the noninverting terminal:

$$\left(\frac{1}{R_2} + \frac{1}{R_1}\right)v^+ - \frac{1}{R_2}v_2 - \frac{1}{R_1}v_1 = 0$$

or $$v^+ = \frac{R1}{R1 + R2}v2 + \frac{R2}{R1 + R2}v1$$

therefore,

$$v3 = (1 + \frac{Rf}{R})\left(\frac{R1}{R1 + R2}v2 + \frac{R2}{R1 + R2}v1\right)$$

and the circuit does indeed compute the weighted sum of the inputs.

11.11

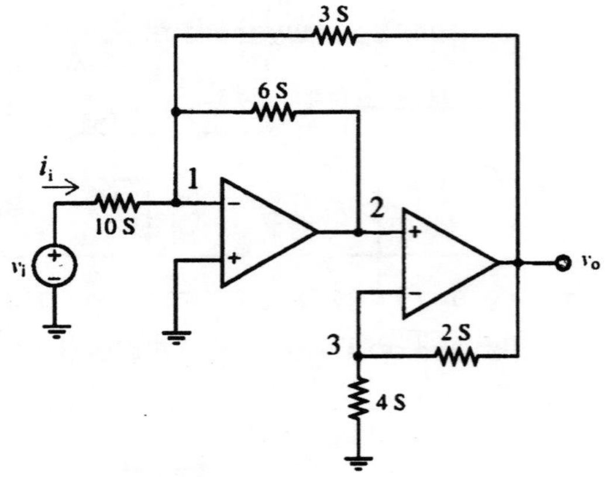

From KCL at node 1:

$$10v_i + 6v_2 + 3v_o = 0$$

Note that $v_3 = v_2$ and, therefore, at node 3:

$$4v_2 + 2(v_2 - v_o) = 0$$

or

$$v_2 = \frac{2}{6}v_o = \frac{1}{3}v_o$$

Combining the two equations,

$$10v_i + 6\left(\frac{1}{3}v_o\right) + 3v_o = 0$$

or

$$\frac{v_o}{v_i} = -\frac{10}{5} = -2$$

$$\therefore A_v = -2$$

Also, note that

$$i_i = 10v_i$$

and

$$G = \frac{10v_i}{v_i} = 10S$$

11.12

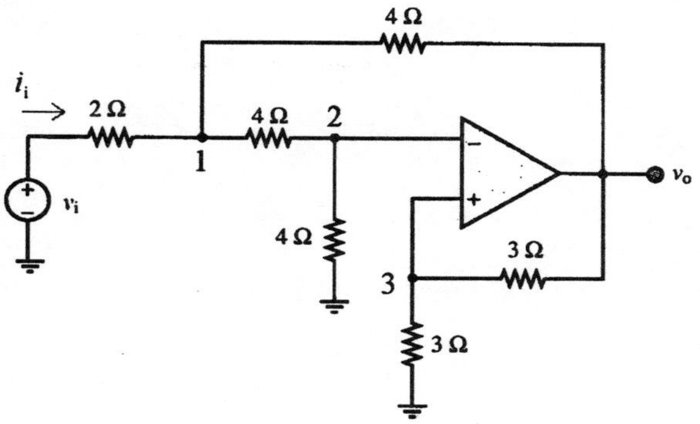

Applying KVL at node 1:

$$\frac{v_1 - v_i}{2} + \frac{v_1 - v_2}{4} + \frac{v_1 - v_o}{4} = 0$$

or

$$-2v_i + 4v_1 - v_2 = v_o \qquad (1)$$

Again, at node 2:

$$\frac{v_2 - v_1}{4} + \frac{v_2}{4} = 0$$

or

$$2v_2 = v_1 \qquad (2)$$

Similarly, at node 3:

$$\frac{v_2}{3} + \frac{v_2 - v_o}{3} = 0$$

or

$$v_2 = \frac{1}{2}v_o \qquad (3)$$

Substituting (3) into (2):

$$v_o = v_1$$

Substituting (2) and (3) into (3):

$$-2v_i = v_o + \frac{1}{2}v_o - 8\left(\frac{1}{2}v_o\right)$$

or

$$\frac{v_o}{v_i} = \frac{4}{5}$$

$$\therefore A_v = \frac{4}{5}$$

Now, since

$$i_i = \frac{v_i - v_1}{2} = \frac{v_i - v_o}{2} = \frac{v_i - \frac{4}{5}v_i}{2} = \frac{1}{8}v_i$$

then

$$G = \frac{i_i}{v_i} = \frac{1}{8}S$$

11.13

Apply KCL at the inverting input:

$$\frac{v_i}{R_1} + \frac{v_{ab,oc}}{R_2} = 0$$

$$\therefore V_T = v_{ab,oc} = -\frac{R_2}{R_1} v_i$$

To find R_T, connect a short circuit between nodes *a* and *b*. Then, KCL yields the following:

$$\frac{v_i}{R_1} + i_{sc} = 0 \Rightarrow i_{sc} = -\frac{v_i}{R_1}$$

$$\therefore R_T = \frac{v_{ab,oc}}{i_{sc}} = \frac{-\frac{R_2}{R_1} v_i}{-\frac{1}{R_1} v_i} = R_2$$

EIT 11.14

(a) The circuit can be reduced to the following form using Thèvenin equivalent circuits:

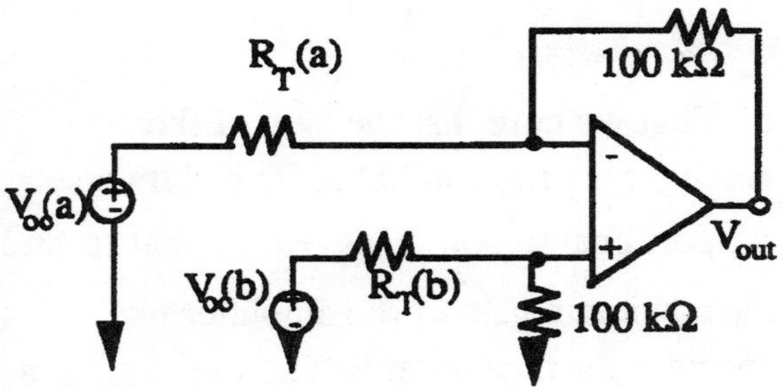

The equivalent circuit seen at the inverting node (node a) is:

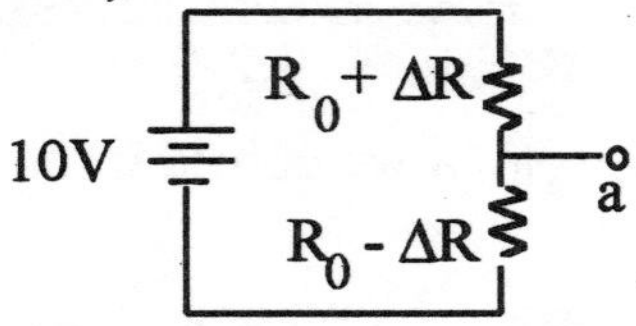

$$R_o - |\Delta R| = R_o(1 - \frac{|\Delta R|}{R_o})$$

$$R_o + |\Delta R| = R_o(1 + \frac{|\Delta R|}{R_o})$$

The Thèvenin (open circuit) voltage is:

$$V_{OC}(a) = \frac{R_o(1 - \frac{|\Delta R|}{R_o})V_S}{R_o(1 + \frac{|\Delta R|}{R_o} + 1 - \frac{|\Delta R|}{R_o})}$$

$$= \frac{(1 + \frac{|\Delta R|}{R_o})V_S}{2}$$

and the Thèvenin resistance is:

$$R_T(a) = R_o(1 + \frac{|\Delta R|}{R_o}) \parallel R_o(1 - \frac{|\Delta R|}{R_o})$$

$$= \frac{R_o}{2}(1 - (\frac{|\Delta R|}{R_o})^2)$$

The equivalent circuit seen at the non-inverting node (node b) is:

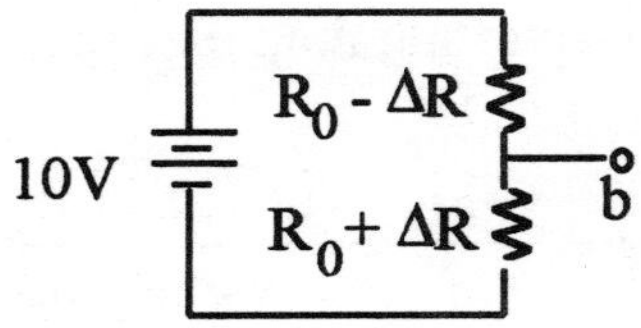

The Thèvenin (open circuit) voltage is:

$$V_{OC}(b) = \frac{(1 + \frac{|\Delta R|}{R_o})V_S}{2}$$

$$R_T(b) = \frac{R_o}{2}(1 - (\frac{|\Delta R|}{R_o}))$$

Assuming $|\Delta R|^2 << R_o$,

$$V_{OC}(a) = (1 - \frac{|\Delta R|}{R_o})\ 5\ \text{V}$$

$$R_T(a) = 500\ \Omega$$

$$V_{OC}(b) = (1 + \frac{|\Delta R|}{R_o})\ 5\ \text{V}$$

$$R_T(b) = 500\ \Omega$$

(b) For a difference amplifier:

$$V_{out} = \frac{R_f}{R_S}(V_{OC}(b) - V_{OC}(a))$$

$$= \frac{10^5}{500}(V_{OC}(b) - V_{OC}(a))$$

$$= 200(5)\{1 + \frac{|\Delta R|}{R_o} - [1 - \frac{|\Delta R|}{R_o}]\}$$

$$= 2|\Delta R|$$

But if $|\Delta R| = K\Delta T$, then

$$V_{out} = 2\ K\Delta T\ \text{V}$$

11.15

For a non-inverting amplifier the voltage gain is given by

$$A_V = \frac{v_{out}}{v_{in}} = \frac{R_f + R_S}{R_S} = \frac{R_f}{R_S} + 1$$

$$A_{Vnom} = 16 = \frac{R_f}{R_S} + 1$$

$$R_S = \frac{R_f}{16-1} = \frac{15K}{15} = 1000 = 1\ k\Omega$$

To find the maximum and minimum R_S we note that $R_S \propto \frac{1}{A_V}$, so to find the maximum R_S we consider the minimum A_V

$$R_{Smax} = \frac{15\ k\Omega}{16(1-0.02)-1} = 1.02\ k\Omega$$

Conversely to find the minimum R_S we must use the maximum voltage gain.

$$R_{Smin} = \frac{15K\Omega}{16(1+0.02)-1} = 980\Omega$$

Since a standard 5% tolerance 1-kΩ resistor has resistance $950 < R < 1050$, a standard resistor will suffice in this application.

11.16

a) The gain of the inverting amplifier is

$$A_V = -\frac{R_f}{R_S}$$

$$= \frac{-33k}{1.2k} = -27.5$$

b) First we note that the gain of the amplifier is proportional to R_f and inversely proportional to R_S. This tells us that to find the maximum gain of the amplifier we consider the maximum R_f and the minimum R_S.

$$|A_V|_{max} = \frac{R_{fmax}}{R_{Smin}} = \frac{33+0.1(33)}{1.2-0.1(1.2)} = 33.6$$

c) To find $|A_V|_{min}$ we consider the opposite case.

$$|A_V|_{min} = \frac{R_{fmin}}{R_{Smax}} = \frac{33-0.1(33)}{1.2+0.1(1.2)} = 22.5$$

EIT 11.17

The key is to recognize that we actually have two inverting amplifiers here and that our output voltage is defined as $v_2 - v_1$.

$$v_1 = -\frac{R_{f1}}{R_{S1}} v_S = -\frac{47}{10} v_S$$

$$v_1 = -4.7 v_S$$

$$v_2 = -\frac{R_{f2}}{R_{S2}} v_1 = -\frac{R_{f2}}{R_{S2}}(-4.7 v_S)$$

$$= -\frac{10}{10}(-4.7 v_S) = 4.7 v_S$$

$$v_0 = v_2 - v_1 = 4.7 v_S - (-4.7 v_S)$$

$$= v_S(4.7 + 4.7)$$

$$\frac{v_0}{v_S} = A_V = 9.4$$

11.18

The simplest way to approach this circuit is to break it up into parts, as shown below.

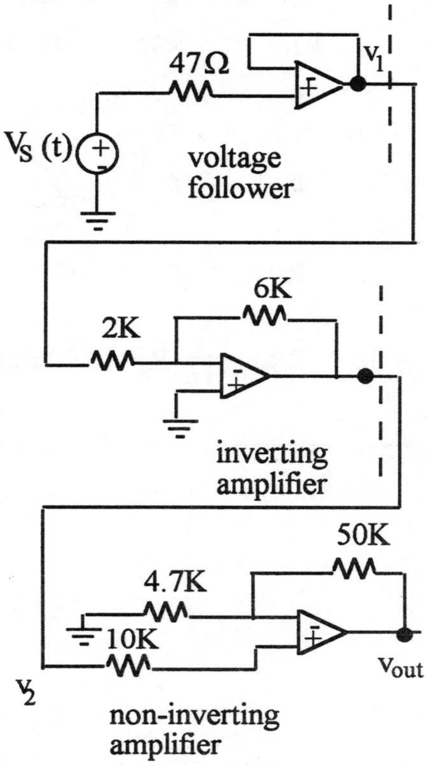

First we note that $v_1 = v_S(t)$ since the op-amp is configured as a voltage follower.

Next, we see that

$$v_2 = v_1\left(-\frac{R_f}{R_S}\right) = v_S\left(-\frac{6}{2}\right) = -3v_S$$

Since no current can flow into the non-inverting terminal of an (ideal) op-amp, the voltage drop across the 10-kΩ resistor is zero. Thus,

$$v_{out} = \left(\frac{R_f}{R_S}+1\right)v_2 = \left(\frac{R_f}{R_S}+1\right)(-3v_S)$$

$$v_{out} = \left(\frac{50}{4.7}+1\right)(-3v_S) = -0.35\cos\omega t$$

11.19

a) The circuit may be modelled as shown:

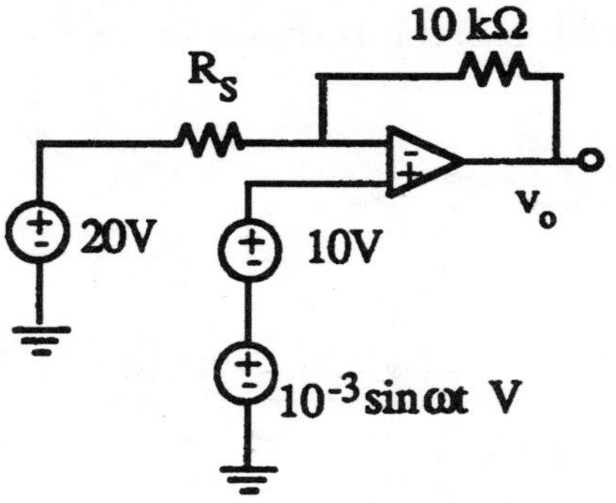

Applying the principle of superposition:

For the 20-V source:

$$v_o\big|_{20} = \frac{-10k\Omega}{R_S}(20)$$

For the 10-V source:

$$v_o\big|_{10} = \left(\frac{10k\Omega}{R_S}+1\right)(10)$$

The total DC output is:

$$v_o\big|_{DC} = v_o\big|_{20} + v_o\big|_{10}$$

$$= -\frac{10{,}000}{R_S}(20) + \left(\frac{10{,}000}{R_S}+1\right)(10) = 0$$

Solving for R_S

$$\frac{10{,}000}{R_S}(10\text{-}20) = -\,10$$

$$R_S = 10\ k\Omega$$

b) Since we have already determined R_S such that the DC component of the output will be zero, we can simply treat the amplifier as if the AC source were the only source present. Therefore,

$$v_o(t) = 0.001\ \sin\omega t\left(\frac{R_f}{R_S}+1\right)$$

$$= 0.001\ \sin\omega t\ (1+1) = 2\times10^{-3}\ \sin\omega t\ \text{V}$$

11.20

Assuming linear operation, an approximate equivalent circuit is shown below:

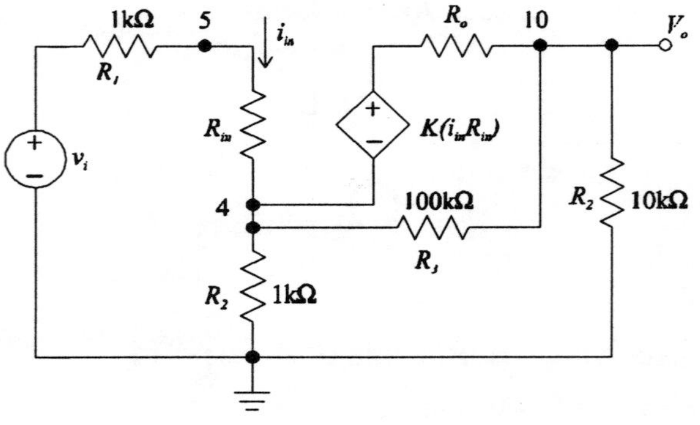

$$i_{in} = \frac{v_i - [-K(i_{in}R_{in})]}{R_{in}+R_1} \Rightarrow i_{in} = \frac{v_i}{(R_1+R_{in})\left(1-\frac{KR_{in}}{R_1+R_{in}}\right)}$$

From KCL at node 4:

$$\frac{v_o}{v_i} = \left(\frac{R_o R_3}{R_o+R_3}\right)\left(\frac{1}{R_1+R_{in}}\right)\left[1+\frac{KR_{in}}{1-\frac{KR_{in}}{R_1+R_{in}}}\left(\frac{1}{R_o}-\frac{1}{R_1+R_{in}}-\frac{1}{R_3}-\frac{1}{R_2}\right)\right]$$

or

$$A_v = \left(\frac{75\times 100k}{75+100k}\right)\left(\frac{1}{1k+1M}\right)\left[1+\frac{(2\times 10^5)2M}{1-\frac{(2\times 10^5)2M}{1k+2M}}\left(\frac{1}{75}-\frac{1}{1k+2M}-\frac{1}{100k}-\frac{1}{1k}\right)\right]$$

$= 0.9235$

11.21

$$v0 = -\frac{1}{4}(v1) - 5(v2) - 2(v3) - 16(v4)$$

$$= -\frac{Rf}{RS1}v1 - \frac{Rf}{RS2}v2 - \frac{Rf}{RS3}v3 - \frac{Rf}{RS4}v4$$

$\frac{Rf}{RS1} = \frac{1}{4}$ $\qquad RS1 = 4\,Rf = 40\text{ k}\Omega$

$\frac{Rf}{RS2} = 5$ $\qquad RS2 = \frac{1}{5}Rf = 2\text{ k}\Omega$

$\frac{Rf}{RS3} = 2$ $\qquad RS3 = \frac{1}{2}Rf = 5\text{ k}\Omega$

$\frac{Rf}{RS4} = 16$ $\qquad RS4 = \frac{1}{16}Rf = 0.625\text{ k}\Omega$

11.22

(a) Apply KCL at the inverting input:

$$\frac{V_i}{R_1}+\frac{V_o}{R}+\frac{V_o}{1/sC}=0$$

Manipulating the above equation yields:

$$-\frac{V_i}{R_1}=V_o\left(\frac{1}{R}+sC\right)=V_o\left(\frac{1+sRC}{R}\right)$$

Then

$$A_v=\frac{V_o}{V_i}=\left(-\frac{R}{R_1}\right)\left(\frac{1}{1+sRC}\right)$$

(b)

$$|A_v|_{dB}=20\log_{10}\left|\frac{V_o(j\omega)}{V_i(j\omega)}\right|=20\log_{10}\left|\frac{1}{-\frac{R_1}{R}-j\omega R_1 C}\right|$$

Note that $\lim\limits_{\omega\to 0}|A_v|_{dB}=20\log_{10}\left(\frac{R}{R_1}\right)$,

the magnitude will be down 3db when

$\omega R_1 C=\frac{R_1}{R}\Rightarrow\omega=\frac{1}{RC}$, and

$\lim\limits_{\omega\to\infty}|A_v|_{dB}=-\infty$

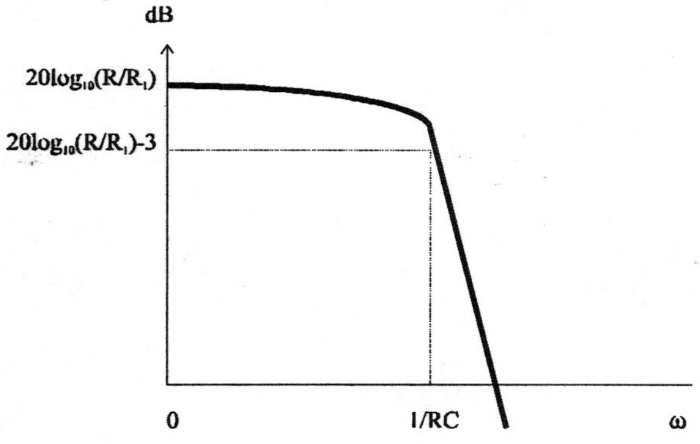

EIT 11.23

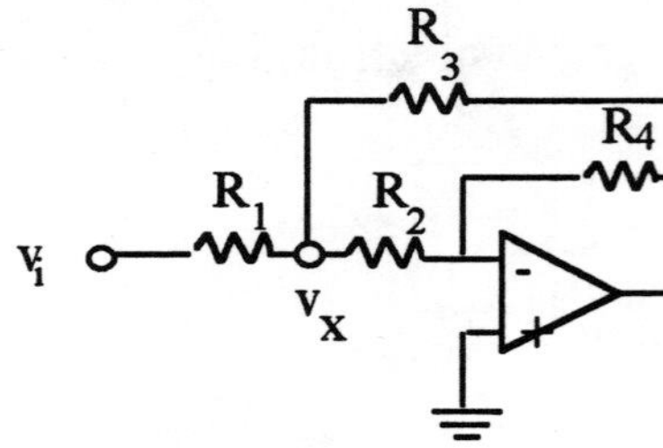

KCL at node v_X

$$\frac{v_X - v_i}{R_1} + \frac{v_X - v_o}{R_3} + \frac{v_X}{R_2} = 0 \qquad (1)$$

KCL at node v^-

$$\frac{v_X}{R_2} + \frac{v_o}{R_4} = 0 \qquad (2)$$

$$v_X = -\frac{-R_2}{R_4} v_o$$

Substituting (2) into equation (1)

$$-\frac{v_i}{R_1} - \frac{v_o}{R_3} - v_o\left(\frac{R_2}{R_4}\right)\left(\frac{1}{R_1} + \frac{1}{R_2} + \frac{1}{R_3}\right) = 0$$

$$\frac{1}{R_1} + \frac{1}{R_2} + \frac{1}{R_3} = \frac{1}{R_{eq}}$$

$$R_{eq} = R_1 \| R_2 \| R_3 = 1000\Omega$$

$$-\frac{v_i}{R_1} - v_o\left(\frac{1}{R_3} + \frac{R_2}{R_4}\frac{1}{R_{eq}}\right) = 0$$

$$\frac{v_o}{v_i} = -\frac{1}{R_1}\left(\frac{1}{R_3} + \frac{R_2}{R_3}\frac{1}{R_{eq}}\right)^{-1}$$

$$= -\frac{1}{R_1}\left(\frac{1}{\frac{1}{R_3} + \frac{R_2}{R_4}\frac{1}{R_{eq}}}\right)$$

$$= -\frac{R_{eq}}{R_1}\left(\frac{1}{\frac{R_{eq}}{R_3} + \frac{R_2}{R_4}}\right)$$

$$= -\frac{R_{eq}}{R_1}\left(\frac{R_3 R_4}{R_{eq}R_4 + R_2 R_3}\right)$$

$$= -\frac{1000}{3000}\left(\frac{3000 \times 1000}{1000 \times 1000 + 3000 \times 3000}\right)$$

$$= -\frac{1}{3}\left(\frac{3}{1+9}\right)$$

$$= -\frac{3}{30}$$

$$\frac{v_o}{v_i} = -\frac{1}{10}$$

11.24

(a)

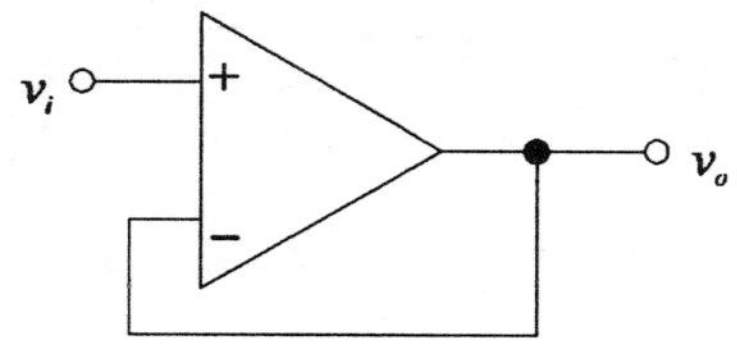

$$v^+ = v_i$$
$$v^- = v_o$$
$$\therefore v_o \approx v_i$$

(b)

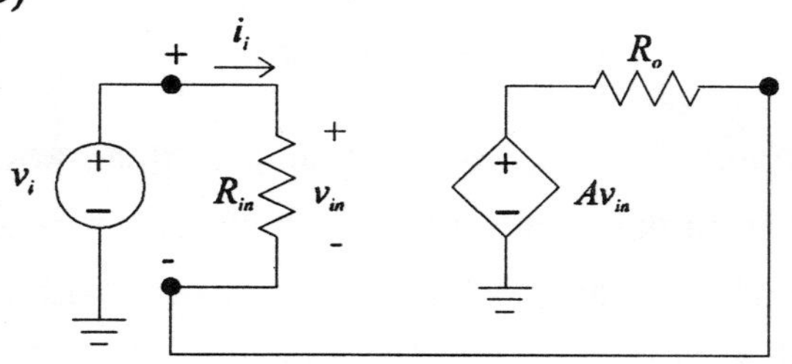

From KVL:

$$-v_i + R_{in}i_i + R_oi_i + AR_{in}i_i = 0$$

But, $R_o \ll R_{in}$ and $A \gg 1$, so that

$$AR_{in}i_i \approx v_i$$

or

$$\frac{v_i}{i_i} \approx AR_{in} = 10^6 \times \left(1 \times 10^6\right) = 1T\Omega$$

11.25

Replacing the components with impedances Z_f and Z_s yields the circuit shown below.

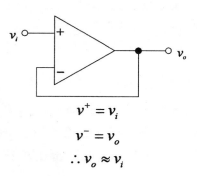

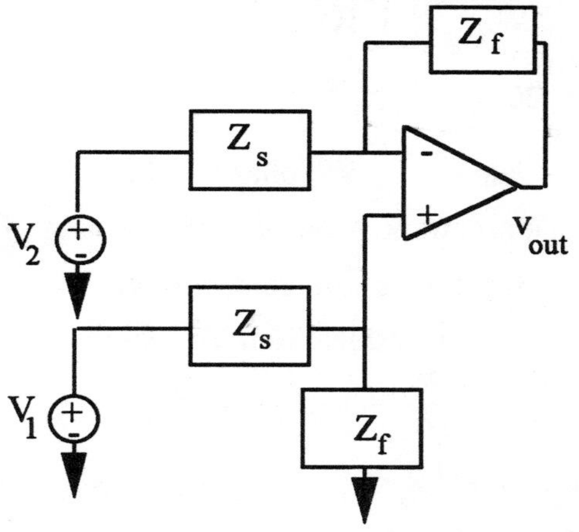

Recognizing that the circuit is a differential amplifier we can directly write:

$$V_{out} = \frac{Z_f}{Z_s}(V_1 - V_2)$$

$$Z_s = 1000 \ \Omega$$

$$Z_f = \frac{10000}{1 + j\omega5\times10^{-3}}$$

$$V_{out} = \frac{10}{1 + j\omega5\times10^{-3}}(V_1 - V_2)$$

(a) Evaluating this voltage at ω=1,000, we have

$$v_{out}(t) = 1.961 \cos (1000t - 78.7°)$$

Thus, the peak value is 1.961 V.

(b) The phase shift of $v_{out}(t)$ is

$$\phi = - \tan^{-1}(\frac{1000(5\times10^{-3})}{1} = - 78.7°$$

EIT 11.26

Applying KCL at the inverting terminal:

a) $$\frac{V_{out}}{V_{in}} = -\frac{j\omega R_2 C}{j\omega R_1 C + 1}$$

b) $$20\log 10 \left|\frac{j10}{j10+1}\right| = -0.04 \text{ dB}$$

c) Gain = - 0.995, phase = -174.3°

d) Since an attenuation of 2 dB (or gain of - 2 dB) corresponds to a gain of 0.7943, we wish to find the values of ω for which

$$\left|\frac{j0.01\omega}{j0.01\omega+1}\right| < 0.7943$$

Solving for ω, we obtain a quadratic equation with solution ω > 130.8 rad/s. A dB plot of the above function will illustrate more clearly the significance of this result:

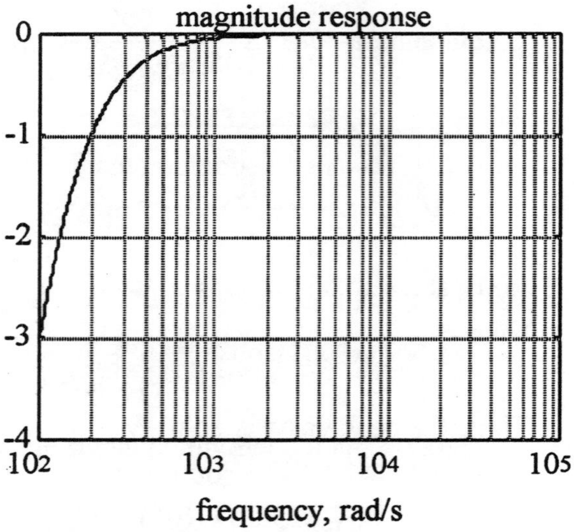

11.27

Applying KCL at the inverting terminal:

a) $$\frac{V_{out}}{V_{in}} = -\frac{j\omega R_2 C}{j\omega R_1 C + 1}$$

b) $$20\log \left|\frac{j5}{j10+1}\right| = -6.06 \text{ dB}$$

c) Gain = - 0.499, phase = -174.3°

d) Since and attenuation of 2 dB (or gain of -2 dB) corresponds to a gain of 0.7943, we wish to find the values of ω for which

$$\left|\frac{j0.005\omega}{j0.01\omega+1}\right| < 0.7943$$

Solving for ω, we obtain a quadratic equation the solution of which, however, is a pair of imaginary numbers. Since no positive real solution exists, we conclude that the condition is either never or always satisfied. A graph of the response reveals that the response is always below or at -6 dB, and therefore the desired condition is not true for any real positive frequencies.

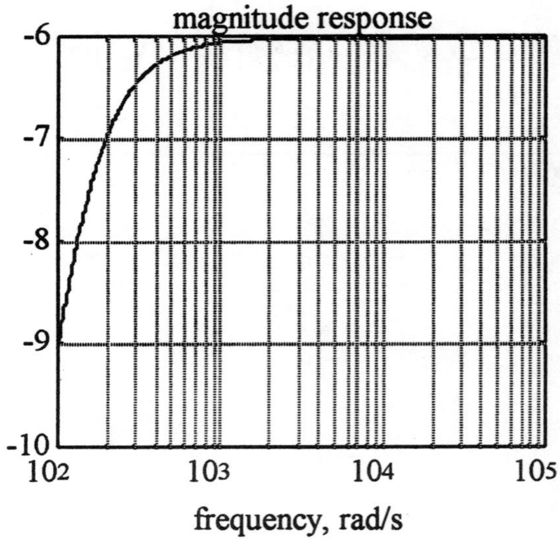

11.28

a) $v_{out} = \frac{-1}{R_S C_F} \int v_{in}(t)\, dt$

$$= \frac{-1}{R_S C_F} \int_0^{\tau} [0.01 + \sin(2000\pi t)] dt$$

$$= \frac{-1}{R_S C_F} \int_0^{\tau} 0.01 dt + \frac{-1}{R_S C_F} \int_0^{\tau} \sin 2000\pi t\, dt$$

The peak amplitude of the AC portion of the output is:

$$V_p = \frac{1}{R_S C_F}\left(\frac{1}{2000\pi}\right) = 1.989 \text{ V}$$

The output will begin to clip when $v_o(DC) - V_p = -15V$ so we need to find at what time the condition

$$-\frac{1}{R_S C_F} \int_0^{\tau} 0.01 dt = -13 \text{ V}$$

is satisfied. The answer is found below.

$$-\frac{1}{R_S C_F} 0.01\tau = -13$$

$$\tau = \frac{13 R_S C_F}{0.01} = 104 \text{ ms}$$

b) Using the results obtained in part (a):

$$\tau = \frac{15 R_S C_F}{0.01}$$

$$\tau = 120 \text{ ms}$$

11.29

a) Replacing the circuit elements with the corresponding impedances:

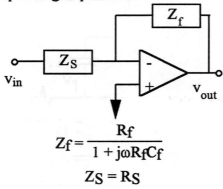

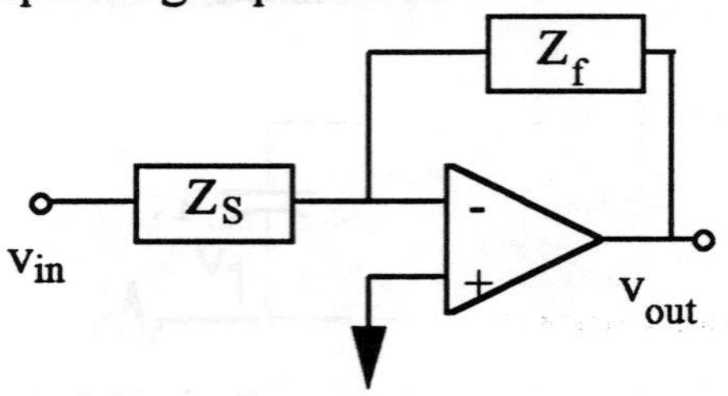

$$Z_f = \frac{R_f}{1 + j\omega R_f C_f}$$

$$Z_S = R_S$$

For the signal component at ω=2,000π:

$$V_{out} = -\frac{R_f}{R_S}\left(\frac{1}{1 + j\omega R_f C_f}\right) V_{in}$$

$$= -200\left(\frac{1}{1 + j\omega/62.5}\right)V_{in}$$

$$= V_{in}\frac{200}{\sqrt{1+(\omega/62.5)^2}} \angle(180° - \arctan(\omega/62.5)$$

$$= 1.9893\angle 90.57° \text{ V}$$

For the signal component at ω=0 (DC):

$$V_{out} = -200\ V_{in} = -2{,}000 \text{ V}$$

Thus,

$$v_{out}(t) = -2000 + 1.9893\sin(2000\pi t + 90.57°)$$

$$Å\ -2000 + 2\cos(2000\pi t) \text{ V}$$

b) <u>R_f = 200 kΩ</u>

For the signal component at ω=2,000π:

$$V_{out} = -\frac{R_f}{R_S}\left(\frac{1}{1 + j\omega R_f C_f}\right) V_{in}$$

$$= 1.9797\angle 95.68° \text{ V}$$

For the signal component at ω=0 (DC):

$$V_{out} = -20\ V_{in} = -200 \text{ V}$$

$$v_{out} = -200 - 1.9797\sin(2000\pi t + 95.68°)$$

$$\approx -200 + 2.0\cos(2000\pi t) \text{ V}$$

<u>R_f = 20 kΩ</u>

For the signal component at ω=2,000π:

$$\mathbf{V}_{out} = -\frac{R_f}{R_S}\left(\frac{1}{1 + j\omega R_f C_f}\right)\mathbf{V}_{in}$$

$$= 1.41\angle 134.8° V$$

For the signal component at ω=0 (DC):

$$V_{out} = -2\ V_{in} = -20 \text{ V}$$

$$v_{out} = -20 + 1.41\sin(2000\pi t + 135°)$$

$$\approx -20 + 1.41\cos(2000\pi t + 45°) \text{ V}$$

c)

R_f	τ	T
2 MΩ	16 ms	1 ms
200 kΩ	1.6 ms	1 ms
20 kΩ	0.16 ms	1 ms

In order to have an ideal integrator, it is desirable to have τ >> T.

EIT 11.30

Applying KCL at the inverting terminal:

a) $$\frac{V_{out}}{V_{in}} = -\frac{R_2 + \frac{1}{j\omega C_2}}{R_1 + \frac{1}{j\omega C_1}} = -\frac{C_1}{C_2}\frac{1 + j\omega R_2 C_2}{1 + j\omega R_1 C_1}$$

b) $$20\log_{10}\left|-\frac{1}{2}\frac{1+j60}{1+j15}\right| = 6.0 \text{ dB}$$

This is actually a gain, not an attenuation.

c) Gain = 1.9977, phase = -177.85°

11.31

The ideal Zener diode can be modeled as shown below:

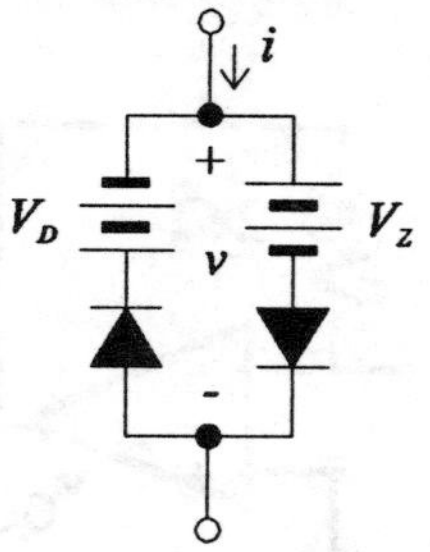

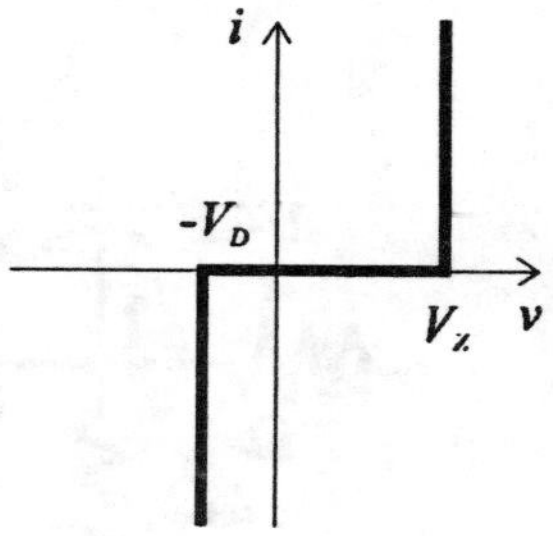

Applying KCL at the inverting input of the op-amp in Figure P11.27, and assuming no current through the Zener diodes, we have:

$$\frac{v_i}{R_1} + \frac{v_o}{R_2} = 0 \Rightarrow v_o = -\frac{R_2}{R_1}v_i$$

The above relationship holds if

$$-(V_Z + V_D) < v_o < (V_Z + V_D)$$

or

$$\frac{R_1}{R_2}(V_Z + V_D) > v_i > -\frac{R_1}{R_2}(V_Z + V_D)$$

If $v_i < -\frac{R_1}{R_2}(V_Z + V_D)$, v_o is clamped at $V_Z + V_D$. If $v_i > \frac{R_1}{R_2}(V_Z + V_D)$, v_o is clamped at $-(V_Z + V_D)$. A sketch of the relationship is shown below:

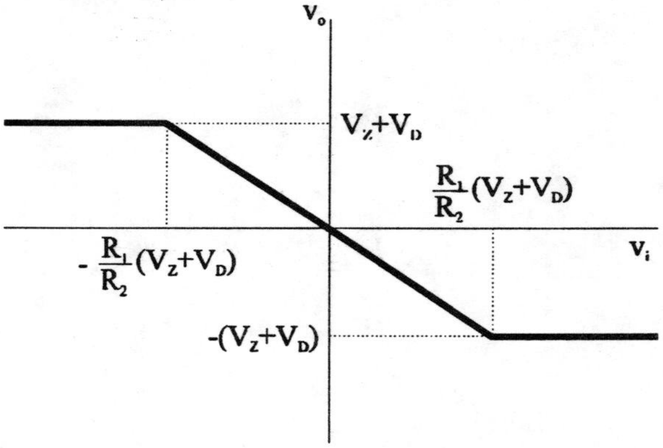

11.32

Applying KCL at the indicated node and at the inverting terminal:

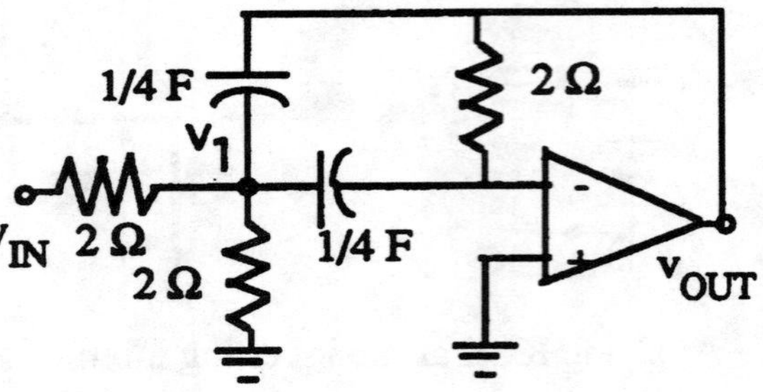

$$-\left(\frac{1}{2}\right)V_{IN} - \left(\frac{j\omega}{4}\right)V_{OUT} + \left(1+\frac{j\omega}{2}\right)v_1 = 0$$

$$-\left(\frac{j\omega}{4}\right)V_1 - \frac{1}{2}\,V_{out} + \left(\frac{1}{2}+\frac{j\omega}{4}\right)v^- = 0$$

and since

$$v^- = 0\ \text{V}$$

Therefore,

$$\frac{V_{OUT}}{V_{IN}} = \frac{j2\omega}{\omega^2 - j4\omega - 8}$$

11.33

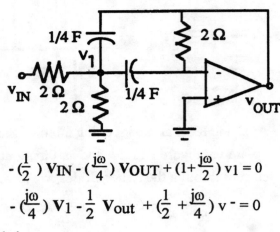

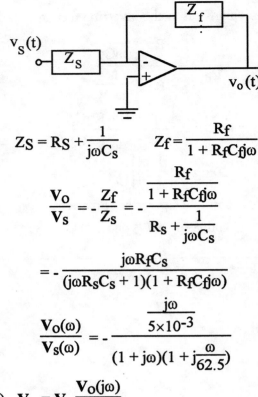

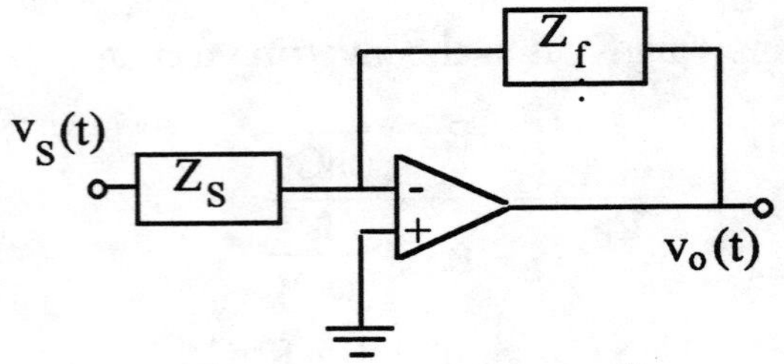

$$Z_S = R_S + \frac{1}{j\omega C_s} \qquad Z_f = \frac{R_f}{1 + R_f C_f j\omega}$$

$$\frac{V_o}{V_s} = -\frac{Z_f}{Z_s} = -\frac{\dfrac{R_f}{1 + R_f C_f j\omega}}{R_s + \dfrac{1}{j\omega C_s}}$$

$$= -\frac{j\omega R_f C_s}{(j\omega R_s C_s + 1)(1 + R_f C_f j\omega)}$$

$$\frac{V_o(\omega)}{V_s(\omega)} = -\frac{\dfrac{j\omega}{5\times10^{-3}}}{(1 + j\omega)\left(1 + j\dfrac{\omega}{62.5}\right)}$$

b) $V_o = V_s \dfrac{V_o(j\omega)}{V_s(j\omega)}$

By superposition,

$$V_o|_{10\ \text{mV}} = \frac{j0\ V_s}{1+1} = 0\ \text{V}$$

$$V_o|_{\omega=2000\pi} = \frac{j1.257\times10^6\ V_s}{(1 + j6283)(1 + j100)}$$

$$= \frac{1.257\times10^6\angle 90^\circ \times 10\times10^{-3}\angle 0^\circ}{6283\angle 89.99^\circ \times 100\angle 89.43^\circ}$$

$$= 20\times10^{-3}\angle(90 - 89.99 - 89.43)^\circ$$

$$= 20\times10^{-3}\angle -89.43^\circ$$

$$v_o(t) = 20\times10^{-3}\sin(2000\pi t - 89.43^\circ)\ \text{V}$$

We can say that the practical differentiator is a good approximation of the ideal differentiator.

11.34

(a) Applying KCL at the inverting node of the op-amp, we have

$$\frac{V_Z}{R_1}+\frac{v_o}{R_2}=0 \quad \text{or} \quad v_o=-\frac{R_2}{R_1}V_Z$$

(b) Applying KCL at the upper end of the Zener diode,

$$i_Z+\frac{V_Z}{R_1}+\frac{V_Z-V_S}{R_S}=0$$

or

$$V_S=R_S\left[V_Z\left(\frac{1}{R_1}+\frac{1}{R_S}\right)+i_Z\right]$$

Then,

$$i_Z\geq 0.1I_Z \Rightarrow V_S\geq V_Z\left(1+\frac{R_S}{R_1}\right)+0.1I_ZR_S$$

EIT 11.35

Applying KCL at the inverting terminal:

a) $$\frac{\text{Vout}}{\text{Vin}}=-\frac{\text{R}2+\frac{1}{\text{j}\omega\text{C}}}{\text{R}1}=-\frac{1+\text{j}\omega\text{R}2\text{C}}{\text{j}\omega\text{R}1\text{C}}$$

b) Gain = .04 dB

c) Gain = -1.0008; Phase = 177.71°

d) To find the desired frequency range we need to solve the equation

$$\left|\frac{1+\text{j}\omega\text{R}2\text{C}}{\text{j}\omega\text{R}1\text{C}}\right|<0.8913$$

since 20 log10 (0.8913) = -1 dB. This yields a quadratic equation in ω, which can be solved to find ω > 196.5 rad/s.

11.36

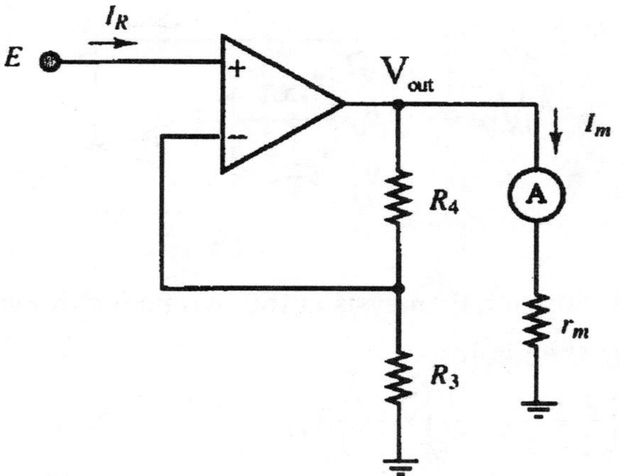

$$V_{out}=I_mr_m=(100\mu A)(10k\Omega)=1V$$

From KCL at the inverting input,

$$\frac{E}{R_3}+\frac{E-V_{out}}{R_4}=0$$

or

$$\frac{V_{out}}{E}=\frac{R_4+R_3}{R_3}=1+\frac{R_4}{R_3}$$

Then,

$$\frac{R_4}{R_3}=\frac{V_{out}}{E}-1=\frac{1}{20\times10^{-3}}-1=49$$

Now, choose R_3 and R_4 such that

$$I_B=\frac{E}{R_3\|(R_4+r_m)}\leq 0.2\mu A$$

At the limit,

$$\frac{20\times10^{-3}}{R_3\|(49R_3+10\times10^3)}=0.2\times10^{-6}$$

Solving for R_3, we have $R_3\approx 102k\Omega$. Therefore, $R_4\approx 5M\Omega$.

11.37

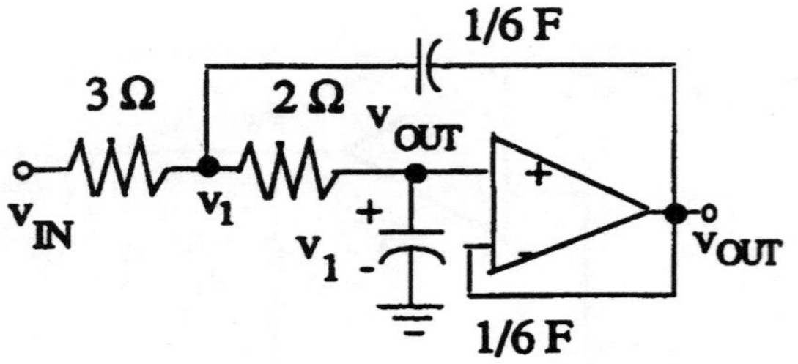

Using nodal analysis at the two nodes shown in the figure,

$$\left(\frac{1}{2}+\frac{1}{3}+\frac{j\omega}{6}\right)\mathbf{V}_1-\frac{1}{3}\mathbf{V}_{IN}-\left(\frac{j\omega}{6}+\frac{1}{2}\right)\mathbf{V}_{OUT}=0$$

$$-\frac{1}{2}\mathbf{V}_1+\left(\frac{1}{2}+\frac{j\omega}{6}\right)\mathbf{V}_{OUT}=0$$

Therefore,

$$\frac{V_{OUT}}{V_{IN}}=-\frac{6}{\omega^2-j5\omega-6}$$

11.38

The summer and the integrator op-amps can be combined. The inputs to the summer will be the inputs to the integrator op-amp. Also, the multiplier $\left(-\frac{B}{M}\right)$ can be eliminated.

EIT 11.39

$$x(t)=-200\int z\ dt$$

or $$z=-\frac{1}{200}\frac{dx}{dt}$$

Also, z = -20 y.

Therefore, $$y=\frac{1}{4000}\frac{dx}{dt}$$

also,

$$y=\int(4f(t)+x(t))\ dt$$ or

$$\frac{dy}{dt}=4\,f(t)+x(t)$$

From the previous expression,

$$\frac{dy}{dt}=\frac{1}{4000}\frac{d^2x}{dt^2}$$

therefore

$$\frac{1}{4000}\frac{d^2x}{dt^2}=4\,f(t)+x(t)$$

or $$\frac{d^2x}{dt^2}-4000\,x(t)-16000\,f(t)=0$$

11.40

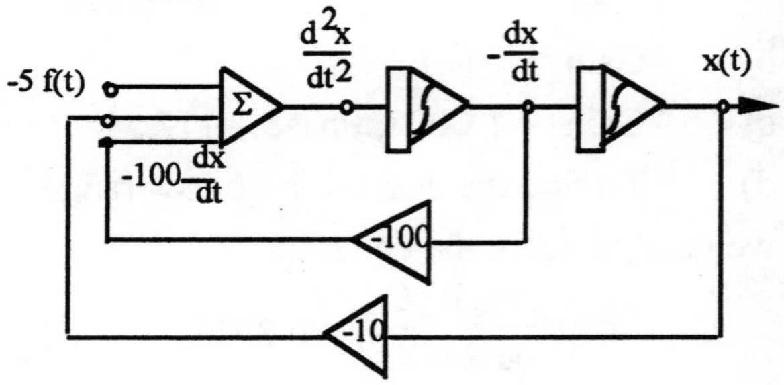

11.41

Applying KCL at the inverting terminal:

$$I + \frac{V_{out}}{R + \frac{1}{j\omega C}} = 0$$

or,

$$\frac{V_{out}}{I} = -\frac{j\omega C}{1 + j\omega RC}$$

This response is clearly that of a high-pass filter, therefore the charge amplifier will never be able to amplify a DC signal.

The low end of the (magnitude) frequency response is plotted below for the three time constants. The figure illustrates how as the time constant decreases the cut-off frequency moves to the right (solid line: R = 10 MΩ; dashed line: R=1 MΩ; dotted line: R=0.1 MΩ.

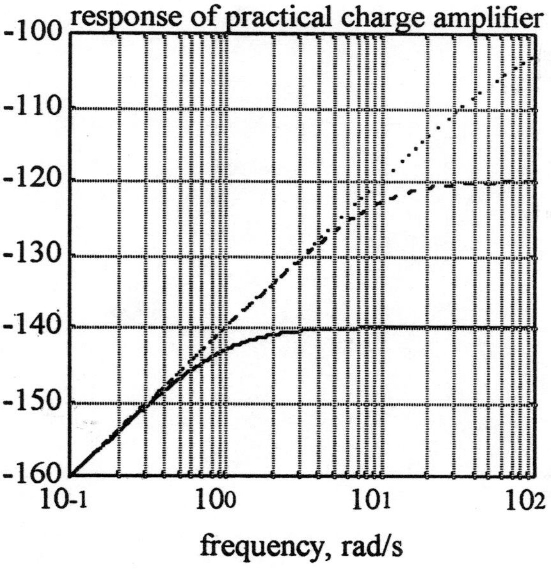

From the frequency response plot one can approximate the minimum useful frequency for distortionless response to be (nominally) 1 Hz for the 10 MΩ case, 10 Hz for the 1 MΩ case, and 100 Hz for the 0.1 MΩ case.

11.42

We first determine which is the common mode and which is the differential mode signal:

$$v_1 - v_2 = 2 \sin 2000\pi t$$

$$\frac{v_1 + v_2}{2} = 0.1 \sin 120\pi t$$

Therefore,

$v_{out} = A_{dm} 2\sin(2000\pi t) + A_{cm}(0.1 \sin(120\pi t))$

Since we desire the common mode output to be less than 1% of the differential mode output, we require

$$A_{cm}(0.1) \le 0.01\ (2)$$

or

$$A_{cm} \le 0.2$$

$$CMRR = \frac{A_{dif}}{A_{cm}}$$

So

$$CMRR_{min} = \frac{1000}{0.2} = 5000 = 74\ \text{dB}$$

11.43

a) $v_{out} = A_{OL}(v^+ - v^-)$ (1)

Writing KCL at v^-:

$$\frac{v^- - v_{in}}{R_S} + \frac{v^- - v_{out}}{R_f} = 0 \qquad (2)$$

Using (1) and (2)

$$\frac{-v_{out}/A_{OL} - v_{in}}{R_S} + \frac{-v_{out}/A_{OL} - v_{out}}{R_f} = 0$$

Re-arranging,

$$\frac{v_{out}}{v_{in}} = A_{CL} = -\frac{R_f}{R_S}\frac{1}{1 + \dfrac{R_f + R_S}{R_S A_{OL}}}$$

b)

A_{OL}	$\lvert A_{CL}\rvert$
1	0.833
10	4.7619
100	9.009
1000	9.8912
10 K	9.9890
100 K	9.9989
1 M	10

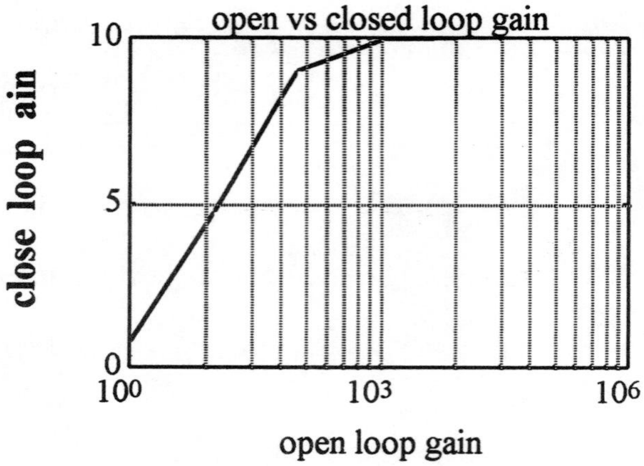

c) As the open loop gain approaches infinity, the amplifier's closed loop gain approaches $-\dfrac{R_f}{R_s}$.

11.44

$$vo = Adm(v2 - v1) + Acm(\frac{v2 + v1}{2})$$

$$v1 = \frac{R2}{R1 + R2} va + \frac{R1}{R1 + R2} vo$$

$$v2 = \frac{R2}{R1 + R2} vb$$

After making the necessary substitutions and re-arranging:

$$vo = \frac{Adm\frac{R2}{R2+R1}(vb-va)+Acm\frac{R2}{R2+R1}(\frac{va+vb}{2})}{1+\frac{R1}{R2+R1}\times(-Acm+Adm)}$$

$$vo = \frac{Adm\frac{R2}{R1}(vb - va) + Acm\frac{R2}{R1}(\frac{va + vb}{2})}{1 - Acm + Adm}$$

using the fact that

$$Adm >> Acm \quad Adm >> 1$$

$$v_o = \frac{R_2}{R_1}\left\{(v_b - v_a) + \frac{A_{cm}}{A_{dm}}\left(\frac{v_a + v_b}{2}\right)\right\}$$

$$v_o = \frac{R_2}{R_1}\left\{(v_b - v_a) + \frac{1}{CMRR}\left(\frac{v_a + v_b}{2}\right)\right\}$$

b) $vo = 2.04 \text{ V}$

EIT 11.45

(a) To determine the frequency response, we first compute $\mathbf{V}^+$, using phasor methods:

$$\mathbf{V}^+ = \frac{Z}{R_2+Z}\mathbf{V}_1$$

where $Z = R_1 \parallel \frac{1}{j\omega C}$; next, we set $\mathbf{V}^+ = \mathbf{V}^-$ and compute the current flowing from $\mathbf{V}_2$ towards the inverting node, $\mathbf{I}_S$:

$$\mathbf{I}_S = \frac{\mathbf{V}_2 - \mathbf{V}^-}{R_2} = \frac{\mathbf{V}_2 - \frac{Z}{R_2+Z}\mathbf{V}_1}{R_2}$$

This current is equal and opposite to the feedback current, $\mathbf{I}_F$:

$$\mathbf{I}_F = \frac{\mathbf{V}_{out} - \mathbf{V}^-}{Z} = \frac{\mathbf{V}_{out} - \frac{Z}{R_2+Z}\mathbf{V}_1}{Z}$$

Setting $\mathbf{I}_S = -\mathbf{I}_F$, we obtain the expression

$$\frac{\mathbf{V}_2 - \frac{Z}{R_2+Z}\mathbf{V}_1}{R_2} = -\frac{\mathbf{V}_{out} - \frac{Z}{R_2+Z}\mathbf{V}_1}{Z}$$

which can be simplified, after a little algebra, to yield:

$$\mathbf{V}_{out} = \frac{Z}{R_2}(\mathbf{V}_1 - \mathbf{V}_2)$$

Thus, the frequency response of the amplifier circuit is:

$$\frac{\mathbf{V}_{out}}{(\mathbf{V}_1 - \mathbf{V}_2)} = \frac{R_1 \parallel \frac{1}{j\omega C}}{R_2} = \frac{R_1/R_2}{1+j\omega CR_1} = H(\omega)$$

This is the response of a low-pass filter, with cut-off frequency $\frac{1}{R_1C}$ and peak gain $\frac{R_1}{R_2}$.

(b) At $\omega = 1{,}500$ rad/s, the dB attenuation is:

$|H(\omega{=}1{,}500)|_{dB} = 20\log_{10}(0.5547) = -5.12$ dB

(c) At $\omega = 2{,}000$ rad/s, the gain and phase shift are:

$$|H(\omega{=}2{,}000)| = 0.4472$$

$$\angle H(\omega{=}2{,}000) = -63.4°$$

(d) To find the range of frequencies over which the attenuation is less than 5%, we must set

$$|H(\omega)| \le 0.95$$

and solve for ω. Since the circuit is a low-pass filter, this range of frequencies will start at $\omega = 0$, and end at the frequency ω which satisfies

$$\frac{R_1/R_2}{\sqrt{1+(\omega CR_1)^2}} = 0.95$$

or

$$(0.95)^2 C^2 R_1^2 \omega^2 = \frac{R_1^2}{R_2^2} - (0.95)^2$$

For the values given in this problem, the solution is:

$$\omega = 328.7 \text{ rad/s}$$

(e) An attenuation of 5% corresponds to:

$$20\log_{10}(0.95) = -0.4455 \text{ dB}$$

11.46

Applying KCL at the inverting input, we have

$$\frac{V_1}{R}+V_2\left(\frac{1}{R}+j\omega C\right)=0$$

or

$$\frac{V_2}{V_1}=\frac{-1}{1+j\omega RC}$$

$$\left|\frac{V_2}{V_1}\right|=\frac{1}{\sqrt{1+(\omega RC)^2}}$$

This function has the form of a low-pass filter with hald-power frequency given by

$$\frac{1}{\sqrt{1+(\omega RC)^2}}=\frac{1}{\sqrt{2}}\Rightarrow\omega=\frac{1}{RC}$$

The function is sketched below.

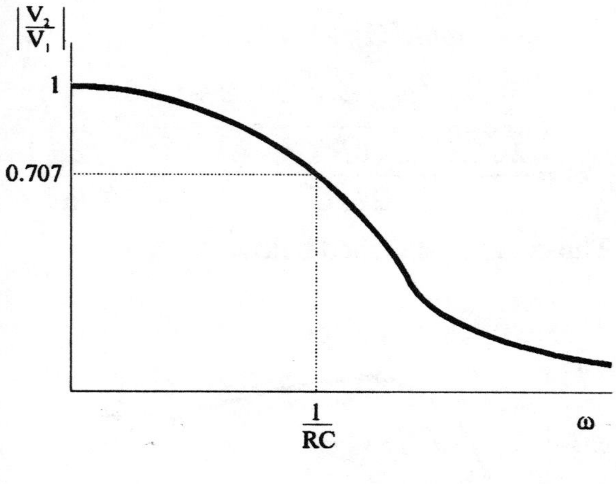

11.47

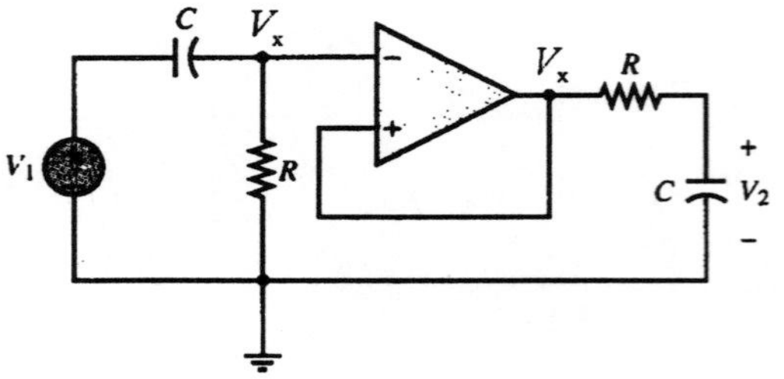

From KCL at the inverting input:

$$\frac{V_x - V_1}{Z_C} + \frac{V_x}{R} = 0$$

$$V_x\left(j\omega C + \frac{1}{R}\right) = j\omega C V_1$$

$$V_x\left(1 + \frac{1}{j\omega RC}\right) = V_1$$

$$V_x = V_1\left(\frac{1}{1 + \frac{1}{j\omega RC}}\right)$$

Similarly, from KCL at the output of the op-amp:

$$\frac{V_2 - V_x}{R} + \frac{V_2}{Z_C} = 0$$

$$V_2\left(\frac{1}{R} + j\omega C\right) = \frac{V_x}{R}$$

$$V_x = V_2(1 + j\omega RC)$$

Combining the above results, we find

$$\frac{V_2}{V_1} = \frac{j\omega RC}{(1 + j\omega RC)^2}$$

or

$$\left|\frac{V_2}{V_1}\right| = \frac{\omega RC}{1 + (\omega RC)^2}$$

This function has the form of a band-pass filter, with maximum value determined as follows:

$$G = \left|\frac{V_2}{V_1}\right| = \frac{\omega RC}{1 + (\omega RC)^2}$$

$$\frac{dG}{d\omega} = \frac{\left[1 + (\omega RC)^2\right]RC - \omega RC\left[2\omega (RC)^2\right]}{\left[1 + (\omega RC)^2\right]^2}$$

Setting the derivative equal to zero and solving for the center frequency,

$$RC + \omega^2 R^3 C^3 - 2\omega^2 R^3 C^3 = 0$$

$$1 - \omega^2 R^2 C^2 = 0$$

$$\omega = \frac{1}{RC}$$

Then $G_{max} = \frac{1}{1+1} = \frac{1}{2}$, and the half-power frequencies are given by

$$\frac{\omega RC}{1 + (\omega RC)^2} = \frac{1}{\sqrt{2}} G_{max} = \frac{1}{\sqrt{2}}\frac{1}{2}$$

$$\omega^2 R^2 C^2 + 1 = 2\sqrt{2}\omega RC$$

$$R^2 C^2 \omega^2 - 2\sqrt{2} RC\omega + 1 = 0$$

$$\omega = \frac{2\sqrt{2}RC \pm \sqrt{8R^2C^2 - 4R^2C^2}}{2R^2C^2} = \frac{\sqrt{2} \pm 1}{RC}$$

The curve is sketched below.

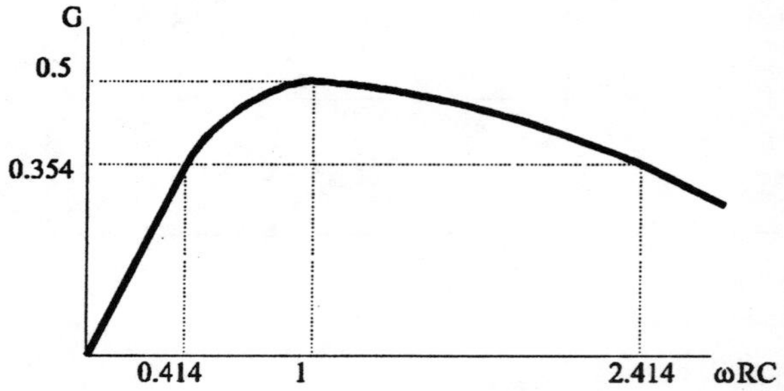

EIT 11.48

a)
$$R_i = v_{in}/i_{in}$$

$$i_{in} = \frac{v_{in} - A_{OL}(R_{in}i_{in})}{R_{in} + r_o}$$

$$v_{in} = i_{in}(R_{in} + r_o)(1 + \frac{A_{OL}R_{in}}{R_{in} + r_o})$$

$$R_i = r_o + (A_{OL} + 1)R_{in}$$

b) $r_o = 75\ \Omega$ $R_{in} = 2\ M\Omega$

$A_{OL} = 10^6$ $R_i = 2\times10^{12}\ \Omega$

11.49

$$\left|\frac{dv_{out}}{dt}\right|_{max} = \frac{V_m(0.9-0.1)}{(14.5-10.1)\times10^{-6}} = \frac{15\times0.8}{4.4}\frac{V}{\mu s} \approx 2.73\frac{V}{\mu s}$$

Therefore, the slew rate is approximately $2.73\frac{V}{\mu s}$.

11.50

$$A_{CL} = -\frac{R_f}{R_s}\frac{1}{1 + \frac{R_f + R_s}{R_s A_{OL}}}$$

a) $A_{CL} = -99.899$

b) $A_{CL} = -990$

c) $A_{CL} = -9091$

d) as $A_{OL} \to \infty$, $A_{CL} = -10{,}000$

11.51

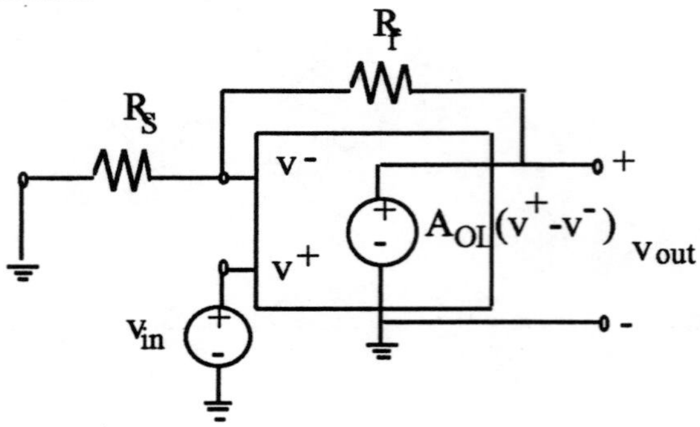

$$v_{in} = v^+$$

and
$$v_o = A_{OL}(v_{in} - v^-)$$

$$v^- = -\left(\frac{v_o}{A_{OL}} - v_{in}\right)$$

Writing KCL at v^-

$$\frac{v^- - 0}{R_s} + \frac{v^- - v_o}{R_f} = 0$$

Substituting,

$$\frac{-\frac{v_o}{A_{OL}} + v_{in}}{R_s} + \frac{-\frac{v_o}{A_{OL}} + v_{in}}{R_f} = \frac{v_o}{R_f}$$

$$v_o\left(-\frac{1}{A_{OL}R_s} - \frac{1}{A_{OL}R_f} - \frac{1}{R_f}\right) = -v_{in}\left(\frac{1}{R_s} + \frac{1}{R_f}\right)$$

$$\frac{v_o}{v_{in}} = \frac{-\left(\frac{1}{R_s} + \frac{1}{R_f}\right)}{-\frac{1}{A_{OL}R_s} - \frac{1}{A_{OL}R_f} - \frac{1}{R_f}}$$

$$= A_{OL}R_sR_f\left(\frac{1}{K_1} + \frac{1}{K_2}\right)$$

where $K_1 = R_fR_s + R_s^2 + R_sA_{OL}R_s$

$K_2 = R_f^2 + R_fR_s + A_{OL}R_sR_f$

$$\frac{v_o}{v_{in}} = \frac{R_f}{R_S}\left(\frac{1}{\frac{R_S + R_f}{R_S A_{OL}} + 1}\right) + \left(\frac{1}{\frac{R_f + R_S}{R_S A_{OL}} + 1}\right)$$

for the conditions of part a) we obtain

$$ACL = \frac{1}{2/45\times10^5 + 1} + \frac{1}{2/45\times10^5 + 1}$$

$$= 1.9999$$

b) $$ACL = 5\frac{1}{6/45\times10^5 + 1} + \frac{1}{6/45\times10^5 + 1}$$

$$= 5.9999$$

EIT 11.52

$$\frac{v_o}{v^+} = \frac{R_4}{R_3}\left(\frac{1}{\frac{R_4+R_3}{R_3 A_{OL}}+1}\right) + \left(\frac{1}{\frac{R_4+R_3}{R_3 A_{OL}}+1}\right)$$

and since we have a voltage divider at v^+

$$\frac{v^+}{v_{in}} = \frac{R_2}{R_1+R_2}$$

we obtain :

$$A_{CL} = \frac{v_o}{v^+}\left(\frac{v^+}{v_{in}}\right) =$$

$$= \left(\frac{R_4}{R_3}+1\right)\left(\frac{1}{\frac{R_3+R_4}{R_3 A_{OL}}+1}\right)\left(\frac{R_2}{R_1+R_2}\right)$$

$$A_{CL} = \left(\frac{R_4+R_3}{R_3}\right)\left(\frac{R_2}{R_1+R_2}\right)\left(\frac{1}{\frac{R_4+R_3}{R_3 A_{OL}}+1}\right)$$

b) Using the numbers given,

$v_o(t) = A_{CL} v_{in}(t) = 4.68 \cos 27.6t$ V

11.53

$$A_0\omega_0 = K = A_1\omega_1$$

$$\therefore K = 1 \times 2\pi \times 5.0MHz = 10\pi \times 10^6$$

$$A_1 = \frac{K}{\omega_1} = \frac{10\pi \times 10^6}{2\pi \times 500} = 10{,}000$$

Digital Logic Circuits

Chapter 12 Instructor Notes

Chapter 12 is a stand-alone chapter, which does not require much more than a general introduction to the idea of analog and digital signals. Thus, the chapter could be covered as early as immediately following Chapter 6. On the other hand, the instructor may find it desirable to first introduce the basics of electronic switching circuits by covering the appropriate sections of Chapters 7-11. In either case, the chapter is self contained.

The first section introduces the ideas of analog and digital signals, and the concepts of sampling and quantization, in an intuitive fashion. Section 12.2 introduces the binary number system, and binary codes; Example 12.2 discusses optical position encoders of the type commonly encountered in many industrial applications (e.g., robotics). The third section presents the foundations of Boolean algebra, and defines the properties of logic gates; combinational logic design through the use of Karnaugh maps is presented in section 12.4. Example 12.21 illustrates a simple application (the safe operation of a stamping press), which can provide an illustration of the usefulness of even the simplest logic circuits in an industrial setting. A brief survey of digital logic could stop here, if desired.

Section 12.5 describes more advanced combinational logic modules, including an example (12.25) of the use of EPROMs as look-up tables; the example is centered around the air-to-fuel ratio control problem in an internal combustion engine, and illustrates a truly wide-spread application of digital logic, since this type of circuit is present in virtually every modern automobile.

In addition to the usual exercises aimed at reinforcing the understanding of the material, the chapter also includes a number of design problems.

Chapter 12 problem solutions

12.1

a) 191, 110010001
b) 111, 100010001
c) F, 1111
d) 26, 100110
e) 38, 111000

12.2

a) 10, 1010
b) 102, 1100110
c) 71, 1000111
d) 33, 100001
e) 19, 10011

12.3

a) 100001111.01
b) 110101.011
c) 100101.01010
d) 110110.010001

12.4

a) F, 15
b) 4D, 77
c) 65, 101
d) 5C, 92
e) 1D, 29
f) 28, 40

12.5

a) 11111010
b) 100010100
c) 110000100

12.6

a) 11100
b) 1101110
c) 1000

12.7

a) -120
b) -31
c) 121

12.8

a) 01111110
b) 11111110
c) 01101100
d) 11100010

12.9

a) 2^4 - 1111 = 10000 -1111 = 1
b) 2^7 - 1001101 = 110011
c) 2^7 - 1011100 = 100100
d) 2^5 - 11101= 100000 - 11101 = 11

12.10

A	B	AB	$\overline{A}B$	$AB+\overline{A}B$
0	0	0	0	0
0	1	0	1	1
1	0	0	0	0
1	1	1	1	1

Comparing the second and fifth columns, it is clear that $B = AB + \overline{A}B$

12.11

ABC	BC	$B\overline{C}$	$\overline{B}A$	$BC+B\overline{C}+\overline{B}A$	$A+B$
0 0 0	0	0	0	0	0
0 0 1	0	0	0	0	0
0 1 0	0	1	0	1	1
0 1 1	1	0	0	1	1
1 0 0	0	0	1	1	1
1 0 1	0	0	1	1	1
1 1 0	0	1	0	1	1
1 1 1	1	0	0	1	1

Comparing the last two columns, it is clear that $BC+B\overline{C}+\overline{B}A = A+B$.

12.12

Using proof by perfect induction, we can see that the two expressions are equal.

X	Y	$\overline{X}$	$(X+Y)(\overline{X}+XY)$
0	0	1	0
0	1	1	1
1	0	0	0
1	1	0	1

12.13

$$F(X,Y,Z) = \overline{X}\,\overline{Y}\,\overline{Z} + \overline{X}\,YZ + X\,(\overline{Y+Z})$$

Applying De Morgan's theorems,

$$= \overline{X}\,\overline{Y}\,\overline{Z} + \overline{X}\,YZ + X\overline{Y}\,\overline{Z}$$

Applying the rules of Boolean algebra,

$$F = \overline{X}\,\overline{Y}\,\overline{Z} + X\overline{Y}\,\overline{Z} + XYZ$$

$$= \overline{Y}\,\overline{Z} + XYZ$$

Therefore,

$$F(X,Y,Z) = \overline{Y}\,\overline{Z} + XYZ$$

12.14

$f(A,B,C) = ABC + \overline{A}CD + \overline{B}CD$

$= ABC(D+\overline{D}) + \overline{A}CD + \overline{B}CD \leftarrow Rule4$

$= ABCD + ABC\overline{D} + \overline{A}CD + \overline{B}CD \leftarrow Distrib.$

$= (ABCD + ABCD) + ABC\overline{D} + \overline{A}CD + \overline{B}CD \leftarrow Rule3$

$= ABCD + ABC\overline{D} + ABCD + \overline{A}CD + \overline{B}CD \leftarrow Comm.$

$= ABC(D+\overline{D}) + CD(AB + \overline{A} + \overline{B}) \leftarrow Distrib.$

$= ABC + CD(AB + \overline{A} + \overline{B}) \leftarrow Distrib., Rule3$

$= ABC + CD(AB + \overline{A} + AB + \overline{B}) \leftarrow Comm.$

$= ABC + CD(B + \overline{A} + A + \overline{B}) \leftarrow Rule18$

$= ABC + CD(\overline{A} + A + B + \overline{B}) \leftarrow Comm.$

$= ABC + CD(1) \leftarrow Rule4$

$= ABC + CD \leftarrow Rule6$

12.15

Applying the rules of Boolean algebra,

$$F = \overline{A}B(C+\overline{C}) + AB(C+\overline{C}) = \overline{A}B + AB$$

Therefore, $F = B(\overline{A} + A) = B$

12.16

From the map, we can see that

$$F = A + C$$

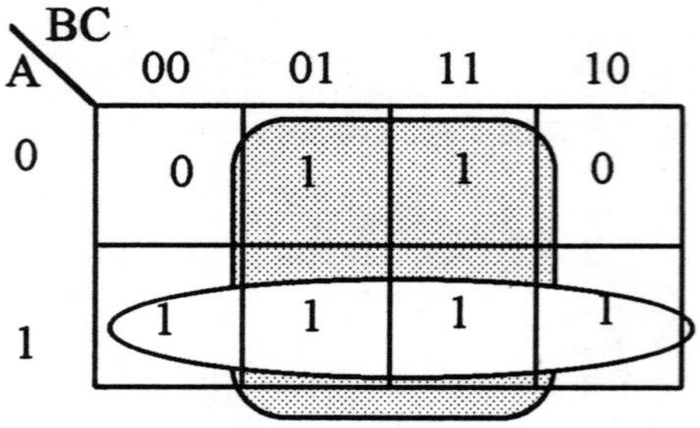

12.17

$$F = \overline{AB} \bullet \overline{CD} \bullet \overline{E}$$

$$= \overline{AB + CD + E}$$

where the second expression is a result of applying DeMorgan's theorem to the first.

12.18

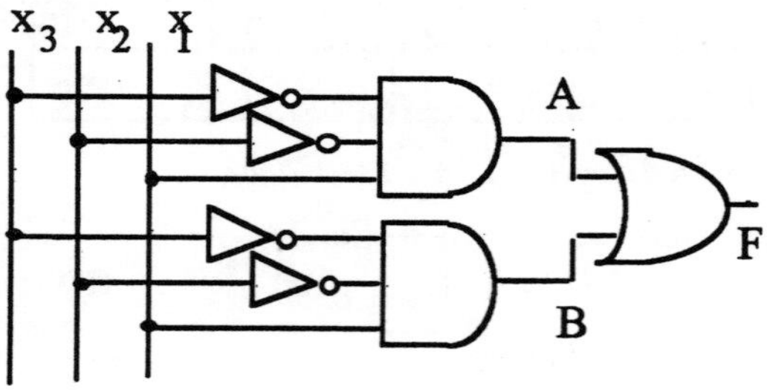

x3	x2	x1	A	B	F
0	0	0	0	0	0
0	0	1	1	1	1
0	1	0	0	0	0
0	1	1	0	0	0
1	0	0	0	0	0
1	0	1	0	0	0
1	1	0	0	0	0
1	1	1	0	0	0

12.19

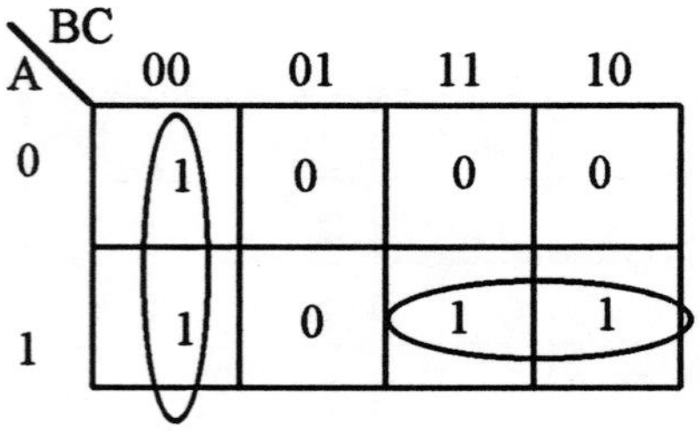

From the map, we can see that

$$F = AB + \overline{B}\overline{C}$$

12.20

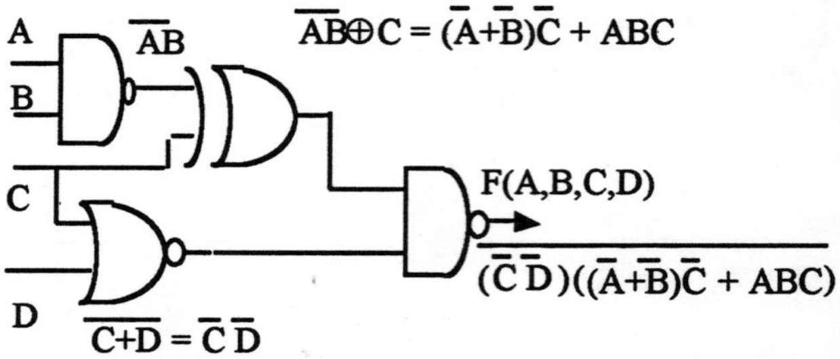

12.21

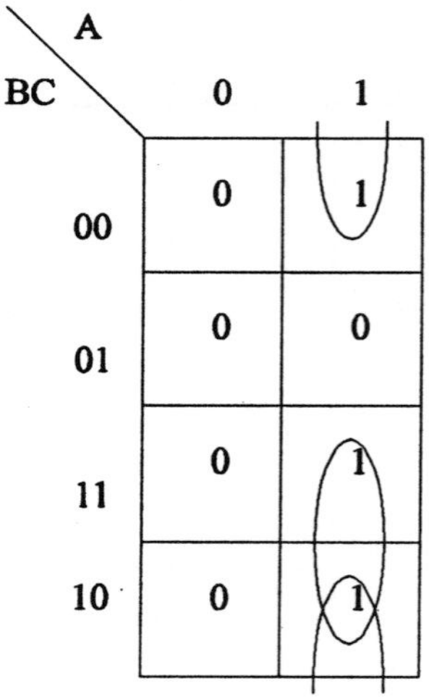

$$f = AB + A\overline{C}$$

12.22

$$f(A,B,C) = (A+B)AB + \overline{A}C + A\overline{B}C + \overline{B}\,\overline{C}$$

$$= AB + \overline{A}C + A\overline{B}C + \overline{B}\,\overline{C}$$

$$= AB + (\overline{A} + A\overline{B})C + \overline{B}\,\overline{C}$$

$$= AB + (\overline{A} + \overline{B})C + \overline{B}\,\overline{C}$$

$$= AB + \overline{A}C + \overline{B}C + \overline{B}\,\overline{C}$$

$$= AB + \overline{A}C + \overline{B} = A + \overline{A}C + \overline{B}$$

$$= A + \overline{B} + C$$

The Karnaugh map is shown below.

A \ BC	00	01	11	10
0	1	1	1	0
1	1	1	1	1

12.23

The Karnaugh map is shown below.

CD \ AB	00	01	11	10
00	1	0	0	1
01	1	0	0	1
11	0	1	0	1
10	1	1	0	1

The map leads to the expression

$$f = \overline{B}\,\overline{C} + A\overline{B} + \overline{A}BC + \overline{B}\,\overline{D}$$

and to the gate realization shown below.

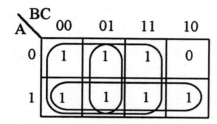

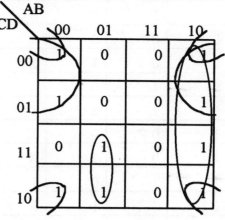

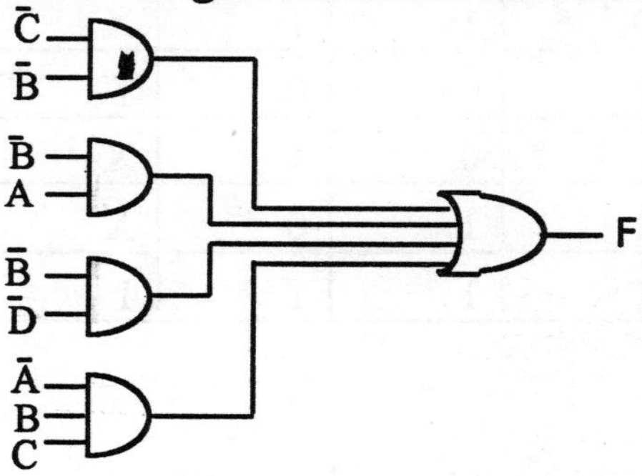

12.24

A \ BC	00	01	11	10
0	0	1	0	1
1	1	0	1	0

$$f(A,B,C) = \overline{A}\,\overline{B}C + \overline{A}B\overline{C} + A\overline{B}\,\overline{C} + ABC$$

12.25

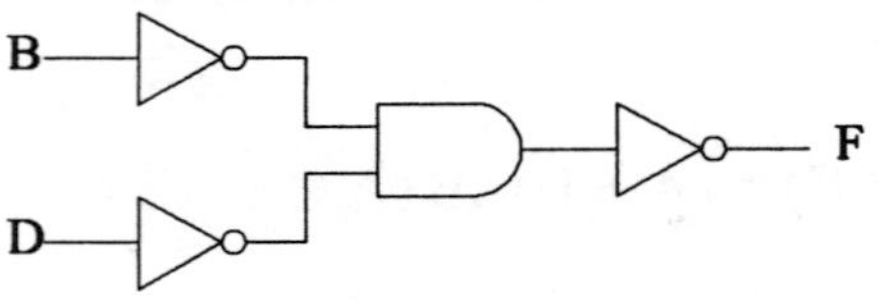

A	B	C	D	F
0	0	0	0	0
0	0	0	1	X
0	0	1	0	0
0	0	1	1	1
0	1	0	0	X
0	1	0	1	X
0	1	1	0	1
0	1	1	1	X
1	0	0	0	0
1	0	0	1	1
1	0	1	0	0
1	0	1	1	X
1	1	0	0	1
1	1	0	1	X
1	1	1	0	X
1	1	1	1	1

CD \ AB	00	01	11	10
00	0	X	1	0
01	X	X	X	1
11	1	X	1	X
10	0	1	X	0

$$F = B + D$$

12.26

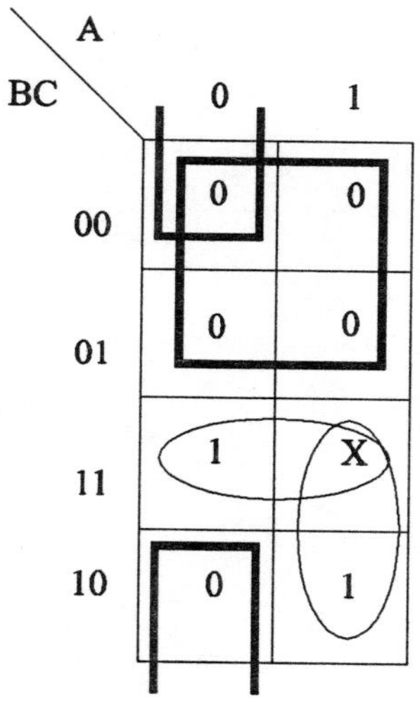

SOP: $F = AB + BC$ $\Rightarrow$ 3 gates

POS: $\overline{F} = \overline{B} + \overline{A}\cdot\overline{C} \Rightarrow F = B(A+C)$ $\Rightarrow$ 2 gates

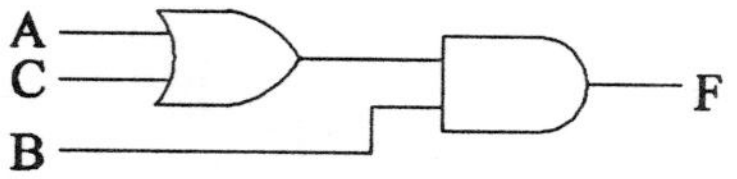

12.27

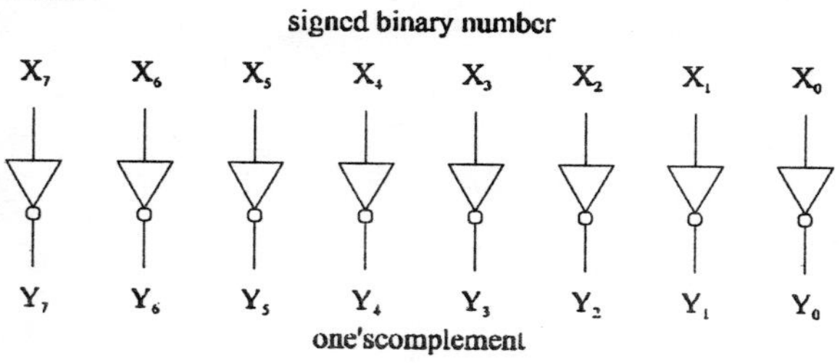

12.28

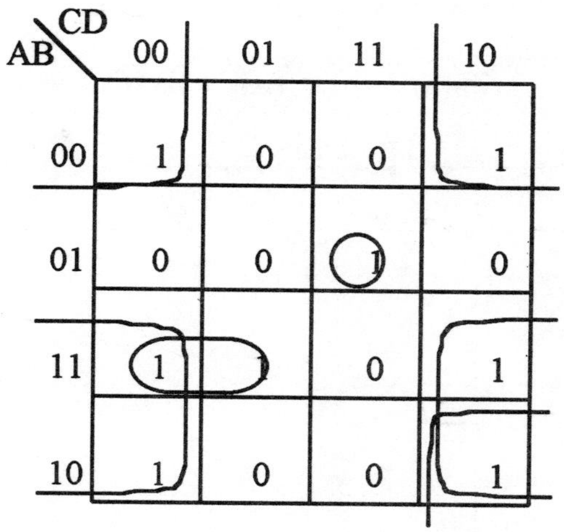

$F = \overline{B}\overline{D} + A\overline{D} + AB\overline{C} + \overline{A}BCD$

12.29

The two's complement is the one's complement plus one.

X	C_{IN}	SUM	C_{OUT}
0	0	0	0
0	1	1	0
1	0	1	0
1	1	0	1

$$SUM = X \oplus C_{IN}$$
$$C_{OUT} = X \bullet C_{IN}$$

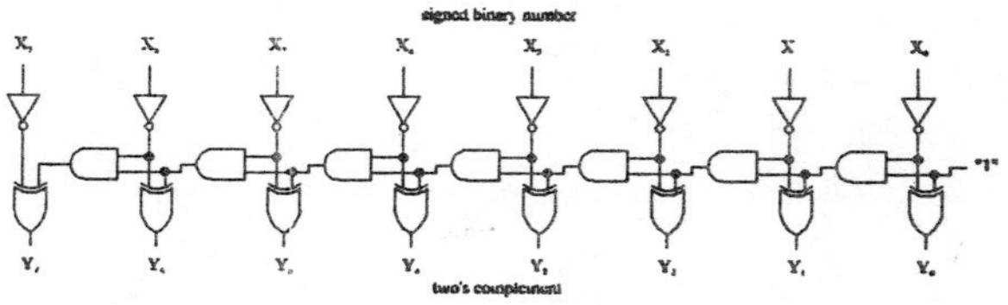

12.30

(a) = $\overline{AB}$ (b) = $\overline{B+C}$

$f = (a) + (b) = \overline{AB} + \overline{B+C}$

$= \overline{A} + \overline{B} + \overline{B}\overline{C} = \overline{A} + \overline{B}$

12.31

A one-bit adder truth table is as follows:

C_{IN}	x	y	SUM	C_{OUT}
0	0	0	0	0
0	0	1	1	0
0	1	0	1	0
0	1	1	0	1
1	0	0	1	0
1	0	1	0	1
1	1	0	0	1
1	1	1	1	1

From this table, we find that:

$$SUM = C_{IN} \oplus x \oplus y$$

$$C_{OUT} = C_{IN} + C_{IN} + xy$$

Simple circuits for these two functions are shown below:

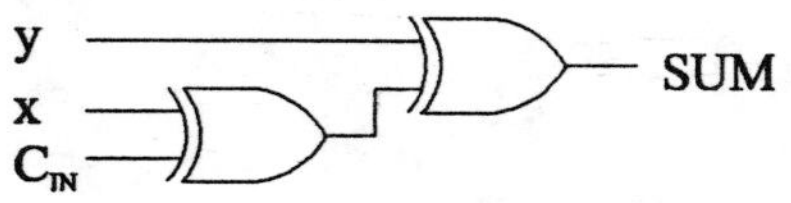

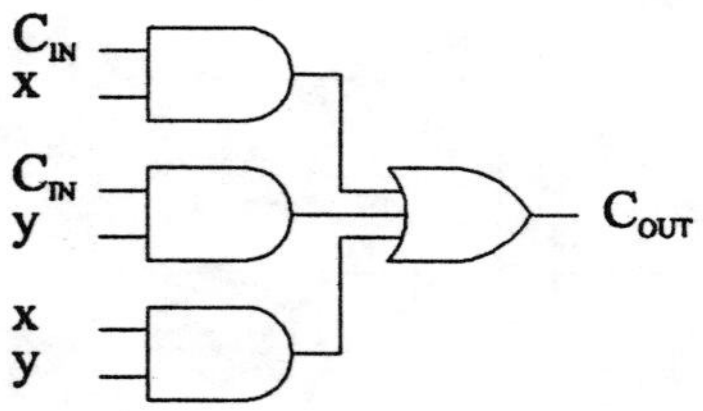

The complete 4-bit adder can be constructed as shown below:

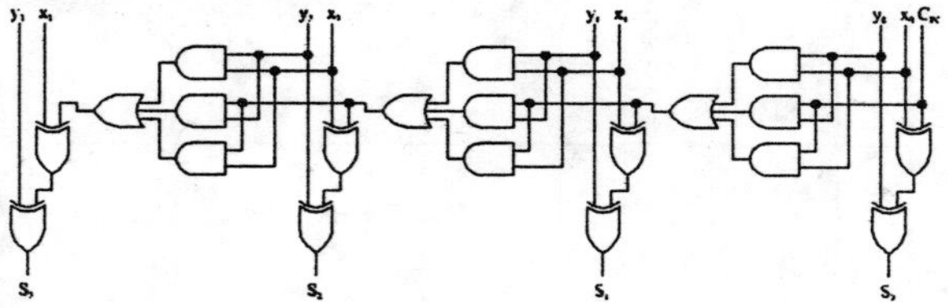

Note that this circuit assumes a carry-in for the lsb. If this is not necessary, then the circuit can be reduced correspondingly.

12.32

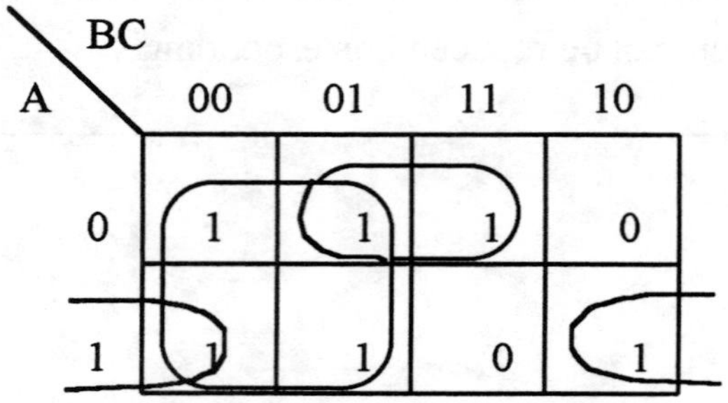

$$F = \bar{B} + \bar{A}C + A\bar{C}$$

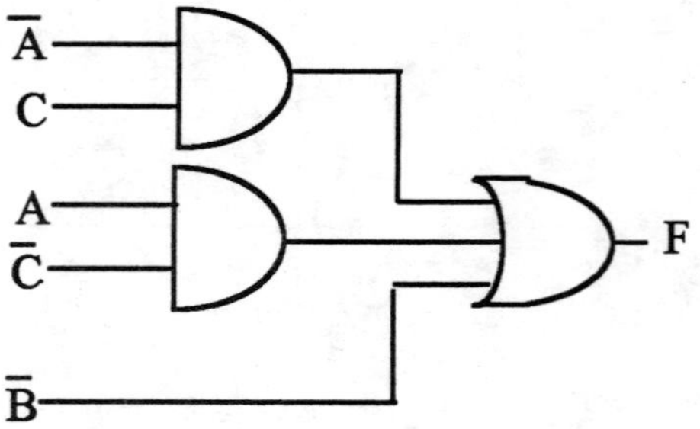

12.33

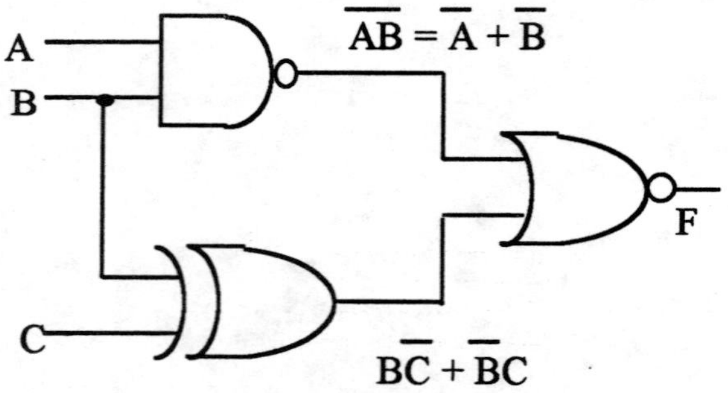

$$f(A,B,C) = ABC$$

12.34

Let WX represent a 2-bit code for the donor blood type, and let yz represent a 2-bit code for the recipient blood type. Then WXYZ will represent a donor-recipient pair. Let F be true if a transfusion can be made. Blood type codes may be assigned as follows:

	WX	YZ
A	00	00
B	01	01
AB	10	10
O	11	11

The truth table is:

Donor→Recipient	WX	YZ	F
A→A	00	00	1
A→B	00	01	0
A→AB	00	10	1
A→O	00	11	0
B→A	01	00	0
B→B	01	01	1
B→AB	01	10	1
B→O	01	11	0
AB→A	10	00	0
AB→B	10	01	0
AB→AB	10	10	1
AB→O	10	11	0
O→A	11	00	1
O→B	11	01	1
O→AB	11	10	1
O→O	11	11	1

And the Karnaugh map, then, is as follows:

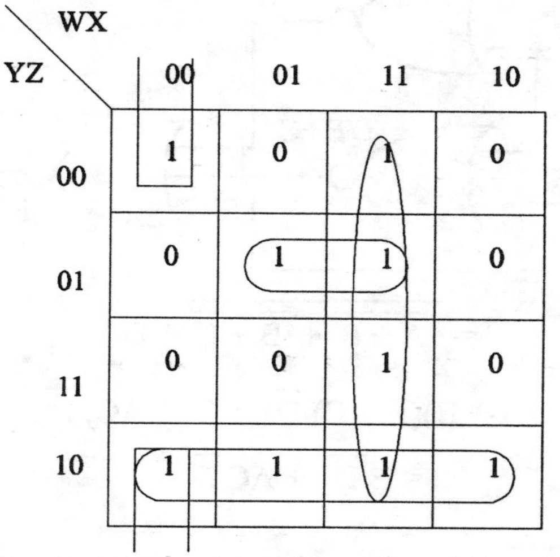

From the Karnaugh map,

$$F = \overline{W}\cdot\overline{X}\cdot\overline{Z} + X\cdot\overline{Y}\cdot Z + WX + Y\overline{Z}$$

and the resulting circuit is shown below:

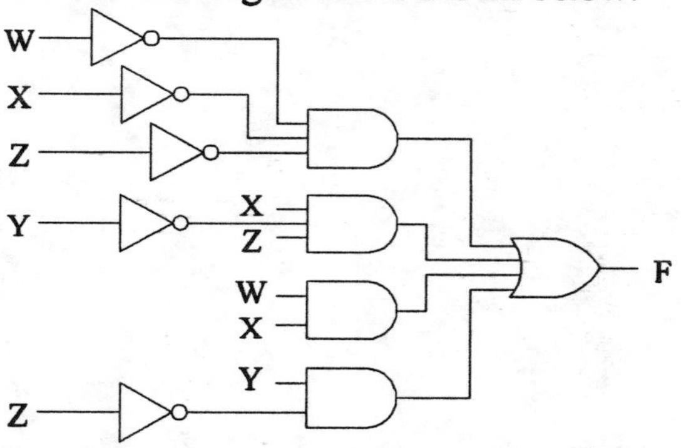

12.35

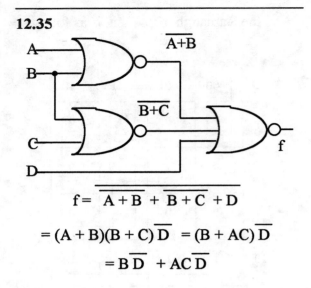

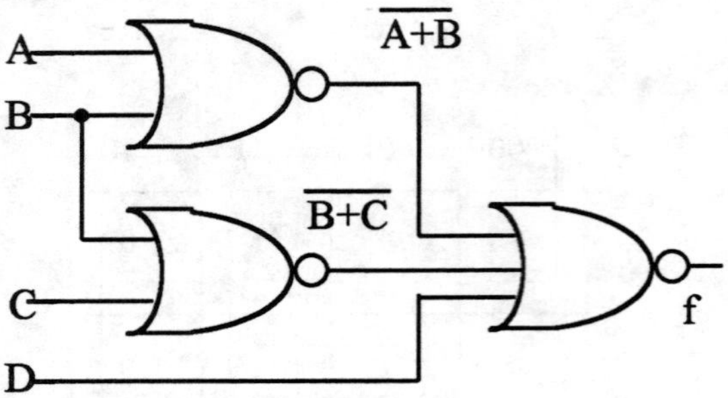

$$f = \overline{\overline{A+B} + \overline{B+C} + D}$$

$$= (A+B)(B+C)\overline{D} = (B+AC)\overline{D}$$

$$= B\overline{D} + AC\overline{D}$$

12.36

The appropriate truth table can be constructed as follows:

A B C D	F4	F3	F2	F1	F0
0 0 0 0	0	0	0	0	0
0 0 0 1	0	0	0	1	0
0 0 1 0	0	0	0	0	1
0 0 1 1	0	0	1	1	0
0 1 0 0	0	0	0	1	0
0 1 0 1	0	1	0	1	0
0 1 1 0	0	0	0	1	1
0 1 1 1	0	1	1	1	0
1 0 0 0	0	0	1	0	0
1 0 0 1	1	0	0	1	0
1 0 1 0	0	0	1	0	1
1 0 1 1	1	0	1	1	0
1 1 0 0	0	0	1	1	0
1 1 0 1	1	1	0	1	0
1 1 1 0	0	0	1	1	1
1 1 1 1	1	1	1	1	0

Next, we construct a Karnaugh map for each bit of the output, and determine its corresponding function.

F_4

CD \ AB	00	01	11	10
00	0	0	0	0
01	0	0	1	1
11	0	0	1	1
10	0	0	0	0

$$F_4 = AD$$

F_3

CD \ AB	00	01	11	10
00	0	0	0	0
01	0	1	1	0
11	0	1	1	0
10	0	0	0	0

$$F_3 = BC$$

F_2

CD \ AB	00	01	11	10
00	0	0	1	1
01	0	0	0	0
11	1	1	1	1
10	0	0	1	1

$$F_2 = AB + A\overline{D}$$

F_1

CD \ AB	00	01	11	10
00	0	1	1	0
01	1	1	1	1
11	1	1	1	1
10	0	1	1	0

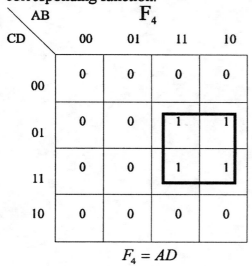

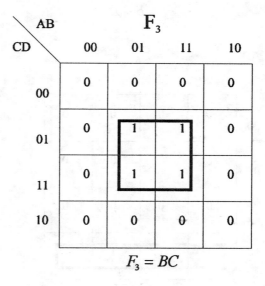

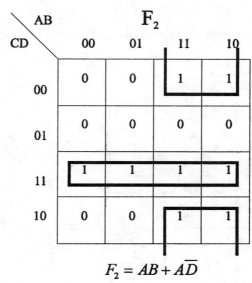

$$F_1 = B + D$$

F_0

CD \ AB	00	01	11	10
00	0	0	0	0
01	0	0	0	0
11	0	0	0	0
10	1	1	1	1

$$F_0 = C\overline{D}$$

The corresponding circuits are shown below:

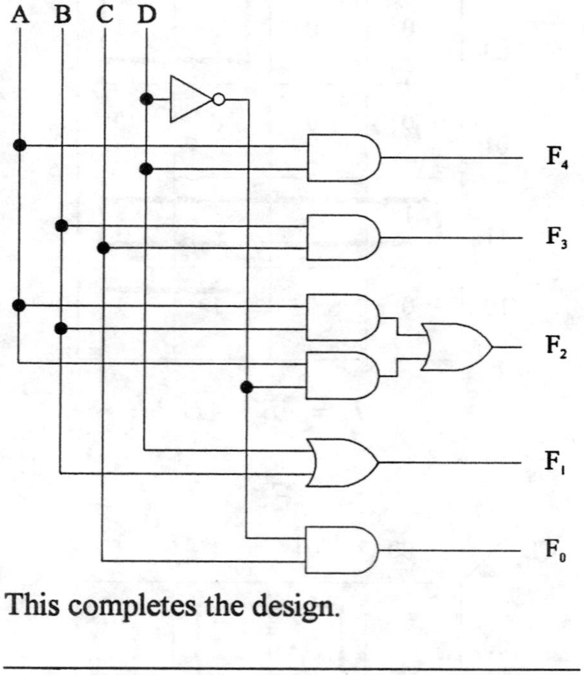

This completes the design.

12.37

a)

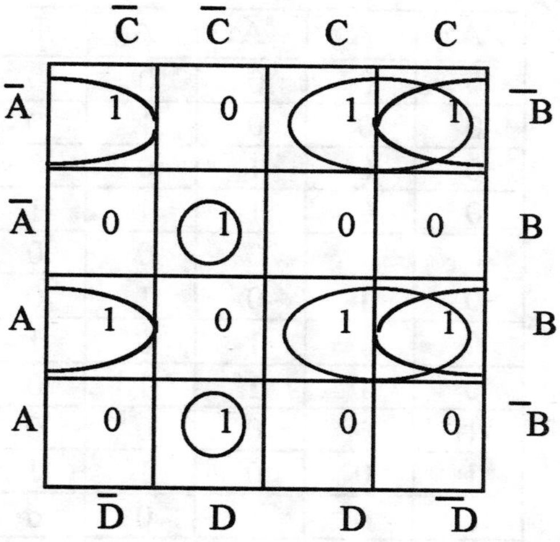

b) $F = \bar{A}\bar{B}\bar{D} + \bar{A}\bar{B}C + \bar{A}BCD +$

$AB\bar{D} + ABC + ABCD$

12.38

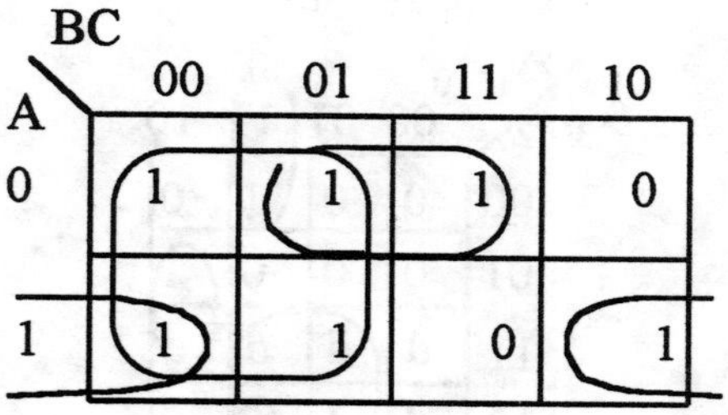

$f = \bar{B} + \bar{A}C + A\bar{C}$

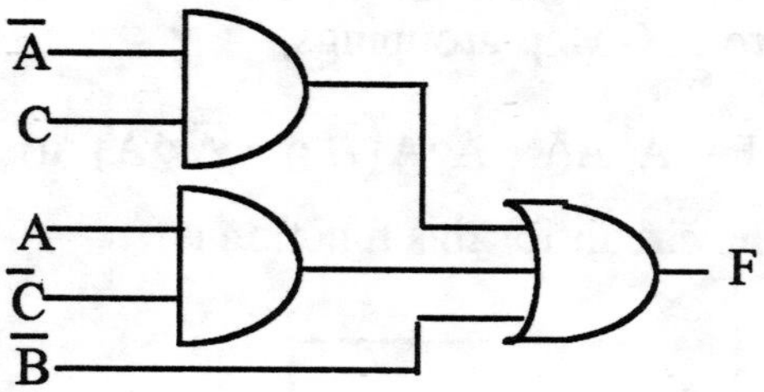

12.39

a)

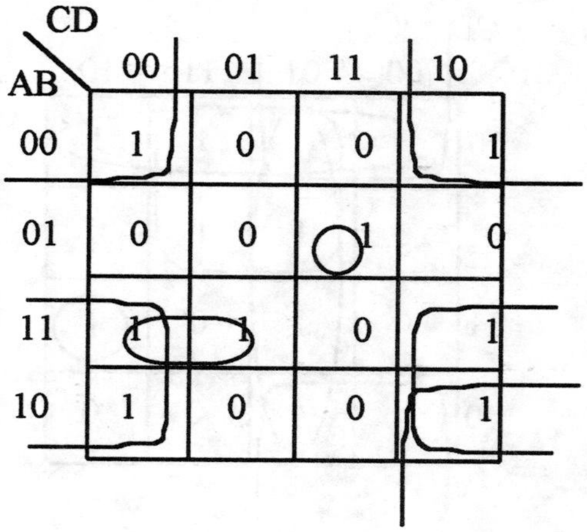

b) $F = \bar{B}\bar{D} + A\bar{D} + AB\bar{C} + \bar{A}BCD$

12.40

a)

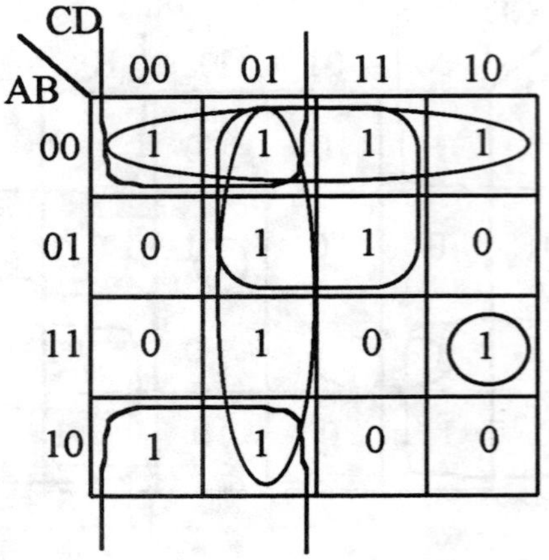

b) $\bar{A}\bar{B} + \bar{A}D + \bar{C}D + \bar{B}\bar{C} + ABC\bar{D}$

c)

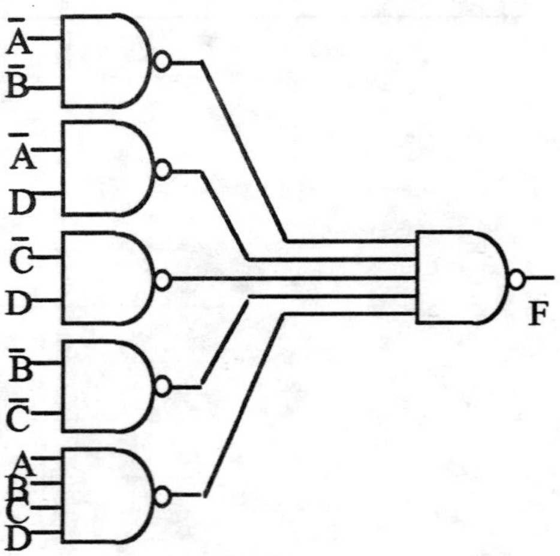

12.41

a)

A_3	A_2	A_1	A_0	F
0	0	0	0	0
0	0	0	1	0
0	0	1	0	0
0	0	1	1	1
0	1	0	0	0
0	1	0	1	0
0	1	1	0	1
0	1	1	1	0
1	0	0	0	0
1	0	0	1	1
1	0	1	0	d
1	0	1	1	d
1	1	0	0	d
1	1	0	1	d
1	1	1	0	d
1	1	1	1	d

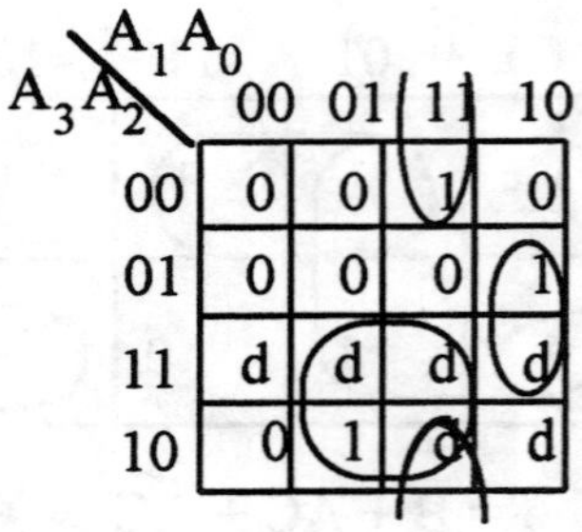

b) From K-Map groupings,

$$F = A_3A_0 + A_2A_1\bar{A}_0 + \bar{A}_2A_1A_0$$

c) The circuit for this function is:

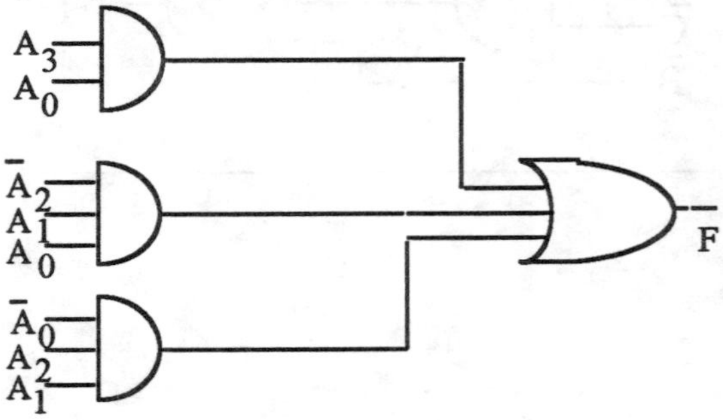

12.42

CD \ AB	00	01	11	10
00	0	1	0	0
01	1	1	0	0
11	0	x	1	0
10	0	0	1	0

$$F = \bar{A}\,\bar{C}\,D + \bar{A}\,B\,\bar{C} + ABC$$

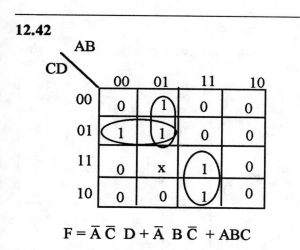

12.43

For this problem, the truth table is as follows:

A B C D	F_4	F_3	F_2	F_1	F_0
0 0 0 0	0	0	0	0	0
0 0 0 1	0	0	0	1	0
0 0 1 0	0	0	0	0	1
0 0 1 1	0	0	1	1	0
0 1 0 0	0	0	0	1	0
0 1 0 1	0	1	0	1	0
0 1 1 0	0	0	0	1	1
0 1 1 1	0	1	1	1	0
1 0 0 0	0	0	1	0	0
1 0 0 1	1	0	0	1	0
1 0 1 0	X	X	X	X	X
1 0 1 1	X	X	X	X	X
1 1 0 0	X	X	X	X	X
1 1 0 1	X	X	X	X	X
1 1 1 0	X	X	X	X	X
1 1 1 1	X	X	X	X	X

Now, we construct the Karnaugh maps and determine the corresponding functions.

F_4

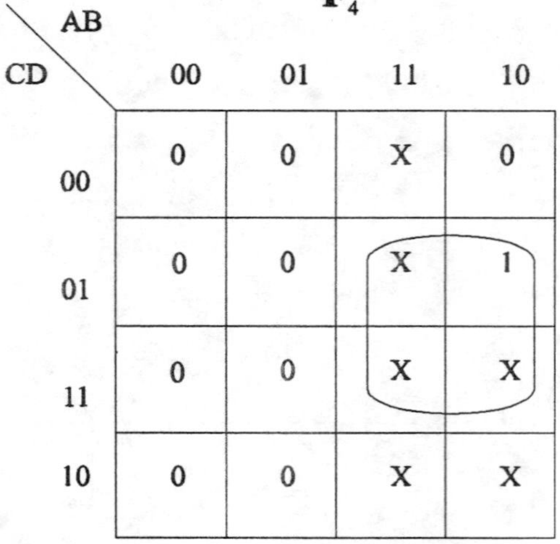

$F_4 = AD$

F_3

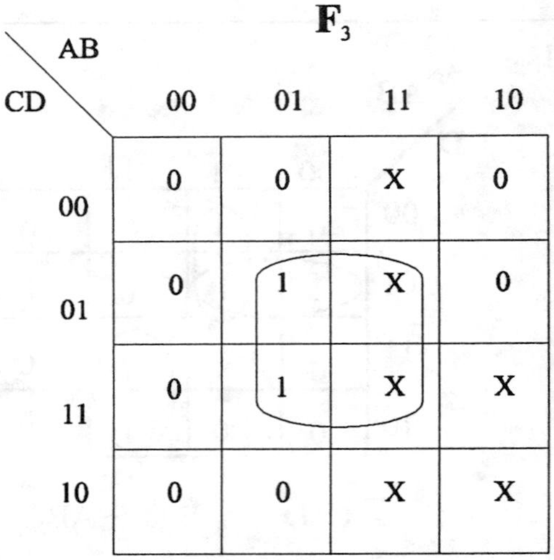

$F_3 = BC$

F_2

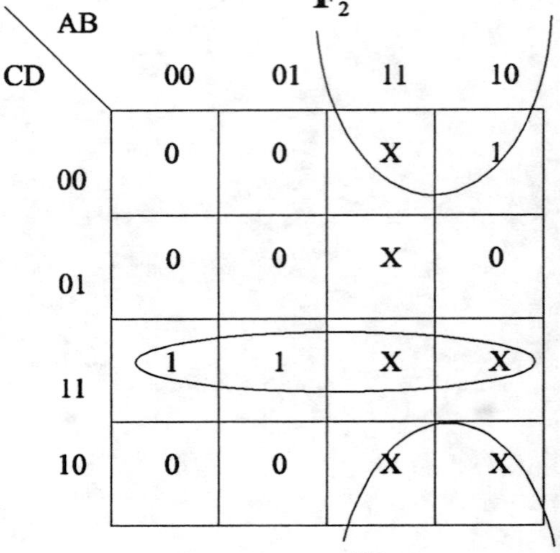

$F_2 = AB + A\overline{D}$

F_1

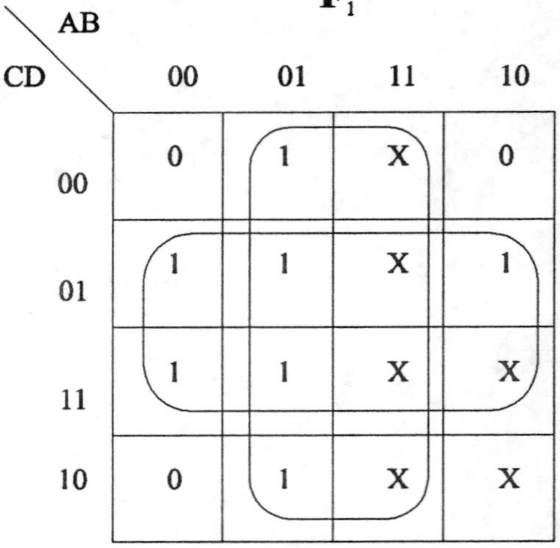

$F_1 = B + D$

F_0

CD \ AB	00	01	11	10
00	0	0	X	0
01	0	0	X	0
11	0	0	X	X
10	1	1	X	X

$F_0 = C\overline{D}$

These expressions are identical to those obtained in Problem 12.36. Suprisingly, the presence of the don't cares did not change (or simplify) the solution.

12.44

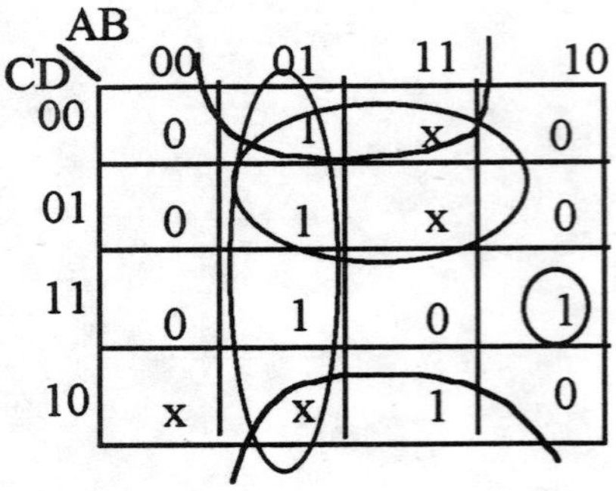

$F = A\bar{B}CD + B\bar{C} + B\bar{D} + \bar{A}B$

12.45

(a)

x	y	C	S
0	0	0	0
0	1	0	1
1	0	0	1
1	1	1	0

(b) Binary Addition - S is the sum, and C is the carry.

12.46

Assuming that the enable input (EN) is active high, when EN is logic 0 (A is logic 1), all decoder outputs of the first decoder are forced to logic 1 independent of the inputs. However, when EN is logic 1 (A is logic 0), all decoder outputs of the second decoder are forced to logic 1 independent of the select inputs. Therefore, A functions as the fourth bit of the select inputs. Thus, the circuit operates as a 4 of 16 decoder.

12.47

We construct the truth table for this circuit as shown below:

Binary Input $B_3B_2B_1B_0$	G_3	G_2 $B_2 \oplus B_3$	G_1 $B_1 \oplus B_2$	G_0 $B_0 \oplus B_1$
0000	0	0	0	0
0001	0	0	0	1
0010	0	0	1	1
0011	0	0	1	0
0100	0	1	1	0
0101	0	1	1	1
0110	0	1	0	1
0111	0	1	0	0
1000	1	1	0	0
1001	1	1	0	1
1010	1	1	1	1
1011	1	1	1	0
1100	1	0	1	0
1101	1	0	1	1
1110	1	0	0	1
1111	1	0	0	0

The output is clearly a Gray code since each number only changes by one bit relative to the previous number.

12.48

(a) Note that:

$B_3 = G_3$

$B_2 = G_3 \oplus G_2 = B_3 \oplus G_2$

$B_1 = G_3 \oplus G_2 \oplus G_1 = B_2 \oplus G_1$

$B_0 = G_3 \oplus G_2 \oplus G_1 \oplus G_0 = B_1 \oplus G_0$

Then, the truth table is:

$G_3G_2G_1G_0$	B3 G3	B2 $G_3 \oplus G_2$	B1 $B_2 \oplus G_1$	B0 $B_1 \oplus G_0$
0 0 0 0	0	0	0	0
0 0 0 1	0	0	0	1
0 0 1 0	0	0	1	0
0 0 1 1	0	0	1	1
0 1 0 0	0	1	0	0
0 1 0 1	0	1	0	1
0 1 1 0	0	1	1	0
0 1 1 1	0	1	1	1
1 0 0 0	1	0	0	0
1 0 0 1	1	0	0	1
1 0 1 0	1	0	1	0
1 0 1 1	1	0	1	1
1 1 0 0	1	1	0	0
1 1 0 1	1	1	0	1
1 1 1 0	1	1	1	0
1 1 1 1	1	1	1	1

The table verifies that the claim is correct.

(b) The circuit is shown below:

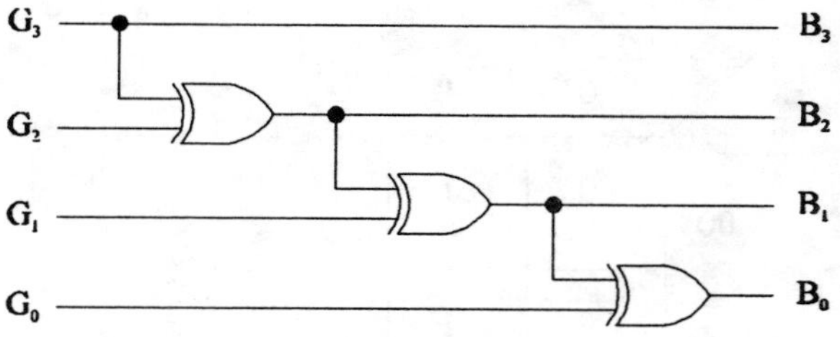

12.49

$f = \overline{A}B\overline{C} + A\overline{B}\overline{C} + AC$

BC \ A	0	1
00	0	1
01	0	1
11	0	1
10	1	0

From the truth table it is clear that:

$I_0 = 0$

$I_1 = \overline{C}$

$I_2 = 1$

and

$I_3 = C$

12.50

CD \ AB	00	01	11	10
00	0	0	0	1
01	0	1	1	1
11	0	0	0	1
10	1	1	1	1

From the truth table it is clear that:

$I_0 = 0$

$I_1 = \overline{D}$

$I_2 = D$

$I_3 = \overline{D}$

$I_4 = 1$

$I_5 = 1$

$I_6 = D$

and

$I_7 = \overline{D}$

Digital Systems

Chapter 13 Instructor Notes

Chapter 13 logically follows the material on combinational digital logic circuits introduced in Chapter 12. It begins with a discussion of sequential logic modules, including a practical example which illustrates the use of a counter to measure the speed of rotation of a slotted wheel; this is a very common measurement in mechanical systems.

The next two sections motivate and briefly introduce digital systems and microcomputer architecture. The third section provides a brief introduction to microprocessors. This introduction is by necessity but a brief survey, and is based on the 80X86 architecture.

In addition to the usual exercises aimed at reinforcing the understanding of the material, the chapter includes a number of design problems.

Chapter 13 problem solutions

13.1

(a) The device is called a MOD-16 ripple counter. It can count clock pulses from 0 to (2^4-1). The outputs divide the frequency by 2^1, 2^2, 2^3, and 2^4 respectively. Therefore, you can use this circuit as a divide by N counter, where N is 2, 4, 8 and 16.

(b)

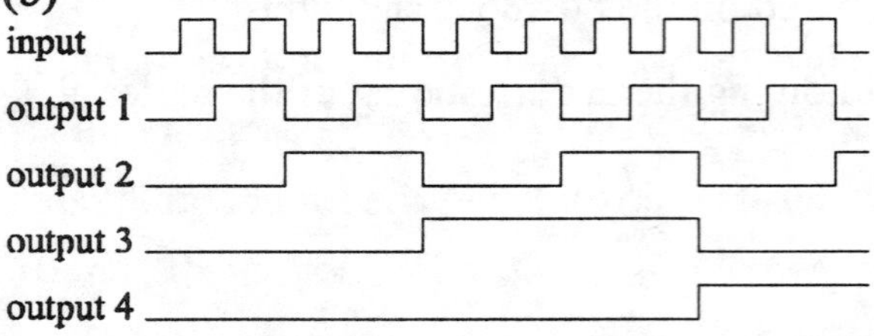

13.2

(a) $100_{10} = 1100100_2 \Rightarrow$ 7 flip flops required

(b)

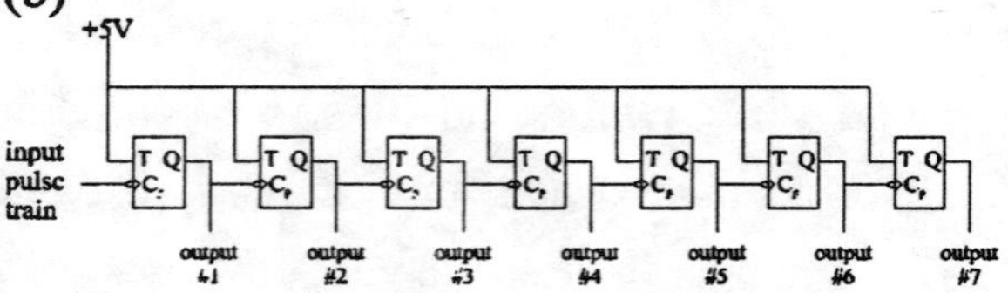

This circuit could be modified with combinational logic if it is desired to have it reset at 100_{10} and start counting again from 0000000_2

13.3

The basic operation of the circuit is to count up when X=0, and to count down when X=1.

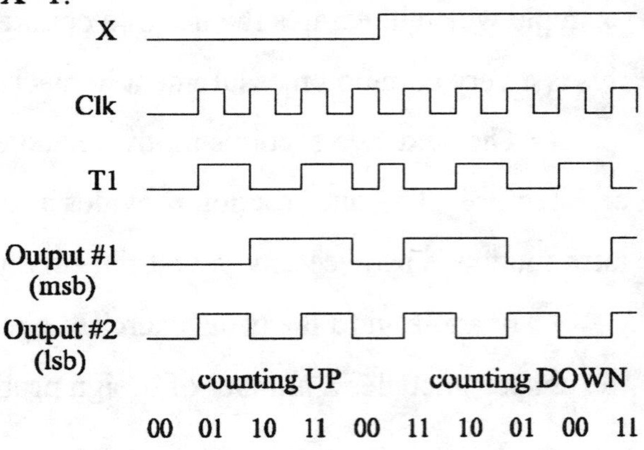

Clock	X	Output #2	T_1	Output #1
↑	0	0	0	No change
↑	1	1	0	No change
↑	0	1	1	toggle
↑	1	0	1	toggle

13.4

(a)

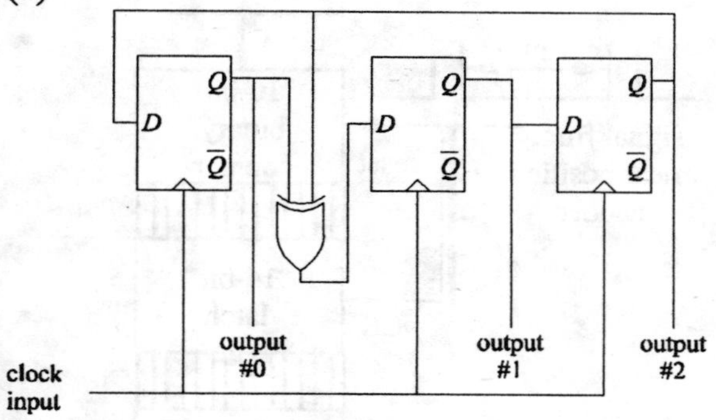

(b)

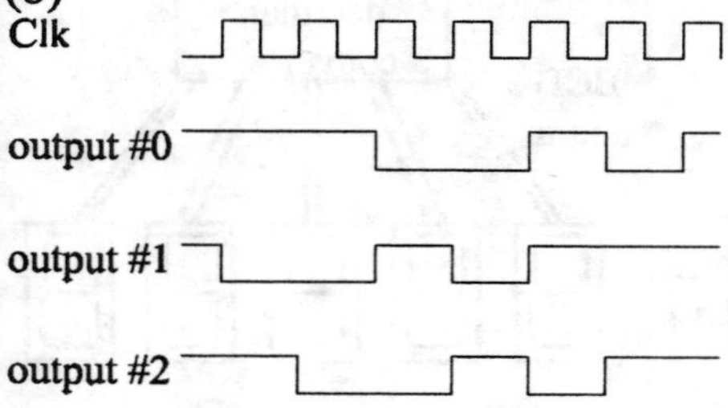

13.5

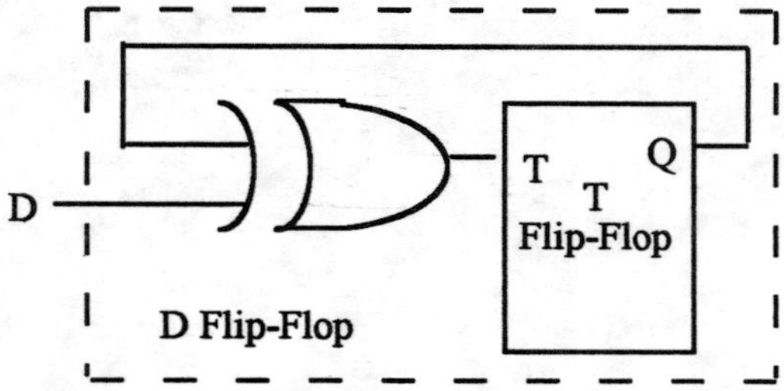

Assume that Q is logic 0 initially. If the input D is logic 0, the output of the gate is logic 0 which means that the output of the T flip-flop will not be toggled (i.e., will remain logic 0). When the input D is logic 1, the output of the gate will be logic 1. Therefore, the output of the flip-flop will be 1. Thus, the circuit will operate as a D flip-flop.

13.6

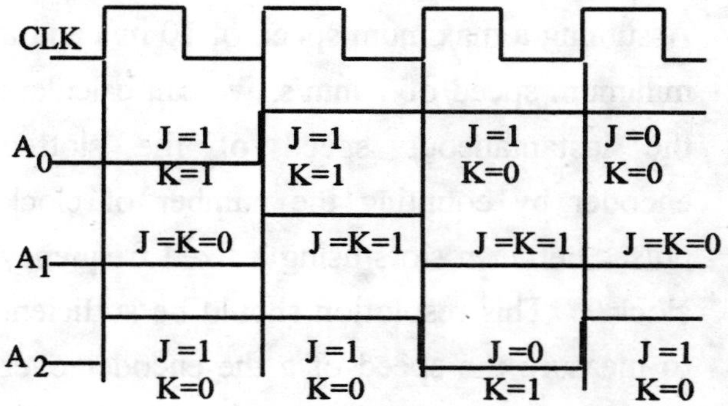

13.7

Assuming a maximum speed of 10 m/s and a minimum speed of 1 mm/s, we can calculate the instantaneous speed of the slotted encoder by counting the number of clock pulses between slots using a fixed frequency clock. This resolution should be sufficient to measure the speed of a the encoder over the range of interest. The figure depicts the arrangement: a 10 kHz clock increments a 16-bit binary counter; the choice for a 16-bit counter is due to the maximum speed requirement: 2^{16} = 65,536, will be the maximum count between slots; at a speed of 10 m/s, the time for one slot to go by is 10^{-4} s, thus the number of counts would be 1 count; at the minimum speed of 1 mm/s the number of counts would be 10^4. A 14-bit counter would be sufficient, but in practice it is easier to cascade two 8-bit counters; thus the choice of a 16-bit counter. The count is held by a latch, and then converted to BCD for use with seven-segment displays. The details of the seven-segment display encoders are not shown (see Example 13.7). If a decimal point is placed to the right of the second seven-segment display (starting from the left in the figure), the display will read the speed in m/s, up to a maximum of 10 m/s, with a resolution of 1 mm/s.

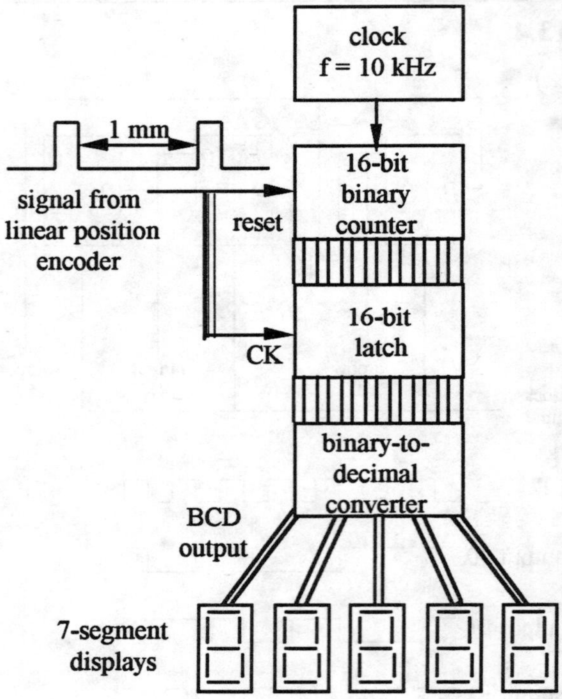

13.8

Output

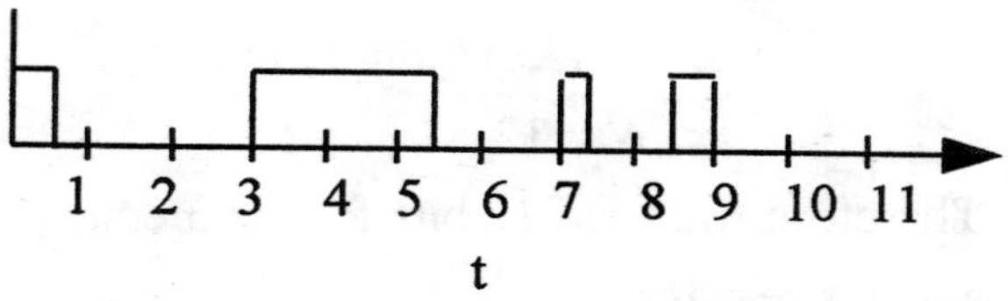

13.9

This is briefly discussed in the digital counters section, on pp. 669-670.

13.10

Knowing that an input to the *R* or *S* line will be effective only when the enable input is *1*, and the outputs are initially 0, the truth table for an R-S flip-flop with set and preset is as follows:

S	R	P	C	Q
0	0	0	0	0
0	0	0	1	0
0	0	1	0	1
0	1	0	0	0
0	1	0	1	0
1	0	0	0	1
1	0	1	0	1

13.11

J_n	K_n	Q_{n+1}
1	1	$\overline{Q_n}$ (toggle)

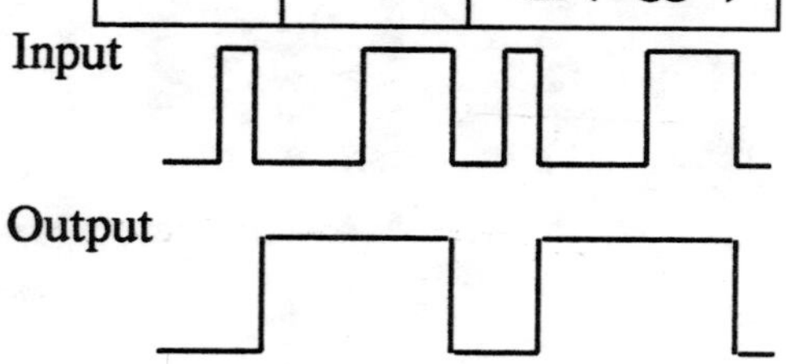

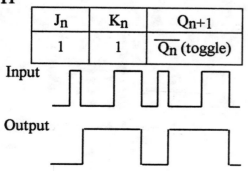

13.12

J_n	K_n	Q_{n+1}
1	1	$\overline{Q_n}$ (toggle)

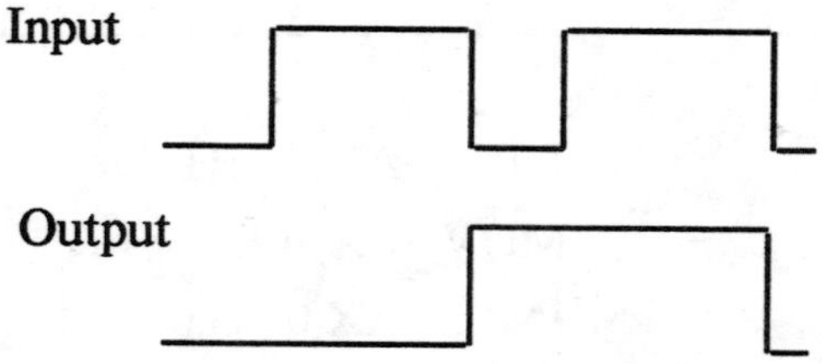

13.13

T	A	B	Q
0	1	0	q
1	0	0	$\bar{q}$

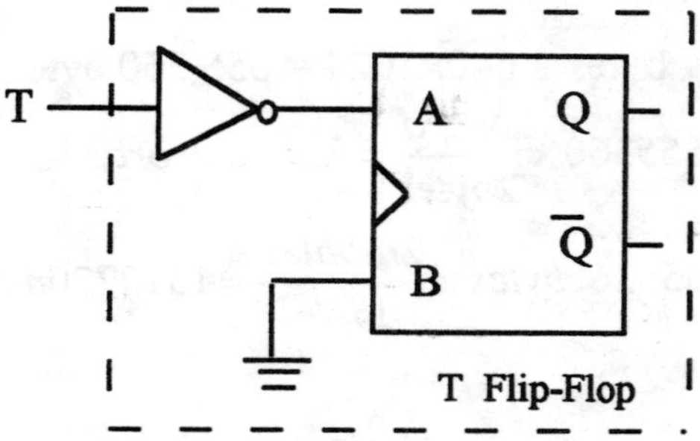

13.14

```
IN    AL,0D1H ;Input from D1H to low byte of accum.
MOV   BL,AL   ;move data to low byte of reg. B
IN    AL,0D2H ;Input from D2H to low byte of accum.
ADD   AL,BL   ;Add both numbers and place in accum.
OUT   0D0H,AL ;Output result to D0H
```

13.15

```
IN    AL,0F5H  ;Input from F5H to low byte of accum.
MUL   0A1H     ;Multiply data by contents of A1H
OUT   0B0H,AL  ;Output result to B0H
```

13.16

```
        IN    AX,0E5H
        MOV   BX,AX
        IN    AX,0C2H
        CMP   AX,BX
        JE    Equal
        MOV   AX,#0H
        JMP   End
Equal:  MOV   AX,#1H
End:    OUT   0B1H,AX
```

13.17

640K bytes = 640×1024 = 655,360 bytes

(a) $655360\times\dfrac{1word}{2bytes}=327680words$

(b) $655360bytes\times\dfrac{2nibbles}{1byte}=1310720nibbles$

(c) $655360bytes\times\dfrac{8bits}{1byte}=5242880bits$

(d) $1Mbyte=1024Kbytes$

$\therefore$ we need $1024-640=384Kbytes$

or $384\times 8=3072Kbits$

or $\dfrac{3072}{256}=12$ of the 256Kbit chips.

Cost = $12\times\$0.20=\$2.40$

13.18

a) n(n-1)

b) 2n

13.19

(a) We need

$$2^N=4Kbytes=4096$$
$$\Rightarrow N=12$$

Therefore, we need 12 bits for the memory address register.

(b) The data register must be at least as large as each word in memory. Therefore, the data register must be 16 bits in length.

13.20

"Volatile" memory is memory whose contents are lost when the power is turned off. This the RAM in a computer. "Nonvolatile" means that the information in the memory is not lost when the power is off. This is a magnetic disk, magnetic tape or ROM in a computer.

13.21

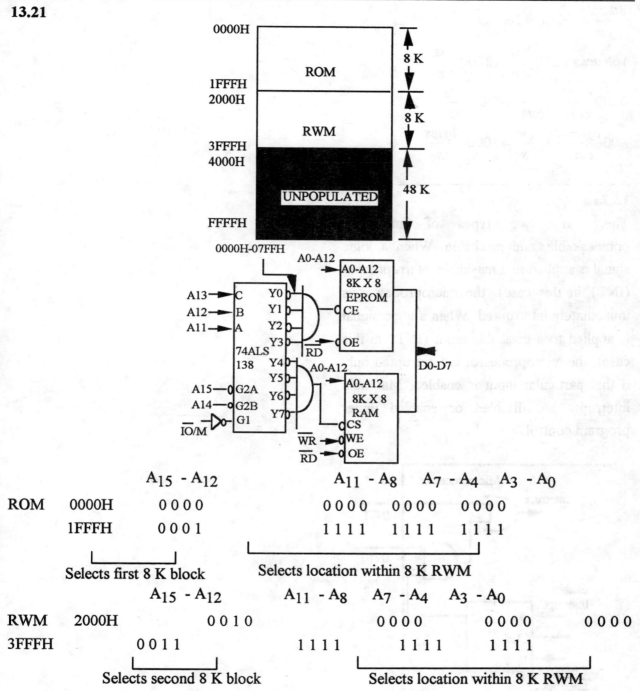

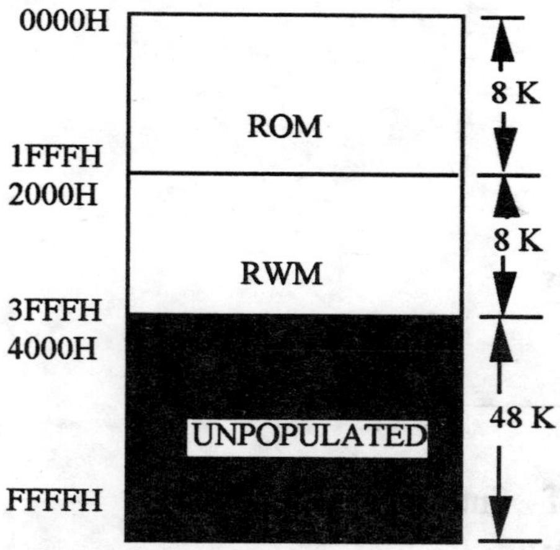

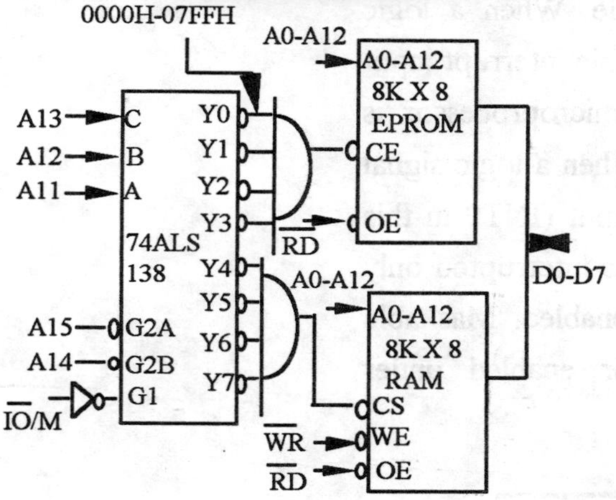

		A_{15} - A_{12}	A_{11} - A_8	A_7 - A_4	A_3 - A_0
ROM	0000H	0 0 0 0	0 0 0 0	0 0 0 0	0 0 0 0
	1FFFH	0 0 0 1	1 1 1 1	1 1 1 1	1 1 1 1

Selects first 8 K block — Selects location within 8 K RWM

		A_{15} - A_{12}	A_{11} - A_8	A_7 - A_4	A_3 - A_0
RWM	2000H	0 0 1 0	0 0 0 0	0 0 0 0	0 0 0 0
	3FFFH	0 0 1 1	1 1 1 1	1 1 1 1	1 1 1 1

Selects second 8 K block — Selects location within 8 K RWM

Using the memory map and address bit map, we can design the required memory system as shown in the figure.

13.22

$$\frac{8tracks}{cm} \times 2cm = 16tracks$$

$$16tracks \times 200\frac{bits}{cm} = 3200\frac{bits}{cm}$$

$$3200\frac{bits}{cm} \times \frac{1byte}{8bits} = 400\frac{bytes}{cm}$$

$$400\frac{bytes}{cm} \times 25\frac{cm}{s} = 10000\frac{bytes}{s}$$

13.23

There are two types of interrupts: nonmaskable, and maskable. When a logic signal is applied to a maskable interrupt input (INT1 in this case), the microprocessor is immediately interrupted. When a logic signal is applied to a maskable input (INT0 in this case), the microprocessor is interrupted only if that particular input is enabled. Maskable interrupts are disabled or enabled under program control.

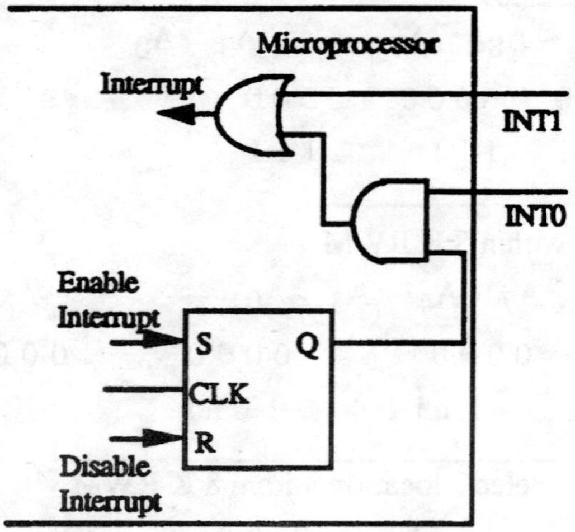

Electronic Instrumentation and Measurements

Chapter 14 Instructor Notes

Chapter 14 continues the discussion of integrated circuit electronics begun in Chapter 11. The Chapter is extremely modular, and the degree of coverage can vary widely, depending on the requirements of each individual Instructor. The first two sections cover measurement systems and transducers, and noise problems. The third covers the instrumentation amplifier (which had been introduced in Chapter 11) in greater depth. This section might be of interest by itself as an extension of Chapter 11. Section 14.3 also discusses practical active filters, focusing on Butterworth and Chebyshev designs; the material in this section is fairly advanced, and will require the student to have had a rigorous introduction to the Laplace Transform and to systems concepts. Thus, this section will be appropriate for a second course on electronics and instrumentation. The active filter design material would be nicely complemented by laboratory exercises; the importance of filter design and analysis in instrumentation problems is not to be underestimated. This material could also be supplemented very effectively by a review of filter design and analysis procedures using computer aids (e.g., MATLAB® or PSpice®).

The material in section 14.4, on the subject of signal interface (A/D, D/A conversion and sample-and-hold amplifiers) is, on the other hand, much more quantitative, and could for example be presented separately, for example, in conjunction with Chapter 11, or Chapter 12, or Chapter 13. There are excellent possibilities for very useful laboratory experiments in connection with this material. The emphasis is on illustrating the important parameters and performance limitations in the application of commercial ADCs, DACs, and sample-and-hold amplifiers. A commercial data acquisition board is also described. It is this Author's opinion that this material is of great practical importance to non-majors, many of whom will at some point make use of a microcomputer-based digital data acquisition system, regardless of their specialty.

Section 14.5 can also be viewed as an extension of Chapter 11, and could be covered in a first course. Again, the section is independent of the other sections in the chapter. In this section, the op-amp comparator and the Schmitt trigger are introduced first; once the analysis methods have been extended to include the possibility of positive feedback, simple oscillators are also introduced, including the astable, and monostable multivibrators. The section closes with a functional description of the NE 555 timer IC.

The last section is somewhat unusual for a textbook of this nature in covering the basic elements of digital data transmission. However, given the pervasive presence of digital instruments and microcomputers in engineering laboratories and in the field, a brief survey of the IEEE 488 and RS-232 standards can prove extremely useful in practice.

The homework problems present a variety of analysis and design problems on instrumentation amplifiers and active filters. Several design problems are also given to complement the section on timing circuits; a few of the problems require the student to explore the data sheets for the AD 625 instrumentation amplifier, the 555 timer, and the 74123 one-shot. Although these problems are fairly simple, they can be used to educate the student to search for design parameters in the data sheets. The data sheets are provided at the end of the chapter.

Also included is a series of problems on DAC and ADC analysis and design. Some emphasis is again placed on reading and understanding the device data sheets of commercial ADCs and DACs. Issues in sampling frequency selection and resolution are approached in a few applied problems, where practical measurement situations pertaining to the measurement of angular position (problem 14.59), torque (problem 14.61), and altitude (problem 14.62) are described. The chapter problems end with a few simple problems on data transmission and coding.

Chapter 14 problem solutions

14.1

1. Frequency - engine speed is normally measured right at the crankshaft prior to any gearing in rpm - typically several thousands. The transducers used with speedometers measure speed at the axle in rpm - typically much lower than at the engine output.
2. Scale factors - the tachometer would require none, the speedometer requires a conversion factor from rpm of the axle (rotational) to mph (linear).

14.2

Audio frequencies: $0 < f \le 15kHz$

Visible frequencies: $3.9 \times 10^{14}\ Hz \le f \le 7.9 \times 10^{14}\ Hz$

Devices used to measure quantities at audio frequencies will be incapable of sensing or measuring accurately those same quantities at frequencies in the visual range.

Various types of photocells are available for use as light sensors. For audio frequencies, more conventional devices like bridges may be used for measuring signals.

14.3

Use a transducer that will convert temperature in degrees Fahrenheit to volts between the values of the 2-sided supply voltage.

Similarly measure the percentage relative humidity and convert the transducer output to the requisite voltage.

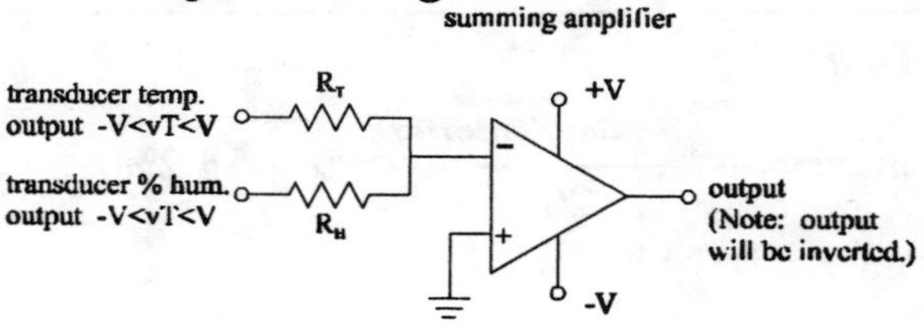

14.4

$$i = C\frac{\Delta e_o}{\Delta t}$$

$$\Delta q = C\Delta e_o$$

$$\frac{\Delta q}{C} = \Delta e_o$$

Assume no change in charge.

$$C_{new} = \frac{2}{3}C_{old} \Rightarrow \Delta e_o = \frac{3}{2}V$$

14.5

(a) $V_{out} = i_D R_L$

Given a large enough value of V_D,

$V_{out} = 0.5 \times 10^{-6} H R_L$; hence, varies linearly with H.

(b) $1 = 0.5 \times 10^{-6}(1500)R_L$

$R_L = 1333\Omega$

14.6

(a) $V_{out} = 0.055\frac{V \cdot m}{N} \times \frac{1in}{0.0254m} \times \frac{1}{0.25in} = 8.66\frac{V}{N}$

(b) $0\frac{V}{N}$

14.7

$$error = \pm\left(10 + \frac{5+2}{2}\right) = \pm 13.5\%$$

14.8

$$mean = \frac{\sum measurements}{20} = 9.945 \pm 2\%$$

$\max. = 10.144$

$\min. = 9.746$

$$average\ deviation = \frac{\sum |deviations|}{20} = 0.225$$

$$standard\ deviation = \sqrt{\frac{\sum |deviations|^2}{20}} = 0.427$$

Measurement #1 exceeds the standard deviation ⇒ probability<0.99 ⇒ roller speed will be adjusted

14.9

(a) This term and instrument accuracy are used interchangeably if only one instrument is involved and if the measurement method is appropriate. Basically, the accuracy of the measurement is given by the instrument's specifications (ordinarily in terms of ±percent of indicated value or full scale value).

(b) See answer to part (a).

(c) Measurement error can be synonymous with measurement accuracy, but can also refer to sloppy methods of data acquisition, use of multiple transducers and/or instruments whose individual errors combine, or simply a lack of reliable, multiple data points.

(d) Precision and resolution are interchangeable terms and refer to the smallest increment of measured quantity that can be detected by the instrument.

14.10

(a) (b) and (c) are precise, (a) and (d) are not.

(b) (a) and (c) are accurate, (b) and (d) are not.

14.11

$$A = 1 + \frac{2R_2}{R_1} = 1 + \frac{1(5k\Omega)}{1k\Omega} = 1 + 10 = 11$$

14.12

$$A = 1 + \frac{2R_2}{R_1}$$

$$\Rightarrow\ R_2 = \frac{1}{2}R_1(A-1) = \frac{1}{2}(1k\Omega)(50-1) = 24.5k\Omega$$

14.13

$$A = 1 + \frac{2R_2}{R_1}$$

$$\Rightarrow\ R_1 = \frac{2R_2}{A-1} = \frac{2(10k\Omega)}{16-1} \approx 1333\Omega$$

14.14

$$\mathrm{A} = 1 + \frac{2\mathrm{R}_2}{\mathrm{R}_1} = 21$$

14.15

$$\mathrm{A} = 1 + \frac{2\mathrm{R}_2}{\mathrm{R}_1} = 107.7$$

14.16

$$\mathrm{A_{dif}} = \frac{\mathrm{R_F}}{\mathrm{R}}\left(1 + \frac{2\mathrm{R}_2}{\mathrm{R}_1}\right) = 110$$

14.17

$$CMRR_{dB} = 20\log_{10}\left|\frac{A_{dif}}{\frac{R_F}{R}\left(\frac{R+R_F}{R_F+R+\Delta R}-1\right)A}\right|$$

$$A_{dif} = A \times \frac{R_F}{R}$$

$$\Delta R = 0.02 \times R = 0.02 \times 1k\Omega = 20\Omega$$

$$CMRR_{dB} = 20\log_{10}\left|\frac{A\frac{R_F}{R}}{\frac{R_F}{R}\left(\frac{R+R_F}{R_F+R+\Delta R}\right)A}\right|$$

$$= 20\log_{10}\left|\frac{1}{\frac{R+R_F}{R_F+R+\Delta R}-1}\right|$$

$$= 20\log_{10}\left|\frac{1}{\frac{1000+200000}{200000+1000+20}-1}\right|$$

$$\approx 80dB$$

14.18

Assume $A = 10$.

Then $A_{dif} = \frac{R_F}{R} A = 2000$

$20\log A_{dif} \approx 66dB$

$CMRR_{dB} = 80dB$ (from Problem 14.17)

$20\log A_{dif} - CMRR_{dB} = -14dB$

14.19

$$A_{dif} = \frac{R_F}{R}\left(1 + \frac{2R_2}{R_1}\right) = \frac{10}{R}\left(1 + \frac{2R_2}{2}\right) = 900$$

Thus, $1 + R_2 = 90R$

Choose $R = 1\ k\Omega \Rightarrow R_2 = 89\ k\Omega$

14.20

$20\log 10\sqrt{1 + \omega_s^{2n}} \geq 40$ @ $\omega_s = 25$ rad/s

Solving the equation, we obtain $n \geq 1.43$.

Thus $n = 2$ is desired.

14.21

This is an inverting amplifier circuit, with

$$V_{out} = -\frac{Z_F}{Z_{in}} V_{in}$$

where

$$Z_F = R_F \left\| \frac{1}{j\omega C_F} \right. = \frac{R_F \times \frac{1}{j\omega C_F}}{R_F + \frac{1}{j\omega C_F}} = \frac{R_F}{1 + j\omega R_F C_F}$$

and $Z_{in} = R_{in}$. Therefore,

$$V_{out} = -\frac{R_F}{R_{in}} \frac{1}{1 + j\omega R_F C_F} V_{in}$$

(a) $\left|\frac{V_{out}}{V_{in}}\right| = \frac{R_F}{R_{in}} \frac{1}{\sqrt{1 + (\omega R_F C_F)^2}}$

(b) $\angle V_{out} - \angle V_{in} = \pi - \tan^{-1} \omega R_F C_F$ rad.

or $= 180° - \tan^{-1} \omega R_F C_F$ deg.

14.22

$$\left|\frac{V_{out}}{V_{in}}\right| = \frac{R_F}{R_{in}} \frac{1}{\sqrt{1 + (wR_F C_F)^2}}$$

$$= \frac{100k}{20k} \frac{1}{\sqrt{1 + \left(2000\pi \times 100 \times 10^3 \times 100 \times 10^{-12}\right)^2}}$$

$$= 4.99$$

$$\angle V_{out} - \angle V_{in} = \pi - \tan^{-1}\left(2000\pi \times 100 \times 10^3 \times 100 \times 10^{-12}\right)$$

$$= \pi - \tan^{-1}\left(62.8 \times 10^{-3}\right)$$

$$= 3.079\, rad.$$

$$v_{out}(t) = 9.98 \sin(2000\pi t + 3.079)\ V$$

14.23

The circuit is shown below:

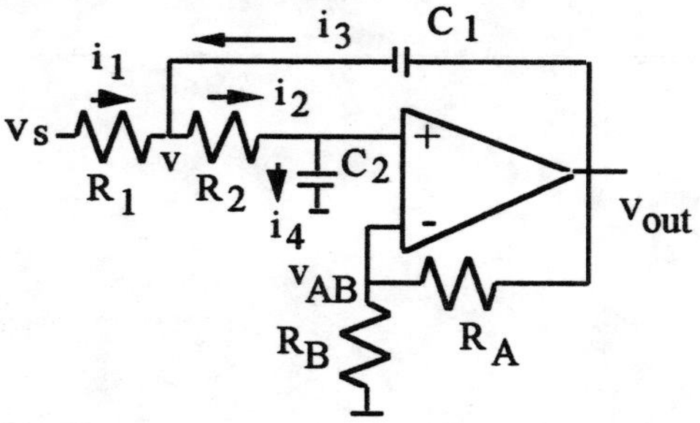

We have

$$v_{AB} = \frac{R_B}{R_A + R_B} v_{out}$$

$$i_1 = \frac{v_s - v}{R_1} \qquad i_2 = \frac{v - v_{AB}}{R_2}$$

$$i_3 = \frac{v_{out} - v}{1/j\omega C_1} \qquad i_4 = \frac{v_{AB}}{1/j\omega C_2}$$

From $i_2 = i_4$, we have

$$v = v_{AB}(1 + j\omega R_2 C_2)$$

From $i_1 + i_3 = i_2$, we have

$$v_{out}\Big(- j\omega C_1 + \frac{R_B}{R_A + R_B} j\omega C_1(1 + j\omega R_2 C_2) + \frac{(1 + j\omega R_2 C_2)}{R_1}\frac{R_B}{R_A + R_B} + \frac{j\omega R_B C_2}{R_A + R_B}\Big) = \frac{v_s}{R_1}$$

Therefore, the frequency response is:

$$\frac{v_{out}(j\omega)}{v_s(j\omega)} = 1/\Big\{\frac{R_B R_1 R_2 C_1 C_2}{R_A + R_B}(j\omega)^2 - \frac{R_1 R_A}{R_A + R_B} j\omega C_1 + \frac{R_1 R_B + R_B}{R_A + R_B} j\omega R_2 C_2 + \frac{R_B}{R_A + R_B}\Big\}$$

$$= \frac{K}{(j\omega)^2 + K_1 j\omega + K_2}$$

where

$$K = \frac{R_A + R_B}{R_B R_1 R_2 C_1 C_2}$$

$$K_1 = \frac{R_1 + 1}{R_1 C_1} - \frac{R_A}{R_B R_2 C_2}$$

$$K_2 = \frac{1}{R_1 R_2 C_1 C_2}$$

14.24

The circuit is shown below:

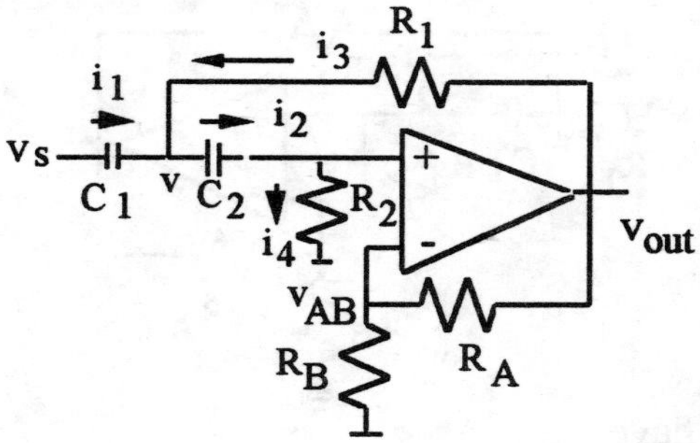

We have

$$v_{AB} = v_{out}\frac{R_B}{R_A + R_B}$$

$$i_1 = \frac{v_s - v}{1/j\omega C_1}, \quad i_2 = \frac{v - v_{AB}}{1/j\omega C_2}$$

$$i_3 = \frac{v_{out} - v}{R_1}, \quad i_4 = \frac{v_{AB}}{R_2}$$

From $i_2 = i_4$, we have $v = \frac{1}{j\omega C_2}\frac{v_{AB}}{R_2} + v_{AB}$

From $i_1 + i_3 = i_2$, we have

$$jwC_1 v_S = v_{out}\left(\left(\frac{jwC_1 R_B}{jwC_2 R_2}\right)\left(\frac{1}{R_A + R_B}\right) + \frac{jwC_1 R_B}{R_A + R_B}\right)$$

$$-\frac{v_{out}}{R_1} + \frac{R_B}{R_1(R_A + R_B)}\left(\frac{1}{jwC_2 R_2} + 1\right)v_{out} + \frac{R_B}{R_2(R_A + R_B)}v_{out}$$

Therefore, the frequency response is:

$$\frac{v_{out}(j\omega)}{v_s(j\omega)} = \frac{(j\omega)^2/K}{(j\omega)^2 + j\omega K_1 - K_2}$$

where $\quad K = \frac{R_B}{R_A + R_B}$

$$K_1 = \frac{1}{K R_1 C_1} - \frac{1}{R_2 C_2} - \frac{1}{R_1 C_1} - \frac{1}{R_2 C_1}$$

$$K_2 = \frac{1}{R_1 R_2 C_1 C_2}$$

14.25

The circuit is shown below:

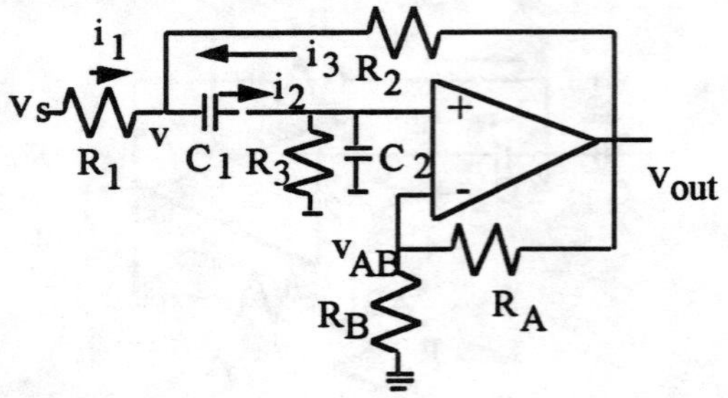

We have

$$v_{AB} = \frac{R_B}{R_A + R_B} v_{out}$$

$$i_1 = \frac{v_s - v}{R_1}$$

$$i_2 = \frac{v - v_{AB}}{1/j\omega C_1}$$

$$i_3 = \frac{v_{out} - v}{R_2}$$

From $i_2 = \dfrac{v_{AB}}{R_3 \| (1/j\omega C_2)} = \dfrac{v_{AB}(1 + j\omega R_3 C_2)}{R_3}$,

we have

$$v = \frac{1 + j\omega C_2 R_3}{j\omega C_1 R_3} v_{AB} + v_{AB}$$

From $i_1 + i_3 = i_2$, we have

$$\frac{v_s}{R_1} = \frac{R_B}{R_1(R_A + R_B)}\left(\frac{1 + j\omega C_2 R_3}{j\omega C_1 R_3} + 1\right) v_{out}$$

$$- \frac{v_{out}}{R_2} + \frac{\left(\frac{1+j\omega C_2 R_3}{j\omega C_1 R_3} + 1\right)}{R_2} \frac{R_B}{R_A + R_B} v_{out}$$

$$+ \frac{1 + j\omega C_2 R_3}{R_3} \frac{R_B}{R_A + R_B} v_{out}$$

The frequency response therefore is:

$$\frac{v_{out}(j\omega)}{v_s(j\omega)} = \frac{j\omega K}{(j\omega)^2 + K_1 j\omega + K_2}$$

where $\quad K = \dfrac{C_1 R_3 (R_A + R_B)}{R_1 R_B R_3 C_1 C_2}$

$$K_1 = \left(\frac{1}{R_1 C_1} + \frac{1}{R_1 C_2} + \frac{1}{C_1 R_2} + \frac{1}{C_2 R_2} - \frac{R_A + R_B}{R_2 R_B C_2}\right)$$

$$K_2 = \frac{R_1 + R_2}{R_1 R_2 R_3 C_1 C_2}$$

14.26

$C_F = 100pF$

$f_C = 20kHz \Rightarrow \omega_C = 2\pi f_C = 40\pi k \dfrac{rad}{s}$

$\omega_C = \dfrac{1}{R_F C_F}$

$\Rightarrow R_F = \dfrac{1}{\omega_C C_F} = \dfrac{1}{40\pi \times 10^3 \times 100 \times 10^{-12}} = 79.6k\Omega$

$\dfrac{R_F}{R_{in}} = 5$

$\Rightarrow R_{in} = \dfrac{R_F}{5} = 15.9k\Omega$

14.27

$K = 1 + \dfrac{R_A}{R_B} = 10$; choosing $R_A = 9$ kΩ

$\Rightarrow R_B = 1k\Omega$.

$f = \dfrac{1}{2\pi\sqrt{R_1C_1R_2C_2}} = 10{,}000$ Hz

$[\sqrt{\dfrac{R_2C_2}{R_1C_1}} + \sqrt{\dfrac{R_1C_2}{R_2C_1}} - 9\sqrt{\dfrac{R_1C_1}{R_2C_2}}\,] = 0.2$

Choose $C_1 = C_2 = 1$ μF and solve for $R_1 = 5.4\ \Omega$ and $R_2 = 47\ \Omega$. Then, substitute the values thus obtained in the high-pass filter of Figure 14.22.

14.28

$K = 1 + \dfrac{R_A}{R_B} = 15$; choosing $R_A = 14$ kΩ

$\Rightarrow R_B = 1k\Omega$.

$f = \dfrac{1}{2\pi\sqrt{R_1C_1R_2C_2}} = 25{,}000$ Hz

$[\sqrt{\dfrac{R_2C_2}{R_1C_1}} + \sqrt{\dfrac{R_1C_2}{R_2C_1}} - 14\sqrt{\dfrac{R_1C_1}{R_2C_2}}\,]=0.1$

Choose $C_1 = C_2 = 1$ μF and solve for $R_1 = 1.8\ \Omega$ and $R_2 = 23\ \Omega$. Then, substitute the obtained values in the high-pass filter of Figure 14.22.

14.29

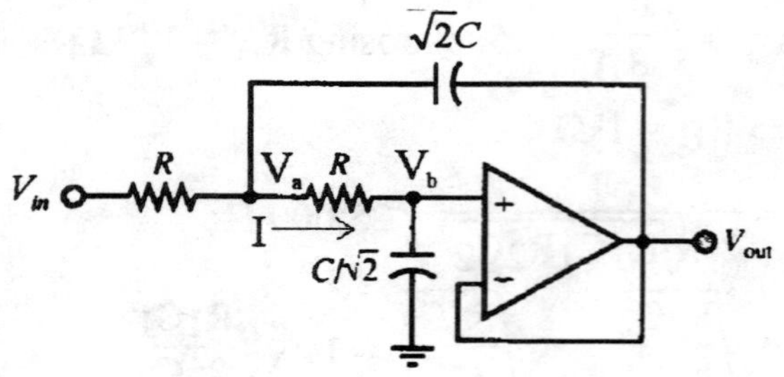

Note that $V_b \approx V_{out}$. Therefore,

$$I = \frac{V_b}{\left(\dfrac{1}{j\omega\dfrac{C}{\sqrt{2}}}\right)} = j\omega\frac{C}{\sqrt{2}}V_{out}$$

and

$$V_a = RI + V_b = R\left(j\omega\frac{C}{\sqrt{2}}V_{out}\right) + V_{out} = \left(1 + j\frac{\omega RC}{\sqrt{2}}\right)V_{out}$$

Now, writing a KCL equation at node a,

$$\frac{V_a - V_{in}}{R} + I + \frac{V_a - V_{out}}{\left(\dfrac{1}{j\omega\sqrt{2}C}\right)} = 0$$

$$\frac{\left(1 + j\dfrac{\omega RC}{\sqrt{2}}\right)V_{out} - V_{in}}{R} + j\omega\frac{C}{\sqrt{2}}V_{out} + \frac{\left(1 + j\dfrac{\omega RC}{\sqrt{2}}\right)V_{out} - V_{out}}{\left(\dfrac{1}{j\omega\sqrt{2}C}\right)} = 0$$

$$\frac{1}{R}V_{in} = \left[\frac{\left(1 + j\dfrac{\omega RC}{\sqrt{2}}\right)}{R} + j\omega\frac{C}{\sqrt{2}} + \frac{\left(1 + j\dfrac{\omega RC}{\sqrt{2}} - 1\right)}{\left(\dfrac{1}{j\omega\sqrt{2}C}\right)}\right]V_{out}$$

$$= \left[\frac{1}{R} + j\frac{\omega C}{\sqrt{2}} + j\frac{\omega C}{\sqrt{2}} - \omega^2 RC^2\right]V_{out}$$

$$V_{in} = \left(1 + j\sqrt{2}\omega RC - \omega^2 R^2 C^2\right)V_{out}$$

$$\frac{V_{out}}{V_{in}} = \frac{1}{1 - (\omega RC)^2 + j\sqrt{2}\omega RC}$$

$$\left|\frac{V_{out}}{V_{in}}\right| = \frac{1}{\sqrt{1 - 2(\omega RC)^2 + (\omega RC)^4 + 2(\omega RC)^2}}$$

$$= \frac{1}{\sqrt{1 + (\omega RC)^4}}$$

which is a second-order Butterworth low-pass function with cutoff frequency

$$\omega_C = \frac{1}{RC}$$

14.30

$$K = 1 + \frac{R_A}{R_B} = 15$$

Choose $R_A = 14\ k\Omega \Rightarrow R_B = 1k\Omega$

$$f = \frac{1}{2\pi\sqrt{R_1C_1R_2C_2}} = 15{,}000\ \text{Hz}$$

$$[\sqrt{\frac{R_2C_2}{R_1C_1}} + \sqrt{\frac{R_1C_2}{R_2C_1}} - 14\sqrt{\frac{R_1C_1}{R_2C_2}}] = 0.2$$

Choose $C_1 = C_2 = 1\ \mu F$ and solve for $R_1 = 2.6\ \Omega$ and $R_2 = 43.9\ \Omega$. Then, substitute the obtained values in the low-pass filter of Figure 14.22.

14.31

$$Q = \frac{\sqrt{f_H f_L}}{f_H - f_L} = 0.6$$

$$K = 1 + \frac{R_A}{R_B} = 2;\ \text{choose } R_A = 1\ k\Omega$$

$\Rightarrow R_B = 1k\Omega$

$$f = \frac{1}{2\pi\sqrt{R_1C_1R_2C_2}} = 1{,}000\ \text{Hz}$$

Choose R1 = R2 and C1 = C2 = 1 μF $\Rightarrow R_1 = R2 = 160\ \Omega$. Then, substitute the obtained values in the high-pass filter of Figure 14.22.

$$K = 1 + \frac{R_A}{R_B} = 2;\ \text{choose:}$$

$$R_A = 1\ k\Omega \Rightarrow R_B = 1k\Omega$$

$$f = \frac{1}{2\pi\sqrt{R_1C_1R_2C_2}} = 200\ \text{Hz}$$

Choose $R_1 = R_2$ and $C_1 = C_2 = 1\ \mu F \Rightarrow R_1 = R_2 = 800\Omega$. Then, substitute the obtained values in the low-pass filter of Figure 14.22. By connecting the output of the high-pass filter to the input of the low-pass filter, we obtain the desired filter.

14.32

$$f_c = 10\,Hz = \frac{1}{2\pi RC}$$

$$\Rightarrow \omega_c = \frac{1}{RC} = 2\pi \times 10 = 20\pi \frac{rad}{s}$$

Choose $R = 20k\Omega$. Then,

$$\frac{1}{(20k\Omega)C} = 20\pi \Rightarrow C = \frac{1}{20 \times 10^3 \times 20\pi} = 796nF$$

and the two capacitors have values given by $\sqrt{2}C = 1.125\mu F$ and $\frac{C}{\sqrt{2}} = 563nF$.

14.33

There is no problem 14.33 in the text.

14.34

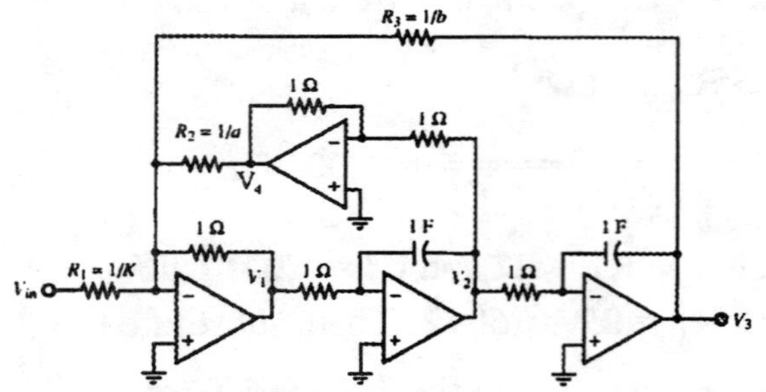

Using Laplace transforms, note that

$$V_2 = -\frac{1}{s}V_1$$

$$V_3 = -\frac{1}{s}V_2 = \frac{1}{s^2}V_1$$

and

$$V_4 = -V_2 = \frac{1}{s}V_1$$

Writing a KCL equation at the inverting input to the leftmost op-amp,

$$-KV_{in} - V_1 - aV_4 - bV_3 = 0$$

or

$$-KV_{in} - V_1 - \frac{a}{s}V_1 - \frac{b}{s^2}V_1 = 0$$

$$\Rightarrow \quad \frac{V_1}{V_{in}} = -\frac{Ks^2}{s^2 + as + b}$$

which is a second-order high-pass function.

Also,

$$\frac{V_2}{V_{in}} = -\frac{1}{s}\frac{V_1}{V_{in}} = \frac{Ks}{s^2 + as + b}$$

which is a bandpass function, and

$$\frac{V_3}{V_{in}} = \frac{1}{s^2}\frac{V_1}{V_{in}} = -\frac{K}{s^2 + as + b}$$

which is a low-pass function.

14.35

The circuit is shown below:

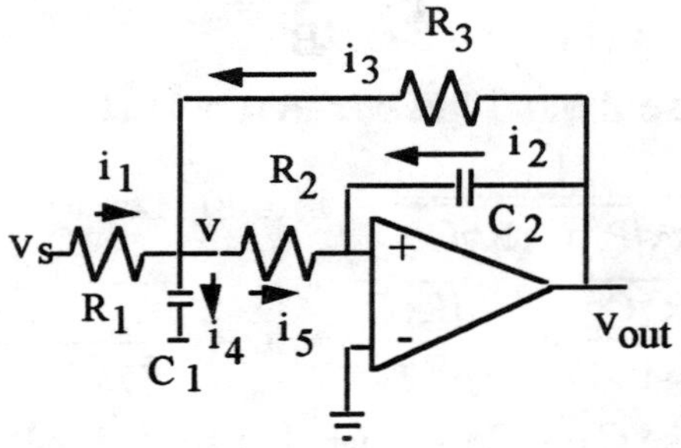

We have

$$i_1 = \frac{v_s - v}{R_1}$$

$$i_2 = \frac{v_{out}}{1/j\omega C_2}$$

$$i_3 = \frac{v_{out} - v}{R_3}$$

$$i_4 = \frac{v}{1/j\omega C_1}$$

$$i_5 = \frac{v}{R_2}$$

From $i_5 = -i_2$, we have

$$v = -j\omega R_2C_2v_{out}$$

From $i_1 + i_3 = i_4 + i_5$, we have

$$\frac{v_s}{R_1} + \frac{j\omega R_2C_2}{R_1}v_{out} + \frac{v_{out}}{R_3} + \frac{j\omega R_2C_2}{R_3}v_{out}$$

$$= -(j\omega)^2R_2C_2C_1\, v_{out} - j\omega C_2\, v_{out}$$

The frequency response therefore is:

$$\frac{v_{out}(j\omega)}{v_s(j\omega)} = \frac{K}{(j\omega)^2 + j\omega K_1 + K_2}$$

where $K = \dfrac{1}{R_1R_2C_1C_2}$

$$K_1 = \frac{1}{R_1C_1} + \frac{1}{R_3C_1} + \frac{1}{R_2C_1}$$

$$K_2 = \frac{1}{R_2R_3C_1C_2}$$

14.36

The circuit is shown below:

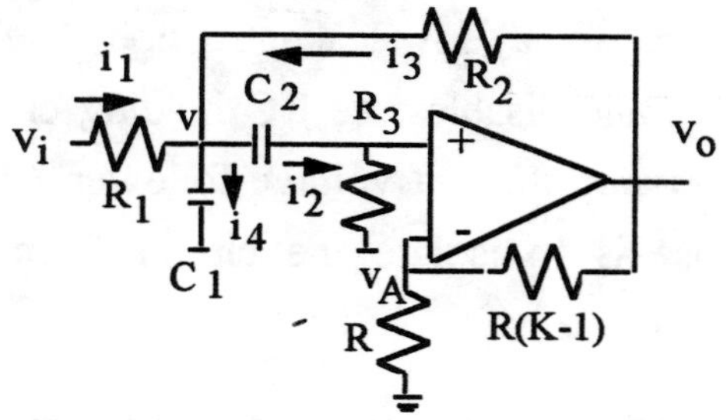

We have

$$v_A = \frac{R\,v_o}{R + R(K-1)} = \frac{v_o}{K}$$

$$i_1 = \frac{v_i - v}{R_1}$$

$$i_2 = \frac{v - v_A}{1/j\omega C_2} = \frac{v_A}{R_3}$$

$$i_3 = \frac{v_o - v}{R_2}$$

$$i_4 = \frac{v}{1/j\omega C_1}$$

From $i_2 = \frac{v_A}{R_3} = \frac{v - v_A}{1/j\omega C_2}$, we have

$$v = \frac{v_A}{j\omega C_2 R_3} + v_A = \left(\frac{1}{j\omega C_2 R_3} + 1\right)\frac{v_o}{K}$$

From $i_1 + i_3 = i_2 + i_4$, we have

$$\frac{v_i}{R_1} - \left(\frac{1}{j\omega C_2 R_3} + 1\right)\frac{v_o}{KR_1}$$

$$+ \frac{v_o}{R_2} - \left(\frac{1}{j\omega C_2 R_3} + 1\right)\frac{v_o}{KR_2}$$

$$= \frac{v_o}{KR_3} + \left(\frac{j\omega C_1}{j\omega C_2 R_3} + j\omega C_1\right)\frac{v_o}{K}$$

The frequency response therefore is:

$$\frac{v_o(j\omega)}{v_i(j\omega)} = \frac{j\omega K/C_1R_1}{(j\omega)^2 + K_1 j\omega + K_2}$$

where

$$K_1 = \frac{1}{C_1R_1} + \frac{1}{C_2R_3} + \frac{1}{R_1C_1} - \frac{K}{R_2C_1} + \frac{1}{R_2C_1}$$

and

$$K_2 = \frac{R_1 + R_2}{R_1R_2R_3C_1C_2}$$

14.37

From the expression, we can see that

$$\omega_c = \sqrt{\frac{1}{R_3R_2C_1C_2}}$$

and

$$\frac{\omega_c}{Q} = \frac{1}{R_1C_1} + \frac{1}{R_2C_1} + \frac{1}{R_3C_1}$$

or

$$\frac{1}{Q} = \sqrt{R_3R_2C_1C_2} \times \left(\frac{1}{R_1C_1} + \frac{1}{R_2C_1} + \frac{1}{R_3C_1}\right)$$

or

$$\frac{1}{Q} = \sqrt{R_2R_3\frac{C_2}{C_1}}\left(\frac{1}{R_1} + \frac{1}{R_2} + \frac{1}{R_3}\right)$$

14.38

1. Digital signals are less subject to noise, since one only needs to discriminate between two voltages.

2. Digital signals are directly compatible with.digital computers, and can therefore be easily stored on a disk, or exchanged between computers. Thus, digital signals are intrinsically more portable than analog signals.

14.39

It sequentially switches a set of analog inputs to the system input.

14.40

Op-amp #1 is an input buffer. The JFET behaves as a low-leakage diode which enables and disables the RC holding circuit, and op-amp #2 is a voltage-follower whose purpose is to isolate the circuit from the load.

14.41

(a)

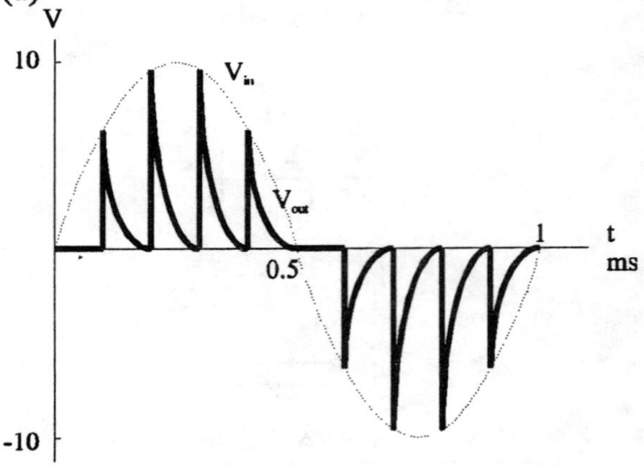

(b)

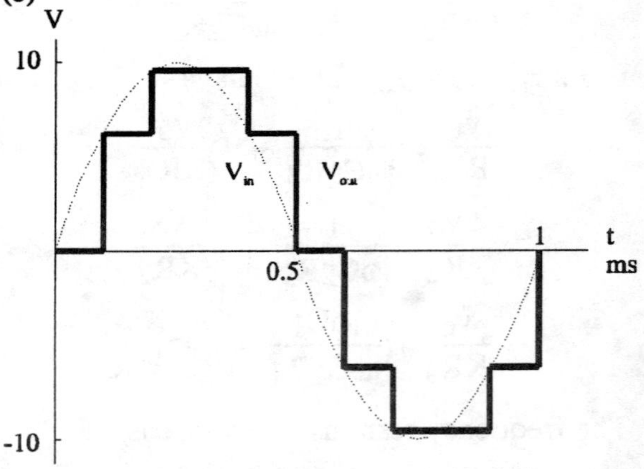

14.42

$$v_a = -4.5\frac{R_f}{R_0}\,[2^3 b_3 + 2^2 b_2 + 2^1 b_1 + b_0]$$

a) $v_a = -4.5(\frac{1}{15})(12) = -3.6\ \text{V}$

b) $(v_a)_{max} = -4.5(\frac{1}{15})(15) = -4.5\ \text{V}$

c) $\delta v = 4.5(\frac{1}{15}) = 0.3\ \text{V}$

d) $$n \geq \frac{\log\left(\frac{|(v_a)_{max} - (v_a)_{min}|}{\delta v} + 1\right)}{\log 2}$$

or $n \geq 7.82$

Therefore, we choose n= 8.

14.43

$$215_{10} = 11010111_2$$

$$v_a = -10\frac{R_f}{R_0}\,[2^7 b_7 + 2^6 b_6 + \ldots + 2^1 b_1 + b_0]$$

a) $v_a = -10(\frac{1}{255})(215) = -8.431\ \text{V}$

b) $(v_a)_{max} = -10(\frac{1}{255})(255) = -10\ \text{V}$

c) $\delta v = 10(\frac{1}{255}) = 39.2\ \text{mV}$

d) $$n \geq \frac{\log\left(\frac{|(v_a)_{max} - (v_a)_{min}|}{\delta v} + 1\right)}{\log 2}$$

or

$$n \geq 11.703$$

Therefore, we choose $n = 12$.

14.44

This circuit is just a summing amplifier, with

$$v_O = -\frac{R_2}{R_1}b_3V - \frac{R_2}{2R_1}b_2V - \frac{R_2}{4R_1}b_1V - \frac{R_2}{8R_1}b_0V$$

$$= -\frac{R_2V}{R_1}\left(b_3 + \frac{b_2}{2} + \frac{b_1}{4} + \frac{b_0}{8}\right)$$

$$= -\frac{R_2V}{8R_1}(8b_3 + 4b_2 + 2b_1 + b_0)$$

14.45

a) $v_a = -4.5(\frac{1}{255})(98) = -1.729\ \text{V}$

b) $(v_a)_{max} = -4.5(\frac{1}{255})(255) = -4.5\ \text{V}$

c) $\delta v = 4.5(\frac{1}{255}) = 17.6\ \text{mV}$

d) $$n \geq \frac{\log\left(\frac{|(v_a)_{max} - (v_a)_{min}|}{\delta v} + 1\right)}{\log 2}$$

or

$$n \geq 13.136$$

Therefore, we choose $n = 14$.

14.46

For the circuit of Figure P14.13, $R_0 = 1\ \text{k}\Omega$ and $n = 4$.

Therefore, $(v_a)_{max} = -10\ \text{V}$

and $-10 = -5\frac{R_f}{1000}(15)$

or $R_f = 133.3\ \Omega$

14.47

The simplest way would be to cascade the circuit of Figure P4.12 with a single-input inverting amplifier like the one shown in Figure 11.5 in the text. The two resistors in that circuit could be chosen equal in value so that all the second amplifier does is change the sign of the output.

14.48

If $b_k = 0$, FET_1 is cutoff and FET_2 is on. Under these conditions, the left-hand end of the resistor is grounded.

If $b_k = 1$, FET_2 is cutoff and FET_1 is on. Under these conditions, the left-hand end of the resistor is connected to V.

14.49

a) $v_a = -10(\frac{1}{4095})(345) = -0.8425$ V

b) $(v_a)_{max} = -10(\frac{1}{4095})(4095) = -10$ V

c) $\delta v = 10(\frac{1}{4095}) = 2.44$ mV

d) $$n \geq \frac{\log(\frac{|(v_a)_{max} - (v_a)_{min}|}{\delta v} + 1)}{\log 2}$$

or $n \geq 14.288$

Therefore, we choose a 15-bit ADC.

14.50

Here, $-15 \leq v_O \leq 0$ V. For the circuit of Figure P14.13, $R_O = 1$ kΩ and n = 4.

Therefore, $(v_a)_{max} = -10$ V

and $$-15 = -5\frac{R_f}{1000}(15)$$

or $R_f = 200\ \Omega$

14.51

From the results of Problem 14.44, we see that we must choose V, R_2 and R_1 such that

$$\frac{R_2 \cdot V}{8 \cdot R_1} = \frac{1}{10}$$

One possible choice is to let $V = 15V$, $R_1 = 30k\Omega$ and $R_2 = 1.6k\Omega$.

14.52

$$n \geq \frac{\log(\frac{30}{0.01} + 1)}{\log 2} = 11.55$$

Choose n = 12.

14.53

$$n \geq \frac{\log(\frac{20}{0.04} + 1)}{\log 2} = 8.96$$

Choose n = 9.

14.54

$$n \geq \frac{\log(\frac{25}{0.004} + 1)}{\log 2} = 12.6$$

Choose n = 13.

14.55

$$n \geq \frac{\log 2501}{\log 2} = 11.29$$

Choose n = 12. With this choice we compute the following resolution:

$$\text{resolution} = \frac{2500}{2^{12}} = 0.61 \text{ rev./min}$$

14.56

(a) $\text{resolution} = 2^{-3} \times 10V = 1.25V$

(b) $\text{resolution} = 2^{-8} \times 10V = 39.0625mV$

(c) more bits ⇒ better resolution

14.57

The range is 15 - (-5) = 20 V

Thus,

$$\delta v = 20(0.0005) = 10 \text{ mV}.$$

$$n \geq \frac{\log(\frac{20}{10 \text{ mv}} + 1)}{\log 2} = 10.97$$

Choose n = 11.

14.58

We assume a data acquisition system of the type shown in Figure 14.32. Therefore, each channel will be sampled at $\frac{1}{8}$ of the external clock rate and the slowest channels will determine the rate.

Thus, sampling rate = 8(100 μs + 500 μs)

= 4.8 ms.

Thus, $f_s = \frac{1}{\text{sampling rate}} = 208.3 \text{ Hz}$

and $f_{max} = \frac{1}{2} f_s = 104.15 \text{ Hz}$

14.59

For a dynamic range of 10 V for 270° of rotation, we compute the following resolution:

$$\frac{10}{270} = 37.04 \text{ mV/1°}$$

or 18.52 mV/0.5°

a) The range for 180° rotation is

$$10(\frac{180}{270}) = 6.67 \text{ V}$$

Thus,

$$n \geq \frac{\log(\frac{6.67}{0.01852} + 1)}{\log 2} = 8.497$$

and we choose n = 9.

b) The voltage gain of the amplifier is

$$\frac{10}{6.67} = 1.5$$

14.60

The conversion time should be no more than 10% of the signal period. For this case, the signal period is

$$T = \frac{1}{250 \times 10^3} = 4\mu s$$

Therefore, the conversion time should be no longer than 400ns.

14.61

Shaft rotation frequency is 800 rev./min or 13.333 rev./sec; therefore, the fluctuation frequency is 26.67 Hz:

$$T_s \leq \frac{1}{2(26.67)} = 18.75 \text{ ms}$$

14.62

The allowable error is $-10 \le e \le 10$. Therefore, an equivalent 20 meter step size is allowable and

$$n \ge \frac{\log\left(\frac{10000}{20}+1\right)}{\log 2} = 8.97$$

Thus, a 9-bit ADC is required.

14.63

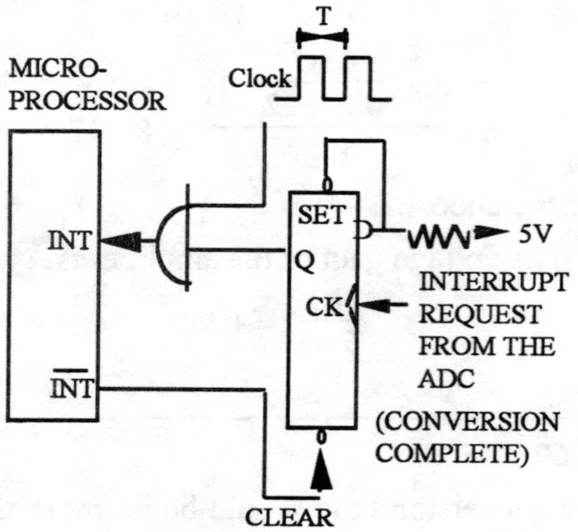

14.64

(a) 5% $\Rightarrow 2^{-n} \le 0.05 \Rightarrow n = 5$

(b) 2% $\Rightarrow 2^{-n} \le 0.02 \Rightarrow n = 6$

(c) 1% $\Rightarrow 2^{-n} \le 0.01 \Rightarrow n = 7$

14.65

This is very similar to Example 14.14,

Therefore,

$$v^{+} = \frac{R_2}{R_2+R_1} V_{OUT} + \frac{R_2}{R_2+R_3} V_S^{+}$$

Since the required noise protection level is ±150 mV, R_1 and R_2 can be computed from:

$$\frac{\Delta V}{2} = \frac{R_2}{R_2+R_1} V_{SAT} = \frac{R_2}{R_2+R_1} 8.5 = 0.15$$

where $\Delta V = 300$ mV.

$$\frac{R_2}{R_2+R_1} = \frac{0.15}{8.5} = 0.018$$

Assuming $R_1 = 100$ kΩ, R_2 can be calculated to be approximately 1.8 kΩ.

Since the required reference voltage is -1 V, we can find R_3 by solving the equation

$$\frac{R_2}{R_2+R_3} V_S^{-} = \frac{R_2}{R_2+R_3} 10 = 1$$

to obtain: $R_3 = 16.2$ kΩ.

14.66

Applying KCL:

$$\frac{v_o}{v_{in}} = 1 + \frac{R_2}{R_1}$$

Therefore, $\frac{v_o}{v_{in}} = 561$

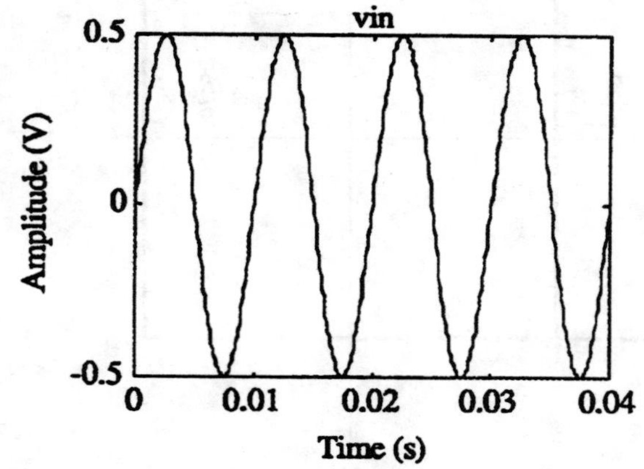

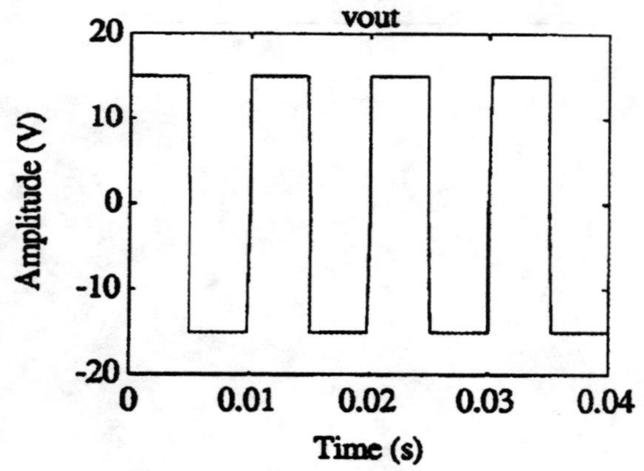

14.67

Operation of this circuit depends on the magnitude of the input voltage, V_{in}, being much larger than zero. When $V_{in} >> 0$, the op-amp will be saturated, and V_{out} will be at its saturation limit, V_R (positive rail).

When the op-amp is saturated, the approximation $V_+ = V_-$ is no longer valid. Writing KCL at the non-inverting input, we have

$$\frac{V_+ - V_{in}}{R_{in}} + \frac{V_+ - V_{out}}{R_F} = 0$$

or $$V_+\left(\frac{1}{R_{in}} + \frac{1}{R_F}\right) = \frac{1}{R_{in}}V_{in} + \frac{1}{R_F}V_{out}$$

The output changes from positive rail $(+V_R)$ to negative rail $(-V_R)$ when $V_+ = V_- = 0$. When V_{in} is small, then $V_+ \approx V_- = 0$, and

$$V_{out} = -\left(\frac{R_F}{R_{in}}\right)V_{in}$$

If $V_{out} = V_R$, then

$$V_{in} = -\left(\frac{R_{in}}{R_F}\right)V_R$$

What this means is the following:

As V_{in} drops from a large positive value, through zero, to a negative value, the output of the op-amp "switches" (from $+V_R$ to $-V_R$) at the point $V_{in} = -\left(\frac{R_{in}}{R_F}\right)V_R$.

Similarly, as V_{in} increases in the opposite direction, the "switch" from $-V_R$ to $+V_R$ occurs at $V_{in} = +\left(\frac{R_{in}}{R_F}\right)V_R$.

This is a form of voltage hysteresis, as shown in the figure below.

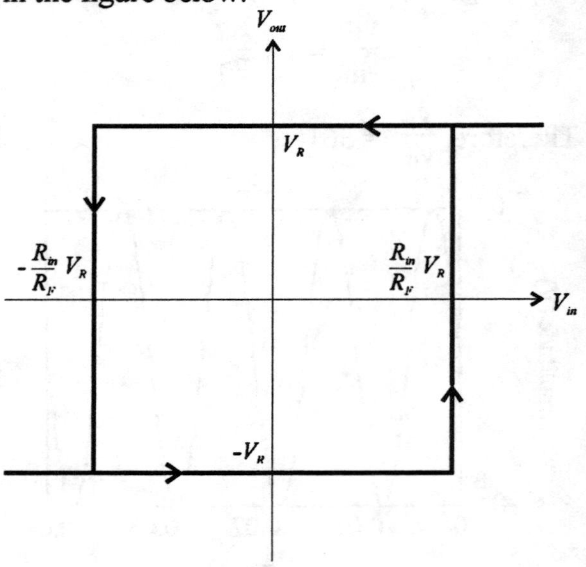

14.68

(a) We know that $V_R \approx 13V$ when the LM741 op-amp is used with $\pm 15V$ bias supplies. Then, from the discussion in the answer to Problem 14.67,

$$V_{in} = -\left(\frac{R_{in}}{R_F}\right)V_{out}$$

$$\Rightarrow R_{in} = \left(\frac{V_{in}}{V_{out}}\right)R_F = \left(\frac{0.25}{13}\right)(104k\Omega) = 2k\Omega$$

(b) The input and output waveforms are sketched below.

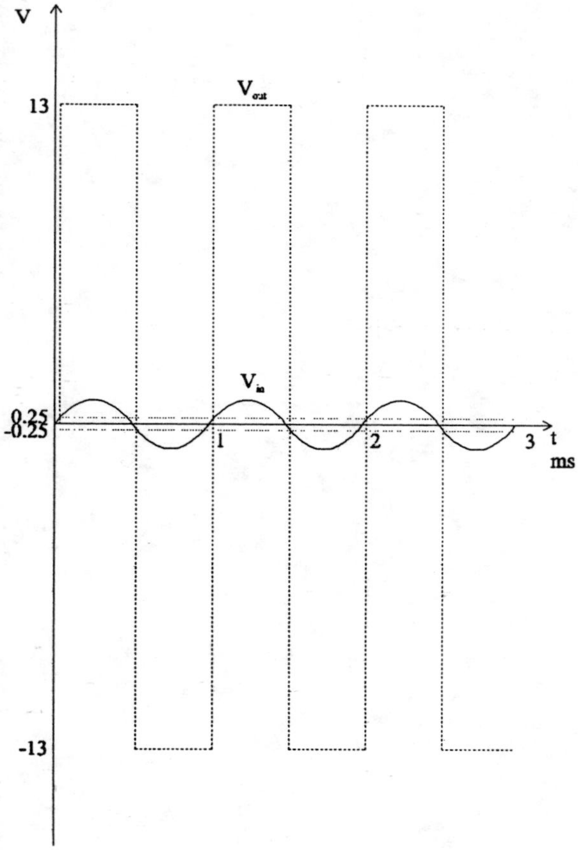

14.69

a)

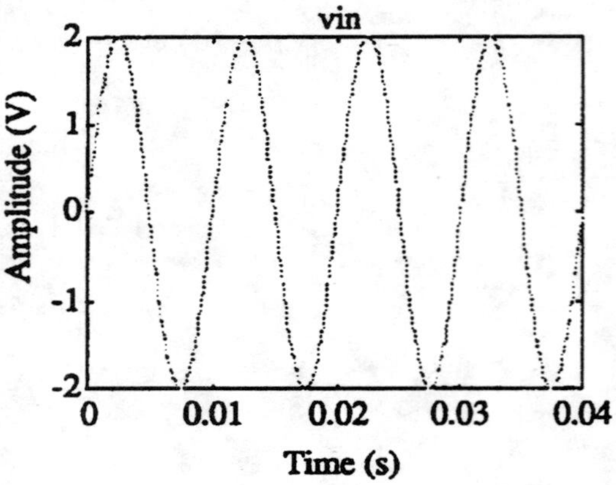
vin
Amplitude (V)
2
1
0
-1
-2
0
0.01
0.02
0.03
0.04
Time (s)

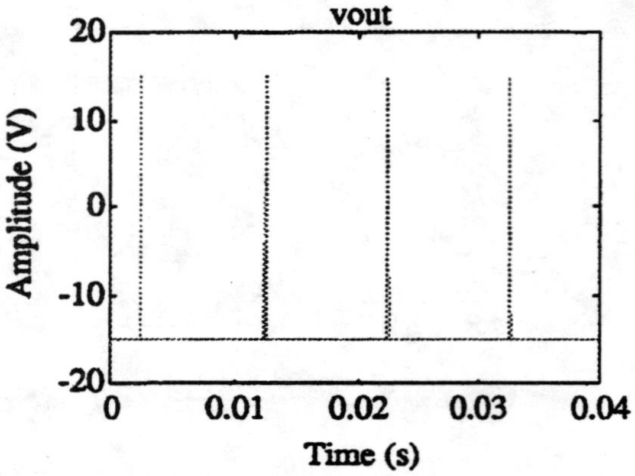
vout
Amplitude (V)
20
10
0
-10
-20
0
0.01
0.02
0.03
0.04
Time (s)

b)

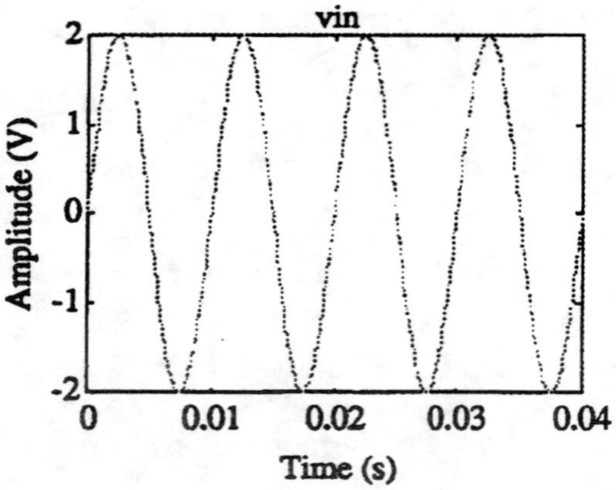
vin
Amplitude (V)
2
1
0
-1
-2
0
0.01
0.02
0.03
0.04
Time (s)

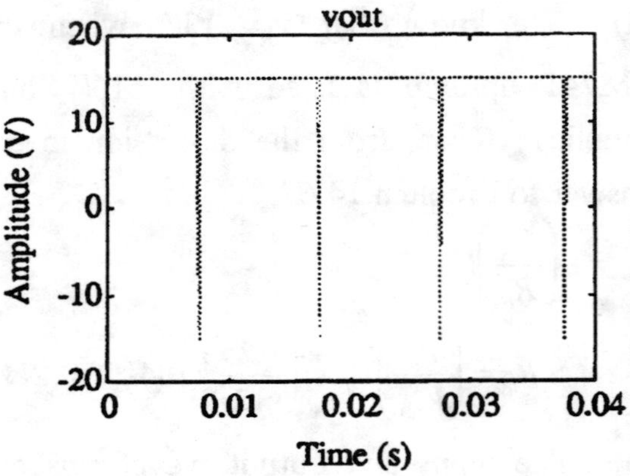
vout
Amplitude (V)
20
10
0
-10
-20
0
0.01
0.02
0.03
0.04
Time (s)

14.70

(a) Define $V_2 = \frac{R_1}{R_2 + R_1}V$ as the voltage at the invertig input of the op-amp. Then:

When $V_{in} > V_2$ the output of the op-amp will be positive and the green LED will turn on (*go*).

When $V_{in} < V_2$ the output of the op-amp will be negative and the red LED will turn on (*no go*)

(b) For this design, $V_2 = 5V$ and $V = 15V$.

$$\therefore \frac{R_1}{R_2 + R_1} 15V = 5V$$

$$\Rightarrow \frac{R_1}{R_2 + R_1} = \frac{1}{3}$$

or $\frac{R_2}{R_1} + 1 = 3$

$$\Rightarrow \frac{R_2}{R_1} = 2$$

Choose $R_1 = 10k\Omega$ and $R_2 = 20k\Omega$ to complete the design

14.71

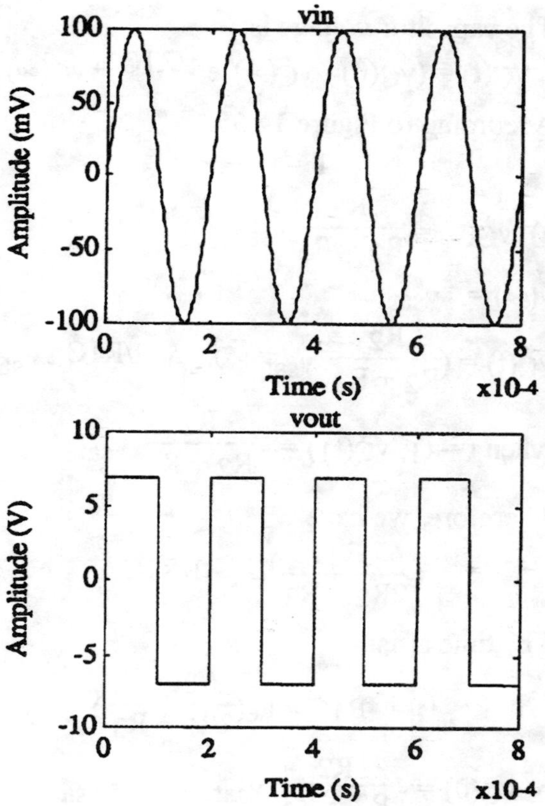

14.72

The capacitor voltage is:

$$v_C(t) = (v_C(0) - v_C(\infty))e^{-t/R1C} + v_C(\infty)$$

According to Figure 14.55,

$$T = t_1 + t_2$$

a) $v_C(0) = \frac{R_2}{R_2 + R_3} v_{sat}$

$v(\infty) = - v_{sat}$

$$v_C(t) = (\frac{R_2}{R_2 + R_3} v_{sat} + v_{sat})e^{-t/R1C} - v_{sat}$$

when $t = t_1$, $v_C(t_1) = - \frac{R_2}{R_2 + R_3} v_{sat}$

Therefore, we have

$$\frac{R_3}{2R_2 + R_3} = e^{-t1/R1C}$$

The time t_1 is:

$$t_1 = -R_1C \log_e(\frac{R_3}{2R_2 + R_3})$$

b) $v_C(0) = - \frac{R_2}{R_2 + R_3} v_{sat}$, $v(\infty) = v_{sat}$

when $t = t_2$, we have

$$v_C(t_2) = \frac{R_2}{R_2 + R_3} v_{sat}$$

We have

$$\frac{R_2}{R_2 + R_3} v_{sat} = (- \frac{R_2}{R_2 + R_3} v_{sat} - v_{sat})e^{-t2/R1C} + v_{sat}$$

From $\frac{R_3}{2R_2 + R_3} = e^{-t2/R1C}$, we have

$$t_2 = - R_1C\log_e(\frac{R_3}{2R_2 + R_3})$$

The period of the square-wave waveform therefore is:

$$T = t_1 + t_2$$

$$= -R_1C \log_e(\frac{R_3}{2R_2 + R_3}) - R_1C \log_e(\frac{R_3}{2R_2 + R_3})$$

$$= - 2R_1C \log_e(\frac{R_3}{2R_2 + R_3})$$

$$= 2R_1C \log_e(\frac{2R_2}{R_3} + 1)$$

14.73

Looking at the data sheet for the 74123 monostable multivibrator, we can see that for a positive going transition, A must be LOW and B must be HIGH.

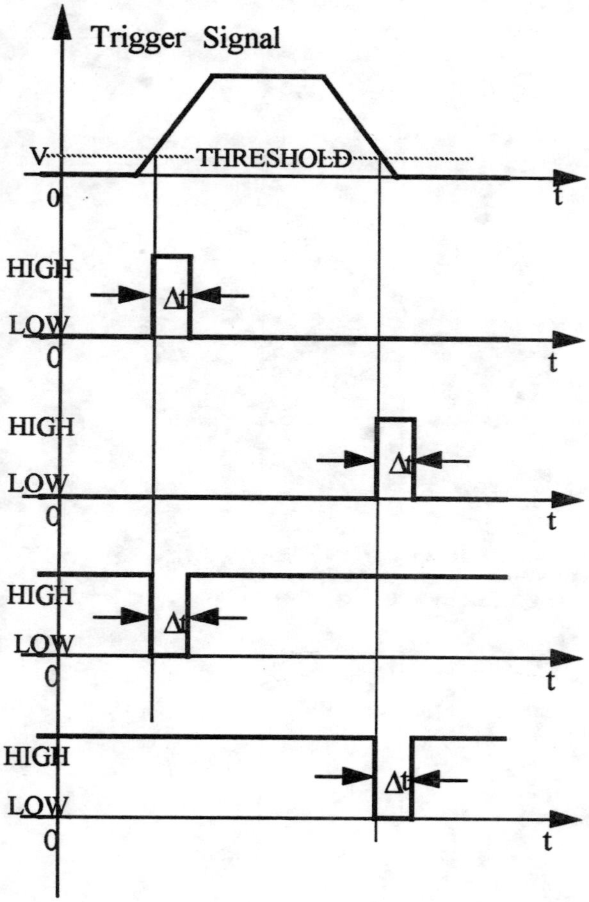

14.74

$T = 1.1\ R_1C$; $T = 10$ ms and $R_1 = 10\ k\Omega$.

Therefore, $C = 0.91\ \mu F$

14.75

ASCII decoding is easy!

14.76

This is a time-consuming problem.

14.77

Decimal	ASCII
12	31 32
345.2	33 34 35 2E 32
43.5	34 33 2E 35

14.78

a) 44 69 67 69 74 61 6C

b) 43 6F 6D 70 75 74 65 72

c) 41 73 63 69 69

d) 41 53 43 49 49

14.79

Serial data transmission requires only a single data path. Parallel requires 16 (or more, depending on word length), and would, therefore, be much more expensive.

14.80

Longest possible delay

$$= 16 \times 1024 \times 5 = 81920 \text{ min.}$$

or

$$= 81920 min \times \frac{1hr}{60min} \times \frac{1day}{24hr} \approx 56.9 days$$

14.81

Three lines are used for handshaking in the IEEE 488 bus to accomplish the following functions: One line is used to declare the bus ready to accept data; another line to declare that data has been accepted, and a third one to declare that the data was indeed valid.

14.82

$$\frac{650\times1024\times1024\frac{bytes}{CD}\times50\frac{CDs}{box}\times100boxes\times400\frac{mi}{hr}}{2500mi}=5.4525952\times10^{11}\frac{bytes}{hr}$$

$$5.4525952\times10^{11}\frac{bytes}{hr}\times8\frac{bits}{byte}\times\frac{1hr}{3600sec}\approx1.21\times10^{9}\frac{bits}{s}$$

or approximately $1.13\frac{Gbit}{s}$

Principles of Electromechanics

Chapter 15 Instructor Notes

The last part of the book presents an introduction to electro-magneto-mechanical systems. Some of the foundations needed for this material were discussed in Chapter 5: the Instructor who wishes to review the polyphase AC power material may do so prior to covering Chapter 15, or together with the AC machine material of Chapter 16.

The emphasis in this chapter (and the next two) is not on the traditional electrical engineering view of electric machines (with much emphasis on electric power generation and steady state analysis), but tries to prepare the student for the use of electro-magneto-mechanical systems as practical actuators for industrial applications. Thus, more emphasis is placed on describing static and dynamic performance characteristics of linear motion actuators and of DC and small AC machines than on a description of the construction details of DC and AC machines and on the analysis of large synchronous generators. The author has used this material over the last several quarters in a course on dynamic system modelling and electromechanics designed for mechanical engineers.

Chapter 15 reviews basic laws of electricity and magnetism, which should already be familiar to the student from an earlier Physics course, in the first section. A practical example is introduced early (Example 15.1) with a discussion of the linear variable differential transformer (LVDT) as a position transducer. Section 15.2 discusses approximate linear magnetic circuits and the idea of reluctance, and introduces magnetic structures with air gaps and simple electro-magnets. The magnetic reluctance position sensor is presented in Examples 15.5 and 15.6. The non-ideal properties of magnetic materials are presented in section 15.3, where hysteresis, saturation, and eddy currents are discussed qualitatively. Section 15.4 introduces transformers in a fairly elementary fashion; more advanced topics are presented in the homework problems.

Section 15.5 is devoted to the analysis of forces and motion in electro-magneto-mechanical structures characterized by linear motion. The author has found that it is pedagogically advantageous to introduce the *Bli* and *Blu* laws for linear motion devices before covering these concepts for rotating machines: the student can often visualize these ideas more clearly in the context of a loudspeaker or of a vibration shaker. Thus, Example 15.10 analyzes the forces in a simple electromagnet, and Examples 15.11 and 15.12 extend this concept to a solenoid and a relay. Finally, Example 15.15 performs a dynamic analysis of a loudspeaker, showing how the frequency response of a loudspeaker can be computed from an electromechanical analysis of its dynamics.

The homework problems present a variety of applied problems, including the analysis of solenoids (15.8, 15.39), and relays (15.26, 15.29). The loudspeaker example is extended in Problem 15.22.

Chapter 15 problem solutions

15.1

a) The current is i = 0.625 A. The energy is:

$$W_m = \int_0^{0.5} (\lambda + 0.5\lambda^2)\, d\lambda = 0.1458 \text{ J}$$

for $\lambda = 0.5$ V s.

The co-energy is then computed from the energy as

$$W_m' = i\lambda - W_m = 0.1667 \text{ J},$$

and the incremental inductance is computed

$$L_\Delta = \frac{d\lambda}{di}\Big|_{i=0.625} = \frac{1}{1+\lambda}\Big|_{\lambda=0.5} = 0.667 \text{ H}$$

b) To compute the voltage, we must add the contribution of the voltage across the resistive part of the inductor plus that generated by the inductance:

$$v_L(t) = R\, i(t) + L_\Delta \frac{di}{dt} = 0.625 + 2.668 \sin(400t + 89.8°) \text{ V}$$

It is important to observe that this is the inductor terminal voltage only for values of flux linkage in the neighborhood of 0.5 V-s.

15.2

(a) $B = \frac{\phi}{A} = \frac{4 \times 10^{-4}}{0.01} = 0.04T$

(b) Viewed from the top:

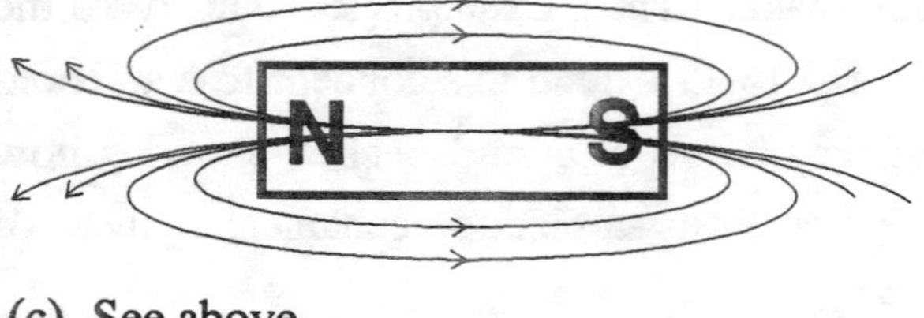

(c) See above.

15.3

(a) The diagram is shown below

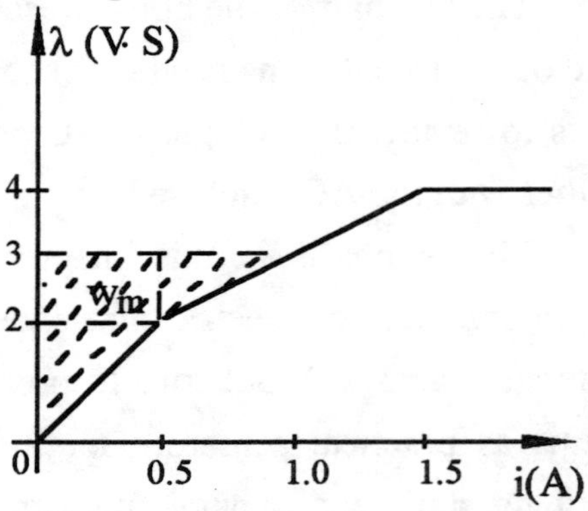

W_m is the area at the left of the curve as shown.

$$W_m = \frac{1}{2} \times 0.5 \times 2 + 0.5 \times 1 + \frac{1}{2} \times 0.5 \times 1 = 1.25 \text{ J}$$

The incremental inductance is:

$$L_\Delta = \frac{\Delta\lambda}{\Delta i}\Big|_{i = 1A} = \frac{2}{1} = 2 \text{ H}$$

(b) For $i = 0.5\sin 2\pi t$ and $R = 2\ \Omega$

$$v = Ri + \frac{d\lambda}{dt}$$

For $|i| < 0.5$, $\lambda = 4i$, therefore,

$$v_L(t) = \sin(2\pi t) + 4 \times 0.5 \times 2\pi\cos(2\pi t) = \sin(2\pi t) + 4\pi\cos(2\pi t)$$

15.4

(a) $\mathfrak{R} = \frac{\mathfrak{F}}{\phi} = \frac{400}{4.2 \times 10^{-4}} = 9.52 \times 10^5 \frac{A \cdot t}{Wb}$

(b) $\mathfrak{H} = \frac{\mathfrak{F}}{6 \times 0.0254 \frac{m}{in}} = 2625 \frac{A \cdot t}{m}$

15.5

(a) $\mathbf{R}_1 = \dfrac{l_1}{\mu A_1} = \dfrac{0.3(3000)(0.01)}{4\pi\times10^{-7}}$

$= 7.96\times10^3\ \text{H}^{-1}$

$\mathbf{R}_2 = \dfrac{l_2}{\mu A_2} = \dfrac{0.1}{(4\pi\times10^{-7})3000(25\times10^{-4})}$

$= 10.671\times10^3\ \text{H}^{-1}$

$\mathbf{R}_3 = \mathbf{R}_1$

The circuit is shown below:

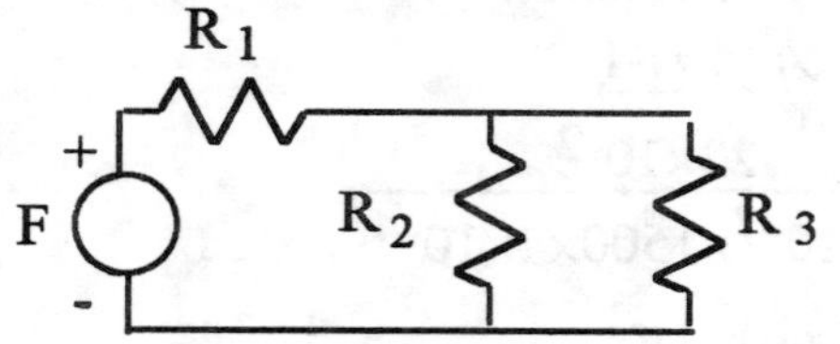

$\mathbf{R}_T = \mathbf{R}_1 + \dfrac{\mathbf{R}_2\mathbf{R}_3}{\mathbf{R}_2 + \mathbf{R}_3}$

$= 12.51\times10^3\ \text{H}^{-1}$

(b) $L = \dfrac{N^2}{\mathbf{R}_T} = \dfrac{100^2}{12.51\times10^3} = 0.8\ \text{H}$

(c) We have

$\mathbf{R}_g = \dfrac{0.0001}{(4\pi\times10^{-7})(100\times10^{-4})}$

$= 7.96\times10^3\ \text{H}^{-1}$

$\mathbf{R}_g$ is in series with $\mathbf{R}_3$ and thus

$\mathbf{R}_T = \mathbf{R}_1 + \dfrac{\mathbf{R}_2(\mathbf{R}_3 + \mathbf{R}_g)}{\mathbf{R}_2 + \mathbf{R}_3 + \mathbf{R}_g}$

$= 14.33\times10^3\ \text{H}^{-1}$

$L = \dfrac{N^2}{\mathbf{R}_T} = 0.7\ \text{H}$

(d) As the gaps get longer, $\mathbf{R}_g$ will get larger and as an extreme case the circuit is made of $\mathbf{R}_1$ and $\mathbf{R}_2$ in series, therefore

$$\mathbf{R}_T = 18.57\times10^3\ \text{H}^{-1}$$

$$L = \frac{N^2}{\mathbf{R}_T} = 0.54\ \text{H}$$

15.6

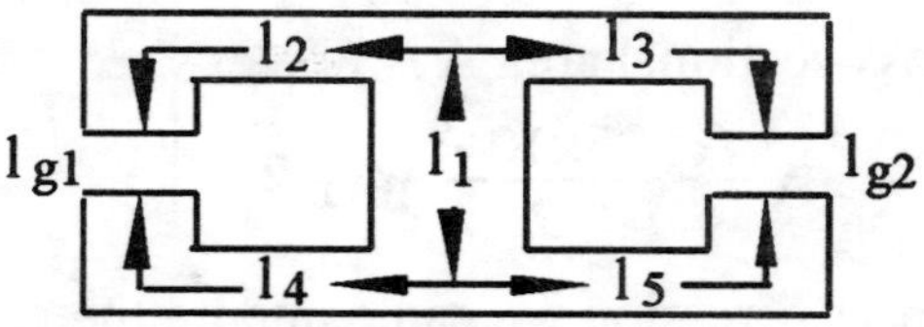

$\mathbf{R}_{g1} = \dfrac{0.0002(0.01)^2}{4\pi\times10^{-7}}$

$= 1.59\times10^6$

$\mathbf{R}_{g2} = 2\ \mathbf{R}_{g1} = 3.18\times10^6$

Assume the reluctance of the material can be neglected when compared to the reluctance of the air gaps; the analogous circuit is shown below:

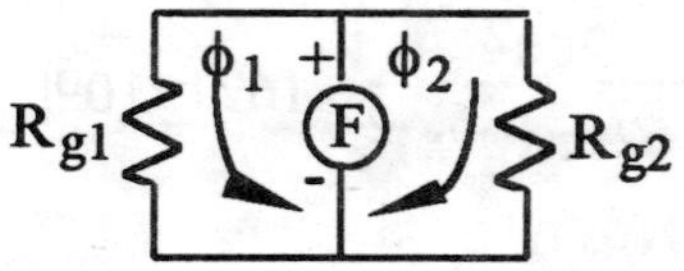

$\phi_1 = \dfrac{N\,i}{\mathbf{R}_{g1}} = 1.26\times10^{-4}\ \text{Wb}$

$B_1 = \dfrac{\phi_1}{A} = 1.26\ \text{Wb/m}^2$

$\phi_2 = \dfrac{1}{2}\phi_1 = 0.63\times10^{-4}\ \text{Wb}$

$B_2 = \dfrac{1}{2}B_1 = 0.63\ \text{Wb/m}^2$

15.7

For a gap area equal to

$$A = A_g = 0.01\ \text{m}^2$$

$$\mathbf{R}_g = \frac{0.005}{(4\pi\times10^{-7})(0.01)} =$$

$$= 398\times10^3\ \text{H}^{-1}$$

From $\phi_g = \dfrac{Ni}{\mathbf{R}_g}$, we can compute the current

$$i = \frac{\phi_g\mathbf{R}_g}{N} =$$

$$= \frac{0.01(398\times10^3)}{1000} = 3.98\ \text{A}$$

15.8

The cross-sectional area A is:

$$A = \pi(\frac{25\times10^{-3}}{2})^2 \ m^2$$

From this expression we can compute the (variable) reluctance of the air gap:

$$\mathbf{R_x} = \frac{x}{4\pi\times10^{-7}\frac{\pi(25\times10^{-3})^2}{4}}$$

$$= 1621\times10^6 x$$

and the resulting force is:

$$f = \frac{i^2}{2}\frac{N^2}{R_x^2}\frac{dR_x}{dx}$$

$$= \frac{7.5^2}{2}\frac{200^2}{(1621\times10^6 x)^2}\times1621\times10^6\Big|_{x=2\times10^{-3}}$$

$$= 173.5 \ N$$

15.9

(a) Assume the material is cast steel.

$$B = \frac{2.4\times10^{-4}}{2\times10^{-4}} = 1.2T$$

$$H_{CS} = 1400\frac{A\cdot t}{m}$$

$$H_{AG} = 9.55\times10^5\frac{A\cdot t}{m}$$

$$100I = 1400(0.1+0.02+0.017)+(9.55\times10^5)(0.003)$$

$$\Rightarrow I = 30.6A$$

(b)

$$\mathfrak{F}_{CS} = 191.8A\cdot t$$

$$\mathfrak{F}_{AG} = 2865A\cdot t$$

Note:

$$\mu_{CS} = 0.0009$$

$$\mu_{AG} = 0.00000126$$

$$\frac{\mu_{CS}}{\mu_{AG}} \approx 700$$

15.10

The analogous circuit is shown below.

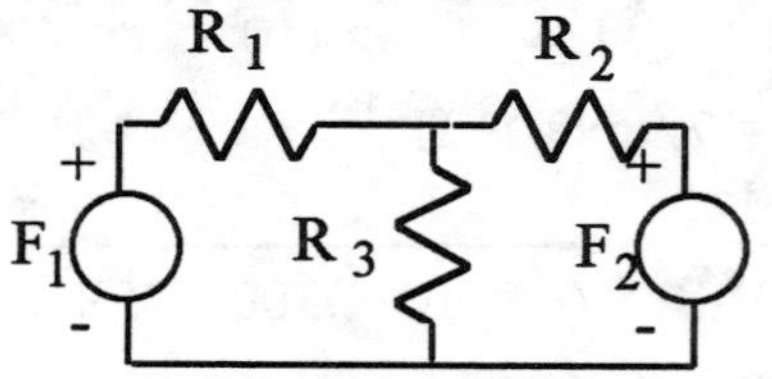

The individual reluctances are:

$$\mathbf{R_1} = \frac{16\times10^{-2}}{4\pi\times10^{-7}\times1500\times4\times10^{-4}}$$

$$= 2.12\times10^5 \ H^{-1}$$

$$\mathbf{R_2} = \frac{22\times10^{-2}}{4\pi\times10^{-7}\times1500\times4\times10^{-4}}$$

$$= 2.92\times10^5 \ H^{-1}$$

$$\mathbf{R_3} = \frac{5\times10^{-2}}{4\pi\times10^{-7}\times1500\times2\times10^{-4}}$$

$$= 1.33\times10^5 \ H^{-1}$$

And the inductances can be computed as follows:

$$L_{m1} = \frac{N^2}{\mathbf{R_1}} = 4.72 \ H$$

$$L_{m2} = \frac{N^2}{\mathbf{R_2}} = 3.43 \ H$$

$$L_{m3} = \frac{N^2}{\mathbf{R_3}} = 7.54 \ H$$

Let $L_T = L_{m1} + L_{m2} + L_{m3} = 15.68 \ H$

$$L_m = \frac{L_{m1}L_{m2}}{L_T} = 1.03 \ H = L_{12} = L_{21} = M$$

$$L_1 = \frac{L_{m1}L_{m3}}{L_T} = 2.27 \ H$$

$$L_2 = \frac{L_{m2}L_{m3}}{L_T} = 1.65 \ H$$

$$L_{11} = L_1 + L_m = 3.3 \ H$$

$$L_{22} = L_2 + L_m = 2.68 \ H$$

15.11

$$I = 2A, \quad r = 0.08m, \quad N = 100,$$
$$A_{cross} = 0.009m^2, \quad \mu_r = 1000$$
$$l = 2\pi r = 0.50265m, \quad \mu = \mu_r \mu_0$$
$$R = \frac{1}{\mu \cdot A_{cross}} = 4.44444 \times 10^4 \frac{A}{Wb}$$
$$mmf = I \cdot N$$
$$\phi = \frac{mmf}{R} = 0.0045Wb$$

15.12

a) The reluctance of the magnetic circuit is:

$$\mathbf{R} = \frac{x}{\mu_0 w^2} + \frac{l_g}{\mu_0 w(w - x)}$$

b) The magnetic energy stored in the air gap is:

$$W_m = \frac{(N_1 + N_2)^2 i^2}{2\mathbf{R}}$$

c) The magnetic force is:

$$f = \frac{i^2}{2} \frac{(N_1 + N_2)^2 \mu_0 w^2}{x^2}$$

15.13

$$A_1 = 2 \times 10^{-4} m^2, \quad A_2 = 5 \times 10^{-4} m^2$$
$$\mu_r = 4000$$
$$l_{gap} = l_{ha} - 2l_{cd} = 0.002m$$
$$R_{gap} = \frac{l_{gap}}{\mu_0 A_2} = 3.1831 \times 10^6 \frac{A}{Wb}$$
$$mmf_{gap} = \phi_1 R_{gap} = 636.61977A$$
$$R_{ef} = R_{cd} = \frac{l_{cd}}{\mu A_2} = 3.93908 \times 10^4 \frac{A}{Wb}$$
$$mmf_{cd} = \phi_1 R_{cd} = 7.87817A$$
$$R_{fg} = R_{bc} = \frac{l_{bc}}{\mu A_2} = 3.97887 \times 10^4 \frac{A}{Wb}$$
$$mmf_{bc} = \phi_1 R_{bc} = 7.95775A$$

To find the mmf in the rightmost leg of the magnetic circuit,

$$mmf_{parallel} = mmf_{gap} + 2 \cdot mmf_{cd} + 2 \cdot mmf_{bc} = 668.29161A$$
$$R_{bg} = \frac{l_{bg}}{\mu A_1} = 1.98944 \times 10^5 \frac{A}{Wb}$$
$$\phi_2 = \frac{mmf_{parallel}}{R_{bg}} = 0.00336Wb$$
$$\phi_T = \phi_1 + \phi_2 = 0.00356Wb$$
$$R_{ab} = \frac{l_{ab}}{\mu A_2} = 7.95775 \times 10^4 \frac{A}{Wb}$$
$$R_{series} = 3 \cdot R_{ab} = 2.38732 \times 10^5 \frac{A}{Wb}$$
$$mmf_{series} = \phi_T R_{series} = 849.69641A$$
$$mmf_{total} = mmf_{series} + mmf_{parallel} = 1.51799 \times 10^3 A$$
$$i = \frac{mmf_{total}}{N} = 7.59A$$

15.14

Yes, the resultant force on the single coil is in the downward direction. If the coils are thought of as electromagnets, there is a north pole from the lower coil attracting a south pole from the upper coil.

15.15

(a) We have $L(x) = \dfrac{N^2}{R(x)}$

$$W_m' = W_m = \frac{L(x)\, i^2}{2}$$

The current is:

$$I_{DC} = \frac{120}{30} = 4\ \text{A}$$

$$W_m = \frac{980^2 \times 4^2}{2 \times 7 \times 10^8 (0.007)} = 1.568\ \text{J}$$

(b) $f = -\dfrac{i^2}{2} \dfrac{N^2}{(\mathbf{R}(x))^2} \dfrac{d\mathbf{R}(x)}{dx} = -224\ \text{N}$

The minus sign indicates that the force f is in a direction opposite to that indicated in the figure.

15.16

$$\mathfrak{F} = \frac{1}{2}\frac{AB^2}{\mu_0}$$

$$= \frac{1}{2}\frac{\pi(10 \times 10^{-3})^2 (1.1)^2}{4(4\pi \times 10^{-7})}$$

$$= 37.8N$$

15.17

The variable reluctance is given by:

$$\mathbf{R}_T(x) = 2\,\mathbf{R}(x) = \frac{2x}{4\pi \times 10^{-7}(0.01)}$$

$$= 159.15 \times 10^6 x$$

The force is related to the reluctance by:

$$f = -10000 = -\frac{N^2 i^2}{2\mathbf{R}_T^2(x)} \frac{d\mathbf{R}_T(x)}{dx}$$

Therefore,

$$i = \sqrt{3.18} = 1.784\ \text{A}$$

15.18

(a) $NI = Hl$

$$250(50 \times 10^{-3}) = H(12 \times 10^{-2}) \Rightarrow H = 104.2$$

$\therefore$ from the curve, $B = 0.75T$

(b)

$$\mathfrak{F} = \frac{1}{2}\frac{AB^2}{\mu_0} = \frac{1}{2}\frac{(0.6 \times 10^{-4})(0.75)^2}{4\pi \times 10^{-7}} = 13.4N$$

15.19

(a) The equivalent circuit is:

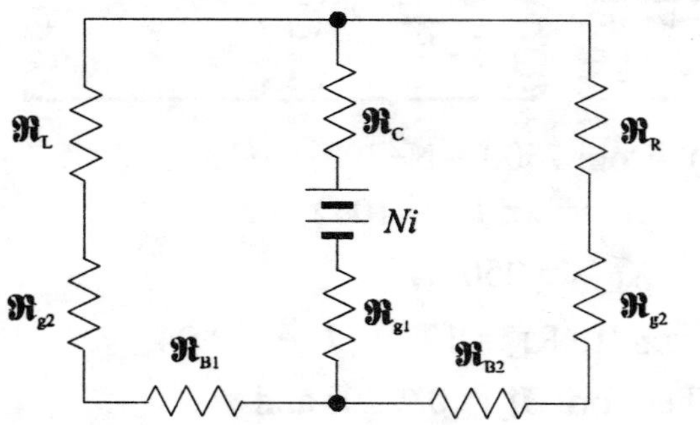

where:

$$\mathfrak{R}_L = \mathfrak{R}_R = \frac{80\times10^{-3}}{\frac{1.2}{260}(35\times17.5)\times10^{-6}} = 28{,}299A\cdot t/Wb$$

$$\mathfrak{R}_C = \frac{80\times10^{-3}}{\frac{1.2}{260}(35\times35)\times10^{-6}} = 14{,}150A\cdot t/Wb$$

$$\mathfrak{R}_{B1} = \mathfrak{R}_{B2} = \frac{61.25\times10^{-3}}{\frac{1.2}{260}(35\times17.5)\times10^{-6}} = 21{,}667A\cdot t/Wb$$

$$\mathfrak{R}_{g1} = \frac{10\times10^{-3}}{(4\pi\times10^{-7})(35\times35)\times10^{-6}} = 6{,}496{,}120A\cdot t/Wb$$

$$\mathfrak{R}_{g2} = \frac{10\times10^{-3}}{(4\pi\times10^{-7})(35\times17.5)\times10^{-6}} = 12{,}955{,}225A\cdot t/Wb$$

$$\mathfrak{R}_T = \mathfrak{R}_C + \mathfrak{R}_{g1} + \frac{\mathfrak{R}_R + \mathfrak{R}_{g2} + \mathfrak{R}_{B2}}{2} = 13.01\times10^6A\cdot t/Wb$$

$$\phi_T = BA = 1.2(35\times35)\times10^{-6} = 1.47\times10^{-3}Wb$$

$$2000I = \mathfrak{R}_T\phi_T \Rightarrow I = 9.56A$$

(b)

$$Hlg = \frac{1.2}{4p\times10^{-7}}\left(10\times10^{-3}\right) = 9549.3A\cdot t$$

$$w_{g1} = \frac{1}{2}\left(1.47\times10^{-3}\right)(9549.3) = 7.02J$$

$$w_{g2} = \frac{1}{2}\left(\frac{1.47\times10^{-3}}{2}\right)(9549.3) = 3.51J$$

$$w_g = w_{g1} + 2w_{g2} = 14.04J$$

(c)

$$w_T = \frac{1}{2}\left(1.47\times10^{-3}\right)(2000)(9.56) = 14.05J$$

$$w_{ST} = w_T - w_g = 0.01J$$

15.20

With $l_1 = 34$ cm, $l_2 = l_3 = 90$ cm and

$A = (8\times10^{-2})^2\ \text{cm}^2$, we compute

$$\mathbf{R}_1 = \frac{0.34}{2000\times4\pi\times10^{-7}\times(8\times10^{-2})^2}$$

$$= 2.114\times10^4\ \text{H}^{-1}$$

$$\mathbf{R}_2 = 5.595\times10^4\ \text{H}^{-1} = \mathbf{R}_3$$

$$\mathbf{R}_T = \mathbf{R}_1 + \frac{\mathbf{R}_2\,\mathbf{R}_3}{\mathbf{R}_2 + \mathbf{R}_3} = 4.91\times10^4\ \text{H}^{-1}$$

$$\phi_T = 0.4\times(0.08)^2 = 2.56\times10^{-3}\ \text{Wb}$$

From $\phi_T = BA = \dfrac{Ni}{\mathbf{R}_T}$, we have $i = \dfrac{BA\mathbf{R}_T}{N}$

(a) $i = \dfrac{2.56\times10^{-3}\times4.91\times10^4}{N} = \dfrac{125.7}{100}$

$= 1.257$ A

(b) Since the current is directly proportional to B, the current will have to be doubled.

15.21

The equivalent circuit is:

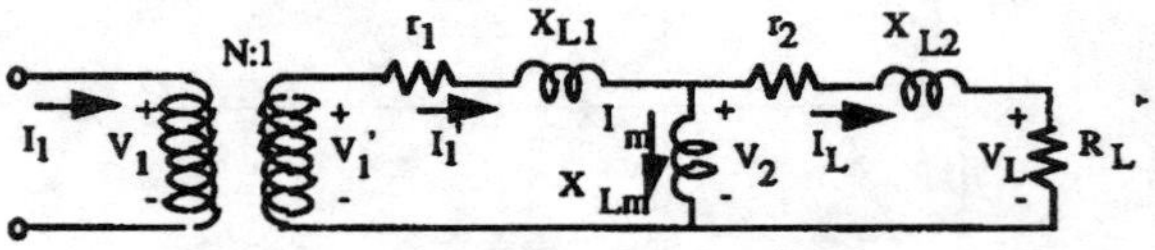

a) From $7500 = N^2 300$, we have $N = 5$

b) $X_{L1} = 2\pi f L_1 = 10\ \Omega = X_{L2}$

$X_{Lm} = 250\ \Omega$

From $I_L^2 R_L = 12$ W, $I_L^2 = 0.04$

Therefore, $\mathbf{I}_L = 0.2\angle0°$ and

$$\mathbf{V}_L = 60\angle0°\ \text{V}$$

$$\mathbf{V}_2 = \mathbf{I}_L(R_L + r_2 + jX_{L2}) = 64 + j2$$

$$= 64.03\angle1.79°$$

$$\mathbf{I}_m = 0.256\angle{-88.21°} = 0.008 - j0.2559$$

$$\mathbf{I}_1' = \mathbf{I}_m + \mathbf{I}_L = 0.33\angle{-50.9°}$$

$$\mathbf{V}_1' = \mathbf{I}_1'(r_1 + jX_{L1}) + \mathbf{V}_2$$

$$= 70.72 - j1.04 = 70.72\angle{-0.84°}\ \text{V}$$

$$\mathbf{V}_1 = N\mathbf{V}_1' = 353.6\angle{-0.84°}\ \text{V}$$

$$\mathbf{I}_1 = \frac{1}{N}\mathbf{I}_1' = 0.066\angle{-50.9°}\ \text{A}$$

$$P_{in} = V_1 I_1 \cos\theta = 14.98\ \text{W}$$

$$\text{efficiency} = \eta = \frac{P_{out}}{P_{in}} = 80.1\%$$

15.22

a) For $k = 5\times10^4$, the transfer function is:

$$\frac{U}{V} = \frac{1845.69\ s}{s^2 + 28375.14s + 5\times10^7}$$

The magnitude frequency response is plotted below for $10^2 \le \omega \le 10^5$ or $16 \le f \le 16$ kHz.

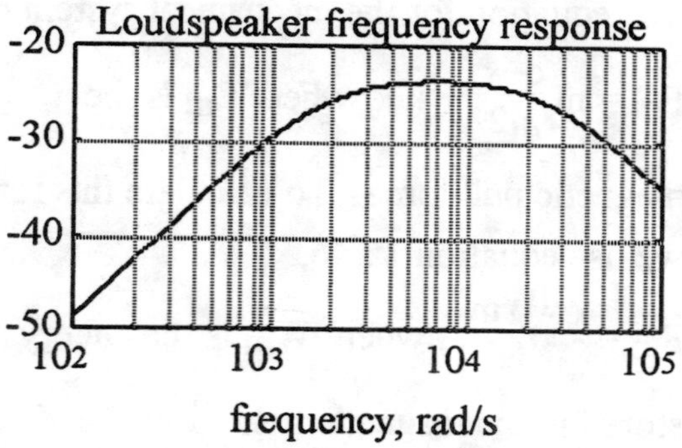

This response would correspond to a midrange speaker.

b) For $k = 5\times10^6$, the transfer function is:

$$\frac{U}{V} = \frac{1845.69\ s}{s^2 + 28375.14s + 5\times10^9}$$

The magnitude frequency response is plotted below.

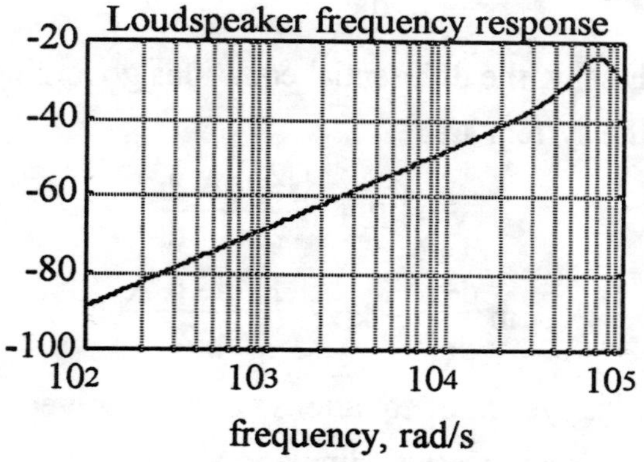

It should be apparent that this response would enhance the treble range, and is the response of a "tweeter".

c) For $k = 0$, the transfer function is:

$$\frac{U}{V} = \frac{1845.69}{s + 28375.14}$$

and the frequency response is plotted below.

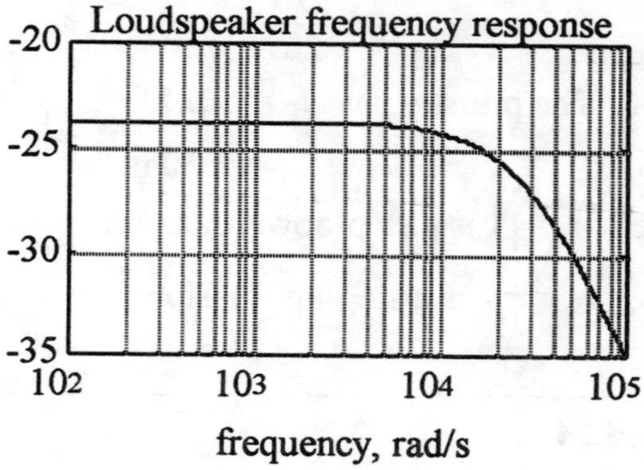

In this case, the speaker acts as a "woofer", emphasizing the low frequency range. In practice, k cannot be identically zero, so the actual response of a woofer would resemble that of a midrange speaker, shifted towards the lower frequencies.

15.23

$$\alpha = \frac{220}{20} = 11$$

a) The primary has $N_p = 50 \times 11$

$= 550$ turns

b) $\alpha = 11$ is a step-down transformer

c) $\alpha = \frac{1}{11}$ is a step-up transformer

15.24

a) $\alpha = \frac{750}{50} = 15$

b) $V_2 = \frac{1}{\alpha} V_1 = \frac{120}{15} = 8 \text{ V}$

c) $R_L = \frac{8}{40} = 0.2\ \Omega$

15.25

a) From $\alpha^2 R_L = 500$, we have $\alpha = 7.91$

b) From $10 = \frac{V_2^2}{R_L}$, we have

$V_2 = 8.94 \text{ V}$

c) $V_1 = \alpha V_2 = 70.7 \text{ V}$

15.26

The equation for the electrical system is:

$v = i\,R + L(x)\frac{di}{dt}$, where

$$L(x) = \frac{N^2}{\mathbf{R}_T(x)} = \frac{N^2 \mu_0 A}{2x}$$

The equation for the mechanical system is:

$F_m = m\frac{d^2x}{dt^2} + k\,x$, where F_m is the magnetic pull force. To calculate this force we use equation 15.46,

$F_m = -\frac{dW_m}{dx}$, where W_m is the energy stored in the magnetic field. Let **F** and **R** be the magnetomotive force acting on the structure and its reluctance, respectively; then

$$W_m = \frac{\phi^2 \mathbf{R}(x)}{2} = \frac{\mathbf{F}^2}{2\,\mathbf{R}(x)} = \frac{N^2 i^2 \mu A}{4x}$$

and $$F_m = -\frac{dW_m}{dx} = \frac{N^2 i^2 \mu A}{4x^2}$$

Finally, the differential equations governing the system are:

$$v = i\,R + \frac{N^2 \mu_0 A}{2x}\frac{di}{dt}$$

$$m\frac{d^2x}{dt^2} + k\,x = \frac{N^2 i^2 \mu A}{4x^2}$$

This system of equations could be solved using a numerical simulation, since it is nonlinear.

15.27

We have

$$\mathbf{V} = \left(R + j\omega L + \frac{K_g U / K_f}{j\omega_m + d + \dfrac{K}{j\omega}} \right) \mathbf{I}$$

where $K_g = Bl$, $K_f = \dfrac{U}{Bl}$

The electrical equivalent circuit of the loudspeaker is shown below:

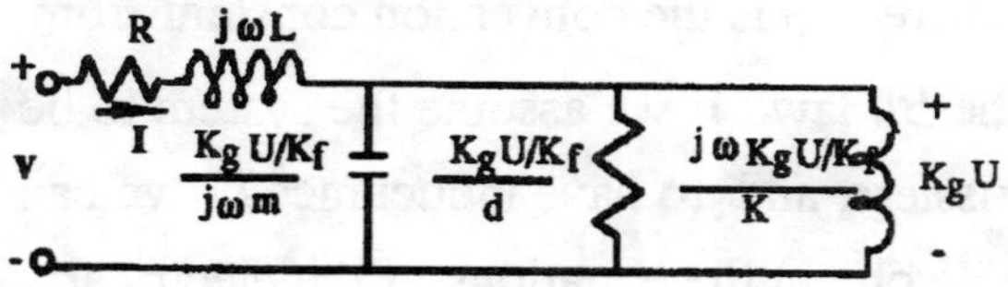

15.28

Assume both secondary windings have resistance R_s and inductance L_s, if M_s is the mutual coupling, we have

$$v1 = M1\frac{di}{dt} - (R_s i_L + L\frac{di_L}{dt}) + M_s\frac{di_L}{dt}$$

$$v2 = M2\frac{di}{dt} + (R_s i_L + L\frac{di_L}{dt}) - M_s\frac{di_L}{dt}$$

$$v_{out} = v1 - v2$$

$$= (M1 - M2)\frac{di}{dt} - 2(R_s i_L + L\frac{di_L}{dt}) + 2M_s\frac{di_L}{dt}$$

$i_L = \dfrac{v_{out}}{R_L}$; therefore,

$$(2(L - M_s)s + 1 + 2\frac{R_s}{R_L})\, V_{out} = (M1 - M2)sI_L$$

and, the transfer function is:

$$\frac{V_{out}}{I_L} = \frac{(M1 - M2)s}{2(L - M_s)s + 1 + 2\dfrac{R_s}{R_L}}$$

15.29

The equation for the electrical system is:

$v = iR + L(x)\dfrac{di}{dt}$, where

$$L(x) = \frac{N^2}{\mathbf{R}_T(x)} = \frac{N^2\mu_0 A}{2x}$$

The equation for the mechanical system is:

$F_m = m\dfrac{d^2x}{dt^2} + kx$, where F_m is the magnetic pull force. To calculate this force we use equation 15.46,

$F_m = -\dfrac{dW_m}{dx}$, where W_m is the energy stored in the magnetic field. Let **F** and **R** be the magnetomotive force acting on the structure and its reluctance, respectively; then

$$W_m = \frac{\phi^2 \mathbf{R}(x)}{2} = \frac{\mathbf{F}^2}{2\,\mathbf{R}(x)} = \frac{N^2 i^2 \mu A}{4x}$$

and $F_m = -\dfrac{dW_m}{dx} = \dfrac{N^2 i^2 \mu A}{4x^2}$.

Finally, the differential equations governing the system are:

$$v = iR + \frac{N^2\mu_0 A}{2x}\frac{di}{dt}$$

$$m\frac{d^2x}{dt^2} + kx = \frac{N^2 i^2 \mu A}{4x^2}.$$

This system of equations could be solved using a numerical simulation, since it is nonlinear.

15.30

We have $v_{ex} = L_p\frac{di}{dt} + R_p i$

$v_{ex}(s) = (L_p s + R_p)I(s)$

$V_{out}(s)(2(L\text{-}M)s+1+ 2\frac{R_s}{R_L}) = MsI(s)$

where $M = M_1 - M_2$. Therefore,

$$\frac{V_{out}(s)}{V_{ex}(s)} = \frac{Ms}{(L_p s + R_p)2(L - M)s + 1 + 2\frac{R_s}{R_L}}$$

To determine the maximum sensitivity of the output voltage to the excitation we could compute the derivative of $H(s) = \frac{V_{out}(s)}{V_{ex}(s)}$ with respect to s, set $\frac{H(s)}{\_s} = 0$, and solve for s. By setting $s = j\omega$, this procedure will yield the excitation frequency for which the sensitivity of the output is maximum. It may, however, be more useful to compute the frequency response $H(j\omega)$ numerically, to visualize the range of frequencies over which the sensitivity is acceptable.

15.31

Figure P15.19 illustrates the interface between the electrical and mechanical parts of a system. The coupling between the two is assumed to be of magnetic origin. The force balance equation for the mechanical side of the system is:

$$f_0 = m\frac{d^2x}{dt^2} + d\frac{dx}{dt} + k + K_m i$$

where K_m is the conversion constant from the *Bli* law. If we assume the system to be lossless, and to have inductance L, we can also obtain the equations of the electrical side:

$$v_O = iR + L\frac{di}{dt} + K_m\frac{dx}{dt}$$

These differential equations are coupled in that the motion of the mechanical system gives rise to an electromotive force (Blu law), and the current in the electrical system gives rise to a mechanical force (Bli law). In this case we have simply modeled the magnetic coupling between systems as being linear and conservative (thus the identical coefficients K_m). Could you sketch an example of a physical device that would behave according to the equations just derived?

15.32

Refer to Problem 15.27.

The mechanical impedance Z_m is:

$$Z_m = (\frac{KgU/Kf}{j\omega m})||(\frac{KgU/Kf}{d})||(\frac{j\omega KgU/Kf}{K})$$

$$= \frac{j\omega KgKf}{-\omega^2 m + j\omega d + K}$$

From $\omega_m = \frac{K}{\omega}$, the angular frequency where Z_m = maximum is:

$$\omega_m = \sqrt{\frac{K}{m}}$$

and $$Z_m = \frac{KgU}{Kfd}$$

15.33

$$\mathbf{R}_T = \frac{x}{4\pi\times10^{-7}(0.025)^2} = 1.27\times10^9 x$$

$$f = -\frac{N^2}{2}\frac{i^2}{\mathbf{R}_T^2}\frac{d\mathbf{R}_T}{dx} = -1.57\times10^{-3}\frac{1}{x^2}$$

For x = 0.001 m, f = - 1574.8 N

The minus sign indicates that the force is in a direction that would decrease the gap.

15.34

We have

$$\alpha = \frac{N_1}{N_2} = 8$$

a) $V_2 = \frac{1}{\alpha} V_1 = 30 \text{ V}$

$I_2 = \frac{V_2}{R_L} = 10 \text{ A}$

b) $I_1 = \frac{1}{\alpha} I_2 = 1.25 \text{ A}$

c) $Z_{in} = \frac{240}{1.25} = 192 \ \Omega$

d) $Z_{in} = \alpha^2 R_L = 192 \ \Omega$

15.35

$$\alpha = \frac{100}{800} = \frac{1}{8}$$

15.36

a) $N_h = \frac{2300}{2.5} = 920$ turns

$N_l = \frac{240}{2.5} = 96$ turns

b) $I_h = \frac{4.6\times10^3}{2300} = 2 \text{ A}$

c) $\alpha = \frac{N_l}{N_h} = 0.1044$

15.37

From e = Blu, we have

$$e(t) = Bl\frac{dx}{dt} = 0.02\cos(10t) \text{ V}$$

15.38

We have

$e(t) = e_1(t) - e_2(t)$

$e_2(t) = (0.1)(0.1)(-1\ \cos 10t)$ V

$e(t) = 0.02\cos(10t) + 0.01\cos(10t)$

$\quad = 0.03\cos(10t)$ V

15.39

$$\mathbf{R}_x = \frac{x}{\mu_0 A_x}$$

$$\mathbf{R}_g = \frac{l_g}{\mu_0 A_g} = 7.96\times10^6\ \text{H}^{-1}$$

$$\mathbf{R}_1 = \mathbf{R}_2 = \frac{0.335}{2000(4\pi\times10^{-7})(5\times10^{-4})}$$

$$= 2.67\times10^5\ \text{H}^{-1}$$

$$\mathbf{R}_3 = \frac{0.055}{2000(4\pi\times10^{-7})(10\times10^{-4})}$$

$$= 2.19\times10^4\ \text{H}^{-1}$$

$$\mathbf{R}_m = \frac{l_x}{2000(4\pi\times10^{-7})(10\times10^{-4})}$$

$$= (3.98\times10^5)(9.5 - x)\ \text{H}^{-1}$$

The circuit is shown below:

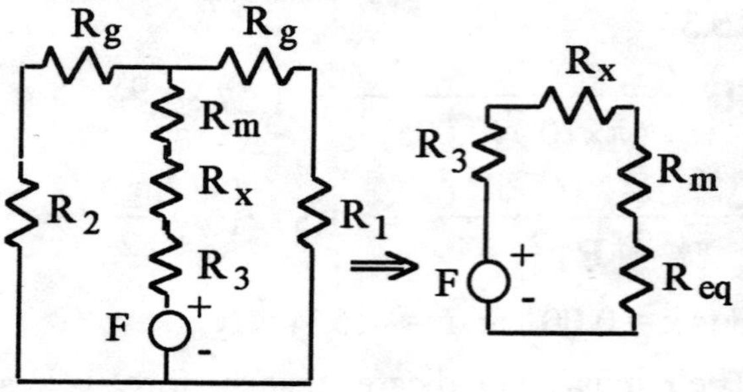

$$\mathbf{R}_{eq} = \frac{\mathbf{R}_g + \mathbf{R}_1}{2} = 4.11\times10^6\ \text{H}^{-1}$$

$$\mathbf{R}_T = 7.91\times10^6 + 7.956\times10^8 x$$

$$f = -\frac{N^2\, i^2}{2\, \mathbf{R}_T^2}\frac{d\mathbf{R}_T}{dx}$$

$$= -\frac{500^2(7.956\times10^8)}{2(7.91\times10^6 + 7.956\times10^8 x)^2}$$

For $x = -0.02$, $f = -1.55$ N

15.40

$$f = Bli = 0.3 \times l \times 4 = 1.2l \text{ N}$$

Force will be to the left if current flows upward.

15.41

$$e = Blu \cos 45° = 2.83 \text{ V}$$

Introduction to Electric Machines

Chapter 16 Instructor Notes

The objective of Chapter 16 is to introduce the foundations for the analysis of rotating electric machines. In the first section, rotating electric machines are classified on the basis of their energy conversion characteristics and of the nature of the electric power they absorb (or generate). Section 16.2 reviews the physical structure of a DC machine and presents a simple general circuit model that is valid for both motors and generators, including dynamic equations. The section also contains a brief discussion of DC generators. Section 16.3 describes the characteristics of the various configurations of DC motors, both of the wound stator and permanent magnet types. The torque speed characteristics of the different configurations are compared, and the dynamic equations are given for each type of motor. The section ends with a brief qualitative discussion of speed control in DC motors.

The second half of the chapter is devoted to the analysis of AC machines. After an explanation of the phenomenon of a rotating magnetic field, the synchronous generator and synchronous motor are discussed. The discussion is brief, but includes the analysis of circuit models of synchronous machines and a few examples. Circuit models for the induction motor are discussed next, as well as general performance characteristics of this class of machines. Although the discussion of the AC machines is not particularly detailed, all of the important concepts that a non-electrical engineer would be interested in to evaluate the performance characteristics of these machines are introduced in the chapter, and reinforced in the extensive homework problem set.

Chapter 16 problem solutions

16.1

$$F = BI \times l = 5.2 \times 10^{-4}\frac{Wb}{in^2} \times \frac{in^2}{(0.0254m)^2} \times 90 \times 6in \times \frac{0.0254m}{in}$$

$$= 11.06Nt$$

EIT 16.2

With B = 4 kG = 0.4 T = 0.4 Wb/m^2
we can compute the flux to be :

$$\phi = BA = 0.4 \times 0.02 \times 0.04 = 0.32 \text{ mWb}$$

16.3

(a) $1800 = \dfrac{220 - 2 - 6(0.32)}{K_a\phi} \Rightarrow K_a\phi = 0.12$

$$n = \frac{220 - 2 - 60(0.32)}{K_a\phi} = 1657rpm$$

(b) $\%reg = \dfrac{1800 - 1657}{1657} \times 100 = 8.65\%$

16.4

v_L at full load is 120 V and

$$E_b = 120 + (2 + 10) \times 0.6 = 127.2 \text{ V}$$

$$R_f = \frac{120}{2} = 60\ \Omega$$

Assuming E_b to be constant, we have

$$i_a = i_f = \frac{127.2}{0.6 + 60} = 2.1 \text{ A}$$

Therefore,

$$v_L = 127.2 - 2.1 \times 0.6 = 125.9 \text{ V}$$

$$\text{Voltage reg.} = \frac{125.9 - 120}{120} = 0.049 = 4.9\%$$

16.5

$$T = K_a\phi I_a \Rightarrow I_a = 0.7(75) = 52.5A$$

$$n_R = \frac{550 - 75(0.36)}{K_a\phi} \Rightarrow K_a\phi n_R = 523$$

$$0.8n_R = \frac{550 - 52.5R_T}{K_a\phi} \Rightarrow 0.8 \times 523 = 550 - 52.5R_T$$

$$\therefore R_T = 2.51\Omega$$

$$R_{add} = 2.51 - 0.36 = 2.15\Omega$$

16.6

If we assume rated output voltage, that is, v_L = 230 V, we have

(a) 230 V

(b) 23 kW

If we assume rated output power, that is, P_{out} = 20 kW, we have

(a) 200 V

(b) 20 kW

If we assume E_b = 230 V, and compute the output voltage to be

$$v_L = 230 - 100 \times 0.2 = 210 \text{ V}$$

we have

(a) 210 V

(b) 21 kW

EIT 16.7

The circuit is shown below

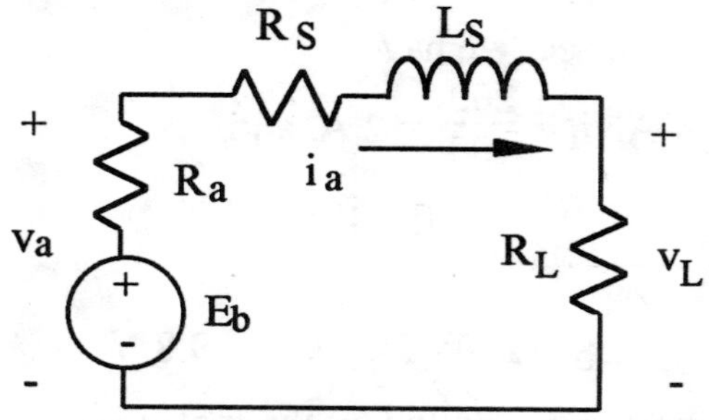

(a) $i_a = \frac{P}{v_L} = \frac{10\times10^3}{120} = 83.33$ A

(b) $v_a = 120 + i_aR_S = 124.17$ V

16.8

The circuit is shown below:

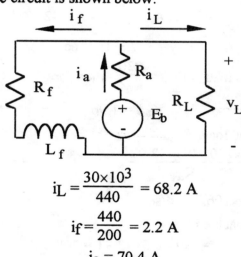

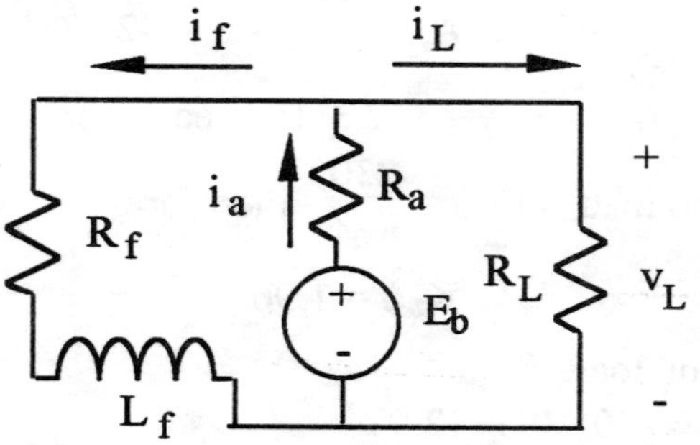

$$i_L = \frac{30\times10^3}{440} = 68.2 \text{ A}$$

$$i_f = \frac{440}{200} = 2.2 \text{ A}$$

$$i_a = 70.4 \text{ A}$$

(a) $E_b = v_L + i_aR_a = 440 + 70.4\times0.1$

$= 447.04$ V

$P = E_bi_a = 31.471$ kW

(b) $i_L = 68.2$ A, $i_f = 2.2$ A, $i_a = 70.4$ A

(c) $P_{loss} = i^2{}_aR_a + i^2{}_fR_f = 1464$ W

16.9

For n = 3600 rev/min, $\omega_m = 377$ rad/sec

$$i_L = \frac{450\times10^3}{4.6\times10^3} = 97.8 \text{ A}$$

$$i_f = \frac{4.6\times10^3}{333} = 13.8 \text{ A}$$

$$i_a = i_f + i_L = 111.6 \text{ A}$$

Using the relation

$$E_b = v_L + i_aR_a = 4823.2 \text{ V}$$

At no-load,

$$v_L = E_b - i_fR_a = 4820.4 \text{ V}$$

At half-load,

$$i_L = 48.9 \text{ A}$$

$$i_a = i_f + i_L = 62.7 \text{ A}$$

$$v_L = E_b - i_aR_a = 4810.7 \text{ V}$$

16.10

At n=1200 rev/min, $\omega_m = 125.7$ rad/sec.

The output power is 100 hp = 74.6 kW

From full-load efficiency of 0.9, we have

$$P_{in} = \frac{74.6}{0.9} = 82.9 \text{ kW}$$

(a) From $P_{in} = i_Sv_S = 82.9$ kW, we have

$$i_S = \frac{82.9\times10^3}{440} = 188.4 \text{ A}$$

(b) $i_f = \frac{440}{400} = 1.1$ A

$i_a = 187.3$ A

(c) $E_b = v_L - i_aR_a = 402.5$ V

(d) $T_{out} = \frac{P_{out}}{\omega_m} = 593.5$ N-m

EIT 16.11

$P_{out} = \frac{1}{2}$ rated load = 15 kW

At an efficiency of 0.85, the input power can be computed to be

$$P_{in} = \frac{15\times10^3}{0.85} = 17.647 \text{ kW}$$

The total loss is:

$$P_{loss} = P_{in} - P_{out} = 2.647 \text{ kW}$$

16.12

$$500 = \frac{240-3-36(0.6)}{K_a\phi} \Rightarrow K_a\phi = 0.431$$

$$n = \frac{240-3-21(0.6)}{\left(\frac{21}{36}\right)(0.431)} = 893 rpm$$

16.13

(a) $E_b = v_L - i_a R_a = 220 - 50\times0.2 = 210$ V

(b) $P = E_b i_a = 210\times50 = 10.5$ kW

$= 14.07$ hp

16.14

$$HP = \frac{2\pi\cdot n\cdot T}{33{,}000}$$

$$75 = \frac{2\pi(820)T}{33{,}000} \Rightarrow T = 480.4 lb\cdot ft$$

$$T = K_a\phi I_a$$

$$480.4 = K_a\phi(112) \Rightarrow K_a\phi = 4.29$$

$$T_n = 4.29(0.85)(84) = 306.2 lb\cdot ft$$

$$n_n = \frac{550-84(0.15)}{0.85(0.65)} = 973 rpm$$

$$HP_n = \frac{2\pi(973)(306.2)}{33{,}000} = 56.7 hp$$

16.15

Since n = 1,100 rev/min corresponds to ω = 115.2 rad/sec, we have

$i_S = 4$ A, $i_f = \frac{200}{100} = 2$ A, and,

$$i_a = i_S - i_f = 2 \text{ A}$$

Also,

$$E_b = 200 - 2\times0.1 = 199.8 \text{ V}$$

The power developed by the motor is

$$P = P_{in} - P_{copper\ loss}$$

$$= 200\times4 - (2^2\times100 + 2^2\times0.1)$$

$$= 399.6 \text{ W}$$

16.16

$i_f = \frac{230}{75} = 3.07$ A, $i_a = i_L - i_f = 42.93$ A

$$\omega_m = 117.3 \text{ rad/sec}$$

At no load, $117.3 = \frac{230}{K_a\phi}$, therefore,

$$K_a\phi = 1.96$$

At full load,

$$\omega_m = \frac{230 - 0.5\times42.93}{K_a\phi}$$

$$= 106.3 \text{ rad/sec}$$

The back emf is

$$E_b = 230 - 0.5\times42.93 = 208.5 \text{ V}$$

The power developed is

$$P_{dev} = E_b I_a = 8.952 \text{ kW}$$

The power available at the shaft is

$$P_o = P_{dev} - P_{rot} = 8952 - 500 = 8452 \text{ W}$$

The torque available at the shaft is:

$$T_{sh} = \frac{P_o}{\omega_m} = 72.1 \text{ N-m}$$

16.17

$i_S = 5$ A, $i_f = \frac{200}{100} = 2$ A, $i_a = i_S - i_f = 3$ A.

The copper loss is

$$P_{copper} = i_f^2 R_f + i_a^2 R_a = 400.9 \text{ W}$$

The input power is

$$P_{in} = 5 \times 200 = 1 \text{ kW}$$

Therefore,

$$P_{rot} + P_{SL} = 1000 - 409 = 599.1 \text{ W}$$

$$\text{at } \omega_m = 2\pi \frac{955}{60} = 100 \text{ rad/sec}$$

Also, E_b at no load is

$$E_b = 200 - 3 \times 0.1 = 199.7 \text{ V}$$

$$k_a \phi = 1.997$$

When $i_S = 40$ A with $i_f = 2$ A and $i_a = 38$ A,

$$E_b = 200 - 38 \times 0.1 = 196.2 \text{ V}$$

$$\omega_m = \frac{E_b}{k_a \phi} = 98.25 \text{ rad/sec} = 938.2 \text{ rev/min}$$

The power developed is

$$P = E_b i_a = 196.2 \times 38 = 7456 \text{ W}$$

The copper loss is

$$P_{copper} = i_a^2 R_a + i_f^2 R_f = 544.4 \text{ W}$$

The input power is

$$P_{in} = 40 \times 200 = 8 \text{ kW}$$

And

$$P_{SH} = 7456 - \frac{98.25}{100} \times 599.1 = 6867.4 \text{ W}$$

$$T_{SH} = \frac{6867.4}{98.25} = 69.9 \text{ N-m}$$

Finally, the efficiency is

$$\text{eff} = \frac{P_{SH}}{P_{in}} = 85.84\%$$

16.18

From the figure, for $I_f > 0.5$A, ω=200 rad/sec

$$E_b = 40 I_f + 100$$

For $\omega = 220$ rad/sec, we have

$$\frac{E_b'}{220} = \frac{100 + 40 I_f}{200}$$

Therefore,

$$E_b' = \frac{220}{200}(100 + 40 I_f) = 110 + 44 I_f$$

For no load, $I_a = I_f$. Therefore,

$$110 + 44 I_f = 101 I_f, \; I_f = 1.93 \text{ A}$$

The terminal voltage is: $V = I_f R_f = 193$ V

16.19

(a) $$I_f = \frac{230}{17.7} = 13.0A$$

$$P_f = (230)(13.0) = 2988.7W$$

$$\frac{P_f}{P_{in}} = \frac{2988.7}{(230)(181)} = 0.072 \text{ or } 7.2\%$$

(b) $$I_f = \frac{230}{(17.7 + 5.3)} = 10A$$

$$P_f = 10^2(17.7) = 1770W$$

$$P_R = 10^2(5.3) = 530W$$

(c) $$P_{in} = (230)(190) = 43{,}700W$$

$$\%P_f = \frac{1770}{43{,}700} \times 100 = 4.05\%$$

$$\%P_R = \frac{530}{43{,}700} \times 100 = 1.21\%$$

16.20

$E_C = K\phi n$; counter emf will decrease

$I_a = \dfrac{V - E_C}{r_a}$; armature current will increase

$T = K\phi I_a$; effect on torque is indeterminate

Operation of a dc motor under weakened field conditions is frequently done when speed control is an important factor and where decreased efficiency and less than rated torque output are lesser considerations.

$$n = \frac{V - I_a r_a}{K\phi}$$

$$1000 = \frac{V - I_a r_a}{K\phi}$$

$$n_{new} = \frac{V - I_a r_a}{0.5K\phi}$$

Assume small change in the steady-state value of I_a. Then

$$\frac{1000}{n_{new}} = \frac{0.5}{1} \Rightarrow n_{new} = 2000rpm$$

EIT 16.21

In Example 15.8, $i_f = 0.6$ A, the mmf F is

$$F = 200\times0.6 = 120 \text{ At}$$

For a series field winding with

(a) $i_{series} = i_a = 8$ A, we have

$$N_{series} = \frac{120}{8} = 15 \text{ turns}$$

(b) $n_m = 120$ rev/min

$\omega_m = 12.57$ rad/sec

$E_b = v_S - i_a(R_a + R_S)$

Neglecting R_S, we have

$$E_b = 7.2 - 8\times0.2 = 5.6 \text{ V} = k_a\phi\omega_m$$

$$k_a\phi = \frac{5.6}{12.57} = 0.446$$

$$T = k_T\phi i_a \text{ and } k_T = k_a$$

$$T = 0.446\times8 = 3.56 \text{ N-m}$$

By using $\phi = ki_a$, we have

$$E_b = k_a k i_a \omega_m = v_S - i_a R_a$$

$$T = k_T(ki_a)i_a = k_a k i_a^2$$

From $i_a = \dfrac{v_S}{R_a + K\omega_m}$

where $K = k_a k = \dfrac{5.6}{8\times12.57} = 0.056$

and $\quad T \propto (\dfrac{1}{R_a + K\omega_m})^2$, we have

$$\frac{T_X}{T} = (\frac{K\omega_m + R_a}{K\omega_X + R_a})^2 = (\frac{\omega_m + \frac{R_a}{K}}{\omega_X + \frac{R_a}{K}})^2$$

We have $\quad \dfrac{R_a}{K} = 3.59$

Therefore,

$$T_X = 3.56\,(\frac{\omega_m + 3.59}{\omega_X + 3.59})^2$$

(1) at $\omega_X = 2\omega_m = 25.12$ rad/sec,

$T_X = 1.13$ NM

(2) at $\omega_X = 3\omega_m = 37.71$ rad/sec,

$T_X = 0.55$ N-m

(3) at $\omega_X = 0.5\omega_m = 6.28$ rad/sec,

$T_X = 9.54$ N-m

(4) at $\omega_X = 0.25\omega_m = 3.14$ rad/sec,

$T_X = 20.53$ N-m

(c) The diagram is shown below:

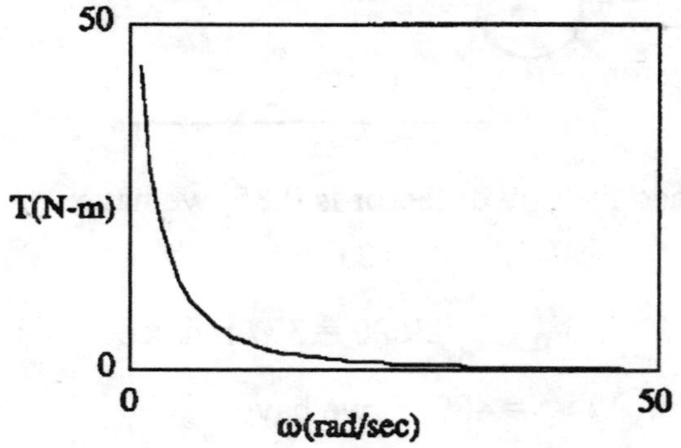

16.22

The per phase circuit is shown below:

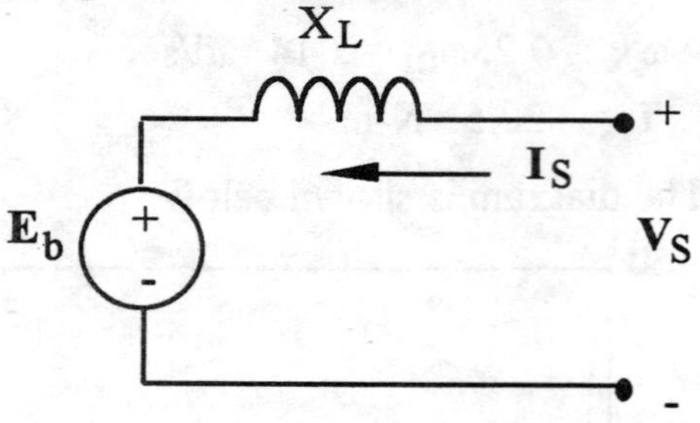

Since the power factor is 0.85, we have:

$$\theta = 31.79°$$

$$\omega_m = \frac{2\pi}{60} 3600 = 377 \text{ rad/sec}$$

From $V_{OC} = 400$ V, we have

$$E_b = 400 \text{ V (open circuit)} = k\omega_m i_f$$

Therefore $k = \dfrac{400}{377 \times 3.32} = 0.3196$

$$\mathbf{E_b} = 400\angle 0° - 50\angle 31.79° \times 7\angle 90° =$$

$$= 400 + 184.38 - j297.49 =$$

$$= 655.74\angle{-26.98°} \text{ V}$$

$$i_f = \frac{E_b}{120.48} = 5.44 \text{ A}$$

$$\theta_T = 31.79° + 26.98° = 58.77°$$

The torque developed is

$$T = \frac{3}{377} |\mathbf{E_b}||\mathbf{I_S}| \cos\theta_T = 135.27 \text{ N-m}$$

δ is the angle from **V** to $\mathbf{E_b}$: $\delta = -26.98°$

The phasor diagram is shown below:

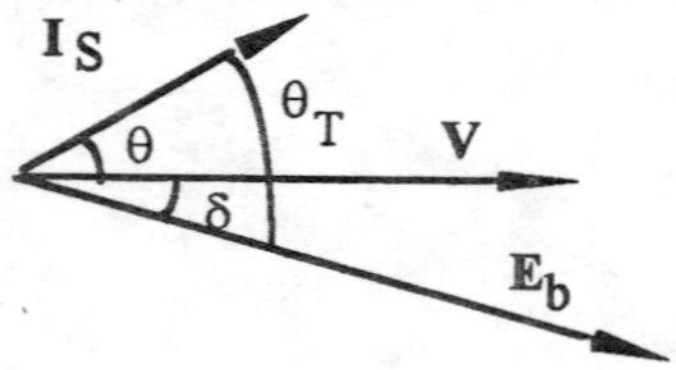

16.23

$P_{old} = 900kW$ $\quad Q_{old} = 1200kVAR$

$P_m = 450kW$

$P_T = 1350kW$ $\quad Q_T = 653.8kVAR$

$Q_m = 653.8 - 1200 = -546.2kVAR$

$$pf_m = \cos\left(\tan^{-1}\frac{Q_m}{P_m}\right) = 0.636 \text{ leading}$$

$$S_m = \frac{P_m}{pf_m} = 708kVA$$

16.24

$$\mathbf{V_L} = \frac{400}{\sqrt{3}}\angle 0° = 230.9\angle 0° \text{ V}$$

$$\mathbf{I_L} = 36\angle 0° \text{ A}$$

$$Z_S = 0.5 + j1.6 = 1.676\angle 72.65° \ \Omega$$

$$\mathbf{E_b} = \mathbf{V_L} + \mathbf{I_L}Z_S = 248.9 + j57.6$$

$$= 255.5\angle 13.03° \text{ V}$$

The power angle is 13.03°

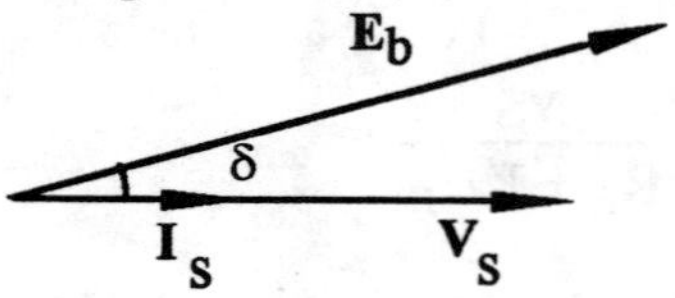

EIT 16.25

The phasor per-phase voltage is:

$\mathbf{V_S} = 127\angle 0°$ V

$$T_{dev} = 50 \text{ N-m} = -\frac{3}{377}\frac{|\mathbf{E_b}||\mathbf{V_S}|}{X_S}\sin\delta$$

Therefore,

$$|\mathbf{E_b}| = -\frac{50(377)2}{3(127)\sin(-30°)} = 197.9 \text{ V}$$

$$\mathbf{E_b} = 197.9\angle -30° \text{ V}$$

For $i_f = 1$ A,

$$\mathbf{I_S} = 49.47 + j22.2 = 54.23\angle 24.16° \text{ A}$$

The load current is:

$$\mathbf{I_L} = 25\angle -\cos^{-1}0.866 = 21.65 - j12.5 \text{ A}$$

and

$\mathbf{I_1} = \mathbf{I_L} + \mathbf{I_S}$

$$= 71.12 + j9.7 = 71.78\angle 7.77° \text{ A}$$

$P_{in\ motor} = 3\times 54.23\times 127\times \cos 24.16 = 18.85$ kW

$P_{in\ total} = 3\times 71.78\times 127\cos 7.77° = 27.10$ kW

The power factor is:

$$pf = \cos 7.77° = 0.991 \text{ leading}$$

16.26

$$I_a = \frac{500}{20} = 25A \qquad P_a = I_a^2 R_a = 31.25W$$

$$P_{out} = 500(0.85) = 425W$$

$$P_f = (2)(12) = 24W$$

$$P_{in} = P_{out} + P_a + 25 + 30 + 24 = 535.25W$$

$$\%\eta = \frac{425}{535.25}\times 100 = 79.4\%$$

16.27

At $\omega_m = 188.5$ rad/sec, we can calculate

$$P_{out} = 30\times 188.5 = 5655 \text{ W}$$

Since $P_{in} = P_{out}$ and

P'_{in}(per phase) = 1885 W = $230\times 15\cos\theta$, we calculate $\theta = \cos^{-1}0.5464 = 56.88°$.

Since $\mathbf{V_S} = 230\angle 0°$ V, $\mathbf{I_S} = 15\angle 56.88°$ A,

$$\mathbf{E_b} = 355.6 - j81.96 = 364.92\angle -12.98° \text{ V}$$

The power angle is:

$$\delta = -12.98°$$

If the load is removed, the power angle is 0° and from

$$364.92\angle 0° = 230\angle 0° - 10\angle 90° \mathbf{I},$$

we have $\mathbf{I} = 13.495\angle 90°$ A

The current is leading the voltage.

16.28

$$P_{out} = 10 \text{ hp} = 7460 \text{ W}$$

From $P_{in} = P_{out} + P_r + P_{copper} = 7740$,

we have

$$P_{in}(\text{per phase}) = 2580 = V_S I_S 0.8$$

$V_S = \frac{230}{\sqrt{3}} = 132.8$ V, therefore,

$$I_S = \frac{2580}{132.8\times 0.8} = 24.3 \text{ A}$$

That is

$$\mathbf{V_S} = 132.8\angle 0°, \mathbf{I_S} = 24.3\angle 36.87° \text{ A}$$

$$\mathbf{E_b} = \mathbf{V_S} - \mathbf{I_S}(6\angle 90°) = 249.2\angle -27.9° \text{ V}$$

a) $\mathbf{I_S} = 24.3\angle 36.87°$ A

b) efficiency = $\frac{7460}{7740} = 0.964 = 96.4\%$

c) power angle = -27.9°

16.29

Q: The setting of R_1 determines the biasing of Q. When Q conducts, the SCR will fire, energizing the alternator's field.

D: This diode serves as a "free-wheeling" element, allowing the field current to circulate without interfering with the commutation of the SCR.

Z: The Zener diode provides a fixed reference voltage at the emitter of transistor Q; i.e., determination of when Q conducts is controlled solely by the setting of R_1.

SCR: The SCR acts as a half-wave rectifier, providing field excitation for the alternator. Without the field, of course, the alternator cannot generate.

16.30

$$I = \frac{500k}{\sqrt{3}(2300)} = 125.5A$$

$$E = \frac{2300}{\sqrt{3}}\angle 0° + (125.5\angle -30°)(0.1 + j0.8)$$

$$= 1327.9 + 101.2\angle 52.9°$$

$$= 1389 + j80.7$$

$$= 1391.3\angle 3.3° V$$

$$E = 1391.3V$$

$$\delta = 3.3°$$

EIT 16.31

$n_s = \dfrac{3600}{15} = 240$ rev/min, $\omega_s = 25.13$ rad/sec

At full load, $P_{in} = 746 \times 2000 = 1.492$ MW

$$V_s = \frac{2300}{\sqrt{3}} = 1327.9\angle 0° \text{ V}$$

For unity power factor,

$$\mathbf{I_s} = 374.5\angle 0° \text{ A}$$

and $\mathbf{E_b} = \mathbf{V_s} - \mathbf{I_s}\mathrm{j}X_s = 1327.9 - \mathrm{j}730.3$

$$= 1515.5\angle -28.2° \text{ V}$$

The maximum power is

$$P_{max} = 3\frac{|\mathbf{E_b}||\mathbf{V_s}|}{X_s} = 3.096 \text{ MW}$$

$$T_{max} = \frac{P_{max}}{\omega_s} = 123.2 \text{ kN-m}$$

16.32

$$\mathbf{V_s} = \frac{1200}{\sqrt{3}} = 692.8\angle 0°$$

The input power per phase is:

$$P_{in(per\ phase)} = 36667 \text{ W}$$

$$\omega_s = 125.7 \text{ rad/sec}$$

The power developed is:

$$P = -3\frac{|\mathbf{E_b}||\mathbf{V_s}|}{X_s}\sin\delta \quad \text{therefore}$$

$\sin\delta = -0.2646$ $\qquad \delta = -15.34°$

$$\mathbf{I_s} = \frac{\mathbf{V_s} - \mathbf{E_b}}{\mathrm{j}10} = 134.4\angle 66.82°$$

The torque developed is:

$$T = \frac{P}{\omega_s} = 875.1 \text{ N-m}$$

16.33

$$\mathbf{V_S} = \frac{600}{\sqrt{3}} = 346.4\angle 0° \text{ V}$$

$$Z_S = 5 + j50 = 50.25\angle 84.29° \ \Omega$$

From pf = 0.707, we have $\theta = 45°$

From $P_{in} = 3|\mathbf{V_S}||\mathbf{I_S}|\cos\theta$, we have

$$|\mathbf{I_S}| = \frac{24\times10^3}{3\times346.4}\times0.707 = 32.67 \text{ A}$$

$$\mathbf{I_S} = 32.67\angle 45° \text{ A}$$

$$\mathbf{E_b} = \mathbf{V_S} - \mathbf{I_S}\mathbf{Z_S} = 1386 - j1270.6$$

$$= 1880.3\angle -42.51° \text{ V}$$

The power angle is:

$$\delta = -42.51°$$

The power developed is:

$$P_{dev} = 3|\mathbf{E_b}||\mathbf{I_S}|\cos 87.51° = 8.006 \text{ kW}$$

The copper loss is:

$$P_{loss} = 3|\mathbf{I_S}|^2 R_S = 16.01 \text{ kW}$$

16.34

$$V_S = \frac{440}{\sqrt{3}} = 254\angle 0° \text{ V}$$

$$Z_{in} = 0.06 + j0.3 + \frac{j5(4 + j0.3)}{4 + j5.3}$$

$$= 2.328 + j2.294 = 3.268\angle 44.59° \ \Omega$$

$$\mathbf{I_s} = 77.7\angle -44.59 \text{ A}$$

$$P_{in} = 3\times254\times77.7\cos(-44.59°)$$

$$= 42.16 \text{ kW}$$

$$\mathbf{I_2} = \frac{j5}{4 + j5.3}\mathbf{I_s} = 58.51\angle -7.55° \text{ A}$$

The total power transferred to the rotor is:

$$P_T = 3\frac{R_s}{s}|\mathbf{I_2}|^2 = 41.1 \text{ kW}$$

$$P_m = P_T - P_{\text{copper loss in rotor}}$$

$$= 41.1\times10^3(1 - s) = 40.26 \text{ kW}$$

$$\omega_m = (1 - s)\omega_s = 0.98\times188.5 = 184.7 \text{ rad/sec}$$

Therefore, the torque developed is:

$$T_{dev} = \frac{P_m}{184.7} = 218 \text{ N-m}$$

The rotational power loss is:

$$P_{rot} = 3240 - 3\times45^2\times0.06 = 2875.5 \text{ W}$$

$$T_{rot} = 15.56 \text{ N-m}$$

The shaft torque is:

$$T_{sh} = 218 - 15.56 = 202.4 \text{ N-m}$$

$$\text{eff} = \frac{P_{out}}{P_{in}} = \frac{202.4\times184.7}{42.16\times10^3} = 0.887$$

EIT 16.35

From $n_s = 1800$ rev/min, we have

$$s = 0.025 \text{ and } \frac{R_R}{S} = 4$$

$$Z_{in} = 0.2 + j0.5 + \frac{j20(4 + j0.2)}{4 + j20.2}$$

$$= 3.972 + j1.444 = 4.226\angle 19.98° \ \Omega$$

Therefore,

$$\mathbf{I_s} = 54.6\angle -19.98° \text{ A}$$

$$P_{in} = 3(54.6)(\frac{400}{\sqrt{3}}\cos(-19.98°)) = 35.6 \text{ kW}$$

$$P_t = P_{in} - 3|\mathbf{I_s}|^2 R_s$$

$$= 35.6\times10^3 - 3(54.6)^2\times 0.2 = 33.81 \text{ kW}$$

$$P_m = (1 - s)P_t = 32.97 \text{ kW}$$

$$P_{sh} = P_{out} = P_m - 800 = 32.17 \text{ kW}$$

$$\omega_m = 183.8 \text{ rad/sec}$$

$$T_{sh} = 175 \text{ N-m}$$

$$\text{efficiency} = \frac{32.17}{35.6} = 0.904$$

16.36

$n_s = 900$ rev/min, $\omega_s = 94.25$ rad/sec

a) $n_m = (1 - s)n_s = 855$ rev/min.

b)The speed of the stator field is 900 rev/min, the rotor speed relative to the stator field is:

- 45 rev/min.

c) +45 revmin

d) 0 rev/min

16.37

a) $P_m = 3(1 - s)P_t = 37$ kW

From $1 - s = 0.925$, $s = 0.075$

$$n_s = 3600 \text{ rev/min}, \omega_s = 377 \text{ rad/sec}$$

$$\omega_m = (1 - s)\omega_s = 348.7 \text{ rad/sec}$$

$$P_{sh} = P_{out} = 37 - 0.8 = 36.2 \text{ kW}$$

$$T_{sh} = \frac{P_{sh}}{348.7} = 103.8 \text{ N-m}$$

b) $P_{in} = 3|\mathbf{I_s}|^2 R_s + P_t$, and

$$3|\mathbf{I_s}|^2 R_s = 5 \text{ kW}$$

Therefore

$$|\mathbf{I_s}| = 57.7 \text{ A}$$

Also

$$P_{in} = 3|V_s||\mathbf{I_s}|\cos\theta = 45 \text{ kW}$$

The power factor is:

$$\cos\theta = 0.65 \text{ lagging}$$

16.38

(a) $$p \approx \frac{120(25)}{720} = 4.17 \Rightarrow p = 4$$

$$n_{sync} = \frac{120(25)}{4} = 750 rpm$$

$$slip = \frac{750 - 720}{750} = 0.04 \quad \text{or} \quad 4\%$$

(b) $$reg = \frac{745 - 720}{720} = 0.035 \quad \text{or} \quad 3.5\%$$

16.39

(a) $n_{sync} = 900 rpm$

$$slip = \frac{900-830}{900} = 0.078 \quad \text{or} \quad 7.8\%$$

(b) $$reg = \frac{895-830}{830} = 0.078 \quad \text{or} \quad 7.8\%$$

(c) $$pf = \frac{20{,}800}{\sqrt{3}(220)(64)} = 0.853 \text{ lagging}$$

(d) $$T = \frac{7.04(25\times 746)}{830} = 158.2 lb\cdot ft$$

(e) $$eff = \frac{25\times 746}{20{,}800} = 0.897 \quad \text{or} \quad 89.7\%$$

16.40

(a) $80 = (0.5)^2 T_{rated} \Rightarrow T_{rated} = 320 lb\cdot ft$

$T_{65\%} = (0.65)^2 320 = 135.2 lb\cdot ft$

(b) $T_{80\%} = (0.8)^2 320 = 204.8 lb\cdot ft$

EIT 16.41

$V_S = 115.5$ V

$\omega_m = (1 - s)188.5 = 181$ rad/sec

a) $$Z_{in} = 0.48 + j0.8 + \frac{j30(10.5 + j0.8)}{10.5 + j30.8}$$

$$= 9.404 + j4.63 = 10.48\angle 26.2°$$

$I_S = 11.02\angle\text{-}26.2°$ A

$P_{in(per\ phase)} = 115.5\times 11.02\times\cos(-26.2°)$

$= 1142$ W

$P_{in(total)} = 3426$ W

$P_t = P_{in(total)} - 3R_S|I_S|^2 = 3251$ W

$P_m = (1 - s)P_t = 3121$ W

$$T_{sh} = \frac{3121}{181} = 17.24 \text{ N-m}$$

16.42

a) For minimum slip, the synchronous speed, $\frac{3600}{p/2}$, should be as close as possible to 1140 rev/min, therefore,

$n_S = 1200$, $p = 6$ poles.

The slip $$s = \frac{1200 - 1140}{1200} = 0.05$$

The rotor current frequency is

$f_{rotor} = 3$ Hz

b) If the line voltage is reduced to half, the starting current is reduced by a factor of 2. The developed torque is proportional to $|I_S|^2$. Therefore, the starting torque is reduced by a factor of 4.

16.43

a) The power at ambient temperature 50°C :

$P_e' = 10 - 10\times 0.125 = 8.75$ kW

b) The power at ambient temperature 30°C :

$P_e' = 10 + 10\times 0.08 = 10.8$ kW

16.44

The characteristic is shown below:

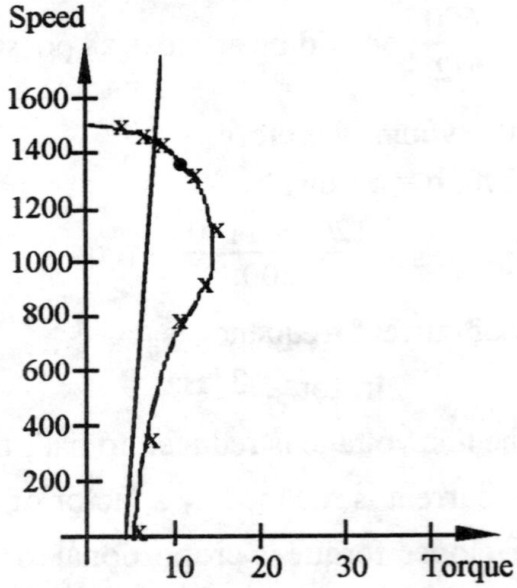

The operating point is

$n_m \approx 1425$ rev/min, $T \approx 7$ N-m

b) From equation 16.95, we have

$$\frac{T_{new}}{T_{old}} = \left(\frac{V_{s,new}}{V_{s,old}}\right)^2$$

or, $$\frac{10}{7} = \left(\frac{KV_s}{V_s}\right)^2 = K^2$$

$\therefore$ K = 1.195

and, $V_{s,new} = 1.195\, V_{s,old}$

EIT 16.45

If the load torque is reduced by one half, the speed will increase and the horsepower delivered will decrease by approximately one half.

16.46

(a) $R_S = \frac{P_{BR}}{3I_{BR}^2}\Big/2 = 0.314\Omega$

(b) $R_R = 0.314\Omega$

(c) $Z_S = \frac{V_{BR}/\sqrt{3}}{I_{BR}} = \frac{48/\sqrt{3}}{18} = 1.54\Omega$

$X_R = \sqrt{Z_S^2 - R^2} = \sqrt{(1.54)^2 - (0.628)^2} = 1.4\Omega$

16.47

(a) $$T = \frac{1}{\omega_S}\frac{q_1 V_1^2\left(R_R/s\right)}{R^2 + X^2}; \qquad s = 1$$

$$T = \frac{1}{377}\frac{3(127)^2(0.314)}{(0.628)^2 + (1.4)^2} = 17.1 N\cdot m$$

(b) $$T = \frac{1}{377}\frac{3(63.5)^2(0.314)}{(0.628)^2 + (1.4)^2} = 4.28 N\cdot m$$

16.48

a) For 60 Hz, $\omega_m = \frac{4\pi f}{P} = 125.7$ rad/sec,

$n_m = 1200$ rev/min

b) For 50 Hz, $\omega_m = 104.72$ rad/sec, $n_m =$ 1000 rev/min

16.49

$$V_s = \frac{440}{\sqrt{3}} = 254\angle 0° \text{ V}$$

For $n_m = n_s = 1200$ rev/min,

$$s = 0(\text{no load}) \text{ and } \frac{R_2}{s} = \infty$$

$$Z_{in} = R_s + j(X_s + X_m) = 0.8 + j35.7$$

$$= 35.71\angle 88.7° \ \Omega$$

$$\mathbf{I_s} = 7.11\angle\text{-}88.7° \ \text{A}$$

The power factor is

$$\cos 88.7° = 0.0224 \text{ lagging}$$

$$P_{in} = 3|\mathbf{I_s}||\mathbf{V_s}|\cos\theta = 121.4 \ \text{W}$$

EIT 16.50

For 8 poles, $n_s = \frac{3600}{4} = 900$ rev/min,

$$\omega_s = 94.25 \text{ rad/sec},$$

$$\omega_m = (1 - s)\omega_s = 92.4 \text{ rad/sec}$$

By using the equivalent circuit of Figure 15.42, we have

$$Z_{in} = 0.78 + j0.56 + \frac{j32(\frac{0.28}{0.02} + j0.84)}{14 + j32.84}$$

$$= 12.03 + j6.17 = 13.52\angle 27.15°$$

$$\mathbf{V_s} = 127\angle 0° \ \text{V}$$

$$\mathbf{I_s} = 9.39\angle\text{-}27.15° \ \text{A}$$

pf = cos(-27.15_) = 0.8898 lagging

16.51

The speed is $n_m = 3565$ rev/min

$$\omega_m = \frac{2\pi \times 3565}{60} = 373.3 \text{ rad/sec}$$

The rated voltxamperes is:

$$\sqrt{3} \times (230 \text{ V}) \times (106 \text{ A}) = 42.23 \text{ kVA}$$

or

$$\sqrt{3} \times (460 \text{ V}) \times (53 \text{ A}) = 42.23 \text{ kVA}$$

The maximum continuous output power is:

$$P_o = 40 \times 746 = 29840 \ \text{W}$$

The rated output torque is:

$$T = \frac{P_o}{\omega_m} = 79.93 \text{ N-m}$$

16.52

(a)
$$T_R = \frac{KV^2(R_2/s_R)}{\left(\frac{R_2}{s_R}\right)^2 + X^2}$$

$$T_{ST} = 1.4T_R \qquad s_{ST} = 1.0$$

$$T_{MT} = 2.1T_R \qquad s_{MT} = \frac{R_2}{X}$$

The above leads to 3 equations in 3 unknowns:

(1) $4.2XR_2 = 1.4R_2^2 + 1.4X^2$

(2) $\frac{R_2^2}{s_R} + s_R X^2 = 1.4R_2^2 + 1.4X^2$

(3) $4.2\frac{XR_2}{s_R} = \left(\frac{R_2}{s_R}\right)^2 + X^2$

Solving, $\frac{R_2}{X} = 0.382$ and $s_R = 0.097$

(b) $s_{MT} = \frac{R_T}{X} = 0.382$

(c) $I_R = \frac{KV}{4.06} \qquad I_{ST} = \frac{KV}{1.07}$

$$\frac{I_{ST}}{I_R} \times 100 = 379\%$$

16.53

(a) $f_R = sf_{ST}$

$$s = 3.0 = \frac{900 - n_R}{900} \Rightarrow n_R = -1800 rpm$$

$$1800 = \frac{120(180)}{p_R} \Rightarrow p_R = 12 \text{ poles}$$

(b) clockwise

(c) 1800 rpm

(d) $n_S = 1800 = \frac{120(60)}{p_S} \Rightarrow p_S = 4$ poles

---

16.54

(a) $n_m = \frac{120(60)}{4} = 1800 rpm$

(b) $n_S = \frac{120(60)}{20} = 360 rpm$

$$s = \frac{360 - (-1800)}{360} = 6.0$$

$$f_R = sf_{ST} = 6.0(60) = 360 Hz$$

Special-Purpose Electric Machines

Chapter 17 Instructor Notes

The content of Chapter 17 is somewhat unusual for a textbook of this nature. The intent of this chapter is to provide a reasonably quantitative overview of the operation of small electric machines (mostly motors). In many practical industrial applications, ranging from servos for robots, to drug delivery systems, to actuation devices for control systems, to manufacturing equipment, to fluid power systems, small motors find widespread application.

The first section discusses the brushless DC motor, including the basics of the electronic circuits that make its operation possible. The second section introduces the stepper motor and its driver circuits. In section 17.3, single phase AC motors are discussed, starting with the universal motor, and continuing with a classification of single phase induction motors, which includes split-phase, capacitor-type and shaded-pole motors. The presentation detail is sufficient to permit quantitative analysis of these motors using circuit models.

The examples given in the chapter are supplemented by a good number of homework problems, some of which are extensions of the examples presented in the text.

Chapter 17 problem solutions

17.1

We know that

$$\lambda_m = 0.1V \cdot s$$
$$p = 6$$
$$m = 2$$
$$\omega_m = 60rev/s = 2\pi \times 60 rad/s$$

Let flux linkage $\lambda = \lambda_m \sin \omega t$ where

$$\omega = \frac{p}{2}\omega_m = 3 \times 60 = 180 rev/s$$
$$= 2\pi \times 180 rad/s = 360\pi rad/s$$

Then, the generated voltage

$$V = e = \left|\frac{d\lambda}{dt}\right| = \frac{d(\lambda_m \sin \omega t)}{dt} = \omega \lambda_m \cos \omega t$$
$$= V_m \cos \omega t$$
$$V_m = \omega \lambda_m = 360\pi \times 0.1 = 113.1V$$

17.2

We know that

$$p = 4$$
$$m = 2$$
$$\omega_m = 3600 rev/min$$
$$\mathbf{V}_n = 50V$$

(a) Let $e = V = \sqrt{2}\mathbf{V}\sin\theta = \sqrt{2}\mathbf{V}\sin \omega t$

$$\omega = \frac{p}{2}\omega_m \cdot 2\pi rad/min = 2 \times 60 \times 2\pi rad/s$$
$$\lambda = \int_0^t e dt = \int_0^t \sqrt{2}\mathbf{V}\sin \omega t dt = \frac{\sqrt{2}}{\omega}\mathbf{V}\cos \omega t$$
$$= \frac{\sqrt{2}}{240\pi} 50 \cos 240\pi t = 0.094 \cos \omega t$$

(b) Symmetric voltages in symmetric windings produce a rotational field in voltage with frequency ω.

Let ω=3600 rev/min. Then, the rotor speed is

$$\omega_m = \frac{\omega}{p/2} = \frac{3600}{2} = 1800 rev/min = \frac{2\pi}{60} \times 1800 rad/s$$
$$= 60\pi rad/s$$

17.3

The equations will have the following form:

$$v = Ri + L\frac{di}{dt} + K_E\omega$$ and

$$T = K_T i = (J_m + J_L)\frac{d\omega}{dt} + D\omega + T_F + T_L$$

17.4

The rotor and stator configuration is shown below:

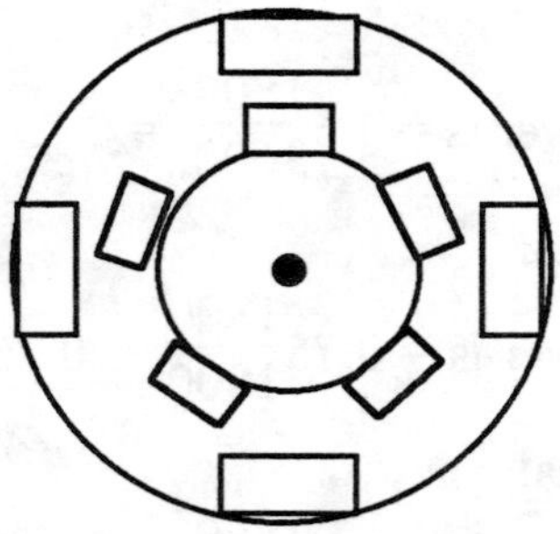

The motor has 5 rotor teeth and 4 stator teeth (2 phases).

17.5

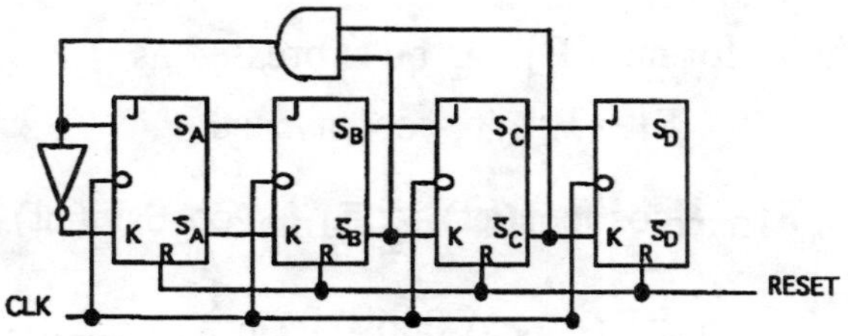

17.6

We know that

$$p = 50$$
$$m = 2$$
$$\omega_m = 100 rad/s$$

Strikes per rev.: $N = p \cdot m = 100$

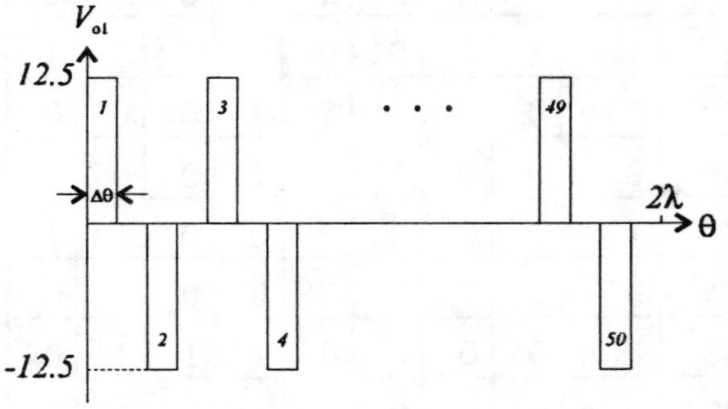

$$\Delta\theta = \frac{2\pi}{N} = \frac{2\pi}{100} = \frac{\pi}{50}$$

$$\lambda = \int_0^t e dt = \int_0^{\frac{\pi}{50}} \frac{V_o}{\omega_m} d\theta$$

$$= \frac{V_o}{\omega_m} \cdot \frac{\pi}{50} = \frac{12.5}{100} \cdot \frac{\pi}{50} = 0.00785 V \cdot s$$

Let the winding resistance be represented by R_w. Then

$$V = k_a \omega_m + R_w I$$
$$T = k_T I$$

where $k_a = k_T = \dfrac{V - R_w I}{\omega_m}$

Then $T = k_a I = \dfrac{V - R_w I}{\omega_m} \cdot I$ N·m

17.7

(a) For full step clockwise rotation is:

Phase 1 → phase 4 → Phase 3 → Phase 2 → Phase 1

(b) The displacement angle of the full step sequence is 90°.

17.8

The motor will require 24 stator teeth and 2 rotor teeth.

17.9

CK	R	1	2	3	4	5	6	7	8
S1	1	1	0	0	0	0	0	1	1
S2	0	0	0	1	1	1	0	0	0
S3	0	0	0	1	1	1	0	0	0
S4	1	1	0	0	0	0	0	1	1
S5	0	1	1	1	0	0	0	0	0
S6	0	0	0	0	0	1	1	1	0
S7	0	0	0	0	0	1	1	1	0
S8	0	1	1	1	0	0	0	0	0

where "1" ⇒ switch is closed

17.10

(a) $steps/revolution = \dfrac{360}{15} = 24$

(b) $d = 0.1" \times \dfrac{15°}{360°} = 0.0042"$

(c) $steps = 17.5rev \times 24\dfrac{steps}{rev} = 420steps$

(d)
$\# pulses = \# steps$

$$\Rightarrow n_{SH} = 220\frac{steps}{s} \times \frac{1rev}{24steps} \times \frac{60s}{min}$$

$$= 550rpm$$

17.11

a) The power is $= 0.75\dfrac{1800}{900} = 1.5$ hp, integral

b) The power is $= 1.5\dfrac{1800}{3600} = 0.75$ hp, fractional

c) The power is $= 0.75\dfrac{1800}{1800} = 0.75$ hp, fractional

d) The power is $= 1.5\dfrac{1800}{6000} = 0.45$ hp, fractional

17.12

The stator mmf $\mathbf{F}_1$ can be expressed as

$$\mathbf{F}_1 = F_{1max}\cos(\omega t)\cos\theta$$

$$= \frac{1}{2}F_{1max}\cos\theta\cos(\omega t) - \frac{1}{2}F_{1max}\cos\theta\sin(\omega t)$$

$$+ \frac{1}{2}F_{1max}\cos\theta\cos(\omega t) + \frac{1}{2}$$

$$F_{1max}\cos\theta\sin(\omega t)$$

$$= F_{CW} + F_{CCW}$$

where

F_{CW} is a clockwise-rotating mmf

F_{CCW} is a counter clockwise-rotating magnetic mmf

17.13

We have: $P_{out} = 746 \times 10 = 7460$ W

$$P_{in} = \frac{P_{out}}{eff.} = 8674.4 \text{ W}$$

From $P_{in} = V_s I_s \cos\theta_s = 8674.4$, we have

$|\mathbf{I_s}| = 48.2$ A, $\theta = 25.84°$ lagging

Therefore,

$$\mathbf{I_s} = 48.2\angle{-25.84°} = 43.38 - j21.01 \text{ A}$$

To get unit power factor, $\mathbf{I_c} = j21.01$.

From $j21.01 = \dfrac{200\angle 0°}{-j\dfrac{1}{\omega C}}$, $\omega = 377$ rad/s,

we have $C = 278.6\ \mu F$

17.14

For a 2 pole machine, the synchronous speed is 3000 rev/min for an excitation frequency of 50 Hz. From s = 0.03, the slip in the opposite direction of rotation is 1.97, the motor speed is 2910 rev/min = 304.7 rad/s.

17.15

$$\omega = 180 \times 15 = 2700°/s = 7.5 rev/s$$

$$t = \frac{28 rev}{7.5 rev/s} = 3.73 s$$

17.16

$0.5Z_b = 0.991 + j1.057) = 0.5(R_b + jX_b)$

$0.5Z_f = 15.93 + j20.07 = 0.5(R_f + jX_f)$

$Z_{in} = 18.94 + j23.93 = 30.52\angle 51.64°$

Therefore, $\mathbf{I_1} = \dfrac{\mathbf{V_1}}{Z_{in}} = 3.60\angle{-51.64°}$ A

$P_f = I_1^2(0.5R_f) = 207.0$ W

$P_b = I_1^2(0.5R_b) = 12.84$ W

$P_{mech} = (1 - s)(P_f - P_b) = 184.45$ W

For a 4-pole machine,

$\omega_s = 188.5$ rad/s, $\omega_m = 179.1$ rad/s

Thus, the rotor speed is:

179.1 rad/s (1710 rev/min)

17.17

$0.5 Z_b = 0.830 + j1.248$

$0.5Z_f = 12.41 + j16.98$

$Z_{in} = 15.1 + j20.79 = 25.7\angle 54.0°$

$\mathbf{I_1} = 4.28\angle{-54.0°}$ A

$P_f = |\mathbf{I_1}|^2(0.5R_f) = 227.5$ W

$P_b = |\mathbf{I_1}|^2(0.5R_b) = 15.2$ W

$P_{mech} = (1 - s)(P_f - P_b) = 201.68$ W

17.18

The synchronous speed is 1800 rev/min, for 1730 rev/min, $(1 - s) = 0.961$, therefore the slip is $s = 0.039$. We have:

$$0.5Z_b = 0.064 + j0.2$$

$$0.5Z_f = 3.034 + j0.747$$

$$Z_{in} = 3.842\angle 20.52°$$

$$\mathbf{I_S} = 29.9\angle\text{-}20.52 \text{ A}$$

$$P_f = 2717.5 \text{ W} \qquad P_b = 57.22 \text{ W}$$

$$P_{mech} = 2660.3 \text{ W}$$

$$\omega_m = 181.2 \text{ rad/s}$$

The torque developed is:

$$T_{dev} = \frac{2551.6}{181.2} = 14.68 \text{ N-m}$$

17.19

At no load, $s \approx 0$, the circuit model is shown below:

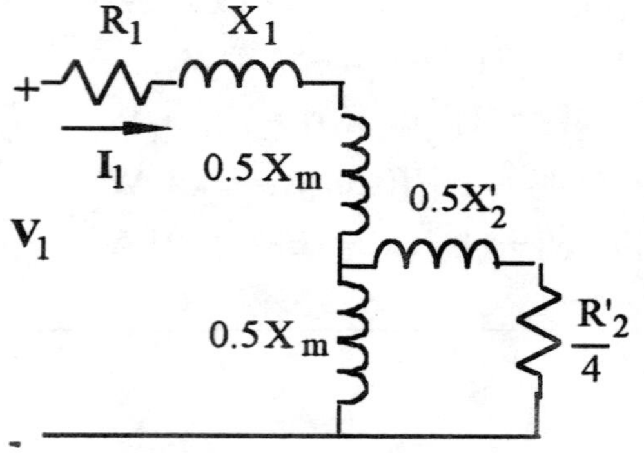

17.20

For locked rotor $\omega_m = 0$, $s = 1$. The circuit is shown below:

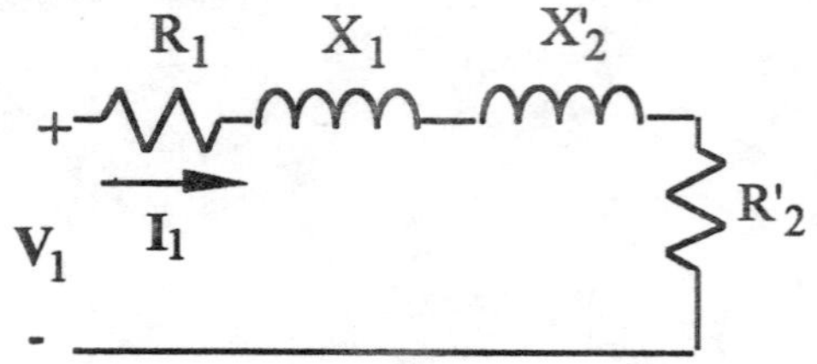

17.21

From pf = 0.88, we have $\theta = -28.4°$ and

$$\mathbf{I_s} = 1.5\angle\text{-}28.4° \text{ A}$$

The rated speed is:

$$\frac{(1/8)\times 746}{0.17} = 548.53 \text{ rad/s}$$

(a) $P_{in} = 151.8$ W and the efficiency is

$$\text{eff} = \frac{93.25}{151.8} = 61.43\%$$

(b) The speed is 5238.1 rev/min

(c) The copper loss is:

$$1.5^2 \times 10 = 22.5 \text{ W}$$

(d) Other loss will be

$$151.8 - 22.5 - 93.25 = 36.05 \text{ W}$$

(e) $P_{in} = (115)(.5)(.88) = 50.6$ W

$$P_{in} = 36.05 + (.5^2 \text{x} 10) + P_{out}$$

$$P_{out} = 12.05 \text{ W}$$

Assume T is proportional to I^2

$$\Rightarrow T_{new} = \left(\frac{0.5}{1.5}\right)^2 (0.17) = 0.019 \text{ N-m}$$

$$\omega = \frac{12.05}{0.019} = 637.9 \text{ rad/s}$$

$$n = 6091.9 \text{ rpm}$$

17.22

From pf = 0.94 (lagging), we have

$$\theta = -19.95°$$

Therefore, $\mathbf{I_s} = 6.5\angle\text{-}19.95°$ A

(a) $\mathbf{E_b} = 146.68 - j53.25$

$$= 156.05\angle\text{-}19.95° \text{ V}$$

(b) $P_{dev} = I_s E_b \cos 0° = 1014.3$ W

(c) $P_{out} = 1014.3 - 65 = 949.3$ W

(d) $P_{in} = 1466.4$ W

$$\text{eff} = 64.7\%$$

17.23

$\mathbf{V_S} = 400\angle 0°$, $\theta = -36.9°$, therefore

$$\mathbf{I_S} = 20\angle{-36.9°} = 16 - j12$$

For a unity power factor, $\mathbf{I_C} = j12$

We have

$$12 = 400\omega C,\ \omega = 314.16 \text{ rad/s}$$

Therefore, $C = 95.5\ \mu F$

17.24

It will work. The *b* and *c* windings will produce a magnetic field similar to a single phase machine, that is, two components rotating in opposite directions and the *a* winding would act as a starting winding. The phase shift provided by the capacitor is needed to provide a nonzero starting torque.

17.25

The universal motor speed is easily controlled and thus it would be used for variable speed, that is, (e) and (g). The vacuum cleaner motors are often universal motors. This motor could also be used for the fan motors.

A single phase induction motor is used for (b) and (c).

The clock should use a single phase synchronous motor.

The tape drive would be a single phase synchronous motor also.

An X-Y plotter uses a stepper motor.

17.26

(a) $P_{out} = \frac{1}{4} \times 746 = 186.5W$

$$eff = \frac{P_{out}}{P_{in}} = 0.602 \text{ or } 60\%$$

(b) $pf = \frac{P}{VI} = \frac{310}{(115)(3.8)} = 0.709$ lagging

(c)

$$T = 7.04\frac{P_{out}}{n_R} = 7.04\frac{186.5}{1725} = 0.761 lb\cdot ft \times 12\frac{in}{ft}$$

$$= 9.13 lb\cdot in$$

17.27

$$n = 230\% \text{ of } 1150 = 2645 \text{ rpm}$$

$$T = 40\% \text{ of } T_{rated}$$

$$= (0.4)\frac{(33{,}000)(5)}{(2\pi)(1150)} = 9.13 lb\cdot ft$$

17.28

(a) reluctance

(b) shaded-pole

(c) capacitor-start

(d) universal

(e) permanent split capacitor

(f) universal

(g) permanent split capacitor

17.29

(a) $HP = (0.8)^3 = 0.512$ or 51.2% of rated

(b) $HP = (0.7)^3 = 0.343$ or 34.3% of rated

(c) $HP = (0.5)^3 = 0.125$ or 12.5% of rated

17.30

$$P_m = \frac{200K}{0.91} = 219.8KW$$

$$P_{new} = 800K + 219.8K = 1019.8KW$$

$$Q_{new} = P_{new}\tan(\cos^{-1}0.92) = 434.4KVAR$$

$$Q_{old} = 800K\tan(\cos^{-1}0.8) = 600KVAR$$

$$Q_m = Q_{old} - Q_{new} = 165.6KVAR$$

$$S_m = \sqrt{P_m^2 + Q_m^2} = 274.8KVA$$

$$pf_m = \cos\tan^{-1}\left(\frac{Q_m}{P_m}\right) = 0.8 \text{ leading}$$